Social Statistics Using SPSS

Social Statistics Using SPSS

Nelson C. Dometrius
Texas Tech University

HarperCollins*Publishers*

To my family: my wife Phoebe and children Chris, Ethan, Natalie, and Alex. Not only did they provide the impetus for writing this book, they also shared the sacrifices entailed in its completion.

Sponsoring Editor: Alan McClare
Project Editor: Art Pomponio
Design Supervisor: Lucy Krikorian
Text Adaptation Design: North 7 Atelier, Ltd.
Cover Design: Jan Kessner
Production Assistant: Linda Murray
Compositor: Circle Graphics Typographers
Printer and Binder: R. R. Donnelley & Sons Company
Cover Printer: New England Book Components, Inc.

SPSS-X, SPSS/PC+, SPSS/PC+ Studentware, SPSS, and SPSS Release 4 are the trademarks of SPSS Inc. for its proprietary computer software.

IBM, IBM PC IBM PC/XT, IBM PC/AT, IBM OS, IBM CMS, OS/2 and PS/2 are registered trademarks of International Business Machines Corporation.

DEC, VAX and VMS are trademarks of Digital Equipment Corporation.

Macintosh is a trademark of Apple Computer Corporation.

Social Statistics Using SPSS

Library of Congress Cataloging-in-Publication Data
Dometrius, Nelson C.
    Social statistics using SPSS / Nelson C. Dometrius.
      p.   cm.
    Includes index.
    ISBN 0-06-041714-5
    1. SPSS (Computer program) I. Title.
  HA32.D66   1992
  300'.1'5195—dc20   91-34190
                                                   CIP

92 93 94 95   9 8 7 6 5 4 3 2 1

Contents

List of Supplements

List of Tables

Preface

I have written this book to help students understand the importance of statistics for research in the social sciences and to help them learn how to use them. To facilitate understanding, key statistical formulas are presented along with explanations of how each is an appropriate approach to different research questions. I reinforce the role of statistics in the research process by continually reminding the reader of the research purposes served by statistical analysis—the nature of the research question being addressed and how a particular statistic might, or might not, be used to answer it.

Statistics is a skill that must be practiced continually to be learned. To provide an opportunity for practice, the text uses the SPSS software to produce the statistics discussed and apply them to appropriate tests of hypotheses. The emphasis on the SPSS software, one of the most widely used programs in business and education, should help students carry the statistical skills learned in class to other classes or job applications.

Two sample data sets are available with the text, subsets of the General Social Survey and the American National Election Study. These are the same data sets from which the examples in the text are drawn, so students can replicate the examples as learning tools. The two data sets provide instructors with flexibility on the types of topics emphasized and give students experience with data they are likely to encounter in professional publications. The data sets are available directly from the publisher. Contact The Software Group, College Division, 10 East 53rd Street, New York, N.Y. 10022 or call (1-800) 677-6337.

This book offers comprehensive coverage of SPSS software. Multiple forms and versions of the SPSS software are discussed from SPSS-X version 2 with its OPTIONS and STATISTICS commands that most instructors were raised on, to the subcommands used by SPSS-X version 3, the innovations of SPSS/PC+, and the new SPSS Release 4 available on many mainframes and microcomputers. This approach should allow students to move from academic mainframes to workplace microcomputers with little difficulty. In addition, instructors using Release 4 do not have to require students to purchase two SPSS manuals, one for the software's command structure and another for its application on a particular computer platform. Users of Release 4 should refer to the notice on page xx.

SPSS/PC+ Studentware is not explicitly covered by this text. The newest version of Studentware requires a hard disk, reducing its attractiveness for users of low cost hardware, and site licensing arrangements with SPSS Inc. can bring the cost of the full SPSS/PC+ program down to very near the cost of the Studentware package. Nonetheless, instructors dedicated to using Studentware will find that most of the discussions of SPSS/PC+ presented in this text apply to Studentware as well. The primary differences involve the use of data modification commands. Instructors using this text with Studentware will need to inform students of these differences.

Next, a note to instructors. Any text that has to be designed to fit a wide variety of teaching needs will not fit any specific need perfectly. Personal preferences are a major factor. Some always cover t tests and analysis of variance while others skip them. I have grouped t tests, analysis of variance, and chi-square together since all deal with statistical significance, but many prefer to leave analysis of variance until later in a course. Finally there is the eternal dispute over whether regression, simple or multiple, should cap a beginning course or be left to advanced statistics. I have tried to build substantial redundancy into many chapters both to repeat topics that typically cause difficulty for students and to allow instructors to modify chapter order or even skip some chapters entirely without a great loss in readability or student comprehension.

Beyond personal preferences, the teaching environment will be a key factor, including student preparation and operating on a quarter versus semester system. Chapter 2 covers the bare bones of research theory and design. It can be skimmed as a refresher or skipped entirely if students are coming straight from a course on social research. Chapter 3 covers information on how to read the text for the particular SPSS application students are using. Instructors may find it more efficient to cover the particulars of their specific software and computer installation via lecture, using this chapter only as an optional reference for students needing extra help. Chapter 17 on partial correlations should be skipped by users of SPSS/PC+ since they are not available in that software. Scatterplots are a favorite teaching tool and I intentionally included in each data set variables with enough values to be useful for scatterplots. None, however, produce particularly clear or neat scatterplots and instructors may wish to either skip the PLOT chapter (Chapter 18) or create some practice variables that will produce clearer pictures. With data massaging, beginning students grasp the SELECT IF and RECODE commands fairly easily but typically avoid the COMPUTE and IF commands. The latter commands are used in later exercises but are not crucial, and thus instructors may wish to skip the last half of the data massaging chapter.

Finally, I gratefully acknowledge the help of those involved in the development and completion of this text, especially David Glenn, the representative of HarperCollins who was willing to send my prospectus on to the home office, and Alan McClare, the editor who kept things going during the writing and review stages and Art Pomponio who helped guide the project to completion. My thanks to SPSS Inc. for allowing me to use illustrations from many of their manuals as well as discuss their proprietary software throughout the book. My thanks also to the Inter University Consortium for Political and Social Research for allowing me to distribute some simplified versions of some of their data holdings as practice data sets to use with the text.

The following reviewers made valuable suggestions: Kenneth W. Eckhardt, University of Delaware; Kevin Fitzpatrick, University of Alabama—Birmingham; David Jaffee, SUNY—New Paltz; Satish Sharma, University of Nevada—Las Vegas; Gregory L. Weiss, Roanoke College; Jack M. Weller, University of Kansas—Lawrence; Barbara A. Zsembik, University of Florida.

Neither teaching nor learning statistics is easy. I hope instructors and students will find this book a useful contribution to their efforts and maybe even introduce a little fun and excitement in the process.

Nelson C. Dometrius

Notice for Users of SPSS/PC+ RELEASE 4

Shortly before this text was printed, SPSS produced a Release 4 version of their SPSS/PC+ software. A quick review of this software shows some significant changes in its technical aspects, but only a few differences in the actual use of the software or its user interface. The major differences are two. First, there are some minor changes in the choices available on the menu/help display to bring SPSS/PC+ closer to the command generator of Release 4 on other computer systems. Second, the CROSSTABS procedure has been changed to use the subcommand and specification keywords discussed in this text to select procedure options instead of the older option and statistic numbers. The CROSSTABS output has also been revised to add the new statistics available with Release 4 on other computer systems.

The net result is that almost all of this text's discussion of SPSS/PC+ still applies to the new version of this software. In the few areas where there are differences, this text's discussion of Release 4 covers those differences and should be used in place of the SPSS/PC+ information.

A cautionary word here to users of SPSS Release 4. This new version of the software is probably pretty free of bugs, but the manuals are not. Here are two examples. At one point the reference manual states that two-tailed tests are the default of the CORRELATION procedure, and later it says one-tailed tests are the default. To produce the Tukey b comparison on the ONEWAY procedure, the manual says to use the keyword BTUKEY, and later it says to use the keyword TUKEYB. I have spoken to people at SPSS about these discrepancies, and they are not too sure what to make of them either. The discrepancies appear to be caused by attempting to integrate the best features of SPSS-X and SPSS/PC+, which have slightly different defaults and keywords, in the new Release 4. This also provides a handy solution. If you occasionally encounter an error with some of the mainframe commands that each chapter emphasizes, look to the slightly different command structure described for SPSS/PC+ for that will probably work.

Chapter 1

Quantitative Social Science

*T*his book is about quantitative social science research—how to do it and how to evaluate it when it is done by others. Three themes will be interwoven throughout the text: the nature of science and scientific research, the quantitative analysis of information, and the use of computers to perform quantitative analyses.

When social science majors first encounter quantitative analysis creeping into their fields of study, they are often a bit put off. They see their chosen avocations as involving the behavior of political leaders, the development of social groups, producing solutions to social problems, and other topics to which numbers and mathematics are irrelevant. Nonetheless, scholars are using mathematical techniques to study social phenomena in ever-growing numbers. There must be some relationship between mathematics and social science topics, but what is it? To explain the connection, let us look briefly at the three topics of this text.

THE NATURE OF SCIENCE

"Science" is a familiar term but remains misunderstood by many. The labels "science" and "scientific" have been bandied about so much in everyday discussion that they have acquired many meanings, most of them wrong. Science is not just a body of knowledge, a collection of facts, working in a white coat in a laboratory, high technology, or a label meaning unquestionable truth. **Science** is a mode of inquiry or the way in which we investigate things. In particular, it is the systematic collection and analysis of observations. This last phrase is quite meaty and deserves further elaboration.

The basis of knowledge is not clear-cut. How do we "know" the things we know? What evidence and thought processes lead us to draw conclusions, such as there is a God, this person is honest, or highly educated people earn higher incomes? Thinking about sources of knowledge has its own label, **epistemology**, which is the study of how we know what we know. Without delving too deeply into epistemology, we can examine four common bases of knowledge to illustrate where science fits.

First is everyday practical knowledge, or **common sense**. While much hallowed by pragmatic U.S. citizens, common sense is a very weak way of knowing the world. A description of common sense attributed to Einstein is "the layers of prejudice laid down in the mind by age 18." While unpleasant, this description is essentially correct, for common sense means nothing more than something consistent with what we already believe. To say of a statement such as "the poor commit most crimes" that it is just common sense means only that it is consistent with what we already believe. Obversely, to say of the statement "the rich commit most crimes" that it is nonsense (lacking common sense) merely means it is inconsistent with our current beliefs.

In everyday life, common sense is necessary and useful. We need habitual patterns of thought and behavior. We cannot approach each situation afresh, searching for ultimate truth—"How do I know I really want mustard on my hamburger? I have never tried it with vinegar or goat cheese." For really important concerns, however, we need to go beyond the "I know what I know and I will not consider anything else" syndrome of common sense.

The second way of knowing can be called **intuition**, which is an inner feeling or sense that some things are true. The founders of this country confidently stated, "We hold these truths to be self-evident, that all men are created equal. . . ." By self-evident they meant something that all people could sense the truth of, something intuitively obvious and thus requiring no further proof or elaboration.

The third source of knowledge is **rational** knowledge, which is the logical derivation of conclusions from premises. One starts with certain statements that are held to be true, for example, thou shalt not kill, or people are motivated by self-interest, and then one is able, by following rigorous rules of logic, to deduce conclusions about everyday life: the death penalty is killing and therefore wrong, or without the death penalty people will kill for personal gain.

Finally, there is **empirical** science. To be empirical is to be based on what we can observe through our senses: touch, sight, smell, taste, and hearing. Science holds that to know the world, observe it. For illustration, consider two different approaches to the question of whether more highly educated people earn larger incomes. We might reason that those with high levels of education are both scarce in number and highly sought after by employers. Corporations compete for such employees by offering high salaries. Therefore, highly educated people receive high incomes. This makes sense, but the conclusion is based solely on logically connected statements or the rational mode of knowing. Science demands a further step—the collection of information from people with varying education levels to see whether they actually have different amounts of income.

Except for placing common sense at the bottom, we do not intend for the ways of knowing the world described above to be in a weak-to-strong hierarchy. Fields such as art, literature, philosophy, and religion make insightful and useful statements about the world, even though these statements are largely based on intuitive or rational modes of knowing. Epistemological debates deal with the supremacy of one method over another, but we need not engage in such debate here. The point is that science is different—different in theory and different in practice.

Observation is a hallmark of science, but observation alone is not enough. All modes of knowing involve some observation of the world. In science, observations must be systematically collected to provide us with **objective** information. When we observe the world, our observations are based on two things: what exists in the world and what exists inside us. As we live out our lives, we develop beliefs about the way the world works and how people behave. When we view the world, we see it in the context of our established beliefs, or through personal **subjective** filters.

Subjectivity is clearly a problem when we conduct research. Suppose a class wants to study the often-raised complaint that television news programs have a liberal bias. To resolve this issue, the class watches a representative sample of videotaped news programs that were broadcast during the 1988 presidential election. At the end of this exercise, the class members discuss what they have watched. One student volunteers that the bias against George Bush was obvious, overwhelming, and quite disgusting. A second class member, however, claims that she saw no discernible bias in any of the programs watched. What have we learned from these reactions? Not much. We want to observe the world, but do these reactions represent what exists in the world or what exists inside each person? Even if the entire class voted 80 percent to 20 percent that no bias existed, does this tell us that television news is really unbiased or merely that this class was composed of a majority of liberals? Science needs to remove personal subjectivity so that observations are based on what is really out there, not what is inside the observer.

Obtaining objective information is not easy. A simplistic strategy might be to search for impartial observers, such as a fair and impartial jury in a criminal trial, who would then render a reliable verdict. This approach is noble, but insufficient. We have all developed prejudices, if not for or against presidential candidates, possibly against people with short hair or shrill voices or wearing suits. Even in a courtroom an impartial jury is not sufficient, which explains why the judge controls the evidence presented by opposing attorneys—to make sure the jury hears only reliable information relevant to the issues of the case.

Objectivity does not inhere in the person, and scientists are not automatons without opinions or feelings. Science seeks objectivity through systematic processes designed to remove the impact of personal biases from observation.

How do we know these procedures work? Objectivity is tested through **replicability**. If two people, regardless of their subjective biases, observe the same phenomenon, it is probably because what they observe is really there, not because their predetermined opinions lead them to see it.

Some of the processes by which objectivity and replicability are ensured include precise definitions of phenomena to be observed, methods of measuring the phenomena's quantity or presence versus absence, and rigorous rules about selecting phenomena to be studied. All this is discussed more thoroughly later in this text. For now, we leave our general discussion of science and turn to the second theme of this text, the quantitative analysis of information.

QUANTITATIVE ANALYSIS

The mere collection of objective information is insufficient to complete the scientific process. Facts do not speak for themselves, nor will simply amassing a large number of facts (objective observations) lead to a correct (or any) conclusion. The observations gathered must be logically and appropriately interpreted, and this is where mathematics enters the picture.

The connections between mathematical techniques and the study of the social world are many. To begin with, mathematics is a highly formalized system of logic providing rules specifying how conclusions can and cannot be drawn. For example, given that the algebraic statement

$$a = b$$

is true, the rules of mathematics tell us that the statement

$$\frac{a}{c} = \frac{b}{c}$$

is also true but that the statement

$$\frac{a}{c} = b$$

is false. Some statements about the world can be translated to an equivalent mathematical form, such as the logical syllogism on the left and its mathematical equivalent in the right in Figure 1.1. Where such equivalences exist, the rules of mathematics can guide our processes of analysis.

A similarity between social and mathematical statements is not a rarity, but a common occurrence. Consider the following statements: Campaign expenditures affect a candidate's chance of winning; education is related to income; and poverty is related to crime. To test these statements through observation, we collect numerical information, such as expenditures in dollars, number of votes, years of education, income in dollars, and frequency of crimes committed. Most statements about the social and political worlds are statements relating

```
A Logical Syllogism              It's Mathematical Equivalent

All humans are mortal.                    a = b
   (a)         (b)

Socrates is a human.                      c = a
  (c)        (a)
-----------------------           -------

Therefore,   Socrates is mortal.     Therefore,  c = b
               (c)        (b)
```

Figure 1.1 Logical statements and mathematical statements.

the quantity of one thing to the quantity of another. They are quantitative statements.

When we seek to test statements such as "higher education leads to higher income," we gather observations about the education and income levels for a number of people, say, 300. Collectively, the information we obtain is called our **data**. The analysis of the data is called, not surprisingly, **data analysis**. Data analysis involves a special subfield of mathematics called statistics. A **statistic** is simply a number summarizing some characteristic of the data. How, for example, would we use our 300 observations to determine whether the statement about education and income was true or false? We could show people a list of all the observations supporting the statement (highly educated with high incomes) as well as a second list of all the observations contradicting it (highly educated with low incomes). However, it is far simpler to use statistics which summarize all the observations in one or two numbers, such as 40 percent of college graduates earn $100,000 or more, but only 15 percent of high school graduates earn that much.

Mathematics in general and statistics in particular are powerful tools in contemporary social science. They give us the means to both describe a large amount of information easily and determine whether that information does or does not support statements made about the world. In later chapters we describe a variety of statistics and how each can be used to draw conclusions from the data.

A note of both caution and assurance is appropriate here. Many people approach a statistics course with trepidation, fearing they will quickly get lost in a maze of numbers and complex mathematical formulas. In one sense, the fear is well grounded. Data analysis courses are different from other social science courses. This text should not be read quickly in hope of gleaning enough key points from each chapter to write a decent essay for the examination. Mathematical analysis is highly structured logic. You must follow it step by careful step to truly understand the material presented. A cursory reading simply will not do. However, the introductory statistics presented in this text do not require familiarity with advanced mathematical techniques. All can be understood with a basic knowledge of high school algebra. What is more, using computers will make our job even easier.

COMPUTER ANALYSIS

Even if you have no intention of conducting any social research after completing this course, you will be constantly inundated with statistical analyses performed by others, from public opinion polls in the daily news media to complex analyses of product quality and production efficiency in the workplace. If nothing else, you need to learn how to interpret this information correctly, and the best way to learn quantitative analysis is to do it.

We have all struggled through plenty of mathematics during our educational experiences. These struggles usually involved working out problems with pencil and paper or occasionally a pocket calculator. The same approach could be used with all the statistics presented in this text, but it is neither necessary nor desirable. When social scientists collect observations to study, they usually obtain hundreds or sometimes thousands of observations. Even simple addition or subtraction with that many numbers is a truly formidable task.

Computers, which can perform thousands of calculations per second, are the preferred tool for analyzing large compilations of data. Instructing computers to perform statistical analyses once required complex programming techniques. Fortunately, current software makes the job much easier. One software program designed with the need of social scientists in mind is the *Statistical Package for the Social Sciences*, referred to by its acronym "SPSS."

In addition to discussing social science and statistics, this text covers use of the SPSS software. As each statistical technique is presented in the text, SPSS commands used to produce that statistic are also covered. To keep this from being merely an abstract exercise, data sets are distributed with the text which cover major social and political issues. You can practice each technique with the sample data set to deepen your comprehension of how quantitative analysis works and how it can be used to draw conclusions about the social and political worlds.

SUMMARY

These, then, are the topics of this text: the processes of science designed to produce objective information, the tools of statistics used to analyze information, and SPSS procedures which produce the statistics. Throughout each chapter, these three threads are constantly interwoven to complete the tapestry that is quantitative social science.

A hoped-for by-product of this effort is the thrill of discovery. Since grade school, your textbooks and instructors have largely provided you with the end results of research—conclusions drawn about what has been studied before. You now begin a journey of selecting your own topics and drawing your own conclusions. The journey is not without its pitfalls of errors and fogs of confusion, but it is both exciting and worthwhile.

REVIEW

Key Terms

Science

Epistemology

Common sense

Intuition

Rational

Empirical

Objective

Subjective

Replicability

Data

Data analysis

Statistic

SUGGESTED READINGS

Babbie, Earl. *The Practice of Social Research*, 5th ed. (Belmont, Calif.: Wadsworth, 1989) Chapter 1.

Hoover, Kenneth R. *The Elements of Social Scientific Thinking*, 4th ed. (New York: St. Martin's, 1988) Chapter 1.

Levin, Jack and James Alan Fox. *Elementary Statistics in Social Research*, 4th ed. (New York: Harper & Row, 1988) Chapter 1.

May, Richard B., Michael E. J. Masson, and Michael A. Hunter. *Application of Statistics in Behavioral Research* (New York: Harper & Row, 1990) Chapter 1.

Nachmias, David and Chava Nachmias. *Research Methods in the Social Sciences*, 3rd ed. (New York: St. Martin's, 1987) Chapter 1.

Chapter 2

An Overview of the Research Process

*B*efore we can analyze data, we must have data. Not just any data will do, for they must both provide the information we want and live up to the scientific goals of objectivity and replicability. To ensure that the research will accomplish these ends, scientists develop detailed designs of research projects before carrying them out.

Numerous works are available which thoroughly describe research design and the social research process. Some elements of the research process—the research focus, definition and measurement of variables, and the collection of data—are critical to a full understanding of the computer analysis of data. These topics are referred to continuously throughout the text and thus are reviewed briefly here. This chapter serves as a refresher for readers who have already taken a course on the research process and allows those without such background to work with and interpret the topics touched on in this text. Note, however, that the treatment of these key elements is highly simplified here, and any standard work on social research should be consulted for a fuller exposition of concepts that remain unclear.

THE RESEARCH FOCUS

To begin at the beginning, we need a topic to investigate. For concrete grounding, let us say we are curious about the topic of sexism. That is well and good, but selecting a topic is merely the first step. Our field of inquiry remains quite broad and uncertain. What, in particular, do we want to know about sexism? What causes it? Has it been increasing or decreasing over time? Does this university have more of it than others?

Observe that each way of describing the topic leads to a need for different information. The causes of sexist attitudes might be found in data covering early life experiences. The historical growth or decline of sexism requires evidence covering a span of years. To study the frequency of sexism at one campus versus another, data must be collected from more than one university. We simply do not know which data to collect until the research focus is clarified.

The Research Question

A handy way to clarify a topic is to state it in the form of a question. After selecting a topic, we ask ourselves, What do we want to know about this topic? The answer comprises the **research question**. The research question guides the data collection process, for we know to collect data which answer the question and to bypass information irrelevant to it.

Scientific research deals with two types of questions: questions of description and questions of explanation. **Descriptive research** seeks to describe what exists. Often this research is directed toward a general audience rather than other scientists. It appears regularly in the mass media: 55 percent of the public believes George Bush is doing a good job, 40 percent of high school students do not know geography, or 70 percent of citizens in Dallas oppose a city tax increase. Of the questions posed earlier, the latter two—has sexism increased or decreased over time and how does its frequency compare at two universities?—require descriptive information.

Description is useful, but scientists want to go beyond description to explanation, or **explanatory research**. Questions of explanation ask *why* things happen or exist as they do. Newton did not just observe an apple falling on his head; he asked why things fall to the earth. Marie Curie observed that photographic plates became fogged when they sat next to radium and asked why.

In the social sciences, we might ask, Why do blacks often fare more poorly on achievement tests than whites? or What factors led people to vote for Bush rather than Dukakis in the 1988 presidential election? Of our original questions, the question of what causes sexism (why some are sexist and others not) is one seeking explanation. The latter two questions could also be rephrased as questions of explanation by asking, Why has the level of sexism changed over time? or Why is sexism seen more frequently at one university than another?

Hypotheses

Having posed a question of explanation, we then do what will seem strange at first: We suggest answers to the question. Why do some people exhibit high levels and others low levels of sexism? It might be due to their level of education, or something in their background such as being raised in a one- versus two-parent family or growing up with opposite-sex versus same-sex siblings. We are suggesting, or hypothesizing, possible answers, and our suggestions are termed **hypotheses**.

Why do we suggest answers? Because neither science nor statistical analysis generates answers for us out of thin air. We do not divide a person's level of sexism by 20, take the cube root, and then watch the answer magically appear—the butler did it. What statistical analysis can do is tell us whether our observations of the world support our hypotheses. After making a number of observations, do we indeed find a relationship (statistical correlation) between the level of education and the level of sexism? Our hypotheses must come first, however, so we will know which data to collect—data on levels of sexism and education.

The statement of the research question points our research in a general direction, but still leaves our task too large to accomplish. The possible explanations for a person's level of sexism are more numerous than any research project could examine. With the statement of specific hypotheses, our research focus receives final closure. These particular explanations—our hypotheses—are what our research will examine to determine whether they are empirically verifiable.

Hypotheses and Variables

A hypothesis is a simple declarative sentence stating a relationship between two things, such as *A* is related to *B*. The explanations suggested earlier for levels of sexism produce three hypotheses.

H_1:   A person's level of education is related to his or her level of sexism.

H_2:   Whether a person was raised in a one- or two-parent family is related to her or his level of sexism.

H_3:   Whether a person was raised with opposite-sex siblings is related to his or her level of sexism.

The two things that hypotheses claim are related are called **variables**. A variable is a characteristic of the object being studied (person, book, rock, or whatever) that varies; it implies differences of degree or kind. Sexism and education involve differences of degree; they are things you can have more of or less of. Other variables represent differences of kind rather than amount, such as a person's race: white, black, Asian, or other. Variables representing the presence or absence of something—were you raised in a two-parent family or did you have siblings of the opposite sex?—are also differences of kind.

Variables are at the heart of the research process, for the questions we pose involve them: Why does some group have more or less of the characteristic (e.g., sexism) than another, or why does a group have this particular characteristic (e.g., voting for George Bush) rather than another? Because of their importance, the two variables contained in a hypothesis are given different names. One is called the dependent variable and the other the independent variable. The **dependent variable** is that variable which we are trying to explain. It is what the research is focused on—explaining levels of sexism. The **independent variables** are the explanations or reasons we suggest for the dependent variable: level of education, one- versus two-parent families, and opposite-sex siblings.

The dependent variable gets its name from the logic of the hypothesis; a person's level of sexism is affected by or *depends upon* that person's level of education. In contrast, the independent variables are just that, independent, for our hypotheses make no claims about what the variables depend on. Although it is not precisely accurate, a useful way to view independent and dependent variables is as cause and effect. The independent variables are the causes, and the dependent variable is the effect.

Research usually tries to explain only one thing at a time. Consequently, most research projects include one dependent variable but many independent variables. If you return to the hypotheses stated earlier, you will observe that each hypothesis contains the focus of our research, the dependent variable, sexism, but each also contains a different independent variable suggested as a possible cause of sexism.

Do not expect to find a bunch of variables running around with tags labeling them dependent or independent. Which is which is determined by the research question. We are investigating sexism, so it is our dependent variable, and level of education is our independent variable. Someone else may be investigating why some people are highly educated and others poorly educated. For that purpose, level of education is the dependent variable, and a suggested explanation, such as a parent's level of education, is the independent variable.

DEFINING AND MEASURING VARIABLES

To test hypotheses, we gather information on the two variables and determine if they are indeed related as the hypothesis claims. Before we collect information, however, we need to pin these variables down further. That involves us in conceptual and operational definitions.

Conceptual Variables

At this stage, the variables in our hypotheses are concepts, or conceptual variables. A **concept** is a mental construction, a word or phrase applied to things that exist which helps us organize the world into categories. We experience a bundle of feelings and call it love. We see that some people have little to live on and call it poverty. Shared concepts help us communicate with one another. When I describe someone as unethical, visions pop into your head of bribery, cheating, and other things you associate with the term "unethical."

While concepts help us communicate, it is not error-free communication. Each of us gives different shades of meaning to the concepts we use. Take the term we have already bandied about in this chapter, "sexism." What is it? Most of us could probably agree that some attitudes are sexist, such as the idea that women do not belong in the workplace or that a woman would not make as good a lawyer or president as a man. However, once we move beyond these extreme situations, we run into far less clear-cut cases. What about the armed services that bar women from combat? Is this a sexist policy or merely a realistic recognition that women are not well suited for combat? Or consider the practice at most universities of having separate athletic teams for women and men; is this sexist or a recognition of real physical differences? How about behavior that seems to benefit women, such as a man holding a door for a woman or insisting on paying for a date? Is this sexism or good manners?

Everyday conversation does not require error-free understanding; pretty close is good enough. But remember that science seeks replicability as a test of objectivity. Research cannot be replicated if everyone sees the variables as meaning different things. To produce replicable tests of hypotheses, first we must define the variables contained in each hypothesis. The defining process involves two stages, providing both conceptual definitions and operational definitions.

A **conceptual definition** uses words to define other words. It is akin to a dictionary type of definition. For example, we might define sexism as any distinction drawn between the sexes not absolutely mandated by physical differences. How does a conceptual definition help? Frankly, that depends on how good the definition is. A good conceptual definition should provide guidelines to what is and is not included in the concept. The definition above helps us make such decisions. Practices such as specialization in obstetrics and gynecology are not sexist because they are based on real physical differences, but for men to hold doors open for women is not required by their physical differences and thus, according to the definition, is sexist.

Take another variable, religiosity. We might define it conceptually as the depth of a person's commitment to a particular religion. Although it is not crystal-clear (no conceptual definition is), this definition does add some information about what religiosity is and is not. It is not the same as morality or spirituality, for one can be either moral or spiritual without adhering to a particular set of religious beliefs. It does include following the teachings and practices of a religion, for we cannot see how someone could be deeply committed to a religion while ignoring its teachings.

Remember, the defining process is an attempt to introduce greater clarity in our research. Defining a vague concept with terms that are equally vague does little good. Defining sexism as an illegitimate bias against one sex does nothing more than move the confusion from what is meant by sexism to what is meant by illegitimate. Similarly, while it is desirable to develop conceptual definitions that everybody agrees on, this is not absolutely necessary. The point of conceptual definitions is that others know what *we* mean by a term in our research. Using our definition, even if they disagree with it, others could replicate our research.

Supplement
2.1

Is It a Variable?

If you have a lot of difficulty in developing conceptual definitions, perhaps your suggested answers, the independent variables, are not really variables. A variable is a particular characteristic of people or things whose categories are both exhaustive and mutually exclusive. "Exhaustive" means that the variable uses up or exhausts all the cases being studied—everybody fits in some category. "Mutually exclusive" means that no single person fits in more than one category. Years of education is a variable, because everybody can be placed in some category from 0 to 20+ years of education and nobody can be placed in more than one category—you cannot have both 5 years and 8 years of education.

Our early and tentative answers to the research question may be global descriptions which are not really variables, such as the idea that a person's level of sexism is determined by her or his background. "Background" is a broad descriptor which includes many things that are not mutually exclusive. A person can be white or black; both blacks and whites can be Episcopalians or Baptists; Episcopalians and Baptists of all races can be raised in the West or the East—these are all parts of a person's background. Each part of the background is in fact a separate variable—race, religion, and region—which can be used to assign people to mutually exclusive categories. It is these particular variables which need to be ferreted out of the broader description and included in the hypotheses.

Operational Variables

Conceptual definitions are a necessary starting place, but only a starting place. They help clarify what we are looking at but are still general enough to allow some different interpretations, and thus individual subjectivity, to creep in. Having completed a conceptual definition, we must follow it with an **operational definition**. Operational definitions are so called because they specify precise operations to be followed in measuring a variable's quantity or presence. An operational measure of sexism might involve giving volunteers a quiz on whether women should or should not be treated differently from men in a series of 10 situations, such as selecting soldiers for combat duty, trying out for the football team, and so on. We define each yes answer as a sexist response, and so someone with 8 yes answers is twice as sexist as someone with only 4 yes answers. The quiz is what we use to collect data on sexism. It is also our operational definition of it, our measure of its presence, absence, or quantity.

It is useful to step back at this point and see what we have done. We began with a variable called "sexism," vague, ill defined, and open to multiple interpretations. We clarified the variable somewhat by providing a conceptual definition which eliminated some of, but not all, the different ways in which the concept could be interpreted. Finally, we moved to a specific set of operations used to measure sexism: If this happens, we call it sexism; if that happens, we do not. With this precise operational definition, our research can now be fully replicated. A woman or a man, young or old, liberal or conservative, literature major or business major, could observe the same group of people and, using our operational definition of sexism (our 10-question quiz), find the same amount of sexism as we did.

To the inexperienced, operational definitions pose problems. They are often seen as capricious, arbitrary attempts to measure the unmeasurable. They are none of these. Operational definitions are attempts to make explicit and clear the things we do unconsciously every day. Let us return to the illustration in Chapter 1, the student who claimed to see bias against George Bush in television newscasts. This student was reacting to some cues or things observed in the broadcast which related to his definition of bias. Such cues or things are usually unconscious, but, digging deep, we can bring them to the conscious level. When we do, we will find that these observable cues constitute operational definitions. "Did you notice how Dan Rather kept interrupting when Bush was talking?" Yes, interrupting is a measure of bias, so we can count how often reporters interrupted Bush and Dukakis to see whether one candidate suffered more bias than the other. "Well, it is not just that. They also gave Dukakis more coverage than Bush." Fine, let us count the seconds of coverage given to each candidate to measure bias. In sum, operational definitions formalize the cues we use to draw conclusions in everyday life.

Operational definitions are also quite familiar to us, just not in the social sciences. We are quite accustomed to them in other fields and do not think twice about using them. However, if we went back to their origins, very common operational measures would seem just as strange as those currently used in the social sciences. Consider distance, a concept dealing with how far apart things are, operationally measured with rulers or yardsticks. One unit of measurement, the foot, was originally based on the length of an English king's foot. Or think about weather reports. Early humans probably only noticed states of being, such as shivering or perspiring. Later names were given to these states—"hot" and "cold"—which are different categories of the variable "temperature." How do we measure how hot or cold we are? By watching mercury expand or contract in a little glass vial which is marked off in units called degrees.

In developing operational definitions or measures we are concerned with two things: their reliability and their validity. The **reliability** of a measure is its ability to produce the same result when used by different people. Operational measures are highly reliable because their specificity allows very little leeway for individual subjective biases to affect observations. What can be far more troublesome is an operational measure's **validity**—the extent to which it really captures the meaning of the concept. Another way to describe validity is as a match between a conceptual variable and an operational variable, as illustrated in Figure 2.1. The terms in our hypotheses are both concepts and variables and thus are labeled "conceptual variables." There is a thing called religiosity which exists in the world, and we readily speak of people being more or less religious. It is a variable represented by a thick middle line in Figure 2.1. We define this variable conceptually and thus end up with a clearer idea of its meaning, but it remains something we cannot measure directly. Consequently, we move to

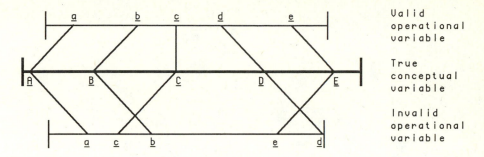

Figure 2.1 The match between conceptual and operational variables.

an operational definition, such as a person's frequency of church attendance. This produces our operational variable, the data we actually collect.

The operational variable is highly reliable, for we can precisely measure each person's position on the operational variable by merely counting how frequently he or she attends church, but is this a valid way to represent the broader concept of religiosity? If our operational variable is a valid one, how it places people in a high-to-low ranking should closely approximate their placement on the underlying conceptual variable. This is shown by the match between the top and middle lines in Figure 2.1. If our operational variable is an invalid measure of the concept, it will not be able to accurately represent people's levels on the conceptual variable, as shown by the mismatch between the middle and bottom lines of Figure 2.1.

Validity is a perennial concern in quantitative research. Hypotheses state relationships between conceptual variables, such as education is related to religiosity. Statistical tests, however, are performed on operational variables—Is the number of years of formal education correlated with the frequency of church attendance? To the extent that the operational variables are valid measures of the conceptual variables, the statistics can be used to draw conclusions about hypotheses.

Understanding this process, illustrated in Figure 2.2, is necessary to do our own research and to understand reports of other investigations. We are inundated with daily statements, such as 20 percent of teachers flunk competency tests or people in the United States favor gun control. We tend to accept such claims at face value, and we should not. Terms such as "teacher competency" and "gun control" are concepts, and we must look at how they are operationally defined before we accept the claims. Does gun control mean banning all firearms or simply requiring a waiting period before purchasing one? Is the ability to spell or do mathematics a good measure of the competency to teach?

Of course, conceptual variables often are not directly measurable, but they are described in our conceptual definitions. We test validity by assessing whether an operational measure seems to capture what is described in the conceptual definition. Since a deep commitment to a religion is probably associated with regular church attendance, we deem the latter to be a good operational measure of the former. This concern with validity is why we do not jump

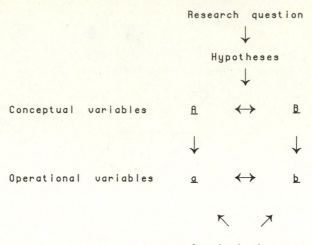

Figure 2.2 The research process.

immediately to operational definitions of a variable. We do not know what the operational variable really measures unless we can compare it to a conceptual definition of what it is supposed to measure.

COLLECTING DATA

The first two sections of this chapter dealt with becoming more and more precise in our research activities. We began with the research topic and moved from that to the basic research question, specific hypotheses, and defining the variables in the hypotheses both conceptually and operationally. We are now ready to begin collecting information. Let us first examine what we hope to end up with and then determine how we get there.

The information collection process consists of selecting a number of objects for study and then obtaining information from each object concerning our operational variables. If the hypothesis being tested is

H_1: Education is related to religiosity.

Then the objects we study will be people, and asking them how many years of education they have completed and how frequently they attend church may be our operational variables.

Once this information is collected, it can be arranged in a table or matrix, as shown in Figure 2.3. Listed on the left side of the matrix or table are the objects, in this case people, from whom we collected data. They are called **cases**. Each case provides information on our variables, which is called that case's **value** on the variable. Case 1 has a value of 4 on the years-of-education variable and a value of "daily" on the church attendance variable. It may seem strange

CASE	YEARS OF EDUCATION	CHURCH ATTENDANCE
1	2	Daily
2	12	Never
3	16	Weekly
4	4	Weekly
.	.	.
.	.	.
.	.	.
300	20	Daily

Figure 2.3 A sample data set.

to refer to a word such as "daily" as a value, a term that usually suggests numbers, but value merely refers to each case's characteristic on a variable. Each variable is contained in a single column and consists of all the values obtained for the cases in the study; the variable varies over these values. The total amount of information obtained by this study, each case's value on each variable, is referred to as our **data** or **data set**.

This is the information we want. Now how do we obtain it? To say that we are "collecting" data is often misleading, for it suggests that data are just lying about waiting to be found. In some cases this is true, as in collecting insects or archaeological artifacts. For many scientific studies, a more accurate term is the "generation" of data. A rock has weight, but there are no tags attached to the rocks with their weights neatly printed on them. The rock's weight must be generated, or made observable, by using a measuring instrument such as a scale. Similarly, a person's attitude toward the sexes is not lying on the street to be picked up. It must be elicited from the person, or generated, through questions. In the social sciences, the two most common ways of generating data are through controlled experiments and surveys. We look briefly at each.

Controlled Experiments

A **controlled experiment** is a research project in which the researcher can directly manipulate the independent variable. Say that a chemistry professor is concerned about student performance in his introductory chemistry course. His students have not been doing as well as he had expected, and he wonders why. His research question is, What factors lead to differences in student performance? One answer that he considers is the textbook being used; it might be too hard, too easy, or just poorly written. This leads to the hypothesis

H_1: Different textbooks are related to differences in student performance.

Since the semester is just about to start, the professor decides to test this hypothesis by using the students in one of his classes as subjects for the study. The class is divided into two groups. One group will use the same textbook that has been required in the past, and the other group will use a different textbook.

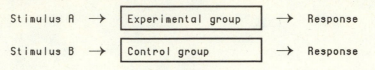

Figure 2.4 A stimulus-response model.

At the end of the semester, the professor will evaluate which group performed better.

This type of experiment is known as the stimulus-response approach or model, and it is illustrated in Figure 2.4. One group receives the **stimulus** or new stimulus (the new textbook), stimulus *A*. This group is designated the **experimental group**, for it is the focus of the experiment: Will the new textbook produce any change? The second group receives the old stimulus, stimulus *B*, or no stimulus at all and is called the **control group**. Each group has a **response**, their level of performance in the class.

Both experimental and control groups are necessary, for any number of factors may affect student performance. This group of students may be more dedicated than others, the professor may have changed his lecture notes, or topics related to chemistry, such as toxic waste or acid rain, may have been common news stories that semester. The two groups are selected to be as alike as possible, and both are affected by the same external forces, such as changed lecture notes and chemistry topics in the news. Since the two groups are the same in all respects save one, the stimulus received, any difference in the response should be due to the difference in the stimulus.

To translate the language of the controlled experiment to more familiar terms, the stimulus and the response are both variables. The stimulus is the independent variable or cause, and the response is the dependent variable or effect. At the end of the experiment we can tally the values of these variables, as shown for six sample cases in Figure 2.5.

Figure 2.5 also shows how we can use data generated through controlled experiments to test the hypothesis. The results suggest that the hypothesis is true: Most of those using textbook *A* performed better than those with textbook *B*. However, if our results were like those in Figure 2.6, we would conclude that the hypothesis was false: The textbooks appear to have no impact since just

CASE	TEXTBOOK (STIMULUS)	PERFORMANCE (RESPONSE)
1	A	High
2	A	High
3	A	Average
4	B	Average
5	B	Low
6	B	Low

Figure 2.5 Data generated by a controlled experiment.

CASE	TEXTBOOK (STIMULUS)	PERFORMANCE (RESPONSE)
1	A	High
2	A	Average
3	A	Low
4	B	High
5	B	Average
6	B	Low

Figure 2.6 Experimental data showing no relationship.

as many performed both well and poorly while using textbook *A* as did with textbook *B*.

Surveys

The essence of a controlled experiment is the researcher's ability to control the conditions of the experiment and to manipulate the stimulus received by each group (the type of textbook used, viewing of selected campaign commercials, or being treated with different therapeutic approaches). Controlled experiments are a highly reliable form of generating information. They are also clearly limited to areas in which the independent variable can be manipulated by the experimenter. In some social science fields, such as psychology and media studies, this is possible, but in other areas it is not.

Many social science questions deal with stimuli that cannot be manipulated in a laboratory, such as whether a person's level of sexism is related to the presence or absence of opposite-sex siblings. Here the stimulus is type of sibling, supposedly leading to different levels of sexism, the response. We cannot divide subjects into two groups and then manipulate the stimulus by waving a magic wand and saying, "People in group 1 now have both brothers and sisters, but those in group 2 have brothers only."

When the stimulus cannot be manipulated, we turn to **surveys** as a source of information. We select a group of people for study and ask them questions about their existing attitudes or characteristics, rather than trying to introduce new ones in a laboratory. We end up with the same things—two variables, as shown in Figure 2.7—which we examine to see whether differences on the first

CASE	OPPOSITE-SEX SIBLINGS	WOMEN TREATED SAME AS MEN
1	Yes	Yes
2	Yes	Yes
3	Yes	No
4	No	No
5	No	No
6	No	No

Figure 2.7 Data collected through a survey.

variable are related to differences on the second. In its broadest meaning, a survey is an assessment of objects in their natural state, rather than in a laboratory setting, for example, a survey of books in the library to evaluate their condition, a survey of the type of plant and animal life in a meadow, or, most common in the social sciences, a survey of people's attitudes.

These abbreviated descriptions of controlled experiments and surveys hardly do justice to the full complexity of either technique. Readers should consult texts on research design for a thorough explanation of these, and other, strategies for generating data. They are included here both as a reminder of where data originate and as background for later references in this text, designed to help illustrate the proper interpretation of our data analysis results.

As an example of the latter, we have already touched on one item relevant to data generation strategies: conceptual and operational variables. The data produced by either strategy are operational variables that we presume reflect a more abstract concept. The chemistry professor uses course grades to measure knowledge of chemistry, a quite reasonable approach as long as these grades are based on fair tests of student knowledge and not irrelevant factors such as biases for or against student athletes, women, or the like. On surveys, the questions asked constitute the operational definitions of concepts, and the answers given are the values for the operational variables in the data set.

The creation of tests in controlled experiments or questions on a survey thus must be sensitive to concerns of validity and reliability. Validity can be undermined by poor wording of the question, a problem plaguing most surveys conducted by amateurs. For example, the question "Should we negotiate arms reductions with the Soviet Union or continue our military buildup?" combines two different things in one question. Someone who wants to negotiate a reduction in nuclear arms but continue our buildup of conventional forces will have difficulty answering. Since we do not know to which part of the question people are responding, the answers tell us little about people's actual attitudes toward defense issues.

The reliability of survey questions depends largely on whether open-ended or close-ended question are used. In an **open-ended question** each person is permitted to answer in her or his own words. This gives people a chance to express their exact feelings, but leads to difficulties in comparing the answers. Asking how people feel about Michael Dukakis may lead two people to give the following open-ended answers: "He seems like a nice person, but he made a number of mistakes as governor of Massachusetts," and "He is not very friendly, but I really like his position on defense spending." Which of these answers shows a greater "liking" for Dukakis? Judgment must be used to answer that question—judgment affected by individual subjectivity.

To produce answers that are easily compared, **close-ended questions** are normally used. These are questions followed by specific answers from which the respondent chooses one. An example is

Would you say you like Michael Dukakis

_____ very much _____ a fair amount _____ a little _____ not at all?

The preset answers can be readily used by people of all ideological stripes without subjective filters affecting their interpretation of the responses.

The surveys included with this text for both illustrations and student exercises were conducted by highly professional organizations and can be relied upon to be fair and accurate. Nonetheless, they remain operational variables, and we must always ask ourselves what concept(s) we are measuring with them. When we ask people whether they find life exciting, routine, or dull, are we measuring how exciting those people's lives really are or their psychological state (well adjusted versus depressed)? Actually, this question might legitimately be used to measure either concept, but we must know in our own minds what we are trying to measure with a particular operational variable if we are to assess that variable's validity and its utility in drawing conclusions about the social or political world.

SELECTING CASES FOR STUDY

One topic we have not yet broached is where our cases, the subjects of our study, come from. Our goal is to be able to draw conclusions about a particular group of individuals or objects. This group is called the **population**. A typical population for social science studies consists of all U.S. citizens over age 18, but other populations are not uncommon, such as all members of Congress, all military veterans, or all women living in Detroit.

Most populations are too large to examine in entirety, so we draw a **sample** from the population for study. The sample itself is not the focus of our interest. We are not particularly curious about how a grandmother in New Orleans or a cab driver from Hoboken voted in the 1988 presidential election. Our sample is a tool used to study the population, and the quality of our study depends on the quality of our sample.

Drawing Samples

What we desire is a **representative sample**, one that matches the population characteristics. If the population consists of 2 percent black college-educated women and 10 percent white blue-collar males who are Republicans, we want our sample to contain the same proportions of each group. Representative samples can be drawn in many ways, but the most familiar is a **simple random sample**, also known as an **equal-probability sample**. In collecting cases for study, each member of the population must have an equal probability of being selected for the sample; there is no bias for or against some population groups. If our selection of cases for the sample is truly random, then we do have an equal-probability sample. The very definition of "random" means that our choices are not affected by personal preferences; one person has as much chance of being selected as another.

We cannot rely on our own judgment to draw a random sample, for subjective feelings will come into play. Sampling students at your university by just talking to people "at random" will not work. Without your realizing it, your

Table 2.1 A RANDOM NUMBER TABLE

Row	A	B	C	D	E	F
1	626	699	096	598	193	844
2	356	174	132	686	047	520
3	406	169	**615**	954	548	674
4	916	791	039	674	536	969
5	038	193	101	068	524	803
6	069	651	032	600	496	034
7	154	656	090	232	418	319
8	721	105	868	162	369	558
9	290	730	896	338	556	529
10	935	457	403	016	433	620
11	612	794	616	761	418	555
12	417	867	677	886	168	290
13	598	347	463	075	092	827
14	759	334	544	253	911	656
15	027	294	100	167	586	099
16	078	508	152	658	753	059
17	172	912	784	470	315	332
18	414	795	878	695	344	611
19	773	353	154	386	742	839
20	109	138	921	038	093	304
21	138	518	594	734	936	265
22	864	787	810	626	236	207
23	374	520	178	060	003	229
24	767	470	182	732	512	429
25	921	642	387	390	264	652

subconscious leads you to avoid certain types of students—those at the far end of the campus where you seldom go, students with evening classes only, or older students your fear might actually be professors. Haphazard techniques will produce a biased sample, one that contains more of some types of population members than others.

An equal-probability sample begins with a **sampling frame**, a complete list of all members of the population. For a sample of students, you might use a student directory or a list of current students provided by the registrar as your sampling frame. From the sampling frame, cases are selected for inclusion in the sample via a table of random numbers, typically generated by a computer (Table 2.1). The table might lead us to pick person 615 in the sampling frame, then person number 39, and so on—all without our personal biases affecting the selections.

Randomization and Controlled Experiments

The random selection of cases is vital in survey research where we usually study attitudes and opinions. Any number of population characteristics might affect opinions, so we need to use random selection techniques to ensure that our sample cases possess these characteristics in proportions representative of the population. Some controlled experiments also require broadly representative samples, but others do not. Many experiments deal with stimuli that should affect all or most people in the same way. We do not expect that Catholics and Episcopalians will differ in their reactions to a new cold remedy, so the cases selected for study do not need to be representative of these groups.

Even though a controlled experiment may not require a perfectly representative sample, it does require something else—that the control and experimental groups be alike in all respects except for the stimulus received. The professor testing the efficacy of different textbooks may have a personal favorite. Subconsciously, he may pick his best students to be in the group treated with that textbook. If this group ends up with the best improvement scores, would it be because of the textbook or because this group contained brighter students?

This problem is dealt with in two ways. One is to match the groups as closely as possible—each contains the same proportions of brighter students, seniors, or chemistry majors. The second solution is to randomize group membership, again using a random number table. Subjects with the lowest numbers comprise group 1, those with the next-lower numbers go to group 2, and so on. Random assignment avoids selection bias and provides a high probability that the members of each group will be similar, except, of course, for the stimulus.

The random selection of cases does not guarantee either that a sample will be perfectly representative or that control and experimental groups will be absolutely identical. What random selection does ensure is that any disparity from these norms is due to random error only, not selection bias. Unlike subjective bias, which we may be unable to measure or even may be unaware of, random error follows clear rules of probability. Later we examine how it is possible to determine the amount of error that samples may possess and thus estimate how closely the cases we study match the ideal of perfectly representative samples or perfectly matched comparison groups.

SUMMARY

The techniques described in this chapter are all devoted to the elimination of subjective bias, eliminating it in making observations and eliminating it in selecting cases to observe. Following these techniques provides objectivity in the data we collect and replicability in the studies we conduct.

The techniques described here also help us to interpret our environment. A good opinion survey requires a clearly identified population and a sample carefully drawn to be representative of that population. Supposed surveys are reported all the time which meet neither criterion. Commercial advertisements are major offenders, relying heavily on **testimonials**, in which people are willing to say that a certain product works well. If you look hard enough, you can always find someone willing to say that almost any product performs brilliantly. Testimonials are clearly not representative samples and tell us little about how the average user feels about a product's performance. Additionally, any survey in which the respondents select themselves is immediately suspect, for only the most motivated will participate, not a representative sample. Surveys in which viewers call in opinions to radio and television stations are common examples.

Along with biased samples, biased questions are not unheard of. Even a slight change in question wording will produce quite different responses. The results from asking the question, "Do you favor increasing teachers' salaries?" will not be the same as the results from asking, "Do you favor *raising taxes* to increase teachers' salaries?" Some groups occasionally take advantage of differences in question wording to produce whatever survey results they want to see.

The brief synopses of research strategies discussed in this chapter illustrate that scientists must take care to obtain data that are reliable, valid, and representative of the group being studied. Having objective information is vital, but not sufficient. The data must now be analyzed in a way that is both practical and logical. Thus in Chapter 3 we introduce computers and the SPSS software.

REVIEW

Key Terms

Research question	Validity	Surveys
Descriptive research	Cases	Open-ended question
Explanatory research	Value	Close-ended questions
Hypotheses	Data	Population
Variables	Data set	Sample
Dependent variable	Controlled	Representative sample
Independent variables	experiment	Simple random sample
Concept	Stimulus	Equal-probability
Conceptual definition	Experimental group	sample
Operational definition	Control group	Sampling frame
Reliability	Response	Testimonials

Exercises

2.1 Below are a number of concepts that appear regularly in everyday discussions. Each can be the focus of a different research project. Pick one and proceed through the steps of the research process: State a research question, develop hypotheses, and define variables both conceptually and operationally.

Racism	Honesty	Athletic ability
Happiness	Liberal	Candidate support
Political information	Political activism	Conservative

2.2 Collect about a half-dozen clippings from newspapers or magazines describing some "scientific" studies. To the best of your ability, try to identify each study's research question, hypotheses, conceptual variables, and operational variables.

2.3 Below are some research topics. Identify the population relevant to each.
  a. Are most southerners religious fundamentalists?
  b. How many books or periodicals in the university library have pages missing?

    c. Why did most voters prefer George Bush to Michael Dukakis in the 1988 presidential election?

    d. What do people in the United States think about Star Wars?

    e. Are homosexuals less religious than heterosexuals?

2.4 Pick one of the topics from Exercise 2.1. Examine, in a descriptive sense only, what the students at your university are like on the topic picked (their level of racism, liberalism, etc.).

    a. Develop survey questions that will assess the students' level on the variable and write them up as a questionnaire.

    b. Select and identify the population that interests you. It can be all the students or just a select group such as seniors or social science majors.

    c. Find a sampling frame to use, and select a random sample of students to examine, using the random number table in Table 2.1.

2.5 Administer the questionnaire described in Exercise 2.4 and develop a data matrix similar to Figure 2.1 based on the data obtained. Keep this data matrix available because it will be used for exercises in later chapters.

2.6 From the clippings collected for Exercise 2.2 try to identify the type of study performed (survey versus controlled experiment), the population, the size of the sample, how people were selected for the sample, and whether the sample appears representative.

SUGGESTED READINGS

Babbie, Earl. *The Practice of Social Research,* 5th ed. (Belmont, Calif.: Wadsworth, 1989) Chapters 2–12.

Converse, Jean M. and Stanley Presser. *Survey Questions,* Quantitative Applications in the Social Sciences, Sage University Papers Series No. 63 (Newbury Park, Calif.: Sage Publications, 1986).

Freedman, David, et al. *Statistics,* 2nd ed. (New York: W. W. Norton, 1991) Chapters 1, 2, 19.

Hoover, Kenneth R. *The Elements of Social Scientific Thinking,* 4th ed. (New York: St. Martin's, 1988) Chapters 2–6.

Kalton, Graham. *Introduction to Survey Sampling,* Quantitative Applications in the Social Sciences, Sage University Papers Series No. 35 (Newbury Park, Calif.: Sage Publications, 1983).

May, Richard B., Michael E. J. Masson, and Michael A. Hunter. *Application of Statistics in Behavioral Research,* (New York: Harper & Row, 1990) Chapter 2.

Nachmias, David and Chava Nachmias. *Research Methods in the Social Sciences,* 3rd ed. (New York: St. Martin's, 1987) Chapters 2–12.

Spector, Paul E. *Research Designs,* Quantitative Applications in the Social Sciences, Sage University Papers Series No. 23 (Newbury Park, Calif.: Sage Publications, 1981).

Chapter
3

Using SPSS

Before delving directly into SPSS commands, we need a brief overview of how computers operate and where the SPSS system fits into this operation. We do that here by reviewing computer hardware and software, including SPSS; features of different operating systems; the unique features of SPSS/PC+ and Release 4; and prompted sessions in SPSS.

COMPUTER HARDWARE AND SOFTWARE

Computers come in two broad types, **mainframe computers** and **microcomputers**, which are also referred to as **personal computers** (PCs). Mainframe computers and personal computers operate similarly, but mainframes are far larger and faster, can handle bigger and more complex tasks, and can serve many users at once. There is also a third type of computer between these two in size, called a "minicomputer," but the differences between minicomputers and mainframe computers are not important for our purpose, so we refer to both as mainframe computers.

A computer is not a single machine, but a group of connected machines and their operating instructions, called a **computer system**. Since each organization has different needs, each computer system will be a little bit different from the others. However, all share similar components, and we begin by looking at the common features of computer hardware.

Computer Hardware

A computer system's **hardware** consists of the actual mechanical or physical features of the system. All computers have three main components: the central processing unit, input and output devices, and storage devices. Figure 3.1 illustrates these components for an average mainframe computer system.

The "brain" of the computer system is the **central processing unit (CPU)**. The CPU is the unit that actually performs the tasks we associate with computers; it calculates numbers, sends messages to different parts of the system, and generally controls the entire system's operation.

We communicate with the CPU through input and output devices. **Input devices** send messages to the CPU, and the CPU gives its response through **output devices**. On a hand calculator, the input device is the keypad. Typing "2 + 3 = " gives messages to the processing chip in the calculator. The messages contain data and commands. The data are the numbers (2 and 3), and the commands are our requests for the computer to do something with the numbers—"+" tells the calculator to add the numbers and " = " tells the calculator

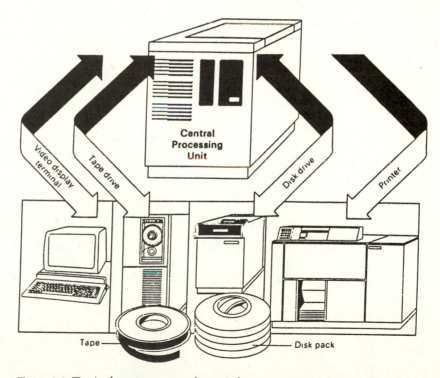

Figure 3.1 Typical components of a mainframe computer system. (*Source*: John Hedderson, *SPSS-X Made Simple*, Figure 1.1, Wadsworth Publishing Co., 1987, p. 11 © 1987 by Wadsworth, Inc. All rights reserved. Reprinted by permission of the publisher.)

to display the result. The result is displayed on an output device, the calculator's visual display.

A variety of input devices exist, including card readers that interpret the punched holes on stiff, heavy paper cards or optical readers that interpret answer sheets from standardized tests or bar codes on retail products. You will probably use a **video display terminal (VDT)**. This terminal contains a typewriter-type keyboard and a television-like screen. The programmer enters data and commands directly on the screen through the keyboard and then sends this information electronically to the CPU. A microcomputer's keyboard and monitor are equivalent to a mainframe terminal. Microcomputers users may work with a second input device as well, a handheld pointer, called a "mouse," discussed more later in this chapter.

Computers use three main types of output devices. First, the same video display terminal that is used for input *to* the CPU can be used for output *from* the CPU. The computer will simply display the results on the screen for you to look at. Second, a printer provides a printed version (called "hard copy") of the results. Third, output may be directed to a storage device for saving and examining at the analyst's leisure. You can select the type of output you wish. The choice is largely a matter of personal preference.

Storage devices are what they sound like, machines and recording media used to store large amounts of information. Let us say that you conducted a survey of 300 college students with each student responding to 50 survey questions. That is a lot of information to type into a VDT every time you want to analyze something from the survey. By using a storage device, you enter the data once and store them in the computer system. At any point in the future, you can then call back and analyze the data. Thus using a storage device is like saving important documents in a file cabinet.

One storage device is the **disk pack**, called a **hard disk** on a microcomputer. Disk packs are quite fast, moving information between the storage device and the CPU very quickly, and they can store enormous amounts of information. However, it is also difficult to move disk packs or hard disks from one computer to another. More transportable forms of storage exist. For mainframes, **computer tapes**—large reels or smaller plastic containers of recording tape—are used for transportable storage. Microcomputers use **floppy disks**, $5\frac{1}{4}$- or $3\frac{1}{2}$-in. disks which can be inserted into and removed from the CPU box, for transportable storage. Transportable storage devices are slower than disks packs or hard disks and cannot store nearly as much information, but they can be moved from computer to computer.

The SPSS Software

We use computers all the time, often without thinking about it, because most are dedicated, single-purpose computers. Hand calculators, automated teller machines at banks, and registers at retail stores are all single-purpose computers that perform specific tasks only. Mainframes and microcomputers are general-purpose computers. Because they can perform a wide variety of different tasks they are both more flexible than special-purpose computers and more difficult to use. To serve many functions, general-purpose computers do not have sets of predetermined tasks performed at the touch of a button, but instead must be instructed, or **programmed**, to perform each task required. Programs are called **software**; they are a series of instructions detailing how the CPU should read, process, and display the output from a task.

To program a computer, you have to learn a language that the computer understands, just as a conversation between you and a non-English-speaking person is not possible until one of you learns the other's language. Computers can speak many languages. At the bottom (called a "low-level language") there is **machine language**. Computers are essentially nothing more than a series of off/on switches, and the computer understands only whether a given switch (out of maybe millions of switches in the entire machine) is off or on. Programming in machine language requires using a binary, or base 2, language; a series of 0s and 1s represents whether a given switch is on or off. For example, the series of numbers 00010101110110101 might be the machine language equivalent of the instructions "2 + 3 = " entered on a hand calculator.

One function of most software programs is to introduce a high-level language to the computer and translate between the high-level language and machine language. A high-level language uses words and symbols which have everyday meaning. For example, to add and subtract numbers in a high-level language, we might write

COMPUTE X = 6 + 8 − 12

which tells the computer to add 6 and 8, subtract 12, and assign the result to the symbol X. The software program then translates these common words and numbers to a set of machine language instructions for the CPU and also translates the result of the CPU's actions from machine language back to words and numbers for display on an output device.

SPSS acts as a translator from high-level to low-level language, but it cannot translate any old word or symbol we care to type. The SPSS software contains a specific set of words that it understands, words such as COMPUTE, FREQUENCIES, and CORRELATIONS. These words are called SPSS **commands**. Upon reading the words we type, SPSS examines an internal dictionary to locate that word. Upon finding it, the computer carries out the actions associated with that command. If SPSS cannot find a word we have entered, it displays an error message, indicating it does not understand what we want it to do.

SPSS commands consist of three main parts: the main SPSS command, one or more **subcommands**, and options or **specifications** for each subcommand. For example, from a survey of 300 college students we may want to determine how many were males versus females. This simple counting function is performed by the SPSS command FREQUENCIES. Once the counting is completed, how do we want the results displayed, as a mere count of *X* males and *Y* females or as a bar chart displaying which group was larger? We can use the FORMAT subcommand, telling SPSS to change the output format, with the specification BARCHART, identifying the display format desired, to produce output as bar charts rather than numerical counts. Each remaining chapter in this text explains a single SPSS command, including an examination of the subcommands and specifications available with it. In addition, we will learn **command syntax**. Just as words must be arranged in a certain pattern to make an understandable sentence, commands, subcommands, and specifications must be entered in a particular fashion for SPSS to fully understand what we want it to do.

One caveat here, SPSS is a very powerful tool. It can perform some quite exotic statistical analyses and can also perform basic procedures in a variety of ways. These aspects of SPSS's power will be slighted by this text, for our purpose is to provide the beginner with enough background to perform rudimentary statistical analyses. The SPSS language is far richer than the content of an introductory text can possibly reveal. Comprehensive reference manuals for the SPSS software exist, and most computer installations have libraries of reference manuals that users may consult. Once you become familiar with basic SPSS commands, you may wish to examine a reference manual for additional features of the software.

SPSS Forms and Versions

SPSS is not a single software program, but multiple programs, depending on the type of computer and version you are using. This text can be used with all SPSS software, but, to keep the narrative neat, it focuses on SPSS-X version 3.0 as it is used on IBM mainframe computers. Separate segments introduced in each chapter describe other implementations of the software. These implementations are briefly described below along with how this text will refer to each.

The SPSS software was developed for use on IBM mainframes and later expanded to other mainframes. Software producers continually update their products to both add improvements and adapt to changing computer hardware. Each change produces a new **version** of the software. Each version is identified by whole and decimal numbers, such as version 1.0 or 2.21. A change in the decimal number of a version usually represents only a small modification of the software; thus the difference between version 1.02 and version 1.16 would usually not require any major adjustments in use of the software. Major changes are indicated when the version's whole number changes, such as from 1.01 to 2.0, and major changes often include new commands or different ways of implementing old commands.

A few years ago SPSS introduced so many changes to the software that it was renamed entirely, from SPSS to **SPSS-X**. Further improvements in the software have led to version changes, and the latest is SPSS-X version 3.0. An earlier version of SPSS-X, version 2.0, is still used at many computer installations and is discussed in this text as well. Whenever differences exist between versions 2 and 3 of SPSS-X, the symbol (v.2) will appear in the text to warn version 2 users that the marked paragraphs do not apply. Immediately following the marked paragraph(s) will be a discussion of how the earlier version differs.

Following the growth of microcomputers, a microcomputer version of SPSS was produced, called **SPSS/PC+**. SPSS/PC+ is available only for IBM microcomputers using the disk operating system. The command structure and syntax of SPSS/PC+ are similar in many ways to those of version 2 of SPSS-X, although differences exist in how the commands are entered. Additionally, SPSS/PC+ is a somewhat stripped-down version of the SPSS software since, at the time it was introduced, microcomputers lacked both memory and speed to use all the features available with the mainframe SPSS-X. Where a difference exists between SPSS-X 3.0 and SPSS/PC+, the symbol (PC) appears to warn readers of the difference. Then, at the end of the chapter is a discussion of how SPSS/PC+ implements the command covered in the chapter.

In 1990, SPSS introduced version 4.0 of the software which is called **Release 4**. Release 4 not only adds some new features, but also integrates the different forms of SPSS. Mainframe versions no longer use the "−X" label, nor do microcomputer versions use the "PC+" label; all are simply called SPSS. SPSS Release 4 contains the same commands and statistical procedures on all computers where it is available—IBM and VAX mainframes as well as Macintosh microcomputers and IBM microcomputers using the OS/2 operating system. Release 4 is not (as of this writing) available for IBM microcomputers using the disk operating system, and users of those microcomputers must still rely on SPSS/PC+.

Release 4 of SPSS on IBM mainframes differs only slightly from SPSS-X version 3. On microcomputers and VAX mainframes, Release 4 differs quite a bit from SPSS-X, primarily in its use of menus to select commands or files. Whenever a discussion of SPSS-X version 3 does not match the command structure or output of Release 4, the (R4) symbol appears in the text. Release 4 differences are then discussed either in a following paragraph or at the end of the chapter, depending on the nature of the difference between Release 4 and SPSS-X version 3. Because the IBM mainframe implementations of SPSS-X and SPSS Release 4 differ so little, the "Release 4" label is used in later chapters to refer to non-IBM mainframe applications, unless explicitly stated otherwise.

Through the use of this marker strategy, the narrative of each chapter should flow smoothly while simultaneously allowing people not using IBM mainframes to quickly find those differences that apply to them. The next section discusses the source of most of the differences—computer operating systems. This section should be of value to most readers, both explaining the nature of the differences mentioned in later chapters and describing the operating system terminology used in those chapters. Following the discussion of operating systems is an introduction to SPSS/PC+; Release 4 for VAX, OS/2, and Macintosh users; and interactive processing with these operating systems and the CMS system on IBM mainframes.

OPERATING SYSTEMS

Along with the SPSS program itself, there is a second software program we need to be familiar with, a computer's operating system. An **operating system** performs the housekeeping tasks needed for a computer's operation and is always present whenever a computer is running, even when another software program, such as SPSS, is being used.

Files

Much of what an operating system does is to organize and manipulate files. A computer **file** is a collection of related items stored under a unique name. A file might be a software program, such as SPSS, data from a survey, or the contents of a term paper. We tell computers to do things with a file by using the file's name for identification. Consequently, no two files are allowed to have the same name, to avoid confusion.

We often describe files as being of different types, such as command files, raw data files, or system files. Each label describes the contents of the file; for example, a command file may contain a series of SPSS commands that we have typed while a data file may contain the results of a particular experiment or survey. These labels are useful ways to think about files and are important to the SPSS software, which does different things with different types of files. At the operating system level, however, a file is a file is a file, and its contents are seldom important.

An operating system acts as a secretary or traffic cop for files stored on a computer. A primary job of the operating system is to manage files—save them, name them, rename them, copy a file from one storage device to another, erase old files, or list the names of all files present on a storage device. The operating system also determines how the CPU receives commands and where CPU output will go. All other software programs must work though a computer's operating system to both manipulate files and communicate with the CPU.

Each operating system is different, and you will need to learn the operating system for your particular computer before using SPSS—information that can be provided by your instructor or computer operator. Fortunately, it does not take long to learn the basics of any operating system. Since all software works through a computer's operating system, SPSS will behave a little differently on each operating system. Below are some key differences between operating systems.

Storing and Using Files

Any storage device can contain a large number of files. When we want to use a particular file, say, some survey data to be analyzed, it is important for the computer to be able to find the file quickly. One way to do this is for each storage device to have a different name. Most IBM microcomputers and compatibles (those made to work as IBM PCs do) use the *disk operating system* (DOS). DOS uses the name "C:" for a hard disk connected to the microcomputer (and "D:" and "E:" if you have two or three hard disks) and "A:" and "B:" for floppy disk drives (most microcomputers have two floppy drives). Thus to refer to file ROSE.DAT on hard disk C:, we type in

```
C:ROSE.DAT
```

Other operating systems use names for disk drives as well, but most allow users to choose storage device names. A disk pack may be named EDPAK1 or A1, and a Macintosh hard disk might be named CHARLIE.

Even with a different name for each storage device, locating a particular file on a hard disk that may contain hundreds of files can be quite tedious. To further ease the process, storage devices can be divided into smaller segments, usually called **directories** or **libraries** and, on Macintosh computers, **folders**. Placing related files within directories, such as all data files in one directory and all term papers created with a text processor in another, allows you to move quickly to find the file you want. Directories can be subdivided further by creating additional directories within them, often called **subdirectories**. For example, a directory of all SPSS files may contain two subdirectories, one for storing data files and the other for storing command files.

Directories are a filing system. Think of yourself sitting in an office that contains a dozen file cabinets with all of your records in them. You want to find a particular item, a receipt for the defective stereo which should be still under warranty if you can find the proof of purchase. Each file cabinet (directory) is labeled by what it contains: lecture notes, rent receipts, automobile records, and the item you want, charge cards. Going to that particular file cabinet, you find each drawer (subdirectory) has a separate label: VISA, Mastercard, and American Express. Opening the VISA drawer, you find it is divided into sections by year (sub-subdirectory). You go to the section for the year in which you bought the stereo and find the receipt (a specific file). Without some organizing system, you would have to examine every slip of paper in all the file cabinets to find that receipt. With everything neatly organized, you go immediately to the right location and find what you want.

Directories divide large storage devices in a similar manner, as illustrated in Figure 3.2. When you first start working with the hard disk, you are in the **root directory**, which is the main directory of the entire hard disk. Some files may be stored at this level, but mostly you will see the names of directories in which groups of related files are stored. Moving to one of these directories, say STATS, shows you what it contains, which may be files or even more directories (subdirectories). Moving deeper still into the SPSS subdirectory allows you to

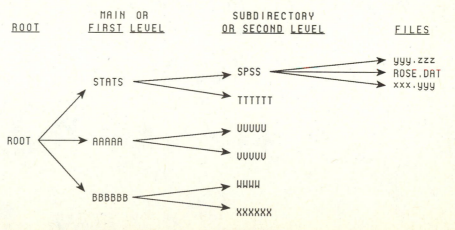

Figure 3.2 Dividing a hard disk into directories.

see what files it contains, which in this case includes the file we are looking for, ROSE.DAT.

We often refer to files while using the SPSS software, fetching a data file we want to analyze or saving some output as a file for printing later. To allow the operating system to find or save files, we may need to specify a **path** to the file. A path is also called a **multilevel file name**, a file name which includes the storage device, directory, and subdirectory containing the file. A path to the ROSE.DAT file in Figure 3.2 is

    C:\STATS\SPSS\ROSE.DAT

It goes from storage device C:, from the root directory (\) to the STATS directory (STATS\) to the SPSS subdirectory (SPSS\) to file ROSE.DAT. Multilevel file names are used by nearly all operating systems, but since each system names and stores files differently, you will need to learn the practices of your operating system to be able to find the file you want.

Command versus Menu-Driven

DOS and most mainframe operating systems are **command-driven**. That is, to perform some function on a file, you must type in a command identifying both the function and the file on which it is to be performed. For example, to make a copy of a file named ROSE.DAT with DOS, use the command

    COPY ROSE.DAT TULIP.DAT

The second file, TULIP.DAT, will be an exact copy of ROSE.DAT but has a different name since no two files with the same name should exist—at least not in the same directory.

Command-driven operating systems usually also receives commands and display files using text (letters or numbers) only. If you asked to see the contents of a particular storage device, the results might look like Figure 3.3: the names of the three files (ROSE.DAT, ROSE.COM, and TULIP.DAT) and two directories (SPSS and TEXT) present in the main directory. Directories are indicated

```
C:\>
C:\>dir

   Directory of   C:\

ROSE      DAT    25276    2-03-88   2:31p
ROSE      COM      162   12-21-90   3:28p
TULIP     DAT      129   12-21-90   3:28p
SPSS            <DIR>    11-14-90   1:47p
TEXT            <DIR>    11-14-90   1:47p
     5 File(s)     8998912 bytes free

C:\>
```

Figure 3.3 A listing of file names on a command-driven system.

with the "⟨DIR⟩" symbol. The total amount of storage space each file uses is also given along with the date that the file was created.

A **menu-driven** operating system contains many file management commands as menu options which you select rather than typing in. Menu-driven systems often have other features as well. Many have a second input device, called a **mouse**, in addition to the keyboard. A mouse is a small object that fits in the palm of your hand. As you move the mouse across a desktop, a pointer on the computer screen moves as well. The mouse and pointer are used to select items such as menu choices. A number of menu-driven systems also use graphics to display files instead of text.

Figure 3.4 shows a Macintosh display which is menu-driven and uses both graphics and a mouse. To the right of the screen are pictures, called **icons**, showing the disk drives currently in use: two hard disks, aProg and bData, and one floppy disk, Floppy #1. The picture in the middle of the screen displays the contents of the hard disk aProg—the same three files and two directories as contained in the command-driven illustration of Figure 3.3 but now represented by icons. The folders are directories containing more files that you will see only if you open the folder (move to the directory).

To work with a file, first you select it by pointing to it with the mouse's arrow and clicking a button on the mouse. The ROSE.DAT file is highlighted, showing that it has been selected for some action. Across the top of the screen is the menu bar, a series of words representing different categories of commands. Moving the mouse pointer to one of these choices and depressing the mouse button will display the choices available within that menu category, such as COPY, PRINT, or DELETE. Picking one of these choices performs that action on the selected file.

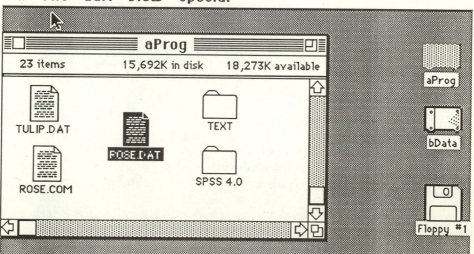

Figure 3.4 A Macintosh display screen.

Command-driven and menu-driven differences extend beyond the operating system into the SPSS software itself. Microcomputer and VAX implementations of Release 4, as well as SPSS/PC+, can use menus to enter commands even when the operating system is command-driven. The menus are only options, and commands can be typed in directly as in a command-driven system. This text will emphasize command-driven implementations of SPSS, but menu choices are also reviewed when available.

Editors

When using a typewriter, you must perform many actions physically; you insert paper, erase mistakes, use a copying machine for copies, and the like. A computer **editor** is the electronic equivalent of these actions, performing them electronically rather than physically.

With an editor you create a **text file**, so called because the computer treats anything entered into the file as text to be stored, *not* as commands to be carried out. The reason is that we do not want the CPU to act immediately on any words entered into a text area, for the command may be unfinished, contain typographical errors to be corrected, or not make sense unless it is part of a complete program. An editor allows us to enter and modify commands (or data). Functions performed by editors include inserting letters into or deleting them from words we have typed and inserting, deleting, moving, or copying entire lines of text or even blocks (multiple lines) of text. When we are satisfied that what we have typed is accurate and complete, then we can send the file to the CPU for it to be read and acted upon.

On some computers, the editor is a program separate from the SPSS software. You use the editor to type your SPSS commands and, when completed, start up the SPSS software to carry out the commands. On other computers, the SPSS software itself contains an editing area in which commands are edited until they are correct before SPSS is instructed to carry them out. In later chapters we assume you are using a separate editor program, although there will be some discussion of other editing approaches.

Batch versus Interactive Processing

Commands can be submitted to SPSS in either batch mode or interactive mode. In batch mode, or **batch processing**, a set of SPSS commands is created with an editor, and then the entire *batch* of commands is sent to the CPU and executed all at once, and the results are returned to us. Interactive mode, or **interactive processing**, can be thought of as command-by-command processing. In interactive processing, each command ends with a special termination mark. As soon as we have completed typing the command and the termination mark, the command is sent immediately to the CPU for action. You can still modify or correct commands with the editor, but only up to the moment when you enter the termination mark. Every time a command is entered, we receive immediate feedback on the results of that command.

All implementations of SPSS can perform batch processing. Many can perform interactive processing as well, which SPSS calls a prompted session. Each processing mode has advantages and disadvantages, some of which are mentioned in later chapters. This text describes batch processing, with additional chapter segments on interactive processing where appropriate.

These, then, are some differences between operating systems. You will need to learn your operating system before using the SPSS software. After you become familiar with it, users of the OS operating system on IBM mainframes should skip to the next chapter while users of CMS on IBM mainframes should go to the discussion of prompted sessions at the end of this chapter. Users of all other systems should proceed with the material below.

SPSS/PC+ AND RELEASE 4

Release 4 of SPSS has all the statistical procedures available in prior versions of the mainframe program SSPS-X, even if you are using it on a microcomputer. The way you use the software, however, is very similar to SPSS/PC+ (version 2.0 and later) for DOS-based microcomputers. In fact, there is little difference between SPSS/PC+ and Release 4 on VAX computers, and the Macintosh and OS/2 implementations differ primarily in their use of menus. We begin by looking at DOS and VAX systems which Macintosh and OS/2 users should read as well. Following this section is a review of the special features of the latter two systems. Finally, there is a discussion of interactive processing including the CMS operating system.

DOS and VAX Computers

To start the SPSS/PC+ program on a DOS microcomputer, enter, at the DOS prompt (⟩), the term SPSSPC and then press the Return (or Enter) key. The opening screen briefly displays the SPSS logo which is soon replaced by a screen that looks like Figure 3.5. Upon starting SPSS/PC+ or Release 4, you will immediately enter an editing environment. This is called **REVIEW** in SPSS/PC+ to distinguish it from another part of the software which processes commands interactively. This distinction and the term "REVIEW" were discontinued with Release 4.

The screen consists of two parts: a menu across the top and a **scratch pad** (called an **input window** in Release 4) across the bottom. SPSS needs to display more information than there is room for on the screen. Consequently, the screen is divided into segments, called **windows**, with each window showing you a part of the SPSS features. Although a screen may have more than one window present, only one may be an **active window**—it allows you to type something into it or select items from it—at a time. The currently active window is always the one containing the cursor.

Windows may be opened, closed, enlarged, shrunk, or moved around the screen. The operators at your installation may have switched the location of the

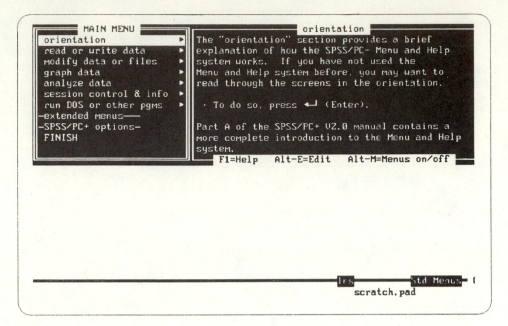

Figure 3.5 The SPSS/PC+ startup screen. (*Source*: *SPSS/PC+ V2.0 Base Manual*, SPSS Inc., Chicago, 1988. Reproduced with permission of SPSS Inc.)

windows (menus on the bottom and scratch pad on the top), but they will still work the same. For now, let us remove the menu from the screen (close its window) by typing Alt-M, the Alt key and the letter M. The menu will disappear, and you will see a third window, the **listing window** (called the **output window** in Release 4), which was hidden by the menu. The listing or output window is where the results of any SPSS commands will be shown.

With VAX Release 4, you start the SPSS software with the command SPSS entered at the DCL prompt followed by pressing the Return key. The opening screen will contain the input and output windows only, not the menu window.

Let us now turn our attention to the scratch pad or input window. This is an SPSS editing area in which we can type in any of the commands mentioned later in this text. A message line at the bottom of the screen keeps us informed of the actions we are taking—the name of the file being edited, the number of the line where the cursor is located, and any editing actions we are currently engaged in. The message line also tells us whether we are in insert mode; the term INS means that letters typed on a line will be inserted, shoving other material on the line to the right. The Insert key (Ins) on the keypad toggles between insert mode and overtype mode. In overtype mode, anything typed on a line will replace (be typed over) what is already there.

Function Keys   We enter, edit, and take action on items in the scratch pad area with special **function keys** available on the keyboard. The primary function keys are numbered F1 to F10 and are located across the top or on one side of the keyboard. Each key controls a group of editing or operating functions that are identified with **mini-menus**.

For example, suppose we type some lines of commands into the scratch pad and then discover that one line was typed twice. One of these identical lines needs to be deleted. So we place the cursor on the extra line and press function key F4, which controls line manipulation commands, and the following mini-menu appears below the scratch pad:

Lines: **Insert after**   insert Before   Delete   Undelete

This mini-menu describes the general command "Lines" and the alternatives available with it. To select an alternative, use the right-arrow ($\rightarrow$) key and left-arrow ($\leftarrow$) key to highlight the action wanted, in this case, "Delete." Once the correct choice is highlighted, pressing the Enter key activates that editing command for whatever line the cursor is on. The first alternative on each list is the most commonly used one and is automatically highlighted when a mini-menu appears.

There is a second way to select a command from a mini-menu. Each alternative has one letter capitalized: Insert after, insert Before, Delete, Undelete. Simply pressing that letter on the keyboard, instead of highlighting the word, and pressing the Enter key also activate that editing function.

Function key F1 is used a lot, for it contains the **help menu**. Pressing F1 produces the following mini-menu:

Info: **Review help and menus**   Var list   File list   Glossary

Selecting the first choice, "Review help and menus" displays the help menu in Figure 3.6 (top). The help menu describes what actions each function key contains and what mini-menus will appear by pressing each F key. Also shown on the help menu are some command key combinations that we will ignore for the present.

Release 4 on VAX computers contains almost identical editing options as SPSS/PC+. The choices are shown in Figure 3.6 (bottom) along with some standard editing keys that activate them. These editing actions are usually accessed through the key combinations PF1-1 to PF1-0, but sometimes functions key F1 to F10 are used and sometimes other special keys, depending on the type of keyboard being used. The help menu that you will see on your screen should show the proper keys to use.

Another option under F1 is the **glossary**. The glossary contains explanations of both SPSS commands and statistical terms. If you select the glossary, you will be asked to type in some term, such as "mean" or "standard deviation." After you do this and press the Enter key, a glossary screen will appear that explains the term. The glossary is also **context-sensitive**. If the cursor is already on a word in the input or output window, selecting the glossary will automatically open it to a description of that term. Thus, if you are scrolling through the output window and find a statistical term you do not understand, place the cursor on that term, open the glossary, and a description of the term will appear in the glossary window. If the glossary does not contain the term, a word close to it

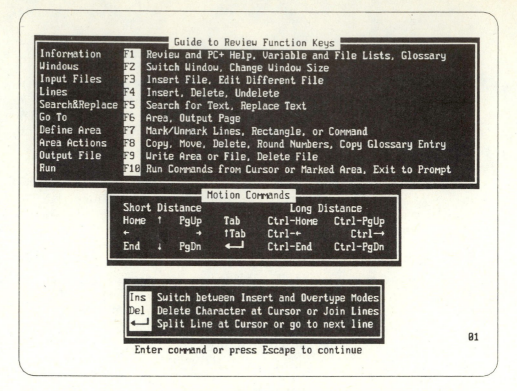

```
┌──────────────── Guide to Review Function Keys ────────────────┐
│ Information      F1   Review and PC+ Help, Variable and File Lists, Glossary │
│ Windows          F2   Switch Window, Change Window Size                      │
│ Input Files      F3   Insert File, Edit Different File                       │
│ Lines            F4   Insert, Delete, Undelete                               │
│ Search&Replace   F5   Search for Text, Replace Text                          │
│ Go To            F6   Area, Output Page                                      │
│ Define Area      F7   Mark/Unmark Lines, Rectangle, or Command               │
│ Area Actions     F8   Copy, Move, Delete, Round Numbers, Copy Glossary Entry │
│ Output File      F9   Write Area or File, Delete File                        │
│ Run              F10  Run Commands from Cursor or Marked Area, Exit to Prompt │
└──────────────────────────────────────────────────────────────┘
       ┌──────────────── Motion Commands ────────────────┐
       │   Short Distance                  Long Distance              │
       │   Home   ↑   PgUp    Tab      Ctrl-Home   Ctrl-PgUp          │
       │   ←          →       ↑Tab      Ctrl-←         Ctrl-→         │
       │   End    ↓   PgDn    ↵         Ctrl-End   Ctrl-PgDn          │
       └───────────────────────────────────────────────┘
            ┌────────────────────────────────────────────┐
            │ Ins  Switch between Insert and Overtype Modes │
            │ Del  Delete Character at Cursor or Join Lines │
            │ ↵    Split Line at Cursor or go to next line  │
            └────────────────────────────────────────────┘
                                                              01
            Enter command or press Escape to continue
```

```
┌──────────────── Guide to Manager Function Keys ────────────────┐
│ Information    Help   Manager Help and Menus, Variable and File Lists, Glossary │
│ Windows        PF1 2  Switch, Change Size, Zoom                                 │
│ Input Files    PF1 3  Insert File, Edit Different File                          │
│ Lines          Ins    Insert, Delete, Undelete                                  │
│ Find&Replace   Find   Find Text, Replace Text                                   │
│ Go To          PF1 6  Area, Output Page, After Last Line Executed, New Output   │
│ Define Area    Selec  Mark/Unmark Lines, Rectangle, or Command                  │
│ Area Actions   Remov  Copy, Move, Delete, Round Numbers, Copy Glossary Entry    │
│ Output File    PF1 9  Write Area or File, Delete File                           │
│ Run            F10    Run Commands from Cursor or Marked Area, Exit SPSS        │
└────────────────────────────────────────────────────────────────┘
      ┌──────────────── Guide to Menu Commands ────────────────┐
      │ ENTER      Paste Selection & Move Down One Level in Menu      │
      │ TAB        Temporarily Paste Selection & Move Down One Level  │
      │ PF1 PF1    Remove Last Temporary Paste & Move Up One Level    │
      │ PF1 J      Jump to Main Menu                                  │
      │ PF1 K      Kill All Temporary Pastes                          │
      │ PF1 T      Get Typing Window                                  │
      │ PF1 E      Switch to Edit Mode                                │
      │ PF1 M      Remove Menus                                       │
      │ PF1 Y      Switch between Standard and Extended Menus         │
      └────────────────────────────────────────────────────────┘
      Enter command or press PF1 R for more help, or PF1 PF1 to continue.
```

Figure 3.6 The help menu. (*Sources*: Marija J. Norusis, *SPSS/PC+ Studentware*, SPSS Inc., Chicago, 1988 and *SPSS for VAX/VMS: Operations Guide*, SPSS Inc., Chicago, 1990. Reproduced with permission of SPSS Inc.)

in spelling will appear. The file list and variable list options for F1 are described in a later section.

Function key F2 is the windows commands, switching the cursor from one window to another, thus making a different window active. The editing commands reviewed here can apply to the output window as well if that window is active. You can also shrink or expand the size of windows. VAX Release 4 includes a zoom option with this command which automatically expands a window to the full size of your monitor screen.

Function key F3 changes the file in the input window, inserting a file which will be *added* to the material already typed there or *erasing* the file in the text area and putting a new one in its place. Both options will ask you for the name of the file you want.

Function keys F5 and F6 move you around a window. Key F5 searches for a specific word or string of text, such as the command FREQUENCIES, that may be difficult to find in a lengthy file. A second option with F5 is to replace a particular text string with another. Either option will open a small area for you to type in the text to be found or replaced. Key F6 moves the cursor to a particular area of the input window or page of the output window.

The F7 key is the block marker. Single characters can be edited with the keyboard's Inscrt and Delete (Del) keys and lines with the line function examined above. You can also edit entire blocks of text, or groups of lines. You must first identify the block by marking its top and bottom. Place the cursor on the top line of the block, press F7, and choose the "mark block" option. Do the same for the bottom line of the block. Having identified a block of lines, you can now use the F8 key to manipulate this block, with its choices of copy, move, and delete. Key F9 writes (saves) all or a marked part of a window as a file. You will be asked to provide a name for the saved file.

Function key F10 activates the run and finishes commands. Commands typed in the input window are only edited and not carried out. The F10 key is used to run the commands or send them to the CPU for processing. You can run an area of commands that have been marked with the marker, or you can position the cursor on a line (including the top line of the file) and run all commands from wherever the cursor is to the last line of the input window. Finally, F10 is also used to quit the SPSS program. Selecting the "exit" option on VAX computers will stop the SPSS software completely and return you to the DCL prompt. On DOS microcomputers, depending on how the SPSS program was started, "exit" may return you to DOS or merely stop the editing part of the program but leave SPSS operating in a prompted mode. If the latter occurs, the screen will change to show an SPSS prompt, SPSSPC), with the cursor next to it. Typing FINISH followed by a period and pressing the Return key will then stop the SPSS program and return you to DOS.

Menu/Help System or Command Generator   The uses of function keys are unique to the DOS and VAX implementations of SPSS. Version 2 of SPSS/PC+ introduced an editing device which we saw earlier, the **menu/help system**. This system has been carried over into the VAX, OS/2, and Macintosh implementations of Release 4. As we discuss the menu/help system below, you should keep something in mind. The system is really quite easy to use, but what you do with it may remain unclear to many readers for a while. If you find yourself in this state, do not worry. It is necessary to describe the editing system before moving to SPSS commands, but since this system deals with the commands themselves, its use and value may remain hazy until you complete later chapters describing the commands. At that point, you may wish to return to this section to refresh your understanding of the system.

To explore this editing tool, we need the menu back on the screen, which is accomplished by pressing Alt-M again. The Alt-M key combination serves as a toggle switch, turning the menu/help system on and off. With the menu/help system back on, let us take a closer look at it. The menu, the box on the left, contains the items that can be selected. The box on the right is the help box which explains whatever menu selection is highlighted in the left box.

In Release 4, the menu/help system is called the **command generator**. The category labels in the Release 4 command generator differ somewhat from the menu choices in SPSS/PC+, but both implementations contain the same functions, except for those commands not available in SPSS/PC+. On VAX computers, you switch the menu on with the PF1-M key combination and off by using the PF1-E key combination.

The prior help screen that we saw dealt with editing commands. The menu/help system deals with SPSS commands, listing commands in the menu area and descriptions of them in the help area. Using the arrow keys, move down from the top choice on the menu, "orientation," to the second choice, "read or write data". (See Figure 3.5.) As you move down the left menu, the text in the help area changes to explain each new topic highlighted. Sometimes there will be more explanatory information that can fit in the area of the help box. When this happens, there will be up or down arrowheads at the right of the help box to show that more information is available. You can scroll this additional information by holding down the Alt key while using any of the motion keys—up arrow ↑, down arrow ↓, PgUp, PgDn, Home, or End. Without the Alt key, these motion keys apply to the menu; used with the Alt key, they apply to the help screen. VAX computers show that more text exists than can fit into a help window with an ampersand in the lower right of the window. The PF3-U and PF3-D key combinations are used to scroll up and down the help window.

Most menu choices in the left box have arrows or ellipses (a series of periods) to the right. These symbols indicate that subtopics are available with the menu options. Pressing either the → or tab key will display these subtopics in the menu area. The subtopics available with the "Read or write data" menu choice are SPSS commands that deal with reading or writing data. Highlighting one of these commands with the ↑ and ↓ keys will produce a description of the command in the help window. The commands will also have arrows to their right, indicating that there are subcommands or options associated with the commands. Pressing the → key again moves you to the subcommand menu. This process can continue deeper and deeper, depending on the number of alternatives available with each SPSS command.

For example, to use the FREQUENCIES command mentioned earlier, you move down the menu to the "analyze data" choice and press the → key, and then the menu will show SPSS commands that can analyze data, including FREQUENCIES. Highlighting the FREQUENCIES command and pressing the → key will then show the subcommands available with FREQUENCIES. Select the /FORMAT subcommand, press the → key, and the menu will display the specifications available with that subcommand, including BARCHART. At each point, the help menu explains what action is performed by the command, subcommand, or specification highlighted. You return to the main menu by backing out one level at a time with the ← or back tab key until the main menu reappears in the menu area.

Working with different levels of menus can be thought of as working with directories. The main menu is the root directory, showing you what first-level directories are available. Moving into any of these directories with the → key shows you what subdirectories that first-level directory contains. Picking a subdirectory and moving deeper show you sub-subdirectories and so on.

On the menu, items in lowercase letters are general topics; those in uppercase (capital) letters are SPSS commands, subcommands, or specifications. When an uppercase term is highlighted, pressing the Enter key pastes that command into the input window without your having to type it.

As you explore the different menu levels with a particular SPSS command, the prior commands and subcommands you have moved through on the menu are placed in a **holding area**. That is, in the example above, after you highlight the FREQUENCIES command and press the → key to see its subcommands, the FREQUENCIES command word is placed in a holding area. Selecting the subcommand /FORMAT and moving with the → key to its specifications add the /FORMAT subcommand to the holding area as well. Highlighting the specification BARCHART and pressing the Return or Enter key will then paste not only that specification into the input window, but also the command and subcommand with which this specification is used (FREQUENCIES and /FORMAT).

Other features of the menu/help system deserve mention. First, most subcommands are optional, but some SPSS commands *require* that a specific subcommand be used. If you select a main command that does have a mandatory subcommand, that subcommand will be preceded by a special symbol, such as an exclamation point or a tilde (˜), to remind you that it is required. A note on the menu will explain the symbol used.

Like the glossary, the menu/help system and command generator are context-sensitive. If you start typing a command in the input window, say, the first three to four letters of the command FREQUENCIES, and then open the menu/help system, SPSS will read the word where the cursor is located and automatically open with that command highlighted.

Some parts of SPSS commands will be unique to each user and cannot be filled in with the menu/help system. Examples are the names of files to be accessed and variables to be analyzed, since each user may choose different names for these items. When a command pasted with the menu requires one of these items, a box will open up, allowing you to type in the needed information which is then pasted into the input window along with any other parts of the command selected with the menu. Depending on the command being used, some implementations of Release 4 will automatically open a **files window** when a file name is needed, allowing you to highlight the file you want and paste its name by pressing the Return key. Similarly, when a command or subcommand needs the names of variables to be analyzed, Release 4 may open a **variables window**, showing you the variables available in the active file which can also be selected (highlighted) and pasted with the Return key. When these two features are not available, you can accomplish essentially the same thing by pressing the F1 function key and then selecting either the "file list" or "variable list" option on the mini-menu. A window will then open, showing you what file or variable names can be pasted into the input window.

Not all editing options are available at all times. The variables window just mentioned, for example, works only after an active SPSS file has been defined for the computer. How such a file is defined is described in the next two chapters. In addition, when the menu/help system is active, you will not be able to use some of the function keys since they might interfere with items that the menu/help system is trying to paste into the input window.

Nor are all commands best entered with the menu/help system or command generator. Those that define a data file to SPSS (tell the software how to read the data) include so many items unique to each user that few can be filled in through menu choices. The commands described in the next two chapters are best typed in directly rather than by using menu choices.

The menus available upon first starting the SPSS software are the **standard menus**. Standard menus contain the most commonly used SPSS commands and subcommands, but not all of them, to avoid clogging the menus with seldom used options. For the topics covered in this text, the standard menus are more than sufficient. As you become more proficient, you may wish to use the **extended menus** which include all SPSS commands, subcommands, and keywords. Pressing Alt-X will change the menus to the extended version, and pressing it again will change back to standard menus. The PF1-Y key combination serves the same function on VAX computers.

Release 4 includes a **syntax window** as well. Select the help function key (PF1-1) and the syntaX option. You will be asked to type the name of a command, and then SPSS will show you the complete syntax for that command—what subcommands are available and required along with the specifications that can be used with each. The syntax window is also context-sensitive and will automatically open to any command to which the cursor points in the input window. Figure 3.7 shows a sample syntax window for the FREQUENCIES command.

SPSS/PC+ automatically creates a **LOG file** and a **LIS file** whenever the software is used. The LOG file is a copy of all the material entered into the input window, and the LIS (listing) file is a copy of all the results that were displayed in the output window. These files are given the automatic names of SPSS.LOG and SPSS.LIS, respectively. Because the same names are always used for these two files, you should rename any you want to save. The next time someone uses

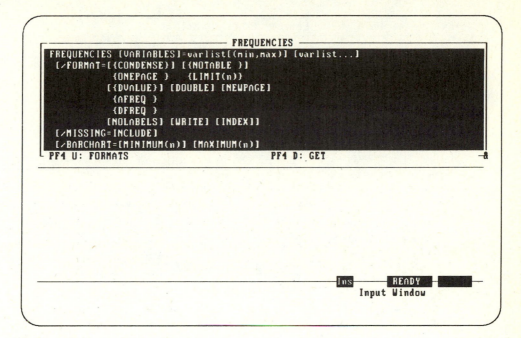

```
                        ┌── FREQUENCIES ──┐
 FREQUENCIES [VARIABLES]=varlist[(min,max)] [varlist...]
  [/FORMAT=[{CONDENSE}] [{NOTABLE }]
           {ONEPAGE }    {LIMIT(n)}]
           [{DVALUE}] [DOUBLE] [NEWPAGE]
           {AFREQ }
           {DFREQ }
           [NOLABELS] [WRITE] [INDEX]]
  [/MISSING=INCLUDE]
  [/BARCHART=[MINIMUM(n)] [MAXIMUM(n)]
 PF4 U: FORMATS                    PF4 D: GET
```

```
                                          Ins    READY
                                              Input Window
```

Figure 3.7 The syntax window. (*Source: SPSS for VAX/VMS: Operations Guide*, SPSS Inc., Chicago, 1990. Reproduced with permission of SPSS Inc.)

the SPSS/PC+ software, new LOG and LIS files will be created and will replace whatever old ones exist from prior sessions.

VAX does not automatically create LOG and LIS files, but, upon quitting SPSS, you will be asked if it is OK to discard the contents of the input and output windows. If you respond no, SPSS will not quit. This gives you a chance to save the contents of either window or both windows by using the PF1-9 key combination and selecting the "write file" option. To save both windows, you must do this twice, once with each window active. You can now quit the software and respond yes to discarding the window contents, since they have been saved.

Macintosh and OS/2

The basic features of SPSS Release 4 have been described above for VAX computers. SPSS Release 4 works very much the same on Macintosh computers and IBM microcomputers using OS/2. The primary difference is that these latter two systems use the mouse and menu bar, instead of functions keys, for editing actions.

For example, let us select an area of text upon which some function will be performed—copying the area, deleting it, saving it as a file, or running the commands contained in the area. On a mouse system, you select an area by dragging the mouse. Dragging is accomplished by pointing the mouse at one end of the area, holding down the mouse button, and then moving the mouse pointer

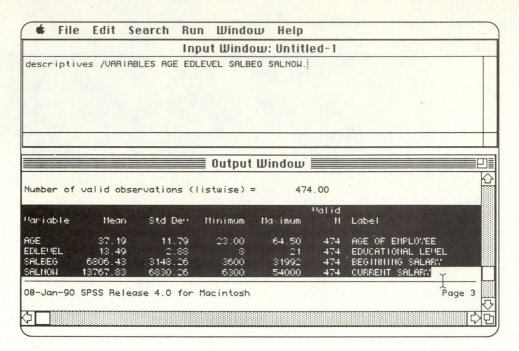

Figure 3.8 An area highlighted with a mouse. (*Source: SPSS for the Macintosh: Operations Guide*, SPSS Inc., Chicago, 1990. Reproduced with permission of SPSS Inc.)

to the other end of the area and releasing the mouse button. The area selected will be highlighted, as in Figure 3.8. Any function command selected will be performed on the highlighted area.

The functions themselves are available as choices on a menu bar across the top of the screen. Figure 3.9 shows an OS/2 screen with the menu bar choices File, Edit, Search, Run!, Window, and Exit. Moving the mouse pointer to one of these menu choices and depressing the mouse button will reveal the choices available under the menu selection. For example, a typical Edit menu would contain, among others, the choices Cut, Copy, Paste, and Clear (or Delete). To move a selected area, you cut it from one part of a window, move the cursor down to another part, and paste the cut area into that part. The mouse is also used to move from one window to another. Place the mouse pointer in the window desired, press the mouse button, and that window becomes the active window.

Virtually all the editing and action commands discussed for SPSS/PC+ and VAX Release 4 are available as menu choices on Macintosh and OS/2 computers. As another illustration, Figure 3.10 shows how selecting the Window choice on the menu bar allows you to open up the command generator, glossary, variables, input, or output windows. To make a menu selection, you point to the menu bar term, depress the mouse button, drag (with the mouse button still pressed) down through the choices to the one you want, and then release the mouse button.

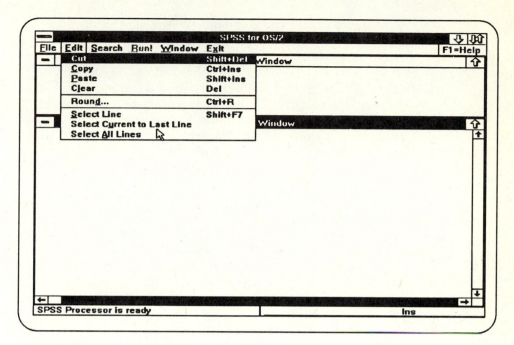

Figure 3.9 An OS/2 menu bar. (*Source: SPSS for the OS/2: Operations Guide,* SPSS Inc., Chicago, 1990. Reproduced with permission of SPSS Inc.)

Window
Arrange All
Command Generator ⌘M
Glossary Window ⌘G
Variables Window ⌘D
Clipboard Window
◇ **Output Window**
◆ **Input Window: User- HD:...:ValuePlot.Commands**
◇ **Input Window: User- HD:...:ValueFreq.Commands**

Figure 3.10 Window choices on the Macintosh menu bar. (*Source: SPSS for the Macintosh: Operations Guide,* SPSS Inc., Chicago, 1990. Reproduced with permission of SPSS Inc.)

There are some minor differences between Macintosh and OS/2 implementations of Release 4 and those discussed for the VAX. The Run! menu bar item contains the selection Run & Close. This selection will run the commands highlighted and simultaneously close the command generator so you can see the output window. Some menus opened up will contain extra buttons on them for further actions. Figure 3.11, for example, shows the command generator window with buttons labeled Prev., Next, Paste, Run & Close, Cancel, and Help. Pushing one of these buttons (moving the mouse pointer to it and pressing the mouse button) carries out that action. In this example, pressing thc help button will put the help window on the screen which explains how to use the window you are working in. Many of the buttons or menu choices will list command key or function key alternatives next to a menu or button label. These alternatives, such as F1 for the help window or Ctrl-V for the variables window, are ways of carrying out the same action without using the mouse. You may experiment with them if you wish, but they are not required.

Macintosh computers offer two other features. First, you can have more than one input window opened at a time, each with a different set of commands. The window choice on the menu bar will list all open input and output windows, and you can drag through this list to the one you want. Also on Macintosh computers the syntax chart of SPSS commands is found by scrolling to the bottom part of the help menu. It is not a separate window as is true for other implementations of Release 4.

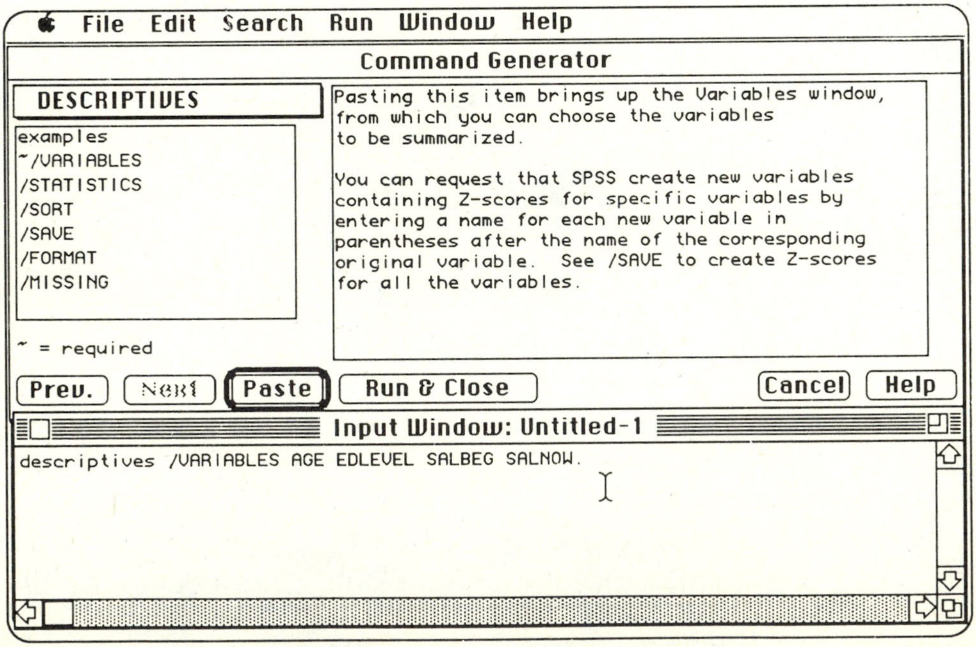

Figure 3.11 Action buttons on windows. (*Source: SPSS for the Macintosh: Operations Guide,* SPSS Inc., Chicago, 1990. Reproduced with permission of SPSS Inc.)

When you are though using the SPSS software, select QUIT from the Macintosh FILE menu or EXIT for the OS/2 FILE menu. Each system will ask you if you want to save the material in your input and output windows. If you respond yes, you will be asked to enter a name for each file being saved.

Prompted Sessions

Using the command generator might be described as a quasi-interactive session since you can run either groups of commands or single commands and then view the output immediately. A true interactive session, command-by-command processing, is called a **prompted session** in SPSS. Prompted sessions are not available on Macintosh computers or IBM mainframes using the OS. They are available with SPSS/PC+, VAX computers, OS/2 computers, and IBM mainframes using the CMS operating system.

To start a prompted session, type SPSS at the OS/2 prompt, SPSS* at the CMS prompt, or SPSS/NOMANAGER at the DCL (VAX) prompt. With SPSS/PC+ you can start the software as before, press F10, and choose the "exit to prompt" option. You will know when you are in a prompted session because a prompt will appear on the screen, SPSS), with the cursor next to it.

In a prompted session, as in SPSS/PC+ and Release 4 on VAX, OS/2, and Macintosh systems, all commands must end with a period. The period is called the **command terminator** and tells SPSS that a command is complete and can be executed. If a command in a prompted session takes more than one line, pressing the Return key to move to the second line changes the prompt to CONTINUE). All successive lines will also contain the CONTINUE) prompt until you end a line with the terminator. At that point, the command will be immediately carried out, and the next line will begin with the SPSS) prompt. Also if a command is entered that indicates you are about to enter data, such as the BEGIN DATA command described in the next chapter, the prompt will change to DATA). The DATA) prompt will continue until you indicate you are through entering data by using the END DATA command, and at that point the SPSS) prompt will return.

Prompted sessions are quite simple—enter a command and view the results. However, there is no command generator, glossary, or syntax chart, so the user needs to be familiar with the SPSS software and its commands. Thus beginning users typically do not engage in prompted sessions. Also editing commands entered in prompted sessions use the editing features available at the operating system level. These will differ from one operating system to another.

There is a help feature with prompted sessions. Typing the command HELP changes the prompt to HELP) and displays a screen of help topics by number. Selecting a number allows you to see subtopics by number, and choosing a subtopic produces an on-screen explanation of a command. The help screen can also be obtained by typing a question mark. If you follow either a question mark or the HELP command with a command name, such as ? FREQUENCIES, the help screen will open to that command.

LOG and LIS files are created in prompted sessions, although not always automatically and not always with these names. CMS automatically produces an output listing file with the name SPSS LISTING. A LOG file is also automatically created by CMS, but it is called a **journal file** and is given the name SPSS JOURNAL. Also OS/2 prompted sessions automatically create listing and journal files with the names SPSS.LST and SPSS.JNL, respectively. VAX computers do not automatically create journal and listing files, but you can request that they be created by adding the /JOURNAL and /OUTPUT options when you begin the prompted session. The full command for starting the session is thus

```
SPSS/NOMANAGER/JOURNAL/OUTPUT
```

The journal and listing files created by VAX will be named SPSS.JNL and SPSS.LIS, respectively.

That is about all there is to a prompted session. The other things that you need to know are the commands themselves, discussed in the following chapters.

SUMMARY

Introduced in this chapter were the major items that you will be working with: the computer system, the SPSS language, operating systems, and some features of SPSS/PC+ and Release 4. Having some familiarity with your computer's operating system, you are now ready to begin examining SPSS commands. Chapter 4 begins at the beginning—having SPSS read the data you have collected.

REVIEW

Key Terms

Mainframe computers	Floppy disks
Microcomputers	Programmed
Personal computers (PCs)	Software
Computer system	Machine language
Hardware	Commands
Central processing unit (CPU)	Subcommands
Input devices	Specifications
Output devices	Command syntax
Video display terminal (VDT)	Version
Storage devices	SPSS-X
Disk pack	(v.4)
Hard disk	SPSS/PC+
Computer tapes	(PC)

Release 4

(R.4)

Operating system

File

Directories

Libraries

Folders

Subdirectories

Root directory

Path

Multilevel file name

Command-driven

Menu-driven

Mouse

Icons

Editor

Text file

Batch processing

Interactive processing

REVIEW

Scratch pad

Input window

Windows

Active window

Listing window

Output window

Function keys

Mini-menus

Help menu

Glossary

Context-sensitive

Menu/help system

Command generator

Holding area

Files window

Variables window

Standard menus

Extended menus

Syntax window

LOG file

LIS file

Prompted session

Command terminator

Journal file

SUGGESTED READINGS

Norusis, Marija J., and SPSS Inc. *SPSS/PC+ V2.0 Base Manual* (Chicago: SPSS Inc., 1988) Chapter 1 and pages 1–28.

SPSS Inc. *Getting Started with SPSS-X on VAX/VMS* (Chicago: SPSS Inc., 1989).

SPSS Inc. *SPSS for IBM CMS: Operations Guide* (Chicago: SPSS Inc., 1990).

SPSS Inc. *SPSS for OS/2: Operations Guide* (Chicago: SPSS Inc., 1990).

SPSS Inc. *SPSS for the Macintosh: Operations Guide* (Chicago: SPSS Inc., 1990).

SPSS Inc. *SPSS for UNIX: Operations Guide* (Chicago: SPSS Inc., 1990).

SPSS Inc. *SPSS for VAX/VMS: Operations Guide* (Chicago: SPSS Inc., 1990).

SPSS Inc. *SPSS Reference Guide* (Release 4) (Chicago: SPSS Inc., 1990) pages 1–32.

SPSS Inc. *SPSS-X User's Guide*, 3rd ed. (Chicago: SPSS Inc., 1988) Chapters 1, 2.

Chapter 4

Entering Data

*B*efore we can analyze data, the data must be entered into the computer through an input device. Many business organizations have staff members devoted to continually updating and adding to the data in their computers. When you mail in a check to pay a credit card bill, a computer operator at the credit card company enters your payment into that company's computer, and when your canceled check reaches the bank, computer operators there debit your account by the amount of the check. An account officer at either institution can look at your account at any time through its computer terminals, and the data will be available because other workers at the organization are continually updating them. The computer can only provide information about the data that have been entered into it—how much money is owed to the credit card company, how many accounts are past due, etc. An account executive cannot analyze data that are not in the computer, such as asking for predictions on the next presidential election.

For the most part, academic computers are used for many different types of research activities, research in biology, physics, astronomy, public policy, history, and the like. Data for all these research activities simply cannot be stored in the computer at one time. Data are entered into the computer each time some analysis is performed and then withdrawn again (erased from the computer's memory) when that analysis is completed. In this chapter, we are going to look at entering our own data since we do not have staff to do this work for us. We examine how to enter data into a computer's editor, issue commands instructing SPSS how to read the data, and take a brief look at analyzing data once they are in the computer.

CREATING A DATA FILE

To illustrate the data-entering process, let us assume that we carried out the sexism survey discussed in earlier chapters. We decided to study sexism just on our university campus through a random sample of 300 students. Each student in the sample was asked to respond to the questions in Figure 4.1, inquiring about their family background and whether women should be treated differently from men in a number of situations. After completing the survey, we organized our results in a table. Figure 4.2 shows such a table for five cases from the sample.

Now that we have the data, we need to enter them into the computer. Before

We are surveying a group of students to discover their opinions on contemporary issues. We would appreciate your cooperation with the survey. It will take only a brief time, and all individual answers will be kept confidential.

1.   What is your name?
         (Print name here):   _____

2.   What is your class in school?
         (Circle one):   Freshman   Sophomore   Junior   Senior

3.   What is your age? (Write age here):   _____

4.   During most of your childhood, did both your parents or only one parent live at home with you?
         (Circle one):   Both   One

5.   Do you have any (for women, brothers) (for men, sisters)?
         (Circle one):   Yes   No

Please tell me whether you approve of, are neutral towards, or disapprove of treating women differently than men in the following situations:

6.   Selecting military personnel for combat duty
         (Circle one):   Approve   Neutral   Disapprove

7.   Selecting members of college athletic teams
         (Circle one):   Approve   Neutral   Disapprove

8.   Selecting candidates to run for high political office
         (Circle one):   Approve   Neutral   Disapprove

         .
         .
         .

15.   In obtaining seats on a crowded bus
         (Circle one):   Approve   Neutral   Disapprove

That is the end of the survey. Thank you for your time.

Figure 4.1 A sample survey questionnaire.

NAME	CLASS	AGE	FAM	SIB	MILITARY	ATHLETICS	POLITICS
ALICE FREER	FRESHMAN	18	ONE	YES	APPROVE	APPROVE	APPROVE
JON BAKER	SOPHOMORE	20	ONE	YES	NEUTRAL	DISAPPROVE	DISAPPROVE
JAMES BROGNAGIAN	SENIOR	24	BOTH	YES	APPROVE	NEUTRAL	DISAPPROVE
PATRICIA STOTT	SENIOR	21	ONE	NO	APPROVE	DISAPPROVE	NEUTRAL
CHRISTY MEYER	JUNIOR	19	BOTH	YES	DISAPPROVE	APPROVE	DISAPPROVE

Figure 4.2 Data collected from the survey.

typing anything into a computer's editor, we need to know how a computer reads information. On this point, it is helpful to remember that, contrary to popular perceptions, computers are quite stupid. We know that the words "Alice Freer" are somebody's name and the word "Freshman" is a person's class in school. Reading these words on a line of data, we know they are items relating to different variables: name and school class. We know this, but the computer does not. A computer reads data by lines, called **records**, and columns. It will keep the information for different variables separate only if we type it in separate columns. This is called the **fixed-format** method of entering data; it is fixed because the values of any variable, such as name or age, will be typed into the same columns on every record.

To enter data in fixed format, we must set aside a certain amount of space (number of columns) for each variable in the data set. Return to the five cases (people) displayed in Figure 4.2. For the first variable (the column of names), the longest name there, James Brognagian, is 16 spaces long (15 letters plus a space between the first and last names); so we assign columns 1 to 16 on each line as the location of the "Name" variable. By the same process, "Sophomore" (9 letters) is the longest response possible for the second variable, so we assign columns 18 to 26 for this variable. We have skipped over column 17 so that the last letters of a person's name will not be right next to their class designation, such as "BrognagianSenior." This is simply for our convenience, to make the data easier to read. The computer does not care whether there is a blank space between the variables.

Continuing this process, we assign columns 28 and 29 for the third variable, columns 31 to 34 for the fourth, 36 to 38 for the fifth, 40 to 49 for the sixth, 51 to 60 for the seventh, and 62 to 71 for the last variable. (You can count the maximum length of responses for each variable to verify that the column assignments are accurate.) Having assigned different columns to each variable, we then type the survey responses (our data) into the appropriate columns in the text area. The computer screen should look something like Figure 4.3.

After completing this process for all the people surveyed, we save the data as a computer file. This does not mean that the computer now "knows" the information in our data file. What we have done is taken our data set and made it **machine-readable**—we translated it from pencil markings on sheets of paper to electronic characters that the computer can read. At this point, *we* know that each case (person) is on a separate row and that our data (the variables) are in distinct columns in each row. What we need to do now is tell this to the computer so that *it* knows what it is reading.

```
0001    ALICE  FREER        FRESHMAN    18   ONE    YES    APPROVE      APPROVE       APPROVE
0002    JON  BAKER          SOPHOMORE   20   ONE    YES    NEUTRAL      DISAPPROVE    DISAPPROVE
0003    JAMES  BROGNAGIAN   SENIOR      24   BOTH   YES    APPROVE      NEUTRAL       DISAPPROVE
0004    PATRICIA  STOTT     SENIOR      21   ONE    NO     APPROVE      DISAPPROVE    NEUTRAL
0005    CHRISTY  MEYER      JUNIOR      19   BOTH   YES    DISAPPROVE   APPROVE       DISAPPROVE
0006
0007
0008
0009
0010
0011
0012
0013
```

Figure 4.3 Data entered in fixed format.

THE DATA LIST COMMAND

Data are not read directly by the computer, but instead through a software program. In SPSS, we describe a data file so the computer can read it through the **DATA LIST** command. For the data we just entered, the DATA LIST command would look like

DATA LIST / RESP 1–16 (A) CLASS 18–26 (A) AGE 28–29
            FAM 31–34 (A) SIB 36–38 (A) Q1 40–49 (A) Q2 51–60 (A)
            Q3 62–71 (A)

Let us examine each part of this statement. The first item is the SPSS command DATA LIST, which tells SPSS to prepare to read some data. Following DATA LIST is a slash (/) which separates the command statement from the specifications or attributes that we add to the statement. The specifications include three pieces of information SPSS must have: each variable's name, its column location, and each variable's type.

Variable Names

First is the **variable name**. Earlier we described SPSS as a language that allows us to communicate with the CPU through understandable English words. The SPSS software contains a number of predefined words that it can understand when we use them, words such as DATA LIST. There are no predefined words, however, that refer to the variables in our data set. The creators of the software have no way of knowing if we are going to analyze 20 variables describing the characteristics of rocks or 20,000 variables dealing with different characteristics of people.

The DATA LIST statement allows us to define new words for SPSS—the names of our variables. When we later use these variable names, SPSS will understand what we mean by these words. Within certain limitations, a variable name in SPSS can be any term we choose. There are five limitations:

1. The variable name must start with a letter, but after that it may consist of any combination of letters and numbers.

Table 4.1   SPSS RESERVED WORDS

ALL	EQ	LE	NOT	TO	AND	GE
LT	OR	WITH	BY	GT	NE	THRU

2. The variable name must be a single word or term without any spaces.
3. The variable name can be no more than eight characters long, although it may be less.
4. Each variable name must be unique so that when we later refer to variables by their names, SPSS will not be confused by two variables with the same name.
5. The variable name cannot be one of the terms reserved by SPSS.

There are a few names or terms that have a special meaning to SPSS. They are some of the predefined words already in its vocabulary, and they cannot be used as variable names lest SPSS again become confused about what command we are giving it. The **reserved words** are listed in Table 4.1. As you can see, they are generally words that we would not think of using anyway.

Within the above constraints, we can select any name we choose. Two conventions are generally followed, although you do not have to use either. First, a starting letter is used, such as V for variable or Q for question, and then each variable is simply numbered sequentially, for example, V1, V2, V3, etc. Second, a variable name is used which indicates the content of the variable, such as RESP (short for respondents or the individuals who were surveyed) to refer to the list or column of names. In our DATA LIST example, we used both types of variable names: RESP, CLASS, AGE, FAM, SIB, Q1, Q2, and Q3.

Locations of Variables

The second type of information contained in the DATA LIST statement is the beginning and ending column numbers of the variable. We have given the variable a name, and now we need to tell the computer where to find it. This information is included immediately after each variable name, such as RESP 1–16. There is at least one space between the variable name and the beginning column number, and the beginning and ending column numbers are separated by a dash. If we had a variable that required only one column (e.g., year in school = 1, 2, 3, or 4), we would specify just one column after the variable name, such as YEAR 13, telling SPSS that the variable named YEAR is in column 13.

Types of Variables

Finally there is the **variable type**. Variables come in two types: numeric (numbers only) and alpha (all letters or a combination of letters and numbers). **Alpha variables** are also sometimes called **string variables** or **alphanumeric variables** because they can contain a string of letters and numbers, such as a person's address: "122 Gilbert Avenue." The key distinction is that numeric variables are numbers only while alpha variables contain at least one character which is not a number.

SPSS distinguishes between two types of string or alpha variables. **Short strings** are alpha variables of eight characters or less, such as the FAM and SIB variables. Alpha variables requiring nine or more columns of characters for its values, such as RESP, CLASS, Q1, Q2, and Q3, are called **long strings**. There is no need to identify short- and long-string variables on the DATA LIST command; the difference is merely in what SPSS can do with them. Short-string variables can be used in almost any SPSS procedure while long-string variables are limited to a few procedures only. For now, this distinction is not vital, but it is discussed again in later chapters.

SPSS expects all variables to consist of only numbers (the contents of the variable, not its name). With the exception of the AGE variable, the contents of our variables contain words and letters, not numbers, so we must tell SPSS to be prepared to read them as alpha variables. We do this by adding the specification (**A**) after the column numbers (be sure to leave a space between the last column number and the left parenthesis). When our variables do consist of numbers only, we can omit this specification since SPSS expects to read numbers unless we tell it differently. Thus no alpha or other designation is included after the column numbers of the AGE variable.

This completes the definition process. From now on, whenever we use the term RESP, SPSS will understand it to refer to columns 1 to 16 of the data file, which contains alphanumeric information.

Including the Data

Before SPSS can read our data, however, we must do three more very simple, obvious things. First, since our data are type alpha (words), how does SPSS know which words in the program are data and which are commands that we are trying to give it? It is very simple. On the line following the DATA LIST command, we type the statement **BEGIN DATA**. Second, we must actually include our data on the lines immediately following the BEGIN DATA statement. Third, after the last line of data we include the statement (surprise!) **END DATA**.

These are the essentials of putting our information into the computer. The term DATA LIST tells SPSS to be prepared to read data; then we tell SPSS each variable's name, the columns where it is located, and which variables contain alpha data. Finally, we tell SPSS where our data begin and end, hopefully not forgetting to actually include our data between these two statements. In its entirety, this part of the program will look like Figure 4.4.

```
0001    DATA LIST /  RESP 1-16 (A)   CLASS 18-26 (A)   AGE 28-29   FAM 31-34 (A)
0002       SIB 36-38 (A)   Q1 40-49 (A)   Q2 51-60 (A)   Q3 62-71 (A)
0003    BEGIN DATA
0004    ALICE FREER        FRESHMAN   18  ONE   YES  APPROVE     APPROVE     APPROVE
0005    JON BAKER          SOPHOMORE  20  ONE   YES  NEUTRAL     DISAPPROVE  DISAPPROVE
0006    JAMES BROGNAGIAN   SENIOR     24  BOTH  YES  APPROVE     NEUTRAL     DISAPPROVE
0007    PATRICIA STOTT     SENIOR     21  ONE   NO   APPROVE     DISAPPROVE  NEUTRAL
0008    CHRISTY MEYER      JUNIOR     19  BOTH  YES  DISAPPROVE  APPROVE     DISAPPROVE
0009    END DATA
0010
```

Figure 4.4 Entering data with the DATA LIST command.

Supplement
4.1
Using JCL

A distinctive feature of OS on IBM mainframe computers is the use of **job language control (JCL)**. JCL consists of a number of lines of computer statements that must be included immediately before and after any SPSS commands. Figure 4.1S shows an SPSS program containing lines of JCL at the top and bottom. The JCL lines are easy to spot because they all begin with at least one or two slashes.

```
0001    //    JOB  (USERID,ACCT*,1min,5sec,3K  lines)
0002    //   EXEC  SPSS
0003    //SYSIN  DD  *
0004    DATA LIST /   RESP 1-16 (A)   CLASS 18-26 (A)  AGE 28-29    FAM 31-34 (A)
0005       SIB 36-38 (A)   Q1 40-49 (A)   Q2 51-60 (A)   Q3 62-71 (A)
0006    BEGIN DATA
  .                   .           .           .         .          .
  .      data         .           .           .         .          .
  .                   .           .           .         .          .
0305    END DATA
0306    FREQUENCIES VARIABLES = SIB
0307    /*
0308    //
```

Figure 4.1S A job requiring JCL.

At first glance, JCL looks intimidating. At second glance, it still looks intimidating. Very briefly, the top JCL line describes you and your program to the computer—your computer account number and how much CPU or printer time to allocate to your program. The operating system needs this information to keep track of the many jobs being submitted almost simultaneously by multiple users. The second JCL line tells the CPU what software program you are using, and line 3—// SYSIN DD *—is essentially a "go" statement, telling the computer to begin executing your program. At the bottom of the file are lines indicating the end of the job. Depending on the type of data you are using, these lines may merely consist of two slashes (//), a slash and an asterisk (/*), or both. In between the top and bottom lines of JCL are your SPSS commands.

Your instructor will provide any JCL statements you need. Since the same JCL commands will probably be used over and over, save them as a file. Thereafter, retrieve this file and use the same JCL, merely changing the SPSS commands in the middle as you request different statistical procedures.

MORE ABOUT THE DATA LIST

There are some other characteristics of the DATA LIST command that we need to be familiar with. Some involve limitations on how DATA LIST is used, while others illustrate how the command can be adapted to meet different characteristics of the data.

Spacing Requirements

Computers can sometimes be very picky about exactly how you enter commands or give it information. Fortunately, SPSS is not as picky as some. You

```
0001    DATA LIST /
0002         RESP 1-16 (A)
0003         CLASS 18-26 (A)
0004         AGE 28-29
0005         FAM 31-34 (A)
0006         SIB 36-38 (A)
0007         Q1 40-49 (A)
0008         Q2 51-60 (A)
0009         Q3 62-71 (A)
0010    BEGIN DATA
0011    ALICE FREER        FRESHMAN  18  ONE   YES APPROVE      APPROVE     APPROVE
0012    JON BAKER          SOPHOMORE 20  ONE   YES NEUTRAL      DISAPPROVE  DISAPPROVE
0013    JAMES BROGNAGIAN   SENIOR    24  BOTH  YES APPROVE      NEUTRAL     DISAPPROVE
0014    PATRICIA STOTT     SENIOR    21  ONE   NO  APPROVE      DISAPPROVE  NEUTRAL
0015    CHRISTY MEYER      JUNIOR    19  BOTH  YES DISAPPROVE   APPROVE     DISAPPROVE
0016    END DATA
```

Figure 4.5 Using different spacing with the DATA LIST command.

can generally add extra spaces in a command statement (but not a single command word) without any problem. For example, we could also have written the DATA LIST statement as in Figure 4.5, with the specification for each variable (name, column locations, and alpha or numeric type) on a separate line. Some people find this latter approach easier to type and understand. The rule of thumb is that whenever a single space is allowed, you can add multiple spaces, or even entire lines, without encountering any problems.

(PC) (R.4) In some statements, however, SPSS demands certain types of spacing. First, all commands must begin in column 1. SPSS looks for commands only in column 1, and if the DATA LIST command were to start in column 2, SPSS would not recognize it as a command. Second, *only* commands should begin in column 1. SPSS reads anything in column 1 as the beginning of a new command. In the DATA LIST illustration in Figure 4.4, if the variable name SIB, which starts the second line of the DATA LIST statement, began in column 1, SPSS would try to read it as a command. It would search through the dictionary of commands that it recognizes, looking for a command called Q1. Since there is no such command, SPSS would give us an error message at this point (a statement saying SPSS cannot interpret our commands) and would fail to execute the rest of our program.

(PC) (R.4) Any list of options or specifications that follows a command can be contained on as many lines as we wish as long as each successive line begins in column 2 or later, until we are ready to enter another command (such as BEGIN DATA). There are a few minor exceptions to this rule, which we discuss in later chapters. The only exception that applies now is that our data *can* clearly start in column 1. The BEGIN DATA statement tells SPSS that the following lines contain data, so SPSS will not try to read anything starting in column 1 as a command until after it sees the END DATA statement.

The logic of this procedure is similar to writing paragraphs in a letter: We begin each new paragraph on a new line, and we indent a few spaces so that it is visually obvious to the reader that we are starting a new paragraph. The logic is the same, although the procedure is reversed with SPSS commands—each new command begins at the left margin (column 1) while continuation lines are indented, so that SPSS knows we are still dealing with the same command rather than starting a new one.

Multiple Records per Case

The characteristics of the data also affect how we describe them on the DATA LIST statement. Conveniently, the data illustrated earlier were brief enough to be contained on only one line. However, suppose we use a sexism quiz with 10 questions instead of just 3. The data we already have for each person take up almost the entire line, so where do we put the responses to the other 7 questions? The responses could be continued on the next line, as in Figure 4.6, but we have already told SPSS that columns 1 to 16 of each line contain the variable RESP. From our current DATA LIST statement, SPSS will read lines 1 and 2 as separate persons (cases), with the first person's name being ALICE FREER and the second person's name being DISAPPROVE NEUTR (columns 1 to 16 of line 2). What do we do about this?

Recall that each line of information is called a record. Up to this point, we have been treating each line or record as if it represented a different case. We do not need to do this. We can use **multiple records** for each case. Figure 4.7 contains another DATA LIST statement, and the differences between it and the one we have been working with so far are shown in boldface type.

(PC) First notice the **RECORDS = 2** statement immediately following the DATA LIST command. This tells SPSS that each case (person) contains two lines or records of information. Following this, **/1** tells SPSS that on the first line of information for each case it will find the variables RESP, CLASS, AGE, FAM, SIB, Q1, Q2, and Q3 in the columns indicated. Then **/2** tells SPSS that it will find variables Q4 and Q5 in columns 1 to 10 and 12 to 21, respectively, on the *second* record or line for each case. If the answers to all 10 questions require more than two lines, we change the RECORDS statement to RECORDS = 3 and add /3 before describing the variables on the third record for each case. We can have as many records per case as we need to hold the information obtained from those surveyed.

```
0001    DATA LIST /  RESP 1-16 (A)   CLASS 18-26 (A)    AGE 28-29  FAM 31-34 (A)
0002     SIB 36-38 (A)    Q1 40-49 (A)   Q2 51-60 (A)   Q3 62-71 (A)
0003    BEGIN DATA
0004    ALICE FREER        FRESHMAN  18  ONE  YES APPROVE      APPROVE      APPROVE
0005    DISAPPROVE NEUTRAL
         .              .       .      .    .     .          .          .
         .              .       .      .    .     .          .          .
         .              .       .      .    .     .          .          .

0304    END DATA
```

Figure 4.6 Data continuing on more than one line.

```
0001    DATA LIST RECORDS = 2 /1 RESP 1-16 (A)  CLASS 18-26 (A)  AGE 28-29  FAM 31-34 (A)
0002       SIB 36-38 (A)  Q1 40-49 (A)  Q2 51-60 (A)  Q3 62-71 (A) /2 Q4 1-10 (A)  Q5 12-21 (A)
0003    BEGIN DATA
0004    ALICE FREER          FRESHMAN  18  ONE  YES APPROVE     APPROVE    APPROVE
0005    DISAPPROVE NEUTRAL
0006    JON BAKER            SOPHOMORE 20  ONE  YES NEUTRAL     DISAPPROVE DISAPPROVE
0007    NEUTRAL      APPROVE
0008    JAMES BROGNAGIAN SENIOR    24  BOTH YES APPROVE     NEUTRAL    DISAPPROVE
0009    APPROVE      DISAPPROVE
0010    PATRICIA STOTT    SENIOR    21  ONE  NO  APPROVE     DISAPPROVE NEUTRAL
0011    APPROVE      APPROVE
0012    CHRISTY MEYER     JUNIOR    19  BOTH YES DISAPPROVE APPROVE    DISAPPROVE
0013    DISAPPROVE DISAPPROVE
          .      .            .     .    .    .   .            .          .
          .      .            .     .    .    .   .            .          .
          .      .            .     .    .    .   .            .          .
          .      .            .     .    .    .   .            .          .

0604    END DATA
```

Figure 4.7 DATA LIST with multiple records per case.

A BRIEF LOOK AT ANALYZING THE DATA

In this final section, we touch briefly on how to analyze the data we have now entered into the computer and how to identify any errors we may have made. This requires the discussion of one new command: FREQUENCIES. This command is examined more thoroughly in a later chapter, but we review a simplified form of it here to see how the computer treats the data we have entered.

The FREQUENCIES Command

Examine Figure 4.8. Lines 1, 2, and 3 contain our DATA LIST and BEGIN DATA statements. Lines 4 through 304 contain the data on the 300 students surveyed as well as the END DATA statement. Line 305 contains a new statement:

FREQUENCIES VARIABLES = Q1

FREQUENCIES is a command and therefore begins in column 1. The FRE-QUENCIES command simply tells SPSS to count the responses on a given

```
0001    DATA LIST / RESP 1-16 (A)  CLASS 18-26 (A)  AGE 28-29  FAM 31-34 (A)
0002       SIB 36-38 (A)  Q1 40-49 (A)  Q2 51-60 (A)  Q3 62-71 (A)
0003    BEGIN DATA
0004    ALICE FREER      FRESHMAN  18  ONE  YES APPROVE     APPROVE    APPROVE
0005    JON BAKER        SOPHOMORE 20  ONE  YES NEUTRAL     DISAPPROVE DISAPPROVE
0006    JAMES BROGNAGIAN SENIOR    24  BOTH YES APPROVE     NEUTRAL    DISAPPROVE
0007    PATRICIA STOTT   SENIOR    21  ONE  NO  APPROVE     DISAPPROVE NEUTRAL
0008    CHRISTY MEYER    JUNIOR    19  BOTH YES DISAPPROVE APPROVE    DISAPPROVE
          .      .          .     .    .    .   .            .          .
          .      .          .     .    .    .   .            .          .
          .      .          .     .    .    .   .            .          .

0304    END DATA
0305    FREQUENCIES VARIABLES = Q1
```

Figure 4.8 Using the FREQUENCIES procedure.

```
Q 1

                                                            VALID        CUM
        VALUE LABEL            VALUE   FREQUENCY  PERCENT   PERCENT    PERCENT

                             APPROVE      143      47.7      47.7       47.7
                          DISAPPROVE      121      40.3      40.3       88.0
                             NEUTRAL       36      12.0      12.0      100.0
                                        ------    -------   -------
                             TOTAL        300     100.0     100.0

VALID CASES    300     MISSING CASES    0
```

Figure 4.9 Sample output from the FREQUENCIES procedure.

variable; for example, how *frequently* did people respond "Approve," "Disapprove," or "Neutral"? OK, count what? The rest of the statement tells SPSS to count the responses for variable Q1 (**VARIABLES = Q1**). This is the first question on the sexism quiz: Should women be treated differently from men in the selection of military personnel for combat duty?

When SPSS sees this variable name, it knows (because we told it so in the DATA LIST) that variable Q1 is in columns 40 to 49 of the data file. SPSS will thus count the contents of these data file columns and print the results, which will look something like Figure 4.9. For now, only two things from Figure 4.9 interest us: the VALUE and FREQUENCY columns. The VALUE column refers to the answers given by our respondents, the values of variable Q1: APPROVE, DISAPPROVE, or NEUTRAL. The FREQUENCY column is the count of how many times SPSS found each of these values in the columns containing the Q1 variable.

Supplement 4.2

The SET WIDTH Command

Contemporary mainframe printers use 132-column paper, and SPSS output is designed to use this wide paper. Most terminal screens, however, are only 80 columns wide. If you want to see some of your output printed in columns 81 to 132, you have to move the terminal's "window," that part of the output your terminal is showing, to the right.

Moving the window to the right and left is clumsy, and it is better to avoid it. You can do this by placing at the beginning of your SPSS program, before the DATA LIST command, the command

SET WIDTH 80

This command tells SPSS to produce output that is no more than 80 columns wide. It will all fit on the terminal screen without having to move the window.

Using only the FREQUENCIES procedure discussed so far, you may not see any difference since the FREQUENCIES output seldom takes more than 80 columns anyway. However, changing the output width will make a significant difference for other procedures discussed later in the text. The SET WIDTH command is not needed for SPSS/PC+ or Release 4 since their output is designed for 80-column computer screens.

In short, once our data are entered, simple commands will instruct the computer to do all our drudgery for us, such as counting responses. The hard part is entering the lines of data, a job we need to do only once. When that is done, we no longer have to shuffle through 300 questionnaires, but can instead tell the computer to do that for us through simple commands.

Errors

One thing needs to be emblazoned in the mind of every new computer user: *You will make errors.* Humans are not perfect, and computers are very stupid (stupid, stupid, stupid). Errors are generally of two types: the obvious spelling errors and the less obvious syntax errors. If you misspell any command, subcommand, specification, or variable name, SPSS will not understand the command and will produce an error message. For example, SPSS understands the command word FREQUENCIES, but it does not know what FERQUENCIES is and will stop processing when it encounters this typing error. Syntax errors occur when you make a logical error in entering a command (such as forgetting to put a slash between the DATA LIST command and the description of the variables), requesting inconsistent subcommands, and either not starting a new command in column 1 in SPSS or failing to end with a command terminator in SPSS/PC+ or Release 4.

When SPSS finds something unusual, it prints out a message describing what it encountered so that you can determine the type of problem you have. These messages come in one of three forms: notes, warnings, or errors. The message is always preceded by one of these terms so you know what kind of message you are reading.

Notes   A **note** represents a minor problem or a situation that may not even be a problem at all. A note is produced when SPSS encounters a situation that it thinks it understands but is not quite sure and wants to advise you of what is happening. For example, a note is produced if SPSS reads a file created by an older version of the software or by a different implementation of SPSS. SPSS generates a note on the output telling you that it is reading a nonstandard file. Notes seldom indicate any problem, but they should be read anyway to ensure that SPSS is doing what you want.

Warnings   A **warning** is a more serious message indicating a situation that will probably affect analyses performed on the data including later commands executed during the same batch job or SPSS session. A warning might occur if SPSS reads an alphabetical or other nonnumeric character in the data file for a variable defined as numeric on the DATA LIST statement. Since the variable is defined as numeric, SPSS will replace any nonnumeric characters with a special symbol, called a system missing value, and print out a warning that it has done so. Such a warning might indicate an error in the DATA LIST command or an error in your data file. Either way, you should check it out to see what is causing it.

Warnings will be produced by data files like those described in this chapter. Any alpha or string variable of more than eight characters can be used with some SPSS commands but not statistical procedures such as the FREQUENCIES procedure. Our earlier illustrations in the chapter contain some string variables longer than eight characters. If asked to perform a FREQUENCIES analysis on these variables, SPSS will carry out the FREQUENCIES procedure but will read only the first eight characters of each long-string variable and will produce a warning message explaining what it has done. For now, just ignore that particular warning. We will learn how to deal with this problem in Chapter 5.

Errors   An **error** is the most serious message that SPSS produces. With notes or warnings, SPSS commands are executed anyway, but you are advised of the unexpected situation that SPSS found. Error messages are produced when the problem is serious enough to prevent SPSS from executing a command. Suppose that on your FREQUENCIES statement you wanted a frequencies table for variable Q1 but typed R1 instead. There is no variable R1 on the DATA LIST statement, so SPSS cannot find the variable, cannot execute the command, and thus issues an error message.

If the error is not too serious, it might affect this one command only but all other commands will be carried out. If the error is more serious, SPSS stops executing all commands at this point, but will go ahead and read the rest of your commands, checking for any other errors and issuing additional error messages if needed. In a few situations SPSS will encounter either too many errors or an error of such magnitude (such as being unable to find the data file) that it simply stops processing immediately and does not check any additional commands for possible errors.

If you encounter an SPSS error message, read it carefully and see if you can identify the error made. The error messages are not always crystal-clear, for if SPSS knew exactly what was wrong, it would correct the problem itself. It can only report a word or symbol that it does not understand and then make a guess as to what mistake you made. About half the time, errors are created by typing mistakes, which you should be able to spot by rereading the command that caused the error. Other errors are usually syntax errors, which you should be able to identify by comparing the command you created with this text's illustrations of how to enter the same command or the syntax charts available with Release 4 of the software.

SPSS/PC+ AND RELEASE 4

There are only a few differences between the commands described here and the SPSS/PC+ or Release 4 versions of them. Each is listed below. Remember, unless explicitly stated otherwise, the Release 4 differences mentioned here and in later chapters apply only to VAX, OS/2, and Macintosh implementations, not to IBM mainframes.

Both SPSS/PC+ and Release 4

Command Terminator　We described commands as beginning in column 1 and continuing on additional lines in column 2 or later, so that SPSS knows when one command ends and another begins. A term starting in column 1 signifies the beginning of a new command.

Instead of taking this approach, SPSS/PC+ and Release 4 use a **command terminator**, which is a period at the end of the command. The command term can begin in any column, and continuations on additional lines can start in column 1 or later. When you reach the end of the command, add the period. This indicates that the command is finished, and then SPSS will read the item starting on the next line, regardless of whether it begins in column 1, as a new command. A new command must begin on a different line, for anything typed on the same line after the terminator is ignored. With SPSS/PC+ and some implementations of Release 4, you could alternatively leave a blank line between the end of one command and the start of another command, which the software would also interpret as a terminator. The one exception to this spacing rule is the END DATA command, which must *always* begin in column 1. SPSS also recommends not using the terminator on the BEGIN DATA command.

Although SPSS/PC+ and Release 4 do not require it, it is desirable to follow the practice described in this chapter of starting commands in column 1 and continuing the command in column 2 or later. This will allow you to use some extra features of the software that are mentioned later. Regardless of the spacing system used, you must include the terminator. The menu/help system and command generator automatically include the terminator whenever any commands are pasted into the input window.

Running Commands　A second difference with SPSS/PC+ and Release 4 is in running commands. The batch processing of OS operating systems on IBM mainframes will run all the commands you enter into the editor and send to the CPU as a batch package. After executing those commands, the CPU clears its memory to be ready for the next user, including erasing any data read with the DATA LIST command. Each command batch sent to the CPU will include a DATA LIST or similar command to read in data before any statistical procedures are executed.

SPSS/PC+ and Release 4 run only the commands selected, those marked with a marker or mouse, or commands beginning with the current cursor position. This difference requires a little extra care with these latter systems. The FREQUENCIES command mentioned in this chapter, for example, will not work until you have instructed the computer to read (run) the DATA LIST command and the data following it. From that point on the data will remain in the computer's memory, allowing you to run the FREQUENCIES or any other command, until you quit the SPSS software.

Command Length　On many implementations of SPSS, if you make a typing error in the command word, such as DATA LISS instead of DATA LIST, the software will not understand the command and will produce an error message. SPSS/PC+ and Release 4 implementations, however, read only the first three letters of each command word and from them can understand what the entire command is. If a command consists of more than one word, such as the two-word command DATA LIST, you must include at least the first three letters of each word. The typing mistake displayed above would not generate an error in these implementations because they would read only the DAT and LIS parts of the command, ignoring the rest.

Despite this feature, it is wise to get used to typing entire commands, not just the first three letters. This makes the command more intelligible to us. It is difficult to remember the meanings of three-letter acronyms such as FRE or CRO; entire words are easier to understand. Using the entire command also makes any transition from one form of SPSS to another quite simple.

SPSS/PC+ Only

Multiple Records   When reading data with multiple records per case, SPSS requires you to specify how many records each case has with the RECORDS = statement. SPSS/PC+ does not accept this statement. Instead you identify the number of records in each case by the number of slashes contained in your description of the variables. The first slash, after the command DATA LIST, tells SPSS/PC+ to read the first record, and a second slash and a third slash tell it to read the second and third records, respectively. Thus the following command is for a case that has three records of information and reads one variable from each record:

DATA LIST / SEX 1 / RACE 1–2 / AGE 1–2

This can be a very important difference. SPSS knows how many records each case has from the RECORDS = statement, but SPSS/PC+ only knows this by the number of slashes in the DATA LIST statement. If each case has three records but you describe data only on records 1 and 2, SPSS knows from the RECORDS = 3 statement that a third record exists for each case which it needs to skip over before reading data for the second case. SPSS/PC+ will not know that a third record exists unless there is a slash in the DATA LIST to tell it so. Thus if you read information only from records 1 and 2, you still need the third slash to tell SPSS/PC+ that the third record exists and should be skipped. The PC+ command is

DATA LIST / SEX 1 / RACE 1–2 /

If there are four records, but you read data from only the first two, you need two slashes at the end.

Note also that SPSS/PC+ does not identify records by number—/1, /2,

/3—only by the number of slashes present. In SPSS you can skip over record 2 in the middle of a case by just identifying the record number, as in

```
DATA LIST RECORDS = 3 / SEX 1 /3 AGE 1–2
```

The SPSS/PC+ form must contain a slash for the record skipped over, so the command is

```
DATA / SEX 1 / / AGE 1–2
```

SPSS also accepts multiple slashes in place of record numbers, but it is usually easier to identify records by number than by multiple slashes.

Alpha Variables   SPSS/PC+ is less flexible in manipulating alphanumeric or string variables. SPSS does have features which allow it to manipulate long-string variables, but PC+ cannot do much with them. This may create some additional error or warning messages for PC+ users, but the illustrations used in this chapter should still work. We find out how to eliminate this problem in Chapter 5.

SUMMARY

Computer analysis requires at least two items—data and commands, to tell the computer what to do with the data. For now, we are concerned with understanding the data to be analyzed. In this chapter we have seen how to enter data into the computer and have SPSS perform a simple analysis. We have also looked at some errors we might make and how SPSS will respond to them. In the next chapter we continue our examination of data, exploring different types of data and how to store data in the computer for maximum ease of use.

REVIEW

Key Terms

Records	Short strings
Fixed format	Long strings
Machine-readable	BEGIN DATA
DATA LIST	END DATA
Variable name	Job control language (JCL)
Reserved words	Multiple records
Variable type	Note
Alpha variables	Warning
String variables	Error
Alphanumeric variables	Command terminator

Exercises

4.1 You developed a data matrix for Exercise 2.5. Enter these data now, using the DATA LIST and other commands discussed in this chapter. Run a FREQUENCIES procedure on some of your variables. Just copy the command as illustrated in Figure 4.8, but change the variable name (Q1) to one that you used on your DATA LIST command. Save the data and commands as a file so they will be available for exercises in future chapters. Readers who skipped Chapter 2 can look briefly at Exercises 2.4 and 2.5 and invent some data to enter as described above. These data are only for practice, so accuracy is not important.

4.2 Below are some sample SPSS program statements which contain errors. Find the errors and correct the program statements. *Note:* Variables beginning with N can be assumed to be numeric while those beginnings with A are alpha variables.

   a. DATA LIST N1 1–2

   b. DATE LIST A1 20–22 (A)

   c. DATE LIST / N1 1–2 N3 4–7
   BEGIN DATA
   data
   FREQUENCIES VARIABLES = N1

   d. DATA LIST / N1 1–2 N3 4–7
   BEGIN DATA
   data
   END DATA
   FREQUENCIES VARIABLES = N2

   e. DATA LIST / N1 1–2 N3 4–7
   data
   END DATA
   FREQUENCIES VARIABLES = N1

   f. DATA LIST / N1 1–2 A3 4–7
   BEGIN DATA
   data
   END DATA
   FREQUENCIES VARIABLES = N1

   g. DATA LIST / N1 1–2 A 3 4–7 (A)
   BEGIN DATA
   data
   END DATA
   FREQUENCIES VARIABLES = A3

   h. DATA LIST N1 1–2 2N 3–4

   i. DATA LIST N1 1–2 GT 3–4 (A)

4.3 Those using SPSS/PC+ and Release 4 should experiment with the menu/help system or command generator. Highlight the "read or write data" menu choice ("data definition" in Release 4), and search deeper into this choice with the arrow keys to find the DATA LIST command. Observe how the help menu describes the command and how pressing Enter when this command is highlighted will paste it into the text area. Once a command has been typed or pasted into the text area, place the cursor on it and select the glossary, then the syntax chart, to see how these features operate.

SUGGESTED READINGS

Norusis, Marija J., and SPSS Inc. *SPSS/PC + V2.0 Base Manual* (Chicago: SPSS Inc., 1988) Chapters 2, 3.

SPSS Inc. *SPSS Reference Guide* (Release 4) (Chicago: SPSS Inc., 1990) pages 72–73, 109–121.

SPSS Inc. *SPSS-X User's Guide*, 3rd ed. (Chicago: SPSS Inc., 1988) Chapter 5.

Chapter 5

Data Coding and Sources

*I*n prior chapters, the DATA LIST command was illustrated by using alpha data, or actual words, to enable beginners to start using SPSS commands in a familiar environment. In addition, the data were included in the same file as the SPSS commands to see how they fit together. Alpha data, however, are rarely used in research, and files of data are often separated from files containing SPSS commands. This chapter covers coding data into numeric format and using external data files rather than combining the data and commands.

DATA CODING

If we do not use alpha data, obviously we use numeric data. We transform, or code, the alpha data by assigning numbers to the responses. In the illustrations of Chapter 4, we surveyed students about how women should be treated in various situations. Those surveyed were to choose one of three responses: APPROVE, NEUTRAL, or DISAPPROVE. Instead of entering these responses as alphabetical strings, social scientists transform them to numeric data by assigning numbers (codes) to each response, such as 1 = APPROVE, 2 = NEUTRAL, and 3 = DISAPPROVE.

Data coding is the process of translating the data from one "language" (English words) to another "language" (numbers) just as we might translate English words to their French or German equivalents. In fact, as we will see later in this chapter, we even develop a dictionary for translating alpha responses to numbers and vice versa. Unless you are particularly mathematically inclined, you would probably much rather deal with words than numbers. In fact, transforming the former to the latter probably seems both rather cumbersome and rather silly. There are very good reasons for coding data, however, and two primary ones are anonymity and statistical power.

Anonymity

In social surveys we often seek intimate, possibly even embarrassing, information. It is important to promise anonymity to the respondents, not only for their protection but also to encourage honest responses. Even with the very simple survey discussed so far, some individuals may not want their family backgrounds broadcast to other students, and other may hide their true feelings about treating women for fear of being labeled sexist. Promising anonymity increases the chance that people will be willing to give us sensitive information and respond as they actually feel instead of giving some socially correct answer.

Since data files may be used by more than one person, it is important not to identify specific individuals in them. Typically, a unique code number is assigned to each completed survey form, and these code numbers become the values of the RESP variable, rather than respondent names. The original survey forms which contain each individual's name are then locked away in a file cabinet or other secure place, accessible only to the director of the research project.

If anonymity is so important, why bother even identifying respondents by code number? Humans make mistakes, including mistakes in entering data. Suppose that we ran across an entry for the AGE variable reading "SF"—an obvious typographical error. We could stare eternally at the keyboard, trying to divine what the response was supposed to be, but there is an easier approach. If this error occurred on the record for respondent 134, we would go back to the original surveys, find the one coded 134, look up the actual response, and correct the information in the data file.

Statistical Power

The greatest value of numeric codes is an enhanced ability to analyze the data. With alpha data, computers essentially can do only three things: The data can be examined for equivalence (equal to or not equal to), the computer can sort the responses in alphabetical order, and the computer can count the number of responses. There is not much else you can do. Even simple arithmetic calculations, such as adding, subtracting, multiplying, and dividing, are forbidden to us. (How do you divide a DISAPPROVE by a NEUTRAL?)

The illustrations at the end of Chapter 4 nearly exhaust the possibilities of alpha data. The FREQUENCIES statement commanded the computer to count the number of times APPROVE, NEUTRAL, and DISAPPROVE occurred on the cases in the data set. The computer did this and then listed the responses in alphabetical order: first, APPROVE, then DISAPPROVE, and finally

NEUTRAL. We want much more, such as finding the "average" response to the question. We also may want to investigate whether there is a connection (relationship) between some of the variables; for example, are seniors less sexist than freshmen? These tasks require numeric data.

Coding data in numeric format does not mean the arbitrary assignment of numbers to words. There are systems for assigning code numbers. Which system we use will depend on the nature of the data. Which system we use will also determine what mathematical operations can be performed on the data. To appreciate how coding provides us with additional statistical power, we need to examine coding systems, more commonly called **levels of measurement**.

LEVELS OF MEASUREMENT

A student's first reaction to the concept of coding is that the responses have no relationship to numbers. This is not necessarily true. Numbers do three things. They indicate a difference: 1 is different from 2; they indicate order: 2 is higher than 1; and they indicate a quantity: 2 is twice as much as 1. The responses to each of our variables have similar meanings, and we can use the properties of numbers to represent these meanings. There are four key levels of measurement: nominal, ordinal, interval, and ratio.

Nominal

Simply identifying similarities or differences is called a **nominal** level of measurement. A nominal coding system, or level of measurement, does not imply any order; it simply indicates that two items with the same number are equal and two items with different numbers are not equal.

We use a nominal system all the time, although without code numbers, whenever we organize anything. Putting socks in the top dresser drawer and sweaters in the second drawer does not indicate that socks are "better" than sweaters; they are just different, and we wish to keep them separate. Probably the most familiar example of a nominal coding system is the Dewey decimal system. Books on philosophy are numbered in the 100s, religious books in the 200s, and so on up to books dealing with geography and history in the 900s. Does this number system mean that a book with the Dewey number 945 is 9 times as "good" as a book with the number 105? Of course not. The numbers are simply a convenient way of separating books on different topics into different groups.

With the data we have, we could assign nominal codes to three of the variables: RESP, FAM, and SIB. As discussed earlier, each respondent could be given a unique identification number for the RESP variable. For the FAM and SIB variables, we could use 1 for the first alternative on each variable and 2 for the second. With variables measured at the nominal level, any numbering system will do as long as the same number is not used for two different categories. For the FAM variable, we could use code 3 for those raised with both parents and 9 for those raised in a one-parent family. We just cannot assign the same code number to both because then we could not distinguish between them.

Ordinal

A second, and more powerful, type of coding is **ordinal**, in which numbers represent some order (higher or lower) in the responses. This level of measurement is appropriate for the approve/disapprove questions asked. Here the conceptual variable is a true continuum, representing differences in degrees; there is such a thing called sexism in the world which people can have a little of, a lot of, or fine gradations in between. Our operational level variable, however, has been able to capture only a limited aspect of this continuum, a greater-than or less-than ordering. Those who approve of treating women differently have more sexism than those who are neutral while those who disapprove have the least.

Although this operational variable allows us to place people in order, we do not know how much each group differs from the other. As illustrated in Figure 5.1*a*, the Disapprove response may represent people at the very low end of the continuum while the Neutral and Approve responses may be close together at the high end. Alternatively, as in Figure 5.1*b*, the three responses may represent people equally spaced across the conceptual variable. An ordinal level of measurement for an operational variable shows us only order, not distance, on the conceptual variable.

This point deserves further elaboration. A good comparison is to use letter grades (A through F) to "measure" results on an examination. There may be

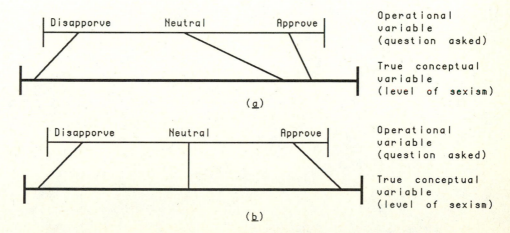

Figure 5.1 An ordinal measure of a conceptual variable.

significant differences among those who received an A on the examination; a few students might have obtained a perfect 100 percent score while others may have barely eked out an A with a 90 percent score. We do know, in an ordinal sense, that students receiving an A performed better than those receiving a B, but we do not know *how much* better. The difference between any two A and B students may be a small difference of 89 versus 90 percent or the A and B may represent a substantial difference of an 80 versus a 100 percent examination score.

For ordinal variables, any coding system is acceptable as long as we maintain the proper order among the responses. In Figure 5.2, the survey responses are arranged in order; Disapprove shows less sexism than Neutral, which reflects less sexism than Approve. The first two coding systems in Figure 5.2 maintain this order: 1 is less than 2 which is less than 3, and 5 is less than 25 which is less than 58. The third coding system, however, violates the order of the responses since 25, the code for the Neutral response, is not less than 10, the code for the Approve response.

At the beginning of this section, we said that an ordinal coding system was more powerful than a nominal one. One illustration of this is that an ordinal system allows us to estimate the "average" attitude of the students toward women. By definition, ordinally measured data rank responses in a high-to-low order. Consider Figure 5.3, responses regarding whether women should be treated differently from men in selecting soldiers for combat. Figure 5.3 is the same as Figure 4.9, except that we have now assigned code numbers representing the order of the responses. For comparison, Figure 4.9 is repeated at the bottom of Figure 5.3

Notice one immediate difference between Figures 5.3 and 4.9: The responses are now in rank order from most approval to least approval. When only alpha data were used, the computer ordered the responses alphabetically with A̲PPROVE coming first, then D̲ISAPPROVE, and finally N̲EUTRAL. Now that we have assigned code numbers to represent low to high sexism, the responses are reported according to their code number ranking, not the sheer happenstance of which responses come first in the alphabet.

For ordinal variables, the average response is represented by the person in the middle of this rank order. Since we surveyed 300 students, we count down 150 students from the top of our ordering to locate the person in the middle. In Figure 5.3 we find there are 143 people in the top category (APPROVE) and 36

Ordinal operational variable:	Disapprove	<	Neutral	<	Approve
Coding system 1	1	<	2	<	3
Coding system 2	5	<	25	<	58
Coding system 3	5	<	25	>	10

Figure 5.2 Coding systems for ordinal variables.

Q1

VALUE LABEL	VALUE	FREQUENCY	PERCENT	VALID PERCENT	CUM PERCENT
	1	121	40.3	40.3	40.3
	2	36	12.0	12.0	52.3
	3	143	47.7	47.7	100.0
TOTAL		300	100.0	100.0	

VALID CASES   300   MISSING CASES   0

Figure 4.9 repeated for comparison:

Q1

VALUE LABEL	VALUE	FREQUENCY	PERCENT	VALID PERCENT	CUM PERCENT
	APPROVE	143	47.7	47.7	47.7
	DISAPPROVE	121	40.3	40.3	88.0
	NEUTRAL	36	12.0	12.0	100.0
TOTAL		300	100.0	100.0	

VALID CASES   300   MISSING CASES   0

Figure 5.3 Sample output from the FREQUENCIES procedure with coded data.

in the next category (NEUTRAL), so person number 150, the middle of our ranking, is in the NEUTRAL category. This approach to calculating the average is called the **median**, and is used with ordinal data.

Observe that we cannot calculate a real average with nominal data. Nominal responses represent no order, so there is no such thing as a middle. Trying to calculate an average with nominal data is like trying to establish the average content of library books—100 books on history combined with 95 on biology and 120 on engineering "average" a book on anthropology, a nonsensical conclusion.

Interval

A more powerful coding system yet is **interval**. An interval level of measurement represents actual quantities of something. Again, the underlying conceptual variable represents differences in degrees, but our operational variable now measures these degrees, allowing us to identify how close or far apart people are on the conceptual variable. From the data we have been working with, the AGE variable can be measured on an interval basis because the numbers represent a quantity—years that a person has lived. This level of measurement is called interval because the interval, or space, between any two numbers is a fixed size

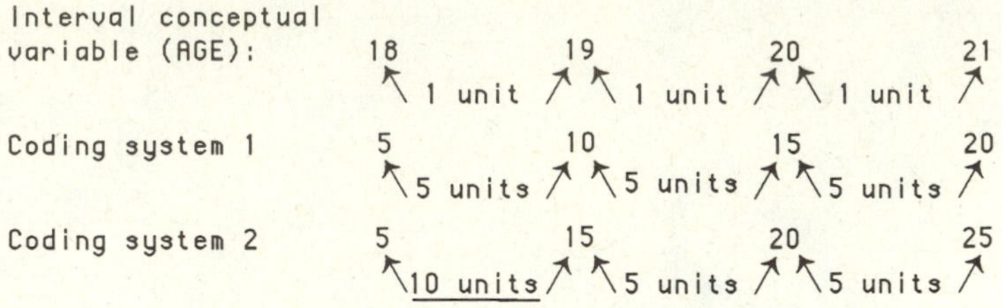

```
Interval conceptual
variable (AGE):        18           19           20           21
                         ↖ 1 unit ↗ ↖ 1 unit ↗ ↖ 1 unit ↗

Coding system 1        5            10           15           20
                         ↖ 5 units ↗ ↖ 5 units ↗ ↖ 5 units ↗

Coding system 2        5            15           20           25
                         ↖ 10 units ↗ ↖ 5 units ↗ ↖ 5 units ↗
```

Figure 5.4 Coding systems for an interval variable.

or distance. The variable AGE is interval because the distance between ages 20 and 21, or 1 year, is equal to the distance between ages 30 and 31.

Any coding system used for interval variables must maintain not only the order of people on the conceptual variable, but also their distances apart. Say that our survey of college students includes respondents between the ages of 18 and 21. Figure 5.4 shows two ways of coding these responses. The first coding system, 5-10-15-20, maintains both the young-to-old order of the respondents and their distances apart; 18- and 19-year-olds are equally as distant from each other (5 units) as 19- and 20-year-olds and 20- and 21-year-olds. The second coding system maintains the proper order, but violates the equal-distance requirement since 18- and 19-year-olds appear farther apart under this coding system (10 units) than 19- and 20-year-olds (5 units), even though they are equally distant from each other on the true conceptual variable.

Usually interval variables are variables with which we associate numbers in everyday life: age, years of education, income, and number of children. Consequently, we simply use these numbers to code the variable, giving 18-year-olds the code number 18. While certainly reasonable, an interval coding system only requires that we maintain the order and distance information that our measure of the conceptual variable provides.

With an interval level of measurement, we can also calculate the **mean**, a more precise indicator of the average than the median. The mean makes use of the actual distances between points to calculate the average of a group of responses, while the median does not. Let us consider a very common example, calculating a grade-point average (GPA). Assume we took five courses in one semester and ended up with grades as portrayed in Figure 5.5: 2 A's, 2 D's, and 1 F. The median merely looks for the grade in the middle, in this case a D, but does not consider how far above or below the middle the other grades are. Distances between the code numbers are assumed to have little meaning with ordinal variables. The mean, however, does take these distances into account; A's are given greater weight than B's or C's because they are farther from the middle and distances are presumed to have a real meaning.

Ratio

The highest level of measurement is ratio. A **ratio variable** is one that has a true zero. Take age and income as examples. These variables are measured not only at the interval level but also at the ratio level, for scores of zero on these variables

```
- - - Median - - - -       - - - - - - - - - Mean - - - - - - - - -

                                                   Grade
Number        Grades       Number     Grades    x  Value   =   Total

   2           A's            2        A's     x   4 pts   =     8
   0           B's            0        B's     x   3 pts   =     0
   0           C's            0        C's     x   2 pts   =     0
   2           D's            2        D's     x   1 pt    =     2
   1           F's            1        F's     x   0 pts   =     0

  ----                      -----                              ----

   5 grades                  5 grades                      10 points


Median = middle value.      Mean = the sum of the values (10 points)
Third grade down from       divided by the number of grades (5), which
the top is a D.             equals 2.0, or a grade of C.
```

Figure 5.5 Calculating a grade-point average by using the median and mean.

really mean zero—a complete absence of age or income. In contrast, variables such as GPA or degrees Fahrenheit may be measured intervally but have no true zero point. Zero degrees Fahrenheit does not mean a complete absence of heat, nor does a zero GPA represent a total lack of learning.

Although ratio deserves mention as the highest level of measurement, we do not refer to ratio variables again in this text. Ratio variables use the same measure of central tendency—the mean—as do interval variables. Similarly, almost all introductory statistics, such as those discussed in this text, draw no distinctions between interval and ratio variables. If you continue your study into advanced statistics, you will encounter some procedures in which the difference between an interval and a ratio variable is crucial. For our purposes, however, we need only distinguish among nominal, ordinal, and interval levels of measurement.

Using the levels of measurement reviewed above, we can now code our data: RESP, FAM, and SIB nominally; CLASS, Q1, Q2, and Q3 ordinally; and AGE intervally. With the data in coded format, our program will now look like Figure 5.6. Numbers have replaced words in the data, and our DATA LIST statement reflects this; fewer columns are used for each variable, and the alpha designation (A) has been removed. Our program is now considerably more compact, which

```
0001    DATA LIST / RESP 1-3 CLASS 5 AGE 7-8 FAM 10  SIBn12 Q1 14 Q2 16 Q3 18
0002    BEGIN DATA
0003    101  1  18  1  1   1  1  3
0004    102  2  20  2  2   3  3  3
0005    103  4  24  1  1   2  3  3
0006    104  4  21  2  1   3  2  2
0007    105  3  19  1  2   1  3  2
  .      .   .   .   .  .   .  .  .
  .      .   .   .   .  .   .  .  .
  .      .   .   .   .  .   .  .  .
  .      .   .   .   .  .   .  .  .

0304    END DATA
```

Figure 5.6 DATA LIST command with numeric data.

can be seen by comparing Figure 5.6 with the identical program using alpha responses in Figure 4.8.

MORE ABOUT LEVELS OF MEASUREMENT

We distinguish between different levels of measurement because this is a fundamental idea that affects many of the topics covered later. It is also a topic about which beginning students of statistics seem to become easily confused. We defined the basic levels of measurement above, but we delve further into them to touch on the aspects of measurement levels that seem to create the greatest confusion.

Using Appropriate Procedures

Later discussions of statistical procedures to analyze data will include different procedures that seem to accomplish basically the same thing. The median and mean briefly described in this chapter are examples, both designed to identify the average. Different statistics exist for the same purpose because each procedure is designed for variables coded at different levels of measurement. Some statistics are useful only for variables measured intervally, others for ordinal variables, and still others for nominal ones. You must use the right tool for the job. It would not be helpful to use a sledge hammer to fix your stereo set. Neither would it be productive to try to tear down a brick wall with a screwdriver. In statistics, as in everything else, the tools you are using (statistical procedures) must be appropriate for the material (variables) you have at hand.

The Computer and Levels of Measurement

We need to recognize that a variable's level of measurement is information that we (the analysts) possess. We examine the operational variables to assess whether the code numbers represent nominal, ordinal, or interval measures of the conceptual variable. The computer, however, simply sees the code numbers and has no idea whether they are nominal categories, ordinal levels, or interval quantities. If we ask the computer to perform an interval-level analysis on nominal data, it will happily do so and give us results—meaningless results, but the computer does not know that. Remember that the computer is a servant, but a stupid one. It is our job to determine the legitimacy of what has been done and the value (if any) of the results.

Our Purpose and Levels of Measurement

Beginning statistics students often treat numbers as though they were sacred. Numbers are a tool and are useful only if they are relevant to our tasks. For different people, numbers can have quite different meanings. Let us go back for a moment to the sexism questions that we originally labeled as ordinal. Our purpose is to use them as indicators of higher or lower rankings on the conceptual variable sexism. Someone else may want to use the same operational variables to measure a different concept, such as the possession of opinions on gender issues. For this latter conceptual variable, the operational variables are but nominal measures of same versus different. The neutral responses represent those who are ambivalent or apathetic, while both the approve and disapprove responses represent a different group, those with opinions.

The same can be true in the opposite direction. We might have asked respondents about their religious preferences, a purely nominal distinction between belonging to one group versus another, to see if levels of sexism might differ among Protestant, Catholics, and Jews. Someone else may take this variable and order the responses to represent a ranking of how each denomination treats women. Episcopalians, who recently ordained a female bishop, would be near the top while fundamentalist Islamic groups that believe women should wear veils in public would be near the bottom.

Such practices are not unusual, for the same item is often used for different purposes. A book can be used as a textbook, in which case its content is of primary importance, or it can be used as a paperweight, where its content becomes less important than its weight. This is also true of information. Used for one purpose, it can be no more than a nominal indication of differences, but when it is used for another purpose, the information may become an ordinal ranking or an interval measure of quantities.

Generally speaking, variables take on one characteristic which changes little from one research purpose to another. It is difficult to see, for example, how our codes for the RESP variable could be anything but nominal. Nonetheless, the reader must remember that the level of measurement of an operational variable depends on how is it used, or what conceptual variable we are trying to measure with it. As you engage in social research, do not blindly treat operational variables as having a fixed and unchanging meaning, but instead always ask what meaning the variable's code numbers have for *your* particular purpose.

The Difference Between Ordinal and Interval

Nominal variables are usually pretty easy to identify because the code numbers associated with the responses do not represent more or less of anything. If we ask respondents to identify their race and code American Indians as 4, this does not mean they have more "race" than blacks who are coded 3. They are just same-versus-different designations.

The difference between ordinal and interval variables is not always clearcut, however. It is a judgment call whether our operational variable represents mere rankings or equal distances on the conceptual variable. Return to Figure 5.1. The only thing we know for sure is that the approve/disapprove responses represent a high-to-low ranking on the conceptual variable of sexism. However, it might be reasonable to conclude that these responses also represent equal distances on the conceptual variable; the difference in the amount of sexism between those who disapprove and those who are neutral is the same as the difference between those who are neutral and those who approve.

The statistics available for interval-level variables are considerably more powerful than those that can be used on nominal and ordinal variables. Consequently, social scientists often use interval statistics on variables that, at first glance, might look like ordinal rankings only. How legitimate this is depends on whether the researcher can make a persuasive case that the code numbers on the operational variable actually do represent distances on the conceptual variable.

A very common example of this practice is the grade-point-average example in Figure 5.5. When a strict definition is used, grades are merely ordinal rankings, but on average the differences between grades A and B are about the same as the differences between grades B and C, and so on through grades D and F. Thus, universities follow the common practice of using the mean, rather than the median, to determine a student's average grade for all courses taken. The mean is more valuable because it provides finer distinctions than the median does. By calling the value of the middle person the average, the median is limited to the five existing categories: A, B, C, D, and F. The mean can take on decimal point values between the categories, enabling us to differentiate between a high C and a low C average or a GPA of 2.2 versus 2.8.

Caution is in order here. Some social scientists are quite lenient in treating variables as interval measures; others are quite strict in insisting that variables be treated as ordinal unless a strong case can be made that they are actually interval measures. In determining which route to follow, ask your instructor what approach he or she prefers. Social science is constantly changing, and books quickly become out of date. Your instructor can provide you with contemporary thinking about this practice.

Dichotomies

Although ordinal versus interval distinctions are sometimes vague, it is virtually never reasonable to treat nominal variables as anything but nominal. There is one exception to this rule, and that occurs when we are dealing with either a nominal or an ordinal variable that is a **dichotomy**—it has only two values, such as 1 = male and 2 = female. Recall the definition of an interval level of measurement: The distance between any two adjacent numbers is the same as the distance between any other pair of adjacent numbers. With dichotomous variables, there is only one distance, and it is equal to itself—this distance between male and female is the same as that between female and male. Thus, since all the distances (there being only one) are of equal size, it is appropriate to treat dichotomies as interval measures of conceptual variables. In statistical analysis, such dichotomies are also called **dummy variables**. With this one exception, however, we reiterate the warning to never use ordinal- or interval-level statistics on nominal variables.

The material in this section may be a bit frustrating to some readers. We started with a clear distinction between the levels of measurement and then proceeded to make these distinctions somewhat fuzzy. At this point, we can only say, "Fear not." We are still at the beginning of our journey through social statistics. As we proceed, we will return many times to the question of how our variables are measured and what statistics are appropriate for them. For now, we turn to the next topic, recalling what the numbers mean.

CODEBOOKS AND EXTERNAL DATA FILES

Coding data in numeric format has a number of advantages but also one serious drawback—what if we forget what the numbers mean? After we complete our survey, it may sit on the shelf for weeks while we work on other class assignments. Returning to the data later, we no longer remember whether 1 represents approve or disapprove.

Codebooks

Clearly, there is a need to keep some record of the coding process, and this record is called a **codebook**. A codebook is developed for each study conducted. Often the first few pages of the codebook describe many of the study characteristics: when it was conducted, who sponsored it, and how many cases there are. Then comes the heart of the codebook: a detailed description of each variable and how it was coded. For our study, the codebook section describing variable Q1 would look like Figure 5.7.

Contained in Figure 5.7 is all the information needed about the data. On the top line there is the variable name (**Q1**), which record for each case (**1**) contains this variable, and in what column(s) on that record (**14**) are found the data for this variable. In short, the top line contains most of the information used in the DATA LIST statement. Following this line is the exact wording of the question asked; then come the possible answers and the code numbers affiliated with each.

If we ever become confused about what a variable or its code numbers mean,

```
VARIABLE = Q1                RECORD = 1              COLUMN(S) = 14

QUESTION:   Please tell me whether you approve of, are neutral toward,
or disapprove of treating women differently from men in the following
situations:

     Selecting military personnel for combat duty

     Code        Response

      1          Approve

      2          Neutral

      3          Disapprove
```

Figure 5.7 Sample codebook entry for the Q1 variable.

reference to the codebook will provide the essential information. Particularly important in interpreting variables is the exact wording of the question. Questions are operational measures of conceptual variables, and some questions may be better measures than others. If the codebook simply described this variable as "a response about using women in combat," we would be asking others who might use the data to trust us that the question was a good measure of this attitude. Including the question's exact wording allows other users to make their own judgments as to how valid a measure the question is.

Corollaries to this reasoning occur regularly in everyday life. When someone presents us with some startling and unbelievable information (e.g., "Did you know that 90 percent of the U.S. public does not know the President's name?"), our reaction is often, "That's crazy! How did you determine that?" This reaction is equivalent to requesting the other person to tell us what his or her measuring instrument was that produced the information. From the other person's answer—"Well, they knew his first and last names, but not his middle names" (George *Herbert Walker* Bush)—we decide for ourselves whether the question was a legitimate measure of the concept (public ignorance).

Secondary Analysis

To this point, we have only described using data that are included as part of the program typed in the text area. More commonly we use a data file that already exists, either one we created or one provided by another source. **Secondary analysis** is a term used to describe the analysis of data collected by someone else. It may seem strange to think of using someone else's data, but this is actually a far more common practice in social research than scholars collecting their own data. A number of profit and nonprofit organizations continually amass files of data on selected subjects. Along with the diennial census, the Census Bureau regularly collects information on family income, housing, living conditions, employment, ethnic composition, and the education levels of U.S. citizens, to name but a few topics. Other government agencies collect information on business conditions, the operation of government programs, crime rates, pollution levels, and birth and death statistics. Major newspapers and TV networks regularly conduct polls of U.S. citizens on current issues, and public and private organizations provide grants for the collection of data by academics.

Once the primary analysis of the information has been completed, the organization collecting the data often releases them for broader use. The original collecting organization may have thoroughly probed the data to obtain all the information *it* needs, but others may be able to use the data to explore different questions. For example, the FBI collects national information on crime rates because it wishes to detect increases or decreases over time. Another individual, however, may wish to use these data to determine whether there is any relationship between a community's crime rate and the quality of the community's schools, the size of its police force, or the local rate of unemployment. Data are essentially raw materials. Like bricks, data can have many uses; one person could build a wall, another could build a garage, and still another could use the bricks for landscaping or paving a patio.

The American National Election Study and the General Social Survey

There are two data sets of particular interest to us because they will be used for numerous examples later in this text. The first is the 1988 **American National Election Study**. Since 1952, the Survey Research Center at the University of Michigan has conducted a major national survey during election years. Unlike surveys commonly reported in the media, the American National Election Study is not designed to primarily predict who will win the presidential contest, but rather to understand what forces lead people to vote as they do (or not vote at all). Thus the American National Election Study asks respondents what issues they consider important, their positions on those issues, their views about the personal qualities of the presidential candidates, their views about government and public groups in general, and a number of items of information about each respondent's background and recent history. The 1988 version of this survey contains about 2000 respondents and about an equal number of variables or items of information on each respondent.

While the American National Election Study is of primary interest to political scientists, the second data set, the **General Social Survey**, is of greater interest to sociologists. The General Social Survey is a broad-based survey of social attitudes, interactions, and behaviors that is conducted at regular intervals by the National Opinion Research Center (NORC) associated with the University of Chicago. The 1988 general Social Survey includes about 1500 respondents and approximately 1000 variables on such items as racial, sexual, political, and religious topics.

From each of these two data sets we have taken as a subset a small number of variables which are distributed along with this text. The codebooks for the variables in these data subsets are included in Appendixes A and B. In the later chapters we use variables from these two data sets for illustrations. Readers should also be able to duplicate the illustrations, or expand upon them, by performing their own analyses of the data.

Raw Data Files

Using already existing data files simplifies the process considerably but also requires a slightly different approach to reading the data. When an organization distributes data to others, the data are generally sent as a **raw data file**. Data-collecting organizations code their data in numeric format and a raw data file consists of these codes. It would look like Figure 5.8, nothing but a series of numbers in rows and columns. The scholar requesting the data also receives a copy of the codebook identifying where in the array of numbers the variables can be found that she or he is particularly interested in and what responses the code numbers stand for.

The original survey we discussed used sheets of paper (the survey form) to record responses. These responses then had to be typed into a text file at the terminal before the computer could read the data. Raw data files, however, are provided in a machine-readable format on tape, disk, computer cards, or any

```
0001    1012567888734002352791123029834729837659283752527375 0
0002    1028837262309482711233418193813956032938217289461832 91
0003    1033243875619386201298376162745891209831235556372888 2
0004    1040066004303030002958438378472811237482317161615551 1
0005    1058837838276273458111928191929192847533276176622222 6
0006    1061929192847533276176622222658912098312355563728898 9
0007    1076788873400235279112302984753327617662222266784532 3
0008    1084729837659283752527375043030300002958438378472823 93
0009    1091929192847533276176622222675619386201298376162745 8
0010    1104303030002958438378472840066004303030002958438375 3
0011    1117561938620129837616274589472983765928375252737509 2
0012    1121298376162745891209831382762734581119281919297372 9
0013    1131929192847533276176622222667888734002352791123029 8
0014    1143324387561938620129837616271298376162745891209831 7
0015    1156788873400235279112302983324387561938620129837616 2
```

Figure 5.8 A typical raw data file.

other medium the computer can read directly. Rather than typing the data ourselves, we simply tell the computer to read this file. To accomplish this, we must instruct the computer to prepare to read data from somewhere else, rather than in the middle of our program, and how to find the data we are interested in. Such a program looks like Figure 5.9.

The DATA LIST statement in Figure 5.10 now includes a new command before the slash and the beginning of the variable listing; a **FILE =** **'computer.file.name'** statement. This added statement tells SPSS that the DATA LIST applies to an **external file** (one stored elsewhere on the computer system), instead of data contained below in the program. The final difference between this program and previous ones is that the data are no longer contained in the program; nor are the associated BEGIN DATA and END DATA statements.

Referring to Files

The term "computer.file.name" stands for whatever file-naming system your computer and version of SPSS uses to refer to external files. The three primary approaches use JCL, exact file names, or a FILE HANDLE command. Your instructor or computer operator can tell you which system you must use to refer to files on SPSS commands. Each is described briefly below.

JCL   IBM mainframes using OS use JCL. When you refer to an external file, additional lines of JCL are needed, as shown in Figure 5.10. Lines 001, 002, and 006 of the JCL were briefly described in Supplement 4.1. The new lines of JCL

```
0001    DATA LIST    FILE = computer.file.name / RESP 1-3   CLASS 5   AGE 7-8   FAM 10
0002            SIB 12   Q1 14    Q2 16   Q3 18
0003    FREQUENCIES  VARIABLES = Q1
```

Figure 5.9 Program statements to access an external data file.

```
0001    //   JOB  (USERID,ACCT#,1min,5sec,3K  lines)
0002    //   EXEC SPSSX
0003    //LARRY       DD      DSN=ELEC88,UNIT=TAPE,VOL=SER=TAPE11,
0004    //    DCB=(RECFM=FB,LRECL=80,BLKSIZE=1600),
0005    //    LABEL=(12,IN),DISP=OLD
0006    //SYSIN DD *
0007    DATA LIST   FILE = LARRY  /  V1  1-2    V2  3    V3  4    V4  5-7    V5  8
0008    FREQUENCIES VARIABLES = V5
0009    /*
0010    //
```

Figure 5.10 JCL for accessing external files.

are numbered 003, 004, and 005. They are called **JCL data definition** (DD) lines for they identify the raw data or other files to which you refer in your program. These lines contain information on the file's name, the tape or disk on which it is stored, and some information about the file's structure. Sometimes you may need only one or two data definition lines, instead of all three; at other times you may need two sets of data definition lines, one for an external file you are reading in and the other for a new file you are going to save. As before, your instructor will provide you with any JCL statements that your institution requires, and you need merely copy them into your command file.

The file name used on SPSS commands refers to the data definition lines in the JCL. For example, the DATA LIST statement in Figure 5.10 uses the file name LARRY. This refers the computer to line 3 of the JCL which begins with this name—the data definition statements instructing the computer how and where to find the file. On IBM mainframes using OS, file names always refer to JCL data definition lines beginning with that name. The actual name under which the file is stored could be—but does not have to be—the same as the name beginning the JCL data definition line.

Exact File Name   All other operating systems, including CMS running on IBM mainframes, normally refer directly to a file through the use of its multilevel name, enclosed in apostrophes or single quotation marks. For example, the file ELEC88.DAT on a floppy disk in drive B: would be referred to on the DATA LIST command with the statement

```
DATA LIST FILE = 'b:ELEC88.DAT'.
```

A file on a hard disk can be referred to just by its name if it is in the current directory, the one the software automatically goes to when looking for files. If the file wanted is in some other directory, a full path name needs to be included when you refer to the file, as in

```
DATA LIST  FILE = '\STATS\DATA\ELEC88.DAT'.
```

On some systems, the apostrophes or single quotation marks can be omitted when a file is in the current directory, but it is wise to get into the habit of always using them.

FILE HANDLE   Finally, if the file you are accessing has a particularly unusual or complex structure, you may need to use a **FILE HANDLE** command before referring to any files on the DATA LIST or other commands. The FILE HANDLE command, illustrated in Figure 5.11, gives a "handle" or nickname to a particular file (just as a CB "handle" is a nickname for a citizen's band radio user). Following the command words FILE HANDLE is the nickname we have given to the file, in this case ELEC88, because the data set in this example comes from a study of the 1988 presidential election. Like variable names, the nickname can be anything you wish, but it is common to use some name that reflects the information in the data file. Following the nickname is a slash, and then comes information explaining to SPSS where the file is located and what its characteristics are. This information may be simply a multilevel file name or a far more complex one with a number of additional statements describing the file.

After you enter the FILE HANDLE command, all later SPSS commands refer to the file by its handle only. Thus the DATA LIST command in Figure 5.11 is

DATA LIST **FILE = ELEC88**

where ELEC88 is the handle defined on the immediately preceding FILE HANDLE command.

Command Files and Data Files

When an external source of data is used, the data themselves reside in a file on one of the computer's storage devices. Because the file contains data only, it is typically, and understandably, called a **data file**. We type in commands telling SPSS how to find the external data and what to do with them. We also typically save these programming commands as a *different* file which is called (any guesses?) a **command file**.

How do all these files get put together? When we run or execute the commands in our command file, the CPU sees that we are requesting data to be read in from a separate data file, so it fetches the data file described. The data file does not appear in the input window, but instead is read, using the DATA LIST command, directly into the computer's internal memory. Once the CPU has read the data, it is ready to carry out any analysis we wish to perform. Whenever we leave an SPSS session, the command and data files are erased from the CPU's memory, making it ready to use another software program, but they remain on their respective storage devices and can be used over and over.

```
0001    FILE  HANDLE    ELEC88   /  'computer.file.name'
0002    DATA LIST   FILE = ELEC88  / RESP 1-3   CLASS 5   AGE 7-8   FAM 10
0003       SIB 12   Q1 14   Q2 16   Q3 18
0004    FREQUENCIES   VARIABLES = Q1
```

Figure 5.11 The FILE HANDLE command.

RELEASE 4

Chapter 4 mentioned that you must instruct the computer to run the DATA LIST command before performing any statistical analyses, such as the FREQUENCIES procedure. On the Macintosh and OS/2 implementations of Release 4, you can access files by using the FILE menu on the menu bar. In most cases when you do this, SPSS will automatically read the data into its memory without you specifically having to instruct it to run a file-accessing command, such as DATA LIST. Messages on the output screen will inform you if this is happening.

If you type a file's name onto a command in the input window, instead of using the FILE menu bar choice, you must instruct SPSS to run whatever file-accessing command you are using. This process is performed automatically only when files are accessed through the menu bar.

SUMMARY

In this chapter we have finally moved from some introductory concerns to actually using data as they typically exist in social science research—as coded, external data files. We have learned how to code data, use codebooks to interpret data that have been coded, and use external data files rather than typing the data into the input window. With the knowledge gained in this chapter, we could begin analyzing data now, but there are ways to make our data easier to use and interpret. That is the subject of the next chapter: describing data and using system files.

REVIEW

Key Terms

Data coding	Codebook
Levels of measurement	Secondary analysis
Nominal	American National Election Study
Ordinal	General Social Survey
Median	Raw data file
Interval	External file
Mean	JCL data definition
Ratio variable	FILE HANDLE
Dichotomy	Data file
Dummy variables	Command file

Exercises

5.1 Return to the sample data file used for Exercise 4.1.
  a. Look at each operational variable and determine whether it is a nominal, ordinal, or interval measure of the conceptual variable.
  b. Code each variable in the data set, and develop a codebook.
  c. Enter the coded data into a data file, as done for the uncoded data in Chapter 4, and run FREQUENCIES on the same variable(s) you used for Exercise 4.1. Compare the results.

5.2 *a.* Examine the codebook descriptions of one or more of the following variables from the GSS88 data set: RACSCHL, TITHING, SPANKING, or PREMARSX. Describe some conceptual variables that you think these operational variables measure. Having done that, determine the level at which the operational variable measures the conceptual variable.
  b. Do the same as in part *a* with the following variables from the ELEC88 data set: V36, V48, V52, and V76.
  (Note: When secondary analysis is used, the research process becomes somewhat turned on its head. Instead of starting with a concept and developing an operational way to measure it, we are presented with a bunch of operational variables but no overarching concept. The tendency is to analyze the operational variables without even considering what concepts we are dealing with—this tendency must be avoided. Since hypotheses are always written at the conceptual level, we need to think of what concepts each operational variable might be used to measure.)

5.3 Identify the problems, if any, that exist in the commands below. You may assume that the file names, variable names, and variable locations are accurate.

SPSS/PC+ and Release 4 computers:
  a. DATA LIST FILE = rose.dat / N1 1 N2 2
  b. DATA LIST FIRE = '/spss/tulip.dat' / N1 1 N2 2
  c. DATA LIST FILE = 'rose.dat' N1 1 N2 2

IBM mainframes using OS:
  d. DATA LIST FILE = 'rose' / N1 1 N2 2
  e. DATA LIST FILE = ROSE N1 1 N2 2
  f. DATA LIST FILE = ROSE / N1 1 N2 2

All computers:
  g. FILE HANDLE / '/spss/tulip.dat'
      DATA LIST FILE = TULIP / N1 1 N2 2
  h. DATA LIST FILE = ROSE / N1 1 N2 2
      FILE HANDLE ROSE / '/spss/tulip.dat'

SUGGESTED READINGS

Babbie, Earl. *The Practice of Social Research*, 5th ed. (Belmont, Calif.: Wadsworth, 1989) Chapter 13.

May, Richard B., Michael E. J. Masson, and Michael A. Hunter. *Application of Statistics in Behavioral Research* (New York: Harper & Row, 1990) Chapter 2.

Nachmias, David and Chava Nachmias. *Research Methods in the Social Sciences*, 3rd ed. (New York: St. Martin's, 1987) Chapters 13, 14.

Kiecolt, J. Jill and Laura E. Nathan. *Secondary Analysis of Survey Data*, Quantitative Applications in the Social Sciences, Sage University Papers Series No. 53 (Newbury Park, Calif.: Sage Publications, 1985).

Chapter
6

Data Description and System Files

*C*oding makes it convenient to enter data and enhances our ability to manipulate information. The obvious cost of data coding is our inability to easily interpret the output. As an illustration, let us run a FREQUENCIES procedure on variables V2, V3, and V4 from the ELEC88 data set to find out how the respondents voted in the 1988 presidential, House, and Senate elections. The output looks like Figure 6.1.

SPSS has done its job—it counted the responses and printed the results. Now we must do our job, which is to interpret what the numbers mean. To do this, we must know what these variable names and code numbers stand for. Is V3 how people voted for president, senator, or members of the House of Representatives? Does the code number 1 represent voting for the Democratic candidate or the Republican one? Of course, we can always consult the codebook, but having to continually flip back and forth between the codebook and the computer printout is a nuisance we prefer to avoid.

Avoidable it is, for SPSS allows us to label data, so that continual references to the codebook are unnecessary, and to save these label descriptions as an SPSS system file. In this chapter we look at commands that label the data—VARIABLE LABELS, VALUE LABELS, and MISSING VALUES—and the SAVE command which creates a system file.

V2

VALUE LABEL	VALUE	FREQUENCY	PERCENT	VALID PERCENT	CUM PERCENT
	0	265	13.0	13.0	13.0
	1	632	31.0	31.0	44.0
	2	563	27.6	27.6	71.6
	3	14	0.7	0.7	72.3
	8	548	26.9	26.9	99.1
	9	18	0.9	0.9	100.0
		-------	-------	-------	
	TOTAL	2040	100.0	100.0	

VALID CASES   2040   MISSING CASES   0

- -

V3

VALUE LABEL	VALUE	FREQUENCY	PERCENT	VALID PERCENT	CUM PERCENT
	0	265	13.0	13.0	13.0
	1	621	30.4	30.4	43.4
	2	433	21.2	21.2	64.7
	7	694	34.0	34.0	98.7
	8	15	0.7	0.7	99.4
	9	12	0.6	0.6	100.0
		-------	-------	-------	
	TOTAL	2040	100.0	100.0	

VALID CASES   2040   MISSING CASES   0

- -

V4

VALUE LABEL	VALUE	FREQUENCY	PERCENT	VALID PERCENT	CUM PERCENT
	0	276	13.5	13.5	13.5
	1	479	23.5	23.5	37.0
	2	359	17.6	17.6	54.6
	3	1	0.0	0.0	54.7
	6	609	29.9	29.9	84.5
	7	302	14.8	14.8	99.3
	8	6	0.3	0.3	99.6
	9	8	0.4	0.4	100.0
		-------	-------	-------	
	TOTAL	2040	100.0	100.0	

VALID CASES   2040   MISSING CASES   0

Figure 6.1 Output from the FREQUENCIES command on coded data.

VARIABLE LABELS

Using numeric sequencing to name variables (for example, V1, V2) indicates nothing about the content of the variables. Even when we try to use variable names with some meaning, that meaning may be difficult to decipher from a variable name that can be no more than eight characters long. It is not immediately obvious, for example, that the variable name SPWRKSTA from the GSS88 data stands for SPouse WoRKing STAtus.

The **VARIABLE LABELS** command allows us to add a label describing the contents of the variable. The command, illustrated in Figure 6.2, begins in column one with the command term VARIABLE LABELS. After the command term comes the name of the variable to be labeled. Following the variable's name is the label we want to attach to the variable. The label, which can be up to 40 characters long, must be enclosed in either single quotes (apostrophes) or double quotes.

The single or double quotation marks indicate to SPSS the beginning and ending of each label. Every character between these marks, including blank spaces, is considered by SPSS to be part of the label you want attached to a variable. SPSS gives you a choice of using either single or double quotation marks to enclose the label because you may want to use one of these symbols as part of the label itself. For example, we might wish to include an apostrophe in the label for variable V2, as in RESP'S PRESIDENTIAL VOTE. Had we done so, enclosing the label in apostrophes would lead SPSS to read the first apostrophe as the starting place of the label and the second apostrophe (between the P and S in RESP'S) as the end of the label. When we use double quotation marks instead to identify the beginning and end of the label, SPSS reads the apostrophe in the middle as a part of the actual label, not a mark indicating the end of the label.

If you are typing a list of labels for many variables, you can mix the symbols, using apostrophes for some labels and double quotation marks for others. Remember, however, that each individual label must begin and end with the same symbol. When you start a label with one symbol, SPSS considers the second appearance of that symbol to indicate the end of the label. If the second symbol is located in the wrong place or is not found at all, an error will result.

As with all SPSS commands, the command can continue on successive lines if you simply begin each additional line in column 2 or later. Note that in Figure 6.2 all the variable names and labels have been aligned to begin in the same column. This is a common practice since it makes it easy to spot each variable

```
001     DATA LIST FILE = ELEC88 / variable names, locations and types
002     VARIABLE LABELS      V2    'PRESIDENTIAL    VOTE'
003                          V3    'VOTE -  U.S.  HOUSE'
004                          V4    'VOTE -  U.S.  SENATE'
```

Figure 6.2 Format of the VARIABLE LABELS command.

```
001    DATA LIST FILE = ELEC88 / variable names, locations and types
002    VARIABLE LABELS      V2  'PRESIDENTIAL VOTE'    V3   'VOTE -
003         U.S. HOUSE'    V4  'VOTE - U.S. SENATE'
```

Figure 6.3 An incorrect format for the VARIABLE LABELS command.

and its associated label, but this is not required by SPSS. While you can continue the *command* for as many lines as you need, you should not split *labels* between lines, including one part of the label on one line and the second part on the next line, as shown in Figure 6.3. Without some additional symbols, which are beyond the scope of this text, splitting labels between lines will cause an error.

VALUE LABELS

Along with adding labels to variable names, we can add labels to variable code numbers. Descriptive labels are attached to the code numbers with the **VALUE LABELS** command. This command follows a similar format to the VARIABLE LABELS command and is illustrated in Figure 6.4. First is the command term VALUE LABELS beginning in column 1, followed by the name of the variable whose values we are going to label. After this, we list the values (codes) for that variable, followed by the labels to be connected with each code number. Like the VARIABLE LABELS command, these labels are enclosed in single or double quotation marks.

Value labels are shorter than variable labels and should take up no more than 20 characters, including spaces between the words comprising the label.

```
001    DATA LIST FILE = ELEC88 / variable names, locations and types
002    VARIABLE LABELS         V2   'PRESIDENTIAL VOTE'
003                            V3   'VOTE - U.S. HOUSE'
004                            V4   'VOTE - U.S. SENATE'
005    VALUE   LABELS          V2  1    "BUSH"
006                 2    "DUKAKIS"        3    "3RD PTY-INDEP"
007                 8    "DID NOT VOTE"   9    "NA"     "INAP" /
008        V3  1    "DEM CAND"    2    "REP CAND"
009                 3    "3RD PTY-INDEP"  7    "DID NOT VOTE"
010                 8    "DK"   9    "NA"   0    "INAP"    /
011        V4  1    "DEM CAND"    2    "REP CAND"
012                 3    "3RD PTY-INDEP"  6    "DID NOT VOTE"
013                 7    "NO SENATE RACE"  8    "DK"
014                 9    "NA"   0    "INAP" /
```

----

*The abbreviations "DK", "NA", and "INAP" are very commonly used in both codebooks and value labels. They stand for "Don't Know", "No Answer", and "Inapplicable" respectively.

Figure 6.4 Format of the VALUE LABELS command.

```
001    DATA LIST FILE = GSS88 / variable names, locations and types
002    VARIABLE LABELS    AIDSSCH  'BAR AIDS STUDENTS FROM SCHOOL'
003                       AIDSADS  'GOVT ADS PROMOTING SAFE SEX'
004                       AIDSSXED 'SCHOOLS TEACH SAFE SEX'
005                       AIDSIDS  'AIDS SUFFERERS WEAR ID TAGS'
006    VALUE  LABELS      AIDSSCH   AIDSADS   AIDSSXED    AIDSIDS
007       1   'SUPPORT'    2   'OPPOSE'    8   'NO OPINION'
008       9   'NO ANSWER'  0   'NA'
```

Figure 6.5 Attaching value labels to a group of variables.

Like the VARIABLE LABELS statement, the VALUE LABELS command can be continued for as many lines as necessary as long as each continuing line begins in column 2 or later and no single label is split between two lines.

(PC) (R4) There are two things about the VALUE LABELS command which are different from the VARIABLE LABELS statement. First, the VALUE LABELS command requires that different variables be separated by a slash (/). Since the VALUE LABELS statement is slightly more complex than the VARIABLE LABELS command, SPSS needs the slash to know when we move from one variable to another. This slash must also appear at the end of the list of value labels.

Second, we can perform on additional trick with the VALUE LABELS command, assigning value labels to a group of variables at one time. Consider the AIDS variables from the General Social Survey—questions about what actions people might support to deal with AIDS. Each policy mentioned has the same set of possible answers, all coded in the same manner: 1 for supporting the mentioned policy, 2 for opposing it, 8 for no opinion, 9 for no answer, and 0 for not applicable. Since the same code numbers have the same meanings for each variable, we want to attach identical value labels to the code numbers of each variable. This can be done by listing the names of multiple variables on the VALUE LABELS command followed by the code numbers and their labels. Then the labels will be applied to the entire list of variables. This process is illustrated in Figure 6.5.

Supplement 6.1

The TO Convention

We often have procedures that we wish to use on an entire group of variables; such as requesting frequencies for a group of variables or attaching the same value labels to a group of variables. One approach is to simply list each variable in the group, as in Figure 6.5. An alternative is to use the **TO convention**. The word TO is one of the key words or reserved words listed in Table 4.1 which have special meaning to SPSS. It is used to refer to any group of adjacent variables by listing the first variable in the group, the key word TO, and then the last variable in the group. Thus, instead of listing all the variables in the VALUE LABELS statement in Figure 6.5, we could have used AIDSSCH TO AIDSIDS, as shown in Figure 6.1S. The key word TO acts as a connector, signifying to SPSS that we are referring to a group of variables. Had we just listed AIDSSCH and AIDSIDS, the value labels would be applied to only those two variables. By separating

```
001    DATA LIST FILE = GSS88 / variable names, locations and types
002    VARIABLE LABELS     AIDSSCH    'BAR AIDS STUDENTS FROM SCHOOL'
003                        AIDSADS    'GOVT ADS PROMOTING SAFE SEX'
004                        AIDSSXED   'SCHOOLS TEACH SAFE SEX'
005                        AIDSIDS    'AIDS SUFFERERS WEAR ID TAGS'
006    VALUE  LABELS       AIDSSCH    TO     AIDSIDS
007         1  'SUPPORT'    2  'OPPOSE'    8  'NO OPINION'
008         9  'NO ANSWER'    0  'NA'
```

Figure 6.1S The VALUE LABELS command using the TO convention.

AIDSSCH and AIDSIDS with the key word TO, SPSS knows we want the labels applied to AIDSSCH, AIDSIDS, and all the variables in between these two.

The phrase "in between" in the previous sentence needs explanation. It implies some order, just as the phrase "from A to Z" implies an alphabetical order and "from 1 to 10" implies a numerical order. To SPSS, the order of the variables is neither alphabetical nor numeric, but rather the order in which the variables were described to SPSS on the DATA LIST command. Let us say that our DATA LIST was as in Figure 6.2S, with the RACE and SEX variables mixed in the middle of the AIDS variables. By using the statement AIDSSCH TO AIDSIDS we would be applying value labels such as "support" to code number 1 for all the variables in the group, including the RACE and SEX variables, where they obviously do not belong.

```
001    DATA LIST FILE = GSS88 / AIDSSCH 1    AIDSADS 2    AIDSSXED 3    RACE 4    SEX 5
002         AIDSIDS 6
003    VARIABLE LABELS     AIDSSCH    'BAR AIDS STUDENTS FROM SCHOOL'
004                        AIDSADS    'GOVT ADS PROMOTING SAFE SEX' .
005                        AIDSSXED   'SCHOOLS TEACH SAFE SEX'
006                        RACE       "RESP'S RACE"
007                        SEX        "RESP'S GENDER"
008                        AIDSIDS    'AIDS SUFFERERS WEAR ID TAGS'
009    VALUE  LABELS       AIDSSCH    TO     AIDSIDS
010         1  'SUPPORT'    2  'OPPOSE'    8  'NO OPINION'
011         9  'NO ANSWER'    0  'NA'
```

Figure 6.2S The TO convention and the order of the variables on the DATA LIST statement.

There is a way around this problem, for SPSS allows us to mix and match the way we list variables on which a procedure is to be performed. For our purpose, we identify the first three variables with the term AIDSSCH TO AIDSSXED, then skip over the RACE and SEX variables, and list just the last AIDS variable, AIDSIDS, as shown in Figure 6.3S.

```
001    DATA LIST FILE = GSS88 / AIDSSCH 1    AIDSADS 2    AIDSSXED 3    RACE 4    SEX 5
002         AIDSIDS 6
003    VARIABLE LABELS     AIDSSCH    'BAR AIDS STUDENTS FROM SCHOOL'
004                        AIDSADS    'GOVT ADS PROMOTING SAFE SEX'
005                        AIDSSXED   'SCHOOLS TEACH SAFE SEX'
006                        RACE       "RESP'S RACE"
007                        SEX        "RESP'S GENDER"
008                        AIDSIDS    'AIDS SUFFERERS WEAR ID TAGS'
009    VALUE  LABELS       AIDSSCH    TO     AIDSSXED    AIDSIDS
010         1  'SUPPORT'    2  'OPPOSE'    8  'NO OPINION'
011         9  'NO ANSWER'    0  'NA'
```

Figure 6.3S Identifying both groups and single variables in a procedure statement.

Many of the procedures examined in this text require us to give SPSS a list of the variables on which to perform the procedures. Whenever such a list of variables is required, the TO convention can be used. This convention is optional and never need be used, but there are occasions when you will find it a considerable time saver.

In Figure 6.4 we described variable and value labels for variables V2, V3, and V4 from the 1988 election data. If we now run a FREQUENCIES procedure on these two variables, the results look like Figure 6.6. Figure 6.6 is a duplicate of Figure 6.1 except that now the variable names and code numbers have the labels we created printed next to them. The added labels make the printout easier to interpret and reduce our need to continually refer to the codebook. In fact, the VARIABLE LABELS and VALUE LABELS commands essentially add codebook information to the printed output.

The labels attached with the VALUE LABELS command will not always match the output perfectly. Compare, for variable V3, the VALUE LABELS command in Figure 6.4 with the output for this variable in Figure 6.6. In Figure 6.4, we created the label "3rd PTY-INDEP" for value 3 of variable V3, but this label does not show up in Figure 6.6. Our VALUE LABELS command worked fine. The reason for the disparity is that none of the respondents gave answer number 3 when this particular survey was conducted, so SPSS will not report either this code number or its label. Similar minor disparities will exist between the output you produce and the codebooks in the appendixes. Since both surveys use closed-ended questions, response codes and their meanings were developed before the surveys were conducted. You will occasionally find a response code described in the codebook which will not show up on your output because no one surveyed gave that answer.

The biggest source of confusion about variable and value labels comes when we think of them as having some importance in the computer's operation or the statistical analyses it performs. They do not. The VARIABLE LABELS and VALUE LABELS commands are for our convenience only, and we are not required to use them. In fact, the computer never uses this information in its calculations—it does not read the label descriptions and say to itself, "Oh, that is what this variable means." The computer merely adds, subtracts, or otherwise manipulates the coded data. The labels are used for printing output because we humans like to know what the numbers stand for. The computer does not care. Labeling variables and their values is like labeling city streets or the buildings on a college campus; the streets and buildings do not care what they are called, but the labeling helps people find their way around.

MISSING VALUES

Using variable and value labels are optional conveniences that we can either use or not, depending on our preference. One thing that always needs to be done, however, is declaring **missing values**. What is this strange-sounding term "missing values"? Missing values are values or code numbers that represent missing information. When conducting a survey, we often run into situations where we were unable to obtain a complete response to all our questions from some of the respondents. Perhaps the interviewer forgot to ask one of the questions, or the respondent had to leave before the survey was completed. More common in social surveys are situations in which the respondent either cannot or will not

```
V2           PRESIDENTIAL  VOTE

                                                  VALID      CUM
      VALUE LABEL          VALUE  FREQUENCY  PERCENT  PERCENT  PERCENT

   INAP                      0      265       13.0     13.0     13.0
   BUSH                      1      632       31.0     31.0     44.0
   DUKAKIS                   2      563       27.6     27.6     71.6
   OTHER                     3       14        0.7      0.7     72.3
   DID  NOT  VOTE            8      548       26.9     26.9     99.1
   NA                        9       18        0.9      0.0    100.0
                                  -------   -------  -------
                         TOTAL     2040      100.0    100.0

VALID CASES   2040      MISSING CASES   0
```

- -

```
V3         VOTE  U.S.  HOUSE

                                                  VALID      CUM
      VALUE LABEL          VALUE  FREQUENCY  PERCENT  PERCENT  PERCENT

   INAP                      0      256       13.0     13.0     13.0
   DEMOC  CAND               1      621       30.4     30.4     43.4
   REPUB  CAND               2      433       21.2     21.2     64.7
   DID  NOT  VOTE            7      694       34.0     34.0     98.7
   DK                        8       15        0.7      0.7     99.4
   NA                        9       12        0.6      0.6    100.0
                                  -------   -------  -------
                         TOTAL     2040      100.0    100.0

VALID CASES   2040      MISSING CASES   0
```

- -

```
V4         VOTE  U.S.  SENATE

                                                  VALID      CUM
      VALUE LABEL          VALUE  FREQUENCY  PERCENT  PERCENT  PERCENT

   INAP                      0      276       13.5     13.5     13.5
   DEMOC  CAND               1      479       23.5     23.5     37.0
   REPUB  CAND               2      359       17.6     17.6     54.6
   3RD  PTY-INDEP            3        1        0.0      0.0     54.7
   DID  NOT  VOTE            6      609       29.9     29.9     84.5
   NO  SENATE  RACE          7      302       14.8     14.8     99.3
   DK                        8        6        0.3      0.3     99.6
   NA                        9        8        0.4      0.4    100.0
                                  -------   -------  -------
                         TOTAL     2040      100.0    100.0

VALID CASES   2040      MISSING CASES   0
```

Figure 6.6 Output of the FREQUENCIES procedure including variable and value labels.

answer some of the questions, such as opinions about a bill before Congress where the respondent does not know anything about the bill, or sensitive personal questions on income or sexual behavior which the respondent refuses to answer. In well-conducted surveys with trained interviewers, the amount of missing data or unanswered questions is kept to a minimum, but some will always occur.

What do we do when we encounter a case with missing responses on some of the variables? Our first reaction might be to consider the interviews containing missing data as worthless and to discard them. Such an approach is unworkable. Major surveys ask hundreds of questions, and we do not want to throw out information that the respondent did provide just because he or she failed to answer four or five questions. Not only is this wasteful, but also it distorts the study. Many citizens feel too uninformed to take a position on some issues. Discarding these cases will bias our sample, leaving us with only a highly educated and politically aware elite instead of a random sample of the entire U.S. population.

So we keep these respondents in the sample even if they did not answer all the questions, but how do we enter data for the cases where some variables have no responses? Merely leaving the columns containing these variables blank is a tactic occasionally used, but it is not the best approach. Sometimes we want to identify different types of missing responses.

Take variable V4, how people voted in their state's senate election. Many respondents told us whether they voted for the Democratic or Republican candidate, but a large number did not. The nonanswers are of three types: those who voluntarily did not vote, those unable to vote because no senate election was held in their state that year, and those who simply refused to tell us whether they voted. Suppose that we were originally curious about whether high-income respondents vote more often for Republicans or Democrats. To answer this question, all those who did not vote are irrelevant since the question deals with only voters. Later we may be curious about a second question: Are highly educated respondents more likely to vote than others? The last two categories of nonvoters are irrelevant to this question, for it requires comparing voters with *voluntary* nonvoters. Those who could not vote or who will not tell us if they voted are irrelevant, but the first group, voluntary nonvoters, should be included in the analysis.

Coding Missing Data

To maximize the value of our data, we want to code missing responses just as we do other responses, using one code number for apathetic nonvoters, a second code number for those unable to vote, and yet a third code number for those who did not answer the question at all. At the same time, we want to indicate that these responses are not "true" answers to our original question (Whom did you vote for?) and should be ignored during most analyses of this variable.

A common convention which deals with both needs is to use extreme, even outlandish, code numbers to represent missing data. Look at the code numbers for variable V4, how people voted in their state's U.S. Senate race. Code number 1 is used for those voting for the Democratic candidate, code number 2 for those voting Republican, and code 3 for those voting for a third-party candidate. We then jump to the other end of the number line for missing responses, using the number 6 for apathetic nonvoters, the number 7 for those who could not vote because there was no U.S. Senate race, and numbers 8, 9, and 0 for other types of nonanswers to the question. We could have used the numbers 4, 5, 6, 7, and

8 for these categories, but that would have given the impression that they were "real" answers to our question. Using numbers far from legitimate response codes symbolizes that these are very different types of responses.

The same procedure is used for variables that are more than one digit wide. Asking respondents how many years of schooling they have had will produce some two-digit responses: 12 years for high school graduates, 16 years for college graduates, and more for those with some postgraduate training. We would thus use code numbers 98 and 99 to represent missing data since not even the most dedicated professional student will have been in school continuously for 99 years. For some variables, extremely high code numbers cannot be used for missing data because they might be legitimate answers. Although not common, it is possible for a respondent to be 99 years old or have a monthly dollar income of 99,999. In such cases, we go to the other end of the spectrum and use negative numbers, since no one can legitimately be a −1 year old.

Declaring Missing Data to the Computer

Using extreme numbers to represent missing information helps us remember that these are missing values which are not to be used for most analyses of the data. However, the computer will perform statistical analyses for us, and *it* needs to know that these are missing responses which should be ignored. Consider Figure 6.7, a FREQUENCIES procedure for the variable SPEDUC from the GSS88 data set—the educational level of the respondent's spouse. There are two missing data codes for this variable: code 97 for those who cannot answer because they are not married and code 98 for those who do not know or otherwise did not answer.

Just looking at the numbers does not cause us any problems. It is obvious that the extreme values, 97 and 98, represent missing information, not real years of education. However, the computer does not know that the extreme numbers represent missing data. If we tell it to calculate the average educational level for spouses, it will include these numbers as legitimate values in its calculations. Consequently, the computer will tell us that the average number of years of education for spouses is 52.5 years—a bit ludicrous.

(PC) We deal with this situation by using the MISSING VALUES command. This command tells SPSS what code numbers (values) for each variable are used to represent missing data. The format of this command is illustrated in Figure 6.8. The command term MISSING VALUES starts in column 1, followed by each variable's name and then the values that represent missing data for that variable enclosed in parentheses. Up to but no more than three code numbers can be declared as missing values for any variable, and different variables must be separated by a slash (/). A slash must also be the last item in the MISSING VALUES command. Where more than one variable uses the same missing-value codes, we can group them rather than repeat the command for each variable, just as was done with the value labels in Figure 6.5. Figure 6.9 illustrates both uses of the command.

```
SPEDUC       HIGHEST YEAR SCHOOL COMPLETED, SPOUSE
```

VALUE LABEL	VALUE	FREQUENCY	PERCENT	VALID PERCENT	CUM PERCENT
2ND GRADE	2	2	0.1	0.1	0.1
3RD GRADE	3	6	0.4	0.4	0.5
4TH GRADE	4	2	0.1	0.1	0.7
5TH GRADE	5	6	0.4	0.4	1.1
6TH GRADE	6	7	0.5	0.5	1.6
7TH GRADE	7	10	0.7	0.7	2.2
8TH GRADE	8	34	2.3	2.3	4.5
9TH GRADE	9	21	1.4	1.4	5.9
10TH GRADE	10	32	2.2	2.2	8.1
11TH GRADE	11	44	3.0	3.0	11.1
12TH GRADE	12	299	20.2	20.2	31.3
1 YR COLL	13	53	3.6	3.6	34.8
2 YRS COLL	14	90	6.1	6.1	40.9
3 YRS COLL	15	29	2.0	2.0	42.9
4 YRS COLL	16	81	5.5	5.5	48.3
5 YRS COLL	17	17	1.1	1.1	49.5
6 YRS COLL	18	26	1.8	1.8	51.2
7 YRS COLL	19	9	0.6	0.6	51.9
8 OR MORE YRS COLL	20	14	0.9	0.9	52.8
NAP-NOT MARRIED	97	696	47.0	47.0	99.8
DK	98	3	0.2	0.2	100.0
		--------	--------	--------	
	TOTAL	1481	100.0	100.0	

Figure 6.7 A FREQUENCIES of variable SPEDUC.

The computer makes no real use of the VARIABLE LABELS or VALUE LABELS commands; they merely label the output and do not affect any calculations. In contrast, the MISSING VALUES command *does* affect the computer's internal calculations. By declaring some code numbers to represent missing data for a variable, we are instructing the computer to ignore these values when it is analyzing the variables.

```
001    DATA LIST FILE = GSS88 / variable names, locations and types
002    VARIABLE LABELS      SPEDUC   "HIGHEST YEAR SCHOOL COMPLETED, SPOUSE"
003    VALUE LABELS      SPEDUC    0    "No formal schooling"
004           1   "1ST GRADE"    2    "2ND GRADE"
005           3   "3RD GRADE"    4    "4TH GRADE"
006           5   "5TH GRADE"    6    "6TH GRADE"
007           7   "7TH GRADE"    8    "8TH GRADE"
008           9   "9TH GRADE"    10    "10TH GRADE"
009           12  "11TH GRADE"   12    "12TH GRADE"
010           13  "1 YR COLLEGE"      14    "2 YRS COLLEGE"
011           15  "3 YRS COLLEGE"     16    "4 YRS COLLEGE"
012           17  "5 YRS COLLEGE"     18    "6 YRS COLLEGE"
013           19  "7 YRS COLLEGE"     20    "8+ YRS COLLEGE"
014           97  "NAP NO SPOUSE"     98    "DK"
015    MISSING VALUES     SPEDUC  (97 98)
```

Figure 6.8 Format of the MISSING VALUES command.

The Separating Slash

```
001    DATA LIST FILE = ELEC88 / variable names, locations and types
002    VARIABLE LABELS          V2    'PRESIDENTIAL VOTE'
003             V3    'VOTE - U.S. HOUSE'      V4    'VOTE - U.S. SENATE'
004    VALUE LABELS      V2   1    "BUSH"      2    "DUKAKIS"      3    "3RD PTY-INDEP"
005             8    "DID NOT VOTE"    9    "NA"    "INAP" /
006      V3   1    "DEM CAND"    2    "REP CAND"      3    "3RD PTY-INDEP"
007             7    "DID NOT VOTE     8    "DK"    9    "NA"    0    "INAP"    /
008      V4   1    "DEM CAND"    2    "REP CAND"      3    "3RD PTY-INDEP"
009             6    "DID NOT VOTE     7    "NO SENATE RACE"    8    "DK"
010             9    "NA"    0    "INAP" /
011    MISSING VALUES          V2    (8, 9, 0)    /
012                            V3    (8, 9, 0)    /
013                            V4    (8, 9, 0)    /
```

Grouping Variables

```
001    DATA LIST FILE = ELEC88 / variable names, locations and types
002    VARIABLE LABELS          V2    'PRESIDENTIAL VOTE'
003             V3    'VOTE - U.S. HOUSE'      V4    'VOTE - U.S. SENATE'
004    VALUE LABELS      V2   1    "BUSH"      2    "DUKAKIS"      3    "3RD PTY-INDEP"
005             8    "DID NOT VOTE"    9    "NA"    "INAP" /
006      V3   1    "DEM CAND"    2    "REP CAND"      3    "3RD PTY-INDEP"
007             7    "DID NOT VOTE     8    "DK"    9    "NA"    0    "INAP"    /
008      V4   1    "DEM CAND"    2    "REP CAND"      3    "3RD PTY-INDEP"
009             6    "DID NOT VOTE     7    "NO SENATE RACE"    8    "DK"
010             9    "NA"    0    "INAP" /
011    MISSING VALUES          V2   V3   V4    (8, 9, 0)    /
```

Figure 6.9 The MISSING VALUES command either using the separating slash or grouping variables.

Figure 6.10 repeats the frequencies for the SPEDUC variable, this time after using the MISSING VALUES command. Observe that the word "MISSING" now appears next to the last two code numbers, showing that SPSS recognizes these values as representing missing data. Also at the bottom of the printout there is a line describing how many cases in the sample had valid responses and missing responses on the variable. When calculating an average for the variable, SPSS will ignore the values declared as missing and, using only the 782 valid cases, produce an average number of years of education for spouses of about $12\frac{1}{2}$. This is far more reasonable than the over-50-year average produced before we told SPSS to exclude the last two values from its calculations. If, as discussed earlier, we later want to include some missing data in the analysis, we can revise what values we want SPSS to consider as missing.

System Missing Values

The MISSING VALUES command allows us to pick values we want to treat as missing data. There are times when SPSS creates its own missing values. These are called **system missing values** because they are created by the SPSS system,

SPEDUC   HIGHEST YEAR SCHOOL COMPLETED, SPOUSE

VALUE LABEL	VALUE	FREQUENCY	PERCENT	VALID PERCENT	CUM PERCENT
2ND GRADE	2	2	0.1	0.3	0.3
3RD GRADE	3	6	0.4	0.8	1.0
4TH GRADE	4	2	0.1	0.3	1.3
5TH GRADE	5	6	0.4	0.8	2.0
6TH GRADE	6	7	0.5	0.9	2.9
7TH GRADE	7	10	0.7	1.3	4.2
8TH GRADE	8	34	2.3	4.3	8.6
9TH GRADE	9	21	1.4	2.7	11.3
10TH GRADE	10	32	2.2	4.1	15.3
11TH GRADE	11	44	3.0	5.6	21.0
12TH GRADE	12	299	20.2	38.2	59.2
1 YR COLL	13	53	3.6	6.8	66.0
2 YRS COLL	14	90	6.1	11.5	77.5
3 YRS COLL	15	29	2.0	3.7	81.2
4 YRS COLL	16	81	5.5	10.4	91.6
5 YRS COLL	17	17	1.1	2.2	93.7
6 YRS COLL	18	26	1.8	3.3	97.1
7 YRS COLL	19	9	0.6	1.2	98.2
8 OR MORE YRS COLL	20	14	0.9	1.8	100.0
NAP-NOT MARRIED	97	696	47.0	MISSING	
DK	98	3	0.2	MISSING	
		-------	-------	-------	
	TOTAL	1481	100.0	100.0	

VALID CASES   782   MISSING CASES   699

Figure 6.10 A FREQUENCIES of the SPEDUC variable after declaring missing values.

not the user. A system missing value is created when SPSS cannot find or interpret a variable's value for one or more cases in the data file. A blank in the data file will cause SPSS to generate a system missing value—it expected a number and did not find one, so it substituted a system missing value instead. Similarly, if the variable were an alpha variable but we forgot to include the symbol (A) on the DATA LIST, SPSS would assume this was a numeric variable and try to read it as such. Upon encountering alphabetical characters instead, SPSS would see this as an error and substitute a system missing value. On the output, a system missing value is represented by a period (.).

What do you do when you encounter a system missing value? The answer depends on whether there are supposed to be any such values. If the data file contains blanks to represent missing values, the appearance of system missing values merely reflects this fact and is no problem. The GSS88 and ELEC88 data files accompanying this text should not contain any blanks. The appearance of a system missing value while you are reading these files indicates that an error has been made somewhere, probably in the DATA LIST statement. System missing values represent an item of data that SPSS could not interpret, and only your knowledge of the data you are working with can tell you whether the appearance of system missing values is a reasonable result or an indication of an error.

Command Order

We are introducing a lot of new commands in this chapter, but are there any rules about which should come first or later in the program? Not really, beyond a little common sense. SPSS is quite flexible in allowing you to enter commands in almost any order *as long as they make sense to the computer.* This last phrase is the obvious catch, so let us explain it further.

The computer starts off as a blank slate. When we enter commands, each is carried out sequentially and one at a time. One requirement of this sequential process is that we neither describe nor analyze data until we have defined the data for the computer. This definition is created by a DATA LIST, GET FILE, or other command instructing SPSS how to read data into the computer's memory. Thus, we cannot refer to a variable on any command until the DATA LIST or GET FILE command has been processed—variables do not exist until they have been explained to SPSS with one of these commands. Similarly, adding or changing a variable's labels will make a difference on a FREQUENCIES command only if the VARIABLE LABELS command comes first (so that it takes effect before the computer starts to process the FREQUENCIES command).

THE SEPARATING SLASH

You probably have noticed that SPSS regularly uses a slash to separate one part of a command from another. There is a logic to the use of the slash, but it is not readily apparent: Sometimes the slash is required, at other times it is merely convenient; sometimes it begins part of a command, at other times it ends part of a command. Since it will continue to appear regularly throughout this text, we discuss the separating slash briefly.

A Requirement Versus a Convenience

The DATA LIST command illustrates the required slash. We must separate the name of the file that the DATA LIST is describing from the description of the variable names and locations. Without the slash as a separator, SPSS would try to read the first item after the DATA LIST command, FILE = , as a variable name. This would produce an error and cause the program to stop because this "variable name" is not followed by either a variable type indicator or a column location.

The VALUE LABELS command illustrates the convenience-use of the slash. If desired, we could repeat the VALUE LABELS command for each variable to which we attach value labels, as in Figure 6.11. This would work just fine. To save typing, however, SPSS allows us to simply continue the command for as many variables as we are labeling, provided we separate each variable with a slash. The slash is necessary here to indicate that we are starting to describe a new variable, and thus the next term that SPSS reads will be a variable's name,

```
001     DATA LIST FILE = ELEC88 / variable names, locations and types
002     VARIABLE LABELS        V2   'PRESIDENTIAL VOTE'
003                            V3   'VOTE - U.S. HOUSE'
004                            V4   'VOTE - U.S. SENATE'
005     VALUE LABELS   V2  1   "BUSH"
006            2   "DUKAKIS"   3   "3RD PTY-INDEP"
007            8   "DID NOT VOTE"   9   "NA"    "INAP"
008     VALUE LABELS      V3  1   "DEM CAND"   2   "REP CAND"
009            3   "3RD PTY-INDEP"   7   "DID NOT VOTE
010            8   "DK"   9   "NA"   0   "INAP"
011     VALUE LABELS    V4  1    "DEM CAND"   2   "REP CAND"
012            3   "3RD PTY-INDEP"   6   "DID NOT VOTE
013            7   "NO SENATE RACE"   8   "DK"
014            9   "NA"   0   "INAP"
```

Figure 6.11 VALUE LABELS without the separating slash.

not a value that we are trying to label. Both the VALUE LABELS command and MISSING VALUES command use the slash as a convenience, eliminating the need to retype the command name for each variable.

The VARIABLE LABELS command does not use the slash at all because it does not need it. There is only one label for each variable, and the label is enclosed in single or double quotation marks. When SPSS reads the second set of quotation marks, it knows that you are through labeling the first variable and are ready to move on to the second.

Beginning Versus Ending Slashes

SPSS commands have more than one part to them. The first part is the command word that identifies the basic procedure you want SPSS to perform, the DATA LIST, VARIABLE LABELS, VALUE LABELS, and MISSING VALUES terms. Commands can contain one or more subcommands and specifications describing how the procedure should be performed and on what variables. So after the command word come the variable names and their column locations (DATA LIST), the variable names and their associated labels (VARIABLE and VALUE LABELS), or the variable names and the values to treat as missing (MISSING VALUES). The slash is used to identify the beginning of each subcommand. We encounter this use in later chapters when discussing subcommands.

(PC) (R4) For two commands only, the VALUE LABELS and MISSING VAL-UES commands, the slash is used to indicate the end of a subpart—the end of the labels to be attached to a variable's values or the end of the values to be considered missing for one variable or a set of variables. This is true only if you are describing multiple variables with one command instead of repeating the command for each variable. Because the slash indicates the end of a subpart for these commands, the slash is also used at the end of the entire command (the end of the last subpart). With these two exceptions, the slash is used at the beginning of subparts and is not required at the end of the entire command.

Do not feel that you have to memorize all these details. Not even the most experienced computer programmer remembers every feature of the computer language that she or he is working with. This text is designed to show you some of the things that SPSS can do and the underlying logic behind the program's operation. At the same time, this book is a reference work. As with any reference work, such as a dictionary, you are not expected to memorize everything it contains, but you are expected to know how to use the reference work to quickly find those details when you need them. You should have this book, your class notes, or other reference material with you when you are working at the computer because you will often need to look up some details about the commands you are using.

SYSTEM FILES

We use computers to make our job easier. That may not be apparent from the material in this chapter, for it seems as if we have to spend an inordinate amount of time just describing the data before we ever get to use them. That is true, but SPSS allows us to simplify things by typing these descriptions of the data only once and then saving them as a system file. A **system file**, sometimes also called an SPSS file, is a file that contains both the data and our descriptions of them.

Most statistical packages, including SPSS, have two different types of commands: data definition commands and procedure commands. The two types of commands do not look different; the difference lies in what they do. **Data definition commands** do what the term sounds like: They define and describe our data. To this point, all the commands we have examined have been data definition commands. With data definition commands we are teaching the computer how to interpret our data. We can enter data definition commands all day long, and nothing will happen; the computer will contentedly learn everything we are teaching it about the data, but will not produce any output because we have not yet asked it to do anything.

By **procedure commands** we actually ask the computer to do something—to perform some statistical analysis of our data and print out the results. We have already made repeated reference to one procedure command, the FREQUENCIES command, to illustrate the impact of our data definition activities because we never see any data definition results until we ask for a statistical procedure to be performed.

Return again to Figure 6.9, our completed command file up to this point. With all the descriptions we have added (VARIABLE LABELS, VALUE LABELS, and MISSING VALUES), the file is becoming somewhat lengthy, even though Figure 6.9 describes only three variables. Major surveys include a minimum of 100 to 2500 or more variables. A file of data definition commands for such surveys would be large indeed. Can we save and use command files this large? Definitely, and they will work just fine, but they are very clumsy to use. It is far easier to save the descriptions of labels and missing values as permanent additions to the data file. This is what a system file is—a file containing both the data and the descriptions of the data discussed in this and prior chapters.

The best way to explain system files is to show how they are created and used. Creating a system file requires the addition of only two commands, illustrated in Figure 6.12. First, after entering the commands which describe our data, we need a procedure, command. The FREQUENCIES procedure is used in Figure 6.12 because we have already discussed it briefly, but any procedure command will do. A procedure command is needed because SPSS is very lazy. It will not carry out any of the data definition commands until it has to, and it does not have to until it actually is required to perform some procedure. Up until it executes a procedure, SPSS does not need to read any of the data or our descriptions of how to read and label the data.

Once SPSS has carried out a procedure, it will have incorporated all our data descriptions into the computer's memory. Now it encounters a second command: SAVE OUTFILE = ELEC88S. The **SAVE** command tells SPSS we want to store some information on a storage device, OUTFILE indicates that what we are saving is an SPSS system file, and ELEC88S is the computer file name under which we are storing this file. Upon encountering this command, SPSS will save the contents of the computer's memory—data and data descriptions together— as an SPSS system file.

Just as it is true in referencing a file on the DATA LIST command, the type of file name used with the SAVE command will differ depending on the type of computer you are using. For IBM mainframes using JCL, the name ELEC88S guides SPSS to a new set of JCL statements describing the actual location and computer file name under which the system file will be stored. SPSS/PC+ and Release 4 implementations use a multilevel name describing the file's actual name and any nondefault directory where it is to be stored, such as

```
SAVE OUTFILE = '/STATS/ELEC88.SYS'
```

On systems requiring the FILE HANDLE command, you will need to have two such commands: one giving a handle to and describing a file being read in with

```
001   DATA LIST FILE = ELEC88 / variable names, locations and types
002   VARIABLE LABELS        V2    'PRESIDENTIAL VOTE'
003          V3    'VOTE - U.S. HOUSE'      V4    'VOTE - U.S. SENATE'
004   VALUE LABELS    V2   1   "BUSH"      2   "DUKAKIS"     3   "3RD PTY-INDEP"
005          8   "DID NOT VOTE"    9   "NA"    "INAP" /
006     V3   1   "DEM CAND"    2   "REP CAND"    3   "3RD PTY-INDEP"
007          7   "DID NOT VOTE"    8   "DK"   9   "NA"   0   "INAP"     /
008     V4   1   "DEM CAND"    2   "REP CAND"    3   "3RD PTY-INDEP"
009          6   "DID NOT VOTE"    7   "NO SENATE RACE"    8   "DK"
010          9   "NA"    0   "INAP" /
011   MISSING VALUES      V2   V3   V4    (8, 9, 0)   /
011   FREQUENCIES   VARIABLES   V2
012   SAVE  OUTFILE  =  ELEC88S
```

Figure 6.12 Commands for saving a system file.

```
001    GET FILE = ELEC88S
002    FREQUENCIES VARIABLES = V2
```

Figure 6.13 Accessing and using an SPSS system file.

a DATA LIST statement and another describing the handle and where and how to save the file. The file name on the SAVE command will be the handle of the file being saved.

The name under which the system file is stored, described in JCL statements, directly on the SAVE command, or on a FILE HANDLE command, should be different from the name used for the raw data file. If the SAVE command used the same name as that used for the data file, the CPU would save the system file in the same place as the old raw data file, erasing this data file in the process. We do not want to do this, for it is risky—a bit like quitting one job before you are sure you can find a new one. The original data file should be preserved until we are sure the new system file has been saved without any errors. Then, and only then, the original data file can be safely erased.

Once a system file has been saved, its use is exceptionally simple. As shown in Figure 6.13, we need only one command to access the file, a **GET FILE** command followed by the computer file name for that file. Using GET FILE instead of DATA LIST tells SPSS that it is reading an SPSS system file which contains both the data and descriptive information about the data.

Since we are now reading in a system file, we can immediately proceed to analyze the data. The FREQUENCIES command in Figure 6.13 asks for frequencies of variable V2. SPSS knows where this variable is in the file because the DATA LIST information about the variable's type and location is included as part of the system file. Similarly, when SPSS prints the results of the FREQUENCIES procedure, it will also print out variable and value labels and will know which values stand for missing data—all information stored as part of the system file.

A system file makes this entire process invisible to the user. Even though the information on the DATA LIST, VARIABLE LABELS, VALUE LABELS, and MISSING VALUES commands has been saved as part of the system file, we never actually see the commands again—they do not show up on the computer screen, nor are they contained on any printed output. While we never see them, they do reside in the system file. The *information* they contain is available to the CPU and will be used by SPSS to read the data and to label the output.

The difference between a system file and a raw data file is similar to the difference between buying a car from a dealer and buying all the parts and building the car. In both situations, we have exactly the same parts. In the latter case (a raw data file) we must put the parts together before we can use the car, whereas in the former case (a system file) we just turn the key and drive off. System files contain only the data and the descriptions of them developed in the commands shown in Figure 6.12. Procedure commands cannot be saved as part of a system file.

Supplement
6.3

The INCLUDE Command

Data sets with a large number of variables can lead to long and complex data definition commands. Many find it easier to create and save a separate file of lengthy data definition commands by using the SPSS input window, a separate editor, or even a word processor with the commands saved as text files that SPSS can read. The file is then processed with the **INCLUDE** command, which has the format

INCLUDE FILE = computer.file.name

When SPSS sees the INCLUDE command, it will fetch the file and immediately carry out any commands contained there.

Files used in this manner can be called *include files* or files processed through the operating system. They can contain any SPSS commands, although data definition and manipulation commands are the most common. Include files must follow a specific format—that described in this text—in which all commands begin in column 1 and continuations of a command start in column 2 or later. This is true even if you are using SPSS/PC+ or Release 4 of the software. The command terminator is optional with an include file.

For greatest flexibility, always enter commands using the spacing described in this text for IBM OS implementations and ending with the command terminator. Such a file can be processed by any implementation of SPSS and avoids the need to modify the commands if you switch from SPSS-X to Release 4 or from using the command generator accessing an include file.

SPSS/PC+ AND RELEASE 4

When multiple variables are described on the VALUE LABELS or MISSING VALUES command, SPSS on OS requires a slash at the end of the last variable described. SPSS/PC+ and Release 4 use the command terminator to end commands and do not require the final slash.

Macintosh and OS/2 implementations of Release 4 can use the FILE choice on the menu bar for saving or fetching system files. When selected, these choices are executed immediately. That is, if you type or paste a GET FILE command into the input window, you must instruct SPSS to run the command for it to read the file. Selecting "Get System File" from the FILE menu bar, however, automatically reads the file into the computer's memory which is then ready for any procedure commands.

SPSS allows users to identify up to three codes for each variable to represent missing values. SPSS/PC+ allows only one data code per variable to represent a missing value.

SUMMARY

This completes our data definition process. We have gone from learning about the DATA LIST command, with or without an external data file, to coding data, describing the variables and codes so they will be understandable on the output, and saving all our efforts as a system file. We can also modify these choices at any time, adding new VARIABLE LABELS, VALUE LABELS, and MISSING VALUES commands to remove old descriptions and replace them with new ones.

More will be said later about further modifications that can be made to the data. For now, however, it is finally time for us to look at how the data can be analyzed—via the procedure commands.

REVIEW

Key Terms

VARIABLE LABELS	System file
VALUE LABELS	Data definition commands
TO convention	Procedure commands
Missing values	SAVE
System missing values	GET FILE
INCLUDE	

Exercises

6.1 Differentiate between
   a. Variable, variable name, and variable label
   b. Variable value and value label
   c. Normal values, missing values, and system missing values
   d. Data description and procedure commands
   e. Data included in the program, an external raw data file, and an external SPSS system file

6.2 a. Using the practice data set from Exercise 5.1, add variable and value labels to the data set. Also identify missing values for each variable where appropriate. Run a FREQUENCIES procedure on some of the variables, and compare the output with what you obtained from the exercises in earlier chapters.
   b. Save the data set, complete with the data description information, as an SPSS system file. When you have finished, use the GET FILE command to access the system file and run a FREQUENCIES procedure on the same variables.

6.3 Identify what errors, if any, you find in the commands below.
   a. VARIABLE LABELS SEX 'RESP'S GENDER' AGE "RESP'S AGE"
   b. VALUE LABELS 1 'FEMALE' 2 'MALE'

    c. VALUE LABELS RACE 1 "WHITE" 2 "NONWHITE" AGE "RESP'S AGE"
    d. MISSING SEX (7)
    e. MISSING VALUES RACE (7,8,9,10)
    f. SAVE OUTFILE
    g. GET ELEC88S

SUGGESTED READINGS

Norusis, Marija J., and SPSS Inc. *SPSS/PC+ V2.0 Base Manual* (Chicago: SPSS Inc., 1988) Chapter 3.

SPSS Inc., *SPSS Reference Guide* (Release 4) (Chicago: SPSS Inc., 1990) pages 197, 225–27, 463–64, 652–57, 710–712.

SPSS Inc., *SPSS-X User's Guide*, 3rd ed. (Chicago: SPSS Inc., 1988) Chapters 5, 6.

Chapter 7

The FREQUENCIES Procedure

We now discuss the actual statistical procedures that SPSS can perform. The first procedure to be examined is our old friend, FREQUENCIES, illustrated many times already. However, our previous illustrations looked at only a small part of the FREQUENCIES procedure, and there are many other features of the command.

The FREQUENCIES procedure performs a **univariate analysis**, so it analyzes only one variable at a time. When we are looking at just one variable, there are three things we may want to know. Looking at the codebooks in the appendixes, you will find the questions asked on each survey and the possible responses. We may wonder how people answered each question. How many people had spouses who were working, unemployed, or students (SPWRKSTA)? The FREQUENCIES procedure can count how many gave each of the possible responses to the question. A second question we may ask in univariate analysis is, What is the "average" or "typical" response to the question? For example, on the ideology variable (V19) we may wonder whether, on average, people in the United States consider themselves to be liberals, conservatives, or middle-of-the-roaders. Finally, we may wonder about the dispersion of the responses. Consider the feeling thermometer about George Bush (V5). Let us say that we found that the average response to this question was 50, a neutral response indicating neither strong positive nor strong negative feelings. Are people closely packed around this average, with most being neutral in their feelings? Alternatively, do one-half the respondents feel strongly positive about Bush and the other half strongly negative, with the two groups canceling each other to produce an average response of neutral? These are the three types of questions to which the FREQUENCIES command can give us an answer.

THE FREQUENCIES COMMAND

By now you are familiar with the format of the FREQUENCIES command, displayed in Figure 7.1. The command word FREQUENCIES starts in column 1, informing SPSS what procedure to perform. Next there is the list of variables on which we want to perform the procedure, the **VARIABLES** = term. Since the list of variables in Figure 7.1 is long, it is continued onto a second line, with the second line indented past column 1. We could have continued the list of variables indefinitely as long as each successive line began in column 2 or later. This is all that is required for the basic FREQUENCIES command.

Earlier we stated that the FREQUENCIES command was for univariate analysis, or looking at only one variable at a time. Despite that, the above paragraph talks about looking at a number of variables by simply listing them all after the VARIABLES = term. This seems like a contradiction, but it is not. You can request a univariate procedure on a large number of variables, even all the variables in the data set. If a procedure is univariate, the computer will report the results for each variable separately and will make no attempt to *compare* the responses for two or more variables, for example, comparing whether men or women (the variable SEX) are more likely to be employed full-time (the variable WRKSTAT). We return to the difference between univariate and other procedures in later chapters.

When we perform a FREQUENCIES analysis on one or more variables, we are telling the computer to count how many people gave answers 1, 2, 3, 4, etc. to the question, or how *frequently* each response was given. However, the output from the FREQUENCIES procedure, displayed in Figure 7.2, gives us more than just a simple count. Let us take a closer look at the output to see what each item of information is.

At the top of the output is the name of the variable being analyzed along with any variable label existing for it. Below that is the frequencies table divided into columns, with each column having a title at the top describing its contents. The first three columns are ones that we have discussed briefly before. On the far left are the labels for the variable's values, followed in the second column by the values, or code numbers, themselves. The third column is the actual frequency, or count, of how often this code number occurs in the sample data for this variable. Thus when the computer read the SPWRKSTA variable in the

```
001    GET FILE = ELEC88S
002    FREQUENCIES VARIABLES =    V2    V3    V4    V5    V6
003          V7    V8    V19
```

Figure 7.1 The format of the FREQUENCIES command.

```
SPWRKSTA   SPOUSE LABOR FORCE STATUS

                                                 VALID      CUM
     VALUE LABEL          VALUE   FREQUENCY   PERCENT   PERCENT   PERCENT

WORKING FULL TIME           1        409       27.6      52.0     52.0
WORKING PART TIME           2         70        4.7       8.9     60.9
TEMP NOT WORKING            3         14        0.9       1.8     62.7
UNEMPL, LAID OFF            4         15        1.0       1.9     64.6
RETIRED                    5        128        8.6      16.3     80.9
SCHOOL                     6          7        0.5       0.9     81.8
KEEPING HOUSE              7        136        9.2      17.3     99.1
OTHER                      8          7        0.5       0.9    100.0
NAP-NOT MARRIED            0        693       46.8    MISSING
NA                         9          2        0.1    MISSING
                                  -------    -------   -------
                         TOTAL     1481      100.0     100.0

VALID CASES      786      MISSING CASES     695
```

Figure 7.2 Output from the FREQUENCIES procedure.

GSS88 data set, it encountered the code number 1 exactly 409 times, code number 2 exactly 70 times, and so on.

The items of information which we have not examined fully to this point are the percentage figures in columns 4, 5, and 6. The actual numerical counts are useful, but often we will want to use the percentages. Finding that 409 spouses were working full-time means little unless you compare it to how many people responded to the question. If the sample contained only 500 people, 409 working spouses would be a lot. For a sample of 50,000, however, 409 working spouses would not be very many. The *percentage* of respondents with working spouses is a number that has meaning regardless of the sample size. Column 4 provides the uncorrected percentage of respondents who gave each particular answer. This column is referred to as the *uncorrected percentage* because it includes the missing values in its calculations—2 people for whom there was no answer and 693 people who never married, are widowed, or are otherwise without spouses.

Sometimes the uncorrected percentage is useful, but most of the time we do not want missing data included in the analysis. The fact that 27.6 percent of the respondents had spouses working full-time is not very helpful information. Does this indicate that most spouses work or very few? We cannot say. If only 27.6 percent of the people surveyed had spouses, then all work full-time. If everyone surveyed had a spouse, then only about one-quarter work full-time. To know what percentage *of the spouses* work full-time, we need the percentage based on only those individuals who had spouses. This figure is reported in column 5, Valid Percent. The valid percent column contains percentages based on only those values not declared to be missing data. Since those who either did not answer or had no spouse (codes 9 and 0) were earlier declared to represent missing data, they are excluded in calculating the column 5 percentages. Column 5 shows that, for the respondents *who had spouses*, 52 percent of those spouses worked full-time.

The final column provides the cumulative percentage, or what percentage of respondents (again, excluding missing values) gave that answer *or lower*. Thus, for row 5 (retired) we find that 80.9 percent of the cases responded with value 5 or lower (values 5, 4, 3, 2, or 1). For nominal variables, which this one is, the cumulative percentage has no meaning. The very notions of lower and higher imply an order, but nominal variables have no order. It means nothing to say that 80.9 percent of the spouses were "retired or lower." If, instead, we were examining an ordinal or interval item, such as variable V5 from the ELEC88 data set (Figure 7.3), the cumulative percentage column would be useful

```
V5              FEELING  THERMOMETER  -  BUSH

                                                      VALID      CUM
     VALUE LABEL           VALUE   FREQUENCY  PERCENT  PERCENT  PERCENT

COLD,HOSTILE                 0         136      6.7      6.9      6.9
                             2           1      0.0      0.1      6.9
                             4           1      0.0      0.1      7.0
                             5           2      0.1      0.1      7.1
                            10          10      0.5      0.5      7.6
                            15          62      3.0      3.1     10.8
                            20          10      0.5      0.5     11.3
                            25           2      0.1      0.1     11.4
                            30          95      4.7      4.8     16.2
                            33           1      0.0      0.1     16.2
                            35           4      0.2      0.2     16.4
                            40         140      6.9      7.1     23.5
                            45           4      0.2      0.2     23.7
                            49           1      0.0      0.1     23.8
NEUTRAL                     50         347     17.0     17.6     41.4
                            55           5      0.2      0.3     41.6
                            60         205     10.0     10.4     52.0
                            65          12      0.6      0.6     52.6
                            70         275     13.5     13.9     66.6
                            75          24      1.2      1.2     67.8
                            80          29      1.4      1.5     69.3
                            85         334     16.4     16.9     86.2
                            90          30      1.5      1.5     87.7
                            92           2      0.1      0.1     87.8
                            95           9      0.4      0.5     88.3
                            97           1      0.0      0.1     88.3
                            98           1      0.0      0.1     88.4
WARM,FRIENDLY              100         229     11.2     11.6    100.0
DSN'T  RECOGNIZE  NAME     997           6      0.3    MISSING
DK,CAN'T  RATE             998          53      2.6    MISSING
NA                         999           9      0.4    MISSING
                                     -------  -------  -------
                          TOTAL       2040    100.0    100.0

VALID CASES      1972     MISSING CASES      68
```

Figure 7.3 A FREQUENCIES of the Bush feeling thermometer (V5).

information. The code numbers for this variable, the George Bush feeling thermometer, do represent an order. Numbers below 50, the neutral point, represent increasingly cool or hostile feelings toward President Bush. Conversely, on the warm side of the neutral point (numbers above 50), the higher the code number, the warmer the feeling toward President Bush. Consequently, the cumulative percentage column tells us that 23.7 percent were on the cool side (answering 45 or below), or 11.4 percent were exceptionally cool toward President Bush (answering 25 or below).

The last item of information provided in the FREQUENCIES table is the line at the bottom listing how many valid and missing cases there were for the variable. For Figure 7.3, there were 1972 valid answers and 68 responses coded as missing data. For Figure 7.2, out of 1481 cases, 786 had valid values (not declared as missing) and 695 people gave responses defined as missing data.

From an examination of the FREQUENCIES output, it is clear that not all the information provided will be useful to us. Why does SPSS provide some unnecessary information? Because the computer is not smart enough to know exactly what information we need. Do we want to know what percentage of the cases is missing (total percentage), or do we need percentages based on only the valid cases? Is this an ordinal or interval variable where the cumulative percentage may be of value or a nominal variable where it is of no utility? The computer does not know the answer to any of these questions, so it provides us lots of information and allows us to pick the items we deem important.

This approach may sound unusual, but it really is not. Try looking up any word in a dictionary. The dictionary will contain not just the spelling of the word, but also how it is syllabified, how it is pronounced, its common definition, its definition within different contexts, which definitions are archaic, and what foreign term (if any) the word is derived from. You may want only the word's common definition, but the dictionary does not "know" this, so it provides you with plentiful information from which you select what you need. Similarly, since different people will be interested in different bits of information, all statistical software programs produce a large quantity of output for each procedure requested and let the users decide which bits of information are relevant to their purposes.

There is an important lesson here for beginning users, one mentioned before but deserving repetition. Computers are large and powerful machines that can perform a multitude of tasks. True social analysis, however, takes place in the human mind, not inside the CPU. We users are the only ones who can decide whether the information the computer provides is useful for answering our questions.

FORMATTING SUBCOMMANDS

All SPSS procedures provide a prespecified output, called the **default**. The default output includes the information most people normally want from the procedure, but, as we have seen, it is not always what *we* want from the procedure. There are ways we can modify the output to produce either more information or less. These modifications are accomplished through the use of **subcommands**.

Again, everyday analogies to commands and subcommands are plentiful. Consider the typical syllabus for a college course. The assignments for a given week may contain one or more primary commands, each specifying a different action to be performed, for example, "Read chapter 5" or "Write a paper summarizing the author's thesis." At times, the syllabus contains additional information (subcommands) telling us particular ways to carry out the primary command, such as "Read chapter 5, *skimming sections 1 and 2, but paying close attention to section 4*," or "Write a paper summarizing the author's thesis *in no more than 5 pages and using direct quotations to substantiate your interpretation.*"

SPSS uses the same approach by providing subcommands with each command, enabling us to tailor the procedure to our particular needs. Most SPSS subcommands perform one of three functions. First, a subcommand can modify the way a procedure is performed. A common example here is a subcommand instructing SPSS to make use of missing data in its calculations, including them, say, in the cumulative percentage columns in Figures 7.2 and 7.3. A second type of subcommand affects the appearance of the output. With this type of subcommand we can request that SPSS present the information as a bar chart rather than in table format or display the table without any of the value labels. The third type of subcommand specifies the statistics we want calculated. We begin with subcommands that affect the output.

Subcommand BARCHART

The default output for the FREQUENCIES command is the FREQUENCIES table shown earlier in Figures 7.2 and 7.3. This FREQUENCIES table is also called a **distribution**. Figure 7.2 shows how the 1481 people in the GSS88 sample are distributed over the 10 possible responses, from working full-time to no answer. There are other ways to portray a distribution of responses for a variable. Sometimes it is helpful to have a graphic display, a picture, rather than just a table of numbers. The **BARCHART** subcommand produces such a graphic display.

A bar chart is what it sounds like, a set of bars illustrating how responses are distributed for a variable; the larger the bar, the more people gave that response. Figure 7.4 shows how to request a bar chart. First, there is a slash (/), so that SPSS will recognize any words following it as subcommands and not merely additional variable names. Second, there is the term BARCHART, indicating what subcommand we are requesting. If we had included a list of variables after the VARIABLES = term in Figure 7.4, SPSS would have produced

```
001    GET FILE = ELEC88S
002    FREQUENCIES VARIABLES = V19    /    BARCHART
```

Figure 7.4 The format of the BARCHART subcommand.

a bar chart for each variable on the list. The BARCHART subcommand can be on the same line as the primary FREQUENCIES command, as in Figure 7.4, or on a second line indented past column 1.

(PC) The output from this revised FREQUENCIES command is shown in Figure 7.5. First is the familiar FREQUENCIES table. Second is the bar chart we

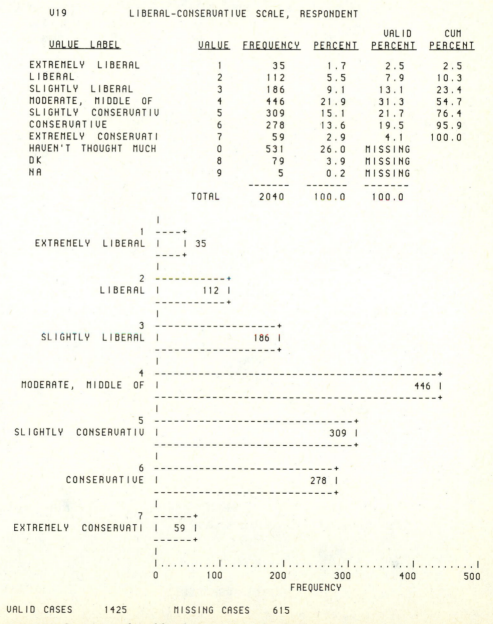

Figure 7.5 Output produced by the BARCHART subcommand.

requested. To the left of the bar chart are the variable's values and their associated labels. Then SPSS has drawn bars to represent how the 2040 people in the ELEC88 data set are distributed over the various values for this variable. Included in each bar (occasionally it is outside if the bar is too small) is the FREQUENCIES count for that code number.

The bar chart is simply a pictorial representation of how people are distributed by political ideology, but the bar chart provides us with less information than the original FREQUENCIES table. Missing values are not included in the bar chart, nor are any of the percentage figures contained in the last three columns of the FREQUENCIES table.

Supplement 7.1   ## The FORMAT NOTABLE Subcommand

FORMAT NOTABLE is an additional subcommand that controls the appearance of the output. The term NOTABLE in this case stands not for "worthy of note," but for "no table." The purpose of this option to the FORMAT subcommand is to instruct SPSS to not print the FREQUENCIES table. Including it with the FREQUENCIES command shown in Figure 7.4 would have changed the output in Figure 7.5 to the bar chart only, not both the bar chart and the FREQUENCIES table.

The bar chart's value is that a graphic portrayal is often easier to grasp quickly than a column of numbers. This value also suggests a limitation in the use of bar charts; they are best used with variables that have only a limited number of response categories, say, five to seven. A bar chart for a variable such as the Bush feeling thermometer (V5) might have as many as 101 different answers, degrees 0 through 100. To see such a large chart would require flipping through numerous pages of printout, and the chart's value—a concise and easily seen picture of the data—would be lost. For variables with a large number of values, it is preferable to use a histogram.

Subcommand HISTOGRAM

The format of the **HISTOGRAM** subcommand is shown in Figure 7.6. It is the same as that for the BARCHART subcommand except obviously we now use the word HISTOGRAM instead of BARCHART.

```
001    GET FILE = ELEC88S
002    FREQUENCIES VARIABLES = V12      /    HISTOGRAM
```

Figure 7.6 Format of the HISTOGRAM subcommand.

(PC) Like BARCHART, the HISTOGRAM subcommand produces a picture of the distribution of responses for a variable. However, instead of the fat bars seen in the BARCHART picture, the HISTOGRAM picture consists of thin rows of asterisks or other symbols. A histogram of variable V5, the Bush feeling thermometer, is shown in Figure 7.7.

While both bar charts and histograms produce graphic portrayals of data, the SPSS histogram is designed for ordinal- or interval-level variables with numerous values. This produces important differences in output from the two subcommands. To begin with, since the purpose of a graphic display is to present the information in a compact form, SPSS sets an arbitrary limit of printing no more than 21 rows for a histogram. If a variable has more than 21 possible values, SPSS will consider this to be too many to make a compact, easily interpretable graphic and will combine some of the values so that no more than 21 rows are produced.

Examine Figure 7.7. The Bush feeling thermometer has 101 possible values, from 0 to 100. SPSS finds the range of values for the variable—the distance between the minimum and maximum values—and then calculates how to divide this distance into no more than 21 groups for the histogram. SPSS prints on the histogram output the count for each *group* as well as the *midpoints* of the groups it created. The boundaries of each group can be easily determined by finding one-half of the distance between the midpoint of one interval (group) and the midpoints of the intervals immediately above and below it. Thus, in Figure 7.7, the group whose midpoint is 50 includes all values between 47.5 and 52.5—one-half the distance between 50 and the midpoints of the groups below it (45) and above it (55). The count for this group is 348. Looking back at the frequencies table, we see that the interval from 47.5 to 52.5 includes none at value 48; 1 person who answered 49; 347 people who answered 50; and none who answered 51 or 52.

Because they may lump some response codes together, histograms should not be used with nominal variables, unless the number of response codes is less than 21, in which case no grouping will take place. Consider Figure 7.8, the frequency table for the religious-preference variable (V83) from the ELEC88 data. The code numbers range from 100 to 800. To produce a histogram with only 21 rows (Figure 7.9), SPSS would combine into groups religious denominations that have nothing in common. For example, the second row in Figure 7.9, the interval whose midpoint is 144, includes such disparate denominations as Pentecostal Christians, Unitarians, Quakers, and Jehovah's Witnesses.

For ordinal or interval variables, such as the feeling thermometer in Figure 7.7, grouping values makes sense since people answering 48 through 52 are all close together around the neutral answer of 50. Codes for nominal variables do not represent any notion of closeness on the underlying conceptual variable—code number 139 (Seventh-Day Adventists) is not "closer" to code number 140 (Southern Baptists) than is code 110 (Presbyterian).

Grouping code numbers creates some other unique features on the histogram output that you should be aware of. SPSS creates histograms by looking

```
V5            FEELING THERMOMETER - BUSH
                                                 VALID      CUM
       VALUE LABEL              VALUE  FREQUENCY  PERCENT  PERCENT  PERCENT
```

VALUE LABEL	VALUE	FREQUENCY	PERCENT	VALID PERCENT	CUM PERCENT
COLD,HOSTILE	0	136	6.7	6.9	6.9
	2	1	0.0	0.1	6.9
	4	1	0.0	0.1	7.0
	5	2	0.1	0.1	7.1
	10	10	0.5	0.5	7.6
	15	62	3.0	3.1	10.8
	20	10	0.5	0.5	11.3
	25	2	0.1	0.1	11.4
	30	95	4.7	4.8	16.2
	33	1	0.0	0.1	16.2
	35	4	0.2	0.2	16.4
	40	140	6.9	7.1	23.5
	45	4	0.2	0.2	23.7
	49	1	0.0	0.1	23.8
NEUTRAL	50	347	17.0	17.6	41.4
	55	5	0.2	0.3	41.6
	60	205	10.0	10.4	52.0
	65	12	0.6	0.6	52.6
	70	275	13.5	13.9	66.6
	75	24	1.2	1.2	67.8
	80	29	1.4	1.5	69.3
	85	334	16.4	16.9	86.2
	90	30	1.5	1.5	87.7
	92	2	0.1	0.1	87.8
	95	9	0.4	0.5	88.3
	97	1	0.0	0.1	88.3
	98	1	0.0	0.1	88.4
WARM,FRIENDLY	100	229	11.2	11.6	100.0
DSN'T RECOGNIZE NAME	997	6	0.3	MISSING	
DK,CAN'T RATE	998	53	0.6	MISSING	
NA	999	9	0.4	MISSING	
	TOTAL	2040	100.0	100.0	

```
COUNT  MIDPOINT  ONE SYMBOL EQUALS APPROXIMATELY  8.00 OCCURRENCES
 137      0      *****************
   3      5
  10     10      *
  62     15      ********
  10     20      *
   2     25
  95     30      ************
   5     35      *
 140     40      ******************
   4     45      *
 348     50      ******************************************************
   5     55      *
 205     60      **************************
  12     65      **
 275     70      ***********************************
  24     75      ***
  29     80      ****
 334     85      ******************************************
  32     90      ****
  10     95      *
 230    100      *****************************
                 I....+....I....+....I....+....I....+....I....+....I
                 0        80       160      240      320      400
                           HISTOGRAM FREQUENCY
```

Figure 7.7 Output produced by the HISTOGRAM subcommand.

V83   RELIGIOUS PREFERENCE

VALUE LABEL	VALUE	FREQUENCY	PERCENT	VALID PERCENT	CUM PERCENT
PROTESTANT, NO DENOM	100	48	2.4	2.6	2.6
NON-DENOM PROTESTANT	101	39	1.9	2.1	4.7
COMMUNITY CHRCH	102	7	0.3	0.4	5.0
OTHER PROTESTANT	109	23	1.1	1.2	6.3
PRESBYTERIAN	110	87	4.3	4.7	11.0
LUTHERAN	111	120	5.9	6.4	17.4
CONGREGATIONAL	112	12	0.6	0.6	18.0
EVANGEL AND REFRMD	113	6	0.3	0.3	18.4
DUTCH CHRISTIAN REFO	114	13	0.6	0.7	19.1
UNITED CHRCH CHRIST	115	11	0.5	0.6	19.6
EPISCOPALIAN	116	52	2.5	2.8	22.4
METHODIST	120	218	10.7	11.7	34.1
AF METHODIST EPIS	121	4	0.2	0.2	34.4
UNITED BRETHREN	122	2	0.1	0.1	34.5
BAPTIST	123	154	7.5	8.3	42.7
DISCIPLES OF CHRIST	124	8	0.4	0.4	43.2
"CHRISTIAN"	125	23	1.1	1.2	44.4
CHURCH OF BRETHREN	127	1	0.0	0.1	44.4
MISSIONARY	130	1	0.0	0.1	44.5
CHURCH OF GOD	131	45	2.2	2.4	46.9
NAZARENE	132	15	0.7	0.8	47.7
CHRCH GOD IN CHRIST	133	6	0.3	0.3	48.0
PLYMOUTH BRETHERN	134	1	0.0	0.1	48.1
PENTECOSTL,ASSEM GOD	135	55	2.7	3.0	51.0
CHURCH OF CHRIST	136	51	2.5	2.7	53.8
SALVATION ARMY	137	1	0.0	0.1	53.8
PRIMITIVE	138	40	2.0	2.1	56.0
SEVENTH DAY ADVENTIS	139	8	0.4	0.4	56.4
SOUTHERN BAPTIST	140	223	10.9	12.0	68.4
MISSOURI SYNOD LUTHE	141	1	0.0	0.1	68.4
OTHER FUNDAMENTALIST	149	8	0.4	0.4	68.9
CHRISTIAN SCIENTIST	150	1	0.0	0.1	68.9
MORMON, LDS	152	11	0.5	0.6	69.5
UNITARIAN	153	6	0.3	0.3	69.8
JEHOVA WITNESS	154	11	0.5	0.6	70.4
QUAKER	155	4	0.2	0.2	70.6
UNITY	156	2	0.1	0.1	70.7
ROMAN CATHOLIC	200	484	23.7	26.0	96.7
JEWISH	300	31	1.5	1.7	98.4
GREEK ORTHODOX	710	5	0.2	0.3	98.7
RUSSIAN ORTHODOX	711	1	0.0	0.1	98.7
SERBIAN ORTHODOX	713	1	0.0	0.1	98.8
MUSLIM	720	2	0.1	0.1	98.9
BUDDHIST	721	1	0.0	0.1	98.9
HINDU	722	1	0.0	0.1	99.0
OTHER RELIGIONS	790	5	0.2	0.3	99.2
AGNOSTICS,ATHEISTS	800	14	0.7	0.8	100.0
REFUSED	996	5	0.2	MISSING	
DK,NONE,NO PREF	998	163	8.0	MISSING	
NA	999	9	0.4	MISSING	
		-------	-------	-------	
	TOTAL	2040	100.0	100.0	

VALID CASES   1863   MISSING CASES   177

Figure 7.8 A FREQUENCIES table for variable V83, the respondent's religious preference.

```
U83              RELIGIOUS PREFERENCE


                              ONE SYMBOL EQUALS APPROXIMATELY 20.00
   COUNT      MIDPOINT        OCCURRENCES

    827         110    ******************************************
    491         144    ************************
      0         178
    484         212    ***********************
      0         246
      0         280
     31         314    **
      0         348
      0         382
      0         416
      0         450
      0         484
      0         518
      0         552
      0         586
      0         620
      0         654
      0         688
     11         722    *
      0         756
     19         790    *
                       I....+....I....+....I....+....I....+....I....+....I
                       0       200      400      600      800     1000
                              HISTOGRAM FREQUENCY
```

Figure 7.9 A histogram for variable V83 combining unrelated religious denominations.

at only the highest and lowest values of a variable and then dividing the range between those values into 21 equal-size intervals. Many of these intervals may be empty, for even though the high-to-low range may go from 0 to 100, not all possible answers may have been given by the people surveyed. For the feeling thermometers, for example, people tend to answer in round deciles (40, 50, etc.), leaving a lot of the numbers in between (e.g., a 41 or a 73) unpicked by anybody in the survey. Both a frequency table and a bar chart will skip over any response codes that were not selected by the people surveyed, but a histogram includes them.

So we have three different ways to look at a variable's distribution: a FREQUENCIES table, a bar chart, and a histogram. Which we use is a matter of personal taste. The FREQUENCIES table presents the most information, but bar charts and histograms are easier to interpret at a quick glance. In most cases, it will not make much difference which approach you use.

BARCHART and HISTOGRAM are two subcommands that affect the way in which SPSS presents the output from the FREQUENCIES command. Other output-modifying subcommands available with this procedure are displayed in Table 7.1. Each subcommand begins with the subcommand term. Most also

<table>
<tr><td>Supplement
7.2</td><td>

Customizing the Histogram

</td></tr>
</table>

Instead of letting SPSS decide how to group codes for a histogram, we can tell it how we want the histogram constructed. This is done with the additional command: MINIMUM (x), MAXIMUM (y), and INCREMENT (z), where the symbols x, y, and z stand for any numbers we choose. The entire HISTOGRAM subcommand thus becomes:

/ HISTOGRAM   MINIMUM (0)   MAXIMUM (100)   INCREMENT (10)

The MINIMUM addition specifies the minimum value of the variable and MAXIMUM the maximum value, 0 and 100 in the example above. These can be different from the variable's actual minimum and maximum. Specifying a minimum of 30 and a maximum of 60 would produce a histogram for this range of values only, ignoring those respondents with higher or lower values.

The INCREMENT term identifies how large each interval should be. The value of 10 shown above would create intervals grouping 10 response codes together. A value of 20 here would create larger groups and consequently a smaller number of rows in the histogram.

There is no slash separating these specifications from the HISTOGRAM term, since they constitute additional options on how to create the histogram, not separate subcommands. These specifications override SPSS's default features, including the limitation of printing only 21 rows. If we asked for intervals of size 1, SPSS would provide a separate row for each of the 101 values of the feeling thermometer.

have more than one specification that can be listed with the subcommand term. Supplement 7.2 illustrates using specifications with a subcommand. BARCHART and HISTOGRAM are the only modifying subcommands that this text covers in detail. Readers interested in other subcommands should consult the SPSS manual for descriptions of their use and impact.

Table 7.1   MODIFYING SUBCOMMANDS AVAILABLE WITH THE FREQUENCIES PROCEDURE

Subcommand	Option	Meaning
FORMAT	NEWPAGE	Begins each FREQUENCIES table on a new page
FORMAT	CONDENSE	Prints a condensed version of the FREQUENCIES table
FORMAT	NOTABLE	Does not print the FREQUENCIES table
BARCHART	PERCENT	Horizontal axis scaled in percentage rather than raw frequency
HISTOGRAM	MIN(#)	Minimum value to be included in plot. Also can be used with BARCHART
HISTOGRAM	MAX(#)	Maximum value to be included in plot. Also can be used with BARCHART
HISTOGRAM	INCREMENT(#)	Sets width of intervals
HBAR		SPSS picks whether a BARCHART or a HISTOGRAM will be printed based on variable's number of values.

SUBCOMMAND STATISTICS

Having looked at a variable's pattern of responses, how do you describe this pattern to someone else? Say that a friend asks us how the people sampled responded to the Bush feeling thermometer. What is our answer? We could read off the results of the FREQUENCIES table from Figure 7.3: 136 people answered 0; 1 answered 2; 1 answered 4; and so on—but our friend would quickly interrupt us and say, "Not all the details, just how people felt on average." What our friend wants is a **statistic**. A statistic is a term that summarizes some characteristic of a sample. Since the FREQUENCIES procedure examines only one variable at a time, the statistics associated with this procedure summarize the responses to a single variable. In univariate analysis, we are interested in two characteristics of the responses to a variable: the variable's central tendency and its dispersion.

The Central Tendency

The **central tendency** of a variable is a number that identifies the typical or average response. It is called the central tendency because it usually reflects the center, or middle, of the distribution of responses. There are three measures of central tendency: the mode, the median, and the mean. We have three, not just one, because each is designed for a different level of measurement: nominal, ordinal, and interval.

The **mode** is the central-tendency measure used for nominal variables. It is nothing more than the answer given by the largest number of respondents. For the SPWRKSTA variable in Figure 7.2, the value 1, working full-time, is the mode because more people gave that answer than any other (except for missing data—respondents without spouses—which does not count).

The mode does not actually describe the middle of anything because with nominal-level variables there is no such thing as a "middle," just a number of groups which are different from each other. Even with nominal-level information, however, we often talk about the characteristic that is typical or most common, and that is exactly what the mode is—the most common characteristic or response. Thus we may speak of the typical American as being brunette or Protestant, not because brunette is the "middle" hair color or Protestant the "middle" religious preference, but because each characteristic is the mode for Americans—the characteristic shared by more people than any other.

The central tendency for ordinal-level variables is the **median**. Since an ordinal variable contains rank-order information, its middle is determined by arranging the respondents from low to high on the variable and then finding the person in the middle of that ranking. The response for that middle person constitutes the median, the point at which one-half of the people gave a higher response and one-half a lower one. Thus, for the ideology variable (Figure 7.5), the respondents are ranked in order of their degree of liberalism (or conservatism), with response 1 being the most liberal (least conservative) and response 7 being the least liberal (most conservative). There were 1425 people who answered the question (ignoring the 615 people who were unable to answer—responses 8, 9, and 0), so the middle person is number 713 down from the top: 712 people saw themselves as more liberal than or just as liberal as person 713, and 712 people responded less than or just as liberal as this person. Counting down from the top, we find that person 713 must be among those who answered 4 (moderate, or middle of the road), so the value 4 is the median value, or average response, for this variable.

A quick way to find the median is to use the cumulative percentage column. Just look down the column until you find the response code where 50 percent or more people gave that response or lower. That response code must contain the person in the middle of the distribution and thus is the median for that variable.

Note two things about the description of the median. First, when we talk about person 713, we are talking about the 713th person down from the top *after* the respondents have been ranked from high to low on the variable. We are not talking about the person or case with identification number 713, for this merely refers to the 713th person interviewed, who may be moderate or extremely conservative or something else. Second, because people may have average or typical attitudes on some issues but extreme attitudes on others, the median person will be different from one variable to another. We have found the average or median *for this variable*, not the typical person for the entire data set.

At this point we can also see why we use different statistics for different types of variables. To calculate the median, we must be able to rank people from high to low on a given variable. For nominal variables, the code numbers have no high or low meaning; they are simply used to group people into similar or different categories. If you ask SPSS to calculate a median for a nominal variable, it will do so, but the median has no meaning for nominal variables.

For interval variables, the appropriate measure of central tendency is the arithmetic **mean**. The mean is the most commonly used measure of central tendency. It is calculated from the formula

$$\overline{X} = \frac{\Sigma X_i}{n}$$

The symbols in this formula have the following meanings:

X = symbol for any variable

$\overline{X}$ = variable symbol with bar over it, read "*X* bar," or symbol for the mean of a variable

X_i = variable symbol with subscript *i* refers to each individual respondent's value on *X* variable

Σ = summation sign which means to add the values on this variable for all cases in the sample

n = number of people in the sample

Let us clarify the formula for the mean through an example. Suppose we want to calculate the average age for all students in a given class. Age is the variable of interest, symbolized by the generic variable X. First we find every student's age, each case's value on the variable, or X_i. Next we add these ages, ΣX_i. Finally we divide by the number of people in the class, $\Sigma X_i / n$. This gives us the average or mean, $\overline{X}$, for the variable AGE for this group of students. In Figure 7.7, there are 136 people with the value 0; 1 with the value 2; 1 with the value 4; and so on up to 229 people with the value 100. Adding these values produces a sum of 119,447 which, when divided by the 1972 responses (ignoring the 68 cases of missing data), produces a mean of 60.572.

Observe how each measure of central tendency is designed to make use of all the information contained in a variable's level of measurement, but no more information than that level of measurement provides. Since the codes for ordinally measured variables contain rank but not distance information, the median uses the rank information but does not make any assumption about distance. In Figure 7.7 (the Bush feeling thermometer) the median is 60 because one-half the respondents are ranked at or below 60 and one-half are ranked 60 or above. In calculating the median, no assumption is made that the values represent distance, how much higher or lower. It makes no difference whether the bottom 712 respondents all have values of 0 or values of 59; the middle person still has a value of 60, and that is the median.

The mean assumes that these values do represent distances, and it uses these distances in determining the average value. Those with a score of 0 are far lower on the feeling thermometer than those with a score of 30. Similarly, those with a score of 100 are far higher in their feelings toward President Bush than those with a score of 80. By including each respondent's actual value, not just his or her rank, in calculating the mean, the distance information contained in the values of interval variables is incorporated.

All statistics are designed for one or another level of measurement. It is not appropriate to use a statistic on a variable measured at a lower level than the statistic was designed for. Calculating a mean for an ordinal variable is not legitimate because the mean assumes the code numbers represent distances which, for an ordinal variable, they do not. Calculating either a mean or a median for a nominal variable is not acceptable because the numbers for the nominal variable represent neither distances nor rankings.

The opposite, however, is legitimate. You can use a lower-level statistic on variables that have a higher level of measurement. The mode is that response that occurs most often. This interpretation is true whether you are talking about the mode for a nominal-, ordinal-, or interval-level variable. The median is the middle response, and this interpretation is accurate even if you calculate it for an interval variable.

Although it is legitimate to use low-level statistics on variables with higher levels of measurement, it is wasteful. The mode makes no use of the rank information that an ordinal variable contains; it throws this information away. The median ignores the distance information available with interval-level variables. It is a bit silly to use these lower-level statistics when a more precise measure, the mean, is available. The difference is like the difference between trying to read a book by using a flashlight or a good reading lamp. If you are out in the woods, you have to use a flashlight because there is no electricity available for the reading lamp. Inside your house or apartment, you could use a flashlight if you wanted to, but why bother when both the reading lamp and the electricity to power it are available?

Measures of Dispersion

The average, or central-tendency, statistics summarize one characteristic of a variable. A second important characteristic is the **dispersion** of answers around this average. Say that we were comparing the average income of U.S. citizens to Swedish citizens, and we found that both countries had average incomes of about $25,000. This would *not* mean that the incomes of the citizens of the two countries were identical. Sweden, a highly socialized country, may have far fewer very poor and very wealthy people than the United States. Most citizens will be closely packed around the average income, ranging from, say, a low of $15,000 to a high of $35,000. The United States, with its more fluid and freewheeling economic structure, may have a large number of very poor people who earn less than $5000 per year, but they are offset by a number of high-income people who earn over $200,000 per year.

In essence, a measure of dispersion tells us how typical the average response is for those in our sample. A small amount of dispersion indicates that most people in the sample are packed closely together around the central-tendency measure. A large dispersion tells us that many respondents gave answers quite different from the central-tendency response. The average is still the average for the entire group, but many in the group gave responses far from this average.

Range For ordinal variables, a measure of dispersion is the **range**, or the difference between the highest response and the lowest one. The range is not a very powerful measure of dispersion for it does not really tell us how most of the responses are distributed, just the highest and lowest responses. The majority of people might answer a question with responses between 3 and 5, but if there is one person who responds 0 and a second who responds 10, then these two extreme cases determine the range for the variable. Nonetheless, for ordinal variables, the range is one of the few measures of dispersion that you can calculate.

For nominal variables we cannot even do this, for no real measure of dispersion exists. The range is not useful because the code numbers represent neither distance nor rank order. A value of 1 is neither lower than nor farther from a mode of 5 than is a value of 4.

Variance For interval variables, a powerful measure of dispersion is available to us, the **variance**. Before we jump straight to the formula for the variance, let us think through what we want as a measure of dispersion. We are interested in the average spread of the respondents around the central-tendency, or mean, value. Because we are dealing with an interval variable here, dispersion can be measured as a distance—how far above or below the mean each case is. This distance is given by $X_i - \overline{X}$, an individual's value on the variable minus the mean of that variable. For the person in Figure 7.7 who answered 31, we subtract the mean (60.6) from this value and obtain a result of -29.6 ($31 - 60.6$). For the person who responded with value 68, subtracting the mean produces 7.4 ($68 - 60.6$). The minus and plus signs show whether the person's response was below (minus) or above (plus) the mean value, and the size of the number shows how far above or below the mean these people were.

The result of the formula $X_i - \overline{X}$ is used so often in statistical analysis that it has its own name: **deviation**. The size of the resulting number tells us how much this one case deviates from the average value, and the plus or minus sign tells us whether the deviation is on the high or low side of the mean. If we add each respondent's deviation from the mean for the entire sample [$\Sigma(X_i - \overline{X})$] and then divide by the size of the sample $\Sigma(X_i - \overline{X})/n$, we ought to end up with a measure of the average deviation around the mean of the variable, which would be an attractive measure of dispersion.

Unfortunately, things are not quite this simple, although we are close. Two changes need to be made in the formula before we have an adequate measure of dispersion. The biggest problem lies in the numerator, the $\Sigma(X_i - \overline{X})$ term. The mean is calculated to be in the exact mathematical middle of a variable's distribution. Because of this, adding all the negative deviations below the mean to positive deviations above it will give a result of zero—always. A formula that always gives a value of zero regardless of whether the respondents are spread widely around the mean value or packed closely near it obviously is not a very useful measure of dispersion.

The problem is that the negative deviations and positive deviations will always cancel each other exactly. We need to eliminate this problem. One way might be to take the absolute value of each deviation, $\Sigma(|X_i - \overline{X}|)$, which would make all the numbers positive. This would work, but mathematicians are interested in statistics with properties—characteristics that make the number useful in more than one formula. Summing the absolute values of the deviations produces a number that you cannot do much else with. Consequently, the preferred way to get rid of the negative signs is to square each deviation and then sum the squared deviations over all the cases in the sample, $\Sigma(X_i - \overline{X})^2$. Squaring the deviations also turns all the negative numbers to positive. Furthermore, as we shall see shortly, squared deviations have some additional properties which make them more useful than the absolute value of the deviations.

The second change is in the denominator of the variance formula. Instead of dividing by the sample size n, we divide by our **degrees of freedom**, which for the variance is $n - 1$. *Degrees of freedom* is a term we will encounter repeatedly in later chapters. The reasons why we use degrees of freedom are too complex to detail in an introductory text, but an analogy may help. Degrees of freedom can be roughly thought of as a correction or safety factor. If engineers determine that a bolt used in building airplanes needs to withstand 1000 lb of tension, you do not use bolts manufactured exactly to that specification. Even the best quality control will err and occasionally produce a bolt that can take only

900 lb of tension. To compensate, you add a safety factor and require bolts built to take 1200 lb of tension so that an occasional weak bolt should still be strong enough to be used without danger.

The same is true in calculating sample statistics. Our sample is merely a tool we use to study the whole population, and we want to draw trustworthy conclusions about that population. The power of the statistics that we calculate is affected by the size of our sample. The net effect of dividing by degrees of freedom is to underestimate the size of our sample marginally, giving us a bit of a safety factor in estimating population characteristics.

With these changes to the numerator and denominator, our measure of dispersion, the variance, is calculated by

$$s^2 = \frac{\Sigma (X_i - \overline{X})^2}{n - 1}$$

where s^2 is the symbol for the variance and the terms on the right-hand side of the equals sign are as discussed above.

Standard Deviation   The variance usually produces very large numbers which are difficult to use. The variance also has no direct interpretation since it deals with squared distances. We may talk about the distance from point A to point B, but we seldom talk about the squared distance between two points. We squared the deviations originally merely to get rid of the negative numbers in our calculation of dispersion. Having accomplished that, we now move back to unsquared distance by taking the square root of the variance. The number that results is called the **standard deviation**, and is represented by the symbol s.

By using either the variance or the standard deviation, we can assess how widely dispersed the responses are around the mean. Returning to our original example, comparing the average incomes of the United States and Sweden, we may find that the means are the same, $25,000, but the standard deviation of incomes in Sweden is $2500 while the standard deviation of incomes in the United States is $7500. The two distributions of income have the same average value, but Swedish incomes are clustered closely around the average value while the distribution of U.S. incomes is dispersed quite broadly around the average point.

We mentioned earlier that mathematicians prefer numbers with more than one property. The standard deviation is a good illustration of this: Not only is it an abstract measure of dispersion, but also, for variables with a normal distribution, it has a more concrete meaning. A **normal distribution** is a distribution of variable values that forms a bell-shaped curve, as in Figure 7.10*a*; each side of the curve is a mirror image of the other. Figure 7.10*a* might be a typical distribution of incomes with most people congregating around the mean value. As we get farther and farther from the average value, the number of people with very low or very high incomes tends to get smaller and smaller. In contrast, Figure 7.10*b* shows a distribution which is not normal, say, the number of days spent on vacation each year. Most people would take about two weeks of

a.   A Normal Distribution

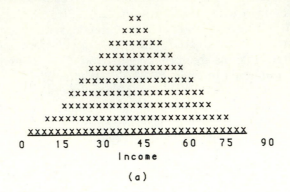

```
                    x x
                   x x x x
                 x x x x x x x
               x x x x x x x x x x
             x x x x x x x x x x x x x
           x x x x x x x x x x x x x x x
         x x x x x x x x x x x x x x x x x
       x x x x x x x x x x x x x x x x x x x
     x x x x x x x x x x x x x x x x x x x x x x
   x x x x x x x x x x x x x x x x x x x x x x x x x
   0      15     30     45     60     75     90
                      Income

                       (a)
```

b.   A Non-normal Distribution

```
                 x x x x x x x
                x x x x x x x x x x x
              x x x x x x x x x x x x x                  x x x
            x x x x x x x x x x x x x x x x             x x x x x
          x x x x x x x x x x x x x x x x x x        x x x x x x x x x
        x x x x x x x x x x x x x x x x x x x x x   x x x x x x x x x x x
      x x x x x x x x x x x x x x x x x x x x x x x x x x x x x x x x x x
   x x x x x x x x x x x x x x x x x x x x x x x x x x x x x x x x x x x x x x x
   0      5      10     15     20     25     30     35     40
                      Vacation  days  per  year

                       (b)
```

Figure 7.10 (a) Normal distribution; (b) nonnormal distribution.

vacation per year, but a sizable group, perhaps students or retirees, take almost three times as many vacation days as others.

Fortunately, many interval variables in the social sciences have normal or near normal distributions. When this is the case, we have found that the standard deviation can be used to determine how many cases are close to the average value. For normal distributions, the region ranging from 1 standard deviation below the mean to 1 standard deviation above the mean includes about 67 percent, or about two-thirds, of all the cases. Furthermore, ±2 standard deviations around the mean includes about 95 percent of the cases, and the region of ±3 standard deviations around the mean includes about 99 percent of all cases. These regions are illustrated in Figure 7.11. Thus, if the Swedish and U.S. incomes are distributed normally, which they probably are, the standard deviation for each group tells us that about two-thirds of all Swedes have incomes between $22,500 and $27,500 while an equal number of Americans are dispersed more widely, from $17,500 to $32,500.

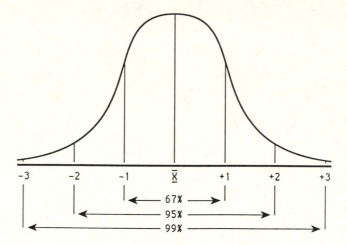

Figure 7.11 The standard deviation and the normal curve.

Requesting Statistics with SPSS

We have seen a lot of formulas in the last few pages, some rather complex. Fortunately SPSS will calculate these statistics for us if we request it. The request is made through the **STATISTICS** subcommand, illustrated in Figure 7.12. We begin with a slash to separate the subcommand from either the main command or other subcommands. Following the slash is the subcommand STATISTICS followed by the list of statistics to be calculated, in this case the mean, median, variance, and standard deviation. This subcommand will produce a list of the requested statistics at the bottom of the frequencies table, as shown in Figure 7.13. If the FREQUENCIES command contains a list of variables after the VARIABLES = term, the statistics requested will be produced for each variable on the list.

Each procedure has a different set of statistics available for it. For the FREQUENCIES procedure, the statistics you can request are displayed in Table 7.2. STATISTICS is the name of the subcommand, and the options available with it are a variety of different statistics such as the ones just discussed. The term or abbreviation used to request each optional statistic is shown in the middle column, and the right column describes the statistic that this term will produce. The statistics we have talked about in this chapter—the ones you are most likely to use—are listed in bold type. The other statistics are used only in rare situations. They are not discussed here, but any common statistics text can describe them.

```
001    GET FILE = ELEC88
002    FREQUENCIES VARIABLES = V19
003         /    STATISTICS      MEAN  MEDIAN  VARIANCE  STDDEV
```

Figure 7.12 Format of the STATISTICS subcommand.

U5   FEELING THERMOMETER - BUSH

VALUE LABEL	VALUE	FREQUENCY	PERCENT	VALID PERCENT	CUM PERCENT
COLD,HOSTILE	0	136	6.7	6.9	6.9
	2	1	0.0	0.1	6.9
	4	1	0.0	0.1	7.0
	5	2	0.1	0.1	7.1
	10	10	0.5	0.5	7.6
	15	62	3.0	3.1	10.8
	20	10	0.5	0.5	11.3
	25	2	0.1	0.1	11.4
	30	95	4.7	4.8	16.2
	33	1	0.0	0.1	16.2
	35	4	0.2	0.2	16.4
	40	140	6.9	7.1	23.5
	45	4	0.2	0.2	23.7
	49	1	0.0	0.1	23.8
NEUTRAL	50	347	17.0	17.6	41.4
	55	5	0.2	0.3	41.6
	60	205	10.0	10.4	52.0
	65	12	0.6	0.6	52.6
	70	275	13.5	13.9	66.6
	75	24	1.2	1.2	67.8
	80	29	1.4	1.5	69.3
	85	334	16.4	16.9	86.2
	90	30	1.5	1.5	87.7
	92	2	0.1	0.1	87.8
	95	9	0.4	0.5	88.3
	97	1	0.0	0.1	88.3
	98	1	0.0	0.1	88.4
WARM,FRIENDLY	100	229	11.2	11.6	100.0
DSN'T RECOGNIZE NAME	997	6	0.3	MISSING	
DK,CAN'T RATE	998	53	2.6	MISSING	
NA	999	9	0.4	MISSING	
	TOTAL	2040	100.0	100.0	

MEAN   60.572   MEDIAN   60.000   STD DEV   27.715
VARIANCE   768.096

VALID CASES   1972   MISSING CASES   68

Figure 7.13 Output from the STATISTICS subcommand.

The statistics shown in Table 7.2 can be requested in one of three ways. First, you can merely include the subcommand / STATISTICS without further specifications. This will produce the default list of statistics: the mean, standard deviation, minimum value, and maximum value. The default list is fine if you are dealing only with interval variables; but if you are examining nominal or ordinal variables, you will also want the mode and median produced. To obtain this information, you list all the statistics you want after the STATISTICS term, as in

/ STATISTICS MEAN MEDIAN MODE STDDEV VARIANCE RANGE

Table 7.2   STATISTICS AVAILABLE FOR THE FREQUENCIES PROCEDURE

Subcommand	Option	Statistic
STATISTICS	**MEAN**	**Mean**
STATISTICS	SEMEAN	Standard error of the mean
STATISTICS	**MEDIAN**	**Median**
STATISTICS	**MODE**	**Mode**
STATISTICS	**STDDEV**	**Standard deviation**
STATISTICS	**VARIANCE**	**Variance**
STATISTICS	SKEWNESS	Skewness of the distribution
STATISTICS	SESKEW	Standard error of the skewness
STATISTICS	KURTOSIS	Kurtosis of the distribution
STATISTICS	SEKURT	Standard error of the kurtosis
STATISTICS	**RANGE**	**Range from minimum to maximum value**
STATISTICS	**MINIMUM**	**Minimum value for the variable**
STATISTICS	**MAXIMUM**	**Maximum value for the variable**
STATISTICS	**SUM**	**Sum of all the variable's values**
STATISTICS	**ALL**	**All the above**

This approach was the one used, although for different statistics, in Figure 7.12. Finally, there is a shortcut approach which is to use the **ALL key word**. When you use the / STATISTICS ALL subcommand, SPSS will produce every statistic listed in Table 7.2. This approach saves typing on the STATISTICS subcommand, but requires a little greater care in interpreting the results since some of the statistics produced will be irrelevant (e.g., a mean for a nominal variable).

Requesting Multiple Subcommands

Subcommands can change many of the ways that SPSS carries out and reports on the results of a procedure. You can request as many different subcommands as you like, as long as they do not call for inconsistent action. You can request both a bar chart and all the available statistics, because these are two different features which do not conflict with each other. You would not want, however, to request both that missing data be included in the cumulative percentage column of the FREQUENCIES table and also that the table not be printed at all.

SPSS/PC+

In SPSS/PC+, the BARCHART subcommand will produce single rows of X's or other symbols to represent each bar rather than drawing boxes as SPSS does. Thus bar charts and histograms will look very similar in the output from SPSS/PC+. Aside from the difference in appearance, the subcommands work the same for both forms of SPSS—histograms group values while bar charts do not.

SUMMARY

In this chapter we have discussed the first SPSS procedure, a command that calculates statistics and produces an output. The FREQUENCIES procedure is highly useful for descriptive information—how respondents answered a specific question, the average response, and the dispersion of the responses. In succeeding chapters we discuss other SPSS procedures, each providing a different way to probe the data in search for answers to our research question.

Before turning to new statistical procedures, we need to explore one further aspect of the data. In earlier chapters we examined how to define the data to SPSS. These data definition commands dealt with the data in their original form, the way they were collected and defined in the codebook. The original form of the data is not always as useful as we might wish. In Chapter 8 we examine how the data can be modified to enhance their value for our particular research question.

REVIEW

Key Terms

Univariate analysis	Mean
Default	Dispersion
Subcommands	Range
Distribution	Variance
BARCHART	Deviation
FORMAT NOTABLE	Degrees of freedom
HISTOGRAM	Standard deviation
Statistic	Normal distribution
Central tendency	STATISTICS
Mode	ALL key word
Median	

Exercises

7.1 The table below contains the values on three variables (V1, V2, and V3) for a sample of 11 cases, *a* through *k*. For each variable, calculate the following six statistics: mode, median, mean, range, variance, and standard deviation. It is usually easiest to calculate the variance in stages by adding extra columns like those shown at the right of the table. After determining the mean, calculate $X_i - \overline{X}$ for each case and then $(X_i - \overline{X})^2$.

Case	V1	V2	V3	$X_i - \bar{X}$	$(X_i - \bar{X})^2$
a	1	9	3		
b	7	8	4		
c	9	4	1		
d	7	2	3		
e	2	1	2		
f	3	3	7		
g	8	7	5		
h	6	7	4		
i	1	7	3		
j	4	6	1		
k	10	9	2		

7.2 Identify the errors, if any, in the commands below.

   a. FREQUENCIES V4
   b. FREQUENCIES VARIABLES = V4 / HISTOGRAM BARCHART
   c. FREQUENCIES VARIABLES = V4 STATISTICS
   d. FREQUENCIES VARIABLES = SEX / BARCHART / STATISTICS
   e. FREQUENCIES VARIABLES = RACE / STATISTICS
   f. FREQUENCIES VARIABLES = RACE SEX WRKSTAT SPW
      RKSTA

7.3 Reproduce the following figures from this chapter: 7.2, 7.3, 7.5, 7.7, 7.8, 7.9, and 7.13. Your output should match these figures exactly.

7.4 SPSS/PC+ and Release 4 users should locate the FREQUENCIES command on the command generator and then move deeper to see how the menu/help screens list both the subcommands and the options as well as explaining each. Remember, whether you are using extended menus will determine how many of the available subcommands or options will appear on the menu. In addition, explore the Glossary to see how it explains the statistical terms (e.g., corrected percent, variance, or mode) on the output.

7.5 Identify the appropriate measure of central tendency and dispersion for the variables listed below. You will need to examine the codebooks carefully to make sure you understand the contents of each variable.

   GSS88: SEX, AGE, WRKSTAT, EDUC, MARITAL, ROTAPPLE, PERMORAL, RINCOME.
   ELEC88: V2, V6, V9, V24, V40, V82, V86

SUGGESTED READINGS

Babbie, Earl. *The Practice of Social Research*, 5th ed. (Belmont, Calif.: Wadsworth, 1989) Chapter 14.

Freedman, David, *et al. Statistics*, 2nd ed. (New York: W. W. Norton, 1991) Chapters 3, 4.

Levin, Jack and James Alan Fox. *Elementary Statistics in Social Research*, 4th ed. (New York: Harper & Row, 1988) Chapters 2, 4–6.

May, Richard B., Michael E. J. Masson, and Michael A. Hunter. *Application of Statistics in Behavioral Research* (New York: Harper & Row, 1990) Chapters 3, 4.

Nachmias, David and Chava Nachmias. *Research Methods in the Social Sciences*, 3rd ed. (New York: St. Martin's, 1987) Chapter 15.

Norusis, Marija J., and SPSS Inc. *SPSS/PC+ V2.0 Base Manual* (Chicago: SPSS Inc., 1988) Chapter 7.

SPSS Inc. *SPSS Reference Guide* (Release 4) (Chicago: SPSS Inc., 1990) pages 219–24.

SPSS Inc. *SPSS-X User's Guide*, 3rd ed. (Chicago: SPSS Inc., 1988) Chapter 29.

Chapter 8

Modifying Data

Some research questions are questions of description: What percentage of the people are Democrats versus Republicans, or how frequently do people attend church? The FREQUENCIES procedure provides the descriptive information of how cases are distributed on a variable and the average value for the cases. It is useful in answering most descriptive questions—most, but not all. Suppose, for example, that we want to know the average income *for women.* The FREQUENCIES procedure, at least by itself, cannot tell us this for its description of the income variable includes both men and women.

To answer some of the descriptive questions we may have, it is often necessary to modify the data in some way. This is particularly true with secondary analysis, for we are using data gathered by others to suit *their* purposes. The data, in their present form, may not be ideally suited to *our* needs. Even with data that we have collected ourselves, we often decide later to do different things from what was originally planned with the data.

Modifying data sounds risky, as though we were cheating to change the results to agree with our preconceived ideas. Clearly, this is not what we have in mind. Data modification is essentially a question of measurement. Are we measuring what we want to measure, or does this operational variable adequately represent the concept we are interested in? There are two general ways we can modify data: by changing the cases being analyzed or by changing the variables being analyzed. In this chapter we examine both and show how the modifications are really attempts to answer questions more accurately.

MODIFYING CASES

When we modify cases, we decide to analyze only some of the cases in the data set, not all. There are two ways to change the number of cases used: the SAMPLE command and the SELECT IF command.

The SAMPLE Command

The **SAMPLE** command draws a computer-generated random sample from the data set. But our data are already a random sample of the population, so why do we want a sample of our sample? In most instances, we do not. The SAMPLE command is of value only in a few limited situations. One example might be the use of a very large data set, such as some of the Census Bureau surveys that can contain up to 150,000 respondents. Analyzing this many cases uses up an enormous amount of expensive computer time. Researchers do not want to bankrupt their research budgets with only one or two exploratory analyses of the data. Consequently, they will draw a random sample of around 2000 to 5000 cases from the data set and use this subsample for preliminary analysis. The entire sample will be used, if at all, only for the polished statistical analysis included in the final research report.

The data sets we will use are nowhere near this large. Even so, there are a few situations in which the SAMPLE command comes in handy. Some are encountered later in this chapter and in Chapter 9. For now, let us look at how the SAMPLE command operates.

Proportional Samples   Two types of samples can be drawn: proportional samples and exact samples. A **proportional sample** involves requesting some percentage of the data set to be included in the sample; say, 5 percent or 20 percent of the cases. To draw a proportional sample, the SAMPLE command is followed by a decimal number telling SPSS what percentage of the cases should be included in the sample. The command

    SAMPLE .10

produces a sample that includes only 10 percent of the cases in the data set. SPSS will generate some random numbers to select cases for the sample and stop when it has randomly selected about 10 percent of the cases.

Proportional samples are not precise. A 10 percent sample of the 1481 respondents in the GSS88 data set will not produce a subsample of exactly 148 cases. The actual sample size may range from around 8 to 12 percent of the entire data set. Drawing an exact-size sample is a difficult procedure which also uses a lot of computer time and would defeat the purpose of trying to cut computer costs. Drawing proportional samples which are pretty close but not exact is far simpler and cheaper. It is also fine for most purposes since seldom do we need a sample that contains exactly 500 or 220 cases.

Exact Samples   In some situations an **exact sample**, a precise number of cases, is needed. The SAMPLE command can also draw exact samples, but the format of the command differs. To draw exact samples, SPSS requires us to specify both the sample size needed and the size of the data set from which the sample is being drawn. Thus, the SAMPLE command is

```
SAMPLE 100 FROM 1481
```

where 100 is the sample size desired and 1481 is the number of cases in the GSS88 data set. Recall that SPSS commands do not include commas in numbers over 1000.

Supplement 8.1 # The SET SEED Command

SPSS uses a starting number, called the **seed number**, from which it generates random numbers to draw random subsamples. If you draw more than one sample during a run or computer session, each sample will be different because SPSS picks up from the last random number generated and continues from there. However, many implementations of SPSS will reset to the same beginning seed number whenever your start a new session at the computer or submit a new job to be run. If your computer installation or form of SPSS does this, the first sample drawn from each run will be exactly the same, as will all second samples drawn during each run, and so on. This is illustrated in Figure 8.1S.

```
_____RUN 1_____                                    _____RUN 2_____
GET FILE = ELEC88                                        GET FILE = ELEC88

SAMPLE .10              ← identical samples →            SAMPLE .10
FREQUENCIES VARIABLES = SEX                              FREQUENCIES VARIABLES = SEX
   ↑                                                        ↑
different samples                                        different samples
   ↓                                                        ↓
SAMPLE .10             ← identical samples →             SAMPLE .10
FREQUENCIES VARIABLES = SEX                              FREQUENCIES VARIABLES = SEX
   ↑                                                        ↑
different samples                                        different samples
   ↓                                                        ↓
SAMPLE .10            ← identical samples →              SAMPLE .10
FREQUENCIES VARIABLES = SEX                              FREQUENCIES VARIABLES = SEX
```

Figure 8.1S Drawing identical and different samples.

The drawing of identical samples during different runs is not a problem if all we wish is to reduce the number of cases analyzed. Sometimes, however, we may be interested in drawing different samples during each run. If so, we can accomplish it by using a different starting seed number at the beginning of each session, thus producing different random numbers to generate the samples. This is done with the **SET SEED** command. This command overrides the computer's default—returning to the same seed number at the beginning of each run—and specifies the starting seed number that SPSS will use instead. Its use is illustrated in Figure 8.2S.

```
            RUN 1                                                    RUN 2
GET FILE = ELEC88                                        GET FILE = ELEC88
SET  SEED  100000000                                     SET  SEED  250000000


SAMPLE .10                      ← different  samples →    SAMPLE .10
FREQUENCIES  VARIABLES = SEX                              FREQUENCIES  VARIABLES = SEX

      ↑                                                         ↑
  different samples                                        different samples
      ↓                                                         ↓


SAMPLE .10                      ← different  samples →    SAMPLE .10
FREQUENCIES  VARIABLES = SEX                              FREQUENCIES  VARIABLES = SEX

      ↑                                                         ↑
  different samples                                        different samples
      ↓                                                         ↓


SAMPLE .10                      ← different  samples →    SAMPLE .10
FREQUENCIES  VARIABLES = SEX                              FREQUENCIES  VARIABLES = SEX
```

Figure 8.2S Drawing different samples with the SET SEED command.

The SET SEED command is followed by a number that we identify as the starting number. SPSS's random number generator works best if the beginning seed number is quite large, at least 1 million or more. The only restriction is that we should not use a number higher than 2 billion (2000000000). As in all numbers used in SPSS commands, no commas are included in the number.

Both versions of the SAMPLE command, as well as the output produced by each, are illustrated in Figure 8.1. Observe that the 10 percent sample is fairly close, producing a sample of 154 cases rather than exactly 148 cases (10 percent of the 1481 respondents in the GSS88 data set). In contrast, the sample in the bottom half of Figure 8.1 is exact—we asked for 100 cases and got 100 cases. Remember also that SPSS carries out commands in the order given. The SAMPLE command comes before the FREQUENCIES command. If these commands were reversed, SPSS would carry out the FREQUENCIES analysis before it drew the sample.

⑫ The SELECT IF Command

Far more common than the need to draw a sample is the desire to analyze only cases selected to meet a specific condition. Return to the information sought at the beginning of this chapter, the average income *for women*. That is, we want to run a FREQUENCIES procedure on the income variable to find its average

```
GET FILE = GSS88
SAMPLE    .10
FREQUENCIES  VARIABLE=SEX
      / STATISTICS ALL


SEX         RESPONDENT'S SEX

                                               VALID    CUM
   VALUE LABEL            VALUE  FREQUENCY  PERCENT  PERCENT  PERCENT

   MALE                     1        56       36.4     36.4     36.4
   FEMALE                   2        98       63.6     63.6    100.0
                                   -------  -------  -------
                          TOTAL     154      100.0    100.0


   MEAN       1.636    STD ERR     0.039    MEDIAN       2.000
   MODE       2.000    STD DEV     0.483    VARIANCE     0.233
   KURTOSIS  -1.694    S E KURT    0.389    SKEWNESS    -0.573
   S E SKEW   0.195    RANGE       1.000    MINIMUM      1.000
   MAXIMUM    2.000    SUM       252.000

   VALID CASES   154      MISSING CASES      0
```

- -

```
GET FILE = GSS88
SAMPLE   100   FROM   1481
FREQUENCIES  VARIABLE=SEX
      / STATISTICS ALL


SEX         RESPONDENT'S SEX

                                               VALID    CUM
   VALUE LABEL            VALUE  FREQUENCY  PERCENT  PERCENT  PERCENT

   MALE                     1        40       40.0     40.0     40.0
   FEMALE                   2        60       60.0     60.0    100.0
                                   -------  -------  -------
                          TOTAL     100      100.0    100.0


   MEAN       1.600    STD ERR     0.049    MEDIAN       2.000
   MODE       2.000    STD DEV     0.492    VARIANCE     0.242
   KURTOSIS  -1.866    S E KURT    0.478    SKEWNESS    -0.414
   S E SKEW   0.241    RANGE       1.000    MINIMUM      1.000
   MAXIMUM    2.000    SUM       160.000

   VALID CASES   100      MISSING CASES      0
```

Figure 8.1 The SAMPLE command and its output.

value, but we want to do this for women only. To take a subset of certain cases for analysis, we use the **SELECT IF** command.

To use the SELECT IF command, we must specify two things: the variable containing the relevant information and the condition (value on the variable) that must be met. The format of the SELECT IF command is

```
SELECT IF (variable name, condition)
```

For the illustration used earlier, the variable SEX includes the needed information—is the respondent male or female? The condition to be satisfied is that the respondent must have a value of 2 on this variable, the respondent is female. To select only women for analysis, the format of the SELECT IF command is

SELECT IF (SEX EQ 2)

In this example, the variable and condition are enclosed in parentheses. This is not required in all forms of SPSS, but it is by some and thus is a good practice to use. It also helps clarify what we are doing with the command by highlighting the variable and condition.

Between the variable and its value is the two-letter term EQ. This is an SPSS **logical operator**, a two-letter term that identifies the relationship between the variable and the condition. Table 8.1 shows the logical operators that can be used and the meaning of each. We used the operator EQ above because we wanted to select only cases whose value equals 2 on the SEX variable.

Figure 8.2 shows the format of the SELECT IF command and the resulting output. Note that the FREQUENCIES table includes only 843 cases, the number of women in the GSS88 data set. The statistics at the bottom of the table now refer to the average income (and dispersion of income) for women only.

Sometimes the condition to be met is represented by more than one value of a variable. For example, suppose that we are interested in how Democrats view the seriousness of the federal budget deficit. We thus want to examine variable V60 (Is the respondent worried about the budget deficit?) but for Democrats only. Variable V74 is the respondent's party identification, but three different code numbers are used to identify Democrats: 0, 1, and 2 for strong Democrats, weak Democrats, and Independents leaning toward the Democratic party, respectively. To include all three groups of Democrats in a single SELECT IF statement, we use the LE or LT logical operators. The command is

SELECT IF (V74 LE 2)

or

SELECT IF (V74 LT 3)

Table 8.1 SPSS LOGICAL OPERATORS

Two-letter operator	Meaning
EQ	Equal to
NE	Not equal to
GT	Greater than
LT	Less than
GE	Greater than or equal to
LE	Less than or equal to

```
SELECT IF (SEX EQ 2)
FREQUENCIES VARIABLES=RINCOME
      /STATISTICS ALL
```

RINCOME   RESPONDENT'S INCOME

VALUE LABEL	VALUE	FREQUENCY	PERCENT	VALID PERCENT	CUM PERCENT
LT $1000	1	27	3.2	5.8	5.8
$1000-2999	2	36	4.3	7.7	13.5
$3000-3999	3	28	3.3	6.0	19.5
$4000-4999	4	12	1.4	2.6	22.1
$5000-5999	5	17	2.0	3.6	25.7
$6000-6999	6	15	1.8	3.2	28.9
$7000-7999	7	27	3.2	5.8	34.7
$8000-9999	8	24	2.8	5.1	39.8
$10000-12499	9	49	5.8	10.5	50.3
$12500-14999	10	36	4.3	7.7	58.0
$15000-17499	11	34	4.0	7.3	65.3
$17500-19999	12	22	2.6	4.7	70.0
$20000-22499	13	26	3.1	5.6	75.6
$22500-24999	14	31	3.7	6.6	82.2
$25000-29999	15	32	3.8	6.9	89.1
$30000-34999	16	24	2.8	5.1	94.2
$35000-39999	17	7	0.8	1.5	95.7
$40000-49999	18	14	1.7	3.0	98.7
$50000-59999	19	2	0.2	0.4	99.1
$60000+	20	4	0.5	0.9	100.0
NAP	97	342	40.6	MISSING	
DK	98	3	0.4	MISSING	
NA	99	31	3.7	MISSING	
	TOTAL	843	100.0	100.0	

MEAN	9.317	STD ERR	0.229	MEDIAN	9.000
MODE	9.000	STD DEV	4.956	VARIANCE	24.565
KURTOSIS	-0.962	S E KURT	0.225	SKEWNESS	-0.065
S E SKEW	0.113	RANGE	19.000	MINIMUM	1.000
MAXIMUM	20.000	SUM	4351.000		

VALID CASES   467   MISSING CASES   376

Figure 8.2 The SELECT IF command and its output.

There may be other occasions where we want to select only cases that meet two or more conditions, say, the incomes of college-educated men. The SELECT IF statement allows us to specify both conditions, as in

SELECT IF (SEX EQ 1 **AND** EDUC GE 13)

The terms AND and OR are used to connect multiple conditions. The **AND connector** requires that only cases meeting *both* conditions, male and 13 or more years of education, be selected. Respondents who are males will not be included in the analysis if they have less than 13 years of education, nor will college-educated women be selected.

There may be occasions when we want to select cases that meet either of two conditions, but not necessarily both. In such situations, we use the **OR connector** between the conditions. If we wanted to identify people who are highly religious, we might begin by selecting those who attend church more than once a week (ATTEND GE 7). However, there may be people who are highly religious but for some reason, perhaps illness, do not attend church frequently. We might thus use the command

> SELECT IF (ATTEND GE 7 **OR** PRAY LE 3)

This SELECT IF command selects for analysis those respondents either attending church more than once a week *or* praying more than once a week. Since cases will be selected if they meet either condition, they will also be selected if they meet both conditions.

MODIFYING VARIABLES

As stated at the beginning of the chapter, data modifications involve questions of how to best measure things. This is clearest when we turn our attention to modifying variables instead of cases. We have some concept that we want to assess, but the operational variables in our data set measure that concept poorly or perhaps not at all. We cannot create information out of thin air, but our operational variables often contain the information we need, but in an indirect way. Modifying variables is similar to a manufacturing process. One plant can take the raw materials available and build an automobile while another plant can use the same raw materials to build sewing machines. The operational variables are the raw materials which can be combined in different ways to measure different things. Three commands which modify variables are RECODE, COMPUTE, and IF.

The RECODE Command

When the data were first collected, the researchers decided to associate particular code numbers with the responses. The **RECODE** command allows us to change the code numbers associated with each response. The format of the command is

> RECODE variable name (old value = new value) (old value = new value)

After the RECODE command word is the name of the variable whose values are to be recoded. Finally, in parentheses, we define some original value(s) of the variable to be equal to some new value. Let us look at three ways in which this command is commonly used.

More Interpretable Code Numbers We sometimes encounter variables for which the original code numbers are somewhat clumsy; different ones would be easier to interpret. The variable PRAY is a case in point. The legitimate responses for this variable (ignoring missing values) range from code 1 through code 6. It is typical to think of organizing things from least to most; those with code 5 pray more often than respondents with code 4. However, that is not how this variable has been coded. The lowest code number, 1, is used for those who pray several times a day, while the highest code number, 6, represents respondents who never pray (Figure 8.3).

The RECODE command can solve this minor inconvenience for us. We can invert the code numbers with the command

RECODE PRAY (1 = 6) (2 = 5) (3 = 4) (4 = 3) (5 = 2) (6 = 1)

Inside the parentheses of this command, the original code number comes first, before the equals sign, and the new code number comes after the equals sign. The results of this change are shown in Figure 8.4

A brief glance at Figure 8.4 may lead you to think that either something is wrong with the table or the recoding did not work—the value label for row 1 still says "Several times a day," just as it did before. Yes, the recoding did take place. Compare the frequency counts in Figures 8.3 and 8.4. You will see that the 346 people who were coded number 1 in Figure 8.3 are now coded number 6 in Figure 8.4, the 450 people coded number 2 originally are now coded number 5, and so on. What did *not* change were the labels attached to these code numbers. Earlier we told SPSS to attach the label "Several times a day" to code number 1 for this variable, and it continues to do so.

What recoding does is similar to changing the contents of any two containers, putting salt in the sugar bin and vice versa. The shifting of contents has been accomplished, but the old labels still remain—the label "Salt" for the salt bin

```
PRAY          HOW OFTEN DOES R PRAY

                                                    VALID      CUM
         VALUE LABEL          VALUE   FREQUENCY   PERCENT   PERCENT   PERCENT

SEVERAL TIMES A DAY             1         346       23.4      23.6      23.6
ONCE A DAY                      2         450       30.4      30.7      54.2
SEVERAL TIMES A WEEK            3         229       15.5      15.6      69.8
ONCE A WEEK                     4         113        7.6       7.7      77.5
LT ONCE A WEEK                 5         326       22.0      22.2      99.7
NEVER                           6           4        0.3       0.3     100.0
DK                              8           5        0.3    MISSING
NA                              9           8        0.5    MISSING
                                        -------   -------   -------
                        TOTAL          1481      100.0     100.0

MEAN          2.751    STD ERR       0.039     MEDIAN        2.000
MODE          2.000    STD DEV       1.476     VARIANCE      2.179
KURTOSIS     -1.210    S E KURT      0.128     SKEWNESS      0.428
S E SKEW      0.064    RANGE         5.000     MINIMUM       1.000
MAXIMUM       6.000    SUM        4039.000

VALID CASES     1468       MISSING CASES      13
```

Figure 8.3 A FREQUENCIES of the PRAY variable.

```
RECODE  PRAY  (1=6)(2=5)(3=4)(4=3)(5=2)(6=1)
FREQUENCIES  VARIABLES=PRAY
        /  STATISTICS  ALL
```

PRAY   HOW OFTEN DOES R PRAY

VALUE LABEL	VALUE	FREQUENCY	PERCENT	VALID PERCENT	CUM PERCENT
SEVERAL TIMES A DAY	1	4	0.3	0.3	0.3
ONCE A DAY	2	326	22.0	22.2	22.5
SEVERAL TIMES A WEEK	3	113	7.6	7.7	30.2
ONCE A WEEK	4	229	15.5	15.6	45.8
LT ONCE A WEEK	5	450	30.4	30.7	76.4
NEVER	6	346	23.4	23.6	100.0
DK	8	5	0.3	MISSING	
NA	9	8	0.5	MISSING	
	TOTAL	1481	100.0	100.0	

MEAN	4.249	STD ERR	0.039	MEDIAN	5.000
MODE	5.000	STD DEV	1.476	VARIANCE	2.179
KURTOSIS	-1.210	S E KURT	0.128	SKEWNESS	-0.428
S E SKEW	0.064	RANGE	5.000	MINIMUM	1.000
MAXIMUM	6.000	SUM	6237.000		

VALID CASES   1468   MISSING CASES   13

Figure 8.4 A FREQUENCIES of the PRAY variable after recoding.

(which now contains sugar) and the label "Sugar" for the sugar bin (which now contains salt). Remember, the value labels are merely for our benefit and have no impact at all on any statistical analyses performed, just as the labels on the salt and sugar bins have no effect on their contents.

Still, it would be nice to have the labels reflect our new coding of the variable. This is easily done by inserting a new VALUE LABELS command to produce labels identifying each code number's new contents. The addition of this command and the revised output are shown in Figure 8.5. Observe that all the numbers—the frequency count for each code number and the summary statistics at the bottom—are exactly the same in Figures 8.4 and 8.5. Only the labels for the code numbers have changed.

Regrouping Responses   Often one of our variables contains information that we want, but the way the variable is structured does not really represent what we are trying to measure. Say we wanted to determine what proportion of the respondents belonged to fundamentalist religious denominations. Variable V83 in the ELEC88 data set contains this information, but in its current state it does not measure what we want. We seek a measure that places respondents in two groups: fundamentalists and nonfundamentalists. Variable V83 divides respondents into about 50 groups based on specific religious identifications.

With the RECODE command we can change the variable so that it measures the phenomena we are trying to capture. We do this by combining the fundamentalist denominations, codes 130 to 149, into one group and the others,

```
RECODE  PRAY  (1=6)(2=5)(3=4)(4=3)(5=2)(6=1)
VALUE LABELS PRAY 1 'NEVER' 2 'LT ONCE A WEEK' 3 'ONCE A WEEK'
    4 'SEVERAL TIMES A WEEK' 5 'ONCE A DAY' 6 'SEVERAL TIMES A DAY'
FREQUENCIES  VARIABLES=PRAY
    / STATISTICS ALL

PRAY        HOW OFTEN DOES R PRAY
```

VALUE LABEL	VALUE	FREQUENCY	PERCENT	VALID PERCENT	CUM PERCENT
NEVER	1	4	0.3	0.3	0.3
LT ONCE A WEEK	2	326	22.0	22.2	22.5
ONCE A WEEK	3	113	7.6	7.7	30.2
SEVERAL TIMES A WEEK	4	229	15.5	15.6	45.8
ONCE A DAY	5	450	30.4	30.7	76.4
SEVERAL TIMES A DAY	6	346	23.4	23.6	100.0
	8	5	0.3	MISSING	
	9	8	0.5	MISSING	
		-------	-------	-------	
	TOTAL	1481	100.0	100.0	

MEAN	4.249	STD ERR	0.039	MEDIAN	5.000
MODE	5.000	STD DEV	1.476	VARIANCE	2.179
KURTOSIS	-1.210	S E KURT	0.128	SKEWNESS	-0.428
S E SKEW	0.064	RANGE	5.000	MINIMUM	1.000
MAXIMUM	6.000	SUM	6237.000		

```
VALID CASES    1468      MISSING CASES    13
```

Figure 8.5 The recoded PRAY variable with new value labels.

nonfundamentalists or no church affiliation, into a second group. The command is

```
RECODE V83 (130, 131, 132, 133, 135, 136, 137, 138, 139, 140, 141, 149 = 1)
    (100, 101, 102, 109, 110, 111, 112, 113, 114, 115, 116, 120, 121, 122, 123,
    124, 125, 126, 127, 150, 151, 152, 153, 154, 155, 200, 300, 710, 719, 720,
    721, 722, 729, 800 = 0)
```

When we are dealing with a large quantity of adjacent code numbers, SPSS has a convenience feature to make recoding easier, the **THRU keyword**. Just as we can refer to a group of adjacent variables with the TO keyword, the THRU keyword allows us to refer to a group of adjacent code numbers. Thus, instead of having to type all the code numbers, as was done in the example above, we could accomplish the same recoding with the command

```
RECODE V83 (130 THRU 149 = 1) (100 THRU 127, 150 THRU 800 = 0)
```

Regardless of which procedure is used, we end up with a variable that now reflects the information we desire—whether the respondent belongs to a funda-mentalist group. A FREQUENCIES table for this revised variable is shown in Figure 8.6.

Because of the RECODE command's ability to combine responses into a smaller number of groups, it is often used to condense the groups that exist on variables with a large number of response categories. AGE might be recoded into young, middle-aged, and older groups, or the feeling thermometer might be

```
RECODE   V83  ( 130 THRU 149 = 1 ) ( 100 THRU 127, 150 THRU 800 = 0)
VALUE LABELS 83 1 'FUNDAMENTALIST'   0   'NONFUNDAMENTALIST'
FREQUENCIES  VARIABLES=V83    / STATISTICS  ALL
```

```
V83           RELIGIOUS PREFERENCE

                                                      VALID      CUM
   VALUE LABEL            VALUE   FREQUENCY   PERCENT  PERCENT  PERCENT

NONFUNDAMENTALIST           0       1408       69.0     75.6     75.6
FUNDAMENTALIST              1        455       22.3     24.4    100.0
REFUSED                   996          5        0.2    MISSING
DK,NONE,NO  PREF          998        163        8.0    MISSING
NA                        999          9        0.4    MISSING
                                   -------    -------  -------
                          TOTAL      2040      100.0    100.0

VALID CASES      1863        MISSING CASES      177
```

Figure 8.6 A FREQUENCIES of V83 recoded to represent fundamentalist and non-funda-
mentalist religious groups.

condensed from 100 response categories to, say, only three groups: positive,
neutral, and negative feelings.

Such condensing of variables into a smaller number of response codes is a
common practice, but should not be undertaken without careful consideration.
Whenever a variable is recoded, what it measures changes. By combining the
AGE variable into young, middle-aged, and older groups, we are no longer
measuring the respondent's absolute age in years; instead we are measuring
the person's membership in one of three groups: under 35 (group 1), over 65
(group 3), and those in the middle (group 2). The difference between what the
recoded version and the unmodified version of the variable measures may be
quite modest, as in the recoding of AGE. At other times, recoding produces a
substantial shift in variable meaning, as in changing V83 from measuring
denominational affiliation to fundamentalist or nonfundamentalist group
membership.

Eliminating Values from Analysis   The third common use of the RECODE
command is to eliminate some cases from the analysis. Again, we are dealing
with a question of what concept we are trying to measure and whether a
variable's current values represent that concept. In some cases, two or three of
a variable's response codes represent what we want, but the variable also
contains one or two others that are irrelevant to our needs. Keeping these
irrelevant code numbers in the analysis creates a measurement problem.

Let us say we wanted to determine the proportion of respondents who voted
for Democratic or Republican candidates for the U.S. Senate during the 1988
election. Variable V4 contains the respondent's Senate voting behavior, but
Democrat and Republican are not the only choices coded for this variable.
Voting for a third-party candidate, choosing not to vote, and being unable to vote
because the respondent's state had no U.S. Senate race that year are also legitimate answers to this question (Figure 8.7). If our interest centers on what
proportion *of the public* voted for Democratic or Republican candidates, then

```
V4              VOTE U.S. SENATE

                                                       VALID     CUM
      VALUE LABEL              VALUE  FREQUENCY  PERCENT  PERCENT   PERCENT

DEMOC CAND                       1       479       23.5     27.4     27.4
REPUB CAND                       2       359       17.6     20.5     47.9
3RD PTY-INDEP                    3         1        0.0      0.1     47.9
DID NOT VOTE                     6       609       29.9     34.8     82.7
NO SENATE RACE                   7       302       14.8     17.3    100.0
INAP                             0       276       13.5   MISSING
DK                               8         6        0.3   MISSING
NA                               9         8        0.4   MISSING
                                      -------   -------  -------
                       TOTAL           2040      100.0    100.0

VALID CASES    1750      MISSING CASES    290
```

Figure 8.7 A FREQUENCIES of V4.

the variable's current composition is fine. If, however, we want to know what proportion *of the voters* chose Republicans or Democrats, then the nonvoters are irrelevant. Similarly, if we are interested in what proportion *of the eligible voters* cast their ballots for Republican or Democratic candidates, then voluntary nonvoters should be kept in the analysis but respondents without a choice (no Senate race) are not relevant.

To eliminate unwanted categories, we do not want to just group them together, for they will be included in the analysis, just under a different code number. How do we eliminate these responses from any of the calculations performed? We already have some code numbers for this variable that SPSS ignores when calculating any statistics—the missing-data codes 8, 9, and 0. Thus, to eliminate any irrelevant groups on a variable, we can just recode these extra groups into one of the missing-data categories, as in

    RECODE V4 (6, 7 = 9)

The result of doing this (Figure 8.8) is a FREQUENCIES table containing only respondents relevant to our question—those who voted in a U.S. Senate race. Now, a quick look at the corrected percentage column tells us that 57.1 percent of the voters chose Democratic candidates while 42.8 percent chose Republican ones.

The same strategy might also have been used in our earlier recoding of variable V83 to represent respondents belonging to fundamentalist versus nonfundamentalist religious denominations. Our earlier recoding of this variable included all those not belonging to fundamentalist Christian groups in the nonfundamentalist category, including Jews, followers of Islam, and atheists. This is just fine if we want to know what proportion of all respondents belongs to a fundamentalist denomination. If, however, we want to know what proportion of Christians or what proportion of Protestants belonged to fundamentalist or nonfundamentalist groups, a different strategy is needed. Only Christian groups should be recoded into the nonfundamentalist category, and non-Christian groups should be folded into one of the missing-data codes.

```
V4              VOTE U.S. SENATE

                                                       VALID      CUM
         VALUE LABEL           VALUE  FREQUENCY  PERCENT  PERCENT   PERCENT

DEMOC  CAND                      1       479      23.5     57.1     57.1
REPUB  CAND                      2       359      17.6     42.8     99.9
3RD  PTY-INDEP                   3         1       0.0      0.1    100.0
INAP                             0       276      13.5   MISSING
DK                               8         6       0.3   MISSING
NA                               9       919      45.0   MISSING
                                       -------   -------  -------
                         TOTAL          2040     100.0    100.0


MEAN          1.430    STD  ERR        0.017    MEDIAN       1.000
MODE          1.000    STD  DEV        0.498    VARIANCE     0.248
KURTOSIS     -1.830    S E  KURT       0.169    SKEWNESS     0.311
S E SKEW      0.084    RANGE           2.000    MINIMUM      1.000
MAXIMUM       3.000    SUM          1200.000

VALID CASES      839     MISSING CASES   1201
```

Figure 8.8 Distribution of voters in the 1988 Senate elections.

Supplement 8.2 # Recoding Multiple Variables

The RECODE command is a data definition command and uses the same features as other data definition commands. For example, the separating slash is available when we are dealing with more than one variable. If we want to recode the two variables EDUC and PRAY, we could write the command as

```
RECODE EDUC (1 THRU 12 = 1)(13 THRU 20 = 2)
RECODE PRAY (1, 2, 3 = 1)(4, 5, 6 = 2)
```

Alternatively, we could write the command as

```
RECODE EDUC (1 THRU 12 = 1)(13 THRU 20 = 2)
     / PRAY (1, 2, 3 = 1)(4, 5, 6 = 2)
```

In the second example, the slash before the name of the second variable tells SPSS we are still continuing the RECODE command, but now describing a second variable to be recoded. Essentially, the slash eliminates the need to retype the RECODE command for each variable we want to modify.

A second feature can be used when two variables contain essentially the same original code numbers and we want to modify them into similarly structured new groups. For example, the variables EDUC and SPEDUC have identical code numbers with identical meanings. Variables like these can be recoded as a group by listing first the names of both variables and then the coding changes that apply to both. For example,

```
RECODE EDUC SPEDUC (0 THRU 12 = 1)(13 THRU 20 = 2)
```

The COMPUTE Command

As we have just seen, the RECODE command modifies the values of an existing variable. A different command, **COMPUTE**, creates a new variable by performing some mathematical operation on one or more existing variables.

Let us begin with the format of the COMPUTE command, which is

```
COMPUTE new variable name = some mathematical expression
```

Since the COMPUTE command creates a new variable, it needs to begin with a name for that variable. We could use the name of an existing variable if desired, but then the COMPUTE command would erase the old variable with this name and put the new one being created in its place. Seldom is there a reason to erase an existing variable, so we generally use a variable name that does not already exist in the data set. After the variable name comes some mathematical expression which creates values for the new variable for each respondent in the data set.

Two simple COMPUTE statements are

```
COMPUTE ONE = 1
```

```
COMPUTE AGE2 = AGE
```

Table 8.2 shows how each of these two COMPUTE statements would work on seven hypothetical cases. The first statement creates a new variable named ONE and sets its value as the number 1 for each respondent. The second statement creates a new variable called AGE2 and sets its value for each respondent to be the same as the value for the existing variable AGE.

There is one difference between the AGE and AGE2 variables, as shown for case 7 in Table 8.2. The COMPUTE statement does not recognize missing-data codes as legitimate numbers. When SPSS encounters missing data on an existing variable being used to create a new variable, it does not calculate a value for that case on the new variable. So when SPSS encountered the missing value of

Table 8.2 HOW THE COMPUTE
COMMAND CREATES
NEW VARIABLES

Case	Variables		
	ONE	AGE	AGE2
1	1	22	22
2	1	76	76
3	1	35	35
4	1	43	43
5	1	51	51
6	1	19	19
7	1	−1	.

−1 on the AGE variable for case 7, it did not copy this value over to the new variable AGE2 for that case, but substituted instead the system missing value, which is a period.

OK, so the COMPUTE statement creates new variables. Why do we want to create new variables? The answer again relates to the question of appropriately measuring concepts. Suppose we want a measure of each respondent's overall view of whether abortions should or should not be legal. We have four questions in the GSS88 data set about abortion, but each deals with it only under specific conditions, such as whether the woman has been raped or is too poor to rear a child. Instead of four different responses, each dealing with a single aspect of abortion policy, we want a measure of the respondent's overall attitude toward abortion regardless of the specific circumstances.

With the COMPUTE statement we can create a **composite measure** by combining the specific measures with the command

```
COMPUTE ABORTION = ABDEFECT + ABPOOR + ABRAPE + ABANY
```

This statement creates a new variable, ABORTION, whose value for each respondent is the sum of the values on the four existing variables to the right of the equals sign. Table 8.3 shows how this process works.

In case 1, we have a person who gave the approve response (1) in all four situations, so his or her value on the new variable ABORTION is 4. Case 2 is the opposite, a person who disapproved in all four situations and thus has a value of 8 on ABORTION. Cases 3 and 4 show gradations in between, people who approved of abortion in some but not all situations. Cases 5 and 6 show respondents with missing data on one or more of the four original variables and thus are given a system missing value for the new variable. In sum, the new variable ABORTION measures a tendency to approve of abortion in a variety of situations. The lower the value on ABORTION, the more the respondent tends to approve of abortion generally. The higher the value on the new ABORTION variable, the more the respondent tends to disapprove of abortion in various situations.

A second example is the COMPUTE statement used with variables V27 and

Table 8.3 USING THE COMPUTE COMMAND TO COMBINE VARIABLES INTO A COMPOSITE MEASURE

Case	ABORTION	=	ABDEFECT	+	ABPOOR	+	ABRAPE	+	ABANY
1	4		1		1		1		1
2	8		2		2		2		2
3	6		2		1		1		2
4	5		1		1		1		2
5	.		2		9		2		1
6	.		9		9		9		9

V29. The first variable is the respondent's view on increasing or decreasing defense spending while the second is the respondent's perception of where George Bush stands on increasing or decreasing defense spending. Each variable is interesting by itself, but they can be combined to represent a new idea—whether George Bush is perceived as sharing or opposing the respondent's preference on defense spending.

The COMPUTE command

```
COMPUTE BUSHDEF = V27 - V29
```

creates a new variable, BUSHDEF, which represents this concept. Table 8.4 shows how the command will work with some hypothetical cases. The first three cases illustrate situations where Bush is perceived as having the same views on defense spending as the respondent and thus produce a difference between them on the BUSHDEF variable of zero. Note that whether Bush is seen as advocating a significant increase or decrease is not the issue (that is measured by V29 in its original form); the issue is whether Bush's position is seen as the same as or different from the respondent's position. Cases 4 and 5 show situations where the respondents want less spending in defense than they believe Bush would support. These become negative numbers on the new BUSHDEF variable; the larger the number the more Bush is seen as farther away from the respondent's position. Cases 6 and 7 are the reverse: Bush is seen as favoring less spending than the respondents want. This produces positive numbers of the BUSHDEF variable, and, again, the larger the number, the greater the difference the respondent sees between her or his position and that of George Bush. Finally, case 8 includes missing data on one of the two variables which leads to BUSHDEF having a system missing value for this case.

Figure 8.9 shows a FREQUENCIES table for the new variable we have just created. The figure shows that only a few people feel Bush desires less defense spending than they do (positive numbers) while a large number of respondents see Bush as favoring more defense spending than they would prefer (negative

Table 8.4   USING COMPUTE TO COMPARE VIEWS ON DEFENSE SPENDING

Case	Variables			
	BUSHDEF	= V27	−	V29
1	0	4		4
2	0	7		7
3	0	1		1
4	−6	1		7
5	−2	2		4
6	2	5		3
7	6	7		1
8	.	4		9

```
COMPUTE BUSHDEF = V27 - V29
VALUE LABELS    BUSHDEF    -6  'MORE DEF, BUSH'    6  'LESS DEF, BUSH'
        0  'SAME DEF,BUSH-RESP'
FREQUENCIES VARIABLES = BUSHDEF  /  STATISTICS ALL
```

BUSHDEF

VALUE LABEL	VALUE	FREQUENCY	PERCENT	VALID PERCENT	CUM PERCENT
MORE DEF, BUSH	-6.00	57	2.8	3.7	3.7
	-5.00	62	3.0	4.0	7.7
	-4.00	92	4.5	6.0	13.7
	-3.00	169	8.3	11.0	24.7
	-2.00	248	12.2	16.1	40.9
	-1.00	358	17.5	23.3	64.2
SAME DEF,BUSH-RESP	0.00	347	17.0	22.6	86.8
	1.00	121	5.9	7.9	94.7
	2.00	42	2.1	2.7	97.4
	3.00	22	1.1	1.4	98.8
	4.00	6	0.3	0.4	99.2
	5.00	6	0.3	0.4	99.6
LESS DEF, BUSH	6.00	6	0.3	0.4	100.0
		504	24.7	MISSING	
		-------	-------	-------	
	TOTAL	2040	100.0	100.0	

MEAN	-1.315	STD ERR	0.051	MEDIAN	-1.000
MODE	-1.000	STD DEV	2.016	VARIANCE	4.064
KURTOSIS	0.710	S E KURT	0.125	SKEWNESS	-0.101
S E SKEW	0.062	RANGE	12.000	MINIMUM	-6.000
MAXIMUM	6.000	SUM	-2020.000		

VALID CASES   1536   MISSING CASES   504

Figure 8.9 A FREQUENCIES procedure of the created variable BUSHDEF.

numbers). However, most people saw Bush as close, preferring about the same amount of spending as the respondents want (values close to or at zero), although with a slight bent toward the higher-spending side. The summary statistics at the bottom show the same thing: an average for all respondents of −1.3, or Bush preferring a bit more defense spending than the average respondent. At the same time, there are a large number of cases with missing data on this variable, respondents unable to identify either their own positions or George Bush's position on whether defense spending should be increased or decreased.

Creating composite measures such as this one can be quite useful but must be done with care. Say we wanted to create a general index of attitudes toward science by using four variables in the GSS88 data set: SCISOLVE, SCICHNG, SCIPRY, and SCIMORAL. All four variables involve only two responses, agree or disagree, but these similar responses do not all mean the same thing in terms of having confidence in or qualms about science. For the first variable, SCISOLVE, an agree answer represents confidence in science and its ability to solve

Table 8.5   QUESTION REVERSALS AND THE CREATION OF NEW VARIABLES

Case		Variables							
	SCIENCE	=	SCISOLVE	+	SCICHNG	+	SCIPRY	+	SCIMORAL
A	4		1 (trust)		1 (distrust)		1 (distrust)		1 (distrust)
B	5		1 (trust)		2 (trust)		1 (distrust)		1 (distrust)
C	5		2 (distrust)		1 (distrust)		1 (distrust)		1 (distrust)
D	7		1 (trust)		2 (trust)		2 (trust)		2 (trust)
E	8		2 (distrust)		2 (trust)		2 (trust)		2 (trust)
F	.		1 (trust)		9 (NA)		2 (trust)		2 (trust)

social problems. For the last three variables, however, an agree answer shows a *distrust* of science, a belief that it creates some problems, while a disagree answer is the one showing *confidence* in science.

Question reversals such as this are very common in surveys. They are intentionally used to avoid a problem called a **response set**, which is the tendency of some respondents to agree to everything, even when they have no real opinion on an issue. Question reversals are a problem when we are creating computed variables, however, as shown in Table 8.5. We cannot just add the responses on these four variables, for the high and low response codes mean opposite things. Consider cases B and C in Table 8.5. Case B is ambivalent about science, giving two trusting and two distrusting answers, while case C gave all distrusting answers. Both cases, however, have a value of 5 on the new variable SCIENCE. This value thus has no real meaning since it could represent a totally distrusting individual or an ambivalent one.

The solution is quite simple: We merely recode the first variable so that it is consistent with the others—a low response code always represents a distrust of science and a high response code represents trust—and then use a COMPUTE statement similar to the one used for the abortion variables. We must be very aware that situations like these exist so we can compensate for them when creating new variables.

Supplement 8.3

The COMMENT Command

The reasoning behind data modifications may be crystal-clear when first developed, but quite hazy when you return to the printout or command file weeks later. If you are creating new variables that you expect to use again, it is wise to add these variables, along with a description of how and why they were created, to the codebook.

An alternative to this strategy is to add a description of the data modifications and their justifications to the command file and printout. This is the function of the **COMMENT** command. The command, beginning in column 1, tells SPSS that any words following the command are to be printed on the output but otherwise ignored. Like any command, the COMMENT command can be continued on multiple lines as long as each successive line begins in column 2 or later. Figure 8.3S illustrates the use of the COMMENT command. On the output, SPSS repeats the command and prints out the comment you entered to explain what you were trying to do with the data modification command.

```
COMMENT RECODE RELIGION VARIABLE SO IT REPRESENTS BEING A
    FUNDAMENTALIST OR NONFUNDAMENTALIST. ONLY STANDARD
    PROTESTANT DENOMINATIONS ARE INCLUDED WITH ALL OTHERS
    ADDED TO CODE 999 - MISSING DATA.
RECODE V83 (130 THRU 149 = 1)( 100 THRU 127, 150 THRU 155 = 0)
    ( 200 THRU 800 = 999)
FREQUENCIES VARIABLES= V83
```

V83   RELIGIOUS PREFERENCE

VALUE LABEL	VALUE	FREQUENCY	PERCENT	VALID PERCENT	CUM PERCENT
	0	861	42.2	65.3	65.3
	1	455	22.3	34.5	99.8
	156	2	0.1	0.2	100.0
	996	5	0.2	MISSING	
	998	163	8.0	MISSING	
	999	554	27.2	MISSING	
	TOTAL	2040	100.0	100.0	

Figure 8.3S Using the COMMENT command.

An alternative to using the word COMMENT is simply to use an asterisk (∗) in column 1, a symbol which stands for a comment. SPSS/PC+ uses only asterisks, never the command term COMMENT. When you add comments in SPSS/PC+, the asterisk must be in column 1, unlike other PC+ commands which can start in column 2 or later. Additionally, SPSS/PC+ will not treat any period contained in your comment as a command terminator unless the period is the last character on that line.

The COMPUTE command can perform any number of mathematical operations on numbers or variables, including addition, subtraction, multiplication, division, absolute value, and square root. The **mathematical operators**, or words and symbols used for common mathematical procedures, are listed in Table 8.6.

The IF Command

The COMPUTE command creates a new variable, using the same formula for every respondent in the data set. Sometimes, however, you want different procedures followed for different groups of respondents. This is where the **IF** command comes in. The IF command is somewhat of a cross between the SELECT IF and COMPUTE commands. The IF command describes a set of mathematical operations to be carried out, as the COMPUTE command does,

Table 8.6   SPSS MATHEMATICAL OPERATORS
AND THEIR MEANINGS

Symbol	Meaning
+	Add
−	Subtract
*	Multiply
/	Divide
**	Raise to a power
SQRT(arg)	Square root of item in parentheses
ABS(arg)	Absolute value of item in parentheses

but IF also specifies a logical condition which must be met before the mathematical operations will be performed.

The format of the IF command is

```
IF (logical condition is true) variable name = value or formula
```

The command begins with the command word IF followed by a logical condition in parentheses. When this logical condition is true, SPSS assigns a value for the respondent as displayed in the last part of the statement: variable name = value or formula. When the logical condition is not true, SPSS does nothing.

Let us say we want to find out if, in most married families, the wife or husband has a higher level of education. We have two variables which contain the necessary information: EDUC, the respondent's level of education, and SPEDUC, the spouse's level of education.

We could start with a simple COMPUTE statement

```
COMPUTE FAMED = EDUC − SPEDUC
```

The FAMED variable will have a positive number if the respondent's education was higher, a negative number if the spouse's education was higher, and a zero if they both had the same level of education. This is clearly insufficient to get the information we want, however, for we have not taken into account whether the respondent is the husband or the wife.

Since this condition, the respondent's gender, affects how we create the FAMED variable, we use the following two IF statements to deal with the condition:

```
IF (SEX EQ 1) FAMED = EDUC − SPEDUC
```

```
IF (SEX EQ 2) FAMED = SPEDUC − EDUC
```

How these IF statements work is illustrated in Table 8.7. If the respondent is male, the degree to which the husband's education is more or less than the wife's is produced by subtracting SPEDUC from EDUC. If, however, the respondent is female, we must reverse the process since EDUC now stands for the wife's level of education and SPEDUC for the husband's. Unmarried respondents will have missing data on the SPEDUC variable which will produce a system miss-

Table 8.7   CREATING A NEW VARIABLE WITH IF COMMANDS

IF (SEX EQ 1)	**FAMED**	**=**	**EDUC**	**–**	**SPEDUC**
Case	SEX	FAMED	EDUC		SPEDUC
A	1	−2	15		17
B	1	4	12		8
C	1	−2	8		12

IF (SEX EQ 2)	**FAMED**	**=**	**SPEDUC**	**–**	**EDUC**
Case	SEX	FAMED	SPEDUC		EDUC
D	2	0	16		16
E	2	7	15		8
F	2	6	18		12

ing value for the FAMED variable whenever this situation is encountered. The FAMED variable now represents what we want, with positive numbers showing how many more years of education the husband has than the wife and negative numbers indicating that the wife has a higher level of education than the husband.

More than one condition can be specified in an IF statement, but when we do this, we have to connect the conditions with either the AND or the OR connector, as described with the SELECT IF command. To show how multiple conditions can be used, let us create a variable showing whether both, only one, or neither of the spouses has a college education. We can create this variable through these statements:

    IF (EDUC LE 12 **AND** SPEDUC LE 12) FAMCOL = 1

    IF (EDUC GE 13 **OR** SPEDUC GE 13) FAMCOL = 2

    IF (EDUC GE 13 **AND** SPEDUC GE 13) FAMCOL = 3

The first IF statement sets the FAMCOL variable equal to 1 if both the respondent and her or his spouse have no college education. The second IF statement sets FAMCOL equal to 2 if either spouse has some college training, and the last IF statement sets FAMCOL equal to 3 if both spouses have some college education. A FREQUENCIES table for this new variable is shown in Figure 8.10.

When the IF command is used, the order of the statements is important. What if the second and third IF statements had been reversed, as in the following?

    IF (EDUC LE 12 **AND** SPEDUC LE 12) FAMCOL = 1

    IF (EDUC GE 13 **AND** SPEDUC GE 13) FAMCOL = 3

    IF (EDUC GE 13 **OR** SPEDUC GE 13) FAMCOL = 2

```
FAMCOL
```

VALUE LABEL		VALUE	FREQUENCY	PERCENT	VALID PERCENT	CUM PERCENT
		1.00	349	23.6	32.3	32.3
		2.00	515	34.8	47.6	79.9
		3.00	218	14.7	20.1	100.0
			399	26.9	MISSING	
		TOTAL	1481	100.0	100.0	

MEAN	1.879	STD ERR	0.022	MEDIAN	2.000
MODE	2.000	STD DEV	0.714	VARIANCE	0.510
KURTOSIS	-1.030	S E KURT	0.149	SKEWNESS	0.181
S E SKEW	0.074	RANGE	2.000	MINIMUM	1.000
MAXIMUM	3.000	SUM	2033.000		

```
VALID CASES    1082     MISSING CASES    399
```

Figure 8.10 A FREQUENCIES procedure of the FAMCOL variable.

This sequence of commands would not produce any 3s on the FAMCOL variable. The second IF statement would set FAMCOL equal to 3 if both spouses had some college training, but the last IF command would then set FAMCOL equal to 2 if either spouse had some college training, including situations where they both did.

MORE ABOUT MODIFYING DATA

These five commands—SAMPLE, SELECT IF, RECODE, COMPUTE, and IF—are the common commands used to modify data. Before ending this discussion, however, we want to discuss three other topics: how long the modifications last, modifying data containing missing values, and cleaning the data after modifications.

Duration of Modifications

Whenever we modify data with any of the commands discussed in this chapter, we are modifying only our current *active file*—the *copy* of the data or system file that has been read into the CPU. The permanent version of the file on the storage device is not changed at all; only the copy of it residing in the CPU memory is altered. Whenever we finish our job or computer session, the active file in the CPU memory is erased, and only the permanently stored version, without any modifications, remains.

If we want to use the same modifications during more than one computer session, we need to repeat the modification commands. This is not difficult to do if you have stored these modification commands as a command file; just fetch the command file and resubmit it to the CPU. If we expect to use the same modifications continuously, it makes sense to save a new file which contains them as permanent additions. This is done with the SAVE command discussed earlier, saving a new system file under a new name. All modifications made before the SAVE command is given, including any recodes, creation of new variables, or selection of a subset of cases, will be saved as part of the new file. This new file can be referred to on a GET FILE command whenever we want to use the modified version of the data, or the original file could be fetched if we want the analyze the data in unmodified form.

(PC) Often we do not want our modifications to last even for an entire computer session or run. Consider the early examples in this chapter of the SAMPLE and SELECT IF commands. The commands below ask for two FREQUENCIES tables for the EDUC variable, first for men only and then for women only.

```
SELECT IF (SEX EQ 1)

FREQUENCIES VARIABLES = EDUC

SELECT IF (SEX EQ 2)

FREQUENCIES VARIABLES = EDUC
```

The first two commands will work just fine, but the second two will not work at all. The first SELECT IF command eliminates all cases containing female respondents from the active file in the CPU memory. The second SELECT IF command asks SPSS to eliminate all cases who are males and to save only the females for later analyses. However, there are no females left in the active file because they were eliminated by the first SELECT IF command. Consequently, SPSS will find no cases meeting the second SELECT IF condition, and the active file will contain zero cases to be analyzed by the second FREQUENCIES command.

(PC) The same situation occurs with the SAMPLE command. If we enter the command series

```
SAMPLE .10

FREQUENCIES VARIABLES = EDUC

SAMPLE .10

FREQUENCIES VARIABLES = EDUC
```

we are probably trying to draw two different 10 percent samples and compare the EDUC variable for each. Again, the first two commands will work fine, leading SPSS to draw a 10 percent sample of the active file (about 150 cases from the GSS88 data set). With the second SAMPLE command, however, SPSS will again draw a 10 percent sample *of the active file*, but this active file now contains only about 150 cases. The second 10 percent sample will thus reduce the active file to only 15 cases.

(PC)   To allow the user greater flexibility, SPSS includes a **TEMPORARY com-mand** that can be used with data modifications. The impact of the TEMPO-RARY command is to restrict the life of data modification commands to the next procedure requested. *Remember*, a procedure command is one that re-quires SPSS to actually produce some output. Thus, in the series of commands

    TEMPORARY

    SELECT IF (SEX EQ 1)

    RECODE EDUC (0 THRU 12 = 1)(13 THRU 20 = 2)

    RECODE AGE (0 THRU 50 = 1)(51 THRU 89 = 2)

    FREQUENCIES VARIABLES = RACE

the SELECT IF and two RECODE commands will be in effect only until SPSS finishes the FREQUENCIES analysis. As soon as that procedure is completed, the active file will again containing all the cases, both men and women, as well as the EDUC and AGE variables as originally coded. It makes no difference that the FREQUENCIES command does not refer to the modified variables; it is still a procedure command and will cancel the effect of any data modification commands between it and the prior TEMPORARY command.

(PC)   To produce separate analyses of men and women in the same run, the following series of commands might be used:

    RECODE EDUC (0 THRU 12 = 1)(13 THRU 20 = 2)

    TEMPORARY

    SELECT IF (SEX EQ 1)

    FREQUENCIES VARIABLES = EDUC

    TEMPORARY

    SELECT IF (SEX EQ 2)

    FREQUENCIES VARIABLES = EDUC

The first FREQUENCIES procedure is based on selecting only men, and when it is completed, the active file will return to containing all the original cases, both men and women. The second set of commands then selects only women and performs the same FREQUENCIES analysis. Finally, the RECODE com-mand comes *before* any TEMPORARY command, so its modification of the EDUC variable will be in effect for the entire session.

Modifications and Missing Data

In modifying data, most of the commands discussed in this chapter do not recognize missing-data codes as legitimate values for a variable. Consequently, if we use a missing data value in a data modification command, SPSS will ignore the command. For example, we might be curious about the respondents who refused to tell us their income levels, wondering if they were predominantly women or men. The commands

```
SELECT IF (RINCOME EQ 97)

FREQUENCIES VARIABLES = SEX
```

seem as if they would provide us this information, but they will not. The value 97 on the RINCOME variable was previously defined as a missing-data code and thus cannot be used in any IF, COMPUTE, or SELECT IF commands. SPSS will search for cases with a legitimate value of 97 on the RINCOME variable, but cannot find any such cases. Code number 97 is defined as representing missing values, and thus SPSS does not read it as a real number. Since no cases meet the SELECT IF condition, the FREQUENCIES procedures will produce an empty FREQUENCIES table.

The one modification command that can refer to missing values is RE-CODE. If, for some reason, we want to analyze people identified by a missing-value code, we can use the RECODE command to do so. This set of commands will select those refusing to tell their incomes:

```
RECODE RINCOME (97 = 96)

SELECT IF (RINCOME EQ 96)

FREQUENCIES VARIABLES = SEX
```

First we changed the coding system so those respondents who used to have code 97 now have code 96 on RINCOME. SPSS still considers code 97 to represent missing data for this variable, but no one has this code number any more—they have all been changed to code 96. As far as SPSS knows, code 96 is a legitimate number to have on this variable, and thus this code number can be used in data modification statements, such as the SELECT IF command in this example.

(R.4) Along with user-defined missing values, system missing values can be recoded. When referring to system missing values, however, you do not use the period, which represents system missing values on the output. Instead, use the keyword **SYSMIS**. Thus, to recode any system missing value that may show up on the FAMCOL variable in Figure 8.10, you can use the command

```
RECODE (SYSMIS = 9)
```

The ability of RECODE to change the code number of respondents with missing data can be a problem. When we recoded V83 earlier to make it an indicator of fundamentalist denominations, we left the missing-data codes alone. Remember, missing data mean just that—no information whatsoever about the religious preference of the respondent. If we had recoded these values to equal zero, we would be treating them as though they were nonfundamentalists. This is wrong. They are not nonfundamentalists just because we are ignorant of their religious preference. They may be fundamentalists or not; we just do not know. A good rule of thumb is to never recode missing data values unless you have thought long and hard about it and decide you have a valid reason for doing so.

Data Cleaning

Data modification commands are not hard to use, but errors are easy to make, particularly with the more complex commands such as IF and COMPUTE. We have already seen some examples of potential problems such as inadvertently listing IF statements in the incorrect order or recoding missing values into numbers that SPSS will treat as legitimate. Errors in data modifications are particularly onerous because the errors are not always easy to spot. SPSS provides us with error messages whenever we enter commands that it cannot understand, but data modification errors do not fall into this category. Dividing a person's age by his or her religious preference is something SPSS can understand—it is stupid, but SPSS understands how to do it and will not produce any error messages.

Whenever we modify data in any way, it is important to check the accuracy of the modifications. This process is called **data cleaning**. When we clean our data, we review them to locate and correct any errors that might have occurred. There is no magical process for cleaning data, for only we know what the data are supposed to look like; but there are a number of procedures that can help locate errors.

First, whenever you are using data modification commands, always run a FREQUENCIES procedure on the relevant variables after the modifications. Why FREQUENCIES? You need a procedure command to activate the data modifications. As with the data definition commands discussed earlier, SPSS will not carry out any of the modification commands, nor will it respond with any note, warning, or error message until you request a procedure.

Second, a number of errors can be caught just by looking at the number of cases existing and their distribution on the variables involved in the modifications. If you select men only, a FREQUENCIES procedure on the SEX variable should not contain any women. If you draw a 10 percent sample, a FREQUENCIES table for any variable should contain only about 10 percent of the cases. If you recode a variable, you should be able to compare before and after frequency tables of the variable to see how the cases changed from one code number to another.

Another important thing to look for when you are using a FREQUENCIES procedure on modified data is the number of missing cases on the FREQUENCIES table. Usually any variable, except for some obvious ones such as SEX, has some cases with missing data. If the FREQUENCIES table does not show any missing cases, you may have inadvertently recoded cases with missing-data codes to values that SPSS is treating as legitimate numbers. For variables you create with IF or COMPUTE statements, you might find the opposite—a very large number of cases with system missing values. Such a finding would be a warning to check your data modifications for logical errors. Two examples will help clarify this.

Let us say we want to create a measure of per capita family income. To do this, we divide the family income by the respondent's number of children:

```
COMPUTE PCINC = FINCOME / CHILDS
```

This COMPUTE command will produce a number of cases with missing data on the PCINC variable. If the respondent has no children, he or she will have a score of zero on the CHILDS variable. Dividing by zero is not an allowable mathematical operation. The command will thus produce a system missing-value code on PCINC for every respondent without children. The solution is to include the respondent as well as her or his children, so that no zero occurs in the denominator, as in

```
COMPUTE PCINC = FINCOME / (CHILDS + 1)
```

A second example involves using the IF statement to create a new variable, COLL, scored 2 if the respondent has attended college and 1 if not. The two commands

```
IF (EDUC GT 12) COLL = 2
```

```
IF (EDUC LT 12) COLL = 1
```

might seem to accomplish this, but again they lead to a large amount of missing data on the new variable. We told SPSS what value to assign to respondents on the COLL variable if they have either less than or more than 12 years of education. We never told SPSS what to do if the respondent's educational level was exactly equal to 12 years. Not knowing what value to assign to such respondents on the COLL variable, SPSS will assign them a system missing value. Changing the logical operator in the second statement to LE instead of LT corrects for this.

Along with a FREQUENCIES table, a second useful cleaning procedure is the **LIST command**. This command produces a list of the cases in the data set and the values of each case for a selected group of variables. The commands

```
TEMPORARY
```

```
SAMPLE .05
```

```
LIST VARIABLES = EDUC SPEDUC FAMCOL
```

produce a list of the values on our newly created variable, FAMCOL, along with the values for the variables used to create it, EDUC and SPEDUC. This enables us to see if FAMCOL has the proper code number based on the values of EDUC and SPEDUC. Checking all 1500 to 2000 cases is quite a chore, so we typically select only a 5 or 10 percent sample of the cases to examine—enough for us to spot any glaring errors.

A partial output from this command is shown in Figure 8.11. Four cases have been highlighted with bold type to show how the checking process works. In the first case, neither spouse has any college training, and the FAMCOL

```
EDUC   SPEDUC   FAMCOL
 12      11      1.00
 17      10      2.00
 14      13      3.00
 12      97       .
 18      16      3.00
  9      97       .
 12      97       .
 16      16      3.00
 15      14      3.00
 14      16      3.00
 11      11      1.00
 12      12      1.00
 11      97       .
```

Figure 8.11 Output from the LIST command.

variable has a value of 1, as it should. The second and third cases show situations where one spouse and both spouses, respectively, have some college education, and again the FAMCOL variable has the appropriate values. The last highlighted case is where the respondent has a missing value on one or more of the variables, in this situation a 97 on the SPEDUC variable because the respondent is not married, and SPSS assigned the system missing value, as it should, to the new FAMCOL variable.

When you modify data, there is about a 50-50 chance that some data modifications will contain errors. Data modification errors are not particularly obvious, and SPSS cannot catch your errors because it has no way of knowing what you are trying to accomplish. The few simple steps outlined in this section allow you to examine your modifications to see if they are working as you planned—a vital step if statistics based on these modifications are to have any meaning.

SPSS/PC+ AND RELEASE 4

Release 4

Release 4 implementations of SPSS can use either two-letter keywords or actual mathematical symbols as logical operators on IF and SELECT IF commands, for example, either = or EQ. In Release 4, the name for system missing values begins with a dollar sign, **$SYSMIS**, not SYSMIS.

SPSS/PC+

TEMPORARY SPSS/PC+ does not use the TEMPORARY command. Instead, some data modifications are always permanent, others are always temporary, and an extra command is added for some situations.

RECODE, COMPUTE, and IF Commands Changes introduced by the RE-CODE, COMPUTE, and IF commands are permanent. They will last the duration of your SPSS/PC+ session. This is seldom a problem with COMPUTE and IF because they are used to create new variables rather than modify old ones. At times, however, we may want to experiment with different ways of recoding a variable, and thus permanent RECODE commands may be a problem.

There is a simple way around this: Create new variables to recode instead of modifying the old ones. The commands

COMPUTE ED1 = EDUC

COMPUTE ED2 = EDUC

COMPUTE ED3 = EDUC

create three new variables—ED1, ED2, and ED3—which are all exact duplicates of the original variable EDUC. You can now recode each of these new variables differently and end up with three different ways of grouping respondents by level of education.

SAMPLE Command In SPSS/PC+, the SAMPLE command always has a temporary impact, in effect for the next procedure only. If you want more than one procedure to be carried out on a sample of the cases, you must repeat the SAMPLE command for each procedure. Remember, this will result in the drawing of different samples each time SPSS encounters a new SAMPLE command. If you want to use the same sample over and over, you must save a permanent file after the first SAMPLE command. This permanent file can then be read in with a GET FILE command and subjected to as many procedures as you want.

SELECT IF and PROCESS IF Commands In SPSS/PC+, the SELECT IF command is a permanent command and cannot be made temporary. To provide for the temporary selection of cases, SPSS/PC+ has a **PROCESS IF** command. This command works as the SELECT IF command does but is always temporary. One difference between the two commands is that the PROCESS IF command is limited to one condition only. You also cannot use the condition connectors OR or AND in the PROCESS IF command, since these are used only to specify two or more conditions.

SUMMARY

Unique interests will lead each of us to approach data analysis with different questions that we want answered. With the commands discussed in this chapter, it is possible to tailor the data analysis to produce the exact information desired. Cases can be sampled or selected to meet certain conditions, and variables can be modified to better measure concepts.

Data modifications should never be done cavalierly or just to simplify things. All modifications involve some change in what the operational variable measures—sometimes a slight change, at other times a substantial one. Using data modification commands is not difficult as long as we keep their purpose—accurate measurement—in mind. We should identify the conceptual variable, determine how to modify the data to create a better operational measure of the concept, and clean the data to verify that the modifications worked as planned. When done properly and carefully, data modifications allow us to make maximum use of the information contained in a data set.

REVIEW

Key Terms

SAMPLE	Response set
Proportional sample	Mathematical operators
Exact sample	IF
SELECT IF	TEMPORARY command
Logical operator	SYSMIS
AND connector	Data cleaning
OR connector	LIST command
RECODE	$SYSMIS
THRU keyword	PROCESS IF
COMPUTE	Seed number
Composite measure	SET SEED
Question reversals	COMMENT

Exercises

8.1 Identify the errors, if any, in these commands.
   a. RECODE (1 = 2)(2 = 3)
   b. RECODE V3 (1, 2, 3 = 4, 5)
   c. IF (V2 EQ 1 OR 2) VOTE = 1
   d. SELECT IF (EDUC EQ 8 AND EDUC EQ 12)
   e. RECODE V83 (100 TO 199 = 1) (200 TO 800 = 2)
   f. IF (V2 = 1) VOTE EQ 1
   g. DIFF = V20 − V21
   h. IF (AGE LT 40) AGE = 1 IF (AGE GE 40) AGE = 2
   i. SELECT IF (AGE EQ − 1)
   j. SAMPLE 200
   k. SAMPLE 1.0

8.2 Use the practice data sets and the commands learned in this chapter to duplicate the computer outputs shown in Figures 8.1 to 8.10.

8.3 *a.* Recode variable V83 in the ELEC88 data set so that its categories match those of the RELIG variable in the GSS88 data set. The distribution of cases will not match perfectly because these are two different samples, but the meaning of the categories should be the same.

b. Using variables ATTEND and SPATTEND, create a new variable to show whether the husband or wife attends church more frequently.

c. Find the average income of blacks, and compare it to the average income of whites.

d. Change variable V74 so that it measures the strength of a person's attachment to *either* political party.

e. Determine whether women pray more frequently than men.

f. Assume that you want to compare whether married people or single people pray more frequently. Change MARITAL or V79 to represent whether the person is or is not single.

g. Change RACE or V85 to represent whether the respondent is or is not black.

h. Change RINCOME or V87 to be an interval measure of income earned by the respondent.

SUGGESTED READINGS

Norusis, Marija J., and SPSS Inc. *SPSS/PC+ V2.0 Base Manual* (Chicago: SPSS Inc., 1988) Chapters 4, 5.

SPSS Inc. *SPSS Reference Guide* (Release 4) (Chicago: SPSS Inc., 1990) pages 85–91, 285–88, 573–76, 650–51, 661–63.

SPSS Inc. *SPSS-X User's Guide,* 3rd ed. (Chicago: SPSS Inc., 1988) Chapters 7–9.

Chapter
9

Drawing Inferences

*I*f we were asked what the average level of education for U.S. citizens was, how would we respond? Earlier we learned the use of the FREQUENCIES command to compute central tendencies, so we apply this command to the education variable V80. Since education is an interval variable, we locate the mean on the printout and declare that U.S. citizens have an average of 12.544 years of education (Figure 9.1).

Finding the mean for variable V80 is a good starting point, but we should not stop there. When students first begin to analyze data, they often get so caught up in the numbers that one important item is forgotten—the sample itself is not what interests us. We do not really care who Jane Porter from Kokomo voted for, how much income Jim Wong from Albany earns, or how frequently Jovita Fontanez from Houston attends church. Our purpose in drawing samples is to estimate some characteristic of the population—the average educational level of all U.S. citizens, not just the few in our sample.

To help differentiate between samples and populations, different terms and symbols are used for each. Population values are termed **parameters**, whereas values produced by samples are called *statistics*. For a sample, a variable's mean is represented by the symbol $\overline{X}$ (called "X bar"), but the mean of the population is referred to by the Greek letter **mu (μ)**. Similarly, a variable's *sample* standard deviation and variance are represented by s and s^2, respectively, but the *population* standard deviation and variance for a variable are represented by the Greek letters **sigma (σ)** and **sigma squared (σ^2)**.

Why this concern with distinguishing between samples and populations? Both the GSS88 and ELEC88 data sets are professionally drawn random samples. Does that not mean that each is representative of the population and thus our sample statistic $\overline{X}$ will match the population parameter μ? Not exactly, no.

```
V80            RESP'S EDUCATION

                                                        VALID      CUM
          VALUE LABEL              VALUE  FREQUENCY  PERCENT  PERCENT  PERCENT

NONE,NO  YRS  CMPLETD                0        5        0.2      0.2      0.2
                                     1        1        0.0      0.0      0.3
                                     2        6        0.3      0.3      0.6
                                     3        7        0.3      0.3      0.9
                                     4       12        0.6      0.6      1.5
                                     5       20        1.0      1.0      2.5
                                     6       21        1.0      1.0      3.5
                                     7       25        1.2      1.2      4.8
8  YRS,  GRADE  SCHOOL               8      102        5.0      5.0      9.8
                                     9       57        2.8      2.8     12.6
                                    10       97        4.8      4.8     17.3
                                    11       76        3.7      3.7     21.1
12  YRS,  HIGH  SCHOOL              12      731       35.8     35.9     57.0
                                    13      176        8.6      8.6     65.7
                                    14      212       10.4     10.4     76.1
                                    15       83        4.1      4.1     80.1
16  YRS,  COLLEGE  GRAD             16      232       11.4     11.4     91.5
17  YRS+,  GRAD  STUDY              17      172        8.4      8.5    100.0
DK                                  98        1        0.0   MISSING
NA                                  99        4        0.2   MISSING
                                          -------  -------  -------
                            TOTAL         2040      100.0    100.0

MEAN        12.544    STD ERR       0.064     MEDIAN       12.000
MODE        12.000    STD DEV       2.885     VARIANCE      8.322
KURTOSIS     1.457    S E KURT      0.108     SKEWNESS     -0.782
S E SKEW     0.054    RANGE        17.000     MINIMUM       0.000
MAXIMUM     17.000    SUM       25527.000

VALID CASES   2035      MISSING CASES       5
```

Figure 9.1 A FREQUENCIES of V80.

Samples, even well-drawn ones, are only partial representations of the population. It is rare for any sample to duplicate, without error, the precise population parameter.

Where does this leave us? Why even bother to draw samples if we know the sample statistics are probably inaccurate? Samples can be used to estimate population parameters, but we need to be aware of the potential for sample error and how to compensate for it. What we did in the first paragraph of this chapter was to make what is called a **point estimate** of the population value, declaring the population mean to be the same as the sample mean. This claim is undoubtedly untrue, for it states that the population mean is not 12.543 or 12.545 or any other number, but instead is exactly 12.544. Sample statistics just do not match the population that neatly.

Although the point estimate is probably wrong as an exact statement, it is probably pretty close to the population parameter. This raises the question of how close. Is the sample statistic off by half a year, a full year, or as much as 3 to 4 years from the population value? Identifying the closeness of a sample result to the population parameter enables us to produce an **interval estimate**, or a range of values within which we are pretty confident that the true population parameter falls. Poll results are usually reported in the media by interval estimates, such as "56 percent of the population currently supports George Bush over Michael Dukakis, but this poll has a margin of error of plus or minus 3 percentage points." The 56 percent figure is the point estimate, the sample statistic, and the pollsters are fairly confident that the population parameter is somewhere in the interval of 53 to 59 percent.

To make a point estimate of the population parameter, we need only be familiar with the FREQUENCIES procedure. The sample statistic, despite its probable inaccuracy, remains our best guess of the population value, a guess based on a randomly selected sample. An estimate based on any other information—a biased sample, a hunch, or consulting chicken entrails—is likely to be even less accurate than the sample statistic. Nonetheless, an interval estimate is clearly superior, for it includes an evaluation of how far off the point estimate might be from the population value. To calculate an interval estimate, we need to examine three topics: probability distributions, sampling distributions, and confidence intervals.

PROBABILITY DISTRIBUTIONS

As we begin the process of making statements about population values from sample results, we move from descriptive statistics to **inferential statistics**—those that allow us to draw inferences about the population. These inferences are never absolute declarations that the population parameter *must be* a certain value or contained within a range of values. Instead, they are *probability* statements, statements that have a high probability of being true for the population. To better comprehend the meaning of such probability statements, we begin by reviewing the notion of probability and then turn to probability distributions with a special emphasis on one type of distribution, the normal curve.

Probability

The term **probability** has a number of interpretations. One way of defining it is as the likelihood that something will happen—what is the probability it will rain tomorrow? If we make a statement about some event, probability can also refer to the likelihood that the statement is true—the statement "It will rain tomorrow" has a high probability of being true. In either case, probability is measured on a scale from 0.0 (something is impossible) to 1.0 (something definitely will happen). Probabilities are referred to either as decimals or percentages between these two endpoints—the probability that it will rain tomorrow is .95, or the statement "It will rain tomorrow" has a 95 percent chance of being correct.

Calculating the probability of any event can depend on a complex number of factors. In the simplest situation there are a finite number of possible outcomes with each outcome being equally likely. In such a case, the probability of getting any single outcome is simply $1/n$; that is, 1 divided by the number of possible outcomes. To illustrate, assume that we toss a fair die, one that is not biased to favor one outcome over another. There are six possible outcomes: the numbers 1, 2, 3, 4, 5, and 6. The probability of getting any one of these outcomes, say, the number 4, is $\frac{1}{6}$.

Often we speak not about the probability of a single event but about some combination of events. If this combination is a group of alternatives—either this will happen *or* that will happen—the probability of the group is determined by the **addition rule**. That is, if we want to know the probability of getting *either* a 1 or a 2 on a single toss of a die, this is determined by adding the probability of the individual events. The numbers 1 and 2 each have a $\frac{1}{6}$ probability of occurring, so the probability that either will occur is $\frac{1}{6} + \frac{1}{6}$, or $\frac{1}{3}$.

On the other hand, if we want to know the probability of a sequence of events occurring—first one and then the other—we use the **multiplication rule**. Say we toss a pair of dice instead of a single die and want to know the probability of getting two 1s. We multiply the probability of getting a 1 on the first die by the probability of getting a 1 on the second. Each 1 has a $\frac{1}{6}$ chance of occurring, so the probability that both 1s will appear is $\frac{1}{6} * \frac{1}{6}$, or $\frac{1}{36}$.

Probability Distributions

So far we have been talking about the probability of specific events or combinations of events. A **probability distribution** is a listing of all possible outcomes from a single action or sequence of actions (rolling one die or a pair of dice) along with the probabilities of each outcome. Let us take the case of rolling a pair of dice. There are 11 possible outcomes, from 2 through 12. A probability distribution would show these possible outcomes and the probability of each.

The probability of the first outcome, the number 2, we calculated above (obtaining two 1s) as $\frac{1}{36}$. What about the second outcome, the number 3? Your first reaction might be that the number 3 has a probability of $\frac{1}{36}$ also, but this is not true. There is only one way to get the number 2 when two dice are rolled: both dice in the pair (we call one A and the other B) have to produce the number 1. However, there are *two* ways that we can get the number 3. First, die A can produce a 1 and die B a 2, with each individual number having a $\frac{1}{6}$ chance of occurring and thus a $\frac{1}{36}$ chance for this outcome. Second, die A could produce the number 2 and die B the number 1, with this combination also having a $\frac{1}{36}$ chance of occurring. We are interested not in how we roll a 3, just in the probability that the number 3 will occur through any combination of the dice. Consequently, the probability of getting a 3 is the probability of either the first or the second outcome which, by the addition rule, is $\frac{1}{36} + \frac{1}{36}$, or $\frac{2}{36}$.

Table 9.1 shows the various ways in which we can achieve outcomes 2 through 12 by tossing a pair of dice. Table 9.1 is also a probability distribution since the rightmost column in the table contains the probability of each outcome. As shown in the table, for any single roll of the dice we have a $\frac{1}{36}$ chance of obtaining the number 2 but a $\frac{6}{36}$ chance of the number 7 showing up.

Table 9.1   A PROBABILITY DISTRIBUTION OF OUTCOMES FROM TOSSING A PAIR OF DICE

Total of both dice	Possible pairings leading to this total	Probability of this total
2	(1, 1)	$\frac{1}{36}$
3	(1, 2) (2, 1)	$\frac{2}{36}$
4	(1, 3) (3, 1) (2, 2)	$\frac{3}{36}$
5	(1, 4) (4, 1) (2, 3) (3, 2)	$\frac{4}{36}$
6	(1, 5) (5, 1) (2, 4) (4, 2) (3, 3)	$\frac{5}{36}$
7	(1, 6) (6, 1) (2, 5) (5, 2) (4, 3) (3, 4)	$\frac{6}{36}$
8	(2, 6) (6, 2) (3, 5) (5, 3) (4, 4)	$\frac{5}{36}$
9	(3, 6) (6, 3) (4, 5) (5, 4)	$\frac{4}{36}$
10	(4, 6) (6, 4) (5 5)	$\frac{3}{36}$
11	(5, 6) (6, 5)	$\frac{2}{36}$
12	(6, 6)	$\frac{1}{36}$

Applying the addition rule to Table 9.1, we can also find the probability of any combination of outcomes. For example, the probability of obtaining a 10 or above on a single roll of the dice is $\frac{1}{6}$: $\frac{3}{36}$ for 10 + $\frac{2}{36}$ for 11 + $\frac{1}{36}$ for 12 = $\frac{6}{36}$ = $\frac{1}{6}$. On the other hand, the probability of getting any number from 5 through 9 is $\frac{24}{36}$, or $\frac{2}{3}$, and the probability of obtaining any number from 2 through 12 is $\frac{36}{36}$, or 1.0.

Like any distribution, the probability distribution in Table 9.1 has a central tendency and a dispersion—topics we will examine shortly in more detail. However, probability distributions are different from distributions obtained with the FREQUENCIES procedure in two ways: They are both known and theoretical.

The distribution of the respondents' educational levels in Figure 9.1 is called an **empirical distribution**. An empirical distribution is one based on collecting observations; for example, from this sample we found in Figure 9.1 that 21.1 percent of the people never graduated from high school (11 or below) while 19.9 percent had a college degree (16 and above). There is no way we could have predicted these outcomes in advance. The only way to discover them was to collect data and examine the results.

In contrast, probability distributions are **known distributions**. Once we know both the number of outcomes and that they are equally likely, we can use the rules of probability to determine the probability distribution for any combination of events. Table 9.1 was not based on any random sampling—tossing a pair of dice a number of times and counting the various outcomes. We do not have to do any sampling at all. Known distributions are ones we can determine without having to draw samples or conduct experiments.

Probability distributions are also **theoretical distributions**. Theoretical distributions describe the outcome over an infinite number of events. If we were to toss a pair of dice 36 times, we probably would not obtain a distribution exactly matching that in Table 9.1—precisely one 2, two 3s, and so on. Our results might be close, or they might be quite far off. However, if we were to toss the dice 100 times, our results would be closer to those in Table 9.1; and 1000 tosses would be closer yet, and 100,000 tosses would be still closer. What the probability distribution in Table 9.1 says is that, over an *infinite number* of tosses, $\frac{1}{36}$ of our results would be the number 2, and $\frac{5}{36}$ of them would be the number 6, and so on. Of course, an infinite number of tosses are impossible, but the more tosses we make, the closer our results will be to the theoretical distribution.

Smooth Curves

An empirical distribution is the distribution of values for a variable. A probability distribution also constitutes a variable. The different outcomes are the values of the variable, and the probability of each outcome constitutes its frequency—over an infinite number of tosses, $\frac{1}{36}$ of them will produce the number 2. Variables can be of two types, discrete or continuous, and the variable's type affects how we calculate the probability of outcomes.

Table 9.1 illustrated a **discrete distribution**, the distribution of a discrete variable with a finite and countable number of categories. Only 11 outcomes are possible from rolling a pair of dice, and Table 9.1 lists them all. In contrast, a continuous variable can take on an infinite number of values. Consider people's heights. As we usually measure this variable, it looks discrete, for we round heights into whole numbers, 6 ft or 5 ft 8 in., rather than using exact measurements. This discreteness, however, is due only to our limited operational measurement. The variable is actually continuous since one can have a height of 5.369832 or 6.194866 ft.

Continuous variables will produce a **continuous distribution**, a smooth curve rather than a series of chunky boxes. As shown in Figure 9.2, there are no clear dividing lines between one height and another, for there are an infinite number of possible heights between any two points on the curve. Between the heights of 5 and $5\frac{1}{2}$ ft, a person might be 5.1, 5.01, or 5.001 ft tall, or any number of other possibilities that can be represented by continuing to add decimal places.

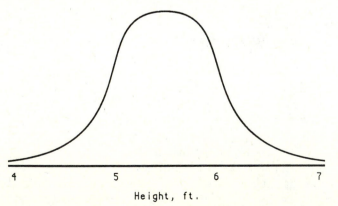

Figure 9.2 A continuous distribution.

Let us say the curve in Figure 9.2 represents the population, the distribution of heights for U.S. citizens. If we randomly select someone from this population, the curve also represents the possible outcomes of this random selection and the probability of each outcome. The curve is at its highest around 5 ft 8 in., showing that many members of the population are this tall, and thus there is a good probability that the person we randomly select will be this tall. The curve gradually sinks lower as we move away from this center point in either direction, showing that few members of the population are below 4 ft 2 in. or above 7 ft 3 in. Consequently, the probability of selecting someone with these unusual heights is small.

When dealing with a smooth distribution, we are faced with a curious mathematical problem: The probability of randomly drawing someone with any *specific value* is always zero, regardless of the value we are talking about. If we are interested in the probability of randomly drawing someone 6 ft tall, we are not talking about someone who is 5.9$\overline{999}$ ft tall (where the bar over the last three numbers means continuing infinitely) or 6.0$\overline{0001}$ ft tall, but instead exactly 6.0$\overline{000}$ ft tall. Recall your basic geometry where a single point was defined as being infinitely small. Any time you thought you had found a point, you could cut it in half and make two smaller points out of it. Similarly, a single point on a smooth curve is infinitely small, and the probability of selecting that exact point (say, 6.0$\overline{000}$ ft) is always zero.

With smooth curves we talk about the probability of selecting a range of values, an area of the curve instead of an exact point on it. We may not be able to identify someone who is exactly 6.0$\overline{000}$ ft tall, but we can identify those who are between 6 and $6\frac{1}{2}$ ft tall. For this area (Figure 9.3), a person's exact height does not need to be determined. Anyone greater than 6.0$\overline{000}$ ft and less than 6.5$\overline{000}$ ft—heights such as 6.010002, 6.238974, and 6.46658—are all included in this area.

To use areas for the purpose of probability statements, we must first recognize that the entire curve represents all the possible outcomes. The probability

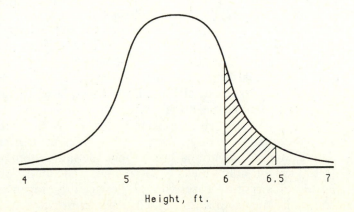

Figure 9.3 An area of a continuous distribution.

of selecting someone who falls under any part of the curve is 1.0—there is a perfect probability that we will select someone who fits somewhere under the curve. If the region from 6 to $6\frac{1}{2}$ ft comprises 30 percent of the curve's area, that is equivalent to saying that 30 percent of all possible outcomes fall into this area. Thus, the probability that someone we select randomly will come from this area is .30.

The Normal Curve

Whenever we must determine the probability of outcomes for a continuous variable, we must base these probabilities on the areas under the curve representing the variable's distribution. Calculating areas under smooth curves can be quite a chore. However, there is one type of curve which has many known and valuable properties, the **normal curve**. Produced by a normal distribution, a normal curve, the type illustrated in Figure 9.2, has the following characteristics:

1. It is bell-shaped.
2. It has a single peak in the exact middle of the distribution.
3. Each half of the curve is a mirror image of the other.
4. Its tails continue indefinitely, almost but never quite reaching the bottom axis.

Many empirical distributions are approximately normal, and, more importantly, a substantial number of theoretical probability distributions can be represented by the normal curve. In addition, the normal curve has an important mathematical property that makes the task of calculating areas relatively simple. It turns out that, regardless of a variable's mean or standard deviation, if its distribution is normally shaped, there will always be a fixed proportion of cases between the mean (the middle of a normal curve) and a particular distance above or below the mean. How can this be? When we are dealing with heights, the range from the average height of 5 ft 8 in. to 10 in. above average, 6 ft 6 in., will include a lot of people. For a distribution of incomes, the range from the average income of, say, $20,000 to $10 above this average surely includes a far smaller number of people. True. We cannot compare apples to oranges or inches to dollars, so we have to use a standard measuring unit to compare distributions. We do this by using the standard deviation as our unit of comparison.

As an illustration, consider the circle. We can calculate the area of any circle, regardless of its size, with the formula πr^2 because all circles have the same geometric shape. Bigger circles will have a larger radius than smaller ones, but the formula πr^2 still determines their areas. Similarly, some normal curves may be quite large and others more compact, with correspondingly large or small standard deviations, but all have the same geometric shape. Thus, regardless of the variable's mean or dispersion, if the distribution is normally shaped, 34.13 percent of the cases will fall between the mean and 1 standard deviation above the mean. In addition, 47.72 percent of the cases will fall between the mean and 2 standard deviations above the mean for normal distributions, and

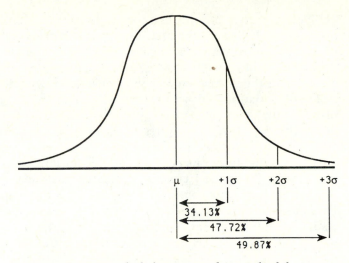

Figure 9.4 Areas included in 1, 2, and 3 standard deviations above the mean of a normal curve.

49.87 percent of the cases will be included between the mean and 3 standard deviations above the mean. These areas are shown in Figure 9.4.

Recall that normal curves are symmetric; each half is a mirror image of the other. Consequently, the area from the mean to 1 standard deviation *below* the mean also includes 34.13 percent of the cases. In fact, areas of the normal curve are usually discussed in terms of regions included by identical distances above and below the mean, such as the mean ± (plus or minus) 1 standard deviation. This area includes 68.26 percent of the cases, or 34.13 percent for each half of the curve. Figure 9.5 illustrates the percentage of cases included in 1, 2, and 3 standard deviations around (above and below) the mean of a normal curve.

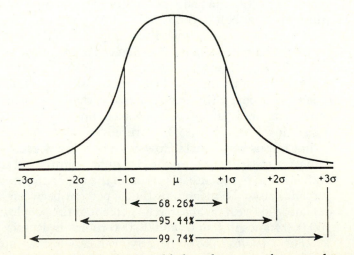

Figure 9.5 Areas above and below the mean of a normal curve.

This property of the normal curve allows us to determine some probabilities quite easily. If a variable's distribution is normal, we have a probability of .95 that any case selected at random will come from the region of 2 standard deviations below the mean to 2 standard deviations above it. Of course, not all areas under the normal curve can be described by using exact multiples of the standard deviation. Say we were dealing with the distribution of IQ scores, a distribution that has a mean of 100 and a standard deviation of 10 and is normally shaped. We are interested in the proportion of cases that fall between 100 and 105, less than a full standard deviation above the mean. To identify areas involving fractions of a standard deviation, we use Z scores.

Z scores are measurements calculated in standard deviation units. Just as we sometimes change our measuring scale from feet to inches or from degrees Fahrenheit to degrees Celsius, a Z score changes the values of a variable from their original measurement base into standard deviation units. To translate the original IQ score of 105 to a Z score, we use the formula

$$Z = \frac{X_i - \overline{X}}{s}$$

In this formula, X_i is the particular value we are interested in, in this case an IQ of 105; $\overline{X}$ is the mean; and s is the standard deviation. The numerator of the formula identifies the distance above or below the mean that the value is; $105 - 100 = 5$, or an IQ of 105 is 5 units above the mean. The denominator then divides by the standard deviation of the distribution, which transforms this distance into standard deviation units $\frac{5}{10} = .5$, or one-half a standard deviation above the mean. Thus an IQ of 105 can also be represented as a Z score of .5, or half a standard deviation above the mean.

The Z scores provide a way to quickly determine the area under any part of a normal curve. Statisticians have been able to identify what proportion of a normal curve's area falls between the mean and fractions of a standard deviation above or below the mean. These proportions of the area of the normal curve are listed in a Z table, illustrated in Table 9.2. For the area that interests us, Table 9.2 tells us that 19.15 percent of the cases will fall between the mean and .5 Z units above the mean in any normal distribution.

Also Z scores are called **standard** or **standardized scores** because they provide ways of comparing results across variables with different means and dispersions, comparing, in effect, apples and oranges. Is an income of 100,000 francs high or low? What about 20,000 rubles? By themselves, these raw income levels do not tell us very much. However, if we knew each was 1 standard deviation above the mean income for the particular country, we could then determine that each income represented a person in the upper 15 percent income level. The 50 percent below the mean plus the 34 percent between the mean and 1 standard deviation above it means that 84 percent of the people have incomes at or below 100,000 francs in France and 20,000 rubles in Russia.

The Z scores take on negative values when we are dealing with distances

Table 9.2 PERCENTAGE OF AREA UNDER THE NORMAL CURVE (Z TABLE)

Z	Area	Z	Area	Z	Area	Z	Area
.10	3.98	1.10	36.43	2.10	48.21	3.10	49.90
.20	7.93	1.20	38.49	2.20	48.61	3.20	49.93
.30	11.79	1.30	40.32	2.30	48.93	3.30	49.95
.40	15.54	1.40	41.92	2.40	49.18	3.40	49.97
.50	**19.15**	1.50	43.32	2.50	49.38	3.50	49.98
.60	22.57	1.60	44.52	2.60	49.53	3.60	49.98
.70	25.80	1.70	45.54	2.70	49.65	3.70	49.99
.80	28.81	1.80	46.41	2.80	49.74	3.80	49.99
.90	31.59	1.90	47.13	2.90	49.81	3.90	49.995
1.00	34.13	2.00	47.72	3.00	49.87	4.00	49.997
		1.96	**47.50**	**2.58**	**49.51**		

Source: Jack Levin and James Alan Fox, *Elementary Statistics in Social Research,* 4th ed., Harper & Row, Publishers, Inc., New York, 1988. Reprinted by permission of the publisher.

below the mean. For example, to determine the area between the mean and 5 units below the mean (IQs from 100 to 95), the Z formula is

$$Z = \frac{X_i - \bar{X}}{s} = \frac{95 - 100}{10} = \frac{-5}{10} = -.5$$

The minus sign merely tells us that the area being dealt with is below, rather than above, the mean. It has no other effect on our calculation. The Z table contains only positive Z scores, but since the two halves of a normal curve are identical, the table can be used for both positive and negative Z scores. A Z score of −.5 represents the same area as a Z score of +.5—19.15 percent of the cases—and the two together (the area from 95 to 105) contain 38.30 percent of the cases.

In Table 9.2 two Z scores regularly used by statisticians, 1.96 and 2.58 are shown in bold. Earlier we mentioned that the mean plus or minus 2 standard deviations included 95 percent of the cases and plus or minus 3 standard deviations included 99 percent. These were only approximations, with 1.96 and 2.58 being the precise numbers used to identify these areas. For normal curves, the area incorporated by the mean ±1.96 standard deviations includes 95 percent of all the cases (47.50 + 47.50 = 95.00), and the mean ±2.58 standard deviations includes 99 percent of the cases (49.51 + 49.51 = 99.02). Let us return to the distribution of IQ scores. With a standard deviation of 10, we see that 1.96 standard deviations below the mean is 19.6 IQ points (1.96 ∗ 10) below 100, or an IQ of 80.4, and 1.96 standard deviations above the mean is an IQ of 119.6. Ninety-five percent of the people in this distribution have IQs between 80.4 and 119.6. This also means that by picking any person from the distribution at random, there is a 95 percent probability that the person selected will have an IQ falling in this range.

With discrete distributions, we can make probability statements about specific numbers, such as "There is a $\frac{5}{36}$ chance of obtaining the number 6 when two dice are tossed." When a variable is continuous, the probability of randomly selecting any particular value is zero because the number of possible values is infinite. We can, however, make a probability statement about randomly selecting someone within a range of values by determining what proportion of all possibilities fits in that range. This is done geometrically, with the curve of the distribution representing all possibilities and the area of one part of that curve representing a portion of the possibilities within a selected range of values. When the continuous curve is a normal curve, our calculations are considerably simplified by the use of Z scores to identify areas under the curve.

SAMPLING DISTRIBUTIONS

From this general discussion of probability and probability distributions we now return to our original question—how to draw inferences about the population from sample results. To do this, we need to look at a different kind of distribution, a **sampling distribution**. A sampling distribution is like any other distribution in that it portrays the frequency with which the values of a variable occur, but it has four characteristic features.

First, a sampling distribution describes the distribution of a sample *statistic*, such as the mean or the variance, not the distribution of cases within a sample or a population. Say we draw one sample of 500 people and calculate the mean level of education for the sample. We then draw a second sample and calculate its mean, a third sample, and so on through 10 samples. A plot of the means obtained from these 10 samples might look like Figure 9.6.

Figure 9.6 is a sampling distribution, for it portrays the distribution of a sample statistic, in this case the mean, obtained from a number of different samples. Observe that knowledge of a variable's sampling distribution is central to the concern expressed at the beginning of this chapter—how much samples will differ from one another in their estimations of the population parameter μ, or how much error samples will have.

A second characteristic of sampling distributions is that, because they deal with sample statistics, they are continuous distributions. This is true even

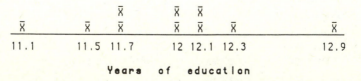

Figure 9.6 Means obtained from 10 samples.

when the variable being examined is discrete. Say the variable of interest is the number of children people have. This variable is clearly discrete, for one might have two children or three, but a family does not have 2.68 children. However, a sampling distribution plots the *mean* for this variable over an infinite number of samples. Samples can produce means of 2.68 or 2.213 or any of an infinite number of possibilities between whole numbers like 2 and 3.

Third, sampling distributions that we will examine are theoretical probability distributions. Random chance dictates what individuals will be selected for each sample, and thus random chance determines whether one sample mean will be higher or lower than another. Random chance behaves according to the rules of probability, making it possible to describe a theoretical sampling distribution based on these rules of probability. Like all theoretical distributions, a theoretical sampling distribution describes the frequency of a sample statistic over an infinite number of samples.

Fourth, sampling distributions are known distributions. Given certain information about the population, we can calculate what a sampling distribution must look like without actually having to draw an infinite number of samples. Our knowledge is summarized in a theorem derived from the rules of probability called the **central limit theorem**. This theorem can be stated as follows:

> If repeated random samples of size n are drawn from any population with mean μ and standard deviation σ, then as n becomes large, the sampling distribution of sample means will approach normality with mean μ and standard deviation $\sigma_{\bar{X}} = \sigma/\sqrt{n}$

In essence, the central limit theorem tells us what the mean, standard deviation, and shape should be for a distribution of sample means. We do not review a formal proof of this theorem here, but we do examine these three points below to explore their meaning and illustrate why the theorem makes sense.

The Central Tendency of a Sampling Distribution

The central limit theorem's first claim is that the central tendency of a distribution of means calculated from an infinite number of random samples will be the same as the population mean. Mathematically, this is equivalent to

$$\bar{\bar{X}} = \mu$$

where $\bar{\bar{X}}$ (called X double bar) represents the mean of the sample means and μ is the mean for the population.

If you think about it for a moment, this statement makes intuitive sense. A random sample is one in which each member of the population has an equal probability of being included in the sample, with random chance dictating exactly which people are selected. This chance factor will lead some samples to include a disproportionate number of cases from the low end of the population, leading to sample means below the population average. However, this same chance factor will also lead other sample means to overestimate the population value. The high and low values will cancel each other, leaving the

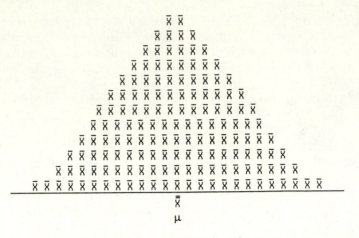

Figure 9.7 The mean of a sampling distribution.

average of all the sample means as the population mean. This statement is graphically represented in Figure 9.7. The mean of any individual sample may be close to or far away from the actual mean of the population, but the theoretical distribution of means from an infinite number of samples will be centered directly over the population mean.

Another way to look at this claim is to ask, How could it not be true? In what way could the distribution of means obtained from a number of samples not be centered over the population parameter μ? This could happen only if we were using a biased sampling procedure, one consistently producing samples that underestimated (or overestimated) the population average, such as trying to determine the average income of the population by sampling only presidents of large corporations or only the unemployed. As long as our samples are random and unbiased, they should, on average, represent the population from which they are drawn.

Dispersion of a Sampling Distribution

It is nice to know that the average of statistics calculated from random samples will be the same as the population parameter. We use, however, only one sample, not the average from an infinite number of samples. How well does our one sample represent the population? We do not really know, because we do not know where in the distribution in Figure 9.7 our particular sample is—right in the middle or at one of the extreme tails.

A measure of dispersion will help here, for it tells us how far away any individual item (such as our specific sample mean) might be from the center of the distribution, the population mean. In essence, the dispersion of the sampling distribution tells us how much error might exist in using a sample mean to estimate the population mean. Again, the laws of probability come to our aid, for the second thing we know about a distribution of sample means is that its standard deviation can be found through the formula

$$\sigma_{\overline{X}} = \frac{\sigma}{\sqrt{n}}$$

First we explain the formula's symbols, and then we illustrate why it works.

Recall that the Greek letter sigma (σ) stands for the standard deviation of the *population*, as opposed to *s*, which represents the standard deviation of the *sample*. The letter *n* we have encountered before. It represents the size of the samples we are dealing with. And $\sigma_{\overline{X}}$ represents the standard deviation of the distribution of sample means. Because it refers to the distribution of a sample statistic rather than the distribution of a variable, it goes by a special name, the **standard error**. The subscript $\overline{X}$ indicates that, in this case, we are dealing with the standard error of the mean, or the standard deviation of the sample statistic $\overline{X}$. The Greek symbol sigma is used for this term because we are actually talking about a population—the population (theoretical distribution) of all possible means for a given variable, such as education, that are produced by samples of size *n*.

Observe that this formula will produce a different result depending on the size of the samples we are dealing with. Our first claim, that the central tendency of the distribution of sample means will be μ, is true for all samples. Samples of size 10, 100, 1000, or 10,000 all have theoretical sampling distributions centered over μ. However, the standard deviation of the sampling distribution will differ for samples of different size. Figure 9.7 might represent the distribution of means for an infinite number of samples, all of size 100. If we were dealing with samples of size 10 or 1000, the dispersion of the distribution would be different.

This explains the symbols in the formula, but why does it work? What the formula says is that the dispersion of sample means will be affected by two things: the dispersion of the variable in the population, σ, and the size of the samples we are taking, *n*. Let us look first at the denominator of the formula, $\sqrt{n}$.

In Figure 9.8*a* we have a hypothetical distribution of the population's level of education. What would our distribution of sample means look like if we took repeated samples of size 1 (each sample included only 1 person) from this population? In this extreme case, the distribution of sample means, shown in Figure 9.8*b*, would be exactly the same as the distribution of the population. By definition, a random sample is one where every member of the population has an equal chance of being selected, so some of our samples will include those people at the extreme high and low points of the distribution of the population. Most will be closer to the middle, not because the middle people have a higher chance of being selected but because there are more of them, each comprising a different sample of size 1.

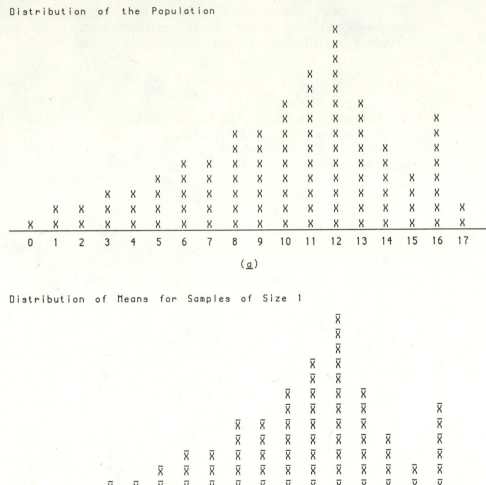

Figure 9.8 The dispersion of a sampling distribution for samples of size 1.

Returning to the formula for the standard error of the mean, we find that taking samples of size 1 produces

$$\sigma_{\bar{x}} = \frac{\sigma}{\sqrt{n}} = \frac{\sigma}{\sqrt{1}} = \sigma$$

This is the point illustrated in Figure 9.8: The distribution of means from samples of size 1 will be the same as the distribution of the population and thus have the same standard deviation as the population.

What happens if we increase our sample size to 2 people per sample? The formula for $\sigma_{\overline{x}}$ tells us the dispersion of these means will be less, $\sigma/\sqrt{2}$ instead of $\sigma/\sqrt{1}$ as was true for samples of size 1. This reduced dispersion for the sample means is illustrated in Figure 9.9.

Let us think through the process of drawing samples to see why an increase in sample size reduces the dispersion of the sample means. For samples of size 2, it might still be the case that the first person included in a sample could be one of these from an extreme tail of the population, a person with 0 or 17 years of education. The second person selected for the sample, however, will probably fall closer to the middle of the population distribution. The average of these two people will be closer to the true mean of the population. In fact, in Figure 9.9 it is mathematically impossible to get some of the extreme sample means we obtained with samples of size 1. Note that there is only one person in the population with 0 years of education. If this were the first person selected for the sample, the second person would have to be a member of the population closer to the mean. At worst, it would be one of the population members with only 1 year of education. Thus, for samples of size 2, the smallest sample mean we could possibly obtain is .5 [(0 + 1)/2 = .5], which is less extreme than the mean of zero 0 that we can get with samples of size 1.

In sum, as samples get larger in size, the distribution of means from these samples becomes more tightly packed around the distribution's central tendency. This is equivalent to saying that larger samples will represent the population more accurately than smaller samples. This becomes most obvious at the other extreme, drawing samples of size N, where capital N refers to the entire population. If we drew multiple samples but each sample included everyone in the population, the distribution of sample means would be a straight line with no variation at all (Figure 9.10b). Each sample of size N would include all members of the population, and each sample would contain the exact same people. Since the samples contain the same people, each sample will produce the same mean.

The denominator of the formula for the standard error of the mean thus makes sense. The larger the size of the samples we draw, n in the formula's denominator, the smaller will be the standard error of the mean, the standard deviation of the distribution of sample means. Now let us look at the numerator of this formula, the standard deviation of the population.

Again, let us begin with an extreme case. If the population had zero variance, it would also have a standard deviation of zero (the square root of the variance) and the means of samples drawn from this population would all be the same (no variation). Assume our population is a country where all the citizens have exactly 12 years of education, no more and no less. Every sample drawn from that population, regardless of its size, will produce the same mean, 12 years of education. The sample means will not vary because all members of the population are identical on this variable.

If we now introduce a little variation into the population, say 10 percent with only 11 years of education and another 10 percent with 13 years of education, the variance of our sample means will also increase. Most samples

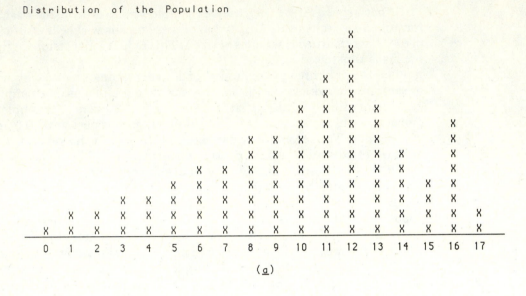

Figure 9.9 The dispersion of a sampling distribution for samples of size 2.

will still include only people with 12 years of education, but some will include a few of the less educated, pulling the mean of the sample group down to about 11.9 years, and a few samples will contain some of the more educated, pulling the sample mean up to about 12.1 years. As we add greater variation to the population, of necessity we add greater variation to the distribution of means for samples drawn from that population.

This aspect of the standard error of the mean is reflected in the numerator

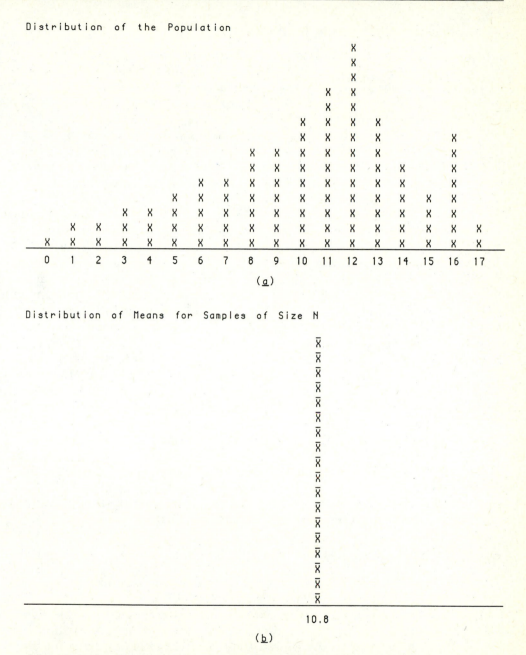

Figure 9.10 The dispersion of a sampling distribution for samples of size N.

of the formula. As the population standard deviation gets larger, the numerator of the formula will increase, producing a larger standard error of the mean. If the population standard deviation is small, so will be the standard error of the means.

The Shape of the Sampling Distribution

To this point we know two things about the distribution of a sample statistic: The average of the distribution will be the same as the population parameter, and the dispersion of the distribution will be given by the formula for the standard error. To these two items of information we add the third piece of the central limit theorem. If we are dealing with large samples (of size 30 or more), the distribution of *means* from these samples will be in the shape of a normal curve *regardless of what the distribution of the population is like.* The distribution of the population may be ragged and nonnormal, as in Figures 9.8 through 9.10, but large samples drawn from that population will produce means that are distributed normally.

This part of the central limit theorem is not obvious. We suspect that a nonnormal distribution of years of education for the population would produce a nonnormal distribution of that variable in our samples as well. In fact, this is the case. However, we are talking here not about the distribution of values for a variable, but about the distribution of means which summarize those values. The sample mean is affected by the number of high and low values in the sample, but not by the normality or nonnormality of the distribution of those values. Random chance leads some sample means to be on the high side and others on the low side of the population parameter, but we are equally likely to get each. As we move farther and farther away from the population mean, we are less and less likely to obtain randomly selected samples that will produce such means. This is true whether we are talking about samples that produce overestimates or underestimates of the population values. The curve representing the distribution of sample means is symmetric in that extreme high values are just as unlikely as extreme low values.

Note that the central limit theorem is not inconsistent with Figure 9.8, which showed samples of size 1 mirroring the distribution of the population, including any nonnormal characteristics of the population distribution. The central limit theorem deals with the distribution of sample means only for large samples, which samples of size 1 definitely are not.

Sampling Distributions and Probability Statements

To what do these three items of information—a sampling distribution's central tendency, dispersion, and shape—lead? They give us a way of estimating how far away our sample value might be from the population value. Recall our earlier discussion of normal curves and Z scores. When a distribution is normally shaped, which the central limit theorem tells us is true for distributions of means from large samples, 95 percent of the cases will fall within the range of 1.96 standard deviations above and below the distribution's mean. What is the standard deviation of this sampling distribution? It is given by the formula for the standard error. What is the mean of the sampling distribution that 95 percent of all sample means will fall within 1.96 standard deviations of? It is μ, the mean for the population on the variable we are examining. In other words, 95 percent of all random samples drawn from the population will have means somewhere in the range of 1.96 standard errors above to 1.96 standard errors below the population mean.

This knowledge allows us to make a probability statement about how closely sample means will match the population value. The probability statement is written mathematically as

$$p = .95 \quad \text{for} \quad \mu - 1.96\sigma_{\bar{X}} \leq \bar{X} \leq \mu + 1.96\sigma_{\bar{X}}$$

In this statement, the first term is the probability level $p = .95$; there is a 95 percent probability that the claim to the right is true. This claim is that any sample drawn from the population will have a mean somewhere in the range of the population mean minus 1.96 standard errors to the population mean plus 1.96 standard errors. This formula is commonly written as

$$p = .95 \quad \text{for} \quad \bar{X} = \mu \pm 1.96\sigma_{\bar{X}}$$

or it is 95 percent probable that our sample mean $\bar{X}$ is in the interval of μ plus or minus 1.96 standard errors.

Supplement 9.1 # Testing the Central Limit Theorem

Some readers may still be uneasy with the claims made in this chapter. Rest assured, the formulas and conclusions presented here are well grounded and accurate. Nonetheless, those who are still doubtful can easily perform their own tests of these claims.

Three of the basic claims made are derived from the central limit theorem:

1. Regardless of any skewness in the distribution of the population, the means of samples will be distributed normally.
2. The center of this distribution will be over the population mean.
3. The standard deviation of the distribution of sample means will be the standard deviation of the population divided by the square root of the sample size.

The central limit theorem leads to our fourth claim:

4. A 95 percent probability interval will contain 95 percent of the means of samples drawn from the population.

How do we test these claims? We begin by assuming that the people in our data set (either one) are the entire population. We then take repeated samples from this "population" to see if the sample means behave in accordance with the above claims. For example, let us use the education variable displayed in Figure 9.1, although any other interval variable would do as well. Since we are assuming this to be the population, our population mean μ is 12.544 and our population standard deviation σ is 2.885. Given this information, we can calculate what the sampling distribution should be like. We know from one of our earlier formulas that

$$P = .95 \quad \text{for} \quad \bar{X} = \mu \pm 1.96\sigma_{\bar{X}}$$

or 95 percent of all sample means should be within a certain range from μ. Recall that the standard error is given by

$$\sigma_{\bar{x}} = \frac{\sigma}{\sqrt{n}}$$

so we cannot calculate it without first identifying the sample size n that we will be using. For simplicity, let us draw repeated samples of size 100. Then we can determine that the standard error of the sampling distribution will be

$$\sigma_{\bar{x}} = \frac{2.885}{\sqrt{100}} = \frac{2.885}{10} = .289$$

Thus, for samples of size 100, of all sample means for the education variable, 95 percent should fall within the range

$$P = .95 \quad \text{for} \quad \bar{X} = 12.544 \pm 1.96 * .289$$

$$= 12.544 \pm .566$$

$$= 11.978 \text{ to } 13.110$$

For samples of size 100, our sampling distribution should be centered over μ (12.544), be normally shaped, and have 95 percent of all sample means fall between 11.978 and 13.110. All that remains to be done is to draw a number of samples and see whether their means indeed fit such a sampling distribution. This is easily done with the SAMPLE command, as illustrated in Figure 9.1S.

```
001    GET FILE = ELEC88

003    TEMPORARY
004    SAMPLE 100 OF 2040
005    FREQUENCIES VARIABLES = V80 / STATISTICS MEAN / FORMAT NOTABLE

006    TEMPORARY
007    SAMPLE 100 OF 2040
008    FREQUENCIES VARIABLES = V80 / STATISTICS MEAN / FORMAT NOTABLE

009    TEMPORARY
010    SAMPLE 100 OF 2040
011    FREQUENCIES VARIABLES = V80 / STATISTICS MEAN / FORMAT NOTABLE

012    TEMPORARY
013    SAMPLE 100 OF 2040
014    FREQUENCIES VARIABLES = V80 / STATISTICS MEAN / FORMAT NOTABLE


       and continuing for as many samples as needed
```

Figure 9.1S Drawing repeated samples of size 100.

You can make a simple chart, as in Figure 9.2S, and plot each sample mean you obtain. You should find that 95 percent of all the sample means fall within the confidence interval range, and the distribution of these means will look approximately normal. Remember that the central limit theorem describes the theoretical distribution of an

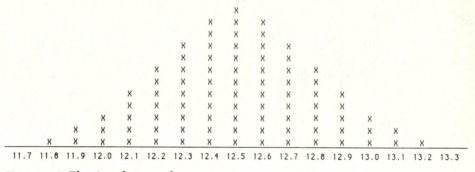

Figure 9.2S Plotting the sample means.

infinite number of samples. You will not be able to duplicate its predictions perfectly with only a few samples, but the more you draw, the more closely your results should match its predictions. Fortunately, computer editors allow us to make multiple copies of single lines or blocks of lines, like those in Figure 9.1S requesting each sample. We can thus type the commands only once and make as many copies as needed to draw 50 to 100 samples.

Drawing multiple samples will produce a lengthy output. To ease our burden somewhat, the commands in Figure 9.1S ask for only the mean to be produced for each sample, instead of all the available statistics. In addition, there is little reason to repeat the FREQUENCIES table with each sample, so the FORMAT NOTABLE subcommand has been added to suppress the printing of the table.

These mathematical formulas still contain many abstract symbols that will eventually have to be replaced with numbers: μ, $\overline{X}$, and $\sigma_{\overline{x}}$. Nonetheless, they move us toward our goal of identifying how close our sample statistic is to the population parameter. If 95 percent of all people have IQs between 95 and 105, then there is a 95 percent probability that any person we draw at random from the population will have an IQ in this range. Similarly, if 95 percent of all sample means fall within a certain distance from the population mean, there is a 95 percent probability that our sample (selected at random from the theoretical distribution of all possible samples) will have a mean within 1.96 standard errors of the population mean.

CONFIDENCE INTERVALS

Having developed a probability formula for sample means, we are now going to modify it a bit. It does us little good to talk about estimating sample values based on our knowledge of the population, that if we know the population's μ and σ, we could identify a sampling distribution's $\overline{X}$ and $\sigma_{\overline{x}}$. We do not have any knowledge of what the population is like. That is why we drew the sample in the first place, to find out something about the population.

What we want to do is reverse the logic of the probability formula so we can estimate the population parameter from information provided by our sample. To accomplish this task, we need to change the formula so that the unknown number to be estimated, μ, is on one side of the equals sign and all the symbols on the other side of the equals sign can be replaced with numbers, allowing us to then complete the calculation of the formula.

The first step in this process is quite simple. We merely exchange the symbols $\overline{X}$ and μ, to produce

$$p = .95 \quad \text{for} \quad \mu = \overline{X} \pm 1.96\sigma_{\overline{X}}$$

At first glance, this looks like mathematical sleight of hand. It is quite legitimate, however, for the formula deals with the distance between two numbers. To say that Los Angeles is 400 mi from San Francisco is exactly the same as saying San Francisco is 400 mi from Los Angeles. It does not matter where you start; the distance to the other point is the same. The earlier equation stated that there was a 95 percent chance that $\overline{X}$ was within 1.96 standard errors from μ, while the equation above says there is a 95 percent chance μ is within 1.96 standard errors of $\overline{X}$. Our claim about how close the two numbers are remains the same.

On the right side of the equals sign we now have two known terms, 1.96, which is already a number, and $\overline{X}$, a statistic that our sample will provide. There remains one unknown: $\sigma_{\overline{X}}$. Recall that the formula for the standard error is

$$\sigma_{\overline{X}} = \frac{\sigma}{\sqrt{n}}$$

We can attach a number to the term n, for that is the size of our sample. Unfortunately, we do not know what the standard deviation of the population σ is. We do, however, have a good estimate for this number—s, the standard deviation of this variable for our sample. We thus estimate the standard error by using the formula

$$\sigma_{\overline{X}} \approx \frac{s}{\sqrt{n}}$$

where the symbol $\approx$ means "approximately equal to" (pretty close, but not necessarily exact).

Because we are using only an estimate of σ, we need to backtrack a little in our development of the probability formula. Using our sample s to estimate the population's σ introduces a possibility of error into the calculations. We must compensate for this by changing another part of the formula, the number of standard errors above and below the mean used to calculate the range of values. To this point we have used Z scores from Table 9.2. The Z table is appropriate only when the population standard deviation is known. When we must estimate this value with the standard deviation from the sample, we use the *t* **statistic** to calculate confidence intervals.

The *t* statistic was developed by W. S. Gosset in 1908. Gosset described the statistic in an article he wrote under the pen name "Student." Hence the statistic is commonly referred to as *Student's t*. Gosset demonstrated that when a sample *s* is used in place of the population σ, probability formulas will still remain accurate as long as the *t* statistic is used in place of the *Z* statistic. The *t* statistic that Gosset developed adjusts for a sample's ability to estimate σ accurately. It does this by making the range of values we claim probably contains the population parameter wider as our ability to accurately estimate σ declines.

As an illustration of this point, consider two people, each trying to determine his or her weight. The first person uses an expensive scale sporting the latest technology. This scale shows person *A* weighing 110 lb. Since few scales are 100 percent accurate, person *A* adds a small margin of error and claims, "It is 95 percent probable that I weigh between 109 and 111 lb." Person *B* uses an old decrepit scale obtained for 75¢ at a garage scale. The scale shows that person *B* also weighs 110 lb, but suspicions about the scale's accuracy lead person *B* to add a large margin of error, claiming, "It is 95 percent probable that I weigh between 105 and 115 lb." Each person has an equal probability of her or his statement being true, but person *B* needs to compensate for the scale's inaccuracy by making a less precise claim (using a larger margin of error).

The *t* statistic developed by Gosset is illustrated in Table 9.3. The table contains three columns. The middle and rightmost columns show what *t* statistic to use for 95 percent and 99 percent probabilities, respectively. Column 1 contains the degrees of freedom available to us, which is nothing more than $n - 1$, the size of our sample minus 1. Look first at the bottom row of the table. This row tells us that for large samples, those above 120 cases, the *t* value used to calculate probabilities is the same as the *Z* value used—1.96 for a 95 percent probability and 2.58 for a 99 percent probability. Samples this large provide an accurate enough estimate of σ with the sample *s* so that no error correction is necessary. As our sample becomes smaller, however, the sample *s* provides a less accurate estimate of σ, which must be compensated for by making our probability interval wider. A sample with only 60 degrees of freedom must use 2 standard errors around the mean for a 95 percent probability level, and one with only 10 degrees of freedom must use 2.23 standard errors above and below the mean for the same level of probability. Any analysis of the GSS88 or ELEC88 data sets will use the *t* value of 1.96 since both data sets contain far more than 120 cases. If, however, you use a smaller sample, such as a data set you might collect yourself, you must consult a *t* table to determine the number of standard errors to use for probability calculations.

With the adjustment of substituting *t* values for *Z* values, we have reached our goal—a formula for estimating the population parameter from sample results. This formula is called a **confidence interval (CI).** The formula provides an interval estimate for the population parameter along with a level of confi-

Table 9.3 VALUES OF *t* USED FOR CONFIDENCE
INTERVALS

Degrees of freedom (df)	Significance level α	
	.95	.99
1	12.71	63.66
2	4.30	9.93
3	3.18	5.84
4	2.78	4.60
5	2.57	4.03
6	2.45	3.71
7	2.37	3.50
8	2.31	3.36
9	2.26	3.25
10	2.23	3.17
15	2.13	2.95
20	2.09	2.85
25	2.06	2.79
30	2.04	2.75
40	2.02	2.70
60	2.00	2.66
120	1.98	2.62
∞	1.96	2.58

Source: Abridged from Table 9 in E. S. Pearson and H. O. Hartley (eds.),
Biometrika Tables for Statisticians, vol. 1, 2d ed. (New York: Cambridge
University Press, 1976). Reproduced with the permission of the trustees of
Biometrika.

dence (probability) that the interval contains that parameter. A CI formula is
usually written as

$$\text{CI} = \alpha \quad \text{for} \quad \mu = \overline{X} \pm t_{\text{df},\alpha} * \sigma_{\overline{X}}$$

where $\sigma_{\overline{X}}$ is given by

$$\sigma_{\overline{X}} \approx \frac{s}{\sqrt{n}}$$

There are two new symbols. First, α (alpha) stands for the level of probability
or confidence that the interval on the right side of the equals sign contains the
population parameter μ. A 95 percent confidence interval is the most common,
although some prefer the 99 percent value, an interval within which we are 99
percent confident the population value falls. Second, instead of including an
actual number for the *t* value in the CI formula, the symbol $t_{\text{df},\alpha}$ is used. The *t*
value will change, depending upon both the degrees of freedom and the alpha
level. From Table 9.3, we see that 25 degrees of freedom and a 99 percent level
of confidence will require using the *t* value of 2.79 while 40 degrees of freedom
and a 95 percent confidence level will require using the *t* value of 2.02.

Let us use this formula to answer our original question: What is the average level of education for the U.S. population? So that you do not have to flip back to the beginning of the chapter, Figure 9.11 repeats Figure 9.1, a FREQUENCIES procedure on variable V80. Our point estimate of the population μ is the sample mean 12.544, but we want to add an interval estimate—information on how close this point estimate might be to μ. The confidence interval is identified by

$$\underset{(\alpha)}{CT = .95} \quad \text{for} \quad \underset{(\overline{X})}{\mu = 12.544} \quad \pm \quad \underset{(t_{df = 2035, \alpha = .95})}{1.96} \quad * \quad \underset{(\sigma_{\overline{X}})}{.064}$$

Carrying out the multiplication in the CI formula (1.96 * .064 = .125) gives

$$CI = .95 \quad \text{for} \quad \mu = 12.544 \pm .125$$

$$= 12.419 \text{ to } 12.669$$

Thus there is a 95 percent probability that the mean education level of the U.S. population is somewhere in the interval of 12.419 to 12.669 years.

V80   RESP'S EDUCATION

VALUE LABEL	VALUE	FREQUENCY	PERCENT	VALID PERCENT	CUM PERCENT
NONE,NO YRS CMPLETD	0	5	0.2	0.2	0.2
	1	1	0.0	0.0	0.3
	2	6	0.3	0.3	0.6
	3	7	0.3	0.3	0.9
	4	12	0.6	0.6	1.5
	5	20	1.0	1.0	2.5
	6	21	1.0	1.0	3.5
	7	25	1.2	1.2	4.8
8 YRS, GRADE SCHOOL	8	102	5.0	5.0	9.8
	9	57	2.8	2.8	12.6
	10	97	4.8	4.8	17.3
	11	76	3.7	3.7	21.1
12 YRS, HIGH SCHOOL	12	731	35.8	35.9	57.0
	13	176	8.6	8.6	65.7
	14	212	10.4	10.4	76.1
	15	83	4.1	4.1	80.1
16 YRS, COLLEGE GRAD	16	232	11.4	11.4	91.5
17 YRS+, GRAD STUDY	17	172	8.4	8.5	100.0
DK	98	1	0.0	MISSING	
NA	99	4	0.2	MISSING	
	TOTAL	2040	100.0	100.0	

MEAN	12.544	STD ERR	0.064	MEDIAN	12.000
MODE	12.000	STD DEV	2.885	VARIANCE	8.322
KURTOSIS	1.457	S E KURT	0.108	SKEWNESS	-0.782
S E SKEW	0.054	RANGE	17.000	MINIMUM	0.000
MAXIMUM	17.000	SUM	25527.000		

VALID CASES   2035   MISSING CASES   5

Figure 9.11 A FREQUENCIES of V80.

Observe that we can calculate the standard error of the mean through the formula

$$\sigma_{\bar{X}} \approx \frac{s}{\sqrt{n}} = \sigma_{\bar{X}} \approx \frac{2.885}{\sqrt{2035}} = \sigma_{\bar{X}} \approx \frac{2.885}{45.111} = .064$$

However, we do not need to bother with this calculation. Conveniently, the summary statistics available with the FREQUENCIES include the standard error, shown in bold in Figure 9.11.

Look closely at the size of the confidence interval calculated above. If, at the beginning of this chapter, you were asked to guess how close the sample mean probably was to the population mean, what would you have said? To allow considerable leeway for errors, most of us would probably have suspected the sampling error to be as much as 2 or 3 years of education—so that the true population mean might have been somewhere between 10 and 14 or 9 and 15 years of education. In reality, we can be far more precise than that. Our confidence interval is quite tight, from only 12.42 to 12.67 years of education. Even if we expanded our level of confidence to 99 percent (substitute a t value of 2.58 for 1.96), the confidence interval would be a compact 12.38 to 12.71. Although random samples cannot pinpoint population parameters with absolute accuracy, they allow us to use the rules of probability to confidently make very precise statements about the population.

Supplement 9.2   Sample Sizes and Prediction Accuracy

The formula for the dispersion of a sampling distribution illustrates why national samples usually include only about 1600 people. The smaller the dispersion of the sampling distribution, the more compact our confidence interval and the more precise our estimates of the population parameter will be. The formula for the standard error

$$\sigma_{\bar{X}} = \frac{\sigma}{\sqrt{n}}$$

shows us that the dispersion of the sampling distribution changes as a function of the population standard deviation σ and the size of the samples $\sqrt{n}$. For any specific variable, σ is an unchanging constant. The population is a set group of people that, no matter how many times you calculate it, will always have the same standard deviation. (The population will change over time as new members are born into it and others die, but we are dealing here with the population at one particular time period.)

With sigma being a constant for any given variable, the only way to narrow the dispersion of a sampling distribution is to increase n, the sample size. However, as samples get larger, the value of increasing their size further declines. We cut the dispersion of sample means in half every time we double the size of the denominator. But the denominator is the square root of n, meaning that we have to increase our sample size by a factor of 4 in order to double the size of the denominator. Thus, the standard error of the mean will have a size of σ ($\sigma/1$) when the sample is size 1, $\sigma/2$ when the sample size is 4, $\sigma/4$ when the sample size is 16, $\sigma/8$ when the sample size is 64, and so on.

By the time we get to larger-size samples, decreasing the variability of sample means requires quite large and expensive increases in the size of the samples. Going from a modest sample of size 400 to one of 1600 only cuts the dispersion of sample means in half. To cut it in half again, our sample would have to increase from 1600 to 6400, and to reduce the dispersion by half again would require using a sample of 25,600. Sampling experts have settled on samples of about 1500 to 2000 as providing a good balance between precise estimates of the population values and the higher costs of drawing larger samples.

SUMMARY

We began this chapter with only some sample results as approximate estimates for population values. We found that the rules of probability determine how sample statistics are distributed around the population parameter. Using the probability rules to create a confidence interval, we can be quite exact in making claims about the population.

Earlier we described social science as proceeding through the development and testing of hypotheses. In this encounter with probability distributions, we have seen one of the key tools used for testing hypotheses, the t statistic. In Chapter 10 we return to a discussion of hypotheses and hypothesis testing, followed in later chapters with an examination of the use of the t statistic in hypothesis testing.

REVIEW

Key Terms

Parameters	Theoretical distribution
Mu (μ)	Discrete distribution
Sigma (σ)	Continuous distribution
Sigma squared (σ^2)	Normal curve
Point estimate	Z scores
Interval estimate	Standard or standardized scores
Inferential statistics	Sampling distribution
Probability	Central limit theorem
Addition rule	Standard error ($\sigma_{\bar{X}}$)
Multiplication rule	Confidence interval (CI)
Probability distribution	t statistic
Empirical distribution	$t_{\text{df},\alpha}$
Known distribution	

Exercises

9.1 When you toss a pair of dice, what is the probability that you will get "doubles" (both dice have the same number)?

9.2 Toss a pair of dice 36 times. Count how often the numbers 2 through 12 appear when you add the faces of the dice. Is this frequency distribution similar to Table 9.1?

9.3 Have every student in the class perform Exercise 9.2, and combine all the results. Does the frequency distribution of this larger number of tosses come closer to matching Table 9.1 than was true for your fewer tosses in Exercise 9.2?

9.4 Do the exercise described in Supplement 9.1.

9.5 Supplement 9.2 describes the impact of sample size on a sampling distribution's standard error. Verify this description by repeating Exercise 9.4 but increasing the size of the samples to 400. Is the distribution of means you obtain now really half of what you got in Exercise 9.4?

9.6 Create 95 and 99 percent confidence intervals for the AGE, EDUC, and SPEDUC variables from the GS88 data set. Do the same for variables V5, V6, V7, and V8 from the ELEC88 data set.

9.7 A 95 percent confidence interval for V83 (religious preference) is 157.041 ± 3.993. How would you interpret this confidence interval?

SUGGESTED READINGS

Freedman, David, *et al. Statistics*, 2nd ed. (New York: W. W. Norton, 1991) Chapters 5, 6, 13, 14, 20, 21.

Levin, Jack and James Alan Fox. *Elementary Statistics in Social Research*, 4th ed. (New York: Harper & Row, 1988) Chapters 7–9.

May, Richard B., Michael E. J. Masson, and Michael A. Hunter. *Application of Statistics in Behavioral Research* (New York: Harper & Row, 1990) Chapters 5, 8, 10.

Chapter 10

Hypothesis Testing

Having learned about probability distributions and confidence intervals, we are now ready for the heart of the statistical analysis process, hypothesis testing. The later chapters in this text review different SPSS procedures used to test hypotheses. Before we look at these procedures, it is useful to have an overview of the essential components of testing hypotheses. Different statistical techniques deal with different research questions and types of variables, but they all provide information on one or more of the key elements needed for testing a hypothesis. These key elements relate to a relationship's existence, strength, or direction.

EXISTENCE—IS THERE A RELATIONSHIP?

To see how hypotheses are tested, let us start with a concrete example. Our research question is, Why do people's incomes differ so much? There could be many reasons for income differences, including disparities in talent, parental income, education, and the like. The explanation that we examine here is gender—sexual discrimination leads to dissimilarities in incomes for men and women. This leads us to hypothesize that a relationship exists between gender and income, the independent and dependent variables, respectively. Our hypothesis states this expected relationship as:

Gender   is related to   income.
independent variable   relationship   dependent variable

This hypothesis is called our **research hypothesis**, a statement which we believe to be true and which we are going to test through our research.

At this point, it might seem that testing the research hypothesis is straight-forward. We divide our sample into female and male groups and then examine the average income of each group. Figure 10.1 does this and shows that a difference does indeed exist: The average male income is 12.217 compared to the average female income of 6.560.

However, Figure 10.1 does not constitute a hypothesis test. Hypotheses make claims about the population. Figure 10.1 shows only that a difference exists in our particular sample. How can we assess whether a difference exists in the population as well? We answer this question with the rules of probability, just as was done in creating confidence intervals. The rules of probability are the same, but they are applied a little bit differently for testing hypotheses. The stages of hypothesis testing include establishing the null hypothesis, assessing its probability level, determining the significance level to use for the hypothesis test, and understanding the errors that can be made in testing hypotheses.

The Null Hypothesis

Return to the sample results in Figure 10.1. There are two reasons why our sample may show income differences between men and women. The first reason is that our research hypothesis is correct; in the population, women and

```
GET  FILE=ELEC88
TEMPORARY
SELECT IF (V87 EQ 1)
FREQUENCIES VARIABLES = V82 / FORMAT = NOTABLE / STATISTICS = ALL


V82          RESPONDENT'S INCOME

MEAN          12.217    STD ERR       0.204    MEDIAN        13.000
MODE          16.000    STD DEV       5.796    VARIANCE      33.590
KURTOSIS      -0.793    S E KURT      0.172    SKEWNESS      -0.371
S E SKEW       0.086    RANGE        22.000    MINIMUM        1.000
MAXIMUM       23.000    SUM        9871.000

VALID CASES      808       MISSING CASES     64


TEMPORARY
SELECT IF (V87 EQ 2)
FREQUENCIES VARIABLES = V82 / FORMAT = NOTABLE / STATISTICS = ALL


V82          RESPONDENT'S INCOME

MEAN           6.560    STD ERR       0.169    MEDIAN         4.000
ODE            1.000    STD DEV       5.507    VARIANCE      30.326
KURTOSIS      -0.670    S E KURT      0.150    SKEWNESS       0.711
S E SKEW       0.075    RANGE        22.000    MINIMUM        1.000
MAXIMUM       23.000    SUM        6927.000

VALID CASES     1056       MISSING CASES    112
```

Figure 10.1 Mean incomes of men and women.

men have different incomes, and our sample is reflecting the population relationship between gender and income. The second explanation is sampling error. Gender and income may not be related in the population, but they appear related in our sample because random chance led the sample to include a disproportionate number of higher-income males or lower-income females or both.

Science always begins conservatively by assuming the latter—that no relationship between variables exists until the evidence demonstrates otherwise. This assumption is called the **null hypothesis**. The research hypothesis and the null hypothesis are exact opposites. The research hypothesis is identified by the label H_R, for research hypothesis, or H_A for alternative hypothesis. The null hypothesis is identified with the label H_0. Examples of the two hypotheses are

Research hypothesis: H_A: Gender **is** related to income.

Null hypothesis: H_0:   Gender **is not** related to income.

In testing hypotheses, it is both simpler and logically sounder to test the null hypothesis rather than the research hypothesis. It is beyond the scope of this text to present the full justification for this statement, but we can illustrate why it is true. To say that gender is related to income is the same as saying that male income differs from female income in some way. Statistics, however, cannot evaluate a vague claim such as "differs in some way." Statistical analysis can only assess specific numerical claims, claims such as "The mean income for males is $500 greater than the mean income for females." However, if we test this claim and find it to be false, that does not mean that the research hypothesis is false. Female and male incomes might differ by $400, or $40, or even 40¢. The research hypothesis simply states that a difference in gender is related to a difference in income, but it does not claim that the income difference is a big one. It would be necessary to test all these numerical implications before we could confirm or refute the research hypothesis, an impossible task.

The null hypothesis, however, makes one clear and precise claim: The difference between male incomes and female incomes is zero in the population. One test can determine the likelihood that the null hypothesis is true. What is more, if the statistical evidence is strong enough to allow us to reject the null hypothesis (conclude it is false), then we can accept the research hypothesis. The two hypotheses are both exact opposites and cover all possible alternatives. Either gender is related to income or it is not; there is no third choice. Rejecting one alternative, such as the null hypothesis, leads inevitably to accepting the other alternative, the research hypothesis.

Tests of the null hypothesis are called tests of **statistical significance**. Statistical significance tests are based on sampling distributions. As illustrated in Figure 10.2, even if female and male incomes are the same in the population, some random samples will show male incomes to be higher and other samples will have female incomes on the high side. However, although sampling error exists, it is not an "anything goes" proposition. Small differences between sample values and population values might be due to sampling error, but substantial disparities between sample results and the claim by the null hypothesis about the population suggest that the null hypothesis is in error. Statistical

Supplement
10.1

A Logical Rationale for the Null Hypothesis

When theories are tested, which scientific research usually does, there is also a logical rationale for testing the null hypothesis rather than the research hypothesis. The null hypothesis is used to avoid a **logical fallacy** in drawing conclusions—a conclusion that may seem reasonable on the surface but is not logically justifiable.

Consider the following hypothetical syllogism:

If it rains	Sue will carry an umbrella
antecedent	consequent

The syllogism contains two parts: the antecedent (or prior condition) and the consequent (or situation that occurs if the antecedent is true). Assuming the syllogism is accurate, we can use evidence to draw conclusions by either **affirming the antecedent** or **denying the consequent**. If the evidence shows that it is raining (affirming the antecedent), we can conclude Sue will be carrying an umbrella. If the evidence shows Sue is *not* carrying an umbrella (denying the consequent), we can conclude that it is not raining. Remember, we assumed that the syllogism is accurate, so Sue must have an umbrella in her hands if it is raining.

A logical fallacy occurs if we attempt to draw conclusions with reversals of these strategies, by **denying the antecedent** or **affirming the consequent**. If evidence shows that it is not raining (denying the antecedent), we do not know what Sue is doing—the syllogism only talks about what Sue will do when it *is* raining. Similarly, if we observe Sue carrying an umbrella (affirming the consequent), we cannot conclude anything about the weather. Sue may always carry an umbrella; the syllogism only says that she definitely will have an umbrella when it rains.

In testing scientific theories, we are using the logic of the hypothetical syllogism; if the theory is true, we should observe a certain relationship between two variables. As an example, if the theory of socialization is true, we should be able to observe a relationship between the respondent's party identification of that of his or her parents. If we test this research hypothesis and find it to be correct, we cannot draw any conclusions about the theory, for that would be affirming the consequent. Parents and children may share similar party identifications for many reasons, and it would be a logical error to claim that the evidence supported the theory of socialization, the antecedent.

Using the null hypothesis, however, is a legitimate way to perform a test of the theory, for this involves denying the consequent rather than affirming it. If we accept the null hypothesis, we deny the consequent that the respondent and parent party identifications are related, and thus we can also deny that the antecedent, the theory of socialization, is true. Any broad theory yields a multitude of testable hypotheses. No single test, or series of tests, will ever prove the theory to be true. But if the theory withstands repeated attempts to deny it—by testing null hypotheses related to it—we are led to an increasing belief in the theory's accuracy.

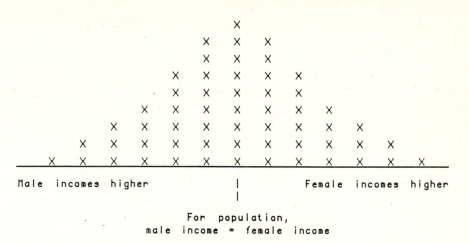

Figure 10.2 Sampling error producing sample relationships between gender and income.

significance tests use the rules of probability to evaluate whether the sample differences are small enough to be sampling error or so large that the sampling error explanation (the null hypothesis) must be rejected as unlikely.

Probability Levels

Tests of statistical significance involve probability calculations similar to those used in creating confidence intervals, but the calculations are both reported and performed differently. To illustrate both the differences and the similarities, we will work through some elementary hypothesis testing with the techniques used to develop confidence intervals.

Let us begin by assuming that the average income reported in Figure 10.1 for females, 6.56, is the real population mean. In claiming no difference in the population between male and female incomes, the null hypothesis is saying that the male income in the population is also 6.56. The observed sample value for males, 12.217, is merely the result of our imperfect sample's overrepresenting high-income males.

We can perform a rudimentary test of the null hypothesis by drawing a confidence interval around the mean income for males and seeing if this interval contains 6.56—which the null hypothesis claims is the population parameter for males. The confidence interval is

$$\text{CI} = \alpha \quad \text{for} \quad \mu = \overline{X} \pm t_{\text{df},\alpha} * \sigma_{\overline{X}}$$

or

$$\text{CI} = .95 \quad \text{for} \quad \mu = 12.217 * \pm 1.96 * .204$$

$$= 11.817 \text{ to } 12.617$$

From this calculation, we are 95 percent confident the population mean income for all males is somewhere between 11.817 and 12.617. Since this interval has a 95 percent probability of being correct, anything outside the interval has only a 5 percent or less chance of being true. The claim of the null hypothesis—that the male income mean for the population is 6.56—does fall outside the confidence interval and thus has a 5 percent or less chance of being correct.

This is the first difference between confidence interval and hypothesis-testing procedures: Tests of statistical significance report **probability levels** instead of confidence levels. With a confidence interval we are trying to identify a *range of values* that probably contains the population parameter. A test of statistical significance, however, determines the probability that *a specific value*, the one claimed by the null hypothesis, is the actual population parameter. Thus, for the test above, we would not report the range which we are 95 percent sure does contain μ, but instead that the null hypothesis has a .05 or less probability (the probability level) of being true.

This leads to a second difference between confidence intervals and significance tests. Confidence intervals are always calculated for a fixed probability value, such as .95. This makes sense when we have no specific claim to test but instead merely want to identify the general location of the population parameter. Since the null hypothesis does make a specific claim, we want to test this claim as accurately as possible.

One way to increase the precision of a statistical significance test is to create successively larger confidence intervals until we find one that almost includes, but does not quite include, the claim of the null hypothesis. The value 6.56 is nowhere near the .95 confidence interval, so we might try a .99 confidence interval. The calculations are

$$CI = \alpha \quad \text{for} \quad \mu = \overline{X} \pm t_{df,\alpha} * \sigma_{\overline{X}}$$

or

$$CI = .99 \quad \text{for} \quad \mu = 12.217 \pm 2.58 * .204$$

$$= 11.691 \text{ to } 12.743$$

This interval still does not contain 6.56, so the null hypothesis has only a .01 chance of being true. We could then move to a 99.9 percent confidence interval, which is

$$CI = \alpha \quad \text{for} \quad \mu = \overline{X} \pm t_{df,\alpha} * \sigma_{\overline{X}}$$

or

$$CI = .999 \quad \text{for} \quad \mu = 12.217 \pm 3.29 * .204$$

$$= 11.546 \text{ to } 12.888$$

Again, the interval containing 99.9 percent of all the possibilities does not contain the value claimed by the null hypothesis. We can thus say that the null hypothesis has .001 or less chance of being true.

Look again at the calculations of the 95, 99, and 99.9 percent confidence intervals:

$$CI = .95 \quad \text{for} \quad \mu = 12.217 \pm \mathbf{1.96} * .204$$

$$CI = .99 \quad \text{for} \quad \mu = 12.217 \pm \mathbf{2.58} * .204$$

$$CI = .999 \quad \text{for} \quad \mu = 12.217 \pm \mathbf{3.29} * .204$$

The formulas are all the same with one exception: The t value used for each is different. Instead of going through the arduous task of creating increasingly larger confidence intervals until we find one containing the null hypothesis, we can calculate directly how large an interval will be necessary. We do this by changing the confidence interval formula a bit to assess how large a t value we will need to use to create an interval containing the null hypothesis. We start with the basic formula

$$\mu_0 = \bar{X} \pm t_{\text{df},\alpha} * \sigma_{\bar{X}}$$

where μ_0 is the null hypothesis that the population mean income for men is 6.56. We then subtract the sample mean for men, $\bar{X}$, from both sides of the equation, producing

$$\mu_0 - \bar{X} = \pm t_{\text{df},\alpha} * \sigma_{\bar{X}}$$

The left-hand side of the equation, $\mu_0 - \bar{X}$, now represents the difference between our sample result, $\bar{X}$, and what the null hypothesis claims to be true, μ_0. Now we divide each side of the equation by $\sigma_{\bar{X}}$, producing

$$\frac{\mu_0 - \bar{X}}{\sigma_{\bar{X}}} = \pm t_{\text{df},\alpha}$$

The effect of this division is to express the difference between the null hypothesis and the sample result in standard error or t units—how many t units wide does a confidence interval have to be for it to contain μ_0?

Note that most of the symbols in the above formula can now be replaced with numbers by using both the null hypothesis and the results from the sample FREQUENCIES procedure in Figure 10.1. The replacements are as follows: μ_0 is 6.560 (from the null hypothesis), $\bar{X}$ is 12.217, $\sigma_{\bar{X}}$ is .204, and df is 807 (the number of men minus 1). This leads to the calculation

$$\frac{6.560 - 12.217}{.204} = -27.73_{807,\alpha}$$

The one remaining unknown, α, is what we seek. For 807 degrees of freedom, what probability is associated with a t value of 27.73? The alpha level can be determined by looking at a t table, though one far more detailed than the simplified version illustrated in Table 9.3. With such a table, one would find the row for 807 degrees of freedom, then move across the columns until the t value 27.73 was located. The heading at the top of that column would give us the probability level of that t value with 807 degrees of freedom. This probability level would be the probability that the null hypothesis is true. Fortunately, the

SPSS procedure used will perform all the necessary calculations and report the results as a probability level.

Not all tests of statistical significance use Gosset's Student *t* statistic to assess the probable correctness of the null hypothesis. Later chapters discuss the *F* test and the chi-square test, both of which are different from the *t* statistic and thus require different tables for assessing probabilities. Nonetheless, the logic of testing the null hypothesis remains the same regardless of which significance test is used. Given the size of our sample and the results from the sample, we can assess with the rules of probability whether a specific claim made about the population has a high probability of being true.

The Significance Level and Decision Error

While statistical significance tests evaluate the probability that the null hypothesis is true for the population, recall that with probabilities we never attain absolute certainty—clear proof that the null hypothesis has to be false. The *t* test calculated in the previous section might lead us to conclude that the null hypothesis only had a .00001 chance of being true. One chance in 100,000 is very unlikely, but still possible. With these odds, most of us would feel very comfortable in rejecting the null hypothesis, but what if the probability level for the null hypothesis were .01 (1 chance in a 100) or .05 (5 chances in 100), or even .10 (1 chance in 10)? At what point do we deem the evidence strong enough to reject the null hypothesis and accept the alternative research hypothesis?

What we are seeking here is a decision criterion, a rule telling us when to reject the null hypothesis and when to accept it. By convention, social scientists usually use .05 as their decision criterion. If the probability of the null hypothesis being true is .05 or less, we reject it and accept the research hypothesis. If the probability level is above .05, we consider the evidence too weak to reject the null hypothesis as an explanation for our findings.

This decision criterion is termed the **significance level**—the level of probability that statistical significance tests must reach in order to reject the null hypothesis. Decisions based on probability always run some chance of error. The significance level is the amount of error we are willing to accept in decision making. A significance level of .05 means we will reject the null hypothesis even when it still has a 5 percent chance of being true.

Why is it common practice to use .05 as the significance level? Why not use a much smaller level, such as .01 or .001, thus making sure that the evidence is overwhelming before deciding to reject the null hypothesis? The answer is that there are two types of errors—rather unimaginatively called Type I errors and Type II errors—that can be made when the null hypothesis is tested. Reducing the chance of making one error increases the chance of making the other.

Our adopted significance level leads us to either one of two decisions: accept or reject the null hypothesis. Each decision has a chance of being right or wrong, as illustrated in Figure 10.3. If we end up in quadrants 1 or 4, we have made the correct decision. Quadrant 2 represents a **Type II error**—deciding to accept the

```
Your Decision          Reality in population is

                       Null            Null
                       hypothesis      hypothesis
                       is true         is false
                     ┌──────────────┬──────────────┐
                     │ 1.           │ 2.           │
   Accept            │              │              │
   null hypothesis   │ Correct      │ Type II      │
                     │ decision     │ error        │
                     ├──────────────┼──────────────┤
                     │ 3.           │ 4.           │
   Reject            │              │              │
   null hypothesis   │ Type I       │ Correct      │
                     │ error        │ decision     │
                     └──────────────┴──────────────┘
```

Figure 10.3 Type I and Type II errors.

null hypothesis based on our sample information when it is actually false in the population. Quadrant 3 is a **Type I error**—deciding to reject the null hypothesis when it is, in fact, true for the population.

The significance level chosen as a decision criterion affects the likelihood of making one type of error versus another. Dropping the significance level criterion from .05 to .01 or to .001 constitutes adopting tougher and tougher standards of evidence before deciding to reject the null hypothesis. In making the null hypothesis more difficult to reject the chances of making a Type 1 error are reduced. At the same time, a lower significance level leads to an increased chance of making a Type II error, failing to reject the null hypothesis when it is actually false for the population.

Supplement 10.2

Probability Levels and Significance Levels

When a null hypothesis is being tested, SPSS procedures may report some very low probability levels, levels such as .001 or less. Does this mean that we are using a significance level of .001 and thus have a high chance of making a Type II error? No. This confuses the significance level that *we use as a decision criterion* with the probability level calculated by the computer.

Let us explain the difference in terms of marketing a new product. A manufacturer develops a new model car that costs $5000 to produce. The manufacturer could charge $20,000 for the car, which would produce a huge profit for each car sold but would lower the number sold since only a few people could afford the car. Instead the manufacturer decides to charge $5500 for the car, which gives a smaller profit, but far more customers are willing to buy the car. Now say that a customer offers to buy one of the cars for $20,000. Is the offer rejected because it is too high? Probably not, but accepting this high offer does not decrease the number of customers because the manufacturer is still willing to sell it to others for $5500.

Similarly, in deciding to use a .05 significance level in determining when to reject the null hypothesis, we have a constant probability of making Type I and Type II errors. We will reject the null hypothesis whenever the probability level is .05 or less and accept it when its probability is above .05. The significance level is the potential for error that *we are willing to accept* in rejecting the null hypothesis. The amount of error that we are willing to accept does not change just because some calculated probability levels are considerably below this amount.

When we are testing hypotheses, there is no way to guarantee we will always make a correct decision. If we knew what was true for the population, we would not need to bother drawing a sample. What we can do, and do quite well, is minimize the chance of making an incorrect decision. For the social sciences, the .05 decision criterion provides a good balance between the risks of making Type I or Type II errors.

THE STRENGTH OF RELATIONSHIPS

Tests of statistical significance enable us to evaluate the claim that a relationship between two variables exists in the population. If a test of the relationship between gender and income leads us to reject the null hypothesis, we conclude a relationship does exist in the population and this conclusion has a high probability of being true. To say that a relationship exists, however, is not the same as saying that it is an important one.

Relationships differ in strength. Some may be quite modest, others very strong. For example, we might research whether time spent studying is related to student grade-point averages (GPAs). The sample we gather shows a difference between those who study a little versus those who study a lot, and a statistical significance test allows us to conclude that this relationship exists for the population of all students as well. The practical size of the relationship, however, may be of little value, such as an average GPA of 2.4 for those studying 30 hours per week versus an average GPA of 2.3 for those who do not study at all. The effect of studying on the GPA is so small that it is not worth the time required. Alternatively, we might find a very substantial relationship, one showing that studying 5 hours per week increases the student GPAs one full grade point. Both relationships are statistically significant, but they differ considerably in substantive importance.

Questions about a relationship's strength are questions dealing with **substantive significance**, how important the relationship is theoretically or practically. Tests of statistical significance do not tell us anything about a relationship's substantive importance. The strength of a relationship is determined by a different statistical test, called a **measure of association**. Sometimes we want to know whether a single relationship is sizable, such as, Does gender have an *important* impact on income? At other times, we wish to compare the impact of different independent variables on the same dependent variable: Does gender or race make a greater difference in a person's income? Questions of this nature are answered through measures of association.

Different measures of association are used, depending on the type of variables being examined. By convention, however, most measures of association use a common scale for assessing the strength of relationships, a range of values from 0.0 to 1.0. A relationship of zero is no relationship—gender makes no difference to a person's income. A relationship of 1.0 is a perfect one, meaning that gender totally determines a person's income—all women have income X and all men have income Y. In practice, measures of association do not reach these theoretical boundaries, but instead take on some value between them, such as .19 or .48

In later chapters we discuss various measures of association that can be used for assessing the strength of relationships, so we do not review them in detail here. We included the concept of a measure of association at this point to remind the reader that different questions require different statistics to be answered. If we only want to know whether gender and income are related at all, a statistical significance test will give us this answer, but it will not tell us whether the association between the two variables is a mild .15 or a quite robust .60. If our question deals with how strongly two variables are related, a measure of association must be used.

THE DIRECTION OF RELATIONSHIPS

Most measures of association also provide us with another item of information, the **relationship's direction**. The values of ordinal and interval variables can be organized along a scale, such as from more to less or higher to lower. Moving along the scale from code numbers 1 to 2 or 5 to 6 represents moving in a direction on the variable—to more years of education or attending church more often. Hypotheses stating relationships between ordinal or interval variables often also state *how* differences on the independent variable are related to differences on the dependent variable. An example is

Greater education	leads to	increased income.
direction on independent variable	relationship	direction on dependent variable

The hypothesis above describes what is called a **positive relationship** between two variables. Positive relationships occur when higher values on the independent variable are related to higher values on the dependent variable—as a respondent's level of education increases, we expect her or his income to increase as well. The hypothesis could be restated as

Education	is positively related to	income.
independent variable	relationship and direction	dependent variable

Between some variables, we would expect a **negative relationship**, where increases in value on the independent variable are related to *decreases* in value on the dependent variable. As an example, we would probably expect highly educated people to be less likely than others to turn to crime and consequently spend time in jail. Thus, we might hypothesize a negative relationship between the two variables as in

<u>Greater education</u>	<u>leads to</u>	<u>fewer years in prison.</u>
direction on independent variable	relationship	direction on dependent variable

Again, the hypothesis can be restated as

<u>Education</u>	<u>is negatively related to</u>	<u>years in prison.</u>
independent variable	relationship and direction	dependent variable

Hypotheses that state a direction are called **directional hypotheses**. Those that do not are **nondirectional hypotheses.** Stating a hypothesis as nondirectional—such as level of education is related to marital status—is necessary when one of the two variables in the hypothesis is nominal. Level of education is an interval variable, but marital status is nominal. One cannot speak of having more or less marital status since the variable's code numbers only represent different categories, such as single, married, divorced, or widowed. Nondirectional hypotheses can be used with ordinal and interval variables as well when we suspect a relationship but are unsure of its direction. We may believe that educational level is related to the number of children a person has, but are doubtful whether the highly educated have more or fewer children.

Measures of association designed for ordinal and interval variables assess both the direction and the strength of a relationship. Such measures of association report values ranging from -1.0 to $+1.0$. The negative numbers show negative relationships and the positive numbers positive ones.

It is common to think of a negative number as representing less of something than its positive counterpart, but this is not so for measures of association. The sign of the relationship, positive or negative, tells us only its direction, not its strength. A relationship's strength is determined by its distance from zero in either direction. Consider flipping a coin 100 times. If the coin is fair, we expect approximately 50 heads and 50 tails. If, instead, we obtained 100 heads, we would conclude that the coin was biased to favor heads. Conversely, obtaining 100 tails would also lead us to conclude that the coin was biased, although this time in favor of tails. Each result shows an equal amount of bias, but in opposite directions. Similarly, a relationship of $-.75$ is as strong as one of $+.75$, but the direction of the relationship differs.

Testing directional hypotheses involves a slightly different approach from nondirectional ones. First, the test is not complete until both the statistical significance test and the measure of association have been calculated. A statistical significance test might show that a relationship found in our sample between years of education and years spent in prison probably exists in the population as well but a directional hypothesis claims *both* that a relationship exists and that it is in a particular direction. A measure of association needs to be calculated to confirm that the direction of the relationship is the same as that claimed in the hypothesis.

Second, testing directional hypotheses modifies somewhat the statistical significance test itself. Up to this point, we have been describing confidence intervals and significance tests using statistics appropriate for nondirectional hypotheses. These statistical significance tests are called **two-tailed tests**. Directional hypotheses, however, require **one-tailed tests** of statistical significance. The two types of test involve the same probability formulas, but use a different logic and different t values.

To return to the hypothesis presented at the beginning of this chapter, gender is related to income. This hypothesis can be expressed mathematically as

$$H_A: \quad \mu_m \neq \mu_w$$

or in the population the average male income is different from the average female income. Conversely, the null hypothesis is expressed mathematically as

$$H_0: \quad \mu_m = \mu_w$$

The logic of testing the null hypothesis begins by assuming it is true. Then we develop a sampling distribution, as illustrated in Figure 10.4. The area in the middle is the 95 percent probability region, showing the most likely sample results if the null hypothesis is true. A sample mean at point X_1 is quite plausible even if the null hypothesis is true, but results at point X_2 or X_3 indicate that the null hypothesis should be rejected—they have less than a 5 percent chance of occurring if the null hypothesis is true. Since the research hypothesis is nondirectional, a sample result in either extreme tail of the distribution—male incomes higher than female incomes *or* female incomes higher than male

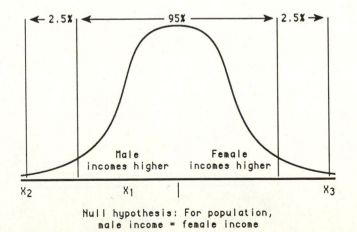

Figure 10.4 Sampling distribution assuming the null hypothesis is true.

incomes—is adequate to reject the null hypothesis. Hence the name *two-tailed test.*

Now let us rephrase the hypothesis to be directional: Men have higher incomes than women. Mathematically, the research hypothesis claims

$$H_R: \quad \mu_m > \mu_w$$

and thus the null hypothesis becomes

$$H_0: \quad \mu_m \leq \mu_w$$

that men have either the same incomes as or lower incomes than women.

Figure 10.5 repeats the sampling distribution for the null hypothesis, but the distribution is used differently. Since the null hypothesis claims that male incomes are either *equal to or less than* female incomes, both points X_1 and X_3 are consistent with it. Only sample results in the extreme part of one tail of the sampling distribution, such as point X_2, would lead to rejecting the null hypothesis and accepting the research hypothesis. Thus the name *one-tailed test.*

The different logic of a one-tailed test also mandates the use of a different *t* value in probability calculations. In identifying sample results that have a .05 or less chance of being true, a two-tailed test eliminates as improbable $2\frac{1}{2}$ percent of the possible outcomes from each side, or tail, of the sampling distribution (Figure 10.4). For a one-tailed test, only one side of the sampling distribution is relevant, and a .05 significance test requires that 5 percent of the least-probable cases be eliminated from that one tail only (Figure 10.5).

As a practical matter, a two-tailed test is commonly used for both nondirectional and directional hypotheses. Two-tailed tests are commonly reported with most statistical procedures and are actually somewhat more stringent than one-tailed tests. The difference between the two types of test is slight, leading to a different decision on rejecting the null hypothesis only when the probability

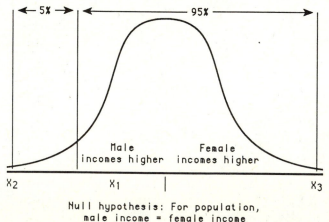

Figure 10.5 Testing the null hypothesis with one tail of the sampling distribution.

level is close to .05, say between .03 and .07. Nonetheless, you will occasionally encounter SPSS procedures reporting statistical significance tests as either one-tailed or two-tailed, and you need to be familiar with the distinction.

PHRASING HYPOTHESES

In the first three sections of this chapter we focused on the technical aspects of testing hypotheses. Before we leave the topic of hypothesis testing, it is helpful to take another look at phrasing hypotheses. Simply put, before we can test a hypothesis, we must have a hypothesis that is testable. Developing a testable hypothesis should not be difficult, for a hypothesis is a very plain little sentence stating a relationship between two variables. Sometimes our ideas seem too complex to be stated so simply, but stating them simply is a must in creating hypotheses. No ironclad rules can be given for this process, but a few examples will help illustrate how complex notions can be stated as clear hypotheses.

One frequently made error is to include irrelevant material in a hypothesis. Usually, the irrelevant material is part of the theory or reasoning behind the hypothesis. An example might be

H_R: Because women are less interested in politics, they will vote less often than men.

The prediction part of the hypothesis—that gender is related to voting frequency—can be tested easily. However, the beginning rationale which led to the prediction—that women are less interested in politics—is part of the theory and not directly testable. We may find women voting less often than men, but this may be due to a lack of candidates who address issues of importance to women, or women may be unable to get to the polls because they are caring for young children, or a host of other reasons. Your rationale for stating a hypothesis is important. It should be discussed in whatever paper you write describing your research. It should not, however, be included in the hypothesis itself.

A second common problem involves including too many variables in the hypothesis. In examining the sources of sexism, we might hypothesize

H_R: People who are older and less educated are more sexist than those who are younger and more educated.

This hypothesis contains three variables, not two: sexism as the dependent variable and both age and educational level as independent variables. What happens if we find that education is related to sexist attitudes, but age is not? Is the hypothesis true or false? What is the null hypothesis we are testing—that neither age nor education is related to sexism, or that one is but the other is not?

The research hypothesis above may be partly true, but hypotheses need to be written so that either the research hypothesis or the null hypothesis is true, not a little of each. This can be done by breaking down this complex hypothesis into two simpler ones, such as

H_R: Level of education is related to level of sexism.

and

H_R: Age is related to level of sexism.

Each hypothesis now has a clear opposite, a corresponding null hypothesis, and each can be tested without difficulty.

A related problem arises when you write a hypothesis with only two variables, but more than one relationship between them. Consider the hypothesis

H_R: Being married is related to higher satisfaction with life for men but lower satisfaction with life for women.

Again, how do we determine if this hypothesis is true? What would our conclusion be if the sample data showed that being married made both men and women more satisfied with life? The hypothesis contains only two variables—marital status and satisfaction with life—but it describes two relationships between the variables—a positive relationship for men but a negative one for women. The solution is the same: Separate the hypothesis into two, as in

H_R: For men, being married is related to higher satisfaction with life.
H_R: For women, being married is related to lower satisfaction with life.

Both these examples illustrate what is called a *conditional hypothesis.* Conditional hypotheses claim a relationship between two variables, but only under certain conditions. Another example is

H_R: <u>For those in the workforce,</u> <u>education is positively related to income.</u>
        Condition   hypothesized relationship

That is, we believe a person's level of education is positively related to her or his income, but only for a certain subset of the population—people in the workforce. The opposite null hypothesis is

H_0: For those in the workforce, education is *not* positively related to income.

Conditional hypotheses are often quite useful, but they also demand a little extra care in testing. What, for example, does the conditional hypothesis above claim is the relationship between education and income for those not in the workforce? Nothing. It does not claim that the relationship is positive, negative, or even zero for that group; it says nothing about them at all. Nonworkers are irrelevant to both the research and null hypotheses and thus are also irrelevant in any statistical test of the hypothesis. Hypothesis tests for conditional hypotheses need to be performed by using only that part of our sample relevant to the hypothesis, the group identified in the condition of the hypothesis. In this case, a SELECT IF statement could be used to isolate those in the workforce, and then the relationship between education and income could be evaluated for just that group.

Writing hypotheses is more an art than a science. It is a skill that improves with practice. This brief discussion illustrates some of the ways you can take ideas about the causes of social attitudes or behaviors and phrase them as testable hypotheses. As you gain experience with social research, the ability to identify testable hypotheses about the social world will become second nature.

SUMMARY

Writing hypotheses and learning statistics go hand in hand. As you learn what types of tests can be performed with statistical analysis, your ability to phrase questions that can be answered with these tests will improve.

This chapter provided a general overview of the central features of hypothesis tests: evaluating the statistical significance, substantive importance, and direction of a relationship as well as making sure that the hypothesis is testable. It is now time to turn to the SPSS procedures that provide the hypothesis tests. In Chapters 11, 12, and 13 we review SPSS commands that produce tests of statistical significance: the t test, the F test, and the chi-square test. The chapters following these examine SPSS procedures which calculate measures of association.

REVIEW

Key Terms

Research hypothesis   Negative relationship
Null hypothesis   Directional hypotheses
Statistical significance   Nondirectional hypotheses
Probability level   Two-tailed tests
Significance level   One-tailed tests
Type II error   Logical fallacy
Type I error   Affirming the antecedent
Substantive significance   Denying the consequent
Measure of association   Denying the antecedent
Relationship direction   Affirming the consequent
Positive relationship

Exercises

10.1 Identify whether the hypotheses below are directional or nondirectional. For directional relationships, identify the direction.
   a. Race is related to voting.
   b. Older people will support premarital sex less often than younger people.
   c. The more favorable a respondent's reaction to Dan Quayle, the less favorable will be his or her feelings toward Lloyd Bentsen.
   d. A person's age is related to her or his income.
   e. People who feel better off financially will have warmer feelings toward George Bush.
   f. More frequent church attendance is related to greater opposition to abortion.
   g. Higher levels of education are related to less frequent TV watching.
   h. Democrats are more liberal than Republicans.

10.2 Write a null hypothesis for each hypothesis in Exercise 10.1.

10.3 Take some of the statements in Exercise 10.1 and rewrite them as conditional hypotheses.

SUGGESTED READINGS

Freedman, David, *et al. Statistics*, 2nd ed. (New York: W. W. Norton, 1991) Chapters 26, 27.

Henkel, Ramon E. *Tests of Significance*, Quantitative Applications in the Social Sciences, Sage University Papers Series No. 4 (Newbury Park, Calif.: Sage Publications, 1976).

May, Richard B., Michael E. J. Masson, and Michael A. Hunter. *Application of Statistics in Behavioral Research* (New York: Harper & Row, 1990) Chapters 8, 9, 12.

Mohr, Lawrence B. *Understanding Significance Testing*, Quantitative Applications in the Social Sciences, Sage University Papers Series No. 73 (Newbury Park, Calif.: Sage Publications, 1990).

Chapter
11

T-TEST

The first question in testing any hypothesis is whether a relationship found in a sample is statistically significant—probably existing in the population as well. How statistical significance is evaluated depends on the nature of the variables in the hypothesis. Are they nominal, ordinal, or interval? When the dependent variable is interval and the hypothesis compares only two groups (e.g., whites and nonwhites or college graduates and people who are not college graduates), an appropriate SPSS procedure is the T-TEST procedure.

Let us take as an example whether the respondent's gender affects the salary that she or he earns. Are employers still paying women lower salaries, or, conversely, are female employees now in high demand and commanding more impressive salaries than men? In prior chapters we explored the relationship between gender and income, but the question above is a little different, focusing on employed respondents only. Women who opt to remain at home, along with the unemployed and retired of both sexes, are not relevant in a comparison of male and female workers. Thus, our research and null hypotheses are conditional ones, stated as follows:

H_R: For those in the workforce, gender is related to income.

versus

H_0: For those in the workforce, gender is not related to income.

The research hypothesis is nondirectional since it will be true if women are earning either more or less than men and false only if the two sexes earn the same.

In this case, the research hypothesis contains an independent variable with only two groups, males and females, and the dependent variable, income, is interval. So the T-TEST can be used to examine it. As you might suspect from its name, the T-TEST is based on the Student's *t* statistic, reviewed during the discussion of confidence intervals. The T-TEST procedure comes in two forms: one for independent groups and the other for dependent groups. Since we are already familiar with confidence intervals, we begin by looking at how they might be used to test hypotheses. After that, we discuss the two forms of T-TEST.

TESTING HYPOTHESES WITH CONFIDENCE INTERVALS

Before jumping to a statistical test of any hypothesis, we must be sure that our test is logically correct, that the data and variables used are relevant to it. The hypothesis above is conditional, referring only to people who are working. Consequently, we must use a SELECT IF command to isolate sample respondents who are working at least part-time (WRKSTAT equals 1 or 2).

Having satisfied the logical requirements, we can turn to a statistical test of the hypothesis, using the commands and output shown in Figure 11.1. Two additional SELECT IF commands are used to separately select women and men from the working respondents. Each is preceded by a TEMPORARY command and followed with a FREQUENCIES request. The temporary SELECT IF commands separate the two groups being compared, while the FREQUENCIES procedure computes the average income for each group. The FORMAT NOTABLE subcommand is used since we are interested in each group's mean, not the FREQUENCIES table showing the distribution of group members.

The results in Figure 11.1 do show an apparent sizable income difference. The sample means are 12.683 for males and 9.841 for females. Now we must determine whether sampling error accounts for this nearly 3-point difference between the sample group means, as the null hypothesis claims, or whether this explanation can be rejected in favor of concluding that an income difference truly exists in the population.

In earlier chapters we used confidence intervals to identify population means, and the same can be done here. Using the 95 percent confidence interval formula

$$\text{CI} = 95\% \quad \text{for} \quad \mu = \overline{X} \pm t_{\text{df},\alpha} * \sigma_{\overline{X}}$$

we replace the symbols with the numbers found in Figure 11.1. For males, we are 95 percent confident that their population mean income is

$$\text{CI} = 95\% \quad \text{for} \quad \mu = 12.683 \pm 1.96 * .230$$
$$= 12.232 \text{ to } 13.134$$

The average income for female respondents (9.841) is outside the range of where we are 95 percent confident the population mean income for males falls. Although we stopped here in Chapter 10, a true test of the hypothesis demands going further. The mean income of women is also a sample estimate with its own variability, so we need to identify the likely range of population mean

```
GET FILE = GSS88
SELECT IF (WRKSTAT LE 2)

TEMPORARY
SELECT IF (SEX EQ 1)
FREQUENCIES VARIABLES=RINCOME / FORMAT NOTABLE / STATISTICS ALL


RINCOME     RESPONDENT'S INCOME

MEAN      12.683     STD ERR      0.230     MEDIAN       14.000
MODE       5.000     STD DEV      4.694     VARIANCE     22.029
KURTOSIS  -0.390     S E KURT     0.239     SKEWNESS     -0.561
S E SKEW   0.120     RANGE       19.000     MINIMUM       1.000
MAXIMUM   20.000     SUM       5276.000

VALID CASES     416        MISSING CASES      34




TEMPORARY
SELECT IF (SEX EQ 2)
FREQUENCIES VARIABLES=RINCOME / FORMAT NOTABLE / STATISTICS ALL


RINCOME     RESPONDENT'S INCOME

MEAN       9.841     STD ERR      0.239     MEDIAN       10.000
MODE       9.000     STD DEV      4.786     VARIANCE     22.907
KURTOSIS  -0.836     S E KURT     0.243     SKEWNESS     -0.174
S E SKEW   0.122     RANGE       19.000     MINIMUM       1.000
MAXIMUM   20.000     SUM       3956.000

VALID CASES     402        MISSING CASES      42
```

Figure 11.1 Average income of working women and working men.

incomes for women as well. Without repeating the formulas or calculations, a 95 percent confidence interval for the mean female income is the range from 9.373 to 10.309. Thus we are 95 percent confident that the average income for males in the population is no lower than 12.232 and 95 percent confident that the average income for females in the population is no higher than 10.309. This confidence-interval test provides substantial evidence for rejecting the null hypothesis that, in the population, the average incomes of the two groups are the same.

Unfortunately, the confidence-interval test is clumsy and does not have the accuracy desired. We seek a test with a .05 significance level, only a 5 percent chance of error in rejecting the null hypothesis. The confidence-interval approach requires us to calculate two intervals, each with a 95 percent probability of accuracy. What, however, is the probability that *both* statements are correct?

Recall from our discussion of probability that when evaluating the probability of a combination of events (both *A* is true and *B* is true), we must multiply the probability of the first event by the probability of the second. This is what we are faced with above. To reject the null hypothesis, we must make two probability statements—one about the population income of females and another about the population income of males. Each claim has a 95 percent chance of being true, but the probability that both are true simultaneously requires multiplying the two probabilities. This multiplication, $.95 * .95$, shows that the probability of both being true is .9025, nearly a 10 percent chance of error when two 95 percent confidence intervals are used to test the null hypothesis. To end up with a .05 probability of error, we would have to use 97.47 percent confidence intervals instead of 95 percent ones.

The logic of using confidence intervals to test for statistical significance is sound, but the need to assess joint probabilities increases the complexity of an already cumbersome procedure. It would be better to have a single statistic that could be used for the hypothesis test. Also it would be preferable to have the computer perform the mathematical calculations for us. Both objectives are achieved in the SPSS T-TEST procedure.

COMPARING MEANS OF INDEPENDENT GROUPS

The logic of the T-TEST procedure is both similar to and different from the comparison of two confidence intervals performed above. The T-TEST approach creates a new hypothetical variable representing the difference between the means of any two groups. This new variable (for simplicity, we will call it MEANDIFF) is produced by subtracting the mean income of men μ_m from the mean income of women μ_w. Mathematically,

$$\text{MEANDIFF} = \mu_m - \mu_w$$

The MEANDIFF variable is directly related to the research hypothesis and null hypothesis which claim that MEANDIFF is *not* zero and that MEANDIFF *is* zero, respectively. We estimate the value of MEANDIFF by using samples, as in

$$\text{MEANDIFF} = \overline{X}_m - \overline{X}_w$$

Note that estimating MEANDIFF requires two samples, a sample of women and one of men, just as in our two samples in Figure 11.1 which produced a difference between the means of 2.842.

Now let us begin by assuming that the null hypothesis is true in the population: the average income of employed females is the same as the average income of employed males, or MEANDIFF = 0. Of course, not all sample estimates will produce a zero difference between the means of the two groups. Random fluctuations will lead some samples to overestimate the mean female income, leading $\overline{X}_m - \overline{X}_w$ to be a negative number. Other samples will underestimate the female population mean, and MEANDIFF will be a positive number. Similar fluctuations will occur in sample estimates for the mean of the second group, men.

In short, although MEANDIFF has a constant value in the population, it will take on a number of different values (it will act as a variable) over repeated samplings from the population. Because it is calculated from two means, the variable MEANDIFF will have a sampling distribution just like the mean of any variable—a distribution centered on the population value (zero, according to the null hypothesis) but having a dispersion of possible sample results above and below this value. If we can identify this sampling distribution, we can use the probability formulas already learned to assess whether our particular sample result, a nearly 3-point difference between male and female incomes, could have been produced by sampling error alone.

We learned earlier how to identify sampling distributions for the means of variables, but how do we identify a sampling distribution for the theoretical variable MEANDIFF? Recall that a sample mean can be considered a variable with its own distribution, a sampling distribution over an infinite number of samples. From the sample information we can identify the sampling distributions for $\overline{X}_m$ and $\overline{X}_w$. Since we can determine how much these sample means might fluctuate around the population value, it is also possible to determine how much the difference between the means might fluctuate—a sampling distribution for the variable MEANDIFF. The mechanics of this process are described more fully later in this chapter. For now, the reader merely needs to recognize that it can be done.

The above description covers the logic of the T-TEST procedure: creating a variable representing the difference between the means of any two groups and then evaluating the probability that this difference is zero (the null hypothesis) in the population. To clarify the strategy, we now turn to the details of the T-TEST procedure, looking first at the command format and then turning to the output produced.

Command Format

The format of the T-TEST command is shown in Figure 11.2. The obvious beginning is the command word **T-TEST**, telling SPSS what procedure to perform. The command can be written either with or without a hyphen, as T-TEST or TTEST. You cannot, however, write the command with a space in the middle (T TEST), for SPSS will not recognize it.

The second item in the command is the keyword **GROUPS**, followed by an equals sign and the name of the **grouping variable**. The T-TEST procedure compares the means of two groups, and SPSS needs to know what these groups are. Providing this information requires two things: the name of the variable containing the grouping information (the independent variable) and the values of that variable identifying the two groups to be compared. Thus, the full specification of the second term is **GROUPS = SEX (1, 2)**; on the variable SEX,

```
001    GET FILE = GSS88
002    SELECT IF (WRKSTAT LE 2)
003    T-TEST    GROUPS = SEX (1,2)    /    VARIABLES = RINCOME
```

Figure 11.2 Command format of the T-TEST procedure.

respondents with code number 1 (males) are to be compared with those having code number 2 (females).

When the grouping variable has only two values, as in the case of SEX, identifying these values in parentheses is not required. Thus, the command could have been written

```
T-TEST GROUPS = SEX / VARIABLES = RINCOME
```

SPSS will recognize that the two values existing on the SEX variable constitute the two groups to be compared. It is a better practice, however, to always include the parentheses and value numbers lest you forget them sometime when they are needed.

Since the command contains the specific values of a variable which identify the groups being compared, the grouping variable does not have to be a dichotomy. For example, V85 (race) has five code numbers identifying different races: 1 for whites, 2 for blacks, 3 for American Indians, 4 for Asians, and 5 for others. Using V85 as the grouping variable, we could compare whites to blacks [GROUPS = V85 (**1, 2**)] or blacks to Asians [GROUPS = V85 (**2, 4**)] just by changing the numbers inside the parentheses. The T-TEST procedure allows for only two code numbers to be identified on the grouping variable. In its original state, we could not use V85 to compare whites with nonwhites because four code numbers are needed to cover all nonwhites (code numbers 2, 3, 4, and 5). Data massaging comes to our aid here. A white/nonwhite comparison could be performed if we first recorded V85 to combine all nonwhites into one group identified by a single code number.

After identifying the two groups, we must inform SPSS what characteristic of the groups should be compared—their average value on the dependent variable. This is done in Figure 11.2 with the / **VARIABLES = RINCOME** statement. This statement tells SPSS to determine whether the means of the two groups on RINCOME are the same or different. Since the T-TEST procedure compares means, it can be used only when the mean is a legitimate statistic, in other words only when the dependent variable is interval. The independent variable can be any type as long as it identifies, in its original or recoded form, two groups to be compared. Possibilities include comparing high- and low-income respondents (interval), strong Democrats to weak Democrats (ordinal), or Catholics to Jews (nominal).

The T-TEST command can specify more than one dependent variable. The command

```
T-TEST GROUPS = SEX (1, 2) / VARIABLES = RINCOME AGE EDUC
```

compares male and female incomes, ages, and educational levels. However, each T-TEST command can include only one grouping specification. To compare more than two groups, such as whites and blacks or whites and Asians, you must use a separate T-TEST command for each group pairing, as shown in Figure 11.3.

```
001    GET FILE = ELEC88
002    T-TEST    GROUPS = V85 (1,2)  /  VARIABLES = V82
003    T-TEST    GROUPS = V85 (1,4)  /  VARIABLES = V82
```

Figure 11.3 Repeating the T-TEST command for multiple group comparisons.

Output

The commands in Figure 11.2 will produce the output in Figure 11.4. The top part of the output is not difficult to comprehend. First, the two groups being compared are identified along with the values of the independent (grouping) variable representing each group. Second, the name of the dependent variable is given along with each group's number of cases, mean, standard deviation, and standard error on that variable. Although it is in a different format, this information is identical to what was produced with the FREQUENCIES commands in Figure 11.1, except that the means are calculated to one extra decimal place.

The bottom row of the output in Figure 11.4 is divided into three sections: an F value and probability level on the far left, a pooled-variance estimate in the middle, and a separate-variance estimate on the right. To explain the meaning of these numbers, we begin by describing how the t value is calculated; then we discuss the pooled-variance estimate, the separate-variance estimate, and finally the F value.

```
- - - - - - - - - - - - - - T  T E S T - - - - - - - - - - - - - - -

GROUP 1 - SEX        EQ          1
GROUP 2 - SEX        EQ          2


VARIABLE              NUMBER                  STANDARD   STANDARD
                      OF CASES      MEAN      DEVIATION  ERROR
-------------------------------------------------------------------

RINCOME     RESPONDENT'S INCOME

      GROUP 1    416        12.6827      4.694      0.230

      GROUP 2    402         9.8408      4.786      0.239


-------------------------------------------------------------------


                 *  POOLED VARIANCE ESTIMATE  *  SEPARATE VARIANCE ESTIMATE
                 *                             *
    F     2-TAIL *    T    DEGREES OF  2-TAIL  *    T    DEGREES OF  2-TAIL
  VALUE    PROB  *  VALUE   FREEDOM     PROB.  *  VALUE   FREEDOM     PROB.
  ------------------------------------------------------------------------
   1.04   0.693  *  8.57      816      0.000   *  8.57    813.64     0.000
  ------------------------------------------------------------------------
```

Figure 11.4 Output from the independent-groups T-TEST.

Calculating the t Value As described earlier, the T-TEST is performed by creating a new variable representing the difference between the means of the groups being compared. For convenience, we called this variable MEANDIFF, although SPSS uses it only for its internal calculations and neither gives the variable a name nor displays it on any part of the output. The null hypothesis claims that the value of MEANDIFF is zero in the population and that any value other than zero in the sample is merely the result of sampling error.

The T-TEST procedure evaluates the claim of the null hypothesis with the formula

$$\frac{D_s - D_0}{\sigma_d} = \pm\, t_{\alpha,\text{df}}$$

where D_s = difference between group means in sample
D_0 = difference between group means claimed by null hypothesis—zero for population
σ_d = standard error of sampling distribution for variable MEANDIFF
$t_{\alpha,\text{df}}$ = value of Student's t statistic produced by formula

The numerator determines the disparity between the sample result D_s and the null hypothesis D_0. This disparity is then divided by the standard error of the sampling distribution σ_d, to determine how large it is in t units.

At this point, the items in the numerator can be identified: D_s is the difference between the means in the sample, $12.6827 - 9.8405$, or 2.8419; and D_0 is zero, the claim of the null hypothesis of no difference between the means. Where, however, do we find the standard error for MEANDIFF, or σ_d? When one variable is produced by combining two others, which is true for MEANDIFF (MEANDIFF $= \overline{X}_m - \overline{X}_w$), the sampling distribution of the new variable is related to the sampling distributions of the variables used to create it.

Figure 11.5 shows hypothetical sampling distributions for female and male income means. The two distributions largely overlap since we are assuming they have the same central tendency, as claimed by the null hypothesis, and approximately the same dispersion. Remember, the two curves represent the distribution of possible means from an infinite number of samples taken from each group, an infinite number of samples of males and an infinite number of samples of females. MEANDIFF is estimated by randomly selecting one sample from each group and determining the difference between the two group means. Under the curve are pairings of male and female sample means—M_1 with W_1 through M_5 with W_5—that might occur through drawing samples at random from each group. The bottom half of Figure 11.5 then shows a resulting distribution of differences obtained when the means of a large number of male and female samples are compared; that is, it is the sampling distribution for the variable MEANDIFF.

Two important principles are illustrated in Figure 11.5. First, since the male and female means being compared are from sampling distributions where it is assumed that the null hypothesis is true ($\mu_m = \mu_w$), the distribution of MEANDIFF in Figure 11.5 also represents the *differences between sample means* that

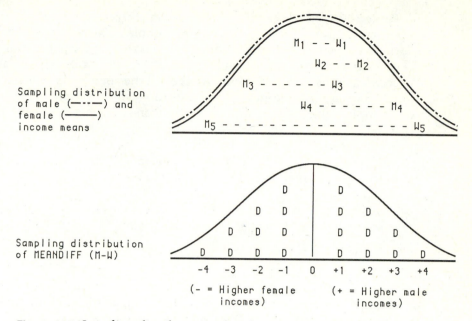

Sampling distribution of male (—·—) and female (——) income means

Sampling distribution of MEANDIFF (M-W)

(- = Higher female incomes)

(+ = Higher male incomes)

Figure 11.5 Sampling distributions of male and female incomes affecting the sampling distribution of MEANDIFF.

we are likely to encounter when the null hypothesis is true. Second, we can readily see the relationship between the sampling distribution of MEANDIFF and the sampling distributions of the two means used to create it. If the distribution of either male or female sample means (or both) becomes more widely dispersed, the sampling distribution for MEANDIFF will grow wider as well. Conversely, if either distribution were more compact, we would no longer be able to find differences as large as the $M_5 - W_5$ distance.

Since we have already learned how to estimate the sampling distribution of the mean of a variable with the central limit theorem, we should be able to also estimate the distribution of the difference between two means. In fact, the distributions of a single mean and the difference between two means have two features in common: They are both normally shaped and centered on the population value. They part company, however, in estimating the standard error of the distribution.

There are two ways of estimating σ_d from the sampling distributions of the two groups. It is not necessary for us to review both formulas in detail, but we need to examine one part of the estimation process. Recall that the dispersion of the sampling distribution of any mean is affected by the amount of variance existing on that variable in the population $\sigma_{\bar{x}} = \sigma/\sqrt{n}$, where σ is the square root of the population variance. In a similar manner, each group's population variance affects the sampling distribution for MEANDIFF. Certain assumptions about these population variances will lead us to use either the pooled-variance estimate or the separate-variance estimate part of the output.

Pooled-Variance Estimate   Variances in the population are unknown but are estimated by using the variances from samples. The best formula for calculating the standard error of the difference assumes that, in the population, the variance of each group on the dependent variable is the same. If this assumption is correct, we have two different estimates of the population variance—the sample variance around the male mean and the sample variance around the female mean. By taking what amounts to an average of these two sample values, we have a more accurate estimate of the true population variance. This gives a better estimate of the standard error of the difference σ_d, which depends on the population variance. This is what is meant by the term **pooled-variance estimate**—an estimate based on pooling the variance information from the two groups.

Let us return to that section of the printout in Figure 11.4 and see how it connects with what we have been discussing. In the formula

$$\frac{D_s - D_0}{\sigma_d} = \pm t_{\alpha,\text{df}}$$

D_s and D_0 are known from the observed sample difference and the null hypothesis, respectively. Since D_0 is zero, subtracting it from D_s leaves the sample difference of 2.8419. As discussed above, SPSS uses the sample variance to calculate σ_d in the denominator (although this value never shows up on the printout). Carrying out the division in the formula produces the t value in the pooled-variance estimate: 8.57.

How probable is it that the null hypothesis and our sample result will differ by as much as $8.57t$ units? To determine the probability of this t value, we must know the degrees of freedom used to calculate the t number. Two samples were involved in creating this t value, one of men and one of women. Each sample has $n - 1$ degrees of freedom, so the degrees of freedom when we are using both samples are $n_w - 1$ plus $n_m - 1$, or $n_w + n_m - 2$. This is the number reported in the pooled-variance estimate—816, the number of men plus the number of women minus 2.

Everything is now identified in the formula except for α, the probability level. Consulting a table of t values contained in the software, SPSS determines that the probability of a t value of 8.57 with 816 degrees of freedom is 0.000. Thus, the probability that the null hypothesis is true—that sampling error could explain why our sample results and the null hypothesis are so far apart—is .000.

Probability levels of zero, like the one in Figure 11.4, must be interpreted with care. A probability level of .000 does not mean that there is no chance at all that the null hypothesis might be true; it means that the probability that it is true is too small to be reported in only three decimal places. The actual probability may be .0000003, or .0001, or any other very small number. SPSS uses standard rounding procedures, so we do know that the fourth digit is less than 5. A probability of .000512 is rounded up to .001 when only three decimal places are reported. In hypothesis testing there is no such thing as perfect confidence that something is true or false; there is only a probability of being wrong that is so low that it can only be measured as zero to the first three decimal places.

We now have all the information needed to evaluate the null hypothesis. In comparing the sample results to the null hypothesis, the T-TEST procedure has determined that the probability of the null hypothesis being true is zero to at least three decimal places. Whatever the exact probability level is, it is below our significance-level cutoff of .05. Thus we reject the null hypothesis and accept the research hypothesis—a person's gender *is* related to his or her salary, both in the sample and in the population.

Separate-Variance Estimate   The pooled-variance estimate is the most efficient way to estimate σ_d but it requires us to assume that the variance of the dependent variable is the same for both groups being compared. Usually this assumption is quite safe. Our reasoning led us to suspect a difference in female and male income *means*, but not in their *variances* as well. There is no obvious reason why men should have a greater (or narrower) range of typical incomes than women.

Sometimes, however, the assumption of similar dependent-variable variances for each group is untenable. Say we want to evaluate, somewhat simplistically, whether Republicans had more favorable views of George Bush than non-Republicans. We naturally expect the average rating on the Bush feeling thermometer (V5) by Republicans to be higher than that of non-Republicans, leading to the following research and null hypotheses:

H_R: Republicans will have more positive evaluations of George Bush than non-Republicans.

versus

H_0:   Republicans will have the same or less positive evaluations of George Bush than non-Republicans.

A little thought, however, would also lead us to expect a difference in the variance of ratings for each group as well. Most Republicans should rate Bush only on the positive end of the feeling thermometer. Non-Republicans, which includes both Democrats and independents, should be more spread out, with a number of Democrats rating Bush negatively, while Independents may group around the moderate to positive end of the scale.

A T-TEST procedure examining the group differences confirms both suspicions (Figure 11.6). The Republicans (group 2, strong and weak Republicans combined) give George Bush a mean rating 26 points higher than that of non-Republicans (group 1, strong Democrats to Republican-leaning Independents). In addition, the Republican distribution on the Bush feeling thermometer has a standard deviation of 18.78. The non-Republicans have a 50 percent greater diversity on the dependent variable with a standard deviation of 27.26.

Supplement 11.1 **Negative t Values**

Beginners are sometimes confused by negative t values, such as those in Figure 11.6, interpreting them as being less important than their positive counterparts. This is not so. In the formula calculating the t value

$$\frac{D_s - D_0}{\sigma_d} = \pm t_{\alpha, df}$$

D_s is produced by subtracting the mean of group 2 from that of group 1 ($\overline{X}_1 - \overline{X}_2$). Which group is which is determined by the GROUPS command, such as GROUPS = RACE (3, 4), where SPSS treats the first code number in parentheses as group 1 and the second as group 2.

In Figure 11.6, group 1 contains the non-Republicans with a low rating of George Bush while group 2 is the Republicans who have a high rating of George Bush. Subtracting the high mean from the low mean produces a negative number for D_s and thus a negative t value in the above formula. If we reverse the order of the code numbers in parentheses—GROUPS = V74 **(2,1)**—the two groups will be reversed in SPSS's calculations, producing positive D_s and t values. The difference between them is just as large, but with a different sign.

Think of this process as people guessing the number of marbles in a jar. Person A guesses 150 marbles, and person B says 200 marbles. If the actual number of marbles is 175, person A's guess is represented by a score of -25 and person B's guess by a $+25$. Each guess was just as accurate (or inaccurate) as the other. The plus and minus signs only show the direction of the error—whether the guess was an over- or underestimate.

When we cannot assume that the variances of the two groups are equal, it is necessary to use the **separate-variance estimate** on the bottom right of the printout. This section contains the same information as that in the pooled-variance estimate: a t value, degrees of freedom, and a two-tailed probability level. The numbers, however, will be a little bit different because SPSS uses a different formula for calculating σ_d, one based on estimating σ_d when each group has a different variance in the population. In addition, the degrees of freedom available for estimating σ_d will also be different. The separate-variance estimate is less efficient than the pooled-variance estimate, but when we cannot assume that the population variances are equal, the separate-variance estimate is more accurate.

The F Value   In most cases the pooled- and separate-variance estimates will be quite close and lead to the same decision regarding the null hypothesis. Nonetheless, in a few situations the probability levels differ enough that one estimate will lead to rejecting the null hypothesis and the other will lead to accepting it. How do we know for sure which estimate to use? The T-TEST

```
RECODE  V74  (O  THRU  4=1)(5,6=2)
T-TEST  GROUPS=V74  (1,2)  /  VARIABLES  =  V5


- - - - - - - - - - - - - - - T  T E S T- - - - - - - - - - - - - - - - -

GROUP  1  -  V74        EQ            1
GROUP  2  -  V74        EQ            2
```

VARIABLE	NUMBER OF CASES	MEAN	STANDARD DEVIATION	STANDARD ERROR
V5	FEELING THERMOMETER - BUSH			
GROUP 1	1397	53.3321	27.256	0.729
GROUP 2	550	79.4309	18.780	0.801

		*	POOLED VARIANCE ESTIMATE			*	SEPARATE VARIANCE ESTIMATE		
F VALUE	2-TAIL PROB	*	T VALUE	DEGREES OF FREEDOM	2-TAIL PROB.	*	T VALUE	DEGREES OF FREEDOM	2-TAIL PROB.
2.11	0.000	*	-20.61	1945	0.000	*	-24.10	1446.02	0.000

Figure 11.6 Republican and non-Republican feelings toward George Bush.

Supplement 11.2

Testing Directional Hypotheses

The T-TEST procedure is designed to test nondirectional hypotheses. Our hypothesis about Republican and non-Republican attitudes toward Bush, however, is directional—we expect Republicans to differ from non-Republicans in a specific (more favorable) direction. The T-TEST procedure can be used with directional hypotheses with just a little bit of extra effort.

No measure of association is calculated with the T-TEST procedure, but since the independent variable contains only two groups, one is not really needed. We only have to look at the top of the output in Figure 11.6 to confirm that the mean Bush rating by Republicans (79.43) is indeed higher than the mean Bush rating by non-Republicans (53.33), consistent with the direction stated in the research hypothesis.

A directional hypothesis also requires a one-tailed test of statistical significance. The T-TEST procedure reports only two-tailed probability levels, but the one-tailed probability level is, in this case, merely the two-tailed figure divided by 2. Since the probability levels in Figure 11.6 are already 0.000, this does not change anything. It would have made a difference if the reported probability level were something like .08, leading us to accept the null hypothesis for a two-tailed test while rejecting it for a one-tailed test (.08 / 2 = .04).

printout provides a helping hand in making this decision. We never know for sure what the population variances are for each group. We do, however, have estimates of them, the sample variances for each group. Are these sample variances similar enough that we can call them equal, or are they so different that we feel compelled to conclude that the population variances are unequal?

To the left of the pooled-variance estimate is an **F test** which examines this very question. The *t* statistic is used to compare means, differences, and similar statistics. The *F* test is used to compare variances. In particular, this test takes the variance of the dependent variable for each group and divides the larger variance by the smaller one. This ratio is the *F* value (2.11) shown in Figure 11.6—the larger variance in this comparison is more than 2 times bigger than the smaller variance. Using an *F* table, similar to a *t* table, SPSS determines the probability of finding this large a difference in sample variances when both population variances are equal (a ratio of 1.0 in the population). This probability is reported in Figure 11.6 to be .000, or almost no chance that the two sample groups came from populations with equal variances. This provides confirmation of our earlier hunch that the separate-variance estimate should be used to compare Republicans with non-Republicans.

Supplement 11.3

Calculating the *F* Value

The *F* value is a ratio of two variances, but the printouts in Figures 11.4 and 11.6 do not show group variances. Still, it is easy to compute the *F* values if we remember that the standard deviation is just the square root of the variance. To turn it around, squaring the standard deviation, which is provided for each group on the printout, will give us each group's variance.

Once we have obtained the needed variances, the *F* value is calculated by dividing the larger of the two variances by the smaller one. Mathematically, the formula is

$$F \text{ value} = \frac{\text{larger variance}}{\text{smaller variance}}$$

Following this formula, you should be able to produce the same numbers as SPSS: 1.04 in Figure 11.4 and 2.11 in Figure 11.6. The probability level associated with each *F* value can be determined by consulting an *F* table. For those interested, a sample *F* table is included in Chapter 12.

In contrast, the *F* value in Figure 11.4 was far smaller at 1.04—the larger variance was only 4 percent greater than the smaller one. The associated probability level showed a 69 percent chance that this difference between the two sample variances was merely sampling error—a .69 probability that the two samples came from populations with equal variances.

In determining which variance estimate to use, do two things. First, do the pooled- and separate-variance estimates lead to different decisions? If not (if both have probability levels above .05 or below .05), it does not matter which you use since your decision regarding the null hypothesis will be the same. Second, if the two estimates do produce different decisions (one probability level is above .05 and the other below it), consult the *F* value and its probability. If the *F* value's probability level is above .05 (there is greater than a 5 percent chance that the two variances are equal in the population), use the pooled-variance estimate. If the *F* value's probability level is below .05, use the separate-variance estimate.

You now have the information needed to test hypotheses related to the means of two independent groups. Using the *F* value, determine whether the pooled- or separate-variance estimate should be used. For the appropriate estimate, find the probability level associated with the null hypothesis, and then make your decision whether to accept or reject it.

This version of the T-TEST procedure, comparing the means of two **independent groups**, is the one most commonly used. The groups are termed *independent* because the composition of one group has no effect on the composition of the other; each is a separate random sample. The women randomly selected to be in one sample do not affect which men are selected for the other. Next we examine a less common form of the T-TEST procedure that compares dependent groups.

DEPENDENT MEANS—THE PAIRED T-TEST

In some research situations, it is necessary to compare two means that are dependent. Means are dependent when the selection of cases for one group is related to (depends upon) the selection of cases for the other group. **Dependent groups** are best explained through some examples.

One way that dependent groups can occur is when data are collected at two different times from the same people, as in a classic scientific experiment. Say we want to determine whether viewing campaign commercials affected people's perceptions of the candidates. A group of subjects is selected randomly and provides, through a questionnaire, their perceptions of candidate X. These subjects then watch some of candidate *X*'s campaign commercials, after which we again assess their perceptions of the candidate to see whether they have changed. We are still comparing two means—the mean perception before to the mean perception after viewing the commercials—but the means are from dependent rather than independent groups. Having randomly selected the group whose perceptions are evaluated before viewing the commercials, we do not then randomly select a second group to assess after-viewing perceptions; the first and second groups are the same people, just at different times.

Another example involving dependent groups might be to compare the respondent's party identification with that of her or his spouse. Once the respondents have been randomly selected, the sample of spouses is fixed. We are not free to choose any subjects at random simply because they are somebody's spouse; instead we must select the particular people who are spouses of the respondents. A comparison of dependent groups is also called a **paired sample** or a **correlated sample** comparison. Each respondent in one group has a pair, or corresponding subject, in the second group. The second subject in the pair may be the same person, as in a before-and-after comparison, or may be a different person who is somehow matched with a respondent in the first sample.

The difference between a comparison of independent and dependent groups is illustrated in Figure 11.7. An independent-groups comparison (the top half of Figure 11.7) splits the *cases* in the sample into two groups and compares the mean of each group on the *same variable*. In a dependent-means T-TEST procedure, each case constitutes a single pair, with each member of the pair being represented by a *different variable*. The two variables might be before and after candidate ratings or, as in Figure 11.7, the educational levels of the respondent and the spouse. A comparison of dependent groups involves assumptions and statistical procedures which are quite different from those used in an

- - - - - Independent means - - - - -

	Case	Gender	Respondent's income
Males	1	1	15
	2	1	9
	3	1	12
	4	1	13
	5	1	12

$\overline{X}$ = 12.2

	Case	Gender	Respondent's income
Females	6	2	4
	7	2	11
	8	2	6
	9	2	14
	10	2	7

$\overline{X}$ = 8.4

- - - - - Dependent Means - - - - -

Case	Respondent's education	Spouse's education
1	12	14
2	9	6
3	18	18
4	12	11
5	12	12
6	8	9
7	18	8
9	15	13
10	11	12

$\overline{X}$ = 11.5 $\overline{X}$ = 10.3

Figure 11.7 Logic of independent- and dependent-group comparisons.

independent-groups comparison. These differences can be illustrated by working through the procedure's command format and output.

Command Format

The **paired T-TEST** will seldom be used on the data sets distributed with this text, for neither contains many pairs. However, there are some. The ELEC88 data set has variables representing the same information on the respondent and the two presidential candidates, such as each one's degree of liberalism. The GSS88 study contains some information on both the respondent and the respondent's spouse, another pairing of individuals. By using the latter study, a possible hypothesis involving a paired comparison might be

H_R: Husbands attend church less frequently than their wives.

versus

H_0: Husbands attend church as frequently as or more frequently than their wives.

Before beginning the test, we must have operational variables representing the concepts in the research hypothesis. The two variables available in the data set, ATTEND and SPATTEND, deal with respondents (male or female) and spouses, not husbands and wives. Using IF commands (Figure 11.8), we can create operational variables matching the concepts. The frequency of the husband's attendance, HATTEND, is equal to ATTEND when the respondent is male and SPATTEND when the respondent is female. The frequency of the wife's church attendance, WATTEND, can be identified in the same way.

Following the statements creating the new variables is the T-TEST command. Note there is no GROUPS term. The GROUPS designation is required only for the regular T-TEST procedure, where SPSS must be instructed how to divide the sample into two groups. Instead, the paired T-TEST contains the term **PAIRS =** followed by the names of the **paired variables** containing the same information (e.g., income, education, or church attendance) for each member of the pair. Naming the paired variables is all that is needed for the paired T-TEST procedure. The two variables identify the groups being compared in the independent-variable part of the hypothesis, one variable for husbands and another for wives, while the values of the variables are the dependent-variable part of the hypothesis, each group's frequency of church attendance.

```
GET FILE = GSS88

IF SEX EQ 1 HATTEND = ATTEND
IF SEX EQ 1 WATTEND = SPATTEND
IF SEX EQ 2 WATTEND = ATTEND
IF SEX EQ 2 HATTEND = SPATTEND

T-TEST PAIRS = HATTEND WATTEND
```

Figure 11.8 Command format for a paired T-TEST.

Usually, only a single matched pair is examined, but the paired T-TEST command allows for other matchings as well. Suppose we have three variables representing matched persons, such as the level of education for the respondent, the respondent's mother, and the respondent's daughter. All three variables could be listed on the same command:

T-TEST PAIRS = RESP MOTHER DAUGHTER

This command produces three comparisons (and three different tables on the output): first between the respondent and her or his mother, a second between the respondent and the daughter, and a third between the respondent's mother and daughter. Instead of having SPSS examine all possible comparisons, you can have only certain comparisons made by using the **WITH keyword**. The command

T-TEST PAIRS = RESP **WITH** MOTHER DAUGHTER

compares the variable(s) on one side of the WITH statement with the paired members represented by the variables on the other side, in this case the respondent compared to the mother and the respondent compared with the daughter. You may include as many variables as needed on each side of the WITH statement. The WITH term is used to avoid unwanted comparisons, such as the mother and daughter, when more than two variables are included on the T-TEST command.

You may also wish to draw a number of different paired comparisons, such as comparing wives and husbands in terms of their church attendance, education, and income. Putting all these variables in a single T-TEST command, such as

T-TEST PAIRS = HATTEND HINCM HEDUC **WITH** WATTEND WINCM WEDUC

leads to a number of unwanted, and some quite silly, comparisons. There is little point, for example, in comparing the mean difference between the husband's level of church attendance and the wife's income. To make a number of different paired comparisons, you can use a separate command for each: one to compare incomes, a second for the education comparison, and a third for any difference in church attendance. An alternative is to use a single T-TEST command but to separate each comparison with a slash. An example of this approach is the command

T-TEST PAIRS = HATTEND WATTEND / HEDUC WEDUC / RESP **WITH** MOTHER DAUGHTER

The slash is a convenience—it allows us to avoid retyping the T-TEST command for each comparison.

Command Output

Figure 11.9 shows the output from the paired T-TEST command. The top of the output describes each variable separately—its *n*, mean, standard deviation, and standard error. The *n* for each variable is the same since we are dealing with

```
- - - - - - - - - - - - - - - -T  TEST- - - - - - - - - - - - - -

VARIABLE         NUMBER                  STANDARD   STANDARD
                 OF CASES      MEAN      DEVIATION  ERROR
-----------------------------------------------------------------
HATTEND
                   784        3.8087       2.767     0.099

                   784        4.4962       2.652     0.095
WATTEND
-----------------------------------------------------------------


(DIFFERENCE) STANDARD   STANDARD  *            2-TAIL  *   T   DEGREES OF  2-TAIL
    MEAN     DEVIATION  ERROR     *  CORR.  PROB.   *  VALUE  FREEDOM    PROB.
-----------------------------------------------------------------
-0.6875       1.988     0.071     *  0.732  0.000   * -9.68    783      0.000
-----------------------------------------------------------------
```

Figure 11.9 Output from a paired T-TEST.

matched pairs. Any case with missing data on either member of the pair (no answer on the attendance variable or no spouse) is deleted from the analysis.

In testing for differences between matched pairs, the paired T-TEST uses a different strategy from an independent-groups T-TEST. The independent-groups T-TEST procedure divided the data set into two separate samples. Since there was no way to match members of one sample with members of the other, the only comparison made was between the means of the two samples. With a paired comparison, however, we can examine directly the difference between the two members of the pair. As shown in Figure 11.10, a new variable is created to represent this difference. We are thus dealing with not two samples, but one sample of pairs and a new variable that is the difference between the two members of the pair—the difference between before and after evaluations of a candidate or between a husband's and a wife's frequency of church attendance.

```
             Husband's         Wife's
             attendance        attendance
             frequency         frequency          Difference:
 Case         HATTEND           WATTEND        HATTEND  -  WATTEND

   1             0                 1                -1
   2             8                 8                 0
   3             8                 1                 7
   4             4                 6                -2
   5             7                 2                 5
   6             0                 0                 0
   7             5                 6                -1
   9             5                 3                 2
  10             1                 2                -1
                                                 ‾‾‾‾‾
                                                 X̄    = 0.9
```

Figure 11.10 Assessing the difference between matched pairs.

Although SPSS does not display its calculation of this new variable (only its results), we can create it ourselves with a COMPUTE statement. The command

```
COMPUTE DIFF = HATTEND - WATTEND
```

creates a new variable, called DIFF, which is the difference between the husband's frequency of church attendance and that of his wife. If the wife attends church more often, this calculation will produce a negative number. If the husband is a more frequent church attender, the result of the COMPUTE command will be a positive number. A zero will be computed if the husband and wife attend with equal frequency.

A FREQUENCIES procedure on the DIFF variable just created (Figure 11.11) shows that it ranges from a low of -8 to a high of $+7$. The mean is $-.688$, or a tendency for wives to attend somewhat more frequently than husbands. If you compare the numbers on the bottom left of the T-TEST printout in Figure 11.9 to the summary statistics in Figure 11.11, you will find that they are the same: a mean difference of $-.6875$ (rounded to $-.688$ in Figure 11.11), a standard deviation of 1.988, and a standard error of .071.

The next step is to determine whether the mean difference found between husbands and wives in our sample is statistically significant. We do this by determining how many standard-error (t) units apart the null hypothesis and the sample results are. The formula is the same as before:

$$\frac{\mathrm{DIFF}_s - \mathrm{DIFF}_0}{\sigma_{\mathrm{DIFF}}} = t_{\alpha,\mathrm{df}}$$

where DIFF_s = sample average (mean) of DIFF variable, $-.688$
           DIFF_0 = claim of null hypothesis about population mean difference, DIFF = 0
           σ_{DIFF} = standard error for sampling distribution of difference, standard error of variable DIFF, .071

Substituting these numbers into the formula

$$\frac{-.688 - 0}{.071} = -9.69_{\alpha,\mathrm{df}}$$

produces a t value of -9.69, where the minus sign means only that the sample result is below the null-hypothesis value instead of above it. In calculating this t value, we used only one sample, a sample of pairs, instead of the two samples used by the independent-groups T-TEST procedure. Consequently, our df is $n - 1$ (instead of $n_1 + n_2 - 2$), or 783.

The remaining unknown in the formula is α, the probability of this large a disparity between the null hypothesis and the sample results—a disparity of $9.69t$ units—when the sample contains 784 cases (783 degrees of freedom). If we had a t table available, we could find this probability ourselves. Happily, this is unnecessary, for SPSS provides the information on the bottom right of the output in Figure 11.9. This part of the output lists a t value of -9.68, differing slightly from the -9.69 calculated above because we used numbers rounded to three decimal places while the computer's internal calculations are substan-

```
GET FILE = GSS88
IF SEX EQ 1 HATTEND = ATTEND
IF SEX EQ 1 WATTEND = SPATTEND
IF SEX EQ 2 WATTEND = ATTEND
IF SEX EQ 2 HATTEND = SPATTEND
COMPUTE DIFF = HATTEND - WATTEND
FREQUENCIES VARIABLES = DIFF
```

DIFF

VALUE LABEL	VALUE	FREQUENCY	PERCENT	VALID PERCENT	CUM PERCENT
	-8.00	8	0.5	1.0	1.0
	-7.00	13	0.9	1.7	2.7
	-6.00	7	0.5	0.9	3.6
	-5.00	25	1.7	3.2	6.8
	-4.00	23	1.6	2.9	9.7
	-3.00	44	3.0	5.6	15.3
	-2.00	32	2.2	4.1	19.4
	-1.00	60	4.1	7.7	27.0
	0.00	518	35.0	66.1	93.1
	1.00	25	1.7	3.2	96.3
	2.00	7	0.5	0.9	97.2
	3.00	12	0.8	1.5	98.7
	4.00	2	0.1	0.3	99.0
	5.00	3	0.2	0.4	99.4
	6.00	2	0.1	0.3	99.6
	7.00	3	0.2	0.4	100.0
	.	697	47.1	MISSING	
	TOTAL	1481	100.0	100.0	

MEAN	-0.688	STD ERR	0.071	MEDIAN	0.000
MODE	0.000	STD DEV	1.988	VARIANCE	3.952
KURTOSIS	3.856	S E KURT	0.174	SKEWNESS	-1.167
S E SKEW	0.087	RANGE	15.000	MINIMUM	-8.000
MAXIMUM	7.000	SUM	-539.000		

VALID CASES   784   MISSING CASES   697

Figure 11.11 A FREQUENCIES of the computed variable DIFF.

tially more precise. The output shows 783 degrees of freedom for the t value, just as in our calculations. Finally, the probability level associated with this t is reported as .000, considerably below our .05 decision criterion. We reject the claim of the null hypothesis of no difference between husbands and wives.

From the left and right parts of the printout, we find the mean difference between the groups and the test of whether that difference is zero in the population. The middle section of the output is the Pearson correlation between the variables HATTEND and WATTEND, along with the correlation's statistical significance. For the present, this correlation is not relevant to our hypothesis testing and can be ignored. The Pearson correlation statistic is reviewed in later chapters.

SUMMARY

We have seen two ways to use the T-TEST command to test a null hypothesis, one approach for independent groups and the other for dependent groups. No subcommands have been discussed with either strategy because they are not needed. There are no additional statistics that can be requested, and the subcommands controlling the procedure's performance and output are so seldom used that they need not concern us.

Remember that the T-TEST procedure can be used for one type of hypothesis only—a hypothesis in which two groups on the independent variable are being compared on an interval-level dependent variable. This is a limited set of circumstances. The independent variables in many hypotheses refer to more than two groups, and many dependent variables are not interval. In the next chapters we examine other techniques for testing the null hypothesis, techniques applicable to hypotheses that the T-TEST procedure cannot be used for.

REVIEW

Key Terms

T-TEST	Paired sample
GROUPS	Correlated sample
Grouping variable	Paired T-TEST
Pooled-variance estimate	PAIRS
Separate-variance estimate	Paired variables
F test	WITH keyword
Independent groups	VARIABLES
Dependent groups	

Exercise

11.1 Correct any errors in the commands.
   a. T-TEST VARIABLES = HAPPY
   b. TTEST GROUPS = SEX (1, 2) / VARIABLES = RINCOME
   c. T-TEST DRUNK (1, 2) / HAPPY RINCOME
   d. T-TEST GROUPS = DRUNK (1, 2, 3) / VARIABLES = HAPPY RINCOME
   e. TTEST GROUPS = SEX (1, 2) / VARIABLES = EDUC RINCOME
   f. T-TEST PAIRS = EDUC SPEDUC / RELIG SPREL
   g. TTEST PAIRS = V19 WITH V20, V21
   h. T-TEST GROUPS = V77 (2, 4)
   i. TTEST PAIRS = V19 (2, 3)
   j. T-TEST GROUPS RACE (1, 2)
   k. TTEST GROUPS = RACE / VARIABLES = HAPPY
   l. T-TEST GROUPS = V87 (1, 2) / VARIABLES = V6 V27 V33

 m. T-TEST PAIRS = V60 V61 / VARIABLES = V6
 n. T TEST GROUPS = SEX (1, 2) / VARIABLES = RINCOME
 o. T TEST PAIRS = V60 V61

11.2 Below are some hypotheses. Determine whether each hypothesis can or cannot be tested with the T-TEST procedure.
 a. Blacks earn lower incomes than whites.
 b. A person's level of education is related to her or his income.
 c. A person's race is related to his or her party identification.
 d. Catholics are more politically conservative than Protestants.
 e. Women favor less spending on defense than men.
 f. A person's marital status affects how often he or she attends church.
 g. Respondents with a college degree will have more favorable attitudes toward science than those without a college degree.
 h. The Republican party is perceived as more conservative than the Democratic party.
 i. In the 1988 presidential election, people perceived Dukakis as more honest than Bush.
 j. In the 1988 presidential election, people perceived Bush as a stronger leader than Dukakis.
 k. Race is related to voting.
 l. More frequent church attendance is related to greater opposition to abortion.
 m. Democrats are more liberal than Republicans.

SUGGESTED READINGS

Levin, Jack and James Alan Fox. *Elementary Statistics in Social Research*, 4th ed. (New York: Harper & Row, 1988) Chapter 10.

May, Richard B., Michael E. J. Masson, and Michael A. Hunter. *Application of Statistics in Behavioral Research* (New York: Harper & Row, 1990) Chapter 11.

Norusis, Marija J., and SPSS Inc. *SPSS/PC+ V2.0 Base Manual* (Chicago: SPSS Inc., 1988) Chapter 11.

SPSS Inc. *SPSS Reference Guide* (Release 4) (Chicago: SPSS Inc., 1990) pages 701–03.

SPSS Inc. *SPSS-X User's Guide*, 3rd ed. (Chicago: SPSS Inc., 1988) Chapter 49.

12

Analysis of Variance (ONEWAY)

Figure 12.1 is a histogram of the Dukakis feeling thermometer (V6). The average evaluation of Dukakis is slightly positive, a mean of 56.76, but many respondents rated him far higher than average, 85 or above, while a sizable number also rated him quite poorly, at 15 or below. Our research question is, Why are respondent evaluations of Dukakis so different?

Numerous possible answers to the research question spring to mind. The respondent's party identification or political ideology may affect the ratings of the candidates, as might respondent views on more specific issues such as defense spending or the environment. Let us focus on just one possibility, each respondent's position on abortion policy. Candidates Bush and Dukakis took very different stands on abortion in the 1988 presidential campaign, and it is thus plausible that how voters felt about this issue affected their ratings of the candidates. This leads to the hypothesis

H_R: Abortion attitudes affect evaluations of Dukakis.

versus

H_0: Abortion attitudes do not affect evaluations of Dukakis.

Our measure of abortion attitudes (V62) divides the respondents into four

```
FREQUENCIES VARIABLES=V6 / STATISTICS ALL / HISTOGRAM
       /FORMAT NOTABLE


V6              FEELING THERMOMETER - DUKAKIS

COUNT MIDPOINT   ONE SYMBOL EQUALS APPROXIMATELY 10.00 OCCURRENCES

    131      0   *************
      2      5
      2     10
     91     15   *********
      9     20   *
      5     25   *
    118     30   ************
      2     35
    172     40   *****************
      0     45
    414     50   *******************************************
     11     55   *
    237     60   ************************
     12     65   *
    231     70   ***********************
     26     75   ***
     30     80   ***
    255     85   **************************
     26     90   ***
      8     95   *
    170    100   *****************
                 I....+....I....+....I....+....I....+....I....+....I
                 0        100      200      300      400      500
                        HISTOGRAM FREQUENCY


MEAN          56.762    STD ERR       0.604    MEDIAN       60.000
MODE          50.000    STD DEV      26.699    VARIANCE    712.848
KURTOSIS      -0.393    S E KURT      0.111    SKEWNESS     -0.348
S E SKEW       0.055    RANGE       100.000    MINIMUM       0.000
MAXIMUM      100.000    SUM     110799.000

VALID CASES    1952       MISSING CASES      88
```

Figure 12.1 Histogram of the Dukakis feeling thermometer.

groups: those who believe that abortion should never be allowed; those who would allow it only in cases of rape or incest or to save the mother's life; those who would allow it for additional reasons as long as there was some justification; and those who would allow it whenever the woman wanted it. We are thus faced with comparing the means of four groups, the mean evaluation of Dukakis for each group of respondents with a different abortion policy preference. A statistical technique that can compare more than two group means is the analysis of variance, also referred to by the acronym **ANOVA**. Like the T-TEST procedure, an analysis of variance allows the independent variable identifying the groups to be any type, but to compare means, the dependent variable must be interval. Since the feeling thermometers are interval variables, an analysis of variance can be used to test this research hypothesis.

Table 12.1 AN EXPERIMENTAL TEST OF THE EFFECT OF THREE DRUGS ON PREVENTING THE COMMON COLD

Stimulus	Group	Response
Drug *A*	1	Average number of colds
Drug *B*	2	Average number of colds
Drug *C*	3	Average number of colds
Placebo	4	Average number of colds

Comparing multiple means is common when the data are gathered through the experimental method. Say we are interested in whether any of three drugs helps prevent the common cold. An experimental study might look like Table 12.1. Subjects are randomly selected for four different treatment groups: one group to receive drug *A*, a second group to receive drug *B*, a third group to receive drug *C*, and a control group to receive a placebo. Our interest lies in any response difference between the groups—do they still suffer from the same average (mean) number of colds, or do one or more groups differ from the others in their frequency of colds?

Although comparing multiple group means is most common in experimental studies, it is done with survey data as well, such as testing the relationship between abortion attitudes and candidate evaluations. The research hypothesis is equivalent to claiming that if the sample is divided into groups based on abortion attitudes, the average evaluation of Dukakis will differ across the groups. This logic, illustrated in Table 12.2, is the same as the comparison of experimental and control groups in Table 12.1. Expressed mathematically, the null hypothesis is

H_0:   For all groups, $\mu_i = \mu_j$.

Here subscripts i and j are symbols for different groups. Stated in words, the population mean evaluation of Dukakis is the same for all groups regardless of their abortion attitude. Conversely, the research hypothesis is written mathematically as

H_R: For some group. $\mu_i \neq \mu_j$.

Table 12.2 RELATIONSHIP BETWEEN ABORTION ATTITUDES AND FEELINGS TOWARD DUKAKIS

Independent variable (V62)	Response code	Dependent variable (V6)
No abortions ever	1	Mean evaluation of Dukakis
Abortions for rape, incest, or to save mother's life	2	Mean evaluation of Dukakis
Abortion if a good reason	3	Mean evaluation of Dukakis
Abortion is woman's choice	4	Mean evaluation of Dukakis

This says that at least one (and maybe more) of the abortion attitude groups has a mean evaluation of Dukakis different from the others.

Figure 12.2 is a preliminary evaluation of the hypothesis, separating each group with a SELECT IF statement and determining its mean. There are some differences between the means which range from a low of 54.8 to a high of 58.3. As always, we are faced with the question of what inferences can be drawn from these sample results to the subject of our interest, the population. To draw conclusions about the μ's, the population ratings of Dukakis for each abortion group, we must determine whether the differences between the sample means, the $\overline{X}$'s in Figure 12.2, are statistically significant or possibly due to sampling error.

Using the T-TEST procedure to answer this question would be both clumsy

```
TEMPORARY
SELECT IF V62 EQ 1
FREQUENCIES VARIABLES = V6 / STATISTICS MEAN / FORMAT NOTABLE


V6             FEELING THERMOMETER - DUKAKIS

MEAN           54.808    VALID CASES    234      MISSING CASES    19




TEMPORARY
SELECT IF V62 EQ 2
FREQUENCIES VARIABLES = V6 / STATISTICS MEAN / FORMAT NOTABLE


V6             FEELING THERMOMETER - DUKAKIS

MEAN           55.459    VALID CASES    632      MISSING CASES    30




TEMPORARY
SELECT IF V62 EQ 3
FREQUENCIES VARIABLES = V6 / STATISTICS MEAN / FORMAT NOTABLE


V6             FEELING THERMOMETER - DUKAKIS

MEAN           58.331    VALID CASES    359      MISSING CASES    11




TEMPORARY
SELECT IF V62 EQ 4
FREQUENCIES VARIABLES = V6 / STATISTICS MEAN / FORMAT NOTABLE


V6             FEELING THERMOMETER - DUKAKIS

MEAN           57.620    VALID CASES    694      MISSING CASES    17
```

Figure 12.2 Mean evaluation of Dukakis by respondent attitudes toward abortion.

and inaccurate, for it can compare only two groups at a time. The research hypothesis claims that at least one group mean is different from the others, but it does not specify any particular group. If a T-TEST procedure found no significant difference between the means of groups 1 and 2 (no abortion ever versus abortion only in cases of rape, incest, or to save the mother's life), this would not be enough information to draw any conclusions about the research or null hypotheses. We would still need to compare group 1 to group 3, group 1 to group 4, group 2 to group 3, group 2 to group 4, and group 3 to group 4. The comparisons required are illustrated in Figure 12.3.

Of course, not all hypotheses will contain independent variables with only four response categories. Some will have fewer and others more. As also shown in Figure 12.3, each additional group on the independent variable adds considerably to the number of comparisons required. Using an independent variable with five categories nearly doubles the number of comparisons needed, from 6 to 10.

To make a large number of comparisons is statistically troublesome, for the probability of error increases exponentially as the number of groups increases. Each T-TEST procedure is performed with a .05 significance level, or a 5 percent chance of error, and six T-TEST comparisons need to be made for the four abortion attitude groups. Using the multiplication rule to determine the probability of making a correct decision about the null hypothesis over *all six* T-TEST procedures (.95 ∗ .95 ∗ .95 ∗ .95 ∗ .95 ∗ .95, or $.95^6$) produces a probability of .735, about a 26 percent chance of drawing an incorrect conclusion about the null hypothesis from at least one of the comparisons. Adding one extra category to the independent variables decreases the probability of making correct decisions over all comparisons to $.95^{10}$, or .599. The multiple T-TEST procedures will not provide a test for any difference between the groups with only a .05 possibility of error. For this reason we must use an entirely different statistical technique, the analysis of variance, for comparing multiple groups.

RELATIONSHIPS AND VARIANCE

Both the research and null hypotheses make claims about the means of groups, a comparison of central tendencies. Why, then, use a technique that analyzes variance, a measure of dispersion? The two are connected, although the connec-

	Group 1	Group 2	Group 3	Group 4
Group 2	X			
Group 3	X	X		
Group 4	X	X	X	
Group 5	X	X	X	X

Figure 12.3 Number of T-TEST comparisons required as the number of groups increases.

tion is not obvious. The hypothesized relationship can be seen as claiming that the independent variable contributes to the amount of variance possessed by the dependent variable. That is, we suspect that the respondents' differences in rating Dukakis stem, at least in part, from the different attitudes they have about abortion. If correct, those who believe abortion should never be allowed (group 1 in Figure 12.4) may be at the low end of the distribution of Dukakis ratings. Those who share Dukakis's perspective (group 4, abortion is the woman's choice) might be at the high end of this distribution while those with middle positions on abortion, group 2 and 3, may have middle values on the Dukakis feeling thermometer.

If the research hypothesis is correct, not only will each abortion group have a different mean evaluation of Dukakis, but also the members of each group will have less variation in their responses. Each group's shared abortion attitude will lead to greater similarity—that is, less dispersion—in its candidate ratings. It is the blending of these groups, together, pro-choice and pro-life combined, which leads to the amount of variation existing in Dukakis evaluations for the entire sample.

In contrast, the null hypothesis claims that each group on the independent variable has the same mean on the dependent variable. In addition, if abortion attitudes do not lead to similar evaluations of the candidates, each group will be just as likely to contain respondents who evaluate Dukakis both poorly and well. Consequently, each abortion subgroup will have just as much variance in its evaluations as is true of the combined sample. This expectation is illustrated in Figure 12.5.

Following this logic, the analysis-of-variance technique tests the null hypothesis by determining whether dividing respondents based on their responses to the independent variable does or does not help explain some of the dependent variable's variance. To describe how this logic is implemented statistically, we

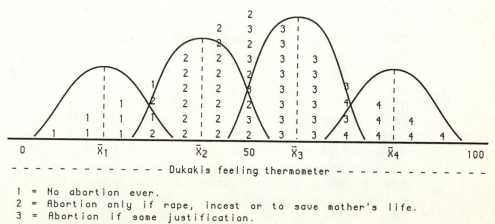

1 = No abortion ever.
2 = Abortion only if rape, incest or to save mother's life.
3 = Abortion if some justification.
4 = Abortion is woman's choice.

Figure 12.4 Separate means and variances in evaluations of Michael Dukakis for each abortion attitude group.

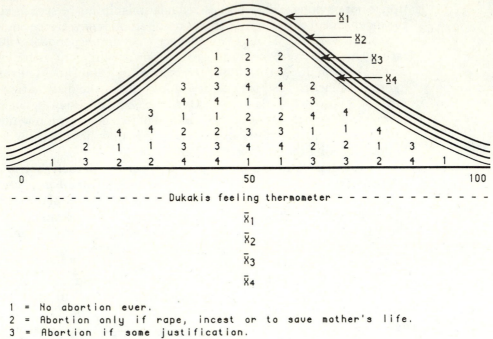

1 = No abortion ever.
2 = Abortion only if rape, incest or to save mother's life.
3 = Abortion if some justification.
4 = Abortion is woman's choice.

Figure 12.5 Similar means and variances in evaluations of Michael Dukakis for each abortion attitude group.

examine three topics: variance as a measure of error, partitioning variance, and the testing of hypotheses with an ANOVA table.

Variance as Error

The variance statistic measures the amount of dispersion in a variable's distribution, but it can also be thought of as a measure of **error**. Populations are described by their central tendency on a variable; the average person in the United States is 36 years old or earns $25,000 per year. A variable's variance (or its square root, the standard deviation) is an indicator of how well the central tendency portrays a typical member of the population. In effect, variance represents the average amount of error we would make if we claimed the central tendency value were true for every member of the population.

To further illustrate how variance represents error, we can play a guessing game, a favorite pastime of statisticians since games of chance, such as poker or blackjack, are essentially the rules of probability in action. In this game we take the 1952 people in the ELEC88 data set who responded to the Dukakis feeling thermometer and guess what each person's response was. That is, we take case 1 and attempt to guess that person's evaluation of Dukakis, then do the same for case 2, case 3, and so on through all the cases. The objective, somewhat like guessing a person's weight or the number of beans in a jar, is to make our guesses as close as possible to each person's actual response on the dependent variable. If two people are competing on this exercise, the winner is the one who makes the smaller amount of guessing error.

In making our guesses, we will use some strategy, perhaps always guessing the middle value of the variable, 50, or, alternatively, guessing low for the first person, high for the second, then back to low for the third, and continuing the pattern for all the cases. Whatever strategy we select, we are bound to make some guessing errors. For a single respondent, the amount of guessing error is

$$\text{Error} = \text{response} - \text{guess}$$

If person A's response was 15 and we guessed 50, we made an error of -35; the person's actual answer was 35 points lower than our guess. If person B responded with a rating of 68 and we guessed 40, our error was $+28$, or an actual response 28 points higher than our guess.

To determine the amount of error made for all 1952 respondents, we use the formula

$$\text{Total errors} = \Sigma \, (\text{response}_i - \text{guess}_i)^2$$

The subscript i represents each individual respondent, and the summation sign Σ tells us to add the errors made over all 1952 respondents. In determining the total error, we do not want positive and negative ones to cancel. Adding errors of -50 and $+50$ would produce zero, making it appear that both guesses were absolutely accurate when in fact we were off by a total of 100 points. Consequently, each error is squared to make them all positive. The formula above provides the sum of the **squared errors**, which is a measure of the total error made when we guess values on V6 for all the respondents in the data set.

Statisticians enjoy games of chance, and they are pretty good at figuring out how to win. In games like this one, it turns out that the best guessing strategy is to use the variable's mean as the guess for every respondent. Because of the way it is calculated, the mean is in the exact mathematical middle of a variable's distribution. While it may not exactly match any single person's response, the mean produces the least amount of error possible when it is used as the guess for all 1952 responses.

When we use the mean as our guess, the amount of error made for a single case is the difference between the mean and that person's actual value on the variable, or

$$\text{Error} = X_i - \overline{X}$$

where the subscript i refers to each individual respondent's value on the variable X. Following the same strategy for each respondent in the data set leads to a total number of errors provided by the formula

$$\text{Total error} = \Sigma \, (X_i - \overline{X})^2$$

Supplement
12.1

The Mean as a Best Guess

You may verify that the mean of a variable is our best (least-error) guessing strategy without too much difficulty. First, pick a small number of cases, say 15, from the data set. There are many ways to do this, but a simple one is to use the familiar SELECT IF command. The first variable in the data set, V1, is each respondent's unique ID number which can be used to select some random cases. For example, respondents 201 to 215 can be selected with the command

   SELECT IF   V1 GE 201   AND   V1 LE 215

Second, obtain values for the two guessing strategies. Use any approach you like for your preferred guessing strategy. As an illustration, you might start with the number 50 for the first case, the middle value of the feeling thermometer, followed by 10 points less (40) for the second case, 10 points higher (60) for the third, then returning to the value of 50 and repeating the cycle. The second strategy requires identifying the mean for the 15 cases selected, which can be produced with a FREQUENCIES command. Then both the mean obtained, which turns out to be 63.93 in this example, and your alternative strategy are entered into a table like Table 12.1S. This table is used to evaluate which strategy produces less error.

Table 12.1S   COMPARING GUESSING STRATEGIES

V1	V6	GUESS G	$X - G$	$(X - G)^2$	$\bar{X}$	$X - \bar{X}$	$(X - \bar{X})^2$
201		50			63.93		
202		40			63.93		
203		60			63.93		
204		50			63.93		
205		40			63.93		
206		60			63.93		
207		50			63.93		
208		40			63.93		
209		60			63.93		
210		50			63.93		
211		40			63.93		
212		60			63.93		
213		50			63.93		
214		40			63.93		
215		60			63.93		
	$\bar{X} = 63.93$			$\Sigma (X - G)^2 =$			$\Sigma (X - \bar{X})^2 =$

Next you need to find the actual responses given on variable V6 by the 15 people selected. This information is obtained with the LIST command, which lists the values of each case for whatever variables we choose. Thus, the command

   LIST VARIABLES V1 V6

```
SELECT IF V1 GE 201 AND V1 LE 215
FREQUENCIES VARIABLES = V6 / STATISTICS MEAN / FORMAT NOTABLE


V6              FEELING THERMOMETER - DUKAKIS


MEAN           63.929

VALID CASES        14        MISSING CASES        1



LIST VARIABLES V1 V6

   V1    V6

  201    50
  202    85
  203    80
  204    85
  205    50
  206    70
  207    60
  208    85
  209    50
  210   998
  211    50
  212    70
  213    40
  214    70
  215    50

NUMBER OF CASES READ =        15    NUMBER OF CASES LISTED =        15
```

Figure 12.1S Selecting 15 cases and obtaining their mean and individual values on the dependent variable.

will list the 15 cases (the SELECT IF command is still in effect), including each case's identification number and evaluation of Dukakis. The SPSS commands and their output are shown in Figure 12.1S.

What remains is to enter the respondents' actual values in the comparison table and then calculate the remaining columns. This is illustrated in Table 12.2S. Note that case 210 has a missing value on V6 which is ignored in subsequent calculations since it is not a real evaluation of Dukakis, just a number representing why this person's answer is missing. The column sums at the bottom of the table show that the total error made in guessing the mean, 3258.86, is indeed less than that produced by the alternative strategy (7575.00).

You can repeat this exercise with any interval variable and number of cases you choose. On rare occasions an alternative guessing system may produce less error than guessing the mean. If this ever happens, it will be due to random chance (also known as luck) only; somehow a set of cases that closely matches your guessing system is

Table 12.2S COMPARING THE MEAN TO AN ALTERNATIVE GUESSING STRATEGY

V1	V6	GUESS G	$X - G$	$(X - G)^2$	$\bar{X}$	$X - \bar{X}$	$(X - \bar{X})^2$
201	50	50	0	0	63.93	−13.93	194.04
202	85	40	45	2025	63.93	21.07	443.94
203	80	60	20	400	63.93	16.07	258.24
204	85	50	35	1225	63.93	21.07	443.94
205	50	40	10	100	63.93	−13.93	194.04
206	70	60	10	100	63.93	6.07	36.84
207	60	50	10	100	63.93	−3.93	15.44
208	85	40	45	2025	63.93	21.07	443.94
209	50	60	20	400	63.93	−13.93	194.04
210	**998**	**50**	—	—	**63.93**	—	—
211	50	40	10	100	63.93	−13.93	194.04
212	0	60	10	100	63.93	6.07	36.84
213	40	50	−10	100	63.93	−23.93	572.64
214	70	40	30	900	63.93	6.07	36.84
215	0	60	−10	100	63.93	−13.93	194.04
$\bar{X} = 63.93$			$\Sigma (X - G)^2 = 7575.00$			$\Sigma (X - \bar{X})^2 = 3258.86$	

chosen. Repeating the process with a different group of cases, or even adding 5 or 10 more cases to your current group, should again lead to the mean being the best guessing strategy.

The formula above takes us back to where we started. Observe that the total error term is the same as that in the numerator of the variance formula

$$s^2 = \frac{\Sigma(X_i - \bar{X})^2}{n - 1}$$

Thus we confirm the statement made at the beginning of this section: A variable's variance is a measure of error. Dividing by the number of cases is necessary in comparing the variance of two or more variables since each may have answers from a different number of respondents. The analysis-of-variance technique examines only one dependent variable at a time and does not need to compensate for a different number of cases. In an analysis of variance the numerator from the variance formula has a unique name, the **total sum of squared errors (TSSE)**.

Partitioning Variance

We now have two things, the mean as the best strategy in guessing respondent values on the dependent variable and the dependent variable's variance, or its TSSE, as a measure of guessing error. If the research hypothesis is correct, the independent variable contributes to the dependent variable's variance and thus to our guessing error. Conversely, if we were able to examine each independent-variable group separately, we should be able to reduce guessing error. Analysis of variance examines the research and null hypothesis by testing for this expectation; whether the pattern is like Figure 12.4 or Figure 12.5. The test requires a process known as **partitioning variance**.

In partitioning variance, we divide the dependent variable's variance into two parts, the amount produced by the independent variable and the variance remaining after the independent variable's impact has been removed. We can illustrate how this is done by partitioning error for two example cases. This formula, also illustrated in Figure 12.6, shows the partitioning of error when we are guessing the value for a single case:

$$\text{Partitioning error: } X_i - \overline{X} = (\overline{G}_i - \overline{X}) + (X_i - \overline{G}_i)$$

where X_i = respondent's actual answer
   $\overline{X}$ = mean answer for all respondents, our guess
   $\overline{G}_i$ = mean answer for all respondents in given independent-variable group (e.g., all respondents with value 1 on V62)

For one case, the total guessing error on the left side of the equals sign is divided into two parts on the equation's right side. The first part, $\overline{G}_i - \overline{X}$, is the difference between the average Dukakis evaluation for the entire sample $\overline{X}$ and the average Dukakis rating of a sample subgroup $\overline{G}_i$. This subgroup consists of all sample cases sharing the respondent's value on the independent variable. Figure 12.6 illustrates two such subgroups; the first (V62 = 1) contains all

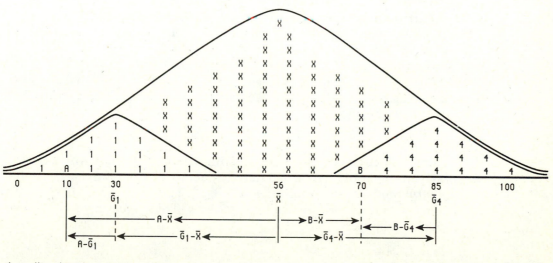

1 = No abortion ever.
4 = Abortion is woman's choice.

Figure 12.6 Partitioning error.

respondents who oppose abortions for any reason, and the second consists of all respondents leaving abortion decisions to a woman's choice (V62 = 4).

The second term on the right side of the equation, $X_i - \overline{G}_j$, is this one respondent's distance above or below the mean of the abortion subgroup to which she or he belongs. Even when respondents are grouped by their answers on the independent variable, we do not expect every member of the group to rate Dukakis exactly the same. This second term is the amount of error produced by variance *within* the subgroup, or the guessing error remaining after the impact of a person's abortion attitude has been taken into account.

Let us describe both the equation and Figure 12.6 in substantive terms. Why does respondent A give Dukakis a rating of 10, which is 46 points below the average rating given by all respondents? Part of the reason is that respondent A is opposed to all abortions, and people with this abortion attitude rate Dukakis lower than others ($\overline{G}_1 = 30$). However, for some additional reason(s), perhaps including Dukakis's defense and health insurance positions, respondent A rates Dukakis even lower than the typical antiabortion respondent, 20 points below this subgroup's mean (A = 10). These two factors, $\overline{G}_1 - \overline{X} = -26$ plus $A - \overline{G}_1 = -20$, add up to the total difference (−46) between respondent A's evaluation of Dukakis and the average rating given by the entire sample. Similarly, person B is a member of group 4 (abortion is a woman's choice) whose average evaluation of Dukakis is 85. However, not everyone in group 4 rates Dukakis the same, and person B rates him at 70, some 15 points below the average of the group. These two factors, +29 points ($\overline{G}_4 - \overline{X} = +29$) and −15 points ($B - \overline{G}_4 = -15$), combine to produce the +14-point difference of person B from the overall mean. Dividing our total error when guessing a respondent's dependent-variable position into the part produced by the independent variable and some remaining error is what the partitioning equation does.

The partitioning equation only represents a single individual respondent's distance from the overall mean. To partition the entire sample's variance, we must partition the total sum of squared errors (TSSE). Observe that squaring and then summing the left side of the equation produces the formula for TSSE, $\Sigma(X_i - \overline{X})^2$. To maintain equivalence on both sides of the equals sign, we must also square the right side of the equation and sum over all cases. The formula thus becomes

$$\text{TSSE} = \Sigma(X_i - \overline{X})^2 = \Sigma[(\overline{G}_j - \overline{X}) + (X_i - \overline{G}_j)]^2$$

At first glance, it appears that squaring the right-hand term will be a complex process, but it can be facilitated by remembering from basic algebra that $(a + b)^2$ produces the result $a^2 + 2ab + b^2$. The same is true of the right term above, where $\overline{G}_j - \overline{X}$ is a and $X_i - \overline{G}_j$ is b. Thus, squaring both sides of the equation produces

$$\text{TSSE} = \Sigma(X_i - \overline{X})^2 = \Sigma(\overline{G}_j - \overline{X})^2 + 2\Sigma(\overline{G}_j - \overline{X})(X_i - \overline{G}_j) + \Sigma(X_i - \overline{G}_j)^2$$

The numbers on the right look quite cumbersome, but they can be further simplified by eliminating the middle group of symbols. Look at the $X_i - \overline{G}_j$ term. This is the deviation of each respondent around the mean of the subgroup to which he or she belongs. We know that the sum of positive and negative deviations around a mean will be zero, which is the reason that most formulas square the deviation. Here, however, we are combining not just the deviations, but each deviation multiplied by another term: $\Sigma(\overline{G}_j - \overline{X})(X_i - \overline{G}_j)$. Fortunately, the $\overline{G}_j - \overline{X}$ term is a constant within each subgroup; $\overline{X}$, the overall mean, which is constant for all respondents, is subtracted from $\overline{G}_j$, the subgroup mean which is constant within each subgroup. For all members of group 1, therefore, $\overline{G}_j - \overline{X}$ will be the constant number -26 ($30 - 56 = -26$). Summing the deviations of group 1 around its mean will still yield zero when each deviation is multiplied by a constant number. Deviations of -1 and $+1$ will cancel, but so will $+26$ and -26, having multiplied each deviation by the constant number -26.

Since the complex middle term will always be zero, it can be deleted from the equation without any harm. The equation now becomes simpler:

$$\text{TSSE} = \Sigma(X_i - \overline{X})^2 = \Sigma(\overline{G}_j - \overline{X})^2 + \Sigma(X_i - \overline{G}_j)^2$$

In addition, the two terms on the right are not just mathematical abstractions; they also have straightforward interpretations. The term $\Sigma(\overline{G}_j - \overline{X})^2$ is referred to as the **treatment sum of squares (TRSS)**. The $\Sigma(X_i - \overline{G}_j)^2$ term is referred to as the **residual sum of squared errors (RSSE)**. Let us look at each.

The research hypothesis claims that part of the dependent variable's original variance is due to the impact of the independent variable, abortion attitudes. The TRSS is this impact, the distance between the overall sample mean and the mean rating of each abortion subgroup. This distance is squared and then summed over all the respondents to determine how much of the original squared error is produced by different abortion attitudes.

The $\Sigma(\overline{G}_j - \overline{X})^2$ term is commonly called the treatment sum of squares because analysis of variance is typically used with scientific experiments in which each experimental group received a different treatment (stimulus). It is also sometimes referred to as the **explained sum of squares** because it represents that part of the deviations around the dependent variable's mean explained or accounted for by the impact of the independent variable. In our original guessing game, we knew nothing at all about the respondents before guessing their dependent-variable values. If, instead, we were first told what abortion stance each respondent took, we could make fewer errors by guessing that *subgroup* mean rather than the overall sample mean. The TRSS term is that part of the original guessing error, the TSSE, that is no longer made if we now use subgroup means as our guesses. This part of the original error has been eliminated, or explained, by the impact of the independent variable.

What about the second term, $\Sigma(X_i - \overline{G}_j)^2$? This is referred to as the *residual*, or remaining, sum of squared errors, for it represents the errors still made even after the impact of the independent variable has been taken into account. Although knowing a person's abortion stance will now lead us to guess the average Dukakis rating of that specific group $\overline{G}_j$, there remain considerable differences of opinion even within each subgroup. This remaining error is the within-group variance, which is given by the $\Sigma(X_i - \overline{G}_j)^2$ term. This is also the amount of guessing error remaining after we account for the impact of the independent variable.

Thus, the equations

$$\Sigma(X_i - \overline{X})^2 = \Sigma(\overline{G}_j - \overline{X})^2 + \Sigma(X_i - \overline{G}_j)^2$$

and

$$\text{TSSE} = \text{TRSS} + \text{RSSE}$$

accomplish exactly what we said analysis of variance does. The original variance of the dependent variable is partitioned into two parts: the treatment sum of squares or variance resulting because respondents belong to different abortion groups and the residual sum of squares or remaining variance unexplained by the independent variable.

An ANOVA Table

Having partitioned the variance, we want to use the partitions to test the null hypothesis

H_0: For all groups, $\mu_i = \mu_j$.

It is easy to calculate the mean of the dependent variable for each independent-variable group; we did just that in Figure 12.2. However, each group constitutes a separate random sample for sections of the population—one random sample drawn from antiabortion members of the population, another from those willing to allow abortions only to save the mother's life, and still a third, and yet a fourth sample from population members with other abortion attitudes. We know that random chance will produce some differences between sample means even when the population means are the same. We need a way to determine whether the differences observed reflect mere sampling error or true differences in the population.

The factors important in making this determination are illustrated in Figure 12.7. In the top part of the figure, each group has such a wide variance that any differences between the group means might easily be due to sampling fluctuations. In the middle part, the distances between the means are the same, but each group's variance is so small that sampling error seems an unlikely reason for the differences. Finally, the bottom part shows the same within-group variance as in the top part, but the means are much farther apart, leading us to again reject sampling error as an explanation.

Note that the two factors illustrated in Figure 12.7 are reflected in the partitioning of variance. The group means are closest when they are all the same, as in Figure 12.5, which only happens when each group mean is also identical to the overall sample mean. As the group means move farther apart from each other, at least some of them must also be moving farther away from the overall sample mean. Consequently, the TRSS, based on the differences between the group mean and entire sample mean $\Sigma(\overline{G}_j - \overline{X})^2$, will become larger. On the other hand, the greater the variance within the groups, the larger

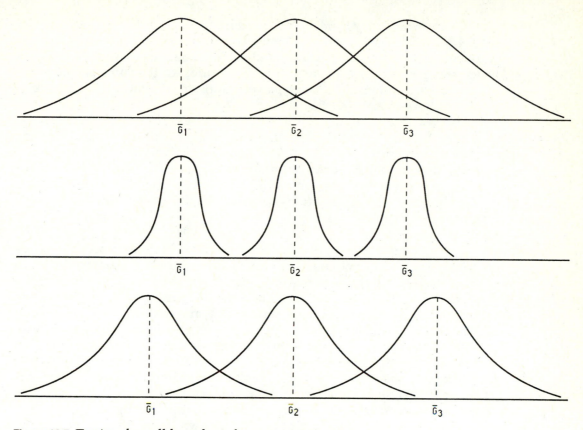

Figure 12.7 Testing the null hypothesis by partitioning variance.

the RSSE term $\Sigma(X_i - \overline{G}_j)^2$ will be. It is the comparison of these two terms that allows us to calculate statistical significance, the disparity between the group means compared to the variance (potential for sample error) within each group.

This comparison is performed through an **ANOVA table**, like the one illustrated in Table 12.3. The first column of the table lists the sources of variance: TRSS, also called the **between-groups sum of squares** since it is the squared error accounted for by the differences between the means of the groups; RSSE, or the **within-groups sum of squares** left after the impact of the treatment has been factored out; and the total, TSSE. In the second column are found the degrees of freedom for each row. For the between-groups row, this number is $G - 1$, the number of groups on the independent variable minus 1. The abortion attitudes variable has four values, so there are 3 degrees of freedom for this row. For the within-groups sum of squares, there are $n - G$ degrees of freedom, the number of cases in the sample minus the number of groups. With 1952 cases providing legitimate (nonmissing) answers on the Dukakis feeling thermometer, the within-groups sum of squares is $1952 - 4 = 1948$ degrees of freedom. The bottom row contains the degrees of freedom for the total variance, or the sum of the two. When $n - G$ and $G - 1$ are added $[n + (-G) + G + (-1)]$, the $+G$ and $-G$ cancel, leaving $n - 1$, the degrees of freedom used to calculate the variance of a variable. Finally, the third column contains the sums of squares calculated for TRSS, RSSE, and TSSE. The figures for the sums of squares in Table 12.3 are fictional, just some picked out of the air, but they will serve to illustrate how an ANOVA table is used.

The last two columns in Table 12.3 allow us to evaluate whether the treatment (abortion attitudes) really leads to significant differences on the dependent variable (evaluations of Dukakis). To do this, we must compare the average difference between the groups to the average difference between people within each group. That is, considering how much variation in the Dukakis ratings exists within each abortion group, are the differences between the groups small enough that they might be explained by merely random error in the four samples?

We begin this process by dividing TRSS and RSSE by their respective degrees of freedom. This produces numbers which are called **mean squares**, shown in the fourth column of Table 12.3. The mean squares represent, roughly, the average impact of the treatment and the average difference between people even after the treatment. A typical respondent has an average squared distance of 1500 from people in other abortion groups, but only an average squared distance of 500 from people with the same abortion attitude as the respondent. To compare these two numbers, we divide the treatment mean square by the residual mean square. This is the **F ratio** in the rightmost column of Table 12.3. This ratio, 3.00, shows that the typical difference between groups is 3 times as large as the average difference between people within each group.

Like other statistics, the F ratio has a known distribution. We begin by assuming that the F ratio for the population is .0—the claim of the null hypothesis of no difference between the means of the groups, which makes the numerator of the F ratio zero. Of course, sample means will differ somewhat through random sampling error. An F ratio of 1.0, 2.0, or even higher might be found in samples even when there is no difference between the groups in the population. How large an F ratio might be found through sampling error depends on both the size of the sample and the number of groups being compared. Small samples provide imprecise estimates of group means and variances, so quite large F ratios might occur solely through sampling error. Larger samples provide more precise estimates, making large F ratios produced only by sampling error less likely.

Table 12.3   AN ANOVA TABLE

Source of variance	Degrees of Freedom	Sums of squares	Mean square	F ratio
Between groups (TRSS)	3	4,500	1,500	3.00
Within groups (RSSE)	1,948	974,000	500	
Total (TSSE)	1,951	978,500		

Similarly, when only two groups are compared, the sampling error could easily lead the two means to be quite different. However, as the number of groups being compared increases, probability tells us that most of the means should be quite close to each other if they were, in fact, drawn from a population for which the null hypothesis is true.

The probability distribution of the F ratio, shown in Table 12.4, reflects these two forces: the sample size and the number of groups. Each column has a title across the top referring to the number of degrees of freedom in the F ratio's numerator (between groups). Down the side the degrees of freedom for the denominator (within groups) are listed. The body of the table contains F ratios that might be produced by sampling error for each degrees-of-freedom combination. These ratios are termed the **critical values**, for they are the values used to determine whether to accept or reject the null hypothesis; larger F ratios lead to rejecting the null hypothesis, smaller ones to not rejecting it.

In Table 12.3 the ANOVA had 3 degrees of freedom for the numerator and over 120 in the denominator. For this degrees-of-freedom combination, the critical F value is 2.60. Any sample F value up to this number might be a product of sampling error, but an F ratio larger than 2.60 would occur less than 5 percent of the time through sampling error only. Since the F value calculated in Table 12.3 is larger (3.0) than the critical number, we can reject the null hypothesis with only a 5 percent or less chance of error, our desired significance level.

Table 12.4 CRITICAL VALUES OF THE F RATIO AT THE .05 LEVEL OF STATISTICAL SIGNIFICANCE

Degrees of freedom for the denominator	\multicolumn{7}{c}{Degrees of freedom for the numerator}
	1	2	3	4	5	6	8
1	161.45	199.50	215.71	224.58	230.16	233.99	238.88
2	18.51	19.00	19.16	19.25	19.30	19.33	19.37
3	10.13	9.55	9.28	9.12	9.01	8.94	8.84
4	7.71	6.94	6.59	6.39	6.26	6.16	6.04
5	6.61	5.79	5.41	5.19	5.05	4.95	4.82
10	4.96	4.10	3.71	3.48	3.33	3.22	3.07
15	4.54	3.68	3.29	3.06	2.90	2.79	2.64
20	4.35	3.49	3.10	2.87	2.71	2.60	2.45
25	4.24	3.38	2.99	2.76	2.60	2.49	2.34
30	4.17	3.32	2.92	2.69	2.53	2.42	2.27
40	4.08	3.23	2.84	2.61	2.45	2.34	2.18
60	4.00	3.15	2.76	2.52	2.37	2.25	2.10
120	3.92	3.07	2.68	2.45	2.29	2.17	2.02
∞	3.84	2.99	**2.60**	2.37	2.21	2.09	1.94

Source: Abridged from Table 18 in E.S. Pearson and H.O. Hartley (eds.), *Biometrika Tables for Statisticians.* vol. 1, 2d ed. (New York: Cambridge University Press, 1976). Reproduced with the permission of the trustees of *Biometrika.*

Because of the complexity of the F table, each F table is for one level of significance only. If we had wanted to use a .01 or .001 significance level, we would have needed to use a different table of F values. Reference works on statistical analysis contain numerous F tables for the commonly used significance levels.

SPSS COMMANDS

Since we have discussed at length how an analysis of variance is conducted, you might think that the SPSS commands needed to perform one are quite complex. In fact, they are very simple. To test the abortion attitude/Dukakis evaluation relationship, the command needed is

    ONEWAY V6 BY V82 (1, 4)

There are actually different types of analyses of variance, depending on the nature of the data being analyzed and the complexity of the analysis. The type discussed in this chapter is called a **one-way analysis of variance**, hence the **ONEWAY command**, which means only one independent variable at a time is being examined. More complex analyses of variance are typically covered only in advanced statistics courses and are not discussed further in this text.

Following the procedure name, there is the name of the dependent variable to be analyzed, V6. Up to 100 dependent variables could be listed here, and the ONEWAY procedure would provide an analysis of variance for each. For example, we could have included both V6 and V5 (the Bush feeling thermometer) as dependent variables, and the ONEWAY procedure would have examined the impact of abortion attitudes on each of the two feeling thermometers.

Following the name of the dependent variable are the **BY keyword** and the name of the independent variable. Multiple dependent variables can be listed, but only one independent variable may be contained on a single ONEWAY command. An analysis of variance requires separating the sample cases into groups by using respondent values on the independent variable. Once the sample is divided in this fashion, the mean of any number of dependent variables can be calculated for the groups. A different independent variable, however, requires resorting the data set into different groups, something too complex for a single command to perform. If you want to examine the impact of more than one independent variable, such as how both abortion attitudes and race affect the Dukakis ratings, it is necessary to repeat the ONEWAY command for each independent variable.

Following the name of the independent variable, SPSS requires that you specify the range of values of the independent variable that will be used to divide the respondents into groups (in our case, different abortion preference groupings). This is done by placing the minimum and maximum values of the range in parentheses. Thus the name of the independent variable is followed by the numbers 1 and 4 in parentheses, which tells SPSS to use response codes 1, 2, 3, and 4 on V62 to divide the respondents into subgroups. Not all the values of

```
GET FILE = ELEC88
ONEWAY   V6   BY   V62   (1,4)


- - - - - - - - - - - - - - O N E - W A Y - - - - - - - - - - - - - -

      VARIABLE   V6        FEELING THERMOMETER - DUKAKIS
   BY VARIABLE   V62       ABORTION LAW

                                 ANALYSIS OF VARIANCE

                           SUM OF          MEAN          F        F
      SOURCE       DF      SQUARES        SQUARES      RATIO    PROB.

   BETWEEN GROUPS   3      3353.9000     1117.9667    1.5708   0.1945
   WITHIN  GROUPS  1915  1362936.404      711.7161
   TOTAL           1918  1366290.304
```

Figure 12.8 A ONEWAY analysis between abortion attitudes and ratings of Dukakis.

the independent variable have to be included here. Say we were interested in only the first three values of V62, each of which identifies respondents wanting some restrictions on abortion, differing only in the severity of those restrictions. Placing numbers 1 and 3 in parentheses would cause an analysis of variance between just three groups to be performed, ignoring those who prefer no restrictions (value 4).

This ONEWAY command is all that is needed for instructing SPSS to calculate an analysis of variance. This command will produce the output shown in Figure 12.8. The top of the output lists the two variables being analyzed, V6 and V62, including the variable labels for each. Below that is an ANOVA table similar to the one shown in Table 12.3. There are only two differences. First, Figure 12.8 analyzes the actual sample data instead of just fictional numbers as in the earlier illustration. Second, it is no longer necessary to consult an F table to determine whether the F ratio leads to accepting or rejecting the null hypothesis. Using an F table stored in its memory, SPSS determines the probability of finding a sample F ratio of 1.5708, assuming no relationship (an F value of zero) in the population. The probability that our F ratio might be the result of sampling error (.1945) is far too high to justify rejecting the null hypothesis. Thus we must conclude that our sample evidence is not strong enough for us to claim that a relationship between abortion policy preferences and evaluations of Dukakis exists in the population.

ANOVA LIMITATIONS AND ASSUMPTIONS

As with any statistical procedure, it is important that we interpret the results correctly. All statistics have certain limitations and involve certain assumptions. We describe these below; then, in the next section, we examine how subcommands can help us adjust to the limitations and assumptions.

Drawing Conclusions from an ANOVA

Interpreting ANOVA results is quite straightforward when, as in the case above, we reject the null hypothesis. We then conclude that none of the independent-variable categories leads to a markedly different position on the dependent variable. The situation is a bit more complicated when the F ratio is statistically significant. For example, Figure 12.9 presents an analysis-of-variance test between the Dukakis ratings and respondent views on the desirability of a national health insurance program (V30). The F ratio is far larger than that in Figure 12.8, and its significance level allows us to reject the null hypothesis.

In interpreting this result, it is helpful to remember exactly what the null and research hypotheses are:

H_0:   For all groups, $\mu_i = \mu_j$.

versus

H_R: For some group, $\mu_i = \mu_j$.

That is, rejecting the null hypothesis does not mean that *each* group with a different position on health insurance also has a different mean evaluation of Dukakis; instead it means that *at least one* of the groups has a mean Dukakis rating different from the others. It may be that all the health insurance groups differ from each other, or that six of them share a common mean but the seventh is different. We do know that in some way attitudes on national health insurance are related to ratings of Dukakis, but the ONEWAY procedure gives us only limited information on the nature of that relationship.

Assumptions

In addition to this limitation, statistical procedures often entail some assumptions about the data or the population. When these assumptions are correct, we can confidently draw conclusions from statistical results. When the assump-

```
GET FILE = ELEC88
ONEWAY V6 BY V30 (1,7)


- - - - - - - - - - - - - O N E - W A Y - - - - - - - - - - - - -


         VARIABLE    V6        FEELING THERMOMETER - DUKAKIS
      BY VARIABLE    V30       HEALTH INS SCALE - RESP


                              ANALYSIS OF VARIANCE


                              SUM OF        MEAN        F         F
        SOURCE       DF       SQUARES       SQUARES     RATIO     PROB.

    BETWEEN GROUPS    6      63520.8575   10586.8096   15.4726   0.0000
    WITHIN  GROUPS  1649    1128293.973    684.2292
    TOTAL           1655    1191814.831
```

Figure 12.9 A ONEWAY analysis between national health insurance preferences and ratings of Dukakis.

tions are in error, our conclusions about the research and null hypotheses may also be in error. Statistical analysis is not unique in this respect, for we continually make assumptions in everyday situations. If told we had just gotten a score of 95 on an English test, most of us would be quite happy. Our happiness is based on the assumption that 100 is a perfect score. If a perfect score on the test were actually 200—if our assumption were wrong—our conclusion that we had done well on the test would also be wrong.

The analysis-of-variance technique makes three assumptions. The first two are fairly easy to justify, but the third requires investigation before acceptance. The first assumption is that each independent-variable group is a random sample from the corresponding population group; the sample respondents favoring a government health insurance plan financed with tax revenues (value 1) must have been randomly selected from the population group holding the same opinion. The same holds for groups 2 through 6. The **random-sample assumption** really means only that there was no systematic bias in the selection of group members. Since the entire sample was randomly selected, any subgroup of the sample was also randomly selected, thus meeting this assumption.

The second assumption is that, in the population, the distribution of group members around its mean on the dependent variable must be normal. The **normality assumption** is needed to estimate sampling distributions for each group's mean, which in turn allows us to determine whether the between-group differences are statistically significant. Again, this is a fairly easy assumption to satisfy as long as each group is big enough, say above 50 cases, so the central limit theorem will apply. Sampling distributions can then be created for each group mean, even if the population distribution of that group is not a normal curve.

The practical impact of the second assumption is that we need to avoid using independent variables containing response values applicable to only a small number of cases. This is most likely to occur when the independent variable has a large number of response categories which then divide the whole sample into some very small groups. For example, using V80 (education) as the independent variable would divide the sample into 18 education groups. Some of these groups, such as the ones for 0 or 1 year of education, have only 2 to 3 respondents—not enough for the central limit theorem to apply, and not even enough for us to call them fair random samples of the corresponding population groups. A simple way to make sure this assumption is satisfied is to run a FREQUENCIES procedure on any independent variable used. If some of the response categories contain very few cases, they can be combined with a RECODE command to produce new groups with a sufficient number of cases.

The third assumption is the most difficult to deal with. It says that, in the population, each group has the same variance around its mean. To determine whether the differences between the groups are statistically significant, ANOVA needs an estimate of the amount of variance existing within each group. Like the T-TEST procedure, ONEWAY pools the information from each group to develop a combined estimate of the within-group variance. This pooled-variance estimate is inappropriate if one independent-variable group has a significantly larger or smaller variance than the others. Over- or underestimating a group's variance is akin to over- or underestimating the amount of sampling error we might encounter in estimating that group's mean. This might cause the F test, and any conclusions drawn from it, to be in error.

The practical importance of violating the **equal-variance assumption** depends on both the seriousness of the violation and the significance level of the calculated F value. If the significance level of the F ratio is close to .05, say between 0.1 and .10, then the impact of some error in calculating the within-group variances might be sufficient to affect our decision about rejecting the null hypothesis. If the significance of the F ratio is quite far from .05, above .10, or below .01, then a modest difference in the variance of one or more population groups probably would not affect the F ratio enough to change our decision about the null hypothesis. Of course, if the variance of one group is radically different from that of the others, it would be unwise to rely on any F value, no matter how significant, as a valid test of the null hypothesis.

SUBCOMMANDS

The ONEWAY procedure has a sizable smorgasbord of subcommands, but most are designed for complex situations that we are unlikely to encounter. Three, however, are useful to us because they enable us to overcome the procedure's limitations and explore the validity of its required assumptions. These three are RANGES, FORMAT, and STATISTICS.

RANGES

The basic ONEWAY procedure determines only whether one group has a different mean from the others, but there are statistics which will make a group-by-group comparison, testing whether *each* independent-variable group has a mean different from the others. As discussed at the beginning of this chapter, performing a simple T-TEST procedure on each pair of groups is undesirable since the chance of making an error increases with the number of groups being compared. There are ways to compensate for an increased number of comparisons so that the overall probability of error in rejecting the null hypothesis remains .05. The techniques by which this can be accomplished are the options available for the **RANGES subcommand**.

This subcommand requests a test to be used over the entire range of groups on the independent variable, hence the name RANGES. There is no need to discuss all the options of this subcommand because the most commonly used one, the **Tukey *b* comparison**, is sufficient for our needs. The Tukey *b* statistic provides a group-by-group comparison of means to determine which are different at a statistically significant level. It does not matter how many groups are being compared, the Tukey *b* comparison maintains a constant .05 probability of erroneously rejecting any null hypothesis (erroneously concluding that two groups are different when their population means are really the same).

(PC) The Tukey *b* comparison is requested by entering the /RANGES = subcommand with the term **TUKEYB** after the equals sign, as in

ONEWAY V6 by V30 (1, 7) / **RANGES = TUKEYB**

Watch your typing here. There is another option on the RANGES subcommand requested with the word TUKEY (no B), and a slight typing error may get you the wrong statistic.

After this subcommand is added, the revised output will look like Figure 12.10. At the top is the familiar ANOVA table followed by the RANGES

```
GET FILE = ELEC88
ONEWAY V6 BY V30  (1,7)    /RANGES=TUKEYB

    - - - - - - - - - - - - - O N E - W A Y - - - - - - - - - - - - -

        VARIABLE   V6        FEELING THERMOMETER - DUKAKIS
     BY VARIABLE   V30       HEALTH INS SCALE - RESP

                                ANALYSIS OF VARIANCE

                            SUM OF          MEAN         F        F
    SOURCE          DF      SQUARES        SQUARES     RATIO    PROB.

  BETWEEN GROUPS     6    63520.8575    10586.8096   15.4726   0.0000
  WITHIN  GROUPS  1649  1128293.973       684.2292
  TOTAL           1655  1191814.831

    - - - - - - - - - - - - - O N E - W A Y - - - - - - - - - - - - -

        VARIABLE   V6        FEELING THERMOMETER - DUKAKIS
     BY VARIABLE   V30       HEALTH INS SCALE - RESP

  MULTIPLE-RANGE  TEST


  TUKEY-B  PROCEDURE
  RANGES FOR THE 0.050 LEVEL -

         3.49    3.75    3.91    4.02    4.11    4.18
  THE RANGES ABOVE ARE TABLE RANGES.
  THE VALUE ACTUALLY COMPARED WITH MEAN(J)-MEAN(I) IS..
        18.4963 * RANGE * DSQRT(1/N(I) + 1/N(J))
  (*) DENOTES PAIRS OF GROUPS SIGNIFICANTLY DIFFERENT AT THE 0.050
  LEVEL
                            G G G G G G G
                            R R R R R R R
                            P P P P P P P

        MEAN      GROUP     7 6 5 4 1 3 2

        47.0852   GRP  7
        48.0000   GRP  6
        52.1875   GRP  5
        58.7788   GRP  4       * * *
        61.2523   GRP  1       * * *
        62.5300   GRP  3       * * *
        63.9771   GRP  2       * * *
```

Figure 12.10 Tukey *b* comparison.

comparison. The first part of the comparison is a technical description of how the Tukey *b* analysis was carried out. We bypass this material, for it contains mathematical details necessary only for advanced data analysis.

The group-by-group comparison, our primary concern, is at the bottom of the output. Each group is identified simply by the label "GRP" followed by a number. This number refers to the value of the independent variable identifying the group. Thus, GRP 7 (group 7) contains respondents who strongly favor a private insurance plan, and members of GRP 1 are those who strongly support a government health insurance program. The groups are listed in order not by their code numbers, but by their means on the dependent variable. Group 7 has the lowest mean rating of Dukakis, followed by groups 6, 5, 4, 1, 3, and 2. The groups are also listed in the same order across the top, providing a matrix which SPSS uses to identify any significant differences between the group means. Differences significant at the .05 level are identified by asterisks in the matrix.

To interpret the matrix, read down each column. The group 7 mean is not sufficiently different from the mean of either group 6 or group 5 for us to conclude that they are different in the population, but the Tukey *b* test shows that group 7 is different from groups 4, 1, 3, and 2 in its evaluation of Dukakis. The same pattern holds for groups 5 and 6. Consequently, the groups for private insurance (7, 6, and 5) are not different from each other in their rating of Dukakis, nor are the groups who are neutral (4) or in favor of government insurance (3, 2, and 1) different from each other. However, all those favoring a private insurance plan, no matter how strongly, do evaluate Dukakis differently from those who are either neutral or favor a government insurance program.

FORMAT

(*v.2*) (*PC*) By default, SPSS identifies each group in the Tukey *b* comparison simply as GRP1, GRP2, and so on. This is not very descriptive information, and it is easy to lose track of whether group 1 is the group favoring government or private insurance. The **FORMAT subcommand** allows us to change this, substituting instead value labels of the independent variable to describe each group. The subcommand is entered as

    / FORMAT = LABELS

It might seem as though you would always want to use this subcommand, but there is a drawback. While value labels may be 20 characters or more in length, there is room on the Tukey *b* analysis for only the first 8 characters of each label. These abbreviated labels may be less useful than the default GRP labels. For example, responses labeled STRONGLY AGREE and STRONGLY DISAGREE would be indistinguishable from each other because the first eight characters of each label are the same—STRONGLY. In our case, the health insurance scale in the ELEC88 data set has labels defined for only three of its seven categories—the two extreme values (1 and 7) and the neutral point (4).

As a result of the eight-character limitation, the FORMAT = **LABELS** subcommand often does not provide any additional clarity to the output. The obvious way around this limitation is to change the value labels of the independent variable so that the first eight characters provide an interpretable label. This is what we have done in Figure 12.11, using the terms GOVT and PRIV with one or more plus signs representing how strongly each position is favored. A simpler alternative favored by many is to keep SPSS's default use of the GRP labels and just write a brief description of each group on the output. Finally, note that adding labels with the /FORMAT = LABELS subcommand is appropriate only when requesting a RANGES comparison. The basic ANOVA table never

```
GET FILE = ELEC88
VALUE LABELS  V30 1 'GOVT+++' 2 'GOVT++' 3 'GOVT+' 4 'NEUTRAL'
    5  'PRIV+'  6  'PRIV++'  7  'PRIV+++'
ONEWAY V6 BY V30 (1,7) / RANGES = TUKEYB /FORMAT = LABELS

- - - - - - - - - - - - - - O N E - W A Y - - - - - - - - - - - - -

        VARIABLE   V6          FEELING THERMOMETER - DUKAKIS
   BY  VARIABLE   V30          HEALTH INS SCALE - RESP

                              ANALYSIS OF VARIANCE

                         SUM OF           MEAN         F         F
   SOURCE        DF      SQUARES         SQUARES      RATIO    PROB.

BETWEEN  GROUPS    6     63520.8575    10586.8096   15.4726   0.0000
WITHIN   GROUPS  1649   1128293.973      684.2292
TOTAL            1655   1191814.831

- - - - - - - - - - - - - - O N E - W A Y - - - - - - - - - - - - -

        VARIABLE   V6          FEELING THERMOMETER - DUKAKIS
   BY  VARIABLE   V30          HEALTH INS SCALE - RESP

MULTIPLE-RANGE  TEST

TUKEY-B  PROCEDURE
RANGES FOR THE 0.050 LEVEL -

         3.49    3.75   3.91   4.02   4.11   4.18
THE RANGES ABOVE ARE TABLE RANGES.
THE VALUE ACTUALLY COMPARED WITH MEAN(J)-MEAN(I) IS..
      18.4963 * RANGE * DSQRT(1/N(I) + 1/N(J))
   (*) DENOTES PAIRS OF GROUPS SIGNIFICANTLY DIFFERENT AT THE 0.050
LEVEL
                           P  P  P  N  G  G  G
                           R  R  R  E  O  O  O
                           I  I  I  U  U  U  U
                           V  V  V  T  T  T  T
                           +  +  +  R  +  +  +
                           +  +     A  +     +
                           +        L  +

      MEAN       GROUP
      47.0852    PRIV+++
      48.0000    PRIV++
      52.1875    PRIV+
      58.7788    NEUTRAL      *  *  *
      61.2523    GOVT+++      *  *  *
      62.5300    GOVT+        *  *  *
      63.9771    GOVT++       *  *  *
```

Figure 12.11 Addition of the FORMAT = LABELS subcommand.

lists each independent-variable group, so there is no need to specify any printing labels for them.

Version 2 The older version of SPSS-X requests subcommands in a manner that is a carryover from SPSS's early days. Alternative ways of presenting the output are referred to as OPTIONS, with each option identified by a number used to invoke that option. Furthermore, the OPTIONS subcommand (without a slash) must begin in column 1, just as the main ONEWAY procedure command must.

For the ONEWAY procedure, the option adding value labels to the output is number 6. Thus, for SPSS-X version 2 the command-subcommand combination

```
ONEWAY V6 BY V30 (1, 7) / RANGES = TUKEYB

OPTIONS 6
```

produces the same output, displayed in Figure 12.11, as the /FORMAT = LABELS subcommand does for SPSS-X version 3 and SPSS Release 4. Version 3 of SPSS-X recognizes the old way of requesting subcommands. Release 4 will not recognize the OPTIONS statement unless your SPSS commands are submitted through the operating system instead of the SPSS software. This is the standard way in which commands are submitted on IBM mainframes using OS, but is not standard for other implementations, except for command files processed with the INCLUDE command and some other ways of submitting command files without going through the command generator.

STATISTICS

The final subcommand to be discussed is the **STATISTICS subcommand**, which produces additional statistics over and above the basic analysis provided by the procedure. A number of alternatives are available with the STATISTICS subcommand, but we only need some descriptive statistics about each of the groups. One of the assumptions required in ANOVA is that each group has an identical population variance on the dependent variable. By looking at how much variability there is in the sample, we can get an idea of whether this assumption is correct.

(v2) (PC) To obtain some summary statistics describing each sample group, we use the **DESCRIPTIVES** option with the STATISTICS subcommand. The complete subcommand and alternative request is entered as

```
/ STATISTICS DESCRIPTIVES
```

The output from the statistics request is shown in Figure 12.12. The bottom of the output lists for each group the count (number of cases), mean, standard deviation, standard error, lower and upper bounds of a 95 percent confidence interval, and minimum and maximum values of the dependent variable. Each

```
GET FILE=ELEC88
ONEWAY V6 BY V30 (1,7) /STATISTICS=DESCRIPTIVES

- - - - - - - - - - - - - - O N E - W A Y - - - - - - - - - - - - - -

        VARIABLE  V6       FEELING THERMOMETER - DUKAKIS
     BY VARIABLE  V30      HEALTH INS SCALE - RESP

                            ANALYSIS OF VARIANCE
                      SUM OF          MEAN        F        F
    SOURCE        DF  SQUARES         SQUARES     RATIO    PROB.

BETWEEN  GROUPS    6    63520.8575   10586.8096  15.4726   0.0000
WITHIN   GROUPS 1649  1128293.973      684.2292
TOTAL           1655  1191814.831
                              STANDARD   STANDARD
GROUP        COUNT     MEAN   DEVIATION   ERROR    95 PCT CONF FOR MEAN

Grp  1        321   61.2523   27.9945   1.5625   58.1783  TO   64.3264
Grp  2        175   63.9771   21.6407   1.6359   60.7484  TO   67.2059
Grp  3        200   62.5300   26.0118   1.8393   58.9030  TO   66.1570
Grp  4        312   58.7788   25.9970   1.4718   55.882   TO   61.6748
Grp  5        240   52.1875   24.2051   1.5624   49.1096  TO   55.2654
Grp  6        185   48.0000   25.8455   1.9002   44.2510  TO   51.7490
Grp  7        223   47.0852   29.1204   1.9500   43.2422  TO   50.9282
TOTAL        1656   56.5266   26.8352   0.6594   55.2331  TO   57.8200

GROUP        MINIMUM    MAXIMUM

Grp  1        0.0000   100.0000
Grp  2        0.0000   100.0000
Grp  3        0.0000   100.0000
Grp  4        0.0000   100.0000
Grp  5        0.0000   100.0000
Grp  6        0.0000   100.0000
Grp  7        0.0000   100.0000
TOTAL         0.0000   100.0000
```

Figure 12.12 Descriptive statistics added to the ANOVA table.

group is again identified with the default GRPx designation since the FORMAT subcommand was not used. If it had been, value labels would have been substituted for the default labels.

Version 2 Like the labels formatting option reviewed earlier, version 2 of SPSS-X uses an old format to request statistics. The keyword STATISTICS must begin in column 1, followed by a number representing the statistics wanted. Alternative 1 on this older version of the statistics subcommand provides the same descriptive statistics as the /STATISTICS DESCRIPTIVES subcommand does in version 3 of SPSS-X or Release 4. For version 2 of SPSS-X, the complete command-subcommand combination is

```
ONEWAY V6 BY V30 (1, 7) / RANGES = TUKEYB

OPTIONS 6

STATISTICS 1
```

Again, both ways of requesting statistics are accepted by version 3 of SPSS-X, but not Release 4 unless you are processing a command file through the operating system. (Qualifications pertaining to version 2 conclude with this paragraph.)

Our concern is with the measure of each group's variability, the standard deviation. We know this will differ across the groups simply because of sampling error, but how do we know when the differences are large enough to question the equal-variance assumption for the population? Unfortunately, there is no exact answer to this question. A very rough guideline is to use the standard deviation for the entire sample (the bottom line of the descriptive statistics) and then see whether the standard deviation of any subgroup differs from it by more than one-third. In Figure 12.12, the sample standard deviation is 27, and one-third of 27 is 9. Thus a range of standard deviations between 18 and 36 would be consistent with assuming that all the variances are equal in the population. Since all the standard deviations in Figure 12.12 are in the 20s, we seem to be on safe ground in meeting the equal-variance assumption. If one or more of the groups are outside this range, the analysis-of-variance technique may be an inappropriate test of the null hypothesis.

Be forewarned, the guideline in the paragraph above is not based on any mathematical formula; it is just one developed by this author which seems to work in most cases. Your instructor may give you different guidance on how to evaluate the equal-variance assumption.

SPSS/PC+ AND RELEASE 4

Both version 2 and version 3 of SPSS-X request the Tukey b comparison with the keyword TUKEYB on the RANGES subcommand. SPSS/PC+ uses instead the keyword BTUKEY on the RANGES subcommand. Release 4 manuals sometimes describe using BTUKEY and at other times TUKEYB. Experimentation should show you which will work with your particular operating system.

SPSS/PC+ requests both value labels, instead of the default GRP designations, and descriptive statistics as done in version 2 of SPSS-X. The OPTIONS and STATISTICS keywords are used with numbers designating the options and statistics desired. The numbers are the same as those described in this chapter—option 6 for formatting labels and statistic 1 for descriptive statistics. There are three differences. First, the OPTIONS and STATISTICS subcommands must be preceded by slashes, as is true of other subcommands. Second, they do not have to begin in column 1, as required by version 2 of SPSS-X. Finally, they can both be contained on the same line, just as other subcommands can.

SUMMARY

Confidence intervals allow us to identify population means for single groups. The T-TEST procedure enables us to compare the means of two groups. In this chapter we have expanded the type of hypotheses that we can test. The basic analysis of variance allows an overall comparison of multiple groups, and adding the Tukey *b* comparison provides for a more detailed group-by-group analysis.

All three of these inferential statistics, however, deal with means and thus are useful only with interval dependent variables. How do we test hypotheses with nominal or ordinal dependent variables? That is the topic of the next chapter, where we discuss contingency tables and the chi-square statistic.

REVIEW

Key Terms

ANOVA	Critical value
Error	One-way analysis of variance
Squared errors	ONEWAY command
Total sum of squared errors (TSSE)	BY keyword
Partitioning variance	Random-sample assumption
Treatment sum of squares (TRSS)	Normality assumption
Residual sum of squared errors (RSSE)	Equal-variance assumption
Explained sum of squares	RANGES subcommand
ANOVA table	Tukey *b* comparison
Between-groups sum of squares	TUKEYB
Within-groups sum of squares	FORMAT subcommand
Mean squares	LABELS
F ratio	STATISTICS subcommand
	DESCRIPTIVES

Exercises

12.1 Correct any errors in the command statements.
   a. ONEWAY V5 V74 (0, 6) / RANGES
   b. ONEWAY V5 BY V74 / RANGES = TUKEYB
   c. ONEWAY V5 BY V74 / RANGES = BTUKEY
   d. ONEWAY V5 V6 V7 BY V74 (0, 6)
   e. ONEWAY V5 V6 V7 BY V74 (0, 6) V84 (1, 5)
   f. ONEWAY V5 V6 V7 BY V74 (0, 6) / RANGES = TUKEYB
   g. ANOVA V5 V6 V7 BY V74 (0, 6)
   h. ONEWAY V5 V6 BY V74 (0, 6) / RANGES = TUKEY
   i. ONEWAY V5 V6 BY V74 (0, 6) / RANGES = TUKEY / FORMAT = LABELS
   j. ONEWAY V5 BY V74 (0, 6) / FORMAT = LABELS
        /STATISTICS = DESCRIPTIVES
   k. ONEWAY V5 BY V74 (0, 6) / FORMAT = LABELS
   l. ONEWAY V5 BY V74 (0, 6) / STATISTICS = DESCRIPTIVES
   m. ONEWAY RINCOME BY MARITAL (1, 5) / OPTIONS 6
   n. ONEWAY RINCOME BY MARITAL (1, 5) / STATISTICS 1

    o. ONEWAY RINCOME BY MARITAL (1, 5)
      OPTIONS 6 / STATISTICS 1
    p. ONEWAY RINCOME BY MARITAL (1, 5)
        OPTIONS 6
        STATISTICS 1
    q. ONEWAY RINCOME BY MARITAL (1, 5)
      OPTIONS 6
      STATISTICS 1

12.2 Below are some ONEWAY commands pairing dependent and independent variables. Determine whether each makes sense in terms of both the logic of hypotheses and the procedure's limitations.

    a. ONEWAY V5 BY V74
    b. ONEWAY V5 BY V84
    c. ONEWAY V4 BY V74
    d. ONEWAY V5 BY V59
    e. ONEWAY V8 BY V87
    f. ONEWAY V24 BY V81
    g. ONEWAY V24 BY V74
    h. ONEWAY V24 BY V74
    i. ONEWAY V5 BY V83
    j. ONEWAY V5 BY V72
    k. ONEWAY V85 BY V84
    l. ONEWAY MARITAL BY CHILDS
    m. ONEWAY EDUC BY RACE
    n. ONEWAY PRAY BY RELIG
    o. ONEWAY PILLOK BY PRAY
    p. ONEWAY MARITAL BY CHILDS
    q. ONEWAY RINCOME BY HAPPY
    r. ONEWAY TVHOURS BY POLVIEWS
    s. ONEWAY XMOVIE BY HAPMAR

12.3 Carry out the exercise described in Supplement 12.1.

12.4 Below are two samples, each divided into three groups, with values on some dependent variable. Carry out an analysis-of-variance test, following these steps: (1) Identify the overall mean. (2) Identify the mean of each group. (3) Calculate the TSSE, TRSS, and RSSE. (4) Fill these values into an ANOVA table, as in Table 12.3. (5) Calculate the F ratio. (6) Use Table 12.4 to determine whether the F ratio is statistically significant. Once the overall and group means have been identified, filling out the table below for all 30 cases will give you the TSSE, TRSS, and RSSE for the ANOVA table.

Case	$(X_i - \bar{X})$	$(X_i - \bar{X})^2$	$(\bar{G}_i - \bar{X})$	$(\bar{G}_i - \bar{X})^2$	$(X_i - \bar{G}_i)$	$(X_i - \bar{G}_i)^2$
1						
.						
.						
.						
30						
Column sums:		TSSE	=	TRSS	+	RSSE

a. Sample 1:

Group 1	Group 2	Group 3
10	30	50
8	22	80
37	75	20
25	40	40
50	60	40
20	35	65
45	55	45
30	30	70
35	48	60
20	30	10

b. Sample 2:

Group 1	Group 2	Group 3
40	30	50
20	80	40
15	94	36
35	76	44
15	60	55
25	30	10
10	50	35
20	65	50
30	70	70
40	65	40

SUGGESTED READINGS

Iversen, Gudmund R. and Helmut Norpoth. *Analysis of Variance*, 2nd ed., Quantitative Applications in the Social Sciences, Sage University Papers Series No. 1 (Newbury Park, Calif.: Sage Publications, 1976).

Levin, Jack and James Alan Fox. *Elementary Statistics in Social Research*, 4th ed. (New York: Harper & Row, 1988) Chapter 11.

May, Richard B., Michael E. J. Masson, and Michael A. Hunter. *Application of Statistics in Behavioral Research* (New York: Harper & Row, 1990) Chapters 13, 14.

Norusis, Marija J., and SPSS Inc. *SPSS/PC+ V2.0 Base Manual* (Chicago: SPSS Inc., 1988) Chapter 14.

SPSS Inc. *SPSS Reference Guide* (Release 4) (Chicago: SPSS Inc., 1990) pages 509–16.

SPSS Inc. *SPSS-X User's Guide*, 3rd ed. (Chicago: SPSS Inc., 1988) Chapter 39.

Contingency Tables (CROSSTABS) and the Chi-Square Test

*T*he last quarter century has seen a continuing controversy over the issue of pornography, both how to define it and the extent to which it should be regulated. The 1988 GSS survey shows a clear division of opinion in the sample (Figure 13.1). Nearly half of the respondents want to ban pornography entirely, a slightly larger proportion support banning it for only those under age 18, and a small number want no restrictions at all.

What are the sources of these disparate views over the regulation of pornography? Religious and civil liberties groups have long been the antagonists in this struggle, but women's groups raised a new issue in the 1970s, claiming that pornography debases women and thus contributes to violence and discrimination against women in the United States. If many women believe this, there may be a connection between a person's gender and view of pornography. We thus hypothesize

H_R: Gender is related to attitudes about pornography.

versus

H_0: Gender is not related to attitudes about pornography.

```
GET FILE=GSS88
FREQUENCIES VARIABLES=PORNLAW / STATISTICS ALL


PORNLAW    'FEELINGS ABOUT PORNOGRAPHY LAWS
```

VALUE LABEL	VALUE	FREQUENCY	PERCENT	VALID PERCENT	CUM PERCENT
ILLEGAL TO ALL	1	429	29.0	44.0	44.0
ILLEGAL UNDER 18	2	499	33.7	51.2	95.2
LEGAL	3	47	3.2	4.8	100.0
NAP	0	484	32.7	MISSING	
DK	8	19	1.3	MISSING	
NA	9	3	0.2	MISSING	
	TOTAL	1481	100.0	100.0	

MEAN	1.608	STD ERR	0.019	MEDIAN	2.000
MODE	2.000	STD DEV	0.579	VARIANCE	0.335
KURTOSIS	-0.738	S E KURT	0.156	SKEWNESS	0.319
S E SKEW	0.078	RANGE	2.000	MINIMUM	1.000
MAXIMUM	3.000	SUM	1568.000		

```
VALID CASES    975      MISSING CASES    506
```

Figure 13.1 Distribution of support for banning pornography (PORNLAW).

RELATIONSHIPS AND CONTINGENCY TABLES

How can we test these claims? Our operational variable measuring pornography regulation, PORNLAW, does not appear to be interval or even approximately so. On the true unmeasured conceptual variable of pornography attitudes, PORNLAW's response code 1, a total ban, is probably at one end of the scale while codes 2 and 3 both represent persons who want little regulation and are probably grouped at the other end of the scale, as shown in Figure 13.2. Since PORNLAW is not an interval variable, it cannot be used as a dependent variable in procedures such as T-TEST or in an analysis of variance (ONEWAY). A highly useful statistic for any type of dependent variable—nominal, ordinal, or inter-

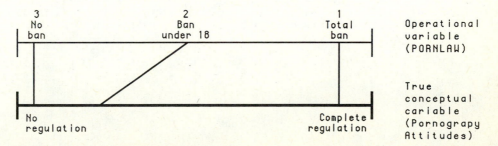

Figure 13.2 Noninterval character of PORNLAW.

val—is the chi-square statistic. Use of this statistic requires that we create a contingency table, a topic that we will examine first. Then we turn to the calculation of chi-square and finally the SPSS command producing contingency tables and the chi-square statistic.

Contingency Tables

A **contingency table** is a way of displaying relationships between two variables. If a relationship exists between gender and attitudes toward pornography, that means that women and men will have different responses on the PORNLAW variable. A contingency table illustrates any such differences by listing the distribution of the dependent variable separately for (i.e., contingent upon) the independent variable. Figure 13.3 shows a contingency table between SEX and PORNLAW for a hypothetical group of 300 people. When a contingency table is developed, accepted practice is to place the independent variable across the top of the table, with its values dividing the table into columns, and the dependent variable down the side of the table, with its values comprising the rows. Together the two variables divide the table into a number of boxes called **cells**.

Before we examine the content of the cells, let us look at the two variables that make up the table. At the right side and across the bottom are the **row totals** and **column totals**. These numbers are also often called the **marginals** since they are written in the margins of the table. They represent the overall (noncontingent) distribution of the independent and dependent variables. Of the 300 cases in the table, 132, 60, and 108, respectively, gave responses 1, 2, and 3 on PORNLAW (row totals). The same 300 cases were also divided on the basis of gender between 120 males and 180 females (column totals). The row and column totals should be nearly identical to the numbers you would find when

```
                              SEX
                              (independent  variable)
                              |
                              |  MALE    FEMALE        ROW
    PORNLAW                   |                        TOTAL
    (dependent               |    1 |      2 |
    variable)  --------- + ------ + ------ +
                         1 |   24 |    108 |      132
    Illegal  to  all        |   20% |    60% |       44%
                         + ------- + ------ +
                         2 |   24 |     36 |       60
    Illegal  under  18      |   20% |    20% |       20%
                         + ------- + ------ +
                         3 |   72 |     36 |      108
    Legal                   |   60% |    20% |       36%
                         + ------- + ------ +
                  COLUMN        120      180         300
                  TOTAL         40%      60%      100.0%
```

Figure 13.3 A contingency table.

examining a FREQUENCIES distribution of each variable separately. The only reason that they may not be exactly the same is that a contingency table includes only cases without a missing value on *either* of the two variables. Thus the column totals for SEX exclude any cases with missing data on *either* SEX or PORNLAW, while a normal FREQUENCIES printout of SEX excludes only those with missing data on SEX.

Inside the cells we find the **contingent distribution** of the dependent variable. The first column shows how 120 males are distributed on PORNLAW; 24 gave answer 1, the same number chose response 2, and 72 men chose answer 3. Similarly, the second column shows the PORNLAW distribution for females. A contingent distribution is sometimes also referred to as a **joint distribution** since the cells divide the respondents based on their values on two variables simultaneously. Out of 300 cases, 24 cases were *both* male and desirous of banning pornography entirely (upper left cell), and 36 cases were *both* female and desirous of no restrictions on pornography (lower right cell).

The columns of a contingency table divide the sample into independent-variable groups, just as the T-TEST and ONEWAY procedures do. However, each group's total distribution on the dependent variable is displayed instead of just the group's mean. Because group means do not have to be used, a contingency table can be utilized even for nominal and ordinal variables for which the mean is an inappropriate statistic.

The rows and columns of a contingency table provide a picture of any relationship between two variables. The pattern in Figure 13.3 does suggest a relationship; only 20 percent of the men versus 60 percent of the women prefer a complete ban on pornography, while the responses are reversed for preferring no restriction—60 percent of the men selected this response compared to only 20 percent of the women.

The Chi-Square Statistic

Although the pattern in Figure 13.3 shows a relationship between SEX and PORNLAW in the sample, we must again ask whether this is a result of sampling error or an accurate reflection of a relationship that exists in the population. We need a statistic summarizing the relationship that has a known probability distribution, allowing us to draw inferences about the likelihood of sampling error. **Chi square** (χ^2), pronounced "kai square," is such a statistic.

To understand the logic of chi square, we start by asking what the data would look like if the null hypothesis were true. Figure 13.4 repeats the contingency table but this time showing only the row and column marginals, leaving each cell blank. If SEX and PORNLAW were not related at all, what numbers would we expect to find in each cell? That is, how would the 120 men and 180 women in each column be distributed over the three categories of the PORN-LAW variable?

Your first reaction might be to distribute the men and women equally across the PORNLAW responses: 40 men each for response codes 1, 2, and 3, and 60 women each for the same responses. Some simple calculations, however, will

```
                                 SEX
                                 (independent  variable)
                                 |
                                 | MALE    FEMALE        ROW
             PORNLAW             |                       TOTAL
             (dependent          |    1  |      2  |
             variable) --------- + ------ + ------ +
                          1  |    |       |       |     132
             Illegal  to  all   |    |       |       |      44%
                                 + ------- + ------ +
                          2  |    |       |       |      60
             Illegal  under  18 |    |       |     . |      20%
                                 + ------- + ------ +
                          3  |    |       |       |     108
             Legal             |    |       |       |      36%
                                 + ------- + ------ +
                     COLUMN         120      180          300
                     TOTAL          40%      60%       100.0%
```

Figure 13.4 A blank contingency table.

show that this is the wrong approach. For the two cells in row 1, the 40 men and 60 women will total 100 respondents for the row, but the marginals show that 132 people in the sample gave this response. Where are the 32 missing cases? It would not help to divide each row total equally between the columns, dividing 132 cases in row 1 into 61 males and 61 females, for that would lead to a 50-50 split between men and women in the column totals when our sample cases actually divide 40-60 between the sexes.

A lack of any relationship between the two variables means not that the respondents have to be distributed equally, but that the pattern of responses on the dependent variable should be essentially the same for all categories of the independent variable. If the overall distribution of opinion is such that 44 percent of the people prefer to ban pornography completely, then 44 percent of the men and 44 percent of the women are expected to give this response when the null hypothesis is true. Similarly, row 2 should contain 20 percent of each gender, and the last row 36 percent.

The cell entries that we expect to find if the null hypothesis is true are called the **expected frequencies**. The expected frequencies for the cells of a contingency table are calculated from the simple formula

Expected frequency = column n * row %

Note that the expected frequency is the *number* of cases in each column times the *percentage* of cases in each row. Thus the expected frequency is 52.8 for the upper left cell (44 percent times 120 males) and 79.2 (44 percent times 180 females) for the upper right cell.

We determine whether a relationship exists by comparing the expected frequencies with the **observed frequencies**, those actually observed in the sample. In the upper left cell, the null hypothesis tells us to expect 52.8 men, but the observed sample frequency in Figure 13.3 was only 24 men. If the differences between the expected and observed frequencies are small, they could easily be the result of an error in sampling from a population where the null hypothesis is true. Large differences between these two numbers would lead us to question the likelihood of the null hypothesis.

Figure 13.5 repeats the contingency table with each cell now containing the expected and observed frequencies along with the differences between them. Note that the difference figures in the two columns are mirror images of each other, such as +28.8 versus −28.8 in row 1. This is a characteristic of contingency tables having only two columns, but it is not necessarily true for larger tables.

The chi-square statistic uses the comparison between expected and observed frequencies to test the null hypothesis. The formula for the statistic is

$$\chi^2 = \Sigma \frac{(f_e - f_o)^2}{f_e}$$

where χ^2 = symbol for chi-square statistic
Σ = summation across all cells in table
f_e = expected frequency of cell
f_o = observed frequency of cell

The first step in the formula is to determine the difference between the observed and expected frequencies for each cell in the table. This difference is then squared, to eliminate any negative numbers canceling positive ones. We do not particularly care whether the observed frequency is above (positive difference) or below (negative difference) the expected frequency. We just want to know the size of the difference in either direction.

Then the squared difference of each cell is turned into a proportion by dividing by the expected frequency. A difference of 20 cases is not very mean-

```
                            SEX
                            (independent  variable)
                            I
                            I  MALE            FEMALE          ROW
        PORNLAW             I                                  TOTAL
        (dependent          I        1    I           2   I
        variable) -------  + ----------- + ----------- +
                    1       I  Exp    52.8 I  Exp    79.2 I
                            I  Obs    24.0 I  Obs   108.0 I    132
        Illegal  to  all    I  Diff   28.8 I  Diff  -28.8 I     44%
                            + ----------- + ----------- +
                    2       I  Exp    24.0 I  Exp    36.0 I
                            I  Obs    24.0 I  Obs    36.0 I     60
        Illegal  under  18  I  Diff    0.0 I  Diff    0.0 I     20%
                            + ----------- + ----------- +
                    3       I  Exp    43.2 I  Exp    64.8 I
                            I  Obs    72.0 I  Obs    36.0 I    108
        Legal               I  Diff  -28.8 I  Diff   28.8 I     36%
                            + ----------- + ----------- +
                  COLUMN           120           180        300
                   TOTAL           40%           60%        100.0%
```

Figure 13.5 A completed contingency table.

ingful if that is only 1 percent off from the expected frequency, but is considerably more noteworthy if it is 30 percent away from the expected frequency. Finally, the proportional squared differences are summed across all the cells in the table to obtain the completed chi-square statistic. Here we apply the chi-square formula to the table in Figure 13.5, getting a chi-square statistic of 58.18:

$$\chi^2 = \Sigma\left[\frac{(52.8 - 24)^2}{52.8} + \frac{(79.2 - 102)^2}{79.2} + \frac{(24 - 24)^2}{24} + \frac{(36 - 36)^2}{36}\right.$$

$$\left. + \frac{(43.2 - 72)^2}{43.2} + \frac{(64.8 - 36)^2}{64.8}\right]$$

$$= \Sigma\left[\frac{(+28.8)^2}{52.8} + \frac{(-28.8)^2}{79.2} + \frac{0^2}{24} + \frac{0^2}{36} + \frac{(-28.8)^2}{43.2} + \frac{(+28.8)^2}{64.8}\right]$$

$$= \Sigma\left(\frac{829.44}{52.8} + \frac{829.44}{79.2} + \frac{0}{24} + \frac{0}{36} + \frac{829.44}{43.2} + \frac{829.44}{64.8}\right)$$

$$= \Sigma\left(15.71 + 10.47 + 0 + 0 + 19.20 + 12.80\right)$$

$$= 58.18$$

Like the t and F statistics, the chi-square statistic has a known distribution, a distribution of values likely to occur through sampling error. The distribution is based on the degrees of freedom available when the statistic is calculated. The degrees of freedom (df) of the chi-square statistic are determined by the formula

$$df = (r - 1) * (c - 1)$$

where df is the number of rows minus 1 times the number of columns minus 1. With 3 rows and 2 columns in Figure 13.5,

$$df = (3 - 1) * (2 - 1) = 2 * 1 = 2$$

Having determined the degrees of freedom of the statistic, we can turn to a table of the chi-square distribution to determine whether the number calculated is statistically significant. A simplified chi-square table is shown in Table 13.1. The table lists the highest chi-square value one is likely to find through sampling error, termed the **critical value**, for each degree of freedom and for the .05 and .01 levels of statistical significance. When the null hypothesis is true in the population, 95 percent of all samples will produce chi-square values of 5.991 or less for tables with 2 degrees of freedom. Our calculated chi-square is far higher than this critical value. We thus reject as implausible the notion that our calculated chi square is the result of sampling error from a population in which the two variables are unrelated.

Table 13.1   CRITICAL VALUES OF CHI SQUARE AT THE .05 AND .01 LEVELS OF SIGNIFICANCE

df	Significance level	
	.05	.01
1	3.841	6.635
2	**5.991**	9.210
3	7.815	11.345
4	9.488	13.277
5	11.070	15.086
6	12.592	16.812
7	14.067	18.475
8	15.507	20.090
9	16.919	21.666
10	18.307	23.209
15	24.996	30.578
20	31.410	37.566
25	37.652	44.314
30	43.773	50.892

Source: Abridged from Table 8 in E. S. Pearson and H. O. Hartley (eds.), *Biometrika Tables for Statisticians,* vol. 1, 2d ed. (New York: Cambridge University Press, 1976). Reproduced with the permission of the trustees of *Biometrika.*

Note that the degrees of freedom and thus the probability distribution of chi square are based solely on the number of rows and columns in the table. This is unlike other distributions in which degrees of freedom were calculated by using the number of cases in the sample. The rules of probability tell us that most samples will be close to the population value, but a few rare ones will be quite far from it. If you draw enough samples, you will eventually encounter some of these rare nonrepresentative ones. Each cell of a contingency table can be thought of as a separate sample from the joint distribution of two variables in the population—for example, the upper left cell is a sample of all population members who are both male and opposed to pornography's being available to anyone. Expanding the number of cells in the table is equivalent to drawing additional samples from segments of the population, some of which are bound to contain large differences between the expected and observed frequencies merely through sampling error. The chi square distribution is based on such possibilities, so larger values of chi square are needed to reject the null hypothesis as the degrees of freedom (table cells) increase.

The sample size is not ignored, but is included in the size of the chi-square statistic itself rather than in its probability distribution. If we increased the size of the row, column, and cell n's in Figure 13.5 by a factor of 10, the difference between the expected and observed frequencies in each cell would be 10 times bigger. Of course, the expected frequencies that we must divide by in the chi-square formula would also be 10 times larger, but each difference in the numerator is squared, to produce a number 100 times larger than the original. The net result is that multiplying the sample size by 10 also leads the calculated chi-square statistic to become 10 times its original size. This effect of the sample size makes sense for measures of statistical significance, since large samples make us more confident that any relationships found are an accurate representation of what is true for the population.

THE CROSSTABS COMMAND

Although calculating the chi square and determining its statistical significance are not exceptionally difficult, they can be cumbersome. In contrast, having SPSS do this work for us is relatively simple. The SPSS command that produces a contingency table is

CROSSTABS TABLES = dependent variable(s) BY independent variable(s)

The command term **CROSSTABS** tells SPSS to produce a contingency table, and the **TABLES** term describes what contingency tables we want. Tables are requested by listing one or more dependent variables first, one or more independent variables last, and separating the two with the **BY keyword**. For example, the command

CROSSTABS TABLES = V2 BY V27 V33

produces two contingency tables. Each has V2 (presidential election vote) down the side comprising the rows, while one table has V27 (defense spending scale) as the table's columns across the top and the other table has V33 (cooperation with Russia scale) in this position.

The specific table that interests us, PORNLAW by SEX, is shown in Figure 13.6. The top of the output lists the names and labels of the two variables in the table. Below is the table itself, showing how the 546 females and 429 males are distributed across the PORNLAW variable. No statistics have been calculated, however, and the table contains only the number of cases falling into each cell. We usually want considerably more information than is provided by the basic table, information that is obtained by adding subcommands.

Formatting Subcommands

In the upper left corner of the contingency table in Figure 13.6 we see the word COUNT. By default, SPSS includes only a frequency count—how many cases fall into each cell of the table. Of what importance is it that only 145 men but fully 284 women want pornography banned completely? Since there are more women than men in the sample, the two numbers may represent the same proportion of each gender, so percentages would provide a clearer picture. We may also want the expected values calculated for each cell. These and other options are available through formatting subcommands, listed in Table 13.2.

```
GET  FILE=GSS88
CROSSTABS  TABLES = PORNLAW  BY  SEX


- - - - - -  C R O S S - T A B U L A T I O N  O F  - - - - - -
PORNLAW  FEELINGS ABOUT PORNOGRAPHY LAWS    BY SEX    RESPONDENT'S SEX
- - - - - - - - - - - - - - - - - - - - - - - - - - - PAGE 1 OF 1

                         SEX
              COUNT   I
                      I MALE      FEMALE      ROW
                      I                       TOTAL
                      I      1 I       2  I
PORNLAW  ---------- + ------ + ------ +
                 1  I    145 I    284  I    429
Illegal  to  all    I        I        I    44.0
                    + ------ + ------ +
                 2  I    257 I    242  I    499
Illegal  under 18   I        I        I    51.2
                    + ------ + ------ +
                 3  I     27 I     20  I     47
Legal               I        I        I    4.8
                    + ------ + ------ +
              COLUMN      429    546      975
              TOTAL      44.0    56.0    100.0
```

Figure 13.6 A cross-tabulation of PORNLAW by SEX.

(v.2) (PC) Most of the subcommands and options are self-explanatory. You can request any of them by beginning with a slash followed by the subcommand name and finally the option selected. For example, the subcommand

/ FORMAT NOLABELS

will eliminate the variable and value labels when the table is printed. You should avoid using the MISSING (including missing data) and WRITE (saving a copy of the table on a storage device) subcommands without first consulting with your instructor; both are used only by experienced analysts.

(v.2) (PC) A subcommand you will use consistently is the **CELLS subcommand**, which determines the information printed in the cells of the table. You will want to request the **COLUMN** and **COUNT** options with this subcommand. The COLUMN option places the column percentages in each cell. The COUNT alternative, the observed frequency, is the default if no CELLS subcommand is added. If, however, you do include a CELLS subcommand, any alternatives requested by that subcommand will replace the count unless you explicitly request that option as well.

(v.2) (PC) Since we previously discussed the chi-square statistic and will return to it again shortly, we include two other CELLS options in the illustrations

Table 13.2   CROSSTABS FORMATTING ALTERNATIVES REQUESTED BY SUBCOMMANDS

Subcommand	Option	Description	Version 2 Option no.
MISSING	INCLUDE	Include missing data in table.	1
MISSING	REPORT	Include missing data in table but not in calculating percentages,	7
FORMAT	NOLABELS	Do not print variable or value labels.	2
FORMAT	NOVALLABS	Print variable but not value labels.	6
FORMAT	DVALUE	Print row variable in descending order.	8
FORMAT	INDEX	Print an index of tables produced.	9
CELLS	ROW	Print row percentage in cells.	3
CELLS	COLUMN	Print column percentage in cells.	4
CELLS	TOTAL	Print total table percentage in each cell.	5
CELLS	COUNT	Print observed frequency in each cell (default).	—
—	—	Do not print observed frequency in each cell.	13
CELLS	EXPECTED	Print expected frequencies in each cell.	14
CELLS	RESID	Print residuals for each cell.	15
CELLS	SRESID	Print standardized residuals for each cell.	16
CELLS	ASRESID	Print adjusted standardized residuals.	17
CELLS	ALL	Print all information available with CELL subcommand.	18
CELLS	NONE	Do not print table (if only summary statistics are desired).	12
WRITE	CELLS	Write count of nonempty cells to a file.	10
WRITE	ALL	Write count of all cells to a file.	11

below: **EXPECTED** prints the expected frequency in each cell and **RESID** prints the residuals (the difference between the expected and observed frequencies) in each cell. Thus the subcommand we will use is

    / CELLS COLUMN COUNT EXPECTED RESID

Normally, however, you will not want to clutter the cells of your contingency table with the EXPECTED and RESID information.

Version 2   Version 2 of SPSS-X requests subcommands in a manner that is a carryover from SPSS's early days. Alternative ways of presenting the contingency table are referred to as OPTIONS. Each option is identified by a number which must be used to invoke the option. The rightmost column of Table 13.2 contains the option numbers associated with each subcommand.

Furthermore, the OPTIONS subcommand (without a slash) must begin in column 1, just as the main CROSSTABS procedure command does. To add column percentages, expected frequencies, and residuals to the count in the cells of the contingency table, the command-subcommand combination for SPSS-X version 2 is

    CROSSTABS TABLES = PORNLAW BY SEX

    OPTIONS 4 14 15

Only three options are included above because version 2 does not eliminate the cell count when other options are requested. Instead a separate option number, 13, is used whenever printing of the observed frequency is to be suppressed. Version 3 of SPSS-X recognizes the old way of requesting subcommands. Release 4 will not recognize the OPTIONS statement unless your SPSS commands are submitted through the operating system instead of the SPSS software. This is the standard way in which commands are submitted on IBM mainframes using OS, but it is not standard for other implementations, except for command files processed with the INCLUDE command and some other ways of submitting command files without going through the command generator.

After you request this additional information to be printed in the cells, the revised output will look like Figure 13.7. Each cell now contains four numbers: the observed frequency, expected frequency, column percentage, and residual. Additionally, the upper left corner of the table lists the cell options you have selected and the order in which they appear in each cell; count is the first

```
GET  FILE=GSS88
CROSSTABS  TABLES=PORNLAW  BY  SEX
           / CELLS  COUNT  COLUMN  EXPECTED  RESID


- - - - - -      C R O S S - T A B U L A T I O N      O F   - - - - - -

PORNLAW FEELINGS ABOUT PORNOGRAPHY LAWS      BY SEX      RESPONDENT'S SEX

- - - - - - - - - - - - - - - - - - - - - - - - - - - PAGE 1 OF 1

                        SEX
              COUNT   I
              EXP VAL I
              COL PCT I MALE      FEMALE      ROW
              RESIDUAL I                      TOTAL
                      I      1 I       2 I
PORNLAW   ------- + ------ + ------ +
            1 I     145 I     108 I
              I   188.8 I   240.2 I     429
Illegal  to all  I    33.8% I    52.0% I   44.0%
              I   -43.8 I    43.8 I
              + ------- + ------ +
            2 I     257 I     242 I
              I   219.6 I   279.4 I     499
Illegal  under 18 I    59.9% I    44.3% I   51.2%
              I    37.4 I   -37.4 I
              + ------- + ------ +
            3 I      27 I      20 I
              I    20.7 I    26.3 I      47
Legal         I     6.3% I     3.7% I    4.8%
              I     6.3 I    -6.3 I
              + ------- + ------ +
         COLUMN       429       546       975
          TOTAL      44.0%     56.0%    100.0%
```

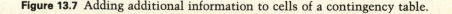

Figure 13.7 Adding additional information to cells of a contingency table.

number, expected value (expected frequency) the second, column percentage the third, and residual the last.

Adding the column percentages clarifies the relationship between SEX and PORNLAW. Only 34 percent of the men want pornography banned completely while 52 percent of the women prefer this policy. The second policy choice, illegal only to those under 18, is preferred by 60 percent of the men but only 44 percent of the women. While the pattern is clearer, it is still a pattern that exists only in the sample. For a chi-square test of whether a relationship also exists in the population, we must use the STATISTICS subcommand.

Statistics

(χ²) (PC) Along with altering the information displayed in the cells of the contingency table, we can request SPSS to calculate a number of statistics summarizing the information in the table. We do this with the **STATISTICS** subcommand. A large number of summary statistics are available, most of which we examine in Chapter 14. The only statistic that interests us at this point is chi square, which is requested with the **CHISQ** keyword added to the STATISTICS subcommand. The complete command-subcommand specification is

        CROSSTABS TABLES = PORNLAW BY SEX

        / CELLS COUNT COLUMN EXPECTED RESIDUALS / STATISTICS CHISQ

Version 2   Like the formatting options, statistics are requested in version 2 of SPSS-X with the STATISTICS subcommand (without a slash), beginning in column 1, followed by a number for the statistic desired. Chi square is statistic number 1. Thus the complete command-subcommand specification for version 2 of SPSS-X is

        CROSSTABS TABLES = PORNLAW BY SEX

        OPTIONS 4 14 15

        STATISTICS 1

(R.4) Figure 13.8 shows the revised CROSSTABS output after the chi-square statistic has been requested. Below the table is the chi-square value, 32.96544. You should be able to calculate this number by squaring the residual value in each cell, dividing by the expected value, and summing over the six cells. Your results will not be exactly the same as those on the output, since SPSS's internal calculations use more decimal places for the expected and residual values than can be shown in the cells, but they should be very close.

Release 4   SPSS produces a different output from the CROSSTABS command for Release 4. The table itself should look the same as illustrations in this chapter, but the organization of the statistics below the table is very different

```
GET  FILE=GSS88
CROSSTABS  TABLES=PORNLAW  BY  SEX
              / CELLS COUNT COLUMN EXPECTED RESID  / STATISTICS    CHISQ


- - - - - - -   C R O S S - T A B U L A T I O N   O F   - - - - - - -
PORNLAW FEELINGS ABOUT PORNOGRAPHY LAWS     BY SEX     RESPONDENT'S SEX
- - - - - - - - - - - - - - - - - - - - - - - - - - - - - PAGE 1 OF 1

                         SEX
                 COUNT  I
                 EXP VAL I
                 COL PCT I MALE    FEMALE       ROW
                 RESIDUAL I                     TOTAL
                         I     1 I      2 I
PORNLAW    -------+ ------ + ------ +
                 1 I    145 I    108 I
                   I  188.8 I  240.2 I       429
   Illegal  to  all I   33.8% I   52.0% I    44.0%
                   I  -43.8 I   43.8 I
                 + ------- + ------ +
                 2 I    257 I    242 I
                   I  219.6 I  279.4 I       499
   Illegal  under 18 I   59.9% I   44.3% I    51.2%
                   I   37.4 I  -37.4 I
                 + ------- + ------ +
                 3 I     27 I     20 I
                   I   20.7 I   26.3 I        47
   Legal         I    6.3% I    3.7% I     4.8%
                   I    6.3 I   -6.3 I
                 + ------- + ------ +
           COLUMN        429      546       975
           TOTAL        44.0%    56.0%    100.0%


CHI SQUARED    DF     SIGNIFICANCE     MIN EF    CELLS WITH EF < 5

  32.96544      2        0.0000        20.680       NONE
```

Figure 13.8 Cross-tabulation of PORNLAW by SEX with the addition of chi-square statistic.

and some additional statistics have been added. The revised output is shown in Figure 13.9. It contains three different chi-square statistics, each using a slightly different way to calculate the statistic. Just use the top number, the Pearson chi square, which is discussed in this chapter. The output will also not contain some of the items mentioned below, such as the number of cells with expected frequencies below 5.

   Let us look further at the statistics below the table. One column to the right of the chi-square value are the degrees of freedom available with the chi square and one column farther to the right is the significance level, or the probability of obtaining this chi-square value with 2 degrees of freedom when the null hypothesis is true in the population. Since the significance level is below our .05 decision criterion, we reject the null hypothesis and accept the alternative.

```
-  -  -  -  -  -  -     C R O S S - T A B U L A T I O N    O F    - - - - - - -
PORNLAW  FEELINGS ABOUT PORNOGRAPHY LAWS      BY SEX      RESPONDENT'S SEX
- - - - - - - - - - - - - - - - - - - - - - - - - - - - - - - PAGE 1 OF 1

                         SEX
              COUNT   I
              EXP VAL I
              COL PCT I MALE      FEMALE      ROW
              RESIDUAL I                      TOTAL
                      I      1 I      2 I
PORNLAW   -------+ ------ + ------ +
             1  I    145 I    108 I
                I  188.8 I  240.2 I    429
Illegal  to all I  33.8% I  52.0% I   44.0%
                I  -43.8 I   43.8 I
                + ------- + ------ +
             2  I    257 I    242 I
                I  219.6 I  279.4 I    499
Illegal  under 18 I 59.9% I  44.3% I   51.2%
                I   37.4 I  -37.4 I
                + ------- + ------ +
             3  I     27 I     20 I
                I   20.7 I   26.3 I     47
Legal           I   6.3% I   3.7% I    4.8%
                I    6.3 I   -6.3 I
                + ------- + ------ +
            COLUMN     429      546      975
            TOTAL    44.0%    56.0%   100.0%
```

Chi Squared	Value	DF	Significance
Pearson	32.96544	2	0.00000
Likelihood ratio	32.49027	2	0.00000
Mantel-Haenszel	26.54495	1	0.00000

```
Minimum expected frequency -   20.680
```

Figure 13.9 Release 4 CROSSTABS output.

The last two columns contain other information relevant to using the chi-square statistic. The chi-square value can be distorted when the expected frequency of one or more cells is very low. Say one cell has an expected frequency of 1 and an observed frequency of 3. While only two cases separate the expected and observed frequencies, dividing this squared difference by a small expected frequency will make this disparity look quite large—a squared difference 400 percent larger than the expected frequency. Were the expected frequency larger, say 10, this same two-case disparity after squaring would be only 40 percent larger than the expected frequency.

Whenever the denominator (the expected frequency) used in the chi-square calculations is very small, any difference between the observed and expected frequencies (the numerator) is exaggerated. To determine whether this might be a problem, SPSS calculates two items: the smallest expected frequency for any of the cells (MIN E.F.) and the number of cells with an expected frequency below 5 (CELLS WITH E.F. < 5). If any cell has an expected frequency less than 1, or more than 20 percent of the cells have expected frequencies less than 5, then the chi-square test of statistical significance will be unreliable. If you encounter either situation, consult with your instructor or an advanced statistics text before drawing any inferences from the contingency table.

When examining 2 by 2 contingency tables, some statisticians believe (although others disagree) that a correction, called the **Yates correction**, is needed to draw valid inferences. Consequently, SPSS produces two different chi-square statistics on the output for 2 by 2 tables. One is the standard chi square following the formula presented in this chapter, and is labeled BEFORE YATES CORRECTION. The other is unlabeled, looking like the chi-square line in Figure 13.8, but it will have been modified with the Yates correction. It is not important to explain the Yates correction here, for usually both chi-square numbers will lead to the same conclusion on whether to accept or reject the null hypothesis. You merely need to be prepared for occasionally encountering additional chi-square statistics on the printout.

APPLICATIONS

Contingency tables are a very powerful and flexible tool in data analysis. You will have already encountered them regularly in numerous situations. For example, whenever the mass media report poll results broken down by age, sex, income, or education, they are presenting you with a contingency table. In using and interpreting contingency tables, two concerns should be kept in mind: uses of the table versus the summary statistics and inclusion of interval variables in a contingency table.

Contingency Tables and Summary Statistics

The CROSSTABS procedure produces an output with two useful features. The first is the contingency table itself, providing a visual portrayal of any relationship between variables in the same manner as a bar chart or histogram provides a visual display of the distribution of a single variable. Graphic displays like a contingency table are very helpful in understanding the data being examined but, by themselves, are imprecise and open to misinterpretation. The summary statistics, such as the mean and variance produced by a FREQUENCIES procedure or the chi square on the CROSSTABS output, provide more useful information when you are drawing conclusions.

It is important to keep this in mind, for people are often tempted to focus on the contingency table itself and to slight the summary statistics below the table. This is like buying a car based solely on how it looks while ignoring such numerical data as its frequency-of-repair record, gas mileage, or price. A contingency table showing that 50 percent of women attend church weekly but only

30 percent of men do appears to exhibit a clear relationship between gender and church attendance. Any conclusions drawn from just this information, however, should be suspect. The data in the female/weekly church attendance cell may be an aberrant sample, misrepresenting the population frequency of female weekly church attenders. Only by considering the patterns in all the cells of the table can we determine if a relationship exists in the population. This is very hard to do by just "eyeballing" the table, but is exactly what is done with the chi square formula. Calculating chi square, something often not done in mass-media reports, will tell us whether the sample pattern is sufficiently strong for us to draw conclusions about the population.

Contingency Tables and Interval Variables

The CROSSTABS procedure is very flexible, allowing our independent and dependent variables to be of any type—nominal, ordinal, or interval. So why do we even bother with the T-TEST and ONEWAY procedures? Both are appropriate for interval dependent variables only, but CROSSTABS can be used for all types of dependent variables; so why not just use CROSSTABS and chi square for all variables?

There are two answers to this question. First, although the chi-square statistic can be used with interval dependent variables, it does not use the interval information that such variables contain. In essence, chi square treats all variables as though they were nominal. This is a mathematically legitimate approach since variables can always be treated as though they were measured at a lower level. An interval variable is, in fact, nominal—it divides respondents in categories of same versus different—but it is also more than that, containing ordinal and interval information as well. Statisticians do not like to waste information, preferring to use the most precise statistics available. Since the T-TEST procedure and analysis of variance make use of the interval information of a dependent variable, they are more efficient and exact than chi square.

Second, because of their nature, interval variables sometimes pose problems for the CROSSTABS procedure. Interval variables typically (though not always) contain a large number of response categories, for example, 15 different categories of income or over 60 code numbers for different ages. A contingency table between income and age would be a 15 by 60 table, or a table with 900 individual cells. Not only is such a table very unwieldy, but also a large proportion of the cells are bound to have expected frequencies less than 5, thus making the chi-square statistic suspect. We could recode interval variables into a smaller number of categories, but then we are back at the beginning, throwing away some of the information that the variables contain.

None of this is to say that interval variables should never be examined with the CROSSTABS procedure; in fact they often are. The point is that the T-TEST procedure and F test also have their uses. They are considerably more precise and can be used in situations where a contingency table would be unwieldy and chi square unreliable.

SPSS/PC+

SPSS/PC+ requests additional statistics or changes in the format of a contingency table as done in version 2 of SPSS-X. The OPTIONS and STATISTICS keywords are used with numbers designating the options and statistics desired. The option numbers are the same as those described in this chapter and listed in Table 13.2. Similarly, statistic 1 is used to obtain the chi-square statistic. There are three differences, the same as those listed at the end of Chapter 12. First, these two keywords must be preceded by slashes, as is true of other subcommands. Second, they do not have to begin in column 1, as required by version 2 of SPSS-X. Third, they can both be contained on the same line, just as other subcommands can.

SUMMARY

With this chapter's review of chi square we have completed our examination of the common measures of statistical significance—the T-TEST procedure, the F test, and chi square. Depending on the nature of the variables we are examining, we will select one of these tests to determine whether our sample data allow us to reject the null hypothesis for the population. We continue to use these three tests of statistical significance in the rest of the text.

It is now time to turn to statistics providing answers to a different kind of question. Given that a relationship exists between two variables, our next concern is with the strength of a relationship, a question that requires the use of a measure of association. The versatile CROSSTABS procedure can also calculate measures of association, and that topic is taken up in Chapter 14.

REVIEW

Key Terms

Contingency table	CROSSTABS
Cells	TABLES
Row totals	BY keyword
Column totals	CELLS subcommand
Marginals	COLUMN
Contingent distribution	COUNT
Joint distribution	EXPECTED
Chi square (χ^2)	RESID
Expected frequencies	STATISTICS
Observed frequencies	CHISQ
Critical value	Yates correction

Exercises

13.1 Correct any errors in the command statements.
  a. CROSSTABS V2 BY V62
  b. CROSSTABS TABLES = V2 BY V62
  c. CROSSTABS TABLES = V2 V62
  d. CROSSTABS TABLES = V2 BY V62 CELLS COLUMN
  e. CROSSTABS TABLES = V2 BY V62 / CELLS
  f. CROSSTABS TABLES = V2 BY V62 /CELLS COLUMN STATISTICS CHISQ
  g. CROSSTABS TABLES = V2 BY V62 /CELLS COUNT
  h. CROSSTABS TABLES = V2 BY V62 /STATISTICS
  i. CROSSTABS TABLES = V2 BY V62 /STATISTICS CHISQ
  j. CROSSTABS TABLES = WRKSTAT BY SEX / CELLS EXPECTED
  k. CROSSTABS TABLES = WRKSTAT BY SEX / CELLS RESID
  l. CROSSTABS TABLES = EDUC BY SEX / CELLS COUNT COLUMN
  m. CROSSTABS TABLES = SEX BY EDUC / CELLS COUNT COLUMN
        / STATISTICS CHISQ
  n. CROSSTABS TABLES = RINCOME BY EDUC /CELLS COUNT COLUMN
        / STATISTICS CHISQ
  o. CROSSTABS TABLES = WRKSTAT BY RACE / CELLS COLUMN
  p. CROSSTABS TABLES = WRKSTAT BY SEX / CELLS 4
  q. CROSSTABS TABLES = WRKSTAT BY SEX
     OPTIONS 4
  r. CROSSTABS TABLES = WRKSTAT BY SEX / OPTIONS 4 14 15
  s. CROSSTABS TABLES = WRKSTAT BY SEX
     /OPTIONS 4, 14, 15
     /STATISTICS 1
  t. CROSSTABS TABLES = WRKSTAT BY SEX
     OPTIONS 4
     STATISTICS 1

13.2 Multiply the *n*'s (row totals, column totals, and cell counts) in Figure 13.5 by 10, and calculate the new chi-square value. Verify that this number gets bigger with larger samples, even though the relationship is the same.

13.3 In the two contingency tables below, fill in the missing information in the blank cells. Calculate the expected frequency for each cell, the chi-square value, and the degrees of freedom. Then use Table 13.1 to determine whether this chi-square value is statistically significant.
  a.

	COUNT	EDUC LOW 1	MEDIUM 2	HIGH 3	ROW TOTAL
RINCOME					
LOW 1			10	5	30 / 30.0%
MEDIUM 2		10		10	40 / 40.0%
HIGH 3		5	5	20	30
COLUMN TOTAL		30 / 30.0%	35 / 35.0%	35 / 35.0%	100 / 100.0%

b.

	COUNT	EXERCISE			ROW TOTAL
HEALTH		NONE *1*	SOME *2*	A LOT *3*	
FAIR	1	75	50	25	150 30.0%
GOOD	2				200 40.0%
EXCELLENT	3	25	75	50	150 30.0%
COLUMN TOTAL		175 35.0%	200 40.0%	125 25.0%	500 100.0%

SUGGESTED READINGS

Babbie, Earl. *The Practice of Social Research*, 5th ed. (Belmont, Calif.: Wadsworth, 1989) Chapter 14.

Freedman, David, *et al. Statistics*, 2nd ed. (New York: W. W. Norton, 1991) Chapter 28.

Levin, Jack and James Alan Fox. *Elementary Statistics in Social Research*, 4th ed. (New York: Harper & Row, 1988) Chapters 3, 12.

May, Richard B., Michael E. J. Masson, and Michael A. Hunter. *Application of Statistics in Behavioral Research* (New York: Harper & Row, 1990) Chapter 17.

Norusis, Marija J., and SPSS Inc. *SPSS/PC+ V2.0 Base Manual* (Chicago: SPSS Inc., 1988) Chapter 9.

SPSS Inc. *SPSS Reference Guide* (Release 4) (Chicago: SPSS Inc., 1990) pages 99–108.

SPSS Inc. *SPSS-X User's Guide*, 3rd ed. (Chicago: SPSS Inc., 1988) Chapter 25.

Contingency Tables (CROSSTABS) and Measures of Association

*T*o a considerable extent, the 1988 presidential election was a referendum on the Reagan presidency. Although other issues were raised as well, evaluations of the Reagan years were a continual part of the rhetoric and campaign strategies of both candidates. Two issues in particular were stressed. George Bush, Reagan's vice president, regularly reminded voters of the economic growth during the prior 8 years and argued that he was the best candidate to continue it. For his part, Michael Dukakis pointed to repeated charges of corruption among high administration officials and contended that he was the best candidate to correct these failings.

As students of the political world, we are curious about the effectiveness of these strategies. Our interest is twofold. First, did citizens' evaluations of the Reagan years affect their decisions to vote for Bush or Dukakis? If we find that they did, our second question is, Which of these issues had the greatest impact on voter decisions? Were the voters very concerned about the corruption issue, or did they feel that the economic successes of Reagan and Bush were considerably more important than any charges of corruption? George Bush's victory in the election suggests the latter explanation, but it is quite possible that voters were concerned about the corruption charges, yet voted for Bush anyway because of other issues (e.g., crime or defense policies) or the personalities of the candidates.

The first question, whether these two issues affected how people voted, can be answered by creating contingency tables and calculating chi-square statistics, as done in Figure 14.1. Values 3 and 8 on V2 (third-party voters and nonvoters) have been recoded in a missing-data category since we are only interested in measuring the choice of voting for Bush or Dukakis. Both of the resulting chi-square values have significance levels below .05, so the issues did make a difference to the population of voters.

What, however, of the second question, Which issue swayed voters more? Does the size of the chi-square values provide an answer? Not really. Chi square, as well as the *t* statistic and *F* ratio, measures **statistical significance**. It is useful to think of statistical significance as a threshold indicator—either a relationship is statistically significant, or it is not. You cannot be a "little bit" statistically significant any more than you can be a little bit pregnant or a little bit dead—you either are or are not, with no gray areas in between. If a relationship is not statistically significant, there is little point in further exploring the nature of the relationship since we are not even convinced that it exists. If, however, we are sure that the relationship exists then we want to probe it further to examine its nature and strength, information provided by measures of association. In this chapter we look at various measures of association that can be calculated from contingency tables.

MEASURES OF ASSOCIATION

Being convinced that a relationship exists in the population is not the same as saying that the relationship is an important one. A relationship's importance is termed its **substantive significance**, and substantive significance is evaluated through **measures of association**. Such statistics determine whether changes in the independent variable lead to large or small changes in the dependent variable. In terms of the questions raised at the beginning of this chapter, did voters who saw the Reagan economic policies as valuable vote for George Bush in far larger, or only slightly larger, numbers than the voters who did not feel those policies were very helpful?

In interpreting measures of association, it is common for people to speak of relationships as either strong or weak. A close connection between an independent and a dependent variable is called a **strong relationship**—only a small change in studying produces a sizable change in grades. A looser connection between the independent and dependent variables—a large amount of studying leads to only a slight improvement in grades—is called a **weak relationship**.

Before looking at selected measures of association, we must again remind the reader that statistics are not based on revealed truth or discovered as laws of nature—statistics are created by humans to deal with specific needs. Measures of association are legion in number, and in the remaining chapters of this text we examine only some of them. Each one has distinctive features. Some are designed for nominal variables, others for ordinal variables, and still others

```
GET FILE = ELEC88
RECODE V2 (3,8=9)
CROSSTABS TABLES = V2  BY  V68  V70  /STATISTICS ALL
   / CELLS COLUMN COUNT
```

```
- - - - - -   C R O S S - T A B U L A T I O N   O F   - - - - - -
V2   PRESIDENTIAL VOTE            BY   V68        REAGAN  IMPACT-ECONOMY
- - - - - - - - - - - - - - - - - - - - - - - - - - - - - PAGE  1 OF  1
```

	V68					
COUNT COL PCT	MUCH BETTER 1	SOMEWHAT BETTER 2	SAME 3	SOMEWHAT WORSE 4	MUCH WORSE 5	ROW TOTAL
V2						
1 BUSH	178 92.2	251 73.4	148 40.0	27 19.6	9 8.6	613 53.4
2 DUKAKIS	15 7.8	91 26.6	222 60.0	111 80.4	96 91.4	535 46.6
COLUMN TOTAL	193 16.8	342 29.8	370 32.2	138 12.0	105 9.1	1148 100.0

CHI SQUARED	DF	SIGNIFICANCE	MIN EF	CELLS WITH EF < 5
346.83451	4	0.0000	48.933	NONE

```
- - - - - -   C R O S S - T A B U L A T I O N   O F   - - - - - -
V2   PRESIDENTIAL VOTE            BY   V70        REAGAN  IMPACT-HONESTY
- - - - - - - - - - - - - - - - - - - - - - - - - - - - - PAGE  1 OF  1
```

	V70					
COUNT COL PCT	MUCH MORE HONEST 1	SOMEWHAT MORE HONEST 2	SAME 3	SOMEWHAT LESS HONEST 4	MUCH LESS HONEST 5	ROW TOTAL
V2						
1 BUSH	15 99.2	43 91.1	466 63.1	49 33.3	26 14.8	599 53.0
2 DUKAKIS	2 11.8	10 18.9	272 36.9	98 66.7	150 85.2	532 47.6
COLUMN TOTAL	17 1.5	53 4.7	738 65.3	147 13.0	176 15.6	1131 100.0

CHI SQUARED	DF	SIGNIFICANCE	MIN EF	CELLS WITH EF < 5
181.85159	4	0.0000	7.996	NONE

Figure 14.1 Relationships between 1988 presidential vote and views about President Reagan's impact on the economy and honesty in government.

for interval variables. Several statistics make use of means, some use variances, and a few statistics use the entire distribution pattern of a variable. Some are designed for predictive purposes, and others are not.

Because of their different features, two measures of association may lead to contradictory results; one may show a sizable relationship between two variables while another shows virtually no relationship at all between the same variables. This happens because each measure of association is designed to detect a specific type of relationship. An analyst's responsibility is to understand what each measure does and how to use the proper one for the analysis being performed. Although no single measure is suitable for all purposes, statisticians look for certain characteristics in a good measure of association. These characteristics are the efficient use of information, a constant measuring scale, and a real-world interpretation or meaning.

When we say that a measure of association makes efficient use of the information, we mean that it effectively utilizes all the information available in the data. In one respect, the chi-square statistic does this because it uses the information in each cell of the contingency table. Not all statistics do. Beyond individual cells, though, the variables themselves contain differing amounts of information: nominal variables contain same-or-different information, ordinal variables contain information about order, and interval variables provide information about distances. Chi square utilizes the first level of information and is thus appropriate for nominal variables, but would be inefficient (not wrong, just inefficient) for ordinal and interval variables since it makes no use of that information. The t test and F test do use interval information and thus are preferred for interval dependent variables. Of course, these three statistics are measures of statistical significance, but we will find similar differences in the measures of association to be discussed.

A constant measuring scale is a second desirable feature, for it enables us to make comparisons between relationships. Say we are interested in purchasing a particular make and model of car, a new BMW with all the trimmings. Being intelligent consumers, we travel to three different dealers to compare prices. The first dealer quotes a price of 20,000 German marks. The second says the price will be 7,000 British pounds, and the third will sell us the car for 50,000 Japanese yen. Which is the best deal? The numbers differ, but so do the measuring scales on which the numbers are based. We cannot draw comparisons until the three prices have been standardized to the same scale, such as by translating each to U.S. dollars.

The same is true for measures of association. If in one situation a relationship of 2.5 is considered weak but in another situation the same number represents a strong relationship, then comparisons become impossible. This is one of the weaknesses of chi square because the importance of a chi-square value of 6 will depend on the size of the table—it is very significant for a 2 by 2 table but not significant at all for a 5 by 5 table.

By convention, statisticians have adopted a scale from 0.0 to 1.0 as the preferred way to measure relationships. An association of 0.0 is no relationship between two variables—dividing respondents by the values of the independent variable uncovers no differences in distributions on the dependent variable. In contrast, an association of 1.0 is a perfect relationship, meaning every value of the independent variable is connected with a unique value on the dependent variable. Hypothetical 0.0 and 1.0 relationships between views on the Bible and abortion attitudes are displayed in Figure 14.2. Relationships at either extreme

A RELATIONSHIP OF 0.0

	COL PCT	BIBLE ALL TRUE	SOME ERRORS	GOOD BOOK	WORTH LITTLE	ROW TOTAL
		1	2	3	4	
NO ABORTION EVER	1	160	80	80	80	400
		40.0	40.0	40.0	40.0	40.0
ABORTION IF RAPE	2	80	40	40	40	200
		20.0	20.0	20.0	20.0	20.0
ABORTION IF NEED	3	80	40	40	40	200
		20.0	20.0	20.0	20.0	20.0
PERSONAL CHOICE	4	80	40	40	40	200
		20.0	20.0	20.0	20.0	20.0
COLUMN TOTAL		400	200	200	200	1000
		40.0	20.0	20.0	20.0	100.0

A RELATIONSHIP OF 1.0

	COL PCT	BIBLE ALL TRUE	SOME ERRORS	GOOD BOOK	WORTH LITTLE	ROW TOTAL
		1	2	3	4	
V36						
NO ABORTION EVER	1	400				400
		100.0	0.0	0.0	0.0	40.0
ABORTION IF RAPE	2		200			200
		0.0	100.0	0.0	0.0	20.0
ABORTION IF NEED	3			200		200
		0.0	0.0	100.0	0.0	20.0
PERSONAL CHOICE	4				200	200
		0.0	0.0	0.0	100.0	20.0
COLUMN TOTAL		400	200	200	200	1000
		40.0	20.0	20.0	20.0	100.0

Figure 14.2 Hypothetical relationships of 0.0 and 1.0 between views on the Bible and abortion attitudes.

seldom exist in the social sciences, but a scale anchored by these endpoints allows for comparisons. The closer the association is to 1.0 (the farther away from 0.0), the stronger the relationship is—an association of .60 is stronger than an association of .45.

The final desirable characteristic of a measure of association is a real-world interpretation. By this we usually mean some form of prediction. Some measures of association are abstract and have meaning only when compared to themselves; for example, a phi of .12 is weaker than a phi of .16. With other statistics, the numbers have an additional interpretation. For example, a lambda of .20 is not only stronger than a lambda of .15, but also means a 20 percent improvement in our ability to predict the dependent variable. The more we can attach a tangible meaning to a measure of association, the more useful it is.

Few measures of association achieve all three of the above purposes well. Some are very efficient at using information, but do not provide any predictive power. Some may be excellent at prediction, but cannot be readily measured on a scale from 0.0 to 1.0. This is why so many are available, to provide maximum freedom for the analyst to select a statistic best suited to both the data available and the question being asked.

We have already examined one statistic available with the CROSSTABS procedure, chi square, which is a measure of statistical significance. Numerous measures of substantive significance can also be requested on the STATISTICS subcommand of CROSSTABS. We will examine them grouped by their efficiency, focusing on their suitability for nominal and ordinal variables (interval variables are covered more fully in later chapters). At the same time, we will also comment about their performance on the other criteria.

NOMINAL MEASURES OF ASSOCIATION

The chi-square statistic is appropriate for nominal-level variables because it requires no assumption that the values of either the dependent or independent variables represent any order or distance information. However, chi square does not use a constant scale to examine relationships, and its size is affected by both the size of the sample and the size of the table. The last two items are acceptable with a measure of statistical significance, for the size of the sample and the number of samples drawn (number of cells in the table) are important in making probability judgments about the population. For a measure of association, however, these two items are completely unsuitable. We should not find a stronger connection between studying and grades just because we added extra cases to the sample or expanded the grades variable (and thus the table) to include plus and minus grades.

Nonetheless, the basic logic of the chi-square statistic can be used to develop a measure of association. The expected frequency of each cell is what we should find when the two variables in the contingency table are unrelated. If a relationship does exist, the observed frequencies will be different from the expected frequencies. The stronger the relationship, the greater the disparity between the two frequencies and thus the larger the chi-square value. Because of the appealing logic of chi square and its efficiency for nominal variables, statisticians have tried to build on this statistic to create measures of association. Their objective is essentially twofold: to transform the statistic to one ranging from 0.0 to 1.0 and to remove the statistic's sensitivity to both sample and table sizes. Statistics developed out of this effort are the contingency coefficient and the combination of phi and Cramer's *V*.

Phi Coefficient

The **phi coefficient** (φ) is a very limited transformation of chi square suitable for 2 by 2 tables. It is calculated by dividing the chi-square value by the sample size N and then taking the square root of the result, as shown in this formula:

$$\phi = \sqrt{\frac{\chi^2}{N}}$$

Dividing by the size of the sample compensates for the increased size of chi square as the sample gets larger. Taking the square root compensates for squaring $f_e - f_o$ for each cell. These two steps adjust the range of phi to be between 0.0 and 1.0. If chi square is zero, so will be the phi coefficient (zero divided by any number is zero). When the two variables are perfectly related, at least in a 2 by 2 table, the chi-square value will be the same as the sample size and the phi coefficient will be 1.0. Less than perfect relationships will produce phis of greater than 0.0 but less than 1.0—in short, a measure of how strongly two variables are related when a constant scale is used.

Cramer's *V*

Unfortunately, the phi coefficient, like the chi square used to calculate it, is also affected by the size of the table. The formula for phi can produce values greater than 1.0 for tables larger than 2 by 2. As a correction, the **Cramer's V** statistic controls for the size of the table. The formula for Cramer's *V* is the same as that for phi with one exception. In the denominator N is multiplied by the term $k - 1$, where k is the smaller of either the number of rows or number of columns in the contingency table, thus compensating for larger tables. This correction restricts Cramer's *V* so that it is possible to have, but not exceed, a value of 1.0:

$$V = \sqrt{\frac{\chi^2}{N(k - 1)}}$$

Note that for tables with either 2 rows or 2 columns, the $k - 1$ term in Cramer's *V* becomes 1, and then the formula for Cramer's *V* becomes exactly the same as that for phi. These two statistics are referred to as the phi–Cramer's *V* combination. When you request phi on the STATISTICS subcommand, SPSS will automatically produce phi for 2 by 2 tables and Cramer's *V* for larger tables.

Contingency Coefficient

The **contingency coefficient (CC)**[1] is another attempt to transform the chi-square statistic to a standardized range from 0.0 to 1.0. It is calculated by dividing chi square by the sum of chi square and the sample size N and then taking the square root of the result. The formula is

$$CC = \sqrt{\frac{\chi^2}{\chi^2 + N}}$$

This statistic can be used on tables of any size, eliminating the need to continually switch between phi and Cramer's V.

The contingency coefficient is partially successful in its purpose, but not completely so. The CC statistic ranges from 0.0 to near 1.0, but it is impossible for it to be as large as 1.0, even when the relationship is perfect. Furthermore, how large it can become depends on the size of the table. This introduces problems in comparing different size tables, for a CC value of .85 may be a perfect relationship in one table but a less-than-perfect relationship for a table of another size. It is a useful statistic, but only for comparing tables of the same size.

PRE Measures

The three statistics just mentioned are all efficient for nominal variables, making use of all the information possible in a contingency table. Phi and Cramer's V, when used in combination, also adhere to a 0.0-to-1.0 scale, while the contingency coefficient comes close to this standard. However, none of the three gives us any predictive information. Each measures how strong a relationship is in an abstract sense, but cannot be otherwise interpreted. To correct for this failing, statisticians have developed an entire class of measures of association, called **proportional reduction of error (PRE)** measures, which have a more understandable interpretation.

PRE measures do not use the chi-square statistic at all. Instead, they are based on a very different logic—the assumption that if two variables are related, the independent variable should help us to predict the dependent variable. If time spent studying is related to course grades, knowing how much a person studies should enable us to predict that person's grade. Naturally, no prediction will be perfect, but a PRE measure assesses how well the independent variable aids in predicting the dependent variable.

To assess the predictive power of an independent variable, we must begin with a baseline—how accurately the dependent variable can be predicted without consulting the independent one. By this we mean being able to predict, or accurately guess, each respondent's position on the dependent variable. That is, a colleague interrogates us about each case in the sample, saying, "Here is case

---

[1]Sometimes the contingency coefficient is denoted simply by C. In this text we use CC.

```
- - - - - - -     C R O S S - T A B U L A T I O N   O F   - - - - - - - -
V2    PRESIDENTIAL VOTE              BY   V68        REAGAN IMPACT-ECONOMY
- - - - - - - - - - - - - - - - - - - - - - - - - - - - - - - - - PAGE 1 OF 1


                        V68
             COUNT   I
             COL PCT I MUCH    SOMEWHAT   SAME   SOMEWHAT  MUCH        ROW
                     I BETTER  BETTER            WORSE     WORSE      TOTAL
                     I     1 I      2 I      3 I      4 I      5 I
V2       ------- + ------ + ------ + ------- + ------ + ------- +
            1 I        I        I        I        I        I       613
       BUSH     I        I        I        I        I        I      53.4%
            + ------- + ------ + ------- + ------ + ------- +
            2 I        I        I        I        I        I       535
     DUKAKIS   I        I        I        I        I        I      46.6%
            + ------- + ------ + ------- + ------ + ------- +
           COLUMN                                               1148
           TOTAL                                               100.0%
```

Figure 14.3 Cross-tabulation of presidential vote by Reagan's economic impact without the cells filled in.

236. Did this person vote for Bush or Dukakis?" After doing this for every person in the sample, we total our correct and incorrect guesses.

Your first reaction might be to guess randomly or even to refuse to participate, believing that there is no rational basis for making any guesses. Consider, however, Figure 14.3, a contingency table (without any cells filled in) between presidential vote and Reagan's perceived impact on the economy. The row marginals constitute a frequencies table for V2 after cases with missing data on either of the two variables in the table have been excluded. The most common answer, the *mode*, is number 1, voting for Bush. If you were to always guess this response for each person in the survey, you would make the smallest number of guessing errors. After completing the guessing for all 1148 people, you would end up with 613 correct guesses and 535 incorrect guesses, or errors.

The guesses just made were based on only one item of information, how the dependent variable itself was distributed. We knew nothing at all about the individual respondents, just the aggregate proportion giving one answer versus another on the dependent variable. Now let us repeat the guessing process but add a second piece of information—each respondent's position on the independent variable. That is, we are again asked how each case responded on variable V2, but before making our guess, we are told how the person responded on V68, Reagan's economic impact. Will this information from the independent variable lead us to improve our guessing accuracy? In this case, yes.

Figure 14.4 repeats the contingency table, but with the cells filled in and the mode of each *column* underlined. The modes differ across the independent-variable groups, and we use this new information in our guessing. That is, if we are first told that case 320 believes that the Reagan policies made the U.S. economy much better, we guess that person's value on V2 to be 1, voting for Bush. Alternatively, if case 583 believed that the Reagan policies made no difference to the economy, we guess that person voted for Dukakis, choice 2. For each case we no longer guess the mode of the entire sample on the dependent

```
- - - - - - -     C R O S S - T A B U L A T I O N   O F   - - - - - - -
V2    PRESIDENTIAL VOTE            BY   V68        REAGAN  IMPACT-ECONOMY
- - - - - - - - - - - - - - - - - - - - - - - - - - - - - - - PAGE  1 OF  1

                     V68
           COUNT    I
           COL PCT  I  MUCH     SOMEWHAT  SAME    SOMEWHAT  MUCH            ROW
                    I  BETTER   BETTER            WORSE     WORSE          TOTAL
                    I     1  I     2  I     3  I     4  I     5  I
   V2      ------ + ------ + ------ + ------- + ------ + ------- +
        1  I        178  I    251  I    148  I     27  I      9  I     613
   BUSH    I       92.2  I   73.4  I   40.0  I   19.6  I    8.6  I    53.4
           + ------- + ------ + ------- + ------ + ------- +
        2  I         15  I     91  I    222  I    111  I     96  I     535
   DUKAKIS I        7.8  I   26.6  I   60.0  I   80.4  I   91.4  I    46.6
           + ------- + ------ + ------- + ------ + ------- +
           COLUMN     193      342      370      138      105      1148
           TOTAL     16.8     29.8     32.2     12.0      9.1     100.0
```

Figure 14.4 Cross-tabulation of presidential vote by Reagan's economic impact with column modes underlined.

variable, but instead the modal response of those who share that respondent's position on the independent variable.

How has this different approach to guessing helped? As illustrated in Figure 14.5, by using the independent variable as our guide in guessing each respondent's value on the dependent variable, we have made 245 additional correct guesses—858 correct guesses after we knew the independent variable,

```
Before knowing views about Reagan's economic impact,
      guess dependent variable's mode (1)

      613  correct  guesses
      535  errors

After knowing views about Reagan's economic impact,
      guess  mode  in  each  independent  variable  column
```

		V2 Presidential Vote	
V68, Reagan's impact On the economy	Guess:	Correct Guesses	Incorrect Guesses
1 = much better	1	178	15
2 = somewhat better	1	251	91
3 = same	2	222	148
4 = somewhat worse	2	111	27
5 = much worse	2	96	9
Total		Correct = 858	Errors = 290

Figure 14.5 Guessing 1988 vote choices before and after knowing each respondent's position on the independent variable.

compared to 613 originally. Phrased in terms of errors, we make 245 fewer guessing errors by using the information contained in the independent variable.

This guessing process is at the heart of what we mean by a relationship. Say that instead of Reagan's economic performance, we are provided with an independent variable that has no logical connection to voters' choices, such as how tall the respondent is or the day of the week on which the respondent was born. We do not expect either item of information to help us guess how a person voted because neither factor has any rational association with the dependent variable. Alternatively, if our reasoning leads us to believe that two variables are related, then a person's position on one variable does affect his or her position on the other. Using the first variable to help us guess responses on the second is a logical extension of this reasoning.

Lambda

Improvement in guessing is the basis of the **lambda** (λ) measure of association. Lambda is calculated with the formula

$$\lambda = \frac{\text{ERRORS 1} - \text{ERRORS 2}}{\text{ERRORS 1}}$$

This formula is nothing more than a mathematical summary of the guessing errors just discussed. ERRORS 1 refers to the number of guessing errors made before we knew the independent variable (i.e., when we always guessed the mode of the whole sample on the dependent variable). ERRORS 2 is the number of errors made after we had the information from the independent variable and thus guessed the mode of each independent-variable group. Thus the numerator (ERRORS 1 − ERRORS 2, or 245) is the reduction in guessing error provided by the independent variable.

The denominator, ERRORS 1, is the number of original errors made. Dividing the reduction in error by the original error gives the proportional reduction of error, or proportion of original error eliminated by adding the information from the independent variable. In Figure 14.5, for example, 245 divided by 535 gives a lambda of .4579—a 46 percent reduction in guessing error that is contributed by the independent variable.

As a measure of association, lambda has two advantages. First, it always ranges between 0.0 and 1.0. If the independent variable does not improve our guessing, then the numerator of the formula for lambda, and thus the resulting lambda statistic, will be zero. If, alternatively, there is a perfect relationship between two variables, it will eliminate all our original guessing errors. The formula will then reduce to dividing ERRORS 1 by itself (no guessing errors means ERRORS 2 will be zero), and dividing any number by itself always gives 1.0. Second, lambda is easy to interpret. Unlike the situation with phi, Cramer's *V*, and the contingency coefficient, we do not need to compare one lambda value to another to draw any conclusions. A lambda of .46 is the proportional improvement (percentage of fewer errors) in our ability to predict the dependent variable by knowing the independent variable.

Where lambda suffers is on the other desirable characteristic of measures of association—efficiency. Lambda does not use all the information in the contingency table; it uses only the modal cell in each column. What this means is that relationships between variables that appear in cells other than the modal cells may go undetected by lambda. For example, consider Figure 14.6, which shows a cross-tabulation of presidential vote by gender. Men show a noticeably greater tendency to vote for Bush than women. Since this is a 2 by 2 table, SPSS calculates the chi-square statistic both with and without the Yates correction, with both numbers showing a high probability that the relationship exists in the population as well. Nonetheless, lambda when calculated from this table would show no relationship, or 0.0.

To understand this result, begin by examining the row marginals. The modal response is 1, a vote for Bush. Now look at each column. The majority (modal response) of each gender is also to vote for Bush (the women are actually evenly divided, which means either vote choice can be considered the mode). Whether we know the independent variable or not, we always guess the same response on the dependent variable, a vote for Bush. There is a relationship between gender and the vote, a relationship that both phi and the contingency coefficient would detect because they use all the cells in the table, not just the mode of each column. The relationship, however, does not improve our prediction of V2, which is what lambda measures, and thus lambda would be 0.0.

Lambda is a very widely used measure of association for nominal variables and is the only one you will need to use in most cases. However, if the pattern in the table suggests a clear relationship but lambda is close to or exactly at 0.0, perhaps lambda is not efficiently measuring the relationship. If such is the case, rely instead on the contingency coefficient or on the combination of phi and Cramer's V.

```
- - - - - - -   C R O S S - T A B U L A T I O N   O F   - - - - - - -
V2    PRESIDENTIAL VOTE              BY    V87                RESP'S SEX
- - - - - - - - - - - - - - - - - - - - - - - - - - -  PAGE  1 OF  1

                  V87
          COUNT  |
          COL PCT | MALE      FEMALE      ROW
                  |                       TOTAL
                  |     1 |      2 |
V2     ------- + ------ + ------ +
              1 |   301 |    331 |      632
     BUSH       |  56.5 |   50.0 |     52.9
                + ------- + ------ +
              2 |   232 |    331 |      563
     DUKAKIS    |  43.5 |   50.0 |     47.1
                + ------- + ------ +
          COLUMN    533     662       1195
          TOTAL    44.6    55.4      100.0

CHI SQUARED     DF     SIGNIFICANCE     MIN EF      CELLS WITH EF < 5
   4.70853      1          0.0300      251.112           NONE
   4.96494      1          0.0259      (BEFORE  YATES  CORRECTION)
```

Figure 14.6 Relationship between gender and presidential vote.

STATISTICS Subcommand and Output

(V.2) (PC) We used the STATISTICS subcommand in Chapter 13 to request a chi-square analysis. We do the same for measures of association, just including different options on the subcommand. A complete list of the statistics available for the CROSSTABS procedure is included in Table 14.1. To add measures of association to the contingency tables in Figure 14.1, we use the command

```
CROSSTABS TABLES = V2 BY V68 V70 / CELLS COLUMN COUNT
   /STATISTICS CHISQ PHI CC LAMBDA
```

Notice that we still request the chi-square statistic because measuring the strength of a relationship is a useless exercise unless we first confirm that a relationship exists with a test of statistical significance.

Version 2   As mentioned in Chapter 13, version 2 of SPSS-X requests statistics through a STATISTICS subcommand, beginning in column 1 and followed by numbers referring to the statistics requested. Table 14.1 also includes the statistic numbers used in version 2. The version 2 form of the command is

```
CROSSTABS TABLES = V2 BY V68 V70
OPTIONS 4
STATISTICS 1 2 3 4
```

(R.4) The revised output is shown in Figure 14.7. Directly underneath each table is the now familiar chi-square statistic. Beneath that is the lambda statistic, and at the bottom of each table's statistic list are the Cramer's *V* and contingency coefficients. Recall that even though our STATISTICS subcommand requested phi, SPSS will print phi only for 2 by 2 tables and Cramer's *V*, instead of phi, for larger tables.

Table 14.1   STATISTICS AVAILABLE WITH THE CROSSTABS COMMAND

Version 2 statistic no.	Subcommand	Keyword	Description
1	STATISTICS	CHISQ	Chi square
2	STATISTICS	PHI	Phi for 2 by 2 tables, Cramer's *V* for larger tables
3	STATISTICS	CC	Contingency coefficient
4	STATISTICS	LAMBDA	Lambda
5	STATISTICS	UC	Uncertainty coefficient
6	STATISTICS	BTAU	Tau-b
7	STATISTICS	CTAU	Tau-c
8	STATISTICS	GAMMA	Gamma
9	STATISTICS	D	Somer's *D*
10	STATISTICS	ETA	Eta
11	STATISTICS	CORR	Pearson's correlation
ALL	STATISTICS	ALL	All the above

```
- - - - - - -    C R O S S - T A B U L A T I O N    O F    - - - - - - - -
V2     PRESIDENTIAL VOTE              BY  V68        REAGAN IMPACT-ECONOMY

             V68
       COUNT  I
       COL PCT I MUCH    SOMEWHAT  SAME    SOMEWHAT  MUCH           ROW
             I BETTER   BETTER            WORSE     WORSE          TOTAL
             I     1 I      2 I      3 I      4 I      5 I
V2     ------- + ------ + ------- + ------- + ------ + ------- +
           1 I   178 I    251 I    148 I     27 I      9 I        613
   BUSH      I  92.2 I   73.4 I   40.0 I   19.6 I    8.6 I       53.4
           + ------- + ------ + ------- + ------ + ------- +
           2 I    15 I     91 I    222 I    111 I     96 I        535
   DUKAKIS   I   7.8 I   26.6 I   60.0 I   80.4 I   91.4 I       46.6
           + ------- + ------ + ------- + ------ + ------- +
       COLUMN      193     342      370      138      105        1148
       TOTAL      16.8    29.8     32.2     12.0      9.1       100.0


CHI SQUARED      DF      SIGNIFICANCE        MIN EF      CELLS WITH EF < 5
346.83451        4        0.0000            48.933            NONE


                                   WITH V2      WITH V68
STATISTIC        SYMMETRIC        DEPENDENT    DEPENDENT
   LAMBDA         0.26504          0.45794      0.13239


STATISTIC                              VALUE         SIGNIFICANCE
CRAMER'S V                            0.54966
CONTINGENCY COEFFICIENT               0.48169
NUMBER OF MISSING OBSERVATIONS =      892



- - - - - - -    C R O S S - T A B U L A T I O N    O F    - - - - - - - -
V2     PRESIDENTIAL VOTE              BY  V70        REAGAN IMPACT-HONESTY

             V70
             I
       COUNT  I MUCH    SOMEWHAT  SAME    SOMEWHAT  MUCH           ROW
       COL PCT I MORE    MORE              LESS      LESS          TOTAL
             I HONEST  HONEST            HONEST    HONEST
             I     1 I      2 I      3 I      4 I      5 I
V2     ------- + ------ + ------ + ------- + ------ + ------- +
           1 I    15 I     43 I    466 I     49 I     26 I        599
   BUSH      I  88.2 I   81.1 I   63.1 I   33.3 I   14.8 I       53.0
           + ------- + ------ + ------- + ------ + ------- +
           2 I     2 I     10 I    272 I     98 I    150 I        532
   DUKAKIS   I  11.8 I   18.9 I   36.9 I   66.7 I   85.2 I       47.6
           + ------- + ------ + ------- + ------ + ------- +
       COLUMN       17      53      738      147      176        1131
       TOTAL       1.5     4.7     65.3     13.0     15.6       100.0


CHI SQUARED      DF      SIGNIFICANCE        MIN EF      CELLS WITH EF < 5
181.85159        4        0.0000             7.996            NONE


                                   WITH V2      WITH V70
STATISTIC        SYMMETRIC        DEPENDENT    DEPENDENT
LAMBDA            0.18703          0.32519      0.00000


STATISTIC                              VALUE         SIGNIFICANCE
CRAMER'S V                            0.40098
CONTINGENCY COEFFICIENT               0.37218
NUMBER OF MISSING OBSERVATIONS =      909
```

Figure 14.7 Contingency tables with measures of association added.

Let us look first at the Cramer's *V* and contingency coefficients. They differ from each other, which is understandable. Although both are based on chi square, they are calculated from different formulas and thus are not comparable. These statistics can be compared only to each other—Cramer's *V* for the first table with that for the second table—or with the absolute 0.0-to-1.0 scale. Both sets of numbers are quite sizable, close to .50 in the top table and near .40 in the bottom one, showing strong relationships between each independent variable and respondents' vote decisions.

More importantly for our purposes, the measures of association enable us to determine which independent variable had a greater impact on individual voter decisions. Both statistics are slightly higher for the top table between Reagan's economic impact and the presidential vote: .55 versus .40 for Cramer's *V* and .48 versus .37 for the contingency coefficient. In sum, views on both the Reagan administration's economic performance and its honesty had sizable effects on voters' choices in 1988. Yet voters were more influenced by the economic issue than by concerns about honesty in government.

When we turn our attention to the lambda statistic, we find not just one number, but three of them. Measures of association come in two forms, known as symmetric and asymmetric. **Symmetric statistics** produce the same number regardless of which of the two variables being analyzed is the dependent one. Lambda, however, is an **asymmetric statistic**, a measure of association in which the measured relationship differs depending on which variable is considered dependent. For asymmetric statistics, SPSS produces three results: one with the row variable as dependent, one with the column variable as dependent, and a quasi-symmetric version roughly akin to an average of the two.

Since we know that V2 is our dependent variable, we look at the number labeled "with V2 dependent." The lambdas here are .46 between the presidential vote and Reagan's economic impact and .33 between the vote and Reagan's impact on honesty in government. This is consistent with the conclusion drawn from the prior statistics, that economic conditions are more important to voters than concerns about integrity in government. Since lambda is a PRE measure, these numbers also tell us that using V68 to help guess voter choice will lead to 46 percent fewer guessing errors (just as we calculated earlier) while V70 would provide less help, only a 33 percent reduction in guessing error.

In Figure 14.7 we have a very comfortable situation; all three statistics lead to the same conclusion about which relationship is the stronger. Generally, the lambda statistic alone will suffice, but it is helpful to examine them all to make sure the relationship is one that lambda can detect.

ORDINAL MEASURES OF ASSOCIATION

Lambda, phi, Cramer's *V*, and the contingency coefficient are useful statistics for analyzing relationships involving nominal variables, variables such as race, religious preference, marital status, and the like. The variables we have been looking at in this chapter, however, are beyond nominal. Both variables about the Reagan presidency are at least ordinal, and some might consider them to even be interval. Since vote choice was recoded to include only the Bush and Dukakis options, it also becomes an interval variable since dichotomies are interval.

Using nominal statistics on higher-level variables is not a problem mathematically—ordinal and interval variables are nominal, just nominal plus some extras—but it is an inefficient use of information. To illustrate this inefficiency, let us look at a relationship in which the dependent variable has more than two values, such as the relationship between a person's level of happiness and the respondent's satisfaction with her or his financial situation (see Figure 14.8). Not surprisingly, chi square shows that the null hypothesis can be safely rejected. Lambda is 0.0 because each column has the same mode, "pretty happy," but the more encompassing Cramer's *V* and contingency coefficients show definite relationships of .20 and .28, respectively.

```
GET FILE = GSS88
CROSSTABS TABLES = HAPPY BY SATFIN
      / CELLS COUNT COLUMN / STATISTICS CHISQ PHI CC LAMBDA

- - - - - - -    C R O S S - T A B U L A T I O N   O F   - - - - - - -
HAPPY GENERAL HAPPINESS            BY SATFIN
                                   SATISFACTION WITH FINANCIAL SITUATION
- - - - - - - - - - - - - - - - - - - - - - - - - - - - PAGE  1 OF  1

                  SATFIN
                  I
          COUNT   I SATIS-   MORE      NOT
          COL PCT I FIED     OR LESS   AT ALL       ROW
                  I                    SAT.         TOTAL
                  I    1 I      2 I      3 I
HAPPY   ------- + ------ + ------ + ------- +
            1 I    211 I    212 I     73 I      496
VERY  HAPPY   I   46.9 I   32.7 I   20.4 I     34.0
              + ------- + ------ + ------- +
            2 I    214 I    404 I    209 I      827
PRETTY HAPPY  I   47.6 I   62.0 I   58.5 I     56.7
              + ------- + ------ + ------- +
            3 I     25 I     36 I     75 I      136
NOT TOO HAPPY I    5.6 I    5.5 I   21.0 I      9.3
              + ------- + ------ + ------- +
         COLUMN    450      652      357       1459
         TOTAL     30.8     44.7     24.5      100.0

CHI SQUARED      DF      SIGNIFICANCE       MIN EF      CELLS WITH EF < 5
 120.99391        4        0.0000          33.278            NONE

                                WITH HAPPY   WITH SATFIN
STATISTIC        SYMMETRIC      DEPENDENT    DEPENDENT
LAMBDA           0.02710        0.00000      0.04833

STATISTIC                            VALUE      SIGNIFICANCE
CRAMER'S V                          0.20363
CONTINGENCY COEFFICIENT             0.27673
NUMBER OF MISSING OBSERVATIONS =     22
```

Figure 14.8 Relationship between financial satisfaction and happiness.

When we contemplate a relationship between ordinal variables, we usually think of it as the *higher* a person is on one variable, the *higher* he or she will be on the other. That translates in this case to the more a person is satisfied with her financial status, the happier she will be. People in column 2, more or less satisfied, should be happier than those in column 3, not satisfied; and the respondents in column 1, satisfied, should be the happiest of all. Nominal measures of association, however, do not capture "the more the *A*, the more the *B*" type of relationship, for they do not assume that the code numbers reflect any more than–less than order. We could recode either variable to destroy its ordinal character, making pretty happy code 1, not too happy code 2, and very happy code 3, and none of our nominal measures of association would change in the slightest.

Many measures of association for ordinal variables use PRE logic similar to that of lambda. Similar, but not identical. Our research hypothesis is that those more satisfied with their financial situations should be happier than those dissatisfied financially—happ*ier*, but not necessarily happy. That is, we do not claim that respondents somewhat satisfied financially (code 2 on SATFIN) are actually very happy or even pretty happy (codes 1 and 2, respectively, on HAPPY), just that they are probably happier than those not satisfied with their financial conditions. This reasoning leads us to compare respondent *pairings* rather than single cases.

Concordant and Discordant Pairs

To illustrate the use of pairs in examining ordinal relationships, consider the hypothetical relationship between financial satisfaction and happiness for the three cases in Figure 14.9. In the pair formed by cases *A* and *B*, we find that person *B* has a higher code number on the independent variable, so is less satisfied financially. Since person *B* is higher on the independent variable, is *B* also higher on the dependent variable? The answer is yes, person *B* has a code of 3 (not happy) versus person *A*'s value of 1 (happy).

When the two cases in a pair are ordered the same on both variables, this is called a **concordant pair**—the same case has the higher value on both the independent and dependent variables. The opposite situation is a **discordant pair**, exemplified by comparing cases *B* and *C*. Respondent *C* is higher than *B* on the independent variable (less satisfied financially), but lower, than *B* on the dependent variable (happier). In examining pairs of cases, **pair ties** are also possible. In pairing cases *A* and *C*, for example, case *C* is higher than case *A*

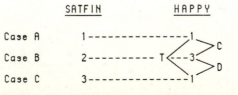

Figure 14.9 Concordant and discordant pairs.

on the first variable, but the two respondents are tied on the second. A tie on one or both variables prevents us from labeling this pair either concordant or discordant.

Note that in determining whether a pair is concordant or discordant, the size of the difference is unimportant. In both parings above, the cases differed by only 1 point on financial satisfaction, but by 2 points on happiness. Distances between variable values have meaning with interval variables, but not ordinal variables. Since we are dealing here with measures of association for ordinal variables, only the higher than–lower than ranking is considered, not distances apart in rank.

However, concordant and discordant pairs do utilize the ranking information available in ordinal variables, determining if the rank order of the respondents is the same or different on the independent and dependent variables. Three measures of association for ordinal variables make use of concordant and discordant pairs: gamma, Kendall's tau-*b*, and Kendall's tau-*c*. All three begin the same way, by calculating the number of concordant and discordant pairs in a two-variable relationship. They differ only in how they handle ties.

Gamma

The simplest measure of association for ordinal variables is **gamma** (**γ**), which is calculated with the formula

$$\gamma = \frac{C - D}{C + D}$$

where C is the number of concordant pairs and D is the number of discordant pairs. By the number of pairs we mean all possible pairings of cases in the sample: case 1 paired with cases 2 through 1481 (GSS88 sample size), case 2 compared with cases 3 through 1481, and so on through case 1480 paired with case 1481.

Look first at the numerator in the formula for gamma. The $C - D$ term determines whether most of the pairings are concordant or discordant. If the variables examined are totally unrelated, such as comparing a person's height to his GPA, then random chance dictates an approximately equal number of concordant and discordant pairs. For every tall person with a higher GPA than a shorter one (concordant) we would probably find another tall respondent who had a lower GPA than a short respondent (discordant). When the numbers of concordant and discordant pairs are approximately the same, the numerator will be close to zero. Conversely, if a relationship does exist between the variables, then the relative position of a case on the independent variable should affect its position on the dependent variable. If being higher on the first variable leads to being higher on the second as well, most pairings will be concordant, leading to a big positive number in the numerator. If the variables are related in such a way that a higher ranking on one leads to a lower ranking on the other, then discordant pairs will be most common, causing the numerator to be a large negative number.

The denominator of the gamma formula, $C + D$, controls for the number of pairs in the data set. A data set containing 1000 people will produce a lot more pairs than one with only 10 people in it. We want to measure the association between two variables, not measure the size of the data set, so we divide by the total number of pairs, thus turning the concordant-discordant plurality in the numerator into a proportion. This allows us to compare statistics across samples of different sizes, such as the GSS88 and ELEC88 data sets. The denominator also standardizes the gamma coefficient to be between 0.0 and 1.0 (or -1.0). Gamma equals 1.0 when all the pairs are concordant. Gamma is -1.0 if all the pairs are discordant, and gamma is 0.0 if the sample shows no particular pattern—an equal number of each.

The formula for gamma is a type of proportional-reduction-of-error formula, except this time it deals with pairs rather than single cases. That is, if you know the order of two people on the independent variable, does this help you guess their order on the dependent variable? If the relationship is random (no relationship), knowing that person *A* is higher than person *B* on the first variable does not help in guessing their order on the second. You could guess that the same person will have higher values on both (concordant pairings) and be right about half the time (number of concordant pairs) and wrong about half the time (number of discordant pairs). As the relationship moves away from zero, you can improve your guessing because a nonzero gamma means that one type of pairing is more common than the other. The size of the gamma statistic represents the proportional reduction of error when you are guessing the order of a pair on the dependent variable by knowing their order on the independent one. Thus a gamma of .36 represents a 36 percent improvement in guessing accuracy, or 36 percent fewer errors.

With ordinal measures of association we have our first encounter with distinguishing between **positive relationships** and **negative relationships**. The plus or minus sign of the gamma coefficient reflects the **direction of a relationship**. When the sign is positive, higher values on one variable lead to higher values on the other. A *higher* score on financial satisfaction leads to a *higher* score on happiness. We do not expect this sort of connection between all sets of variables. For example, if we had a variable measuring the time spent in prison, we would naturally expect that the *more* time spent in prison, the *less* happiness the respondent has—a higher value on one variable leads to a lower value on the other.

The possibility of a negative number does not undermine our desire to use a constant 0.0-to-1.0 scale. In measures of association, the sign of the statistic tells us only the direction of the relationship while the absolute value of the statistic measures the strength of the relationship. A gamma of -36 is just as strong as a gamma of $+.36$; both show a 36 percent proportional reduction of error. The only difference is how we guess, not our guessing improvement. A positive relationship means guessing a similar order on both variables while a negative relationship means guessing that a pair's order on the second variable is the reverse of its order on the first.

Recall that phi, Cramer's *V*, the contingency coefficient, and lambda range only from 0.0 to 1.0. They do not produce any negative numbers because the notion of direction (moving higher or lower) does not apply to nominal variables. Ordinal and interval variables do represent higher than–lower than rankings, so measures of association for these variables can produce either positive or negative numbers.

Kendall's Tau

Gamma is a versatile and widely used statistic, but it has characteristics that make it a bit generous in measuring relationships. Gamma's denominator $(C + D)$ does not count any pairs tied on one or both of the variables. Thus, to say that a gamma of .36 (or $-.36$) represents a 36 percent proportional reduction of error is a bit misleading—it does, but only if we do not count tied pairs. If the number of pairs tied on one or both of the variables is high, gamma might show a large proportional reduction of error when, in fact, we will still make considerable guessing errors affecting the tied pairs.

Kendall's tau compensates for this fact by including ties in the denominator. The formula for **Kendall's tau-*b*** is

$$\tau_b = \frac{C - D}{\sqrt{(C + D + T_x)(C + D + T_y)}}$$

where T_x is the number of ties on the independent variable and T_y is the number of ties on the dependent variable. The numerator for tau-*b* is the same as that for gamma, but with ties included in the denominator the tau statistic comes closer to showing our proportional reduction of error over all cases—concordant, discordant, and tied—than gamma does.

There are two versions of Kendall's tau. Tau-*b*, described above, is used with square contingency tables: 2 by 2, 3 by 3, and so on. Rectangular tables require a slightly different approach to counting ties. Consequently there is a second tau statistic, **Kendall's tau-*c***, defined by

$$\tau_c = \frac{2m(C - D)}{N^2(m - 1)}$$

where m is the smaller of the number of rows or columns in the contingency table and N is the size of the sample. In a pure sense, tau-*b* and tau-*c* are not PRE measures, but they are close enough that they can occasionally be interpreted as such.

STATISTICS Subcommand and Output

(v.2) (PC) Requesting statistics should be familiar now. The STATISTICS subcommand is used in the same manner, but with different keywords for requesting the ordinal statistics, as in

```
CROSSTABS TABLES = HAPPY BY SATFIN / CELLS COLUMN COUNT
        / STATISTICS CHISQ GAMMA BTAU CTAU
```

Version 2   In version 2 of SPSS-X the STATISTICS subcommand (no slash) begins in column 1 and uses numbers 1, 8, 6, and 7 in place of the keywords CHISQ, GAMMA, BTAU, and CTAU, respectively.

(R4)   The contingency table showing these ordinal measures of association is displayed in Figure 14.10. As expected, gamma is the largest of the three. The inclusion of ties in the denominator will always make Kendall's tau smaller than gamma. Since the table is square, tau-c is not relevant, and tau-b should be used instead to measure the relationship. The relationships are also positive, indicating that increased financial security leads to increased happiness. Although noteworthy, neither the tau-b value of .23 nor the gamma of .37 is an exceptionally large relationship. The two variables are definitely related, but given the emphasis in U.S. culture on financial success, it is interesting that the association between finances and happiness is not up in the .40-to-.60 range.

```
CROSSTABS   TABLES = HAPPY BY SATFIN
     / CELLS   COUNT COLUMN   / STATISTICS   CHISQ GAMMA BTAU CTAU

- - - - - - -   C R O S S - T A B U L A T I O N   O F   - - - - - - -
HAPPY   GENERAL HAPPINESS          BY SATFIN
                                   SATISFACTION WITH FINANCIAL SITUATION
- - - - - - - - - - - - - - - - - - - - - - - - - - - - - - - PAGE  1 OF  1

                  SATFIN
                    I
          COUNT     I SATIS-   MORE     NOT
          COL PCT   I FIED     OR       AT ALL       ROW
                    I          LESS     SAT.         TOTAL
                    I     1 I     2 I      3 I
HAPPY   -------+ ------ + ------ + ------- +
        1 I     211 I   212 I     73 I       496
VERY  HAPPY  I  46.9 I  32.5 I   20.4 I      34.0
            + ------- + ------ + ------- +
        2 I     214 I   404 I    209 I       827
PRETTY HAPPY I  47.6 I  62.0 I   58.5 I      56.7
            + ------- + ------ + ------- +
        3 I      25 I    36 I     75 I       136
NOT TOO HAPPY I  5.6 I   5.5 I   21.0 I       9.3
            + ------- + ------ + ------- +
          COLUMN    450     652     357      1459
          TOTAL     30.8    44.7    24.5     100.0

CHI SQUARED      DF    SIGNIFICANCE     MIN EF    CELLS WITH EF < 5
 120.99391        4      0.0000         33.278         NONE

STATISTIC                         VALUE      SIGNIFICANCE
KENDALL'S TAU B                  0.22610       0.0000
KENDALL'S TAU C                  0.20286       0.0000
GAMMA                            0.36898

NUMBER OF MISSING OBSERVATIONS =    22
```

Figure 14.10 Relationship between financial satisfaction and happiness with ordinal measures of association.

For comparison, Figure 14.11 shows the relationship between happiness and satisfaction with family life. The relationship here is somewhat stronger; gamma is .47 as opposed to .37 in SATFIN, and the tau-*c* value (this is a rectangular table) is .27 compared to the tau-*b* value of .23 in Figure 14.10. Satisfaction with family life is more important to an individual's happiness than financial satisfaction.

Given that gamma and taus both measure ordinal relationships, which statistic does one use? The answer again is that it is a matter of personal preference. Gamma is simple both to calculate and to interpret. A gamma of +.25 is 25 percent more concordant than discordant pairs. In addition, gamma is a pure PRE measure and may thus be compared to other PRE measures. This is true even when the other PRE statistic is based on a different level of measurement, such as lambda, since all PRE statistics have a similar interpretation. Using a nominal variable to predict vote choice leads to a certain reduction in guessing error (lambda) while an ordinal variable predicting vote choice leads to a different reduction in guessing error (gamma). The ability of PRE measures to be compared with one another is a useful feature that will be mentioned again in later chapters.

```
CROSSTABS   TABLES = HAPPY BY SATFAM
   / CELLS   COUNT COLUMN   / STATISTICS   CHISQ GAMMA BTAU CTAU


- - - - - - - - - - - C R O S S - T A B U L A T I O N   O F - - - - - - - - - - -
HAPPY      GENERAL HAPPINESS                        BY   SATFAM                FAMILY LIFE
- - - - - - - - - - - - - - - - - - - - - - - - - - - - - - - - - - -  PAGE  1 OF  1
```

	SATFAM VERY GREAT DEAL 1	GREAT DEAL 2	QUITE A BIT 3	A FAIR AMOUNT 4	SOME 5	A LITTLE 6	NONE 7	ROW TOTAL
COUNT COL PCT								
HAPPY								
1 VERY HAPPY	208 48.4	106 32.0	19 22.4	8 13.8	2 6.7	2 7.1	2 10.0	347 35.3
2 PRETTY HAPPY	204 47.4	207 62.5	57 67.1	39 67.2	20 66.7	15 53.6	8 40.0	550 56.0
3 NOT TOO HAPPY	18 4.2	18 5.4	9 10.6	11 19.0	8 26.7	11 39.3	10 50.0	85 8.7
COLUMN TOTAL	430 43.8	331 33.7	85 8.7	58 5.9	30 3.1	28 2.9	20 2.0	982 100.0

```
CHI SQUARED      DF      SIGNIFICANCE       MIN EF    CELLS WITH EF < 5
 165.61684       12         0.0000           1.731     3 OF 21   (14.3%)
```

STATISTIC	VALUE	SIGNIFICANCE
KENDALL'S TAU B	0.29285	0.0000
KENDALL'S TAU C	0.26990	0.0000
GAMMA	0.46513	

```
NUMBER OF MISSING OBSERVATIONS = 499
```

Figure 14.11 Relationship between satisfaction with family life and happiness.

Supplement
14.1
How Strong Is Strong?

Beginning students of statistics always seek rules to follow in labeling a relationship as strong or weak. Unfortunately, no such absolute criteria exist. Some general guidelines can be provided, but remember that these are only rough rules of thumb which do not apply in all circumstances.

First, do not expect any relationships close to perfect, 1.0 or −1.0. Even relationships of .50 and above are uncommon. Given a little thought, this is not surprising. Political and social behaviors are complex things not easily explained by one factor only. Many items affect our attitudes toward political candidates. Experience with prior presidents may be one, but other important factors include issues of the campaign, personalities of the candidates, and the attitudes of friends or spouses. To expect one variable to perfectly or nearly perfectly determine a second variable is to say that all other factors are unimportant. Human behavior is seldom that simple.

Although a little more common, relationships of 0.0 are also unusual. Most variables are related to one another in some way, but many such relationships are too small to be noteworthy. Regularly eating breakfast may affect a person's GPA—being hungry may marginally affect test performance—but the grade difference between those who do and those who do not eat breakfast may be an insignificant 2 hundredths of a point (.02).

In general, associations below .10 are not large enough to be important and may even be due to sampling error. Relationships between .10 and .20 are small but consequential. Relationships between .20 and .40 are moderate to strong, definitely large enough to be substantial and important. Any relationship above .40 can usually be considered quite strong.

Finally, rather than using some absolute standard to determine the strength or weakness of a relationship, it is often more helpful to think of relationships as interesting or uninteresting. A relationship can be considered strong or weak in comparison with what we think it ought to be. We probably expect a very strong relationship, say .45 or better, between education and income. If we then find a gamma of only .30, this is an interesting result; it challenges our preconceived notions of the education-income connections. Similarly, we might not expect frequency of church attendance to be connected with attitudes on defense spending, so finding a small but clear relationship of about .12 would also be an interesting result. In contrast, finding a strong .60 relationship between party identification and vote choice is a rather inconsequential result despite its size—of course Democrats vote for Dukakis and Republicans for Bush. What else do you expect?

This author has a slight preference, however, for the taus for two reasons. First, they provide a more conservative estimate of the relationship strength. As the number of ties becomes large, gamma tends to make relationships appear stronger than they actually are. If the number of ties is small, the impact of counting ties in the denominator is also small and the tau statistic will be nearly identical to gamma.

(R4) The taus have an added advantage—their own sampling distributions and significance levels. Some measures of association either have no easily determined sampling distribution or share the same sampling distribution as chi square. In either case, we need to look at two different places on the printout—chi square for statistical significance and the measure of association for substantive significance. Other measures of association, however, have identifiable sampling distributions, typically *t* or *F* distributions, and can thus be used to determine both statistical and substantive significance. Kendall's tau is one such statistic. In Figures 14.10 and 14.11, the values of tau are followed by significance levels, which are the probabilities that a tau of 0.0 (the null hypothesis of no relationship) exists in the population. When the taus are used, it is no longer necessary to consult chi square for an evaluation of statistical significance.

MORE ABOUT MEASURING ASSOCIATION

The nominal and ordinal measures of association examined so far do not exhaust the statistics available with the CROSSTABS procedure. They are, however, the ones most commonly used. Nonetheless, you will be consumers as well as producers of quantitative analyses, and you may encounter these other statistics in some situations. Consequently, we discuss each briefly below. In addition, other features of measures of association deserve attention, including the assumptions required and some problems of interpretation. These topics are also covered in this section.

Other Statistics

(R4) Instead of typing out each specific statistic desired on the STATISTICS subcommand, analysts frequently just use the **ALL** keyword, requesting all the statistics that the CROSSTABS procedure can produce. Then analysts focus on just the specific statistics desired from the output. Figure 14.12 displays the output received after /STATISTICS ALL has been requested. Look at the organization of the output. There are three groups of statistics, organized not by whether they are nominal or ordinal, but by the information that each provides. First, at the top the chi-square statistic is set off by itself. This statistic includes information, such as the degrees of freedom, which the others do not. The second group consists of all the asymmetric statistics in which different coefficients must be used depending on which variable is considered dependent. The third group at the bottom consists of the symmetric statistics in which only one coefficient is reported to measure the relationship between two variables. Many of the statistics in this last group also have tests of statistical significance listed next to the coefficient. Also, there are four new statistics in Figure 14.12: the uncertainty coefficient, Somer's *D*, eta, and Pearson's *r*.

```
CROSSTABS TABLES = HAPPY BY SATJOB
      / CELLS COUNT COLUMN / STATISTICS ALL
```

```
- - - - - -     C R O S S - T A B U L A T I O N    O F   - - - - - - -
HAPPY  GENERAL HAPPINESS           BY SATJOB                JOB OR HOUSEWORK
- - - - - - - - - - - - - - - - - - - - - - - - - - - - - PAGE  1 OF  1
```

	SATJOB				
COUNT COL PCT	VERY SATIS- FIED 1	MOD. SATIS- FIED 2	A LITTLE DISSAT- ISFIED 3	VERY DISSAT- ISFIED 4	ROW TOTAL
HAPPY					
1 VERY HAPPY	252 47.5	111 24.6	17 14.8	9 20.5	389 34.1
2 PRETTY HAPPY	248 46.7	306 67.8	76 66.1	23 52.3	653 57.2
3 NOT TOO HAPPY	31 5.8	34 7.5	22 19.1	12 27.3	99 8.7
COLUMN TOTAL	531 46.5	451 39.5	115 10.1	44 3.9	1141 100.0

CHI SQUARED	DF	SIGNIFICANCE	MIN EF	CELLS WITH EF < 5
113.24525	6	0.0000	3.818	1 OF 12 (8.3%)

STATISTIC	SYMMETRIC	WITH HAPPY DEPENDENT	WITH SATJOB DEPENDENT
LAMBDA	0.05920	0.00820	0.10000
UNCERTAINTY COEFFICIENT	0.04695	0.05168	0.04300
SOMER'S D	0.25958	0.24549	0.27539
ETA		0.27723	0.27076

STATISTIC	VALUE	SIGNIFICANCE
CRAMER'S V	0.22277	
CONTINGENCY COEFFICIENT	0.30048	
KENDALL'S TAU B	0.26001	0.0000
KENDALL'S TAU C	0.22666	0.0000
PEARSON'S R	0.27070	0.0000
GAMMA	0.43311	

```
NUMBER OF MISSING OBSERVATIONS =   340
```

Figure 14.12 CROSSTABS output when STATISTICS ALL is requested.

Uncertainty Coefficient   The **uncertainty coefficient** is a PRE-type measure like lambda that is used for nominal variables. However, instead of measuring improvement in guessing, as lambda does, the uncertainty coefficient measures the reduction in uncertainty. Uncertainty is a probabilistic concept—the probability of guessing correctly. Determining probability requires the use of information in each cell of the contingency table whereas lambda involves the use of only the modal cell in each column. The uncertainty coefficient is thus more efficient than lambda, but does not have lambda's simplicity of interpretation.

Somer's *D* Somer's *D*, used for ordinal variables, is similar to gamma and the taus. Essentially, Somer's *D* is an attempt to provide an asymmetric measure of association for ordinal variables in which the result differs depending on which variable is considered dependent. The numerator for Somer's *D* is the same as that for gamma and tau—$C - D$—but the denominator includes only ties on the independent variable. The reasoning is that it does not make any difference if we guess that a pair is tied on the dependent variable, but a tie on the independent variable prevents us from making any guess.

Eta Eta (η) is a statistic used when the independent variable is nominal and the dependent variable is interval. It essentially compares how different the mean of the dependent variable is for each category of the independent variable. This strategy is very similar to a T-TEST or analysis of variance, but is used here as a measure of substantive rather than statistical significance. Eta squared can also be interpreted as the proportion of variance explained on the dependent variable, a concept discussed more in Chapter 16.

Pearson's *r* Pearson's *r* is a measure of association used when both variables are interval. It is so widely used that when analysts speak of a correlation or a correlation coefficient without any other designation, they typically mean Pearson's *r*. Because of the power and common use of this statistic, a separate chapter is devoted to it.

Release 4 Release 4 includes some additional statistics not listed in Table 14.1, which we briefly mention here but leave to the instructor or reader to explore in greater depth. Requesting lambda will produce Goodman and Kruskal's tau as well, a measure of the probability of making an error before and after knowing the independent variable. Requesting CORR will produce Spearman's correlation coefficient, a correlation for ordinal variables, in addition to the Pearson correlation used for interval variables. There are also two new specifications on the STATISTICS subcommand. Requesting KAPPA will produce a kappa coefficient for square tables which is a test of agreement between two observers over the same group of objects (e.g., the extent to which respondents and spouses agree on religious preferences). RISK is a test of the relative risk between two groups, such as smokers and nonsmokers, on some dependent variable such as heart disease.

Release 4 also prints statistics in a different format. This new format is illustrated in Figure 14.13, although many of the numbers are fictional. The measures of association, below the chi-square statistics, are reported in five columns. In the first two columns, labeled "Statistic" and "Value," are the name of each statistic and its calculated size. In the "ASE1" column is the asymptotic standard error, a measure of the standard error of the sampling

```
- - - - - - -    C R O S S - T A B U L A T I O N   O F   - - - - - -
HAPPY   GENERAL HAPPINESS          BY SATJOB               JOB OR HOUSEWORK
- - - - - - - - - - - - - - - - - - - - - - - - - - - - - PAGE  1 OF  1


                SATJOB
                |
         COUNT  | VERY     MOD.     A LITTLE  VERY
         COL PCT| SATIS-   SATIS-   DISSAT-   DISSAT-       ROW
                | FIED     FIED     ISFIED    ISFIED       TOTAL
                |     1 |      2 |      3 |       4 |
HAPPY   -------+-------+-------+-------+------+
           1   |   252 |   111 |    17 |     9 |        389
VERY  HAPPY    |  47.5 |  24.6 |  14.8 |  20.5 |       34.1
               +-------+-------+-------+------+
           2   |   248 |   306 |    76 |    23 |        653
PRETTY HAPPY   |  46.7 |  67.8 |  66.1 |  52.3 |       57.2
               +-------+-------+-------+------+
           3   |    31 |    34 |    22 |    12 |         99
NOT TOO HAPPY  |   5.8 |   7.5 |  19.1 |  27.3 |        8.7
               +-------+-------+-------+------+
         COLUMN    531     451     115     44         1141
         TOTAL    46.5    39.5    10.1    3.9        100.0


CHI SQUARED               VALUE           DF        SIGNIFICANCE
PEARSON               113.24525            6          0.00000
LIKELIHOOD RATIO      115.49088            6          0.00000
MANTEL-HAENSZEL        98.87273          • 4          0.00000

MINIMUM EXPECTED FREQUENCY -    5.6943

                                                          APPROXIMATE
STATISTIC                  VALUE      ASE1     T VALUE   SIGNIFICANCE

LAMBDA :
   SYMMETRIC            0.05920    0.03864    1.53209
   WITH HAPPY  DEPENDENT 0.07820   0.04599    1.70037
   WITH SATJOB DEPENDENT 0.10000   0.03098    3.22788

GOODMAN & KRUSKAL TAU :
   WITH HAPPY  DEPENDENT 0.08265   0.02707               0.00000 *2
   WITH SATJOB DEPENDENT 0.02808   0.00970               0.00000 *2

KENDALL'S  TAU-B        0.26001    0.11273    2.30650
KENDALL'S  TAU-C        0.22666    0.09827    2.30650
GAMMA                   0.43311    0.18777    2.30650

SOMER'S D :
   SYMMETRIC            0.25958    0.11254    2.30650
   WITH HAPPY  DEPENDENT 0.24549   0.11038    2.30650
   WITH SATJOB DEPENDENT 0.27539   0.13523    2.30650

*2 Based on chi-square approximation

Number of Missing Observations:   240
```

Figure 14.13 CROSSTABS output for Release 4.

distribution for the statistic which can be used for confidence intervals or hypothesis testing. The fourth column, labeled "T-value," is the distance in t (standard-error) units between the calculated measure of association and zero. Zero is the claim of the null hypothesis—no relationship between the variables. Finally, the column entitled "Approximate Significance" identifies the statistical significance level associated with the statistic. Sometimes this can be calculated exactly, and at other times it can be only roughly approximated.

Assumptions

Many measures of association make certain assumptions about the data, as do measures of statistical significance. When these assumptions are violated, the statistics may lead the user to draw an erroneous conclusion. For the statistics discussed in this chapter, the important assumptions are logical, not mathematical.

First and foremost, you must use the correct statistic for the variables being analyzed. For ordinal-level statistics it is assumed that *both* variables are ordinal, and for interval-level statistics it is assumed that *both* variables are interval. If you have an interval independent variable and a nominal dependent variable, you must use a nominal measure of association. There are a few statistics that are exceptions, such as eta, discussed above, which allows for an interval dependent variable and a nominal independent one. Unless an exception is explicitly stated, however, the rule is this: The measure of association used is determined by the variable with the *lowest* level of measurement.

Second, different statistics are sensitive to different types of relationships. Nominal measures of association detect any deviation from randomness. Ordinal measures of association, however, detect a specific type of pattern in the data, a **monotonic relationship**. In a monotonic relationship, as the value of the independent variable increases, the average value of the dependent variable *consistently* increases (or decreases) as well. That is, a monotonic relationship between education and income means that as education increases, so does income—sometimes a little, at other times a lot—but income does not increase through the primary grades then drop with each additional year of high school and increase again with every extra year of college. Such a pattern is a **nonmonotonic relationship**; that is, it is positive over some values of the independent variable and negative over others. Even if we are looking at a strong relationship between two ordinal variables, if it is nonmonotonic, ordinal measures of association will not detect it.

Consider the hypothetical relationship in Figure 14.14 between age and income. During a person's early years, with increasing age the person gains seniority, climbs the organizational ladder, and consistently obtains increased income as well. However, past middle age, the relationship changes direction. Once the person has reached the top of the ladder or the peak of his or her abilities, the pay raises become fewer and smaller. After retirement, the respondent's income drops as salary checks are replaced by pension payments. Increas-

```
- - - - - - - - -   C R O S S - T A B U L A T I O N   O F   - - - - - - - - -
  INCOME                                                              BY  AGE
- - - - - - - - - - - - - - - - - - - - - - - - - - - - - - - -  PAGE  1 OF  1

                 AGE
        COUNT   I
        COL PCT I VERY      YOUNG    MIDDLE    NEARING   RECENT-   VERY
                I YOUNG               AGE      RETIRE-   LY        OLD          ROW
                I                               MENT     RETIRED                TOTAL
                I      0  I     1  I      2  I      3  I      4  I      5  I
  INCOME ------ + ------ + ------ + ------- + ------ + ------- + ------ +
              1 I      0  I     0  I    100  I    100  I      0  I      0  I    200
       HIGH     I    0.0  I   0.0  I  100.0  I  100.0  I    0.0  I    0.0  I   33.3
                + ------ + ------ + ------- + ------ + ------- + ------ +
              2 I      0  I   100  I      0  I      0  I    100  I      0  I    200
     MEDIUM     I    0.0  I 100.0  I    0.0  I    0.0  I  100.0  I    0.0  I   33.3
                + ------ + ------ + ------- + ------ + ------- + ------ +
              2 I    100  I     0  I      0  I      0  I      0  I    100  I    200
       LOW      I  100.0  I   0.0  I    0.0  I    0.0  I    0.0  I  100.0  I   33.3
                + ------ + ------ + ------- + ------ + ------- + ------ +
        COLUMN     100      100      100       100       100       100         600
        TOTAL     16.7     16.7     16.7      16.7      16.7      16.7       100.0
```

Figure 14.14 A fictional and nonmonotonic relationship between age and income.

ing age may also lead individuals to sell income-producing assets to meet expenses such as medical bills, thus leading to even greater income decreases.

The fictional relationship portrayed in Figure 14.13 is not only strong; it is perfect. Knowing the respondent's position on the independent variable enables us to perfectly determine her or his position on the dependent variable. The variables are also ordinal (in fact, interval), yet ordinal statistics such as gamma or tau will be close to zero because the relationship is not monotonic. On the right half of the contingency table, all the pairs are concordant. On the left half of the table all the pairs are discordant. The numbers of concordant and discordant pairs will cancel. Since the $C - D$ term is the numerator for both gamma and the taus, these statistics will have zero in the numerator and 0.0 as the size of the relationship.

The assumption that the relationship between two ordinal variables is monotonic is not very stringent. Virtually all relationships between ordinal variables are monotonic. You may encounter a few, however, which are non-monotonic and for which ordinal measures of association will seriously underestimate the size of the relationship. You should suspect this whenever most of the nominal measures of association show strong relationships but the ordinal measures are close to zero. If you do encounter a nonmonotonic relationship, use a nominal measure of association since it is not based on the monotonic assumption.

Directional Relationships and Operational Variables

One source of confusion in interpreting ordinal relationships stems from confusing operational and conceptual variables. For example, consider the connection between family income and happiness shown in Figure 14.15. FINCOME

```
RECODE FINCOME (1 THRU 10=1)(11 THRU 15=2)(16 THRU 20=3)
VALUE LABELS FINCOME 1 'LOW' 2 'MIDDLE' 3 'HIGH'
CROSSTABS TABLES = HAPPY BY FINCOME    / STATISTICS ALL
    / CELLS COLUMN COUNT


- - - - - -   C R O S S - T A B U L A T I O N   O F   - - - - - -
HAPPY   GENERAL HAPPINESS              BY FINCOME    TOTAL FAMILY INCOME
- - - - - - - - - - - - - - - - - - - - - - - - - - - - - PAGE  1 OF  1

                  FINCOME
                       |
            COUNT      |
            COL PCT  I LOW      MIDDLE    HIGH        ROW
                     I                                TOTAL
                     I     1 I      2 I      3 I
HAPPY     ------- + ------ + ------ + -------- +
              1  I    115 I    124 ,I    217 I       456
VERY  HAPPY    I   26.1 I   32.9 I   41.0 I      33.9
               + ------- + ------ + ------- +
              2  I    263 I    223 I    281 I       767
PRETTY HAPPY   I   59.8 I   59.2 I   53.1 I      57.0
               + ------- + ------ + ------- +
              3  I     62 I     30 I     31 I       123
NOT TOO HAPPY  I   14.1 I    8.0 I    5.9 I       9.1
               + ------- + ------ + ------- +
            COLUMN      440      377      529       1346
             TOTAL     32.7     28.0     39.3      100.0
```

CHI SQUARED	DF	SIGNIFICANCE	MIN EF	CELLS WITH EF < 5
36.76326	4	0.0000	34.451	NONE

STATISTIC	SYMMETRIC	WITH HAPPY DEPENDENT	WITH FINCOME DEPENDENT
LAMBDA	0.02221	0.00000	0.03794
UNCERTAINTY COEFFICIENT	0.01348	0.01484	0.01235
SOMER'S D	-0.14347	-0.13173	-0.15751
ETA		0.16077	0.16165

STATISTIC	VALUE	SIGNIFICANCE
CRAMER'S V	0.11686	
CONTINGENCY COEFFICIENT	0.16305	
KENDALL'S TAU B	-0.14405	0.0000
KENDALL'S TAU C	-0.13046	0.0000
PEARSON'S R	-0.16047	0.0000
GAMMA	-0.23729	

NUMBER OF MISSING OBSERVATIONS =   135

Figure 14.15 Relationship between family income and happiness.

has been recorded into low-, medium-, and high-income groups so the contingency table will not be too large. We saw earlier that satisfaction with financial status was positively related to happiness, but gamma and tau-*b* in Figure 14.15 both have minus signs. How can this be?

When we think of variables conceptually, we typically equate low numbers with a small amount of the concept and high numbers with more of it—60 in. is shorter than 70 in., and a happiness score of 30 reflects a "happier" state than a score of 10. This approach is used with FINCOME: Code 1 is the lowest-income group, and code 3 is the highest-income group. It is not unusual, however, for operational variables to have a different numbering system; 1 represents the greatest amount of something, and higher code numbers represent smaller amounts of it. This is true with the HAPPY variable; code 1 is greatest happiness, and code 3 is least happiness.

It is helpful to remember here that the computer makes no use of value labels at all; it just compares code numbers without understanding what they mean. The negative relationship in Figure 14.15 reflects that as one increases in *value* on FINCOME (has a higher income), one decreases in *value* on HAPPY (becomes happier). This situation is fairly common when you are dealing with secondary analysis. Those who collected the data coded them for their individual purposes, which may not be the same as our purposes. This is a problem only if the analyst is being lazy, blindly interpreting measures of association without thinking closely about the nature of the variables being analyzed.

The problem of **reverse coding** in a variable can be dealt with in one of two ways. The first approach is to change the code numbers of the offending variable. The command

    RECODE HAPPY (1 = 3) (3 = 1)

makes this variable's highest code number represent those who are happiest while code 1 now represents those who are least happy. Remember that the value labels will not be changed and will no longer fit the recoded variable. Adding new labels with a VALUE LABELS command will eliminate this possible source of confusion.

A second approach is to simply change the sign of the affected statistic from a minus to a plus or vice versa. Examine, in Figure 14.16, a repetition of the earlier case pairing of concordant and discordant pairs. After the code numbers on the HAPPY variable are reversed, all previously concordant pairs become discordant and all prior discordant pairs are now concordant. The gamma and tau measures of association will end up being exactly the same size, but their signs will be reversed.

Any time one of the variables is coded "backward," at least in terms of how you want to use it, merely writing in a different sign for the statistic is legitimate. There are two caveats here. First, never change the sign of a nominal

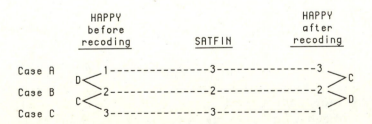

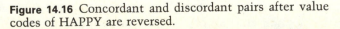

Figure 14.16 Concordant and discordant pairs after value codes of HAPPY are reversed.

measure of association, for positive and negative relationships make no sense with nominal variables. Second, change the sign if only *one* of the variables has reverse coding, but not if both do. The problem with reverse coding is that high code numbers on the independent and dependent variables mean different things—large amounts of the first concept in one case and small amounts of the second concept in the other. When both variables are coded in the same way, either both "forward" or both "backward," no problem arises. Look back at the relationship between HAPPY and SATFIN in Figure 14.12. Low code numbers represent both high happiness on HAPPY and high satisfaction on SATFIN. With both coded consistently, even though this is the reverse of what we might expect, the measures of association work just fine and show the expected positive direction of the relationship.

SPSS/PC+

As mentioned in prior chapters, in SPSS/PC+ you can request additional statistics or changes in the format of a contingency table as in version 2 of SPSS-X. The OPTIONS and STATISTICS keywords are used, with numbers designating the options and statistics desired. The statistic numbers are the same as those described in this chapter and listed in Table 14.1. There are three differences, the same as those listed in prior chapters: First, the OPTIONS and STATISTICS subcommands must be preceded by slashes. Second, they do not have to begin in column 1, as required by version 2 of SPSS-X. Third, they can both be contained on the same line, just as other subcommands can.

SUMMARY

In this chapter we have had our first encounter with measures of association—statistics identifying the substantive importance of a relationship between variables. These measures deal with questions quite different from those for measures of statistical significance. A variety of measures of association exist for different variables and relationship types. A few have been examined in this chapter, and more are examined in later chapters.

In addition to their primary function of measuring the strength of a relationship, measures of association allow for an enormously richer examination of the data. Some measures of association enable us to branch out into multivariate analysis, which involves the joint impact of two or more variables on the dependent variable. Other measures enable us to develop a predictive model, predicting, with a high degree of accuracy, success in college by knowing a student's SAT score along with GPA and class rank at high school graduation. In Chapter 15 we look at one of these additional applications of measures of association, the inclusion of control variables.

REVIEW

Key Terms

Statistical significance	Pair ties
Substantive significance	Gamma (γ)
Measures of association	Positive relationship
Strong relationship	Negative relationship
Weak relationship	Direction of a relationship
Phi coefficient (ϕ)	Kendall's tau-b (τ_b)
Cramer's V	Kendall's tau-c (τ_c)
Contingency coefficient (CC)	ALL
Proportional reduction of error (PRE)	Uncertainty coefficient
	Somer's D
Lambda (λ)	Eta (η)
Symmetric statistic	Pearson's r
Asymmetric statistic	Monotonic relationship
Concordant pair	Nonmonotonic relationship
Discordant pair	Reverse coding

Exercises

14.1 Correct any errors in these command statements.
  a. CROSSTABS TABLES = V15 BY V77 STATISTICS ALL
  b. CROSSTABS TABLES = V13 BY V70 /STATISTICS GAMMA
  c. CROSSTABS TABLES = V15 BY V77 /STATISTICS BTAU
  d. CROSSTABS TABLES = V13 BY V70 /STATISTICS CTAU
  e. CROSSTABS TABLES = V15 BY V77 /STATISTICS GAMMA
  f. CROSSTABS TABLES = V11 BY V35 /STATISTICS CHISQ GAMMA
  g. CROSSTABS TABLES = V11 BY V35 /STATISTICS ALL
  h. CROSSTABS TABLES = V11 BY V35 /STATISTICS CHISQ PHI
  i. CROSSTABS TABLES = ABRAPE BY RACE /STATISTICS CHISQ GAMMA
      CTAU
  j. CROSSTABS TABLES = ABRAPE BY RACE /STATISTICS ALL
  k. CROSSTABS TABLES = PARTNERS BY SEX
      /STATISTICS CHISQ PHI CC
  l. CROSSTABS TABLES = SATFIN BY SEX /STATISTICS CHISQ GAMMA
      BTAU CTAU
  m. CROSSTABS TABLES = WRKSTAT BY SEX /STATISTICS CHISQ PHI CV CC
      LAMBDA
  n. CROSSTABS TABLES = WRKSTAT BY SEX /STATISTICS CHISQ PHI CC
      GAMMA
  o. CROSSTABS TABLES = SATFIN BY SEX /STATISTICS CHISQ PHI CC
      LAMBDA GAMMA BTAU CTAU

p. CROSSTABS TABLES = ABRAPE SATFIN WRKSTAT BY SEX
/STATISTICS ALL
q. CROSSTABS TABLES = ABRAPE BY SEX RACE PRAY /STATISTICS ALL
r. CROSSTABS TABLES = ABRAPE BY SEX /STATISTICS 7 8
s. CROSSTABS TABLES = ABRAPE BY SEX
STATISTICS CTAU GAMMA
t. CROSSTABS TABLES = ABRAPE BY SEX
/STATISTICS 7,8
u. CROSSTABS TABLES = ABRAPE BY SEX
STATISTICS ALL

14.2 Below are the values of chi square and n for the relationships between the variables listed. Using the formulas in this chapter, calculate phi or Cramer's V and the contingency coefficients. You can check your answers by analyzing these relationships with the CROSSTABS procedure.
a. ABRAPE BY SEX, chi square = 1.36340, n = 924
b. XMOVIE BY SEX, chi square = 29.43806, n = 992
c. RACCHNG BY SEX, chi square = 6.18845, n = 900
d. V11 BY V35, chi square = 51.15629, n = 1380
e. V13 BY V70, chi square = 305.13287, n = 1591
f. V15 BY V77, chi square = 34.16561, n = 1599

14.3 Will any of the relationships below produce the wrong sign for the measures of association (i.e., one of the variables will have reverse coding)?
a. V11 BY V35
b. V13 BY V70
c. V15 BY V77
d. ABRAPE BY SATFIN
e. ABRAPE BY PRAY
f. ABRAPE BY RACE

14.4 Recode some ordinal variables so that their code numbers no longer reflect order (the variable becomes nominal). Run a CROSSTABS procedure with the variables before and after the recoding, and examine any changes in the nominal and ordinal measures of association.

SUGGESTED READINGS

Hildebrand, David K., James D. Laing and Howard Rosenthal. *Analysis of Ordinal Data,* Quantitative Applications in the Social Sciences, Sage University Papers Series No. 8 (Newbury Park, Calif.: Sage Publications, 1977).

Levin, Jack and James Alan Fox. *Elementary Statistics in Social Research,* 4th ed. (New York: Harper & Row, 1988) Chapter 13.

Liebetrau, Albert M. *Measures of Association,* Quantitative Applications in the Social Sciences, Sage University Papers Series No. 32 (Newbury Park, Calif.: Sage Publications, 1983).

Nachmias, David and Chava Nachmias. *Research Methods in the Social Sciences*, 3rd ed. (New York: St. Martin's, 1987) Chapter 16.

Norusis, Marija J., and SPSS Inc. *SPSS/PC+ V2.0 Base Manual* (Chicago: SPSS Inc., 1988) Chapter 9.

Reynolds, H. T. *Analysis of Nominal Data*, Quantitative Applications in the Social Sciences, Sage University Papers Series No. 7 (Newbury Park, Calif.: Sage Publications, 1977).

SPSS Inc. *SPSS Reference Guide* (Release 4) (Chicago: SPSS Inc., 1990) pages 99–108.

SPSS Inc. *SPSS-X User's Guide*, 3rd ed. (Chicago: SPSS Inc., 1988) Chapter 25.

Chapter 15

Control and Elaboration

*I*n prior chapters we investigated the hypothesis that gender is related to income. The source of the research hypothesis was our theoretical suspicion that sex discrimination in employment and earnings still existed. In testing the hypothesis we found definite income differences both when looking at all respondents and when restricting our attention to just women and men employed half-time or more. The relationship between gender and income is repeated in Figure 15.1, this time in a contingency table with income recoded into three groups so that the table is a manageable size.

The quantitative results are clear. Gender is related to income. Can we then conclude that income differences are the result of gender bias? Not necessarily, for the statistical results show only that the two variables are related, not *why* they are related. Factors other than gender bias might cause the gender-income relationship. Perhaps women are too new in the workforce, and thus we are comparing women at junior management positions with men at middle or senior management positions. If so, the management levels, not gender, might be producing the income differences. Another problem in the comparison may be different levels of education. Until recently, a large proportion of women did not graduate from, or even attend, college. We are comparing not just respondents in their twenties and thirties, but all women with all men, including older women raised during a time when entering college and the professions was reserved for males.

Our theories are theories of causation, that one factor causes another, studying is a cause of improved grades, or gender bias causes females to earn lower salaries. The question of causation is a logical or theoretical one, not a statistical one, but statistics help in this logical process. To establish causality requires, at a minimum, three things: The cause must come before the effect,

```
RECODE RINCOME (1 THRU 10=1)(11 THRU 15=2)(16 THRU 20=3)
VALUE LABELS RINCOME 1 'LOW' 2 'MEDIUM' 3 'HIGH'
CROSSTABS TABLES = RINCOME BY SEX / CELLS COUNT COLUMN
        / STATISTICS BTAU CTAU GAMMA


- - - - - - - -  C R O S S - T A B U L A T I O N   O F  - - - - - - -
RINCOME   RESPONDENT'S INCOME        BY SEX        RESPONDENT'S SEX
- - - - - - - - - - - - - - - - - - - - - - - - - - - - PAGE  1 OF  1


                 SEX
        COUNT  I
        COL PCT I MALE    FEMALE       ROW
                I                      TOTAL
                I      1 I       2 I
RINCOME  ----- + ------ + ------ +
        1  I     157 I     271 I     428
      LOW   I    32.8 I    58.0 I    45.3
                + ------ + ------ +
        2  I     176 I     145 I     321
      MEDIUM  I   36.8 I    31.0 I    34.0
                + ------ + ------ +
        3  I     145 I      51 I     196
      HIGH    I   30.3 I    10.9 I    20.7
                + ------ + ------ +
        COLUMN       478     467     945
        TOTAL       50.6    49.4   100.0


STATISTIC                   VALUE        SIGNIFICANCE

KENDALL'S TAU B            -0.27104      0.0000
KENDALL'S TAU C            -0.30578      0.0000
GAMMA                      -0.46201

NUMBER OF MISSING OBSERVATIONS = 536
```

Figure 15.1 Relationship between gender and income.

the cause and effect must be correlated, and other possible explanations for the correlation must have been eliminated.

The first condition is apparent. An individual's gender may be a cause of her income, but your adult income hardly determines your sex at conception. The "cause comes first" requirement is the same as determining which variable is independent (cause) and which dependent (effect). This condition is a logical one about which statistics say very little, but statistical evidence is relevant to the second and third conditions.

The second requirement, that the cause and effect be correlated, is a little less obvious but equally necessary. If a cause is truly a cause, then whenever it is present, the effect should be present as well. If we reason that a high level of education is one cause of high income, then there should be an observable positive relationship between education and income. If the data instead show that highly educated people earn no more than poorly educated people, then higher levels of education cannot be causing higher earnings. The measures of both association and statistical significance examined so far help us determine whether this condition of causality is met.

The third requirement for causality is the one to which this chapter is devoted—eliminating other possible explanations for the potential cause-effect correlation. We will look at how third variables might confound examinations of two-variable relationships and how to control for the impact of third variables.

CONFOUNDING VARIABLES AND CONTROLS

Variables can be correlated for a variety of reasons, including reasons which have nothing to do with causality. There is a long-established relationship between the number of storks in a region and that region's birthrate. Based on this evidence, do we conclude that the old tale of storks bringing babies is true? Of course not, but then we must explain why a correlation exists if there is no cause-effect relationship.

The reason for this seemingly irrational correlation is the presence of a **confounding variable** which is a third variable in addition to the two in the hypothesis being tested that interferes with our ability to accurately measure the relationship between the independent and dependent variables. In the example above, the confounding variable is the urban versus rural character of the regions. Rural areas have both higher birthrates and a greater amount of wildlife, including storks, while urban areas have a lower number of both. If we look at only the number of storks and the birthrate in a region we will find a relationship between them, but the relationship exists because both are caused by a third factor, the region's urban or rural status.

It is easiest to understand how confounding variables operate by first examining an illustration from a scientific experiment. Say an experimenter wants to test whether a particular drug leads white rats to gain weight. The scientist gathers a group of rats, injects them with the drug (the stimulus), and periodically measures their weights (the response).

To determine if the drug was the cause of any change in response, a control group that does not receive the drug is also needed. Perhaps the experiment is being conducted in the fall when most animals instinctively add fat to nourish them through the lean winter. To avoid being misled into attributing such a weight gain to the drug, the experimental and control group responses are compared. Both groups may gain weight for extraneous reasons, but if the drug is having the expected effect, the experimental group receiving it should be gaining more weight than the control group.

A possible confounding influence on this study could be the age of the rats used. Young rats will gain weight more rapidly than fully mature rats. If most rats in the experimental group are young and those in the control group are mature, the experimental group will gain weight more rapidly, not because of the stimulus but because of the confounding variable of age. The researcher would again be led to erroneously believe that the drug was having an effect when, in fact, age was the cause of the response.

What a confounding variable does is to introduce a second stimulus into the experiment. The control and experimental groups differ in two ways: receipt of the drug and age. If a response difference is then found between the groups, we do not know which stimulus is producing it. The same problem exists with variables obtained through survey or other research means. If there is a confounding influence, a single operational variable in effect may be representing two concepts simultaneously. If we divide respondents on the basis of sex, might we also be dividing them into high and low education groups? If so, are any income differences between the groups the result of the variable we are studying, sex, or the interfering variable, differences in education?

For a third variable to confound a relationship, it must be correlated, either positively or negatively, with *both* the independent and dependent variables being examined. A third variable correlated with only one of them, but not both, cannot confound attempts to measure a two-variable relationship. Men and women differ on many factors—such as height, weight, dress styles, and social attitudes—but these are correlated with only gender, not income, and will not interfere with our attempt to measure the gender-income connection. Similarly, age may be strongly correlated with income but only weakly correlated (if at all) with gender and again will not confound the independent variable–dependent variable relationship.

Experimental researchers control for confounding variables by randomly assigning subjects to the experimental and control groups. **Random assignment** creates a high probability that possible confounding factors will be present equally in both experimental and control groups. This removes any correlation between the stimulus and the confounding variable—both groups now contain an approximately equal number of young and old rats, so age differences between the groups no longer exist and cannot be a cause of any weight differences. Since a third variable can confuse a relationship only if it is related to both the independent and the dependent variables, severing the relationship of the third variable with the independent variable (stimulus) through random assignment removes its confounding impact on the stimulus-response relationship.

The experimental approach to research (and eliminating confounding variables) works well in many fields of study, but can be used only rarely in most of the social sciences. Consider the relationship that interests us between gender and income. We could gather a number of volunteer respondents and even randomly assign them to experimental and control groups. However, subjecting them to a stimulus while we examine their responses is a bit difficult, given the kinds of stimuli and responses of interest to social scientists. We cannot tell the experimental group, "You people will now all be female so we can study your incomes." People are helpful, but not quite that helpful.

Instead of first dividing respondents into control and experimental groups and then providing the stimulus, in survey research we identify sample respondents who have already received or not received the stimulus (males and females) and divide them accordingly. The problem faced by survey researchers is that they are not able, as experimental researchers are, to control for confounding factors by randomly assigning subjects to experimental and control groups before introducing the stimulus. In fact, we must do the opposite, systematically assign respondents to the groups based on the presence or absence of the stimulus. How, then, do we control for confounding variables?

The answer lies in how a confounding variable operates to confuse a relationship. Without the presence of confounding variables, the experimental and control groups differ in one respect only—the experimental group has received the stimulus and the control group has not—so any differences in the responses of the two groups must be due to the stimulus. When a confounding variable is present, the experimental and control groups differ on more than one characteristic: Not only is the experimental group of a different gender, but also it probably has a different educational level from the control group. Since confounding variables may produce more than one difference between the groups, our job is to remove those extra differences so that only the stimulus, or positions on the independent variable, remains as the difference between groups.

We can remove the possibly confounding impact of education by holding this variable **constant**—by making sure that everyone we examine has either a high or low educational level so that the experimental and control groups will not differ in educational attainments. One way to do this involves the SELECT IF command. We can select only college-educated respondents and then conduct the CROSSTABS analysis. Since all the respondents in the contingency table now have the same educational level, there cannot be any significant difference between the experimental group (women) and control group (men) on the confounding variable of education. Education is held constant—not allowed to vary—for this analysis.

When we remove the impact of a confounding variable in this manner, it is called a **statistical control**; the confounding variable is controlled for by the way in which we statistically analyze the data, rather than before the data are even collected, as in the random assignment of subjects in an experiment. The confounding variable we are controlling for is also called our **control variable**.

CONTROL VARIABLES ON THE CROSSTABS COMMAND

While the SELECT IF command can accomplish the goal of controlling for education, it is a bit clumsy to use for this purpose. If we look at just college-educated respondents, any conclusions that we draw will be applicable to only that group; the gender-income hypothesis has not been tested for other educational groups. To fully test the hypothesis, we must use multiple SELECT IF commands and CROSSTABS statements to perform the contingency table analysis for each educational level.

There is an easier way to introduce a control: Simply add the possible confounding variable to the CROSSTABS statement. This is accomplished through the following commands:

```
RECODE EDUC (0 THRU 12 = 1) (13 THRU 20 = 2)
VALUE LABELS  EDUC 1 'HS OR LESS' 2 'COLL'
CROSSTABS TABLES = RINCOME BY SEX  BY EDUC /CELLS COUNT COLUMN
    / STATISTICS CTAU
```

Most of the CROSSTABS command is the familiar request for a contingency table with column percentages and summary statistics. What is new is that the independent and dependent variables are followed by a second BY keyword and then the name of the control variable, EDUC. This form of the CROSSTABS command holds education constant by producing separate contingency tables for each value of the control variable, as shown in Figure 15.2. Each contingency table between RINCOME and SEX is for one educational level only, with education held constant. With education constant, there cannot be differences in education between women and men, thus removing such a difference as a possible confounding influence on the RINCOME-SEX relationship.

EDUC is a variable with many values, ranging from 0 to 20 in the GSS88 data set. If the variable is kept in its original form, the command will produce 20 different contingency tables between RINCOME and SEX, one for each value of EDUC. This is far too many to reasonably interpret. Breaking the sample into 20 smaller subsamples will also produce a number of tables with zero cases in some cells, distorting the summary statistics. Consequently, it is common practice to recode the control variable to only two or three values so that the resulting tables can be easily examined and interpreted. This was done in the commands above, by combining EDUC into two categories. Of course, this means that education is not held completely constant since group 1 varies from 0 years to a high school diploma while group 2 ranges from 1 year of college to a graduate degree. Nonetheless, the most crucial educational factor affecting income—whether the respondent has any college training—is constant in each of the two contingency tables.

The CROSSTABS output after a control variable is added is largely self-explanatory. The legend at the top of the first table in Figure 15.2 shows that RINCOME is being cross-tabulated with SEX *while controlling for* EDUC. The table includes only people whose value on recoded EDUC is 1, which is 12 or fewer years of education. The bottom table in Figure 15.2 is the same, but it includes only respondents with a value of 2 on EDUC, which is 13 or more years of education.

When control variables are included, a different nomenclature is used to refer to the resulting measures of association. The tau statistics at the bottom of each table are based on the respondents in that table only. As a result, they are called **partial correlations** because we have eliminated the possibly confounding impact of one or more control variables. More precisely, the partial taus are called **first-order statistics**, or **first-order partial correlations**, to indicate that they are measures of association produced while one other variable is controlled for. The original tau statistic in Figure 15.1 is called a **zero-order correlation** because no (zero) variables were controlled for in producing the correlation. These terms will not appear on the printout, but they are regularly used in reporting statistical results so that readers will know whether and how many confounding variables have been controlled for.

Second-order, third-order, or higher-order partial correlations are produced when two, three, or more possible confounding variables are controlled for. This is done in the CROSSTABS procedure by adding additional *controls*. The word

```
RECODE RINCOME (1 THRU 10=1)(11 THRU 15=2)(16 THRU 20=3)
       /EDUC (0 THRU 12=1)(13 THRU 20=2)
VALUE LABELS RINCOME 1 'LOW' 2 'MEDIUM' 3 'HIGH'
           /EDUC 1 'HS OR LESS' 2 'COLL'
CROSSTABS TABLES = RINCOME BY SEX BY EDUC /CELLS COUNT COLUMN
      / STATISTICS CTAU
```

```
- - - - - -  C R O S S - T A B U L A T I O N  O F  - - - - - -
RINCOME   RESPONDENT'S INCOME      BY SEX       RESPONDENT'S SEX
CONTROLLING FOR   EDUC   HIGHEST YEAR OF SCHOOL COMPLETED
VALUE = 1   HS OR LESS
- - - - - - - - - - - - - - - - - - - - - - - - - PAGE  1 OF  1
                 SEX
          COUNT  I
          COL PCT I MALE    FEMALE      ROW
                 I                     TOTAL
                 I    1  I     2 I
RINCOME ----- + ------- + ------ +
          1  I    94  I   164  I     258
      LOW    I  41.6  I  69.2  I    55.7
             + ------- + ------ +
          2  I    90  I    64  I     154
    MEDIUM   I  39.8  I  27.0  I    33.3
             + ------- + ------ +
          3  I    42  I     9  I      51
      HIGH   I  18.6  I   3.8  I    11.0
             + ------- + ------ +
          COLUMN    226     237      463
          TOTAL    48.8    51.2    100.0
```

```
STATISTIC                 VALUE        SIGNIFICANCE
KENDALL'S TAU C          -0.31094        0.0000
```

```
- - - - - -  C R O S S - T A B U L A T I O N  O F  - - - - - -
RINCOME   RESPONDENT'S INCOME      BY SEX       RESPONDENT'S SEX
CONTROLLING FOR   EDUC   HIGHEST YEAR OF SCHOOL COMPLETED
VALUE = 2 COLL
- - - - - - - - - - - - - - - - - - - - - - - - - PAGE  1 OF  1
                 SEX
          COUNT  I
          COL PCT I MALE    FEMALE      ROW
                 I                     TOTAL
                 I    1  I     2 I
RINCOME ----- + ------- + ------ +
          1  I    63  I   107  I     170
      LOW    I  25.0  I  46.5  I    35.3
             + ------- + ------ +
          2  I    86  I    81  I     167
    MEDIUM   I  34.1  I  35.2  I    34.6
             + ------- + ------ +
          3  I   103  I    42  I     145
      HIGH   I  40.9  I  18.3  I    30.1
             + ------- + ------ +
          COLUMN    252     230      482
          TOTAL    52.3    47.7    100.0
```

```
STATISTIC                 VALUE        SIGNIFICANCE
KENDALL'S TAU C          -0.29622        0.0000
NUMBER OF MISSING OBSERVATIONS = 536
```

Figure 15.2 CROSSTABS output when a control variable is added.

"controls" is emphasized because adding additional *control variables* is not the same as adding additional *controls*. Consider the command set

```
RECODE EDUC (0 THRU 12 = 1) (13 THRU 20 = 2) / WRKSTAT (3 THRU 8 = 3)
CROSSTABS TABLES =  RINCOME BY SEX  BY EDUC  WRKSTAT
   /CELLS COUNT COLUMN   /STATISTICS CTAU
```

This command includes two control variables, EDUC and WRKSTAT, with the latter recoded into working full-time (1), part-time (2), or not at all (3). Because of the way the variables are listed on the command, SPSS will control for each variable *separately*. That is, contingency tables between RINCOME and SEX will be produced for the two values of EDUC and then for the three values of WRKSTAT. The statistics for each table will be first-order partial statistics because they were produced by controlling for only one variable at a time, first for EDUC and then for WRKSTAT. While EDUC is controlled for, employment differences between men and women may still exist, and while working status is controlled for, educational differences between women and men may exist.

To produce a second-order partial correlation simultaneously controlling for both variables, the command has to read

```
RECODE EDUC (0 THRU 12 = 1) (13 THRU 20 = 2) / WRKSTAT (3 THRU 8 = 3)
CROSSTABS TABLES =  RINCOME BY SEX  BY EDUC  BY WRKSTAT
   /CELLS COUNT COLUMN   / STATISTICS CTAU
```

Notice that EDUC is now separated from WRKSTAT with an additional BY keyword, indicating that we want to analyze RINCOME and SEX while also controlling for both EDUC and WRKSTAT. This command will produce six contingency tables, one for each possible combination of EDUC and WRKSTAT values. The first table includes only those respondents for whom *both* EDUC equals 1 *and* WRKSTAT equals 1. The second table still contains only the less-educated respondents, but now for cases in which WRKSTAT equals 2; and the third table is for EDUC equals 1 and WRKSTAT equals 3. The fourth, fifth, and sixth tables are for different values of WRKSTAT, but including only college-educated respondents (EDUC = 2). In each table, both variables are being held constant, for there is neither an educational nor an employment difference between women and men when their respective incomes are examined. The statistics for each table are second-order partial correlations since two variables are being controlled for concurrently.

Using higher-level controls on the CROSSTABS command introduces difficulties. The number of tables produced increases exponentially with each additional level of control. Consequently, the number of cases in each table becomes increasingly small, rendering the calculation of measures of association less reliable. For this reason, analysts seldom move beyond first- or second-order controls on the CROSSTABS command. Procedures that we examine later can handle higher levels of controls with far greater ease and less difficulty in interpreting the output.

Let us return to the analysis that interests us. Having suspected education as a confounding influence on the gender-income relationship, we controlled for education and got two contingency tables with associated first-order partial tau-c statistics. Interpreting partial correlations involves a different strategy from interpreting zero-order correlations. Below we examine the various interpretations that can be made from partial correlations, and then we return to the results of Figure 15.2 to see what they tell us.

ELABORATION—INTERPRETING PARTIAL CORRELATIONS

In one sense, interpreting a partial correlation is straightforward. The two statistics in Figure 15.2 are the relationships between gender and income with the effect of attending college removed. More interesting and useful, however, is the determination of the impact of the control variable by comparing the zero-order correlation in Figure 15.1 with the partial correlations in Figure 15.2. This comparison is termed **elaboration**, for we expand or elaborate upon our analysis of what affects the respondent's income. We are now performing a **multivariate analysis** (instead of a bivariate one), examining how two or more variables jointly affect differences in income (the dependent variable). After a control variable is introduced, four types of changes—differences between the zero-order and partial correlations—might occur in the statistical results. Each change leads to a different interpretation, interpretations that expand our understanding of the independent variable–dependent variable relationship.

No Change

The first possibility is that the zero-order and partial correlations are essentially the same, say, .40 for the zero-order relationship and .37 and .43 for the two partial correlations. The zero-order and first-order relationships will seldom be identical, for they are based on different samples—the entire sample for the zero-order correlation and smaller subsamples of college educated and non-college educated only for the first-order correlations—with each sample containing some random error. Differences ranging from 5 percentage points up to 20 percent of the size of the zero-order correlation (or 10 percentage points for a zero-order correlation of .50) could easily be due to sampling fluctuations.

When no sizable difference exists between the zero-order and partial relationships, we have a **replicated relationship**, a reproduction of the original correlation under more stringent conditions (the control variable). The interpretation of this result is illustrated in Figure 15.3. The relationship hypothesized between X and Y has been confirmed, represented by the arrow connecting the variables. The suspected confounding variable C is not interfering with the

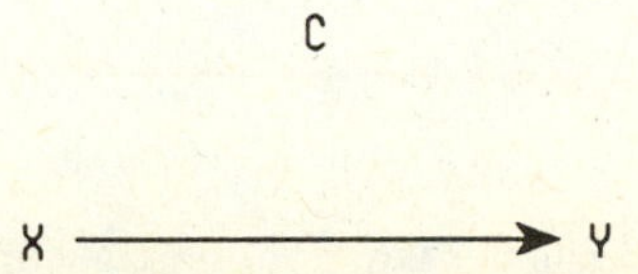

C

X ⟶ Y

Figure 15.3 Relationships between the three variables when the partial correlations show little change.

relationship, illustrated by the lack of arrows between it and *X* or *Y*. Having controlled for variable *C* and finding it makes no difference in the measures of association, we now have greater confidence that variable *X* is a cause of (leads to differences in) variable *Y*.

This might be what happens with our relationship between gender and income. We suspect women and men have different college attendance rates, but this may not be the case. Educational differences between the sexes, if they exist at all, may be only at the lower educational levels or just a difference in the proportion of graduate degrees earned—both differences with less impact on income than the division between college and no college.

Consistent Increase or Decrease

A second possible outcome is that the partial correlations may all be smaller (or larger) than the original zero-order correlations, such as a zero-order correlation of .40 and partial correlations of .25 and .30, or a zero-order correlation of .40 and partial correlations of .55 and .60. This result means that the independent and control variables are both correlated with each other and affect the dependent variable, as diagramed in Figure 15.4. In the zero-order correlation,

Correlations with C leading to a positive impact on the X-Y relationship

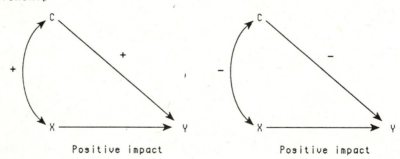

Correlations with C leading to a negative impact on the X-Y relationship

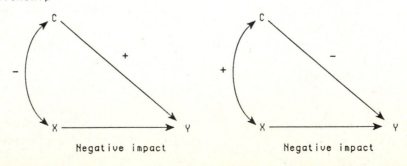

Figure 15.4 Relationships between the three variables when the partial correlations show a consistent change.

variable X is "picking up" some of the effect of variable C on Y, leading the zero-order relationship to distort how strongly X and Y are correlated.

A sports analogy may help illustrate this phenomenon. Say we wish to determine how much the quality of a quarterback affected the winning margin of a football team. We find two teams that are evenly matched except that team A has a better quarterback than team B, and we run the teams through a series of 10 games against the same opponents. The result is that team A scores, on average, 20 points more per game than team B. So we attribute all this relationship, all 20 points, to the impact of the quarterback.

Now comes a fly in the ointment. After the games have been played, we discover that team A also had a better running back than team B and that this second difference between the teams contributed to some of the winning margin of team A. In short, we attributed all the winning margin to the difference in quarterbacks when part of the winning points were due to the difference in running backs. If we were able to control for, or eliminate, the point difference contributed by the running back, we might find that the better quarterback added an average of only 10 extra points to the winning margin—still significant, but not as big a relationship as we originally thought.

A confounding variable has a positive impact on the relationship between X and Y if C is correlated with the independent and dependent variables in the same direction, either positively or negatively. This is diagramed in the top half of Figure 15.4. Alternatively, a confounding variable has a negative impact if it is correlated negatively with the first variable and positively with the second variable in the original hypothesized relationship, diagramed in the bottom half of Figure 15.4.

If the original correlation is positive, then adding a positive impact from the confounding variable leads to an **exaggerated relationship**, a correlation larger than it should be. On the other hand, if a confounding variable is exerting a negative impact on an essentially positive relationship, then we have a **suppressed relationship**, a correlation appearing smaller than it ought to be. If the pure X-Y relationship is negative, the results above will be reversed; a positive impact depresses it while a negative impact exaggerates it.

Let us return to the football analogy. Say we discover no difference in the winning margins between teams A and B. We later find, however, that team B had a better running back, which canceled the benefit that team A was receiving from its better quarterback. The quarterback was contributing additional points to the score of team A, but this impact was hidden by extra points earned by the running back of team B. If we rerun the tests after equalizing the running backs of both teams, we might find team A now scoring 10 points more on average—the quarterback–winning margin relationship is suppressed by the confounding influence of the running back.

This type of problem might also be affecting our gender-income relationship. Education is positively related to income. If it is also negatively related to gender (women have lower values on EDUC but a higher code number on SEX), it could be leading us to underestimate the impact of gender on income. If so, we will find the first-order partial correlations to be much larger than the zero-order correlation.

Inconsistent Increase or Decrease

Another result from using a control variable is to find that the partial correlations move in different directions—some decline from the zero-order value while others increase or remain the same. For example, we might find a zero-order relationship of .40 between gender and income, and controlling for education leads the relationship to jump to .60 for the low education group but drop to .15 for highly educated respondents.

This result typically leads to a **conditional interpretation** of the research hypothesis. We might conclude that the X-Y relationship exists and is strong for one group on the confounding variable, exists but is far weaker for a second confounding-variable group, and does not exist at all for a third group. In the gender-income relationship, we may find a strong relationship for those with a high school education or less, because men may have highly paid factory or construction jobs while women with the same educational level may have the lower-pay occupations of secretary, government worker, or food handler or service person. Among the college-educated, however, there may be little or no difference in the incomes of men and women—all may be employed in professions such as the law, medicine, architecture, and so forth; management positions; or other lucrative endeavors.

This type of pattern would lead to a conditional explanation because we conclude that the research hypothesis is true only under certain conditions. If the respondent belongs to group 1, the relationship has this strength; but if the respondent belongs to group 2, the relationship is weaker or does not exist at all. Consequently, gender may be a cause of income differences for only certain groups of the population.

Relationship Drops to Zero

The final possible outcome from using a control variable is that the partial correlations will drop to zero or near zero. The prior three situations led to only a single interpretation of the results. When the partial correlations decline to near zero, however, there are two possible interpretations. The first is that the original correlation was a spurious one. A **spurious relationship**, diagrammed in Figure 15.5, is the explanation for the correlation between a region's number of storks and its birthrate, the example used at the beginning of this chapter. There is no rational reason to expect a correlation between variables X and Y but since each is correlated with the confounding variable C, variables X and Y will appear

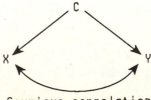

Figure 15.5 A spurious relationship between two variables caused by a confounding variable.

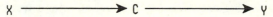

Figure 15.6 An intervening variable between the
x-y relationship.

related to each other unless C is controlled for. In the gender-income case, it may be that sex discrimination no longer exists in the marketplace, but the possibility that women have lower levels of education might lead gender and income to appear correlated if differences in education are not controlled for.

While the spurious relationship explanation is one possibility, a second interpretation is that C is an **intervening variable**, one that intervenes between X and Y and is the reason that they are related. This possibility is diagramed in Figure 15.6. An intervening variable represents a causal chain or process. Gender discrimination in society may lead women to be excluded from educational opportunities which in turn leads to women's being restricted to lower-pay jobs. Controlling for an intervening variable will cause the X-Y relationship to drop to zero because we are controlling for the very process by which X is correlated with Y. Studying leads to an increase in GPAs, but if we were to control for grades made on tests, the studying-GPA relationship would decline to zero because we would be controlling for the mechanism by which studying produces higher GPAs.

In determining whether a decline of the partial correlations to zero is the result of a spurious relationship or an intervening one, the statistics are of little help. Choosing one explanation over another is a matter of theory and logic, not statistics. In making this determination, observe that the intervening pattern in Figure 15.6 is really two causal connections—X causes C and C causes Y—each of which must follow the criteria of causality discussed earlier. In particular, remembering that the cause must come before the effect helps to determine whether a relationship is spurious or intervening. Region cannot intervene between storks and the birthrate, for storks (variable X) do not come first and cause a region to become rural (variable C). This conjures up the ridiculous vision of giant storks uprooting homes and skyscrapers to transform an urban area to a rural one. Similarly, if a relationship between education and income drops to zero when gender is controlled for (a reverse of our independent and confounding variables), the original relationship was probably spurious. Sex cannot intervene between education and income without our assuming that increases in educational levels lead respondents to change from female to male. Education, however, can intervene between sex and income. That does not mean that it does, but it is a plausible explanation for the results and does meet the causality criteria.

Interpreting Figures 15.1 and 15.2

This discussion of control variables reemphasizes the interplay between reasoning and empirical analysis when you are investigating a research question. Statistical results, such as the correlation between storks and the birthrate, that appear illogical probably are. When encountering them, we should search for why they exist. Are they possibly due to variables coded in a reverse direction, the presence of a confounding variable, or a mismatch between conceptual and operational variables? The computer merely plugs variables into formulas and prints results. Only we can determine what, if anything, the results mean.

On the other hand, armchair theorizing is seldom sufficient. In the sections above we discussed four possible ways that education might impinge on the gender-income relationship: not at all, suppressing its size, leading to a conditional interpretation of the research hypothesis, or as an intervening variable. Each possibility was quite plausible, and reasoning alone could not tell us which was correct. Statistical analysis shows us that some possibilities are more likely than others.

In Figure 15.1, we found the zero-order correlation between RINCOME and SEX to be $-.306$. Controlling for education in Figure 15.2 led to two partial tau-c values of $-.311$ and $-.296$—virtually no change from the original relationship. We have replicated the relationship and thus pick an alternative one. Education, at least as we have recoded it to measure having some college experience, is not confounding the connection between gender and income.

At this point we may wish to test for other possible confounding variables such as a respondent's work status or marital status, to see if they have any impact on the original relationship. If we exhaust all plausible confounding variables and find that gender and income are still related, we will have met the third criterion for causality—eliminating other possible explanations for the X-Y correlation. At that point we will have increased confidence in concluding that sex, by itself, is a cause of income differences between respondents.

FINDING AND USING CONTROL VARIABLES

The discussion above explains how to interpret the statistics after control variables have been used. Before ending this chapter, we look at topics related to control variables and the broader research process: determining which variables should or can be used, and comparing statistical versus substantive significance.

What Variables to Control For

The experimental researcher has it easy. She or he merely needs to randomly assign subjects to experimental and control groups. All possible confounding variables are then controlled for, even if the experimenter has no idea what these variables might be. Random assignment makes it highly likely that the groups will be similar on all characteristics except for receipt of the stimulus. The use of control variables is more difficult in the survey research process. The survey researcher uses statistical controls after the data have been generated. That means we need to have an idea of what variables might exert a confounding impact so we will know which ones to control for.

Some confounding variables may be obvious, others far less so. Our best guide to performing a complete and careful analysis is to become familiar with other research on the same topic. This should always be done anyway, for there is little point in investigating a research question that another analyst has already satisfactorily answered. Even when the research question deserves further probing, past research efforts will provide us with a richer understanding of the topic, including confounding variables identified by other scholars.

Confounding Variables and the Research Design

There may be many factors confounding the gender-income relationship that we would like to control for. In addition to education and work status, factors might include the type of occupation (e.g., teacher, architect, or attorney); years of seniority on the job, union membership, etc. Unfortunately, we cannot control for them because no variables representing these concepts exist in either of our data sets.

This is another good reason for always reviewing the existing literature early in the research process. We can identify what independent and control variables other scholars deemed important and include them in the survey. Once the data have been collected, we cannot go back and add variables that were forgotten. Even if we can locate the respondents again and they are willing to sit through another interview, the passage of time will corrupt any efforts to add new data. Some respondents may have lost their jobs and others may have been promoted, leading us to correlate current employment status with income that the respondent earned 6 months earlier when holding a different job.

We are faced with a different situation: performing secondary analyses of data that we had no part in collecting. Inevitably a number of key variables that we would like to examine will not be available in the data set. This is an inherent limitation of most research, but it should not lead us to ignore important factors just because we have no operational measures of them. Science seeks to be cumulative, building on past research to steadily expand our understanding of the world. Just as you may improve your research efforts by incorporating ideas suggested by others, future analysts may use your ideas when designing new research projects.

We cannot analyze variables that we do not have, but we can include them in reports made about our results. It is not only common but also expected for scientific reports to include a section, usually in the conclusion, discussing suggestions for future research. Ignoring deficiencies in the data, such as possible unmeasured confounding variables, gives the impression that our analysis is more conclusive than it actually is. Each scholar does the best she can with the data available, but also clearly points out any gaps in the data and recommends that future research fill in these gaps. Another scholar reading this report may develop a research project that does just that. Few individuals ever answer any research question completely. The sharing of ideas, both successes and failures, may lead the community of scholars to accomplish what a lone individual cannot.

Variables Not to Control For

In the research process, theory always comes first. Theory yields hypothesized relationships which the quantitative analysis of empirical data will then support or refute. Without a strong theory to guide us, data analysis can produce any number of nonsensical results. In investigating confounding variables, this reminder should help us to avoid introducing inappropriate control variables. Whenever a third variable is correlated with the dependent and independent variables, it is a mathematical given that controlling for it will affect the original relationship. This is true even when the relationship of the third variable to the other two is not logically a confounding one.

This problem commonly occurs when we are controlling for a third variable that amounts to a second measure of the independent or dependent variable. Suppose we want to determine whether gender leads to different religious behaviors as measured by frequency of church attendance. We then decide to control for how frequently the respondent prays, which is obviously correlated with church attendance and, if the research hypothesis is correct, is related to sex as well. Controlling for PRAY would definitely affect the correlation between SEX and ATTEND, not because PRAY is a confounding variable but because it is a second measure of the dependent variable, religious behavior. We are actually controlling for the dependent variable.

To avoid making this error, keep theoretical concerns in the forefront of your thinking. Does the operational variable that you are thinking of controlling for measure a different concept from the independent and dependent variables? If so, is this third conceptual variable something that logically could confound the original relationship? If the answers to both questions are yes, proceed—the control process is grounded in theory, and the results can be interpreted intelligently. If the answer to either question is no, stop and rethink what you are doing. You may read some meaning into the statistical results that is not justifiable.

Comparing Statistical and Substantive Significance

In examining the impact of control variables, we focused on measures of association, not measures of statistical significance. There is a reason for this. Introducing control variables in the CROSSTABS procedure involves dividing the data set into subgroups, each smaller than the entire sample. All statistical significance formulas—the t test, F test, and chi square—incorporate the size of a sample in their calculations. This makes sense, for the larger the sample, the greater our confidence that it faithfully reflects the population. It also means, however, that dividing the sample into subgroups will usually increase the chi-square significance level for each subgroup, even when the control variable has no effect on the relationship.

In contrast, measures of association are not affected by the sample size. If a subsample is too small, less than 50 cases, any statistic may become unreliable; but as long as the subgroups are of decent size, measures of association should be unaffected. We may thus compare taus, lambdas, gammas, and other measures of association across samples of different size with greater confidence that any differences observed are due to the control variable, not to a smaller number of cases.

Some changes in the level of statistical significance of a relationship are important. It is even possible for the significance level to go down (become more statistically significant), instead of up, if the control variable is suppressing the relationship. Usually, however, meaningful changes are also reflected in the measures of association. Focusing on measures of association alone should provide all the information needed without the risk of being misled by changes in sample size.

SUMMARY

A simple zero-order correlation between two variables is seldom sufficient to identify the strength and nature of their relationship. Elaborating our research through the introduction of control variables enables us to more completely comprehend the social forces at work. Are confounding variables operating which distort the relationship or act as intervening mechanisms between the independent and dependent variables? Investigating this topic is not just a statistical nicety, it is at the heart of the analyst's desire to understand which items are related to each other as well as how and why.

In this and prior chapters we have learned how to portray a relationship with a contingency table, identify strong and weak relationships with measures of association, and expand our analysis to remove confounding variables. In all these activities we used one SPSS procedure only: CROSSTABS. The CROSSTABS procedure is well suited for studying nominal and ordinal variables. Contingency tables can also be used for interval variables, but considerably more powerful procedures are readily available and easy to use. In the next few chapters we look at procedures designed exclusively for interval variables.

REVIEW

Key Terms

Confounding variable	Elaboration
Random assignment	Multivariate analysis
Constant	Replicated relationship
Statistical control	Exaggerated relationship
Control variable	Suppressed relationship
Partial correlations	Conditional interpretation
First-order statistics	Spurious relationship
First-order partial correlations	Intervening variable
Zero-order correlations	

Exercises

15.1 Correct any errors in the command statements below. All should include control variable(s), and you may assume that all variables have been condensed into a small enough number of categories to permit a reasonable contingency table analysis.
- *a.* CROSSTABS TABLES = V2 V27 V74 /STATISTICS ALL
- *b.* CROSSTABS TABLES = V36 BY V55 V87 /STATISTICS ALL
- *c.* CROSSTABS TABLES = V2 BY V27 BY V74 BY V87 BY V85 /STATISTICS ALL
- *d.* CROSSTABS TABLES = BY V2 BY V27 BY V74 /STATISTICS ALL
- *e.* CROSSTABS TABLES = V2 BY V27 BY V74 V87 V85 /STATISTICS ALL
- *f.* CROSSTABS TABLES = V2 V27 V74 BY V87 V85 /STATISTICS ALL
- *g.* CROSSTABS TABLES = RINCOME BY EDUC BY WRKSTAT /STATISTICS ALL
- *h.* CROSSTABS TABLES = PILLOK BY SEX BY AGE /STATISTICS ALL
- *i.* CROSSTABS TABLES = PREMARSX BY SEX EDUC /STATISTICS ALL
- *j.* CROSSTABS TABLES = FEHOME FEFAM FEPOL BY EDUC BY SEX /STATISTICS ALL
- *k.* CROSSTABS TABLES = FEHOME BY EDUC BY POLVIEWS /STATISTICS ALL
- *l.* CROSSTABS TABLES = RINCOME BY EDUC SEX BY WRKSTAT /STATISTICS ALL
- *m.* CROSSTABS TABLES = RINCOME BY EDUC SEX BY WRKSTAT

15.2 Identify the commands in Exercise 15.1 by the order of the correlations that they will produce: zero-order, first-order, etc.

15.3 Below are some variables (dependent, independent, and control) as they might be listed on the CROSSTABS command, with hypothetical zero- and first-order partial correlations. Interpret these results. All control variables have been condensed into two or three categories.
- *a.* V2 BY V27 BY V74; zero = .40, partials = .02, .05
- *b.* V13 BY V87 BY V74; zero .20, partials .10, .12, .11
- *c.* V16 BY V28 BY V32; zero .43, partials .05, .03, .06
- *d.* V36 BY V55 BY V87; zero .32, partials .25, .24
- *e.* V47 BY V74 BY V87; zero .36, partials .44, .42
- *f.* PILLOK BY SEX BY AGE; zero .25, partials .40, .10
- *g.* RINCOME BY EDUC BY WRKSTAT; zero .40, partials .66, .14, .00
- *h.* PILLOK BY SEX BY AGE; zero .25, partials .22, .28
- *i.* PREMARSX BY EDUC BY SEX; zero .36, partials .06, .07
- *j.* PREMARSX BY EDUC BY SEX, zero .36, partials .45, .08
- *k.* RINCOME BY EDUC BY AGE; zero .25, partials .36, .36

SUGGESTED READINGS

Babbie, Earl. *The Practice of Social Research*, 5th ed. (Belmont, Calif.: Wadsworth, 1989) Chapter 16.

Nachmias, David and Chava Nachmias. *Research Methods in the Social Sciences*, 3rd ed. (New York: St. Martin's, 1987) Chapter 17.

Correlation
(Pearson Corr)

Many issues were raised during the 1988 presidential campaign. The American National Election Study measures respondents' opinions on some of the key issues, including government spending in general (V24), spending on defense (V27) and health insurance (V30), cooperation with the Soviet Union (V33), and the equality of women in society (V36). Which of these issues had the greatest impact on public perceptions of George Bush, as measured by the Bush feeling thermometer (V5)? Were the defense or foreign policy issues most important, or domestic concerns such as health insurance and sexual equality, or were voters most attentive to government spending and Bush's "no new taxes" pledge?

As we have learned, such questions are answered through measures of association. We merely correlate attitudes concerning each issue with the Bush feeling thermometer and discover which correlation is the largest. The statistics examined thus far, however, would not do justice to these variables. The Bush feeling thermometer is interval. So, too, are the issue variables, each measured as a 7-point scale anchored at the endpoints (that is, 1 = greatly decrease defense spending and 7 = greatly increase) with respondents picking a number representing their location on the scale. As presented to respondents during the interview, each number on the scale represents an equal distance away from one endpoint and toward the other.

Ordinal measures of association (and, clearly, nominal ones as well) are inefficient when both variables in a relationship are interval. Table 16.1 illustrates this inefficiency. The right and left parts of the table each compare eight

Table 16.1 TWO RELATIONSHIPS BETWEEN DEFENSE SPENDING ATTITUDES AND FEELINGS TOWARD GEORGE BUSH

Case	Defense spending X	Feeling thermometer Y	Defense spending X	Feeling thermometer Y
A	1	15	1	23
B	1	25	1	24
C	1	35	1	25
D	1	45	1	26
E	7	55	7	73
F	7	65	7	74
G	7	75	7	75
H	7	85	7	76

cases widely apart on the defense spending scale—values 1 (greatly decrease) and 7 (greatly increase)—but with different values on the Bush feeling thermometer. For interval variables, these pattern differences are quite important. The right-most pattern is the stronger relationship. All respondents wanting a large decrease in defense spending are grouped very close together on the feeling thermometer and also are quite far away in their evaluations of Bush from the respondents wanting a large defense spending increase. The pattern on the left, however, shows considerable variety in feelings toward Bush even when the cases are grouped by their defense attitudes. There are also smaller differences between the defense spending groups; cases *D* and *E* have radically different defense spending postures, but are only 10 points apart in their evaluations of Bush.

Ordinal measures of association will not reflect these pattern differences, for notions such as "small" versus "large" or "close" versus "far apart" are distance concepts which the code numbers of an ordinal variable do not represent. As far as gamma and tau are concerned, both sides of Table 16.1 are the same relationship, concordant pairs. This would be entirely appropriate if the code numbers for the feeling thermometer represented only rankings, for then codes 23, 24, and 25 would not represent any "closeness." Code 25 is higher than 24 which is higher than 23, but codes 25 and 24 may represent people close together on the conceptual variable while respondents with codes 24 and 23 may be quite far apart. When, as is true here, the numbers do represent closeness, we prefer a measure of association that captures this, recognizing that the right pattern is a stronger connection between defense attitudes and perceptions of Bush than the left pattern. One measure that does so is the Pearson correlation.

PEARSON CORRELATION

The term **correlation** is often used, as it has been in this text, to refer to any measure of association. When it is used in this way, the context surrounding the term clarifies whether the author is talking about lambda, gamma, or another statistic. In the absence of a specific reference to any statistic, the term "correlation" usually means the **Pearson correlation**, also referred to as **Pearson's r** (where *r* is the symbol for the statistic).

The Pearson correlation is based on the simple idea of measuring a relationship by multiplying the values of the independent and dependent variables. Why this works is not obvious, and calculating the statistic involves much more than simple multiplication, but the multiplication of the two variables is at the heart of the process. Below we will show how the multiplication process can be used to measure the direction and strength of a relationship on a scale from −1.0 to +1.0.

Measuring Direction

Table 16.2 contains eight hypothetical cases and their values on two variables, *X* and *Y*. In the left columns variable values have been created to be a perfect positive relationship. As *X* declines from 3 to 2 to −2 to −3, variable *Y* declines in lockstep, from 5 to 4 to −4 to −5. The relationship is positive since large positive values on one variable are connected with large positive values on the other, and the same holds for negative values on each variable. The relationship is perfect since knowing the value of a case on *X* allows us to predict, without any error, its value on *Y*. The *X* ∗ *Y* column is the result of multiplying the values of each case on the two variables. These products are summed over all eight cases at the bottom of the table. The sum of the products is a large positive number, 92, because we are always multiplying a positive number by a positive number (which produces a positive product) or a negative number by a negative number (also producing a positive product).

Now look at the right side of the table. Here we have created a perfect negative relationship between *X* and *Y*. Large positive values of *X* go with large *negative* values of *Y*, and vice versa. Similarly, smaller positive values of one variable are linked with smaller negative numbers on the other. This relation-

Table 16.2   PERFECT POSITIVE AND NEGATIVE RELATIONSHIPS BETWEEN *X* AND *Y*

Case	Perfect positive			Perfect negative		
	X	*Y*	*X* ∗ *Y*	*X*	*Y*	*X* ∗ *Y*
A	3	5	15	3	−5	−15
B	3	5	15	3	−5	−15
C	2	4	8	2	−4	−8
D	2	4	8	2	−4	−8
E	−2	−4	8	−2	4	−8
F	−2	−4	8	−2	4	−8
G	−3	−5	15	−3	5	−15
H	−3	−5	15	−3	5	−15
			Σ(x ∗ y) = 92			Σ(x ∗ y) = −92

ship is just as strong as the first one, since knowing the value of a case on X allows us to perfectly predict its value on Y, but this relationship goes in the opposite direction. Multiplying the values of the two variables now produces consistently negative $X * Y$ products, since we are always multiplying a negative number by a positive one. In turn, the sum of these products is a large negative number.

Measuring Strength

The purpose of the brief exercise above is to show that multiplying variable values can indicate the direction of a relationship. The sum of the products is negative for a negative relationship and positive for a positive one. In the same manner, the multiplication process can provide a representation of the strength of a relationship. We illustrate this point with the data in Table 16.3. The left side of Table 16.3 contains a less-than-perfect relationship between X and Y. A relationship exists and is both strong and positive—all cases with positive values on X have positive values on Y as well—but there is not a one-to-one correspondence between the two. Of the two cases with a value of 3 on X one has a value of 5 on Y and the other has a value of 4. There is a similar Y variation for cases C and D, each with a value of 2 on X.

When the relationship is less than perfect, the sum of the $X * Y$ products will necessarily be a smaller number, here 90 instead of 92. The sum of the products will be largest, either positively or negatively, when the most extreme values of one variable are multiplied by the most extreme of the other (e.g., all 3s on X associated with all 5s on Y). A less-than-perfect relationship dilutes this by multiplying some of the highest values on X with lower numbers on Y, thus producing both smaller products and a smaller sum of products. Consequently, the sum of the $X * Y$ products reflects both the direction and the strength of a relationship, being greatest (farthest away from zero either positively or negatively) when the relationship is perfect and smaller with imperfect relationships.

The right columns in Table 16.3 illustrate this point most clearly. Here we have a zero correlation between the two variables. For every high value of X connected with a high value on Y, there is another case having a high value on X and a low value on Y. Knowing a respondent's position on variable X does not help us guess his or her position on Y. For a high value on X we can be just as right (or just as wrong) by guessing high, low, or even randomly on Y. When this type of pattern exists, for every large positive $X * Y$ product there will be a correspondingly large negative $X * Y$ product. The positive and negatives will cancel, leading the sum of the products to be close to zero.

A Constant Scale

Multiplying the values of the independent and dependent variables looks like a promising way to measure the direction and strength of a relationship, but it encounters some obvious problems. The first is that, contrary to the hypothet-

Table 16.3   LESS-THAN-PERFECT AND ZERO RELATIONSHIPS BETWEEN X AND Y

	Moderate positive			Zero		
Case	X	Y	$X * Y$	X	Y	$X * Y$
A	3	5	15	3	5	15
B	3	4	12	3	−5	−15
C	2	5	10	2	4	8
D	2	4	8	2	−4	−8
E	−2	−4	8	−2	4	−8
F	−2	−5	10	−2	−4	8
G	−3	−4	12	−3	5	−15
H	−3	−5	15	−3	−5	15
			90			0
		$\Sigma(x * y) = $	90		$\Sigma(x * y) = $	0

ical examples above, none of the variables in our data sets possess any negative values, except for occasional missing-data codes, which are never included in statistical calculations. Without negative values, all $X * Y$ products will be positive even when the relationship might be negative. Remember, a negative relationship occurs when having a high value on one variable leads to having a low value on another variable, even when that low value is a low *positive* number.

The solution to this problem lies in not using the original values of the two variables, but instead in translating the X and Y values for each case to **deviation format**, which is a value's distance above or below the variable's mean, given by the formula $X_i - \overline{X}$. As illustrated in Table 16.4, for each case, subtracting the mean of a variable from the original value on the variable produces negative

Table 16.4   TRANSFORMING ORIGINAL VARIABLE VALUES TO DEVIATION FORMAT

	Original values		Deviation values		
Case	Defense spending X	Feeling thermometer Y	$X - \overline{X}$	$Y - \overline{Y}$	$(X - \overline{X}) * (Y - \overline{Y})$
A	1	15	−3	−30	90
B	2	25	−2	−20	40
C	3	35	−1	−10	10
D	4	45	0	0	0
E	5	55	1	10	10
F	6	65	2	20	40
G	7	75	3	30	90
	$\overline{X} = 4$	$\overline{Y} = 45$			

numbers when the case is below the mean and positive numbers when above it. Then the deviation values are used in the multiplication process, and they can produce both positive and negative $X * Y$ products. This transformation to deviation format does not affect what each variable measures at all; it just applies a different measuring scale. It is similar to translating a distance originally measured in feet to inches or yards. In a similar vein, for a respondent rating her or his feeling toward Bush as 95 on the feeling thermometer, we can describe this rating either by its original value on the absolute scale (95) or as a deviation above the mean value (say 55) of +40 points. Either description communicates the same information, although each uses a different base of measurement.

Actually, deviation format communicates more information about the respondents. We cannot speak of a case having a high or low value on a variable without using a reference point—high or low compared to what? The endpoints of a scale are often ineffective reference points, for the evaluation of a respondent as high or low will change if one of the endpoints changes. If we measure income up to a maximum of $500,000 per year, then anyone at the top of the scale would appear, quite appropriately, to have a high income. Say we expand the top of the scale to represent incomes of $100 million per year, an amount actually earned by a junk bond trader recently. Someone earning only $500,000 would be so far away from the top of the scale as to appear a pauper. In contrast, deviation format uses a reference point common to our everyday thinking: Is a person above or below average, and how much above or below average? Someone with an annual income of $500,000 will be considerably above average regardless of the scale's endpoints.

Because of this added value, deviation format is regularly used to analyze interval variables. What, after all, does a value of 51 or 82 on a feeling thermometer really mean? Reporting the same scores as deviations of −4 and +27 tells us two things: whether the person is above or below the sample average and how far above or below that average—a Bush evaluation close to but slightly below average in the first case and an evaluation far more positive than average in the second. Widespread use of deviation format leads us to represent it with a special symbol, a lowercase script version of the variable symbol. The letters X and Y represent variables as they are originally measured in the data set while x and y represent the same variables measured in deviation format. Using these symbols, we can write the mathematical term $\Sigma(X - \overline{X})(Y - \overline{Y})$ as Σxy without any loss of meaning.

The sum of the products from multiplying the deviations of two variables, $\Sigma(X - \overline{X})(Y - \overline{Y})$, or Σxy, also has a special name, the **covariance** of two variables. The covariance term captures the extent to which two variables covary, whether a variation in values from low to high on one variable is connected with a variation in values on another variable. Covariance also reflects the distance information contained in interval variables since the deviations being multiplied are distances above or below the mean of a variable.

Translating variable values to deviation format enables the multiplication process to reflect both positive and negative relationships as well as corresponding distances above or below means, but problems still remain. The size of the covariance term is affected by the strength of the relationship, but also by two other factors completely unrelated to this strength: the range of values of a variable and the number of cases being analyzed. A variable ranging only from 1 to 10 with a mean of 5 will have a maximum deviation of 5, while a second variable ranging from 1 to 100 with a mean of 50 can have a maximum deviation of 50. Very different covariances arise from each variable. Similarly, summing covariances over a sample of 100 will produce a much smaller term than summing covariances over a sample of 2000. Clearly both problems are unacceptable. The solution is to divide the covariance by another term that is also influenced by both the value range and the number of cases, the sum of squared deviations, $\Sigma(X - \overline{X})^2$, which gives

$$r = \frac{\Sigma(X - \overline{X}) * (Y - \overline{Y})}{\sqrt{\Sigma(X - \overline{X})^2 * \Sigma(Y - \overline{Y})^2}}$$

In deviation format symbols this is

$$r = \frac{\Sigma xy}{\sqrt{\Sigma x^2 * \Sigma y^2}}$$

The two sums-of-squared-deviation terms in the denominator compensate for both the range of values on each variable and the number of cases in the data set.

Either formula above produces the Pearson correlation coefficient which ranges, as desired, between -1.0 and $+1.0$. The closer to $+1.0$ or -1.0, or the farther away from zero in either direction, the stronger the relationship. There are numerous features of the Pearson r statistic which we examine shortly, but first let us look at the SPSS commands used to produce it.

THE CORRELATION COMMAND

(v2) Pearson correlations are obtained with the **CORRELATION** procedure. The basics of the command are quite simple. The command word CORRELA-TION begins in column 1, followed by a list of the variables to be correlated. For the variables of interest to us, the command is

```
CORRELATION V5  V24  V27  V30  V33  V36
```

In the list of variables following the command name, there is no need to draw any distinction between independent and dependent variables. The Pearson correlation is an symmetric statistic, so it makes no difference which variables are independent and which dependent; the resulting correlation will be the same. *You* need to know the difference to properly interpret the results, but SPSS does not need to know this to calculate the statistic.

Version 2   The name of this procedure was changed between versions 2 and 3 of SPSS-X. Version 2 uses PEARSON CORR instead of CORRELATION. Except for the different term and the approach to the subcommands, discussed later, the two commands work the same. All later versions of SPSS recognize the old command name.

(R.4) (PC) The output from the CORRELATION command is shown in Figure 16.1: a square table with the variables listed both across the top and down the side. Reading across the top row, for example, shows the correlations of the Bush feeling thermometer (V5), first with itself (obviously 1.0) and then with the five issue variables. The same information can be found by reading down column 1. This output, called a **correlation matrix**, shows the correlations of all possible combinations of the variables listed on the CORRELATION command.

For each variable pair, the matrix includes three numbers. A legend at the bottom of the table explains what the numbers are. The top number is the Pearson correlation coefficient. The second is the degrees of freedom used to calculate the correlation, essentially the same as the number of cases without missing data on either variable in the pair. The bottom number (for example,

```
CORRELATION   V5   V24   V27   V30   V33   V36


-  P E A R S O N   C O R R E L A T I O N   C O E F F I C I E N T S  -

                 V5         V24         V27         V30         V33         V36

U5          1.0000     -0.2757      0.3438      0.2742      0.1107      0.0699
           ( 1972)     ( 1589)     ( 1726)     ( 1672)     ( 1679)     ( 1866)
           P=  .       P= 0.000    P= 0.000    P= 0.000    P= 0.000    P= 0.001


U24        -0.2757      1.0000     -0.0878     -0.3353     -0.0616     -0.0873
           ( 1589)     ( 1615)     ( 1498)     ( 1434)     ( 1456)     ( 1569)
           P= 0.000    P=  .       P= 0.000    P= 0.000    P= 0.009    P= 0.000


U27         0.3438     -0.0878      1.0000      0.1322      0.2921      0.0620
           ( 1726)     ( 1498)     ( 1752)     ( 1543)     ( 1575)     ( 1693)
           P= 0.000    P= 0.000    P=  .       P= 0.000    P= 0.000    P= 0.005


U30         0.2742     -0.3353      0.1322      1.0000      0.1098      0.0297
           ( 1672)     ( 1434)     ( 1543)     ( 1707)     ( 1505)     ( 1641)
           P= 0.000    P= 0.000    P= 0.000    P=  .       P= 0.000    P= 0.115


U33         0.1107     -0.0616      0.2921      0.1098      1.0000      0.2052
           ( 1679)     ( 1456)     ( 1575)     ( 1505)     ( 1703)     ( 1650)
           P= 0.000    P= 0.009    P= .0000    P= 0.000    P=  .       P= 0.000


U36         0.0699     -0.0873      0.0620      0.0297      0.2052      1.0000
           ( 1866)     ( 1569)     ( 1693)     ( 1641)     ( 1650)     ( 1908)
           P= 0.001    P= 0.000    P= 0.005    P= 0.115    P= 0.000    P=  .

(COEFFICIENT / (CASES) / 1-TAILED SIG)
" . "  IS PRINTED IF A COEFFICIENT CANNOT BE COMPUTED
```

Figure 16.1 Output from the CORRELATION command.

$p = .001$) is the significance level or the probability that the null hypothesis is true for the population. Like the tau statistic from the CROSSTABS procedure, the Pearson correlation coefficient has an identifiable sampling distribution, a t distribution. This allows us to evaluate the statistical and substantive significance of a relationship with a single statistic.

The bottom legend also explains that a period is printed in the matrix if a correlation cannot be computed. If this happens, usually it is the result of one of two problems. First, there are no cases left to analyze. Perhaps you used a series of nontemporary SELECT IF commands that led to deleting all the cases in the data set. Second, a combination of data-massaging commands may have transformed a variable to a constant. If a period does show up in a correlation matrix (other than when a variable is correlated with itself), search through any data-massaging commands to see whether they are causing the problem.

What of the questions we posed at the beginning of this chapter regarding the impact of the five issue positions on respondents' feelings about George Bush? Using the leftmost column or top row will provide our answers. We look first at the probability levels for each variable pair. All are below .05, allowing us to conclude that each issue variable affects attitudes toward Bush in the population as well as in the sample. We turn then to the top numbers in each variable pairing, the correlation coefficient showing the strength of the relationship. Variable V27, the defense spending scale, has the strongest correlation with evaluations of Bush, .34. Slightly lower, but still sizable correlations with Bush evaluations exist for variables V24, government services and spending $(-.28)$, and V30, the health insurance issue $(+.27)$. The signs differ because all the issue variables are coded so that larger numbers reflect conservative positions on the issue, except for V24 where the low code numbers represent the most conservative positions.

Considerably weaker in their impact on Bush evaluations are variables V33 and V36 with correlations of .11 and .07, respectively. Although small, these correlations remain theoretically interesting because they are different from what we might expect. Each variable has significance statistically, but only marginal impact substantively on the Bush ratings. Interestingly, both candidates repeatedly raised the issue of U.S. relations with the Soviet Union during the 1988 campaign. Candidate Bush argued for the need to be tough with the Soviet leadership, while candidate Dukakis argued for greater cooperation with Soviet leaders to reduce international tensions. Nonetheless, this issue was apparently not a major concern in selecting a president since it has a low correlation with respondents' attitudes toward George Bush.

Variable V36, attitudes about a woman's role in society, reflects the opposite situation. Both candidates voiced support for government assistance for child care, and both made the U.S. family a theme of their campaigns. Aside from differences over abortion, there was little separating the candidates on how government should support women in society. Despite this apparent sameness of the candidates, how respondents felt about a woman's role in society did make a difference in their evaluations of Bush. The variable's impact was small, but statistically significant and thus not to be ignored.

The CORRELATION procedure provides a simple and effective way to explore relationships between interval variables. The Pearson correlation coefficient can also be requested on the CROSSTABS command and was mentioned briefly during the discussion of that procedure. Regardless of the procedure used, the statistical results will be the same, but contingency tables produced by CROSSTABS will be quite large and unwieldy for many interval variables. The variables examined here, for example, would produce contingency tables containing 101 rows (V5) and 7 columns (V24 to V36). Recoding these variables to produce smaller contingency tables causes some of the distance information provided by the variables to be lost. This will also affect the resulting Pearson correlation since it will be calculated from variables in their recoded form. The CORRELATION procedure does not require the condensing of variables into a small number of categories and thus retains all the original information that the variables contain.

The WITH Keyword

Using the correlation matrix output is not difficult at all, but the matrix does contain a sizable amount of repetitive and, for us, irrelevant information. We are concerned about only the correlations between the issue variables and the Bush feeling thermometer. The correlations between the issue variables themselves are not relevant to our research question. We can always ignore the superfluous information, but it is also possible to modify the CORRELATION command to produce only the correlations desired.

This is accomplished by separating the independent and dependent variables by using the keyword WITH. Suppose we want to compare the impact of the five issues on both Bush and Dukakis evaluations, but we do not want to create an even larger correlation matrix. We use the command

```
CORRELATION V5 V6 WITH V24 V27 V30 V33 V36
```

In this form of the command, each variable listed to the right of the keyword is correlated with only each variable to the left of it. This produces the simpler output in Figure 16.2. The variables before the WITH keyword, in this case our dependent variables V5 and V6, are listed down the side; their correlations with those after the WITH keyword, our independent variables, are listed across the top.

The results of this analysis are simpler to view and interpret than a crowded correlation matrix. Substantively, the Dukakis pattern is very similar to the Bush pattern except that the signs are reversed; liberal positions on these issues help Dukakis as opposed to conservative ones helping Bush. There are two notable exceptions, however. Bush is helped quite a bit by his defense spending position (V27), but attitudes on defense spending have a much weaker connection with respondent ratings of Dukakis—correlations of +.34 versus −.18. On the other hand, Dukakis's ratings are more strongly affected by views on cooperating with the Soviet Union than Bush's ratings are.

The comparison above helps us to again clarify the meaning of relationships

```
CORRELATION V5 V6  WITH  V24 V27 V30 V33 V36


- P E A R S O N   C O R R E L A T I O N   C O E F F I C I E N T S -

           V24          V27          V30          V33          V36

U5       -0.2757       0.3438       0.2742       0.1107       0.0699
         ( 1589)      ( 1726)      ( 1672)      ( 1679)      ( 1866)
         P= 0.000     P= 0.000     P= 0.000     P= 0.000     P= 0.001


U6        0.2664      -0.1846      -0.2105      -0.1735      -0.0586
         ( 1573)      ( 1712)      ( 1656)      ( 1662)      ( 1849)
         P= 0.000     P= 0.000     P= 0.000     P= 0.009     P= 0.006


(COEFFICIENT / (CASES) / 1-TAILED SIG)
" . " IS PRINTED IF A COEFFICIENT CANNOT BE COMPUTED
```

Figure 16.2 Adding the WITH keyword to the CORRELATION command.

and their signs. A positive correlation does not mean that the variable helps a candidate while a negative one hurts him; the signs tell us only whether evaluations of the candidates increase or decrease as we go up or down the issue scales. A positive relationship for all but V24 means that more conservative positions (higher code numbers) on the issue scales are connected with more positive evaluations of Bush (and negative evaluations of Dukakis), while more liberal positions on these scales (lower code numbers) are connected with lower evaluations of Bush (and higher ones for Dukakis). The size of the correlation (distance from zero) tells us how strongly attitudes on the issues affect candidate evaluations. Respondents' positions on the defense spending, government services, and health insurance scales affect their ratings of the candidates quite a bit. Alternatively, the lower correlations between the scales of the feeling thermometers and the cooperation with Russia and women's role in society mean that respondents' positions on these issues, whether liberal or conservative, have very little impact on their evaluations of the candidates.

Nothing in the correlations themselves indicates whether a candidate is being helped or hurt by a given issue. To determine that, we would need to know where a majority of the respondents locate themselves on the issues. Attitudes toward gun control might also be strongly related to candidate evaluations, but whether this helps Bush or Dukakis will depend on whether most voters support or oppose gun control. A correlation shows only the direction and strength of the relationship between attitudes and candidate evaluation, not whether most of the respondents hold liberal or conservative positions on these attitudes.

Subcommands

The subcommands available with the CORRELATION procedure are listed in Table 16.5. Some are needed only for advanced analyses, but others are useful in basic data analysis: FORMAT, PRINT, and STATISTICS.

Table 16.5 SUBCOMMANDS AVAILABLE WITH THE CORRELATION PROCEDURE

Subcommand	Option	Description	Version 2 option no.
MISSING	PAIRWISE	Excludes missing values for each variable pair (default)	—
MISSING	LISTWISE	Excludes cases with missing values for any variable on the CORRELATION variables list	2
MISSING	INCLUDE	Includes missing data in the statistical computations	1
FORMAT	MATRIX	Prints correlations in matrix format (default)	—
FORMAT	SERIAL	Prints correlations in serial string format	6
PRINT	ONETAIL	One-tailed statistical significance tests (default)	—
PRINT	TWOTAIL	Two-tailed statistical significance tests	3
PRINT	SIG	Prints number of cases and significance levels (default)	—
PRINT	NOSIG	Does not print number of cases and uses asterisks for significance levels	5
STATISTICS	DESCRIPTIVES	Mean, standard deviation, and number of nonmissing cases	1
STATISTICS	XPROD	Cross-product deviations and covariance	2
STATISTICS	ALL	Both groups of statistics above	ALL
MATRIX	OUT	Writes correlation matrix to a file	4
—	—	Writes correlation matrix to a file without the case counts	7

(V.2) (PC) **FORMAT**   The **FORMAT** subcommand has one option, **SERIAL** (the MATRIX option is the default). Use of the subcommand

```
/FORMAT = SERIAL
```

eliminates all redundant pairs when the correlations are printed regardless of whether the keyword WITH is used. When /FORMAT = SERIAL is specified, SPSS lists one pair of variables after another across the page (serially) until the number of possible correlation pairs has been exhausted. The WITH keyword is actually more useful because it eliminates both redundant and irrelevant correlations, but the FORMAT subcommand still comes in handy on occasion. Figure 16.3 illustrates the output when the /FORMAT = SERIAL subcommand is used.

(V.2) (PC) (R.4) **PRINT**   A second subcommand is **PRINT**, which has two options besides the defaults. The first is **TWOTAIL**. By default, the CORRELA-TION procedure calculates and prints one-tailed tests of statistical significance. This is usually desirable since hypotheses involving interval variables are typically directional. Nonetheless, on some occasions we may test a nondirectional hypothesis containing interval dependent and independent variables, a hypothesis for which a two-tailed test of statistical significance is appropriate. The /PRINT = TWOTAIL subcommand can then be used to instruct SPSS to calculate two-tailed significance tests. In most cases, the difference between one- and

```
CORRELATIONS   V5   V24   V27   V30 V33   V36
    /FORMAT = SERIAL

- - - -  P E A R S O N   C O R R E L A T I O N   C O E F F I C I E N T S  - - - -

VARIABLE              VARIABLE              VARIABLE              VARIABLE
PAIR                  PAIR                  PAIR                  PAIR
--------              --------              --------              --------

V5        -0.2757     V5         0.3438     V5         0.2742     V5         0.1107
WITH      N( 1589)    WITH      N( 1726)    WITH      N( 1672)    WITH      N( 1679)
V24    SIG 0.000      V27    SIG 0.000      V30    SIG 0.000      V33    SIG 0.000

V5         0.0699     V24       -0.0878     V24       -0.3353     V24       -0.0616
WITH      N( 1866)    WITH      N( 1498)    WITH      N( 1434)    WITH      N( 1456)
V36    SIG 0.003      V27    SIG 0.001      V30    SIG 0.000      V33    SIG 0.019

V24       -0.0873     V27        0.1322     V27        0.2921     V27        0.0620
WITH      N( 1569)    WITH      N( 1543)    WITH      N( 1575)    WITH      N( 1693)
V36    SIG 0.001      V30    SIG 0.000      V33    SIG 0.000      V36    SIG 0.011

V30        0.1098     V30        0.0297     V33        0.2052
WITH      N( 1505)    WITH      N( 1641)    WITH      N( 1650)
V33    SIG 0.000      V36    SIG 0.230      V36    SIG 0.000

(COEFFICIENT / (CASES) / 1-TAILED SIG)
" . " IS PRINTED IF A COEFFICIENT CANNOT BE COMPUTED
```

Figure 16.3 CORRELATION output when FORMAT = SERIAL is used.

two-tailed tests will be minor, but if the significance level is close to the .05 decision point, then it is necessary to carefully select the statistical significance test appropriate to the hypothesis.

(V.2) (PC) (R.4) The second PRINT option is /PRINT = **NOSIG.** This option suppresses the printing of both the number of cases and the statistical significance levels. Statistical significance tests are a vital part of the output, so they are not ignored completely. Instead of the default printing of exact significance or probability levels, the NOSIG option substitutes asterisks next to the correlation coefficients. One asterisk represents a .01 significance level, and two asterisks are used when the significance level is less than .001. A legend is printed at the bottom of the table to remind the user what the asterisks mean.

Release 4   Release 4 implementations of SPSS use NOSIG as the default or standard output. To produce tables similar to the illustrations in this chapter, you must use the /PRINT SIG subcommand and specification. Release 4 implementations also produce two-tailed significance tests as the default output. One-tailed tests can be obtained by adding the ONETAIL specification to the /PRINT subcommand. The default output for Release 4 prints one asterisk for a .05 significance level and two asterisks for a .01 significance level, instead of the .01 and .001 significance levels used in earlier versions of the software.

```
CORRELATIONS V5 V24 V27 V30 V33 V36 / PRINT = TWOTAIL NOSIG


- P E A R S O N   C O R R E L A T I O N   C O E F F I C I E N T S -

           U5          V24         V27         V30         V33         V36

U5      1.0000      -0.2757**    0.3438**    0.2742**    0.1107**    0.0699*
U24    -0.2757**     1.0000     -0.0878**   -0.3353**   -0.0616     -0.0873**
U27     0.3438**    -0.0878**    1.0000      0.1322**    0.2921**    0.0620
U30     0.2742**    -0.3353**    0.1322**    1.0000      0.1098**    0.0297
U33     0.1107**    -0.0616      0.2921**    0.1098**    1.0000      0.2052**
U36     0.0699*     -0.0873**    0.0620      0.0297      0.2052**    1.0000


* - SIGNIF. LE 0.01        ** - SIGNIF. LE 0.001      (2-TAILED)
" . " IS PRINTED IF A COEFFICIENT CANNOT BE COMPUTED
```

Figure 16.4 Output when TWOTAIL and NOSIG are requested with the PRINT subcommand.

Figure 16.4 shows the resulting output when both PRINT options are included (although each may be requested individually). Suppression of the case counts and of exact probability levels simplifies the printout enormously, probably too much for our needs. If we are using the .05 decision level, we know that any correlation with an asterisk meets (exceeds actually) that cutoff. Coefficients without asterisks might or might not be significant at the .05 level; we know only that their significance level is above .01. The TWOTAIL option does not produce much of a change in the output. There are only two observable differences. The probability levels themselves will be somewhat different, although close to the one-tailed values, and the legend at the bottom now contains the notation "2-tailed."

(v.2) (pc) **STATISTICS** The final subcommand is **STATISTICS**, which asks for additional statistics to be printed with the CORRELATION output. The one option we might be interested in using here is /STATISTICS = **DESCRIP-TIVES**. This subcommand adds the mean, standard deviation, and number of nonmissing cases for each variable to the top of the printout. Figure 16.5 illustrates its use and output.

Version 2 In version 2 of SPSS-X, the options are invoked through the OP-TIONS subcommand, beginning in column 1, followed by the appropriate option number from Table 16.5. Option 6 requests a serial printing of the correlations, option 3 requests a two-tailed significance test, and option 5 suppresses the case count and significance level. Similarly, additional statistics are requested with the STATISTICS subcommand, starting in column 1. Alternative number 1 requests descriptive statistics.

```
CORRELATION  V5  V24  V27  V30  V33  V36  /  STATISTICS=DESCRIPTIVES


VARIABLE        CASES          MEAN          STD DEV

V5              1972         60.5715         27.7145
V24             1615          4.1486          1.5962
V27             1752          3.9344          1.5865
V30             1707          3.8424          2.0182
V33             1703          3.7798          1.7859
V36             1908          2.5954          1.8436
```

- P E A R S O N   C O R R E L A T I O N   C O E F F I C I E N T S -

	V5	V24	V27	V30	V33	V36
V5	1.0000	-0.2757	0.3438	0.2742	0.1107	0.0699
	(1972)	(1589)	(1726)	(1672)	(1679)	(1866)
	P= .	P= 0.000	P= 0.000	P= 0.000	P= 0.000	P= 0.001
V24	-0.2757	1.0000	-0.0878	-0.3353	-0.0616	-0.0873
	(1589)	(1615)	(1498)	(1434)	(1456)	(1569)
	P= 0.000	P= .	P= 0.000	P= 0.000	P= 0.009	P= 0.000
V27	0.3438	-0.0878	1.0000	0.1322	0.2921	0.0620
	(1726)	(1498)	(1752)	(1543)	(1575)	(1693)
	P= 0.000	P= 0.000	P= .	P= 0.000	P= 0.000	P= 0.005
V30	0.2742	-0.3353	0.1322	1.0000	0.1098	0.0297
	(1672)	(1434)	(1543)	(1707)	(1505)	(1641)
	P= 0.000	P= 0.000	P= 0.000	P= .	P= 0.000	P= 0.115
V33	0.1107	-0.0616	0.2921	0.1098	1.0000	0.2052
	(1679)	(1456)	(1575)	(1505)	(1703)	(1650)
	P= 0.000	P= 0.009	P= .0000	P= 0.000	P= .	P= 0.000
V36	0.0699	-0.0873	0.0620	0.0297	0.2052	1.0000
	(1866)	(1569)	(1693)	(1641)	(1650)	(1908)
	P= 0.001	P= 0.000	P= 0.005	P= 0.115	P= 0.000	P= .

```
(COEFFICIENT / (CASES) / 1-TAILED SIG)
"  .  " IS PRINTED IF A COEFFICIENT CANNOT BE COMPUTED
```

Figure 16.5 Adding descriptive statistics to the CORRELATION output.

ASSUMPTIONS AND INTERPRETATION

The Pearson correlation coefficient is a very powerful statistic that we can use for interval variables. It does, however, entail more stringent assumptions than some of the other statistics we have considered, assumptions which may limit its use. In this section we first discuss those assumptions and then turn to the features of the statistic that lead us to call it "powerful."

The Bivariate Normal Assumption

The first assumption made is that the two variables being correlated have a **bivariate normal** distribution in the population. What this unwieldy term means is that each variable has a normal distribution for every value of the other variable. If we isolate all members of the population desiring a large defense spending increase and examine their distribution on the candidate feeling thermometer, that distribution will have the shape of a normal curve. Similarly, all population members giving Bush a 50 rating on the feeling thermometer will have a normally shaped distribution of attitudes on the defense spending scale.

This is a tricky assumption, for there is no simple way of determining whether it is likely to be true; essentially we have to take it on faith. Fortunately, our faith is not often misplaced, for it is common for two interval variables to have a bivariate normal distribution in the population. There is little that people new to data analysis can do about this assumption, and you should not let it bother you. It is mentioned here because you may encounter reports by other statistical analysts that discuss this assumption as a reason for using or not using the Pearson *r*.

The bivariate normal assumption is made in order to estimate the sampling distribution of the statistic, so a violation of it means that the statistical significance tests on the printout may be in error. The more the population violates the assumption, the more the calculated significance level may be inaccurate.

The Linear Assumption

The second assumption made by the Pearson correlation statistic is that the relationship between the two variables is a linear one: as *X* increases, *Y* increases (or decreases) at a constant rate. A **linear relationship** is illustrated in Figure 16.6, which contains a **scatterplot** of two variables. In a scatterplot a dot is placed on a graph for each case based on its joint values on the *X* and *Y* variables. The points in the lower left part of Figure 16.6*a* have low values on both *X* and *Y* while those in the upper right sector have high values on each variable. The relationship between the two variables can be summarized by the line drawn through the points, which shows that, on average, increases in *X* are related to increases in *Y*. A similar linear relationship is shown in Figure 16.6*b*, although this time the relationship is a negative one with high values on one variable associated with low values on the other.

Relationships between interval variables, when they exist at all, are often linear, so this assumption is also not a terribly difficult one to meet. Nonetheless, there are occasions when a strong but **nonlinear relationship** exists between interval variables, relationships like those in Figure 16.7. Figure 16.7*a* shows one variable continually increasing as the other does, but not at a constant rate. Increases from low to medium values of *X* are associated with mild increases in *Y*, while changes from medium to high values of *X* lead to very large increases in *Y*. Figure 16.7*b* shows a different situation; low to medium values of *X* are paired with increases in *Y* while medium to high values of *X* are

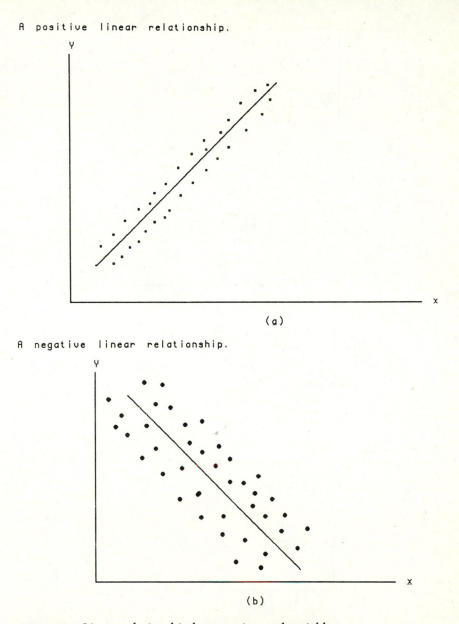

Figure 16.6 Linear relationship between interval variables.

negatively related to changes in Y. Both relationships are quite strong, since knowing the value of a case on X allows us to predict its value on Y quite accurately; but the attempt of the Pearson correlation to draw a line through the points seriously misrepresents the nature of the relationship. Pearson correlation coefficients will underestimate the strength of nonlinear relationships.

How do we know if a relationship is linear? We make this decision on two grounds. First, is there any theoretical or logical reason to believe that some

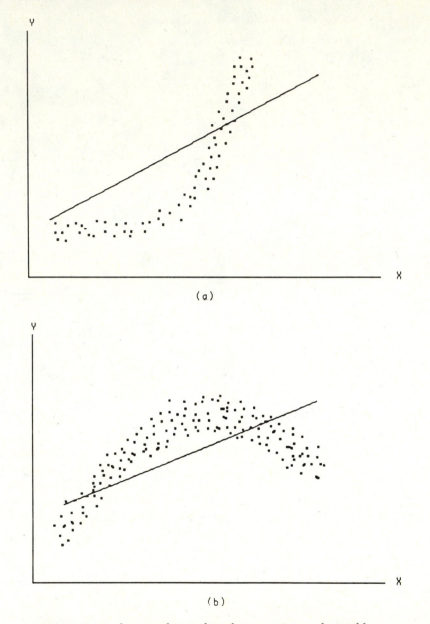

Figure 16.7 Nonlinear relationships between interval variables.

changes in X are related to larger changes in Y than others, as in Figure 16.7a, or relate positively to Y in some situations but negatively in others, as in Figure 16.7b? If we cannot think of any sensible reason why either pattern should occur, then we can feel more comfortable with the linear assumption. Second, we can actually view a scatterplot between two variables and see what the relationship looks like. How to do this is the subject of Chapter 18 on the PLOT procedure.

Supplement
16.1

Is the Relationship Linear?

A common error made with the Pearson correlation coefficient is to conclude that a nonzero correlation implies a linear relationship between the variables. This is not so. The linear assumption is verified either through theory or by viewing a scatterplot of the variables. A substantively and statistically significant Pearson correlation cannot be used as evidence of a linear relationship.

Recall the curve in Figure 16.7*a*. The relationship is clearly nonlinear, but it is monotonic. An imaginary line drawn through the scatterplot can be used to improve our guess of the *Y* variable since increasing values of *X* are related to increasing values of *Y*. Hence the Pearson *r* formula will produce a positive nonzero correlation for this relationship even though there will be large guessing errors wherever the curve moves away from the correlation line.

Despite a Pearson correlation that would probably be both sizable and statistically significant, a line does not accurately represent the relationship between the variables, and neither would Pearson's *r*. A technique that matched the curvilinear pattern between the variables would more accurately represent the strong relationship that exists. In sum, you cannot interpret a nonzero Pearson correlation as proof of a linear relationship. Instead Pearson's *r* is interpreted as a correct measure of the strength of a relationship *if* that relationship is a linear one, and an incorrect measure of strength (by some unknown amount) if it is nonlinear.

If the relationship is nonlinear, you will need to use a measure of association that does not make the linear assumption. Ordinal measures of association, such as gamma and tau, assume only that the relationship is monotonic; as *X* increases, *Y* changes (increases or decreases) consistently, but not necessarily at a constant rate. Figure 16.7*a* is a monotonic relationship since all increases in *X* are related to increases in *Y*—sometimes small increases, sometimes large ones, but all increases. If the relationship is not even monotonic, as in Figure 16.7*b*, a nominal measure of association, such as lambda or Cramer's *V*, will do. Nominal measures of association do not make even the monotonic assumption. Of course, lower-level statistics will be inefficient for interval variables, but they will measure the strength of the relationship more accurately than Pearson's *r* when the relationship is not linear.

A second approach is used with nonlinear relationships. It is more cumbersome, but it also retains the ability to use the distance information in interval variables. Many nonlinear relationships can be divided into two or more parts where, within each part, the relationship is close to linear. We could thus divide a relationship into its parts (using the SELECT IF command, for example) and conduct separate Pearson correlation analyses on each part. This is illustrated in Figure 16.8, where we have repeated the relationships from Figure 16.7 but with different lines drawn through parts of each curve. For low to medium values of *X* there is one linear relationship for each curve, and there is a different linear relationship for medium to high values of *X*. This leads to a conditional

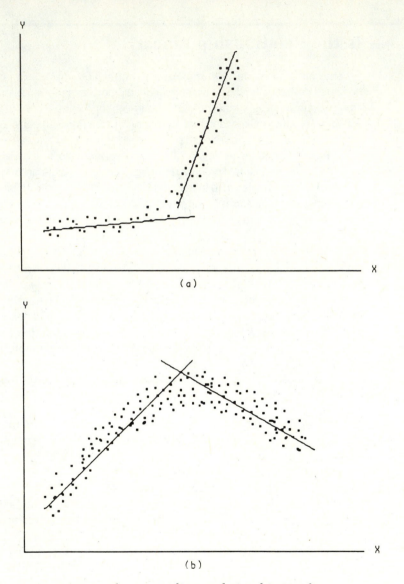

Figure 16.8 Dividing a non-linear relationship into linear parts.

interpretation of the relationship: one correlation between *X* and *Y* for a selected range of values on *X* and a different correlation for another range of *X* values.

Pearson's *r* as a PRE Measure

When we feel the linear assumption is a safe one, which should be most of the time, the Pearson *r* statistic is preferred because of its efficiency and straightforward interpretation. Pearson's *r* is a proportional-reduction-of-error (PRE) measure, as are lambda and gamma. The size of the coefficient can be used to determine an improved ability to predict *Y* based on a knowledge of *X*. To

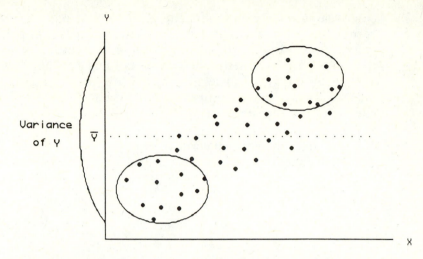

Figure 16.9 Vertical axis represents the distribution of the Y variable.

illustrate the PRE character of this statistic, consider Figure 16.9, a graph of variable Y compared with variable X but without a correlation line drawn in. By itself, the Y (vertical) axis is a FREQUENCIES distribution of the Y variable. As explained in Chapter 12, if we were to guess each case's value on Y when knowing only the Y distribution, we would use the mean of Y as our guess for all cases. The points circled on the graph are some of the large guessing errors we would make when always guessing the mean. Although these errors are sizable, they are also unavoidable since the mean is still the best (least-error) strategy available to us when the distribution of Y is all that we know.

Now let us add the information for variable X—before we have to guess a person's value on Y, we are told her or his value on X. If both variables are interval and the relationship is linear, the line summarizing the relationship constitutes our guessing strategy. As illustrated in Figure 16.10, once given a

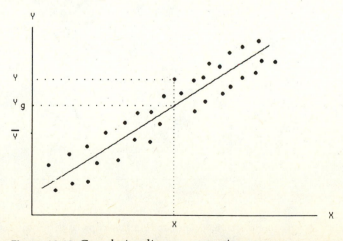

Figure 16.10 Correlation line as a guessing strategy.

case's value on X, we go straight up from that point on the X axis to the correlation line and then straight across to the Y axis. The point where this line crosses the Y axis constitutes our guess for that case's Y value, represented by the symbol Y_g. The distance between this guess and the actual case value on Y constitutes our current guessing error, while the distance between Y_g and the mean of Y is our guessing improvement. When using the correlation line as our guessing strategy instead of the mean, we no longer make the large errors shown in Figure 16.9.

The larger the Pearson correlation coefficient, the more the points on the graph will cluster close to the correlation line. Figure 16.11a shows a perfect X-Y

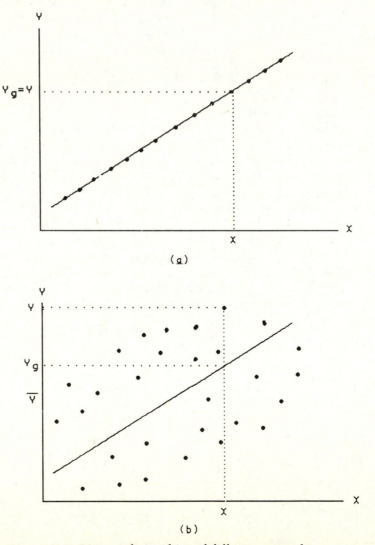

Figure 16.11 Linear relationships of different strengths.

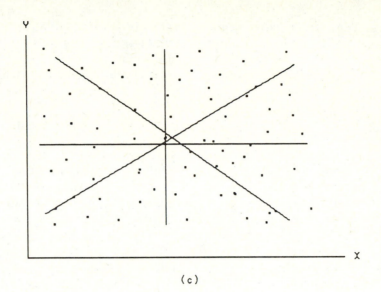

(c)

Figure 16.11 (continued)

relationship with all points exactly on the line. Using the line as a guessing strategy would produce zero guessing errors in this case, and the Pearson correlation would be a perfect 1.0. Figure 16.11*b* shows a wider spread of points around the line than existed in Figure 16.10. Consequently, using the line as the guessing strategy produces more errors and a lower correlation coefficient than would be true for Figure 16.10. Finally, Figure 16.11*c* displays no relationship between *X* and *Y*. We could draw any number of lines through the scattered points and not make any improvement in guessing over consistently guessing the mean of *Y*. The correlation coefficient for this graph would be 0.0.

Coefficient of Determination

Although Pearson's *r* is a PRE-based statistic, the correlation coefficient itself cannot be interpreted as a direct measure of error reduction. The stronger the coefficient, the greater the reduction in error; but the coefficient number does not exactly measure the amount of error reduction. To identify the proportional reduction of error, we use the squared value of the Pearson *r*. This number is called the **coefficient of determination**, and it represents the proportional reduction of error when *X* is used to predict *Y*. This is also called the **explained variance**, or the amount of original variance in *Y* explained by cases having different values on *X*. For example, the correlation between respondents' defense spending preferences and their evaluations of Bush was .34. Squaring this number gives .1156, or 12 percent of the original variation in Bush evaluations is due to differences in respondents' defense spending attitudes.

As a PRE measure, the coefficient of determination can be compared directly with other PRE measures from different relationships, such as lambda or gamma. Squaring Pearson's r, however, eliminates any minus signs and thus our ability to identify the direction of a relationship. It is needed for comparison with other PRE measures, but when not making such a comparison, most analysts use just the original Pearson correlation and do not bother to calculate the coefficient of determination.

SPSS/PC+

As is true of other procedures, SPSS/PC+ adds options and additional statistics to the correlation output in a manner similar to version 2 of SPSS-X. The OPTIONS and STATISTICS subcommands, each beginning with a slash, are used with numbers designating the options and statistics desired. However, SPSS/PC+ uses different defaults, a practice that affects the options and what they mean.

There are two basic differences in the PC+ defaults. First, SPSS defaults to pairwise deletion of missing data where each two-variable correlation is based on all cases with valid values for these two variables. SPSS/PC+ defaults to listwise deletion of missing data where cases are not used to calculate any correlation coefficient if they have a missing value for any variable listed on the CORRELATION command. Each version can perform the other missing-data deletion strategy by adding an option, but since the defaults differ, so do the options. Option 2 requests listwise deletion of missing data in SPSS-X version 2.0, but the same option number is used for pairwise deletion in SPSS/PC+.

Second, SPSS/PC+ defaults to the /PRINT NOSIG option (number 5), printing only the correlations without case counts and using asterisks for significance levels. Option 5, which requests this alternative in SPSS-X version 2.0, is used by SPSS/PC+ to request a printing of the case counts and exact significance levels.

Finally, options 6 and 7 are not available in SPSS/PC+. The other options (1, 3, and 4) as well as the statistics alternatives (1, 2, and ALL) are the same for SPSS/PC+ as they are for SPSS-X version 2.0 and are listed in Table 16.5.

SUMMARY

When examining hypotheses containing only interval variables, we can use more powerful measures of association than ones available with nominal and ordinal variables. The Pearson correlation coefficient incorporates interval information in measuring association, thus being efficient, and uses the scale from -1.0 to $+1.0$; and its square, the coefficient of determination, is a PRE measure of reduced guessing error.

Pearson's r does make some restrictive assumptions, including the fact that the two-variable relationship is linear. This is a common assumption for techniques used to analyze interval variables, one also made by the regression procedure discussed in Chapter 19. The assumption is a reasonable one, and it can often be checked by creating a scatterplot between the variables, something done with the PLOT command, discussed in Chapter 18. Before turning to either of these procedures, however, we will examine another feature of the power of the Pearson correlation in Chapter 17, its ability to easily control for confounding variables.

REVIEW

Key Terms

Correlation	TWOTAIL
Pearson correlation	NOSIG
Pearson's r	STATISTICS
Deviation format	DESCRIPTIVES
Covariance	Bivariate normal
CORRELATION	Linear relationship
Correlation matrix	Scatterplot
FORMAT	Nonlinear relationship
SERIAL	Coefficient of determination
PRINT	Explained variance

Exercises

16.1 Correct any errors in the command statements given.
  a. CORRELATION V74 / FORMAT = SERIAL
  b. CORRELATION V74 V66 FORMAT = SERIAL
  c. CORRELATION V74 V66 /FORMAT = SERIAL MATRIX
  d. CORRELATION V74 WITH V66
  e. CORRELATION V2 WITH V74 / FORMAT = SERIAL
  f. CORRELATION V6 WITH V74 V13
  g. PEARSON CORR V9 WITH V17 /FORMAT = SERIAL
  h. CORRELATION EDUC SEX /PRINT TWOTAIL
  i. CORRELATION EDUC SEX WITH AGE POLVIEWS
       /PRINT = TWOTAIL NOSIG
  j. CORRELATION EDUC SEX / PRINT = ONETAIL
  k. CORRELATION EDUC SEX /FORMAT = MATRIX
  l. CORRELATION EDUC SEX / MISSING = INCLUDE / PRINT = SIG
  m. CORRELATION EDUC SEX /PRINT = TWOTAIL NOSIG DESCRIPTIVES

16.2 a. Below is a table of 10 cases (A through J) and their values on variables X and Y. Calculate a Pearson correlation between the variables. The easiest way to do this is to add columns to the table for the terms you need to calculate—x, y, $x * y$, x^2, and y^2—and then use the sums of the columns for the Pearson correlation formula.

Case	X	Y	x	y	x * y	x^2	y^2
A	1	15					
B	2	13					
C	6	12					
D	5	11					
E	4	14					
F	3	18					
G	8	18					
H	9	18					
I	7	16					
J	5	15					

b. Repeat part *a* for these 10 cases.

Case	X	Y	x	y	x * y	x^2	y^2
A	4	7					
B	9	3					
C	3	15					
D	3	13					
E	9	4					
F	4	16					
G	8	2					
H	6	8					
I	7	3					
J	7	19					

SUGGESTED READINGS

Freedman, David, *et al. Statistics*, 2nd ed. (New York: W. W. Norton, 1991) Chapters 8, 9.

Levin, Jack and James Alan Fox. *Elementary Statistics in Social Research*, 4th ed. (New York: Harper & Row, 1988) Chapter 13.

May, Richard B., Michael E. J. Masson, and Michael A. Hunter. *Application of Statistics in Behavioral Research* (New York: Harper & Row, 1990) Chapter 6.

Norusis, Marija J., and SPSS Inc. *SPSS/PC+ V2.0 Base Manual* (Chicago: SPSS Inc., 1988) Chapter 13.

SPSS Inc. *SPSS Reference Guide* (Release 4) (Chicago: SPSS Inc., 1990) pages 92–96.

SPSS Inc. *SPSS-X User's Guide,* 3rd ed. (Chicago: SPSS Inc., 1988) Chapter 24.

Chapter 17

Partial Correlation*

Let us return to the topic investigated in Chapter 16, the relationship of respondents' attitudes on issues to evaluations of George Bush. The five issues examined were all related to respondent positions on the Bush feeling thermometer, some strongly and some weakly, but each at a statistically significant level. We could reject the null hypothesis for each relationship. Before we conclude that the correlations uncovered reflect a causal process—positions on issues lead to positive or negative evaluations of the candidates—the possible impact of confounding variables needs to be examined.

One potential confounding influence might be party identification. Most people in the United States are not politically active, nor are they even particularly attentive to political issues, but a large proportion have developed attachments to one of the two major political parties. Research has found that party identifications are often developed in adolescence, learned from the leanings of family members or the community one was reared in, and are likely to change only grudgingly, if at all, during adult years. Psychological identification with a political party may lead respondents to be sympathetic to both the candidates put forward by that party and the issue positions adopted by the candidates or the party platform.

Given the nature of party identification, the correlations found in Chapter 16 may not represent the real impact of issues on evaluations of candidates. Instead we may have discovered only that Republicans (Democrats) both express Republican (Democratic) positions on the issues and favor Republican (Democratic) candidates. If we control for the influence of party affiliation, we

---

*Note: *SPSS/PC+* The PARTIAL CORR procedure is not available in SPSS/PC+.

may find that issues have less of an impact (maybe even none at all) on evaluations of candidates. Democrats will support Democratic candidates regardless of any similarities or differences on issues between the respondents and the candidates.

We learned about confounding variables earlier and how to control for them via either the CROSSTABS command or SELECT IF statements. Both control techniques are not without problems, especially for interval variables. First, they require that we look at not just one summary measure of association, but two, three, or more—a different one for each group on the confounding variable. This is clumsy at best, and at worst it makes it difficult to interpret what the relationship is if the summary measures of association differ between the groups.

Second, if our confounding variable contains numerous values, as many interval variables do, practical necessity requires that we recode the variable into only two or three groups. In doing this, we are cutting down on the variance of the confounding variable, but not holding it completely constant. When we examined the gender-income relationship earlier while controlling for education, we were forced to recode education into only two groups, those with and those without some college education. Absent recoding, we would have obtained 20 different contingency tables, most containing very few cases. With recoding, however, educational differences still existed within each group, from 0 to 12 years of education in the first group and from 1 year of college to a graduate degree in the second group. It is possible that educational differences could still have been affecting the gender-income relationship within each group.

One way to solve the above problem is to try different recoding strategies for the confounding variable, perhaps separating respondents into two other groups, those having some high school training and those having none, or using four groups for elementary graduates, high school graduates, college graduates, and those with graduate degrees. This can be done fairly easily for variables with a small number of values to begin with, something true of most nominal and ordinal variables, but it is usually a bit troublesome with interval variables. Whenever the confounding variable has a large number of possible values, any recoding into groups will still leave a sizable amount of variation within each group. The confounding variable is being held somewhat constant, but not perfectly constant.

In contrast, consider how simple it would be if we could merely subtract from any two-variable relationship whatever impact the confounding variable might have. In an earlier example we wanted to determine the impact of a quarterback on a football team's average score, but we found that our strong quarterback–weak quarterback comparison was confounded by one of the teams having a better running back than the other. Generally, we would have to redo our experiment after equalizing the running backs of both teams to control for this confounding influence.

What, however, if we knew exactly what impact the different running back made—the better running back contributed 10 extra points to his teams? We could subtract this impact directly from our quarterback comparison. That is, say the team with the better quarterback scores 25 points more on average than the team with the weaker one. If the quarterback and running back are both on the same team, we subtract the running back's 10-point contribution from the difference between the teams and determine the quarterback's impact to be 15 points. If the running back is on the other team, this leads us to underestimate the quarterback's influence by 10 points, so we add this confounding impact back in and conclude that the better quarterback (when the teams are evenly matched in all other respects) contributes 35 points to his team.

The approach described above is essentially what is accomplished by the **PARTIAL CORR** procedure. This procedure mathematically removes the impact of one or more confounding variables without the need to divide the sample into multiple subgroups for analysis. The result is a single number representing the **partial correlation** between two variables rather than multiple measures of association for each control-variable group.

THE PARTIAL CORRELATION

The PARTIAL CORR procedure uses the following formula to produce a partial Pearson correlation:

$$r_{id.c} = \frac{r_{id} - r_{ic}\, r_{dc}}{\sqrt{1 - r_{ic}^2}\,\sqrt{1 - r_{dc}^2}}$$

where r = symbol for Pearson correlation coefficient
i, d = independent and dependent variables
c = variable being controlled for
$r_{id.c}$ = symbol for a partial correlation between variables i and d while controlling for variable c

The key to understanding the formula lies in its numerator, $r_{id} - r_{ic}\,r_{dc}$. The r_{id} term is the zero-order correlation between the independent and dependent variables, a correlation we suspect is affected by confounding variable c, as illustrated in Figure 17.1. To remove the impact of c, we identify its correlation with the independent (r_{ic}) and dependent (r_{dc}) variables and multiply these two correlations. The two correlations with c are multiplied because it is the interaction of c with the independent and dependent variables that confounds their

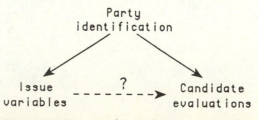
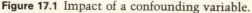

Figure 17.1 Impact of a confounding variable.

zero-order relationship. If those who drink and drive have a 50 percent chance of being in an automobile accident and 50 percent of automobile accidents produce at least one fatality, we multiply the probabilities to find the 25 percent chance that a drunk driver will be involved in a fatal accident.

Having identified the interaction of c with i and d, we subtract this interaction from the original zero-order correlation (r_{id}) and are left with a pure (unconfounded) correlation between variables i and d $(r_{id.c})$. The denominator of the formula

$$\sqrt{1 - r_{ic}^2} \ \sqrt{1 - r_{dc}^2}$$

is essentially a correction term. Without going into detail, its function is to retain for the partial correlation statistic the ability to range between, but not beyond, the values of -1.0 to $+1.0$.

A closer look at the numerator of the partial correlation formula illustrates how confounding variables influence zero-order correlations. If the confounding variable is either positively or negatively related to *both* the dependent and independent variables, then the $r_{ic}r_{dc}$ term will be positive, a product of two positive or two negative numbers, which is a positive number. Subtracting a positive number from a positive zero-order correlation will produce a partial coefficient that is closer to zero, while subtracting a positive number from a negative zero-order correlation will produce a partial coefficient that is farther away from zero. If a confounding variable is related negatively to the first variable but positively to the second variable in the original relationship, the $r_{ic}r_{dc}$ term will involve multiplying a negative number by a positive one, resulting in a negative product. Subtracting a negative number is the same as adding a positive one, so the partial correlation will be farther from zero if the original relationship is positive and closer to zero if the original relationship is negative.

Remember that a confounding variable can either exaggerate or suppress a zero-order relationship. If we believe that two variables should be correlated but find no relationship in the data, it is quite possible that a confounding variable is hiding the relationship. Controlling for it should lead the hidden relationship to appear. Similarly, we may find a relationship, such as the one between the presence of storks and the birthrate of an area, which is not a cause-effect connection. The correlation appears in the data set only because there is another difference between the cases—the confounding variable—which is the source of the differences on the dependent variable.

Two other items are also illustrated by the partial correlation formula. First, for a third variable to confound a relationship, it must be correlated with *both* the independent and dependent variables. If either r_{ic} or r_{dc} is zero, then the $r_{ic}r_{dc}$ term will also be zero and nothing will be either added or subtracted for the zero-order correlation. Second, the formula contains Pearson correlations (r's) between the independent, dependent, and control variables. The partial correlation formula can be used only when Pearson's r is a legitimate statistic—when all the variables, including the confounding one, are linearly related interval variables.

SPSS COMMANDS

Having briefly looked at the mathematics of the partial correlation statistic, we need to know how to instruct SPSS to carry it out for us. Instead of using the CORRELATION command, we use PARTIAL CORR. In most respects, the PARTIAL CORR procedure has the same format and subcommands as CORRELATION. There are only a few differences, and much of the discussion below focuses on these differences.

The PARTIAL CORR procedure begins, like CORRELATION, with the command term starting on column 1, followed by a **correlation list**, a list of variables to be correlated, separated by the WITH keyword or not, depending on our preference. The difference between the commands is twofold. The PARTIAL CORR procedure must include a list of variables to be controlled for, followed by an inclusion level for the control variables.

A **control list** is nothing more than a list of one or more variables to be used as controls. This list is separated from the correlation list by using the **BY keyword** so that SPSS will know which variables are to be correlated and which controlled for. For the variables of interest to us, the command with the correlation and control lists is

```
PARTIAL CORR    V5 V24 V27 V30 V33 V36    BY    V74
                correlation list                 control list
```

The command above is not complete, for we must add an **inclusion level**, also called **an order level**, after the control list. Recall when control variables were first discussed. A zero-order relationship is a correlation without using control variables; a first-order partial correlation is a correlation controlling for one variable; a second-order partial correlation is a correlation controlling for two variables; and so on. We must specify what order partial correlation we want by adding the order number in parentheses after the last control variable. Since we are controlling for only one variable here, we add the order number (1) after the control list. The entire command is thus

```
PARTIAL CORR V5 V24 V27 V30 V33 V36   BY  V74 (1)
```

The output from the PARTIAL CORR command is shown in Figure 17.2. It is quite similar to the CORRELATION output, a correlation matrix with a legend at the bottom describing the meaning of the numbers in the matrix. The only noticeable difference is at the top of the output which now contains the title *"Partial* Correlation Coefficients," and immediately below this line is a statement saying what variable is being controlled for.

Of course, another difference is in the correlation coefficients themselves. If you compare the correlations in Figure 17.2 with those from Figure 16.1—correlations between the same variables without controlling for party identification—you will find that the partial correlation coefficients are consistently smaller than the zero-order ones. The correlations with V5 have dropped a sizable amount for V24 and V30, from $-.28$ to $-.13$ and $.27$ to $.14$, respectively.

```
PARTIAL CORR V5 V24 V27 V30 V33 V36 BY V74 (1)


- P A R T I A L   C O R R E L A T I O N   C O E F F I C I E N T S -

CONTROLLING FOR..      V74

              V5          V24          V27          V30          V33          V36

V5         1.0000      -0.1338       0.2760       0.1360       0.0971       0.0509
          (    0)      ( 1215)      ( 1215)      ( 1215)      ( 1215)      ( 1215)
          P= .         P= 0.000     P= 0.000     P= 0.000     P= 0.000     P= 0.038


V24       -0.1338       1.0000       0.0229      -0.2704      -0.0486      -0.0953
          ( 1215)      (    0)      ( 1215)      ( 1215)      ( 1215)      ( 1215)
          P= 0.000     P= .         P= 0.213     P= 0.000     P= 0.045     P= 0.000


V27        0.2760       0.0229       1.0000       0.0921       0.3014       0.0724
          ( 1215)      ( 1215)      (    0)      ( 1215)      ( 1215)      ( 1215)
          P= 0.000     P= 0.213     P= .         P= 0.001     P= 0.000     P= 0.006


V30        0.1360      -0.2704       0.0921       1.0000       0.1211       0.0455
          ( 1215)      ( 1215)      ( 1215)      (    0)      ( 1215)      ( 1215)
          P= 0.000     P= 0.000     P= 0.001     P= .         P= 0.000     P= 0.056


V33        0.0971      -0.0486       0.3014       0.1211       1.0000       0.1640
          ( 1215)      ( 1215)      ( 1215)      ( 1215)      (    0)      ( 1215)
          P= 0.000     P= 0.045     P= 0.000     P= 0.000     P= .         P= 0.000


V36        0.0509      -0.0953       0.0724       0.0455       0.1640       1.0000
          ( 1215)      ( 1215)      ( 1215)      ( 1215)      ( 1215)      (    0)
          P= 0.038     P= 0.000     P= 0.006     P= 0.056     P= 0.000     P= .

(COEFFICIENT / (DF) / SIGNIFICANCE)
(" . " IS PRINTED IF A COEFFICIENT CANNOT BE COMPUTED)
```

Figure 17.2 Output from the PARTIAL CORR command.

They also dropped, although by lesser amounts, for V27, V33, and V36 as well: from .34 to .28, from .11 to .10, and from .07 to .05, respectively. Thus all our original correlations were being inflated by the confounding impact of party identification, some only a little and others a great deal. The partial correlations in Figure 17.2 retain a high level of statistical significance, so issues still apparently affect evaluations of candidates but the sizes of the relationships are not as strong as originally thought.

Different Inclusion Levels

Selecting an inclusion level may seem almost automatic; just enclose in parentheses the number of variables on the PARTIAL CORR control list. However, the inclusion level is more flexible than this. Say we want to control for two variables while examining the connection between issues and evaluations of candidates—party identification and sex (V87)—suspecting that women may differ from men in both attitudes toward issues and evaluations of candidates, thus also potentially confounding this relationship.

One way to control for both variables is with the command

```
PARTIAL CORR V5 WITH V24 V27 V30 V33 V36  BY  V74 V87 (1)
```

The output from this command is two different tables, shown in Figure 17.3. Our order level, 1, asks for first-order partial correlations only, correlations controlling for one variable at a time. SPSS will thus produce two correlation tables, the first while controlling for V74 only and the second while controlling for V87 only. The legend at the top tells us which variable is being used as a control for each correlation table.

If we want to control for both party identification and gender at the same time, an inclusion level of 2 is used, as in the command

```
PARTIAL CORR V5 WITH V24 V27 V30 V33 V36  BY  V74 V87 (2)
```

This command requests SPSS to perform a second-order partial correlation, producing a single correlation matrix while controlling for both variables together. The output, shown in Figure 17.4, contains only one table with the notation that both V74 and V87 are being controlled for simultaneously.

```
PARTIAL CORR V5 WITH V24 V27 V30 V33 V36 BY V74 V87 (1)


- P A R T I A L    C O R R E L A T I O N   C O E F F I C I E N T S  -

CONTROLLING FOR..      V74

           V24        V27         V30         V33         V36

V5        -0.1338     0.2760      0.1360      0.0971      0.0509
          ( 1215)    ( 1215)     ( 1215)     ( 1215)     ( 1215)
          P= 0.000   P= 0.000    P= 0.000    P= 0.000    P= 0.038


 (COEFFICIENT / (DF) / SIGNIFICANCE)
 (" . " IS PRINTED IF A COEFFICIENT CANNOT BE COMPUTED)


- P A R T I A L    C O R R E L A T I O N   C O E F F I C I E N T S  -

CONTROLLING FOR..      V87

           V24        V27         V30         V33         V36

V5        -0.2876     0.3653      0.2759      0.1229      0.0641
          ( 1215)    ( 1215)     ( 1215)     ( 1215)     ( 1215)
          P= 0.000   P= 0.000    P= 0.000    P= 0.000    P= 0.013


 (COEFFICIENT / (DF) / SIGNIFICANCE)
 (" . " IS PRINTED IF A COEFFICIENT CANNOT BE COMPUTED)
```

Figure 17.3 Controlling for two variables by using an inclusion level of 1.

```
PARTIAL CORR V5 WITH V24 V27 V30 V33 V36 BY V74 V87 (2)


- P A R T I A L    C O R R E L A T I O N    C O E F F I C I E N T S -

CONTROLLING FOR..      V74      V87

             V24         V27         V30         V33         V36

V5        -0.1341      0.2761      0.1360      0.0972      0.0509
          ( 1214)     ( 1214)     ( 1214)     ( 1214)     ( 1214)
          P= 0.000    P= 0.000    P= 0.000    P= 0.000    P= 0.038


(COEFFICIENT  /  (DF)  /  SIGNIFICANCE)
("  .  " IS PRINTED IF A COEFFICIENT CANNOT BE COMPUTED)
```

Figure 17.4 Controlling for two variables by using an inclusion level of 2.

We also can, and sometimes want to, specify more than one order level. Say we suspect that gender might confound the relationship between how one views a woman's role in society and evaluations of candidates, but not necessarily the other issue evaluation correlations. We could conduct two PARTIAL CORR analyses, the first between V5 and V36 while controlling for both party identi-fication and gender and the second between V5 and the other issue variables while controlling for party identification only. Alternatively, we could use a single command containing all the issue variables, but two inclusion levels, such as

```
PARTIAL CORR V5 WITH V24 V27 V30 V33 V36  BY  V74 V87 (1,2)
```

The output from this command is a combination of Figures 17.3 and 17.4. There are three correlation tables; the first and second control for V74 and V87 separately, and the third controls for both simultaneously.

Common Subcommands

The subcommands that can be used with the PARTIAL CORR procedure are listed in Table 17.1. Many mirror those used with CORRELATION. In partic-ular, /FORMAT = SERIAL requests the serial printing of correlation pairs instead of a matrix containing redundant correlations, and /STATIS-TICS = DESCRIPTIVES requests the printing of the mean, standard deviation and number of nonmissing cases for each variable before the correlation table.

Version 2   For the following paragraph and all other paragraphs in this chapter, users of SPSS-X version 2 will need to substitute the OPTIONS and STATIS-TICS subcommands, beginning in column 1 and followed by the option or statistic number desired. These numbers are included in Table 17.1.

(R.4)   Other subcommands are requested slightly differently for the PARTIAL CORR procedure. One example is the request for two-tailed rather than one-

Table 17.1 SUBCOMMANDS AVAILABLE WITH THE PARTIAL CORR PROCEDURE

Subcommand	Option	Description	Version 2 option no.
MISSING	EXCLUDE	Excludes user-defined missing data (not SYSMIS) (default)	—
MISSING	INCLUDE	Includes user-defined missing data (not SYSMIS) in calculations	1
MISSING	ANALYSIS	Excludes missing data pairwise from zero-order correlations	2
MISSING	LISTWISE	Excludes cases with missing values listwise from any zero-order correlations calculated (default)	—
FORMAT	MATRIX	Prints correlations in matrix format (default)	—
FORMAT	SERIAL	Prints correlations in serial string format	8
FORMAT	CONDENSED	Does not print case *n*'s and uses asterisks for significance levels	7
SIGNIFICANCE	ONETAIL	One-tailed statistical significance tests (default)	—
SIGNIFICANCE	TWOTAIL	Two-tailed statistical significance tests	3
MATRIX	OUT	Writes correlation matrix to a file	4
MATRIX	IN	Reads correlation matrix in from a file	5
MATRIX	NONE	Neither of the above (default)	—
STATISTICS	DESCRIPTIVES	Mean, standard deviation, and number of nonmissing cases	2
STATISTICS	CORR	Zero-order correlations with case *n*'s and significance levels	1
STATISTICS	NONE	No additional statistics (default)	—
STATISTICS	ALL	All statistics available	ALL
STATISTICS	BADCORR	Zero-order correlations only if some cannot be computed (to discover problem correlations)	3

tailed significance tests. For the CORRELATION procedure, **TWOTAIL** was an option on the /PRINT command, while for PARTIAL CORR the TWOTAIL option is used with the **/SIGNIFICANCE** subcommand. Second, the /PRINT = NOSIG combination was used with CORRELATION to eliminate the case count and to print asterisks for significance levels. For PARTIAL CORR, this result is achieved with the **/FORMAT = CONDENSED** subcommand-option combination.

Release 4 In contrast with the CORRELATION procedure, the default output in Release 4 is the same as that with SPSS-X version 3, a one-tailed level of statistical significance and the full correlation matrix instead of using asterisks for significance levels. Additionally, if the /FORMAT = CONDENSED subcommand and specification are used, then one asterisk stands for a .01 significance level and two asterisks stand for a .001 significance level.

In addition to the differences noted above, the default options differ for the two procedures. This is not of enormous significance to us, but it does affect our use of the options unique to PARTIAL CORR. Two of these unique options are discussed here, one each for the STATISTICS and MISSING subcommands.

Zero-Order Correlations

Whenever a partial correlation analysis is performed, a common practice is to compare the partial and zero-order correlations to determine the impact of controlling for a third variable on the original relationship. We did this when we first looked at partial correlations in Figure 17.2. It is inconvenient, though, to rely on two commands for this comparison, CORRELATION for zero-order correlations and PARTIAL CORR for the partial correlations. A simple alternative is the **CORR option** on the STATISTICS subcommand.

The subcommand /STATISTICS = CORR produces a zero-order correlation matrix printed along with the partial correlation table. The output is illustrated in Figure 17.5. Observe that the zero-order correlations are always printed as a full matrix even if the WITH keyword is used in the PARTIAL CORR command.

Along with eliminating the need to use two procedures for the comparison of zero-order and partial correlations, the CORR option has another advantage. It aids us in identifying how and why a control variable is or is not affecting the original relationship. To understand this point, we repeat an analysis performed in Chapter 15 on the relationship between gender and income while controlling for education. In that earlier chapter, using contingency tables, we found that controlling for education did not affect the original relationship.

The partial correlation printout in Figure 17.6 reconfirms this finding, and the zero-order correlation matrix helps explain why. Remember that a third variable can have a confounding effect only if it is correlated with both the independent and dependent variables. The zero-order correlation matrix in Figure 17.6 shows that education is highly correlated with income, but the correlation of education with gender is neither statistically significant nor substantively large. Our suspicion that gender and education are correlated was reasonable, but turns out to be wrong. Apparently women are no longer disadvantaged compared to men when it comes to years of education.

Missing Data

Above we described the STATISTICS = CORR subcommand as replicating the zero-order correlation matrix produced by CORRELATION. This is not completely accurate. A comparison of Figure 16.1 and Figure 17.5 will show marginal differences between the matrices. The differences stem from the way in which each procedure handles missing data. The default practice of the CORRELATION procedure is to use **pairwise deletion** of cases with missing data, deleting a case from the analysis only if it has missing data on one of the variables in the pair currently being correlated. The number of cases differs for each correlation since a case with missing data on one variable may contain a valid response for a different variable in the matrix. The default practice of the

```
PARTIAL CORR V5 WITH V24 V27 V30 V33 V36 BY V74 (1)
        / STATISTICS CORR
```

ZERO-ORDER PARTIALS

	V5	V24	V27	V30	V33	V36	V74
V5	1.0000	-0.2907	0.3670	0.2781	0.1217	0.0656	0.5961
	(0)	(1216)	(1216)	(1216)	(1216)	(1216)	(1216)
	P= .	P= 0.000	P= 0.000	P= 0.000	P= 0.000	P= 0.011	P= 0.000
V24	-0.2907	1.0000	0.0602	-0.3376	-0.0693	-0.1035	-0.3167
	(1216)	(0)	(1216)	(1216)	(1216)	(1216)	(1216)
	P= 0.000	P= .	P= 0.213	P= 0.000	P= 0.045	P= 0.000	P= 0.000
V27	0.3670	0.0602	1.0000	0.1599	0.3094	0.0805	0.2563
	(1216)	(1216)	(0)	(1216)	(1216)	(1216)	(1216)
	P= 0.000	P= 0.018	P= .	P= 0.000	P= 0.000	P= 0.002	P= 0.000
V30	0.2781	-0.3376	0.1599	1.0000	0.1370	0.0555	0.2913
	(1216)	(1216)	(1216)	(0)	(1216)	(1216)	(1216)
	P= 0.000	P= 0.000	P= 0.001	P= .	P= 0.000	P= 0.056	P= 0.000
V33	0.1217	-0.0693	0.3094	0.1370	1.0000	0.1665	0.0736
	(1216)	(1216)	(1216)	(1216)	(0)	(1216)	(1216)
	P= 0.000	P= 0.045	P= 0.000	P= 0.000	P= .	P= 0.000	P= 0.000
V36	0.0656	-0.1035	0.0805	0.0555	0.1665	1.0000	0.0415
	(1216)	(1216)	(1216)	(1216)	(1216)	(0)	(1216)
	P= 0.011	P= 0.000	P= 0.002	P= 0.026	P= 0.000	P= .	P= 0.074
V74	0.5961	-0.3167	0.2563	0.2913	0.0736	0.0415	1.0000
	(1216)	(1216)	(1216)	(1216)	(1216)	(1216)	(0)
	P= 0.000	P= 0.000	P= 0.000	P= 0.000	P= 0.005	P= 0.074	P= .

```
(COEFFICIENT / (DF) / SIGNIFICANCE)
(" . " IS PRINTED IF A COEFFICIENT CANNOT BE COMPUTED)
```

- - - P A R T I A L   C O R R E L A T I O N   C O E F F I C I E N T S - - -

CONTROLLING FOR..   V74

	V24	V27	V30	V33	V36
V5	-0.1338	0.2760	0.1360	0.0971	0.0509
	(1215)	(1215)	(1215)	(1215)	(1215)
	P= 0.000	P= 0.000	P= 0.000	P= 0.000	P= 0.038

```
(COEFFICIENT / (DF) / SIGNIFICANCE)
(" . " IS PRINTED IF A COEFFICIENT CANNOT BE COMPUTED)
```

Figure 17.5 Adding a zero-order correlation matrix with the STATISTICS = CORR subcommand.

```
PARTIAL CORR RINCOME SEX BY EDUC (1)   / STATISTICS = CORR

- P A R T I A L   C O R R E L A T I O N   C O E F F I C I E N T S -

ZERO-ORDER PARTIALS

                  RINCOME          SEX            EDUC

RINCOME           1.0000         -0.2954         0.3468
                  (    0)        (   943)        (   943)
                  P= .           P= 0.000        P= 0.000

SEX              -0.2954          1.0000        -0.0202
                  (   943)       (    0)         (   943)
                  P= 0.000       P= .            P= 0.268

EDUC              0.3468         -0.0202          1.0000
                  (   943)       (   943)        (    0)
                  P= 0.000       P= 0.268        P= .

   (COEFFICIENT / (DF) / SIGNIFICANCE)
   (" . " IS PRINTED IF A COEFFICIENT CANNOT BE COMPUTED)

- P A R T I A L   C O R R E L A T I O N   C O E F F I C I E N T S -

CONTROLLING FOR..      EDUC

                  RINCOME          SEX

RINCOME           1.0000         -0.3095
                  (    0)        (   942)
                  P= .           P= 0.000

SEX              -0.3075          1.0000
                  (   942)       (    0)
                  P= 0.000       P= .

   (COEFFICIENT / (DF) / SIGNIFICANCE)
   (" . " IS PRINTED IF A COEFFICIENT CANNOT BE COMPUTED)
```

Figure 17.6 Partial correlation between income and gender while controlling for education.

PARTIAL CORR procedure is to use **listwise deletion** of cases with missing data; a case with missing data on any variable in the correlation or control lists is deleted from the entire analysis including any partial or zero-order correlations calculated.

Listwise deletion of missing data is a sound practice in partial correlation analyses. Say we request a zero-order correlation between the respondent's educational level and family income, as shown in Figure 17.7. Upon consideration, we suspect that the spouse's educational level may confound this relationship, since people tend to marry those with similar educational attainments and the spouse's education affects family income as well. We thus follow up our original analysis with a partial correlation controlling for the spouse's education, shown in Figure 17.8. The numbers of cases in the two analyses differ

```
CORRELATION FINCOME WITH EDUC


- P E A R S O N   C O R R E L A T I O N   C O E F F I C I E N T S -

                EDUC

FINCOME     0.4121
           ( 1354)
           P=  0.000


(COEFFICIENT / (CASES) / 1-TAILED SIG)
" . " IS PRINTED IF A COEFFICIENT CANNOT BE COMPUTED
```

Figure 17.7 Zero-order correlation between FINCOME and EDUC.

```
PARTIAL CORR FINCOME WITH EDUC BY SPEDUC (1)
     / STATISTICS = CORR


- P A R T I A L   C O R R E L A T I O N   C O E F F I C I E N T S -

ZERO-ORDER  PARTIALS

            FINCOME       EDUC        SPEDUC

FINCOME     1.0000       0.4605       0.3902
           (    0)      (  721)      (   721)
           P=  .        P= 0.000     P= 0.000

EDUC        0.4605       1.0000       0.6025
           (  721)      (    0)      (   721)
           P= 0.000     P= .         P= 0.000

SPEDUC      0.3902       0.6025       1.0000
           (  721)      (  721)      (    0)
           P= 0.000     P= 0.000     P= .


 (COEFFICIENT / (DF) / SIGNIFICANCE)
(" . " IS PRINTED IF A COEFFICIENT CANNOT BE COMPUTED)


- P A R T I A L   C O R R E L A T I O N   C O E F F I C I E N T S -

CONTROLLING FOR..     SPEDUC

              EDUC

FINCOME     0.3068
           (  720)
           P= 0.000


 (COEFFICIENT / (DF) / SIGNIFICANCE)
(" . " IS PRINTED IF A COEFFICIENT CANNOT BE COMPUTED)
```

Figure 17.8 Partial correlation between FINCOME and EDUC while controlling for SPEDUC.

substantially because nearly half of the respondents in the data set (47 percent) are not currently married and thus have a response defined as missing data on the SPEDUC variable. These cases are removed from the partial correlation analysis, including the zero-order correlation table requested.

The correlations in Figures 17.7 and 17.8 are actually based on two different samples. The zero-order correlations in Figure 17.7 are based on all respondents, while those in Figure 17.8 are based on married respondents only. If we find a difference between the zero-order correlations in the first figure and the partial correlations in the second, is the difference based on the impact of the control variable or the impact of using a different sample? We have no way of knowing. We can make a comparison, however, by looking at the zero-order and partial correlations in Figure 17.8 only, for both use listwise deletion and thus both are based on the same sample—just respondents with spouses. Any differences between the zero-order and partial correlations must thus be due to the control variable.

The impact of the sample differences can be seen by comparing Figures 17.7 and 17.8. The zero-order correlation between education and family income is actually larger for respondents with spouses than for all respondents, .46 versus .41. Consequently, we find a larger impact from the control variable while using listwise deletion than we might have found when comparing the two different samples.

Despite the value of listwise deletion, there are times when pairwise deletion is useful. Say we want to examine whether political ideology is correlated with attitudes about how to deal with AIDS victims. We thus correlate the four AIDS variables with POLVIEWS. Suspecting gender may be correlated with both POLVIEWS and AIDS attitudes, we also control for it. When we do this, however, SPSS does not produce any correlations at all, neither zero-order nor partial correlations. All that shows up on the output are some messages (Figure 17.9). The first one is a technical message produced by most SPSS procedures merely informing us how much computer memory is currently available and how much is needed for the procedure. We typically ignore this information since exceeding the computer's memory capacity is a rare occurrence. The second part of the message, however, tells us that there are zero cases left for this list of variables and that the partial correlation coefficients cannot be calculated.

This message has appeared because the listwise deletion of missing data led to the elimination of all cases in the data set. Major survey organizations

```
PARTIAL CORR  POLVIEWS  WITH  AIDSSCH  TO  AIDSIDS  BY  SEX (1)
       / STATISTICS= CORR


THERE ARE 1077000 BYTES OF MEMORY AVAILABLE.
THE LARGEST CONTIGUOUS AREA HAS 1077000 BYTES.
PARTIAL CORR WILL ALLOCATE 360 BYTES.
ONLY        0.000 CASES   FOR THIS VARIABLE LIST.
PARTIAL  CORRELATION  COEFFICIENTS  WILL  NOT  BE  CALCULATED.
```

Figure 17.9 Partial correlation between AIDS attitudes and POLVIEWS while controlling for SEX.

Table 17.2   IMPACT OF LISTWISE DELETION OF MISSING DATA

	Variable			Correlation		
Case	X1	X2	X3	X1 * X2	X1 * X3	X2 * X3
A	Miss	1	6	Deleted	Deleted	Deleted
B	Miss	2	10	Deleted	Deleted	Deleted
C	Miss	3	12	Deleted	Deleted	Deleted
D	8	Miss	6	Deleted	Deleted	Deleted
E	9	Miss	5	Deleted	Deleted	Deleted
F	7	Miss	4	Deleted	Deleted	Deleted
G	6	3	Miss	Deleted	Deleted	Deleted
H	10	4	Miss	Deleted	Deleted	Deleted
I	9	3	Miss	Deleted	Deleted	Deleted

continuously experiment with new questions that might improve the measurement of social attitudes. To avoid making the survey too long, some questions are asked of only half the respondents while the other half answer different experimental questions. Each group is given missing-data values for the questions not asked. Trying to correlate some of the split half variables leads to every case in the sample having a missing value for at least one of the variables on the correlation or control lists. Table 17.2 illustrates how listwise deletion of cases with a missing value for any variable on either list can lead to the deletion of all cases in the sample.

Which of the variables on the correlation or control lists are the problems? We can determine this by using pairwise deletion of missing data. Pairwise deletion allows for correlations to be produced between any set of variables where some cases in the sample have legitimate values for that set, regardless of any missing values for other variables on the correlation or control lists. The impact of pairwise deletion is illustrated in Table 17.3.

Table 17.3   IMPACT OF PAIRWISE DELETION OF MISSING DATA

	Variable			Correlation		
Case	X1	X2	X3	X1 * X2	X1 * X3	X2 * X3
A	Miss	1	6	Deleted	Deleted	6
B	Miss	2	10	Deleted	Deleted	20
C	Miss	3	12	Deleted	Deleted	36
D	8	Miss	6	Deleted	48	Deleted
E	9	Miss	5	Deleted	45	Deleted
F	7	Miss	4	Deleted	28	Deleted
G	6	3	Miss	18	Deleted	Deleted
H	10	4	Miss	40	Deleted	Deleted
I	9	3	Miss	27	Deleted	Deleted

Supplement 17.1   **Cases Versus Degrees of Freedom**

We have repeatedly referred to the second number in correlation matrices as the number of cases included in the analysis. This is a general rule-of-thumb interpretation, but it is not precisely accurate. The middle number in a correlation matrix is actually the degrees of freedom available for that calculation—the number of cases minus a certain number based on the type of correlation analysis performed and the number of variables being controlled for. Thus you will find a slight discrepancy in these numbers between a CORRELATION printout and a PARTIAL CORR printout, even when the same missing-value deletion methods are used for both procedures. With the large data sets we are working with, these slight differences are not of real importance and do not affect the correlations calculated.

The pairwise deletion of missing data is requested with the /**MISSING** subcommand using the **ANALYSIS** option. The output is shown in Figure 17.10. This subcommand produces partial correlations based on only the cases containing valid values for the variables in that specific correlation [dependent, independent, and control(s)]. For this reason, each partial correlation in Figure 17.10 displays a different number of cases used in its calculation.

When pairwise deletion is used to avoid eliminating all cases, it is advisable to request a zero-order correlation matrix as well to spot the variable combinations producing the problem. From the zero-order correlation matrix in Figure 17.10 we find that AIDSSCH and AIDSADS can be correlated with each other, so there are some respondents who answered both questions. Neither of these variables, however, can be correlated with AIDSSXED or AIDSIDS, questions apparently asked of different respondents in the sample. Once the problematic variable combinations have been identified, the preferred practice is to redo the partial correlation analysis separately for each set of variables—the first PARTIAL CORR contains only the first two AIDS variables and the second contains the last two—using listwise deletion for each PARTIAL CORR command.

ASSUMPTIONS AND INTERPRETATION

Like all procedures, PARTIAL CORR requires certain assumptions about the nature of the data and the relationships between the variables. The output from this procedure is also slightly different from both the Pearson correlation and the use of a control variable on the CROSSTABS command. We first look at the primary assumptions made and then turn to interpreting the output.

```
PARTIAL  CORR   POLVIEWS  WITH   AIDSSCH   TO  AIDSIDS  BY  SEX (1)
     /STATISTICS = CORR    /MISSING = ANALYSIS
```

```
- P A R T I A L   C O R R E L A T I O N   C O E F F I C I E N T S -
ZERO-ORDER PARTIALS
```

	POLVIEWS	AIDSSCH	AIDSADS	AIDSSXED	AIDSIDS	SEX
POLVIEWS	1.0000	-0.1051	0.2194	0.2000	-0.0348	-0.0262
	(0)	(621)	(649)	(702)	(662)	(1414)
	P= .	P= 0.004	P= 0.000	P= 0.000	P= 0.186	P= 0.163
AIDSSCH	-.1051	1.0000	-.0525	.	.	-0.0179
	(621)	(0)	(622)	(0)	(0)	(645)
	P= 0.004	P= .	P= 0.095	P= .	P= .	P= 0.325
AIDSADS	0.2194	-0.0525	1.0000	.	.	0.0597
	(649)	(622)	(0)	(0)	(0)	(676)
	P= 0.000	P= 0.095	P= .	P= .	P= .	P= 0.060
AIDSSXED	0.2000	.	.	1.0000	-0.0020	-0.0144
	(702)	(0)	(0)	(0)	(676)	(730)
	P= 0.000	P= .	P= .	P= .	P= 0.479	P= 0.349
AIDSIDS	-0.0348	.	.	-0.0020	1.0000	-0.0058
	(662)	(0)	(0)	(676)	(0)	(685)
	P= 0.186	P= .	P= .	P= 0.479	P= .	P= 0.439
SEX	-0.0262	-0.0179	0.0597	-0.0144	-0.0058	1.0000
	(1414)	(645)	(676)	(730)	(685)	(0)
	P= 0.163	P= 0.325	P= 0.060	P= 0.349	P= 0.439	P= .

```
(COEFFICIENT / (DF) / SIGNIFICANCE)
" . " IS PRINTED IF A COEFFICIENT CANNOT BE COMPUTED.
```

```
- P A R T I A L   C O R R E L A T I O N   C O E F F I C I E N T S -
```

CONTROLLING FOR..   SEX

	AIDSSCH	AIDSADS	AIDSSXED	AIDSIDS
POLVIEWS	-0.1057	0.2214	0.1997	-0.0349
	(620)	(648)	(701)	(661)
	P= 0.004	P= 0.000	P= 0.000	P= 0.185

```
(COEFFICIENT / (DF) / SIGNIFICANCE)
" . " IS PRINTED IF A COEFFICIENT CANNOT BE COMPUTED.
```

Figure 17.10 A PARTIAL CORR using pairwise deletion.

Assumptions

In all statistical procedures it is assumed that the data analyzed consist of a representative sample, an assumption necessary to draw inferences about the population. In addition, the partial correlation statistic makes essentially the same assumptions as the Pearson correlation: The independent, dependent, and control variables are measured at the interval level and should be linearly related. For PARTIAL CORR, however, there is one additional level of stringency not required by CORRELATION, the **multivariate normal** assumption.

To develop a sampling distribution for hypothesis testing, we had to assume in the CORRELATION procedure that the two variables had a bivariate normal distribution in the population—for each value of one variable, the other variable was normally distributed. With the PARTIAL CORR procedure, it is necessary to go one step further and assume that the variables are multivariate normal. This means, if we are using only three variables (one independent, one dependent, and one control), that for each combination of two variables the third is normally distributed. That is, respondents who want a large defense spending increase (independent) and are also weak Democrats (control) are normally distributed on the Bush feeling thermometer (dependent). In turn, for respondents with a neutral evaluation of Bush (dependent) who also want a small defense spending decrease (independent) their distribution of party identifications (control) is shaped like a normal curve.

As was true for the bivariate normal assumption of the Pearson correlation, it is difficult to verify whether the multivariate normal assumption is true for the population. However, experience has shown that it is generally a reasonable assumption in most cases. The practical impact of this assumption occurs on the inclusion level. As we control for more variables simultaneously (use a larger inclusion level), it becomes increasingly tenuous to assume that variable A is distributed normally for all combinations of variables B, C, D, and E, our one independent variable and multiple control variables. A general rule of thumb is that we can control for two variables and probably three fairly safely, but controlling for more than three variables runs a serious risk of violating the multivariate normal assumption. Note that the crucial issue is not the *number* of variables on the control list, but the *inclusion level*, which determines how many of those variables will be controlled for concurrently.

If your research needs require controlling for a large number of variables together, you will be better off using a procedure with less restrictive assumptions. Later we discuss the regression procedure, which does allow for multiple control variables without the multivariate normal assumption needed for the PARTIAL CORR procedure.

Interpretation

Recall Chapter 15 where we discussed control variables and elaboration. For the CROSSTABS procedure, adding a control variable could produce one of four outcomes: (1) The zero-order and partial correlations are approximately the same, indicating the control variable does not significantly confound the zero-order relationship. (2) The partial correlations may be significantly lower or higher than the zero-order correlation, showing that the control variable was confounding the zero-order relationship—either inflating or deflating it—but a relationship remains even after the confounding variable is controlled for. (3) The relationship may increase for one group on the control variable, but decrease for the other group, leading to a conditional interpretation of the hypothesis—the relationship is one type for group *A*, but a different type for group *B*. (4) The partial correlation may drop to zero, which means that either the original relationship was spurious or we are looking at a causal chain where one of the variables intervenes between the others.

The output from the PARTIAL CORR procedure can also lead to interpretations 1, 2, or 4 above, but not 3. The partial correlation statistic is one number, not the two or more measures of association that result from adding a control variable (and thus obtaining multiple contingency tables) to the CROSSTABS command. One number cannot reflect both an increase and a decrease at the same time. In fact, an inconsistent increase or decrease is the same as saying that there is a nonlinear relationship, a relationship of one type for some cases but of a different type for other cases. The Pearson correlation, whether a zero-order or partial correlation, simply will not produce reliable results for nonlinear relationships. If you suspect the relationship might be nonlinear, you can use one of the strategies discussed at the end of Chapter 16, including using the CROSSTABS procedure and its ordinal statistics, which do not require the linear assumption.

A second difference in interpreting the output involves the statistical significance levels. We did not pay much attention to statistical significance when using a control variable on the CROSSTABS command because splitting the sample into smaller subgroups affects the statistical significance tests even when the control variable is not confounding the relationship. The PARTIAL CORR procedure, however, uses all the cases in the sample to calculate its statistics, and thus it is quite reasonable to compare significance levels, as well as the substantive size of the correlation, before and after the control variable is added. You are not required to do so, for comparing the size of the correlation coefficient should be sufficient, but it is at least a valid comparison with PARTIAL CORR while it was not for CROSSTABS.

SUMMARY

The Pearson correlation coefficient is an example of a powerful statistic. A number of statistics provide only limited information, do not make full use of the information contained in a variable, or require a number of steps to perform such tasks as controlling for confounding variables. Pearson's correlation uses all the distance information possessed by interval variables, and its squared coefficient of determination is a PRE measure of guessing improvement. In addition, it has a simple yet effective way to control for confounding variables while testing relationships.

The assumptions it makes—that the relationships are linear and the variables have a multivariate normal distribution—are occasionally troublesome. In the remaining chapters we show how to both examine the linear assumption and use it in an even more powerful statistical procedure—regression.

REVIEW

Key Terms

PARTIAL CORR	FORMAT
Partial correlation	CONDENSED
Correlation list	CORR option
Control list	Pairwise deletion
BY keyword	Listwise deletion
Inclusion level	MISSING
Order level	ANALYSIS
TWOTAIL	Multivariate normal
SIGNIFICANCE	

Exercises

17.1 Correct any errors in the command statements given.
   a. PARTIAL CORR V5 V6 V7
   b. PARTIAL CORR V5 V6 V7 BY V74
   c. PARTIAL CORR V5 V6 V7 BY V74 (1)
   d. PARTIAL CORR V5 V6 V7 BY V74 V87 (1)
   e. PARTIAL CORR V5 V6 V7 BY V74 V87 (3)
   f. PARTIAL CORR V5 WITH V6 V7 BY V74 V87 (2)
   g. PARTIAL CORR V5 V6 V7 BY V74 (1) FORMAT = SERIAL
   h. PARTIAL CORR V5 V6 V7 BY V74 (1) /STATISTICS = CORR
   i. PARTIAL CORR V5 WITH V74 BY V24 V27 V30 V33 V36 (5)
   j. PARTIAL CORR V5 V74 BY V24 V27 V30 V33 V36 (1, 3)
   k. PARTIAL CORR V5 V74 BY V24 V27 V30 V33 V36 (1, 2)
   l. PARTIAL CORR POLVIEWS WITH SEX WITH EDUC (1)
   m. PARTIAL CORR POLVIEWS SEX BY EDUC (1) /MISSING = ANALYSIS
   n. PARTIAL CORR POLVIEWS SEX BY EDUC (1) /MISSING = ANALYSIS
        /STATISTICS = CORR
   o. PARTIAL CORR POLVIEWS SEX BY EDUC (1) /MISSING = LISTWISE
        /STATISTICS = CORR
   p. PARTIAL CORR POLVIEWS SEX BY EDUC (1) /STATISTICS = LISTWISE
   q. PARTIAL CORR POLVIEWS WITH SEX BY EDUC (1) /PRINT = TWOTAIL
   r. PARTIAL CORR POLVIEWS BY SEX EDUC (1) /STATISTICS = CORR
   s. PARTIAL CORR POLVIEWS WITH SEX BY MARITAL (1)

17.2 Conduct a partial correlation analysis using any set of variables, being sure to request a matrix of zero-order correlations as well. Using the zero-order correlation matrix, calculate your own partial correlations. That is, identify r_{id}, r_{ic}, and r_{dc} and use them and the partial correlation formula to calculate $r_{id.c}$. Except for minor rounding errors, your results should match the partial correlations calculated by SPSS. There are two caveats: Be sure to use listwise deletion of missing data and first-order partial correlations only. Pairwise deletion of missing data or higher-level correlations require different formulas from that given in the beginning of this chapter.

SUGGESTED READINGS

SPSS Inc. *SPSS Reference Guide* (Release 4) (Chicago: SPSS Inc., 1990) pages 517–22.

SPSS Inc. *SPSS-X User's Guide*, 3rd ed. (Chicago: SPSS Inc., 1988) Chapter 40.

Chapter
18

Plot

*L*et us return to the CROSSTABS procedure for a moment. That procedure accomplishes two things. First, it produces a host of summary statistics, such as chi square, lambda, gamma, and tau, measuring statistical and substantive significance. Second, CROSSTABS produces pictures of relationships between variables in the contingency table. The contingency table is not actually necessary, for it is the summary statistics that we use to measure relationships and test hypotheses. Nonetheless, having a visual portrayal of relationships often aids in understanding and interpreting them.

The visual display is one reason that we may use CROSSTABS rather than CORRELATION to examine some interval variables. For example, the relationship between vote choice (recoded as an interval Bush-Dukakis dichotomy) and respondent's party identification is easily portrayed in a contingency table (Figure 18.1), and the Pearson correlation produced by CROSSTABS is identical to what CORRELATION would produce between these variables. Contingency tables are limited not to nominal and ordinal variables, just to variables with a small number of values. Even when you are dealing with variables deemed to be interval, if the variables contain only a limited number of response values, you may prefer to use CROSSTABS over CORRELATION to obtain the contingency table display.

Many interval variables, however, contain a large number of response choices, such as income, age, education, or the candidate feeling thermometers. When this is the case, contingency tables become too large and unwieldy to be easily interpreted. All is not lost, however, for relationships between interval variables with numerous values can be portrayed with a different technique, a **scatterplot** instead of a contingency table.

A scatterplot can be thought of as a contingency table with very small cells,

```
RECODE V2 (3,8=9)
CROSSTABS TABLES = V2 BY V74    /CELLS=COLUMN / STATISTICS=CORR


- - - - - - - - - - - C R O S S - T A B U L A T I O N   O F - - - - - - - - - - - - -
V2     PRESIDENTIAL VOTE                          BY   V74      RESP'S PARTY IDENTIFICATION
- - - - - - - - - - - - - - - - - - - - - - - - - - - - - - - - - - - PAGE  1 OF  1

                 V74
                   I
         COUNT     I STRONG   WEAK     INDE-    INDE-    INDE-    WEAK     STRONG
         COL PCT   I DEMO-    DEMO-    PENDENT  PENDENT  PENDENT  REPUB-   REPUB-      ROW
                   I CRAT     CRAT     DEMO.             REPUB.   LICAN    LICAN     TOTAL
                   I     0  I     1  I     2  I     3  I     4  I     5  I     6  I
V2       ------- + ------ + ------ + ------ + ------ + ------ + ------ + ------ +
              1  I        I        I        I        I        I        I        I       630
      BUSH      I   6.3  I  28.1  I  12.0  I  64.6  I  84.9  I  83.4  I  98.2  I      52.9
               + ------- + ------ + ------ + ------ + ------ + ------ + ------ +
              2  I        I        I        I        I        I        I        I       562
      DUKAKIS   I  93.7  I  71.9  I  88.0  I  35.4  I  15.1  I  16.6  I   1.8  I      47.1
               + ------- + ------ + ------ + ------ + ----- + ------ +
        COLUMN     238      192      133       79      146      181      223      1192
        TOTAL     20.0     16.1     11.2      6.6     12.2     15.2     18.7     100.0


PEARSON'S R               -0.71093      0.0000

NUMBER OF MISSING OBSERVATIONS = 848
```

Figure 18.1 A CROSSTABS between vote choice and party identification.

somewhat like the illustration in Figure 18.2. The X and Y axes represent the two variables being examined, and each cell is the *joint position* of a case on the two variables. Since each cell is very small, the size of one character (letter or number) only, there is no room for the information typically printed in a contingency table, such as the case count or column frequency. Instead, a dot, X, or other character is placed in the cell if a case has the combination of X and Y values represented by the cell. To illustrate, two cells are emphasized in Figure 18.2. The first represents cases with a value of 10 on the Y axis and 12 on the X axis. One or more cases do exist with this combination of X and Y values, so the cell is filled in with an X. The other emphasized cell is for cases with a value of 6 on the Y axis and 12 on the X axis. This cell is empty (represented here by a zero), showing that none of the cases plotted had that particular combination of X and Y values.

A scatterplot is interpreted by looking at the pattern of the filled-in cells. A strong relationship between two variables should lead most of the filled cells to congregate in a pattern, like the general linear pattern in Figure 18.2. A weak or zero relationship between two variables will lead to no visible pattern, as shown in Figure 18.3.

A scatterplot is not a statistical tool in the same sense as the other procedures we have examined. It has no unique statistics for determining substantive or statistical significance, although it can display some limited statistics from the REGRESSION procedure. Nor can we use scatterplots, no matter how

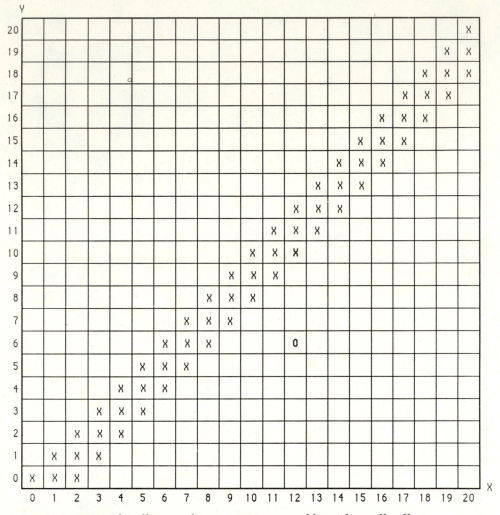

Figure 18.2 Scatterplot illustrated as a contingency table with small cells.

striking the pattern, to draw conclusions about the nature of relationships. A scatterplot is merely a visual aid, but visual aids are often valuable resources for interpreting numerical measures of association.

THE PLOT COMMAND

To produce a scatterplot, we start with the PLOT command, beginning in column 1. This command instructs SPSS to carry out the PLOT procedure, but it must also be followed by a **PLOT subcommand** that tells SPSS what variables

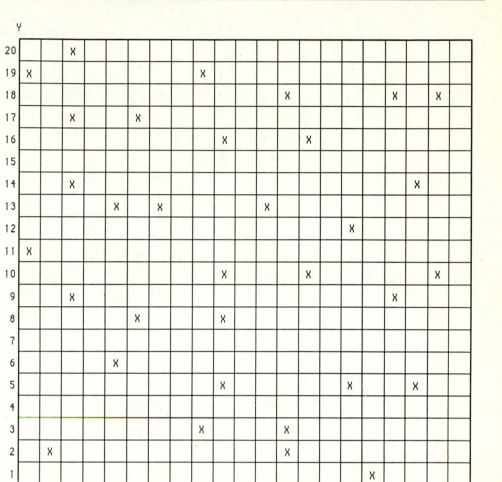

Figure 18.3 Scatterplot showing no visible pattern.

to plot. To produce a scatterplot between the education of respondents and their spouses, the command is

```
PLOT /PLOT SPEDUC EDUC
```

It appears redundant to use the PLOT term twice, once to initiate the procedure and again to start the subcommand, but there is a reason for this practice. Requesting scatterplots via a subcommand allows us to produce different plots with the same command. For example, if we also wish a plot of income by age, we can request this with a second PLOT subcommand, as in

```
PLOT / PLOT SPEDUC EDUC
     / PLOT RINCOME AGE
```

The PLOT subcommand follows the same basic format as the CORRELA-TION command. If more than two variables—say, RINCOME, EDUC, and SPEDUC—are included on a single command, SPSS will produce scatterplots for all combinations of the variables: RINCOME by EDUC, RINCOME by SPEDUC, and EDUC by SPEDUC. In addition, the **WITH keyword** can be used to separate the variables on the PLOT list. The command

PLOT / PLOT RINCOME **WITH** EDUC SPEDUC

will plot RINCOME by both EDUC and SPEDUC, but will not produce a scatterplot between the two variables following the WITH keyword. In creating scatterplots, it is customary to use the vertical axis for the dependent variable and the horizontal axis for the independent variable. It is thus desirable to always use the WITH keyword, since it allows you to control the axis used for each variable. Variables listed before the WITH keyword will appear on the vertical axis, and those after it will be on the horizontal axis.

Let us turn to the output obtained from plotting SPEDUC by EDUC, shown in Figure 18.4. The SPEDUC variable is placed on the vertical axis while EDUC occupies the horizontal axis. The label of each variable is printed next to the axis representing it. Numbers for the values of each variable are also printed next to the axes.

Locations on scatterplots can be occupied by more than one person. Our sample may contain 25, 50, or more people who have 12 years of education and whose spouses also have 12 years of education. To indicate that some positions on the plot are occupied by more than one person and other positions by only one person, SPSS uses different symbols for the plotted points, depending on the number of respondents occupying that point. A legend appears at the top of each scatterplot describing the nature of the plot and the symbols used. This information, displayed in Figure 18.5, explains that the numbers 1 through 9 represent 1 through 9 cases, respectively, and letters A through Z are used for points containing 10 through 35 respondents, respectively. An asterisk (*) at any point on the plot stands for 36 or more people.

Now let us examine the plot itself. It is quite congested. Points are scattered everywhere and exhibit no obvious pattern. A pattern does exist; it is just difficult to pick out. If you look closely, you will see that the symbols representing a large number of cases, 4 through the asterisk, are congregated close to each other in an upward trend. Figure 18.6 clarifies this by repeating the plot with those points underlined. Why is the pattern so difficult to detect? Because we are trying to plot too many cases onto too few points. Each education variable contains 21 values, ranging from 0 for no formal education to 20 for 8 years or more of college. Consequently, the maximum number of plottable locations on the graph is $21 * 21 = 441$ combinations of values for these two variables. Into these 441 spaces we are cramming 782 respondents from the General Social Survey (half the cases are deleted because they have no spouses). With this many respondents, it is not surprising for us to find cases that fit into most of the possible locations of the plot.

```
PLOT / PLOT SPEDUC WITH EDUC


* * * * * * * * * * * * * *  P L O T  * * * * * * * * * * * * * *

                    PLOT OF SPEDUC WITH EDUC

         ++---+----+----+----+----+----+----+----+----+----+----++
H    20  +------------------------------------1----------3-1-4----5+
I        I                                                        I
G        I                                 1  1       2  1 2   2  I
H        I                                                        I
E        I                                 1   1 4   1 6     6 3 4I
S   17.5 +                                                        +
T        I                      1 1        1 3     2     7 1    1 I
         I                                                        I
Y        I                            2       J  5 4   4 *  2 2 3 1I
E        I                                                        I
A    15  +                 1          1       1 6  3 2  4 4  4 1  1 1+
R        I                                                        I
         I                    1 1       2     4 T  9 G  7 C  4 3  2 I
S        I                                                        I
C        I                            1     2  2 K  9 7  5 5  2     I
H   12.5 +                                                        +
O        I                 1 1      2  5 8  B B  F *  U U  4 K  1 6  2 I
O        I                                                        I
L        I                      1 1  2 5  7 4  8 B  1 2  2        I
         I                                                        I
C    10  +                 1 1      2  3 5  5 B  1 2        1     +
O        I                                                        I
M        I                         1  3 5    8  1 2  1          I
P        I                                                        I
L        I                    3  1 A  1 4  3 7  3 2            I
E   7.5  +                                                        +
T        I              1      1 1 2       1 3      1          I
E        I                                                        I
D        I              1      1    1 1    1 2             I
         I                                                        I
     5   +              1  2      1 1      1               +
S        I                                                        I
P        I                  1              1                I
O        I                                                        I
U        I        1        1      1 1      1               I
S   2.5  +                        1       1                +
E        I                                                        I
         I                                                        I
         I                                                        I
     0   +                                                        +
         ++---+----+----+----+----+----+----+----+----+----+----++
         -4      0      4       8      12     16            20

              HIGHEST YEAR OF SCHOOL COMPLETED

        782 CASES PLOTTED.
```

Figure 18.4 PLOT between SPEDUC and EDUC.

```
PLOT / PLOT SPEDUC WITH EDUC


* * * * * * * * * * * * *  P L O T  * * * * * * * * * * * * * *

DATA   INFORMATION

     1481 UNWEIGHTED CASES ACCEPTED.

SIZE OF THE PLOTS

    HORIZONTAL SIZE IS 65
      VERTICAL SIZE IS 40

FREQUENCIES AND SYMBOLS USED (NOT APPLICABLE FOR CONTROL OR OVERLAY
PLOTS)

        1 - 1        11 - B        21 - L        31 - U
        2 - 2        12 - C        22 - M        32 - W
        3 - 3        13 - D        23 - N        33 - X
        4 - 4        14 - E        24 - O        34 - Y
        5 - 5        15 - F        25 - P        35 - Z
        6 - 6        16 - G        26 - Q        36 - *
        7 - 7        17 - H        27 - R
        8 - 8        18 - I        28 - S
        9 - 9        19 - J        29 - T
       10 - A        20 - K        30 - U

followed by the plot shown in Figure 18.4.
```

Figure 18.5 Explanatory output from the PLOT command.

The nature of the problem suggests two solutions. We can either expand the number of plottable points on the graph or reduce the number of cases to plot. The first option means creating more value categories for each variable— measuring education in semesters or months instead of years. If we could do this, each variable might represent 40 semesters instead of 20 years, expanding the number of possible locations on the plot to 41 * 41 = 1681 combinations of the two variables. Unfortunately, this option is not open to us. The number of values that a variable assumes is a decision made at the data collection stage. We can reduce the number of values on a variable by grouping some with the RECODE command, but we cannot expand the variety of responses on a variable beyond those available in the data set. While this option is not possible for us, it is an important consideration if you ever collect your own data. It is usually advisable to collect information in as much detail as possible, for you can always condense the information later, but you can never expand upon it.

The second alternative, reducing the number of cases to be plotted, is something we can do. The SPSS SAMPLE command, discussed earlier in Chapter 8 on data massaging, draws a random sample of any size needed from the respondents in the data set. How does drawing a sample simplify the scatterplot? Consider the hypothetical plot between two variables shown in Figure 18.7. Most of the respondents are in the plot positions represented by the

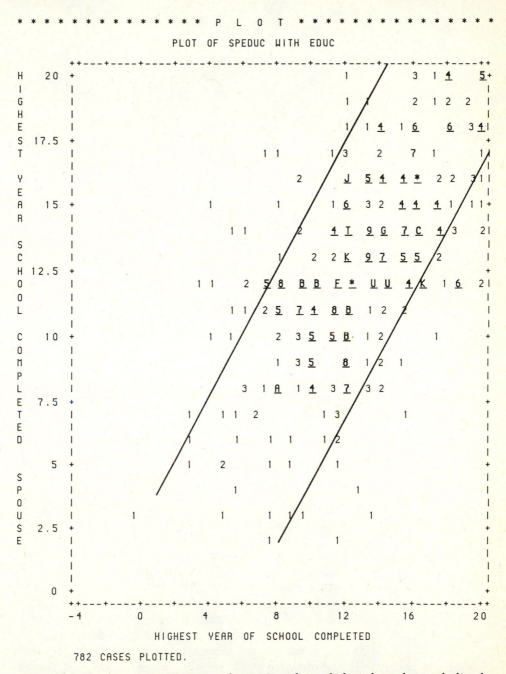

Figure 18.6 Plot between SPEDUC and EDUC with symbols 4 through * underlined.

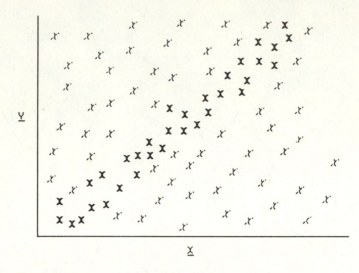

Figure 18.7 Scatterplot trend hidden by visual "noise."

bold **X**'s, with each **X** being a location occupied by 20 or more cases. The **X**'s show a general linear trend upward. However, there are a few scattered individuals at other points on the graph, depicted by the italicized *X*'s, who tend to hide the upward trend in the data. These *X*'s constitute visual "noise." If you draw a large enough sample, it is bound to contain some cases with abnormal combinations of values on the two variables, abnormal combinations which hide what is generally true for most respondents. An SPSS scatterplot does use different symbols for locations occupied by a few versus many cases, but it is very difficult to train yourself to see only the symbols representing a large number of cases. Either you need to identify them with some clearly observable mark, as we did in Figure 18.6, or you need to eliminate the aberrant and unusual points so that the general trend can be easily seen.

If we draw a 10 percent sample from the data, we eliminate 90 percent of our cases—but which 90 percent? The answer is that the unusual cases are the most likely ones to be eliminated, leaving only the cases showing the general pattern remaining in the plot. To understand this, we have to dip briefly into a topic called the **expected value**. The expected value is the average or typical outcome of some operation performed. It is the probability of a given outcome times the number of times we carry out the operation. For example, if we toss a fair coin, the probability of obtaining a head on each toss is .5. If we flip the coin 100 times, we should expect to find 50 heads, the probability of the outcome (.5) multiplied by the number of operations (100 flips). Now let us say each bold **X** in Figure 18.7 contains 2 percent of the cases and each italicized *X* contains only .1 percent. If we have a random sample of 1000 people, we expect to end up with 1 case for each italicized position (.001 * 1000 = 1) and 20 cases for each bold position (.02 * 1000 = 20). If, instead, we draw a sample of 100, we expect less than 1 case to show up for each italicized position (.001 *

100 = .1), but 2 cases for every bold position (.02 * 100 = 2). In short, a smaller sample will eliminate most of the visual noise, leaving only the most common value combinations in the scatterplot.

What size sample should we draw? There is no easy answer to this question, for it depends on the size of the data set, the number of plottable locations on the graph, and the strength of the relationship. A rough guideline is to draw a sample no larger than about 25 to 50 percent of the number of plottable graph locations—the number of values on variable X times the number on variable Y. For the SPEDUC-EDUC relationship, there are 441 plottable locations, so we want a sample containing between 110 and 220 cases. We will use a 15 percent sample for this relationship since nearly half of the cases are eliminated anyway (respondents without spouses), and 15 percent of the approximately 800 cases remaining is about 120 cases. For other variable combinations from the entire GSS88 data set or the larger ELEC88 data set, samples of 5 to 10 percent would be more common. Our 15 percent sample produces the scatterplot shown in Figure 18.8, a plot based on only 114 cases. The sample clarifies the visual relationship; the upward linear trend is far more visible than it was in the plot containing all the cases.

SUBCOMMANDS

Table 18.1 contains a partial list of the subcommands used with the PLOT procedure. A scatterplot's primary function is to provide a visual portrayal of a relationship. As such, there are few optional statistics available with this procedure, but there are a large number of subcommands, whose purpose is to change the graphical features of the display. We examine four of these features here: changing the plot size, adding reference lines, identifying the regression line, and using control variables.

Before we delve into the details of the subcommands, it is necessary to comment on one overall difference between PLOT and the procedures examined previously. Most SPSS procedures require that we identify the analysis to be performed first (e.g., the correlation or contingency table to be produced) and later add the subcommands modifying the output or requesting additional statistics. In the PLOT procedure, it is reversed. All subcommands modifying the output must be described first, and *then* the PLOT subcommand is used to request specific plots. This difference is illustrated as we discuss specific subcommands.

Scatterplot Size

By default, SPSS uses an entire printer page to produce the scatterplot. The descriptive information accompanying each plot, shown in Figure 18.5, lists the number of horizontal spaces across the page (65) and vertical lines up and down the page (40) used for that plot. These numbers vary between types of mainframes and microcomputers used since SPSS adjusts the plot size to the type of

```
TEMPORARY
SAMPLE  .15
PLOT / PLOT SPEDUC WITH EDUC


 * * * * * * * * * * * * * P  L  O  T  * * * * * * * * * * * * * * * *
                    PLOT OF SPEDUC WITH EDUC
      +----+----+----+----+----+----+----+----+----+----+----++
H   20 +                                          1      1       +
I      |                                                         |
G      |                                 1          1            |
H      |                                                         |
E      |                                          2    2  1 1    |
S 17.5 +                                                         +
T      |                   1 1                     1  1          |
       |                                                         |
Y      |                       1        2  2       4  1          |
E      |                                                         |
A   15 +                                1          1             +
R      |                                                         |
       |                                5  1 4  1 2         1     |
S      |                                                         |
C      |                                6  1    1 1            |
H 12.5 +                                                         +
O      |                   1  4 1   1 H  3 6     3    1          |
O      |                                                         |
L      |                     1 1  1 2     1 1                   |
       |                                                         |
C   10 +                       1  2 3    1                       +
O      |                                                         |
M      |                       1    2                            |
P      |                                                         |
L      |             1         1 1  2 1  1                       |
E  7.5 +                                                         +
T      |                                                         |
E      |                                                         |
D      |                             1                           |
       |                                                         |
    5  +             1                                           +
S      |                                                         |
P      |                                                         |
O      |                                                         |
U      |             1                                           |
S  2.5 +                                                         +
E      |                         1                               |
       |                                                         |
       |                                                         |
       |                                                         |
    0  +                                                         +
      +----+----+----+----+----+----+----+----+----+----+----++
           0         4         8        12        16        20
              HIGHEST  YEAR  OF  SCHOOL  COMPLETED
```

    114 CASES PLOTTED.

Figure 18.8 PLOT between SPEDUC and EDUC after a 15 percent sample is drawn.

Table 18.1   SELECTED SUBCOMMANDS AVAILABLE FOR THE PLOT PROCEDURE

Subcommand	Option	Description
MISSING	PLOTWISE	Excludes missing data pairwise from plot (default)
MISSING	LISTWISE	Excludes missing values listwise from plot
MISSING	INCLUDE	Includes user-defined missing data (not SYSMIS) on plot
TITLE	'.....'	Uses description between single quote marks as a title for the plot
VERTICAL	REFERENCE (n)	Draws references lines at points identified in parentheses
VERTICAL	STANDARDIZE	Plots standardized versions of the variables
VERTICAL	'.....'	Uses description between single quote marks for axis label; default is variable's predefined label
HORIZONTAL	----	Same options as for VERTICAL
FORMAT	DEFAULT	Bivariate plot between two variables (default)
FORMAT	REGRESSION	Calculates regression statistics and identifies where the regression line crosses each axis
HSIZE	= n	The number sets the horizontal width of the plot.
VSIZE	= n	The number sets the vertical height of the plot.

computer system being used. The size of the printed plot can also be adjusted with the **HSIZE** and **VSIZE** subcommands. Each subcommand is followed by an equals sign and then a number identifying the horizontal or vertical dimensions of the plot we desire. The command sequence

```
PLOT  / HSIZE = 42  /  VSIZE = 21  /PLOT SPEDUC WITH EDUC
```

will produce a much smaller plot (illustrated in Figure 18.9) than the ones examined earlier.

Note that the horizontal size is larger than the vertical size in the command sequence above. This is because horizontal spaces on a printer are smaller than vertical ones. Look at any letter printed on this page and you will notice that character widths are typically smaller than character heights. A 20 by 20 plot appears not as a square, but as a rectangle, since vertical spaces are larger than horizontal spaces. A good rule of thumb, followed in Figure 18.9, is to make a plot's vertical size about one-half of its horizontal size.

The sizes specified with the HSIZE and VSIZE subcommands refer to the number of spaces that will appear on each axis. These sizes do not include the axes themselves or the axis numbers or titles. You can use the HSIZE and VSIZE subcommands to produce plots of any size, but the horizontal width of the graph should leave at least 15 spaces available for these descriptive items and the vertical height should leave 20 lines. This is a concern only if we want to make the graph larger than the default size. Another concern is to avoid reducing either axis to a size smaller than the number of values existing on a variable. If, for example, we change the vertical height to 15, SPSS will have to

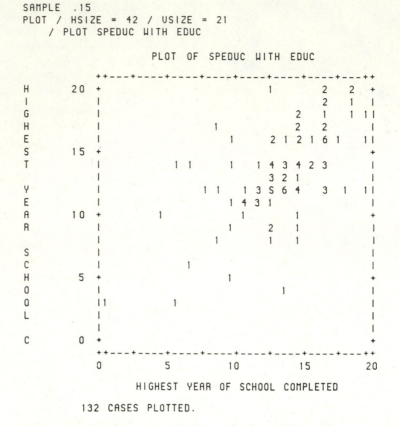

Figure 18.9 Condensing a PLOT with the HSIZE and VSIZE subcommands.

combine some of the 21 values on the SPEDUC variable in order to print them in the 15 spaces available. This undermines what we did with the SAMPLE command, which was to try to achieve a balance between the number of plottable points and the number of cases to be plotted.

Reference Lines

Sometimes there are some critical "break points" in the data that we wish to visually emphasize. Say we are examining the relationship between the Bush and Dukakis feeling thermometers. We suspect that most people behave in a highly partisan manner; those favorable to Bush are hostile to Dukakis and vice versa. When we examine this relationship visually on a scatterplot, the critical values of each variable are the neutral points, 50. Our belief is that those above 50 on one feeling thermometer are below 50 on the other. To highlight these critical values, SPSS allows us to draw **reference lines** on a plot, lines bisecting the graph to separate the points above or below a given value.

Reference lines are created with the **HORIZONTAL** and **VERTICAL** sub-commands. Each subcommand has a number of options, shown in Table 18.1. To create reference lines, we use the **REFERENCE (n)** option for each subcommand. The (n) identifies one or more values of the variable where SPSS should add reference lines. The command-subcommand combination

```
PLOT /HSIZE = 50 / VSIZE = 25 /VERTICAL REFERENCE (50)
      / HORIZONTAL REFERENCE (50) /PLOT V5 WITH V6
```

will produce a plot with reference lines at the neutral values of each variable. If you wish more than one reference line per axis, you can include two or more numbers between the parentheses, separating them with a comma or space. The option REFERENCE (30,60) adds two reference lines to the vertical or horizontal axis.

You may have noticed that we seemed to have violated our own dictum with the above command, reducing the plot size with HSIZE and VSIZE below the number of values contained in the variables. This is not exactly the case. While V5 and V6 each have 101 (0 to 100) *theoretically* possible values, most respondents tend to answer these questions in round numbers such as multiples of 5 or 10. Thus each variable contains only 25 to 30 values actually selected by respondents, not the 101 values theoretically possible.

The plot with reference lines added is shown in Figure 18.10. The lines allow us to quickly pick out certain value combinations and thus examine our expectation that most cases will group in the upper left and lower right quadrants, quadrants representing high values on one variable and low values on the other. Our expectation is somewhat confirmed, although not completely so. A number of respondents do appear to be acting in a highly partisan manner; having warm feelings toward one candidate is connected with cool feelings toward the other. Nonetheless, a substantial number of cases also appear in the upper right quadrant, representing favorable feelings toward both candidates. In addition, despite the commonly heard complaint during elections that neither candidate is worth voting for, there are almost no cases in the lower left quadrant, representing negative feelings toward both candidates.

A simple correlation between the feeling thermometers shows a sizable negative relationship ($-.3831$, $p = .000$), supporting our suspicion of a highly partisan electorate. Examining a scatterplot, however, adds depth when we are interpreting the relationship. Some respondents are quite partisan, but many others like both candidates and very few dislike both. People in the United States seem both less partisan and more content with their candidates than we might believe from listening to the heated rhetoric during campaigns.

Regression Lines

When discussing the CORRELATION and PARTIAL CORR procedures earlier, we repeatedly mentioned the linear assumption made by the Pearson correlation statistic. Pearson's *r* assumes that a line reasonably summarizes the relationship between two variables, but neither of the above procedures identifies

```
TEMPORARY
SAMPLE  .05
PLOT /HSIZE = 50 / VSIZE = 25   /VERTICAL REFERENCE (50)
       / HORIZONTAL REFERENCE (50)   /PLOT V5 WITH V6

                          PLOT OF V5 WITH V6

               ++---+----+----+----+----+----+----+----+----+--++
       F   100 +2      1                3                      +
       E       I                        I                      I
       E       I            1           I  1                   I
       L       I                        I                      I
       I       I           1   1     3  3    1    2       4   1 I
       N    80 +                         I                      +
       G       I              1          I                      I
               I           1          2  I  3            3      I
       T       I                         I                      I
       H       I                         I                1    I
       E    60 +           1           1  1    4    1       5   1+
       R       I                     1   I                      I
       M       +----------------------- 7----1----2-------1---- 4+
       O       I                         I                      I
       M       I                         I                      I
       E    40 +                 1     3  3    2  1              +
       T       I                         I                      I
       E       I                         1                2    I
       R       I                         I                      I
               I                         I                      I
       -    20 +                         I                      +
               I                         I                      I
       B       I                         I      1            1 I
       U       I                         I                      I
       S       I                         I                      I
       H     0 +1                      3  1         1  1       4 +
               ++---+----+----+----+----+----+----+----+----+--++
               0        20        40        60        80       100

                      FEELING THERMOMETER - DUKAKIS

           94 CASES PLOTTED.
```

Figure 18.10 PLOT with reference lines added.

what that line is. Correlation lines are called **regression lines** which the PLOT procedure can calculate and print. The **FORMAT** subcommand with the **REGRESSION** option instructs SPSS to do this. The command

```
PLOT /HSIZE = 42 /VSIZE = 21 /FORMAT = REGRESSION
     / PLOT SPEDUC WITH EDUC
```

produces the output shown in Figure 18.11.

Computer printers can create horizontal and vertical lines without a problem, but many are unable to create diagonal lines. Consequently, SPSS makes no attempt to actually draw the regression line. Instead, it places the letter **R** on an axis to show where the regression line crosses it, at 5 on the left axis and 18 on the right one. With this information it is a simple task to draw in the line

```
TEMPORARY
SAMPLE .15
PLOT / HSIZE = 42 / VSIZE = 21  /FORMAT = REGRESSION
     / PLOT SPEDUC WITH EDUC
```

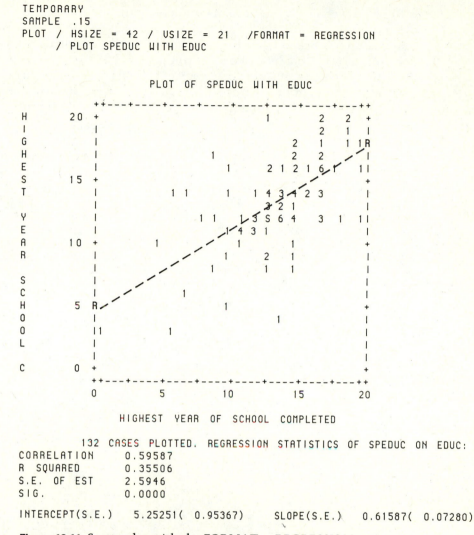

```
            PLOT OF SPEDUC WITH EDUC
```

Figure 18.11 Scatterplot with the FORMAT = REGRESSION option.

```
        132 CASES PLOTTED. REGRESSION STATISTICS OF SPEDUC ON EDUC:
CORRELATION      0.59587
R SQUARED        0.35506
S.E. OF EST      2.5946
SIG.             0.0000

INTERCEPT(S.E.)   5.25251( 0.95367)    SLOPE(S.E.)   0.61587( 0.07280)
```

ourselves, as has been done in Figure 18.11. At the bottom of Figure 18.11 are the regression statistics that SPSS uses to create the regression line. We bypass these for now because in Chapters 19 and 20 we review regression analysis in detail, including the meaning of these statistics and how the lines are created.

Control Variables

We may wish to examine the impact of a third variable on the two being plotted. For example, the historical tendency in this country is for males to have higher levels of education than their spouses. Is this what is happening with our plots of SPEDUC versus EDUC? If so, respondents in the upper left quadrant (spouse has more education) should be females and those in the lower right quadrant (respondent has higher education than spouse) should be males. This expectation can be evaluated by using a **control plot**.

SPSS allows one, and only one, control variable to be included on the PLOT subcommand. As in other procedures, the control variable is added after the PLOT list and separated from it with the BY keyword. The command sequence

PLOT /HSIZE = 42 /VSIZE = 21 / PLOT SPEDUC WITH EDUC **BY SEX**

produces the output shown in Figure 18.12. The scatterplot in Figure 18.12 is basically the same as the others we have examined except that the symbols used are different. As explained by the legend at the bottom of the plot, the symbol M is used for points occupied by male respondents, the symbol F is for points

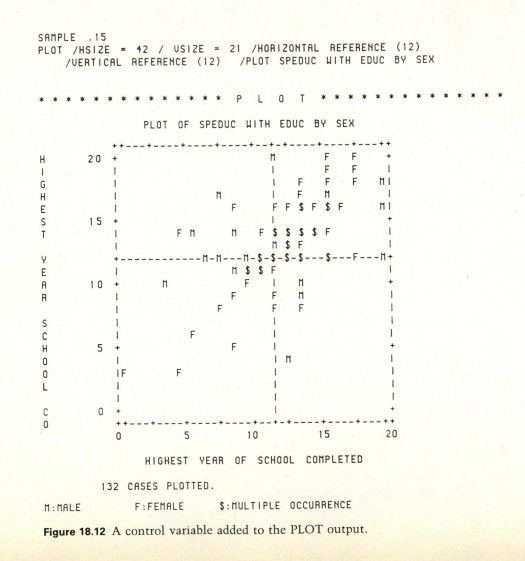

Figure 18.12 A control variable added to the PLOT output.

occupied by females, and the dollar sign ($) is for any plot location shared by respondents of both sexes. In producing these symbols, SPSS uses the first letter of the value label associated with each value of the control variable (1 = **M**ale, 2 = **F**emale). If you control for a variable for which some of the value labels start with the same letter, such as WRKSTAT (1 = **W**orking full-time, 2 = **W**orking part-time), you will not be able to distinguish between these control variable values; a W will represent each. To correct such a situation, change the value labels of the control variable so that each label starts with a different letter. If we look at the letters in the plot of Figure 18.12, our expectation does not seem to be borne out. The upper left and lower right quadrants appear to be occupied by equal numbers of both male and female respondents.

Adding control variables to the PLOT subcommand is satisfactory in some cases, but not all. First, this tactic allows you to control for only one variable at a time, and there may be occasions when you want to control for more than one, say, both gender and age. Second, control plots are not always easily interpreted. You have to search for the symbols representing different values of the control variable and attempt to perceive whatever pattern may exist.

A second way of introducing a control variable into a plot is by use of the SELECT IF command, producing separate plots for each value of the control variable. We might select just older and then younger respondents, plotting the relationship separately for each age group. The SELECT IF command also allows us to control for two or more variables simultaneously, say, selecting both young and female respondents (SELECT IF AGE LE 35 AND SEX EQ 2). When using SELECT IF, however, you will need to adjust the SAMPLE command since the SELECT IF command will also eliminate some cases from the analysis. A 15 percent sample of just younger females will be a considerably smaller number of cases than a 15 percent sample drawn from the entire data set, and the percentage of the sample will need to be increased proportionally to compensate for the decrease in cases produced by SELECT IF.

Introducing a control variable into a scatterplot is not simple, but it can be done. Both approaches described above work well, and the selection of one strategy over another depends on the specific circumstances of the analysis you want to perform. They can even be used together, by using SELECT IF to isolate younger respondents and then adding SEX as a control variable on the PLOT subcommand.

SUMMARY

Statistics are exact measures of the statistical significance and substantive strength of a relationship. It is often useful, however, to see a relationship as well as measure it. The PLOT command draws such a picture. It does not calculate any statistics, and consequently it makes no assumptions about the data. However, for reasonably interpretable graphics, two conditions should be met. First, the independent and dependent variables should be interval. Scatterplots show trends, and trends are characteristics of interval variables. Second, each variable in the plot must contain a large number of actual values. The party identification and liberalism-conservatism scales may both be considered interval, but each has only 7 response categories. Consequently, any plot between them will contain only 49 plottable locations. It will be difficult to see any trend from so few plot locations unless we reduce the sample size to an unacceptably small number of cases, somewhere around 20 or 25. When these conditions are met, a scatterplot can be an eminently useful aid to understanding the relationship between variables.

An added value of displaying a relationship via a scatterplot is that we can check on the linear assumption made by correlation analysis. The lack of clear patterns in a scatterplot does not mean that the linear assumption is wrong; it may be merely a weak relationship that can still be summarized with a line even when points are spread all over the plot. Scatterplots are used more for negative checks on the linear assumption than positive ones. If the scatterplot clearly shows that a curve better represents a relationship, then the linear assumption becomes untenable. If there is not strong evidence of a curve, then the linear assumption is probably reasonable.

In Chapters 19 and 20 we expand on the use of lines to analyze relationships. We examine the REGRESSION procedure, a procedure that creates lines to represent bivariate and multivariate relationships.

REVIEW

Key Terms

Scatterplot	HORIZONTAL
PLOT subcommand	VERTICAL
WITH keyword	REFERENCE (n)
Expected value	Regression lines
HSIZE	FORMAT
VSIZE	REGRESSION
Reference lines	Control plot

Exercises

18.1 Correct any errors in the command statements.
   a. PLOT V5 V6 V7
   b. PLOT V5 V6 WITH V7
   c. PLOT /VSIZE = 30 /PLOT V5 V6
   d. PLOT /VSIZE = 30 /HSIZE = 60 /PLOT V5 WITH V6
   e. PLOT /VSIZE = 30 /HSIZE = 60 /HORIZONTAL REFERENCE (50)
   f. PLOT /HORIZONTAL REFERENCE (50) /VERTICAL REFERENCE (50)
        /PLOT V5 WITH V6
   g. PLOT /HSIZE = 40 /HORIZONTAL REFERENCE (50) /PLOT V5 V6
   h. PLOT /HSIZE = 40 /VSIZE = 20 /PLOT EDUC WITH RINCOME
   i. PLOT /HORIZONTAL (12) /PLOT RINCOME EDUC

j. PLOT /VSIZE 40 /HSIZE 20 /PLOT RINCOME WITH EDUC
k. PLOT /PLOT RINCOME WITH EDUC /FORMAT = REGRESSION
l. PLOT /FORMAT = REGRESSION /VSIZE = 30 /PLOT RINCOME EDUC
m. PLOT /PLOT HAPPY WITH RINCOME
n. PLOT /HAPPY WITH RINCOME BY SEX
o. PLOT /PLOT RINCOME WITH EDUC BY SEX BY AGE
p. PLOT /PLOT RINCOME BY EDUC BY SEX

18.2 a. Create a scatterplot of the *wife's* educational level by that of her *husband*.
   b. Create scatterplots of the difference in evaluations of Bush and Dukakis by the respondents' income and education.

18.3 Below are age and income values for 20 respondents.

Case	Age	Income (in thousands)	Case	Age	Income (in thousands)
A	25	50	K	64	58
B	18	19	L	45	36
C	20	23	M	33	32
D	30	30	N	28	26
E	50	45	O	65	69
F	42	60	P	50	38
G	38	39	Q	30	48
H	60	58	R	26	52
I	34	29	S	35	30
J	21	34	T	47	38

a. If you were to plot these two variables, which would go on which axis?
b. Using graph paper or a graph you draw on plain paper, create a scatterplot between the variables. Is there a visible pattern?
c. Recode the two variables into 10-year age groups (10 to 19 = 1, 20 to 29 = 2, etc.) and $10,000 income groups ($10,000 to $19,000 = 1, and so on). Create a scatterplot between the recoded variables. Is the pattern still visible?
d. Recode the two variables into 20-year age groups (10 to 29 = 1, 30 to 49 = 2, etc.) and $20,000 income groups ($10,000 to $29,000 = 1, etc.). Plot the recoded variables. Is any pattern still visible?

SUGGESTED READINGS

Freedman, David, *et al. Statistics,* 2nd ed. (New York: W. W. Norton, 1991) Chapter 7.

Norusis, Marija J., and SPSS Inc. *SPSS/PC + V2.0 Base Manual* (Chicago: SPSS Inc., 1988) Chapter 12.

SPSS Inc. *SPSS Reference Guide* (Release 4) (Chicago: SPSS Inc., 1990) pages 523–28.

SPSS Inc. *SPSS-X User's Guide,* 3rd ed. (Chicago: SPSS Inc., 1988) Chapter 41.

Creating Lines with Simple Regression

We have talked a great deal in this book about prediction, predicting the dependent variable by knowing the independent variable. For nominal and ordinal variables we were able to provide some guidelines. Without any other information, the best prediction for a nominal variable is its mode. When adding the information from an independent variable, as in a contingency table, we switch our guessing strategy to the mode for each independent-variable group (contingency table column), and lambda tells us the proportional reduction of guessing error contributed by the independent variable. For ordinal variables, we compare pairs. If we know pair order on the independent variable, does that help in guessing which member of the pair is higher on the dependent variable? A statistic like gamma answers this question. A positive gamma tells us to guess that the same person is higher on both variables (concordant pairs predominate). A negative gamma indicates that discordant pairs are more common, and thus we guess that the person who is higher on the first variable is lower on the second.

For relationships between interval variables, we use the Pearson correlation as a measure of association, but this statistic does not provide an explicit guessing strategy. Pearson's r assumes that the relationship between two variables can be summarized with a line. The closer the points fit around the line, the closer the correlation coefficient is to $+1.0$ or -1.0. Squaring the correlation coefficient produces the coefficient of determination, a PRE measure when the line is used as a guessing strategy. In this respect, Pearson's r is similar to other PRE measures such as lambda or gamma, but there is one major difference. The

Pearson correlation never tells us what line to use for a guessing strategy. A correlation of .60 between income and age is quite strong, and its squared coefficient of determination indicates a 36 percent reduction of guessing error when we know a person's age before guessing her or his income. However, if we choose a respondent at random and discover her age to be 42, what do we guess her income is? The Pearson correlation does not give us the slightest clue. Somewhere out there is an imaginary line used by the correlation coefficient, but it is one we never see and thus cannot use as a guessing guide.

In this chapter we talk more about lines and linear relationships. We begin by reviewing the equation for a line and illustrating how that equation matches nicely with our understanding of variable relationships. We then turn to the procedure which uses the linear formula, REGRESSION, to both examine relationships and create explicit lines.

RELATIONSHIPS AND THE LINEAR FORMULA

The formula for a line is no mystery. It is

$$Y = a + bX$$

where Y is the dependent variable and X is the independent variable. When it is covered in high school mathematics, the formula is sometimes written as

$$Y = bX + a$$

or $Y = mX + b$

The formulas are all the same; they just use different symbols for the various parts. One term is multiplied by the X variable, b or m, and a second term is off by itself, a or b. We will use the symbols in the first formula listed, a and bX.

The meaning of the formula becomes clearer if we illustrate it on a graph, as in Figure 19.1. The Y and X axes are the values of the Y and X variables, respectively. The term multiplied by X, or b, is the **slope** of the line. The slope is the amount that the Y value changes for every unit change in X. Figure 19.1 contains segments drawn up to the line from values 1 and 2 on the X axis. Where these segments intercept the line, we draw corresponding segments over to the Y axis to discover the Y values for these points, which are 2 and 2.5, respectively. Thus, as X changes 1 unit, from 1 to 2, variable Y changes only $\frac{1}{2}$ unit, from 2 to 2.5. The slope of this line is .5, meaning that as X increases 1 unit, Y increases $\frac{1}{2}$ unit. What of a? The symbol a is called the **intercept** of the line, or the **constant**. This is the point at which the line crosses the Y axis, or the value of Y when X equals zero. When X equals zero, bX will also be zero, and we are left with $Y = a$, in this case, 1.5. Thus the formula for this line is

$$Y = \underset{a}{1.5} + \underset{b}{.5X}$$

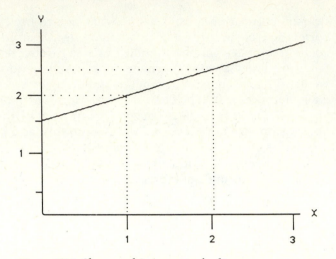

Figure 19.1 Slope and intercept of a line.

The linear formula nicely reflects the nature of relationships. To say that X is related to Y is to say that Y changes as X changes. The slope b is that change. For every 1-unit change in X, variable Y changes by an amount b: Y increases if b is positive and decreases if b is negative. Additionally, a slope of zero means there is no relationship between the variables; X can change an enormous amount, and Y is completely unaffected. The intercept a also has a real-world interpretation. Say we are examining income as the dependent variable and education as the independent variable. Furthermore, let us say that the line representing their relationship is Y (income in thousands) $= 12 + 1.5 * X$ (education in years). The slope, 1.5, tells us that each additional year of education adds, on average, $1500 to a person's income. However, when $X = 0$ (no formal education at all), a person's income will still average $12,000 per year. This makes sense, for we do not expect someone with no education to have absolutely no income—such a person can still get a job and have an income, just not a very large one. The intercept captures this notion—the average value of the dependent variable when the independent variable is zero.

The linear equation provides us with what is missing from other interval measures of association—an explicit predicted value of the dependent variable for each value of the independent variable. For example, if a respondent has 12 years of education, the linear formula above leads us to predict that person's income to be $30,000: $12 + 1.5 * 12 = 12 + 18 = 30$.

The predictive power of a linear equation is an exceptionally valuable characteristic. It enables us to go beyond our data and predict values of Y for some potential future value of X. Say a city budget director knows that her city's annual revenues are determined by the formula

Income (in millions) $= 1 + .05 *$ property value (in millions)

The intercept, 1, is the average income received from nontax sources, such as parking meters or traffic fines. The slope, .05, is the property tax rate, the percentage of the property value that its owners pay annually in taxes. Knowing this formula, the budget director can predict next year's revenues based on an educated guess about increases in city property values due to inflation, new buildings, or annexing an area into the city. In short, the linear model not only enables us to predict values of Y for current values of X, but also allows us to ask "what if" questions. If we increase or decrease X by a certain amount, how much will Y change?

So far we have discussed the linear formula, but we have not described where the numbers in the equation come from. To this point, we have just been picking numbers out of the air. We now need to determine what line best summarizes the relationships actually found in our data. Upon examining the linear equation

$$Y = a + b * X$$

you should realize that we already have information on two of the four symbols in the formula, Y and X. Variable Y is our dependent variable and X is the independent variable; both are present in our data set. What remains is to calculate estimates for the intercept a and the slope b.

There are many ways to draw a line through points on a scatterplot to summarize that relationship. We need a criterion for selecting one line over another. Since our emphasis is on prediction, the criterion followed by statisticians is to select the line that minimizes prediction error. Such a line is called the **least-squares line**. The logic of the least-squares approach was touched on briefly in Chapter 16, and we expand upon it here. The regression line constitutes our guessing strategy. We take the value on variable X for each respondent, plug it into the linear formula (say, $Y = 12 + 1.5 * X$), and carry out the calculations on the right side of the equals sign. The result is an estimate of Y for each respondent, our guess of that person's Y value. This mathematical process is identical to the graphical process illustrated in Figure 19.2. For a given value on the X axis, we draw one segment up to the regression line and then another segment from the line over to the Y axis. The point at which the latter segment crosses the Y axis constitutes our guess of Y, denoted Y_g, for any case with that X value.

The line represents the average relationship between X and Y. Unless the correlation between the variables is a perfect $+1.0$ or -1.0, most of the points on the scatterplot will not fit exactly on the line. The difference between an actual case value on variable Y and the value predicted by the line constitutes our guessing error, represented by

Error = actual Y − predicted Y

Some errors will be positive and others negative, depending on whether a respondent's actual Y value is above or below our guess; so we square each error to prevent the positive and negative errors from canceling. Thus our total

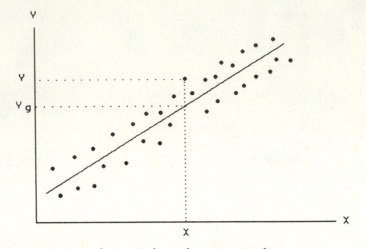

Figure 19.2 Predicting Y from the regression line.

amount of error, when using the line as our guess, for all the cases in the data set is

Total error = Σ (actual Y − predicted Y)^2

The least-squares strategy makes use of the total guessing error to create a line summarizing a relationship. Any number of different lines might reasonably be drawn through a scatterplot to represent a relationship. The least-squares criterion chooses the one specific line that produces a smaller total guessing error than any other possible line. Hence the name "least squares," the line producing the lowest sum of squared guessing errors.

Statisticians have determined how the least-squares line for any two-variable relationship (one independent, one dependent) can be identified. The slope b of the least-squares line is calculated with the formula

$$b = \frac{\Sigma(X - \overline{X})(Y - \overline{Y})}{\Sigma(X - \overline{X})^2}$$

or, written in deviation form,

$$b = \frac{\Sigma xy}{\Sigma x^2}$$

Once the slope has been identified, the intercept a can be calculated with the formula

$$a = \overline{Y} - b * \overline{X}$$

Or a is the mean of Y minus b times the mean of X. If you were to use any other line to summarize the same two-variable relationship—a different slope, a different intercept, or both—the sum of the squared guessing errors would be larger than that produced by the least-squares line.

THE REGRESSION PROCEDURE

We know from correlation calculations in earlier chapters that respondents' views about the need to increase or decrease defense spending affect their ratings of George Bush. What we do not know is by how much. What is the difference in evaluations of Bush between a respondent preferring a large decrease in defense spending and another respondent preferring a modest increase? This question asks about the slope of the linear relationship, the amount of change in V5 for every unit change in V27. To answer it, we calculate a regression line.

SPSS has a procedure, called REGRESSION, for calculating the slope and intercept of regression lines. The commands needed for the procedure are

```
REGRESSION VARIABLES = V5  V27
     /DEPENDENT = V5
     /METHOD = ENTER
```

We start with the command term REGRESSION, beginning in column 1 and followed by a list of the variables, both dependent and independent, to be analyzed. Following the variable list are two subcommands. We usually think of subcommands as adding optional features, but these two are required parts of the REGRESSION procedure. The first, **/DEPENDENT = ** V5, identifies to SPSS which variable on the list is the dependent one. Despite many similarities between regression statistics and correlation coefficients, REGRESSION is an asymmetric procedure. The slope and intercept in a two-variable relationship will differ depending on which variable is Y (dependent) and which is X (independent).

Second is the **/METHOD subcommand**. There are different ways to include independent variables in the REGRESSION procedure. Most are designed for advanced forms of analysis and need not concern us here. The simplest and most common way to treat independent variables is to enter all simultaneously into the calculations, although in this case there is only one, and that is accomplished with the **ENTER option** for the /METHOD subcommand. Because the ENTER option is so commonly used, SPSS allows you to skip the subcommand name when using this option and just use **/ENTER**. In this chapter, we follow the practice of using the full subcommand and option specification.

The format of the REGRESSION procedure looks complex, but the basic approach is actually simple. The REGRESSION command must be followed by the VARIABLES term and the list of independent and dependent variables. We then use the /DEPENDENT = subcommand to identify the dependent variable and the /METHOD = ENTER subcommand to enter the independent variable into the analysis.

The output from the procedure, shown in Figure 19.3, both looks complex and is complex. REGRESSION is the most powerful procedure examined so far. It can be used in many situations to answer a variety of questions, so the output contains an abundance of information. In this chapter, we discuss what is called **simple regression**. A simple regression contains only one independent variable, as opposed to multiple regression, the topic of Chapter 20, which uses more than one independent variable. For a simple regression, many of the statistics on the output are repetitive. We will examine them all nonetheless, both as a precursor to the next chapter and so nothing on the output remains mysterious to the reader.

The output in Figure 19.3 consists of three separate sections, each of which is identified separately in Figure 19.4. At the top is a **descriptive section** including a list of the dependent and independent variables, along with their labels, and the notation that listwise deletion of missing data is in effect. This section also talks about blocks or steps, which is the result of using the ENTER option on the METHOD subcommand, entering all independent variables as a block or in a single step. This top section is merely a reminder of how the procedure is being performed and is usually bypassed when the output is examined.

The middle part of the output contains statistics describing the *entire* regression equation $Y = a + b * X$. We will refer to this as the **model section** of the output because the regression equation is commonly referred to as a model. Models are discussed in more detail in Chapter 20. A dashed line with the title "Variables in the Equation" separates the middle from the bottom part of the output. The information below the dashed line analyzes the independent

```
REGRESSION  VARIABLES=V5 V27 /DEPENDENT =V5 /METHOD=ENTER


           * * * *   M U L T I P L E   R E G R E S S I O N   * * * *

LISTWISE  DELETION  OF  MISSING  DATA
EQUATION  NUMBER  1
DEPENDENT  VARIABLE..    V5     FEELING  THERMOMETER  -  BUSH

BEGINNING  BLOCK  NUMBER   1.   METHOD:   ENTER

VARIABLE(S)  ENTERED  ON  STEP  NUMBER
     1..     V27          DEFENSE  SPENDING  SCALE  -  RESP

MULTIPLE  R            0.34379
R  SQUARED            0.11819
ADJUSTED  R  SQUARED  0.11768
STANDARD  ERROR      26.08596

ANALYSIS  OF  VARIANCE
                DF         SUM  OF  SQUARES       MEAN  SQUARE
REGRESSION       1            157238.11651      157238.11651
RESIDUAL      1724           1173143.08685         680.47743
F  =   231.07029        SIGNIF  F  =   0.0000


-------------------- VARIABLES  IN  THE  EQUATION --------------------
VARIABLE         B            SE B          BETA         T       SIG T

V27          6.035908      0.397073      0.343788    15.201    0.0000
(CONSTANT)  36.976886      1.689945                  21.881    0.0000

END  BLOCK  NUMBER   1    ALL  REQUESTED  VARIABLES  ENTERED.
```

Figure 19.3 Output from the REGRESSION procedure.

```
* * * *   D E S C R I P T I V E   S E C T I O N   * * * *

LISTWISE DELETION OF MISSING DATA
EQUATION NUMBER 1
DEPENDENT VARIABLE..    V5    FEELING THERMOMETER - BUSH

BEGINNING BLOCK NUMBER  1.  METHOD:  ENTER

VARIABLE(S) ENTERED ON STEP NUMBER
   1..   V27        DEFENSE SPENDING SCALE - RESP


        * * * *   M O D E L   S E C T I O N   * * * *

MULTIPLE R            0.34379
R SQUARED             0.11819
ADJUSTED R SQUARED    0.11768
STANDARD ERROR        26.08596

ANALYSIS OF VARIANCE
                  DF       SUM OF SQUARES      MEAN SQUARE
REGRESSION         1          157238.11651    157238.11651
RESIDUAL        1724         1173143.08685       680.47743
F =   231.07029       SIGNIF F =  0.0000


* *   I N D E P E N D E N T   V A R I A B L E S   S E C T I O N   * *

------------------- VARIABLES IN THE EQUATION ---------------------
VARIABLE          B          SE B         BETA         T       SIG T

V27          6.035908     0.397073     0.343788    15.201     0.0000
(CONSTANT)  36.976886     1.689945                 21.881     0.0000

END BLOCK NUMBER  1    ALL REQUESTED VARIABLES ENTERED.
```

Figure 19.4 Three parts of the REGRESSION output.

variables and is thus referred to as the **variables section** of the output. The bottom two sections contain substantial amounts of information and deserve thorough reviews. We begin by discussing the variables section and then return to an examination of the model section.

VARIABLES SECTION

We are interested in estimating the linear equation $Y = a + b * X$, where Y and X are our dependent and independent variables, respectively. What needs to be calculated are the a and b terms. This is the information contained in the variables section of the printout. In this section there are six columns spread across the page. The first column, titled "Variables," is simply the name of the variable to which the statistics in that row apply. The second column, labeled "B," is the b statistic calculated for that variable, called the **b coefficient**.

Let us look at just these first two columns for a minute. The first item listed in column 1 is V27, the name of our independent variable. Looking over to column 2, we find the *b* coefficient calculated for the variable, 6.036. The second row down in column 1 contains the word "Constant." This is the intercept *a*. SPSS has calculated the value of the intercept in column 2 to be 36.977. With these two pieces of information, we can complete the estimate of the linear model

$$\frac{V5}{Y} = \frac{36.977}{a} + \frac{6.036}{b} * \frac{V27}{X}$$

Testing Hypotheses

The first two columns allow us to complete the linear formula, but there are other things that we want to know besides the calculated values of **a** and **b**. We noted earlier, for example, that if the *b* coefficient is different from zero, that indicates that a relationship exists between variables *X* and *Y*. Since the *b* coefficient in Figure 19.4 is different from zero, we are tempted to conclude that V5 and V27 are related.

Recall, however, that any hypothesis claiming a relationship between two variables refers to what is true for the population, not for a sample. That is, we are really interested in

$$Y = \alpha + \beta X$$

where **α** (alpha) and **β** (beta) are symbols for the population parameters. If our sample statistic *b* is different from zero, what does that tell us about the population parameter β?

Like all sample statistics, the *b* coefficient has a sampling distribution. Statisticians have determined that the sampling distribution of the *b* coefficient is the same as that for the mean or Pearson's *r*, a *t* distribution. Thus, if we were to take an infinite number of samples from the same population, 95 percent of all the sample *b* values would be within plus or minus 1.96 standard errors of the population β. SPSS uses this knowledge to test the null hypothesis of no relationship in the population.

The test is the same as that performed by the T-TEST procedure, although with different symbols:

$$t = \frac{b_s - \beta_0}{\text{se}_b}$$

where b_s = *b* calculated from our sample
    β_0 = claim of null hypothesis that population β is zero
    se_b = standard error of sampling distribution for *b*

This formula will tell us how large a difference in *t* (standard-error) units exists between our sample statistic and the claim of the null hypothesis. If this difference is less than 1.96 *t* units, it is quite possible that our sample *b* came from a population for which the null hypothesis is true. If the t distance is greater than 1.96, there is a less than a 5 percent probability that the null hypothesis is an accurate description of the population.

In the variables section of the output, columns 2 and 3 provide the information needed to carry out this test, and columns 5 and 6 are the results when SPSS conducts the test for us (for the moment, we skip over column 4). Column 2 contains the sample b coefficient, and column 3 is the standard error of the sampling distribution for this coefficient. Since the null hypothesis contends that the population β is zero, we can complete the t formula as follows:

$$t = \frac{b_s - \beta_0}{se_b} = \frac{6.035908 - 0}{.397073} = \frac{6.035908}{.397073} = 15.201$$

Our sample b is 15.201 t units away from zero, a very unlikely sample result if the population β is actually zero.

We do not need to personally perform this hypothesis test. SPSS does it for us and produces the results in column 5, labeled "T," which contains the same t value calculated above. In column 6, "SIG T," SPSS determines the probability of finding this large a t value when the null hypothesis is true. This probability is zero to at least four decimal places, or less than .00005. Although columns 3 and 5 provide information on how SPSS tests the null hypothesis, standard practice is to jump straight to column 6. If the probability that the null hypothesis is true is below .05, we reject it; otherwise we decide the evidence is too weak to reject the null hypothesis.

Observe that SPSS carries out the same exercise—testing statistical significance—on the constant as well. In rare cases this may be of importance, but for the most part we are not interested in this test. It only tells us the probability that α is different from zero, but seldom do we state a hypothesis about the constant, the average value of Y when X is zero. Consequently, it is common practice to just accept the calculated sample a as part of the linear formula without testing its statistical significance.

Beta Coefficient

The b coefficient has a variety of applications. Not only can we use it to test the null hypothesis, but also it has a very straightforward interpretation; it is the average change in the dependent variable for every unit change on the independent variable. Respondents with the lowest defense spending preference (1 on V27, greatly decrease) give Bush an average evaluation on the feeling thermometer of

$$V5 = a + b * V27 = 36.977 + 6.036 * 1 = 36.977 + 6.036 = 43.013$$

Respondents one value higher on defense spending preferences (a 2 on V27) evaluate Bush on average at 49.049 on V5:

$$V5 = a + b * V27 = 36.977 + 6.036 * 2 = 36.977 + 12.072 = 49.049$$

Finally, respondents wanting the largest defense spending increase (7 on V27) evaluate Bush the highest:

$$V5 = a + b * V27 = 36.977 + 6.036 * 7 = 36.977 + 42.252 = 79.229$$

Despite its strengths, the b coefficient has one significant deficiency: It cannot be used to compare the substantive size of relationships. Consider Figure 19.5, the independent-variables sections of two regression analyses. The respondent's income is the dependent variable in both analyses, but the independent variables differ. In the top output, the independent variable is RACE, recoded into a white-nonwhite dichotomy so that it can be used as an interval variable. The b coefficient is $-.867$, or a decline of nearly a full unit of income as we move from white to nonwhite respondents (moving from code number 1 to 2 on RACE). In the bottom output, the independent variable is EDUC, with a b coefficient of .629, an increase of slightly over half a step in income for every additional year of education.

If we looked at the b coefficients alone, we might be led to conclude that race, with the larger (farther from zero) coefficient, has a stronger connection to income than education does. However, when we think of unit changes in the

```
RECODE RACE (3=2)
REGRESSION VARIABLES=RINCOME RACE /DEPENDENT =RINCOME /METHOD=ENTER

     * * * *    M U L T I P L E    R E G R E S S I O N    * * * *

EQUATION NUMBER 1      DEPENDENT VARIABLE..    RINCOME
RESPONDENT'S INCOME

-------------------- VARIABLES IN THE EQUATION --------------------
VARIABLE          B              SE B            BETA          T      SIG T

RACE          -0.866767       0.445648        -0.063210     -1.945   0.0521
(CONSTANT)    11.885973       0.549546                       21.629   0.0000

END BLOCK NUMBER    1    ALL REQUESTED VARIABLES ENTERED.



REGRESSION VARIABLES=RINCOME EDUC /DEPENDENT=RINCOME /METHOD=ENTER

     * * * *    M U L T I P L E    R E G R E S S I O N    * * * *

EQUATION NUMBER 1      DEPENDENT VARIABLE..    RINCOME
RESPONDENT'S INCOME

-------------------- VARIABLES IN THE EQUATION --------------------
VARIABLE          B              SE B            BETA          T      SIG T

EDUC          0.629353        0.055428        0.346802      11.354   0.0000
(CONSTANT)    2.548000        0.749795                       3.398   0.0007

END BLOCK NUMBER    1    ALL REQUESTED VARIABLES ENTERED.
```

Figure 19.5 Regression analyses of RACE and EDUC with RINCOME.

independent variable, we have to remember how many unit changes are possible. Race has only two possible values: 1 for whites and 2 for nonwhites. Consequently, the biggest impact that race can have on respondents' income is a change of only .867 unit, as we change from respondents of race 1 to race 2 or vice versa. In contrast, education has a smaller b coefficient of .629, but a larger range of values, from 0 to 20. With so many different values on this variable, the most educated person will be 12.58 points higher (20 $*$ .629 = 12.58) in income than the least educated (0 $*$ .629 = 0). In short, the b coefficient for race is larger, but education can produce a greater overall change in income.

Since the comparison problem is due to the fact that variables have different value ranges, the solution is to transform the measuring scales so that each variable has a similar value range. This is done by using **standardized variables**. The formula for standardizing a variable is

$$Y^* = \frac{Y - \bar{Y}}{S_Y}$$

where Y^* = symbol for Y variable in standardized format
  Y = original value of variable Y for any case
  $\bar{Y}$ = mean of Y
  S_Y = standard deviation of Y

The standardizing process first identifies for a case the deviation above or below the mean of the variable ($Y - \bar{Y}$) and then transforms that distance to standard deviation units (divides by S_Y). As in other transformations discussed earlier, this change does not affect what the variable measures; it just modifies the scale used for the measurement. Instead of a raw score of, say, 45 on the Bush feeling thermometer, a standardized format of the variable might represent that score as a value of 1 standard deviation below the mean. Variables in standardized format have two valuable characteristics: Their means are always 0, and their variances are always 1. Consequently, standardized format eliminates the problem of variables having different value ranges.

Once the independent and dependent variables have been standardized, a new linear equation can be estimated:

$$Y^* = b * X^*$$

Note that this linear equation does not include the intercept symbol a. Recall that a is calculated with the formula

$$a = \bar{Y} - b * \bar{X}$$

When variables are standardized, their means are always zero and thus the formula for the intercept will always be zero.

When standardized versions of the X and Y variables are used, the b coefficient of the equation is called the **beta coefficient**. It is not actually necessary to reestimate the linear equation to calculate beta since it represents the same X-Y relationship as b but merely with a different measuring scale applied to the variables. The beta coefficient can be calculated directly from the *b* coefficient with the formula

$$\text{Beta} = b * \frac{S_X}{S_Y}$$

Multiply *b* by the standard deviation of *X* divided by the standard deviation of *Y*.

Readers need to be aware that the beta coefficient is not the same as β. The Greek symbol β refers to a population parameter, the slope between X and Y in the population. The *beta coefficient* is a statistic calculated from a sample where the variables have been standardized. In this text, whenever we spell out beta, it refers to the beta coefficient calculated from a sample. The population parameter will be referred to with the β symbol or the added description, "population beta."

The beta coefficient is contained in column 4 of the variables section of the output. Since standardized variables have exactly the same variance, 1, any difference in the size of the beta coefficients between two independent variables is due to the strength of the *X-Y* relationship, not to different ranges of the two *X* variables. In fact, for simple regression, the beta coefficient is identical to the zero-order Pearson correlation coefficient between *X* and *Y*. Beta always ranges between +1.0 and −1.0, and its distance from zero reflects the strength of the relationship. Also observe that column 4 does not contain a beta term for the constant since, as shown above, this will always be zero when standardized variables are used.

Using *b* Versus Beta

With two different measures of the relationship, *b* and beta, which do you use? The choice, as always, depends on the question you are trying to answer. Usually the *b* coefficient is preferred. First, hypothesis tests that are conducted use *b*, not beta. The two statistics are merely mathematical transformations of each other, but the standard error reported on the SPSS output is for the *b* coefficient, not beta. Second, *b* has a direct interpretation: the amount of change in *Y* for every unit change in *X*. The interpretation of beta is similar, but only for standardized versions of the variables—the change in the standardized value of *Y* for every 1-standard-deviation change in the standardized value of *X*—a far more cumbersome interpretation.

Beta is necessary if you want to compare the substantive strength of the relationships between the dependent variable and two or more independent variables. In Figure 19.5, the *b* value for RACE was larger than *b* for EDUC, but the betas are the opposite, .347 for EDUC versus only −.063 for RACE. Consequently, educational differences have a stronger impact on income than racial differences do.

MODEL SECTION

The model section of the output examines the entire regression model, the equation $Y = a + bX$. The statistics in this section are often called **goodness-of-fit statistics**, for their primary purpose is to test how well the model fits the data. Our model says $V5 = a + b * V27$, so we can predict ratings that respondents give to George Bush by looking at respondents' positions on the defense spending scale. How well does this model work, or how accurately can we predict V5 with the calculated equation $V5 = 36.977 + 6.036 * V27$?

Observe that this is a very different question from our examination of the null hypothesis. If, in the variables section, the significance value for the b coefficient leads us to reject the null hypothesis, then we can conclude that X is related to Y; so V27 does help in predicting V5. However, this does not tell us how much V27 aids in predicting V5. Have we reduced our guessing error (increased our guessing accuracy) by only a small amount or by a large amount? The independent variables section does not tell us this, but the model section does.

With a simple regression analysis, the model section is not especially crucial, for its statistics tend to duplicate information available in the variables section. The model statistics are more important in multiple regression analysis. Nonetheless, the model statistics do provide a different perspective on the results even in the simple regression case and thus deserve some attention.

Predicted Y

A value of REGRESSION over CORRELATION is that the regression equation provides predicted values of Y. How well does it perform its predictive function? A direct evaluation of this question can be provided by calculating a predicted Y value for each case in the data set and comparing that value to each respondent's actual value on the Y variable. A special symbol is used for Y values predicted by the regression equation, $\hat{Y}$, rather mundanely called **Y-HAT** since the small symbol on top of the Y looks like a hat. We can create a Y-HAT variable containing the predicted Y for each case with the command

```
COMPUTE  YHAT =  36.977 + 6.036 * V27
```

The numbers in the COMPUTE statement come directly from the REGRESSION output, the intercept (36.977) plus the b coefficient times the independent variable (6.036 * V27).

How well do the Y-HAT values produced by the regression equation match the actual value on the Y variable for each case? Answering this question is quite simple; we just calculate a Pearson correlation between Y and $\hat{Y}$, the actual Y values and the predicted Y values. The substantive size of this correlation coefficient will tell us how closely the Y and $\hat{Y}$ variables correspond.

Multiple *R*

Comparing the predicted *Y* to the actual *Y* is the basis of the model section. SPSS does not display the $\hat{Y}$ variable, but does calculate it internally to produce the statistics in the model section. The first statistic reported in this section (see Figure 19.4) is entitled **multiple R**. This statistic, often represented by just the capital letter ***R***, is the analysis mentioned in the paragraph above, the Pearson correlation between *Y* and $\hat{Y}$. The size of this correlation, .344, shows there is a sizable, but far from perfect, match between the predictions of the regression model and the dependent variable.

In the simple regression case, the multiple *R* will be the same number as you would obtain if you calculated a Pearson correlation coefficient between the dependent and independent variables, V5 and V27. Remember, the Pearson correlation statistic is based on drawing a line to summarize a two-variable relationship, but the CORRELATION procedure does not tell you what that line is. The REGRESSION procedure produces the formula for the line, the same line as that used by CORRELATION, so the resulting statistics will be identical. With a simple regression the beta coefficient in the variables section is also identical to the zero-order correlation between the independent and dependent variables, so it will also match the multiple *R*. There is one difference between the multiple *R* and either beta or the correlation coefficient: The sign of the multiple *R* is always positive. The signs of the *b* and beta coefficients in the variables section tell us whether the relationship is positive or negative, but the model section only evaluates prediction accuracy, not the direction of the prediction.

R Square

The second term in the model section is entitled ***R* square**, symbolized as R^2. As its name implies, this is nothing more than the squared value of the multiple *R*. Why square the multiple *R*? Recall our discussion of Pearson correlation coefficients a few chapters ago. The Pearson correlation is a PRE measure, but not a direct one. If you square the correlation coefficient, you obtain the coefficient of determination, which has a direct PRE interpretation. The coefficient of determination is the amount of error reduction obtained when the correlation line is used to guess *Y*, as opposed to always guessing the mean of *Y*. Another interpretation of the coefficient of determination is as the explained variance of the dependent variable, the proportion of variance in *Y* explained (accurately predicted) by its relationship with *X*. The R^2 is the coefficient of determination (although *R* square is the more common term) for the entire regression model, the extent to which the model explains the dependent variable. In this case, 12 percent of the variance in respondents' ratings of George Bush can be attributed to the respondents' different defense spending preferences.

The R^2 is the most common, and in many cases the only, statistic used from the model section of the REGRESSION output. The variables sections allows us to test the null hypothesis (SIG T), determine the direction of a relationship (the sign of b or beta) and the strength of the relationship (beta), and compute a predicted value for Y (b and constant). The R^2 tells us how good a prediction this is—our reduction of error when we use Y instead of $\bar{Y}$ for our prediction. There is also an adjusted R^2 statistic which is a slight modification of R^2. This statistic is not important for a simple regression, and it is discussed fully in Chapter 20.

Standard Error

Another statistic calculated is the **standard error of regression**, a goodness-of-fit indicator for the accuracy of the regression prediction. The prediction error for each case can be identified with the formula

$$\text{Error} = Y - \hat{Y}$$

The distance between the actual case value on Y and the value predicted by the linear equation is the error. Errors will be negative if our prediction is too high and positive if it is too low. If we were to graph a distribution of these errors, it would look something like Figure 19.6; a number of errors are close to zero (high prediction accuracy), but some cases spread out toward the positive or negative extremes (high prediction error). The standard error of the regression is the standard deviation of this distribution of errors.

We can use the standard error as an estimate of prediction accuracy much as we did when creating a confidence interval for the mean. About 68 percent of all the cases will have predicted Y values within plus or minus 1 standard error of the actual Y values (plus or minus 26.086), and 95 percent of the predicted Y values will be within plus or minus 1.96 standard errors (± 51.129) of the actual Y values. This is a fairly large range of prediction error, but then again our R^2 was only .12, meaning that 88 percent of the variation in Y remains unexplained by its linear relationship with X.

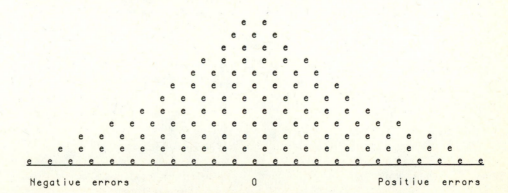

Negative errors   0   Positive errors

Figure 19.6 A distribution of the prediction errors.

ANOVA

The final part of the model section is an analysis-of-variance test. The dependent variable for this test is the same as the dependent variable for the regression equation, Y. The independent variable is $\hat{Y}$, the predicted value of Y. This test allows us to determine whether Y-HAT is related to Y at a statistically significant level, the significance level of the F ratio. The ANOVA test is not discussed further here because it is a seldom-used part of the model statistics and because you can explore it further by referring to the analysis-of-variance discussion in Chapter 12.

SUBCOMMANDS

A partial listing of the subcommands available with the REGRESSION procedure is given in Table 19.1. Subcommands, beyond the required DEPENDENT and METHOD subcommands, are not a critical feature of this procedure. The

Table 19.1   SELECTED SUBCOMMANDS AVAILABLE WITH THE REGRESSION PROCEDURE

Subcommand	Option	Description
MISSING	INCLUDE	Includes user-defined missing data (not SYSMIS) in calculations
MISSING	PAIRWISE	Excludes missing data pairwise from calculations
MISSING	LISTWISE	Excludes missing data listwise from calculations (default)
VARIABLES	varlist	Lists dependent and independent variables to be used
VARIABLES	COLLECT	Creates variable list from variables mentioned on DEPENDENT and METHOD subcommands (default). *Note:* Useful only if METHOD subcommand contains a list of variables
METHOD	ENTER	Uses as independent variables all those on VARIABLES list not referred to on DEPENDENT subcommand
METHOD	ENTER varlist	Uses as independent variables those explicitly listed after ENTER keyword. In both uses, term METHOD may be omitted.
DEPENDENT	varlist	Uses variable(s) listed as dependent
STATISTICS	DEFAULTS	Beta, *b*, *t* test, multiple *R*, *R* square, and ANOVA table (default)
STATISTICS	ZPP	Zero-order, part, and partial correlations between variables
STATISTICS	CI	Prints 95 percent confidence intervals for *b* coefficients
STATISTICS	SES	Prints standard error for beta instead of *b*
DESCRIPTIVES	NONE	No descriptive statistics (default)
DESCRIPTIVES	CORR	Zero-order correlation matrix between variables
DESCRIPTIVES	SIG	One-tailed significance levels for correlation coefficients
DESCRIPTIVES	DEFAULTS	Means, standard deviations, and correlation matrix; default if DESCRIPTIVES subcommand is used without further options

default output already contains a substantial amount of detail and requires few modifications or additions. Two subcommands, DESCRIPTIVES and STATISTICS, add further material to the output and occasionally may be useful. When either is used, as in the PLOT procedure, it must come before the identification of the regression model—before the DEPENDENT and METHOD subcommands.

Descriptive Statistics

The **DESCRIPTIVES subcommand** adds descriptive information about the variables being used in the regression analysis. It has three standard options: DEFAULTS, CORR, and SIG. The **DEFAULTS option** calculates the mean and standard deviation for each variable on the VARIABLES = list. A table of zero-order correlations between the variables is also produced with this option. The modified output is shown in Figure 19.7.

There are some slight differences between the correlation matrix produced by the DESCRIPTIVES subcommand and one you would obtain from the CORRELATION procedure. The major difference is that the correlation matrix in Figure 19.7 uses listwise deletion of missing data, the system used by the REGRESSION procedure, instead of the pairwise deletion method used by the CORRELATION procedure. This ensures that the descriptive information and regression statistics are calculated from the same cases. Another difference is that the correlation matrix includes no significance calculation, just the correlations.

The second alternative for the DESCRIPTIVES subcommand is the **CORR option**. Using this option produces just the correlation matrix without the other descriptive information. The output is the same as that shown in Figure 19.7 except that for each variable the mean and standard deviation are not printed. Finally, there is the **SIG option**, which is used in conjunction with either the DEFAULTS or CORR option. Adding this option causes one-tailed significance levels to be included in the correlation matrix, as shown in Figure 19.8. Obviously, if you have not requested a correlation matrix with either CORR or DEFAULTS, there is no point in requesting significance levels with the SIG option.

Added Statistics

The DESCRIPTIVES subcommand adds information to the descriptive section of the output. In contrast, the **STATISTICS subcommand** adds statistics, sometimes the same as in the DESCRIPTIVES options, to the variables section of the output. The standard options with this subcommand are ZPP, CI, SES, and DEFAULTS.

The **ZPP option** requests zero-order, part, and partial correlations between the variables. As shown in Figure 19.9, the three correlations appear in the variables section of the output. The part and partial correlations are different methods for removing the impact of other variables from a two-variable corre-

```
REGRESSION VARIABLES = V5 V27    /DESCRIPTIVES DEFAULTS
   /DEPENDENT = V5   /METHOD = ENTER


         * * * *   M U L T I P L E   R E G R E S S I O N   * * * *

LISTWISE DELETION OF MISSING DATA

                 MEAN   STD DEV  LABEL
V5            60.827    27.771   FEELING  THERMOMETER  -  BUSH
V27            3.951     1.582   DEFENSE  SPENDING  SCALE  -  RESP

N  OF  CASES  =    1726

CORRELATION:
               V5          V27
V5           1.000        0.344
V27          0.344        1.000



         * * * *   M U L T I P L E   R E G R E S S I O N   * * * *

EQUATION NUMBER 1
DEPENDENT VARIABLE..    V5     FEELING THERMOMETER - BUSH

BEGINNING BLOCK NUMBER   1.   METHOD:   ENTER
VARIABLE(S) ENTERED ON STEP NUMBER
    1..    V27         DEFENSE SPENDING SCALE - RESP

MULTIPLE R            0.34379
R SQUARED            0.11819
ADJUSTED R SQUARED   0.11768
STANDARD ERROR       26.08596

ANALYSIS OF VARIANCE
                  DF      SUM OF SQUARES        MEAN SQUARE
REGRESSION         1         157238.11651       157238.11651
RESIDUAL        1724        1173143.08685          680.47743
F =      231.07029   SIGNIF F =   0.0000


-------------------- VARIABLES IN THE EQUATION --------------------
VARIABLE         B           SE B         BETA         T       SIG T

V27          6.035908      0.397073     0.343788     15.201    0.0000
(CONSTANT)  36.976886      1.689945                  21.881    0.0000

END BLOCK NUMBER    1    ALL REQUESTED VARIABLES ENTERED.
```

Figure 19.7 REGRESSION output with default statistics added to the descriptive section.

lation. Statisticians disagree over which method should be used to control for third variables, so SPSS provides both statistics, allowing the user to choose whichever is preferred. The part correlation is the same statistic as that produced by the PARTIAL CORR procedure. The partial correlation is a slightly different statistic which produces a result close to, but not exactly the same as, the part correlation. In Figure 19.9, of course, all three correlations are identical because only two variables are being analyzed and none are being controlled for.

```
REGRESSION VARIABLES = V5 V27    /DESCRIPTIVES CORR SIG
      /DEPENDENT = V5    /METHOD = ENTER


         * * * *   M U L T I P L E   R E G R E S S I O N   * * * *

LISTWISE DELETION OF MISSING DATA

N OF CASES =   1726

CORRELATION,   1-TAILED  SIG:

                V5          V27
V5            1.000       0.344
              0.999       0.000

V27           0.344       1.000
              0.000       0.999



         * * * *   M U L T I P L E   R E G R E S S I O N   * * * *

EQUATION NUMBER 1
DEPENDENT VARIABLE..    V5    FEELING THERMOMETER - BUSH

BEGINNING BLOCK NUMBER  1.   METHOD:   ENTER

VARIABLE(S) ENTERED ON STEP NUMBER
    1..     V27         DEFENSE SPENDING SCALE - RESP

MULTIPLE R         0.34379
R SQUARED          0.11819
ADJUSTED R SQUARED 0.11768
STANDARD ERROR     26.08596

ANALYSIS OF VARIANCE
                   DF         SUM OF SQUARES        MEAN SQUARE
REGRESSION          1          157238.11651      157238.11651
RESIDUAL         1724         1173143.08685         680.47743
F =    231.07029      SIGNIF F =  0.0000


-------------------- VARIABLES IN THE EQUATION --------------------
VARIABLE          B            SE B          BETA         T      SIG T

V27          6.035908      0.397073      0.343788     15.201    0.0000
(CONSTANT)  36.976886      1.689945                   21.881    0.0000

END BLOCK NUMBER    1    ALL REQUESTED VARIABLES ENTERED.
```

Figure 19.8 REGRESSION output with CORR and SIG options.

The **CI option** creates a confidence interval for the *a* and *b* coefficients. The default *t* test examines the null hypothesis only (the probability that the population parameters are zero). Instead of testing for what these parameters are *not*, sometimes we want to determine what they probably *are*. Just like a sample mean, the *a* and *b* coefficients are point estimates of the population parameters α and β, respectively. Each has the same type of sampling distribution as a mean,

```
REGRESSION VARIABLES = V5 V27    / STATISTICS DEFAULTS ZPP
    /DEPENDENT = V5 /ENTER


                * * * *  M U L T I P L E   R E G R E S S I O N  * * * *

LISTWISE DELETION OF MISSING DATA
EQUATION NUMBER 1      DEPENDENT VARIABLE..    V5    FEELING THERMOMETER - BUSH

BEGINNING BLOCK NUMBER  1.   METHOD:  ENTER

VARIABLE(S) ENTERED ON STEP NUMBER  1..      V27        DEFENSE SPENDING SCALE - RESP

MULTIPLE R         0.34379   ANALYSIS OF VARIANCE
R SQUARED          0.11819                 DF     SUM OF SQUARES     MEAN SQUARE
ADJUSTED R SQUARED 0.11768   REGRESSION      1      157238.11651    157238.11651
STANDARD ERROR    26.08596   RESIDUAL     1724     1173143.08685       680.47743
                             F =    231.07029    SIGNIF F =   0.0000

--------------------------------- VARIABLES IN THE EQUATION ---------------------------------
VARIABLE        B         SE B      BETA      CORREL    PART COR    PARTIAL       T     SIG T

V27        6.035908   0.397073  0.343788  0.343788   0.343788   0.343788   15.201   0.0000
(CONSTANT) 36.976886  1.689945                                             21.881   0.0000

END BLOCK NUMBER    1    ALL REQUESTED VARIABLES ENTERED.
```

Figure 19.9 REGRESSION output with ZPP statistics added.

a t distribution. Consequently, a confidence interval can be created for each statistic by adding plus and minus the appropriate t value times the statistic's standard error. For a 95 percent confidence interval, the t value is 1.96, giving

$$CI = 95\% \quad \text{for} \quad \beta = b \pm 1.96 * se_b = 6.036 \pm 1.96 * .397$$
$$= 6.036 \pm .778$$
$$= 5.258 \text{ to } 6.814$$

The CI option instructs SPSS to calculate a 95 percent confidence interval for us. The output shown in Figure 19.10, contains the upper and lower bounds of the confidence interval, numbers which are identical (except for minor rounding errors in the last decimal place) to the boundaries we calculated above. SPSS calculates only a 95 percent confidence interval, the most commonly used one. For other levels of confidence we have to do the calculations ourselves, a very simple process once we locate the appropriate t value in a t table.

The **SES option** adds the standard error of the beta coefficient to the output. The default standard error is for the b coefficient. Beta is produced from standardized versions of the variables, which have different variances from the original versions. Because of their different variances, the two versions of the variables will have different standard errors. If we want to calculate a confidence interval for the beta coefficient, we need to use the standard error for that statistic, not the standard error of b. The SES option adds the standard error of beta to the output (Figure 19.11), allowing us to carry out significance calculations on beta.

The DEFAULTS option requests the default statistics for the variables section: b, standard error, beta, t value, and the significance of t. SPSS will

```
REGRESSION VARIABLES =V5 V27     / STATISTICS DEFAULTS CI
    /DEPENDENT = V5 /ENTER


              * * * *   M U L T I P L E   R E G R E S S I O N  * * * *

LISTWISE DELETION OF MISSING DATA
EQUATION NUMBER 1      DEPENDENT VARIABLE..   V5   FEELING THERMOMETER - BUSH

BEGINNING BLOCK NUMBER  1.  METHOD:  ENTER

VARIABLE(S) ENTERED ON STEP NUMBER  1..     V27      DEFENSE SPENDING SCALE - RESP

MULTIPLE R         0.34379    ANALYSIS OF VARIANCE
R SQUARED          0.11819                     DF    SUM OF SQUARES     MEAN SQUARE
ADJUSTED R SQUARED 0.11768    REGRESSION        1      157238.11651   157238.11651
STANDARD ERROR    26.08596    RESIDUAL       1724     1173143.08685      680.47743
                              F =  231.07029    SIGNIF F =   0.0000


----------------------------------- VARIABLES IN THE EQUATION -----------------------------------
VARIABLE        B        SE B      95% CONFDNCE      INTRVL B     BETA         T     SIG T

V27         6.035908  0.397073    5.257113         6.814703   0.343788   15.201   0.0000
(CONSTANT) 36.976886  1.689945   33.662332        40.291440              21.881   0.0000

END BLOCK NUMBER   1   ALL REQUESTED VARIABLES ENTERED.
```

Figure 19.10 Adding confidence intervals to the REGRESSION output.

```
REGRESSION VARIABLES =V5 V27     / STATISTICS DEFAULTS SES
    /DEPENDENT = V5 /ENTER


              * * * *   M U L T I P L E   R E G R E S S I O N  * * * *
LISTWISE DELETION OF MISSING DATA
EQUATION NUMBER 1
DEPENDENT VARIABLE..   V5   FEELING THERMOMETER - BUSH

BEGINNING BLOCK NUMBER  1.  METHOD:  ENTER

VARIABLE(S) ENTERED ON STEP NUMBER
    1..    V27        DEFENSE SPENDING SCALE - RESP

MULTIPLE R              0.34379
R SQUARED               0.11819
ADJUSTED R SQUARED      0.11768
STANDARD ERROR         26.08596

ANALYSIS OF VARIANCE
                      DF      SUM OF SQUARES      MEAN SQUARE
REGRESSION             1        157238.11651     157238.11651
RESIDUAL            1724       1173143.08685        680.47743
F =   231.07029       SIGNIF F =   0.0000

--------------------- VARIABLES IN THE EQUATION ----------------------
VARIABLE        B        SE B       BETA      SE BETA     T     SIG T

V27         6.035908  0.397073   0.343788   0.022616  15.201   0.0000
(CONSTANT) 36.976886  1.689945                         21.881   0.0000
END BLOCK NUMBER   1   ALL REQUESTED VARIABLES ENTERED.
```

Figure 19.11 REGRESSION output including beta's standard error.

automatically use this option if no STATISTICS subcommand is used. When a STATISTICS subcommand is included, however, SPSS replaces the default statistics with those requested on the subcommand. Thus, for example, using the subcommand /STATISTICS SES will lead SPSS to print just the standard error of beta in the output, but nothing else, not even the beta coefficient itself. Since most of the optional statistics are items we want *in addition to*, not in place of, the regular output, you should include the DEFAULTS specification along with any other specification requested on the STATISTICS subcommand. If you look at Figures 19.9 through 19.11, you will see that this practice was followed for those outputs.

ASSUMPTIONS

We might expect regression analysis, a highly complex procedure, to entail assumptions about the data which are both greater in number and more highly restrictive than those for other statistics. This is only partially true. Regression analysis does involve more assumptions than other statistical procedures, but they are not necessarily more restrictive.

We do not describe all the regression assumptions here, but we briefly discuss a few of the most important ones. These assumptions concern the nature and behavior of the **error term**. The model we estimate statistically is

$$Y = a + b * X$$

We know, however, that our Y-HAT predictions will not be exactly equal to the real Y values. For this model to be a true equation, both sides of the equals sign must have the same value. Thus, in precise terms, the regression equation is

$$Y = a + b * X + e$$

where e is the error term, or the difference between Y-HAT $(a + b * X)$ and Y. Three key assumptions about our prediction error are required by regression analysis:

1. Error e is uncorrelated with X.
2. Error e is normally distributed with a mean of zero.
3. Error e has a constant variance.

No Correlation Between e and X

The first assumption amounts to assuming the absence of a confounding variable. The e term is the residual variation in Y not accounted for by the X variable. If e is systematically correlated with X—it increases or decreases in value as X increases or decreases—then there is at least a third variable out there correlated with both Y and X, which is our definition of a confounding variable. If a confounding variable exists, the b coefficient will not represent the true relationship between X and Y.

This assumption is not too restrictive, for it is the same assumption that we must make for any measure of association. Confounding variables will distort the true lambda, gamma, tau, or Pearson r relationships as well. We discuss how to control for confounding variables in Chapter 20 on multiple regression.

Zero Mean and Normal Distribution

The second assumption is also not too restrictive. To claim that e has a mean of zero is to say that our prediction errors are not systematically too high (most errors are negative with a negative mean) or too low (mostly positive errors with a positive mean). Note that this does not say that our predictions are close to accurate, just that any predictions by the model are in the middle of the real Y values with positive and negative errors (large or small) canceling, to produce a mean of zero.

To assume that e is normally distributed is equivalent to assuming that Y is normally distributed for every value of X. Observe that this is actually a less restrictive assumption than the bivariate normal assumption of Pearson's r (that each variable is normally distributed for every value of the other). Bivariate normality is necessary for correlation coefficients because they are symmetric statistics in which either variable might be considered dependent. Regression is an asymmetric technique in which we must identify the dependent variable. We do assume that the dependent variable Y is normally distributed for every value of X, but we do not have to make any assumption about the distribution of X.

Constant Variance

The third assumption is that e has a constant variance, or that our prediction errors do not get larger or smaller as the value of X changes. This assumption is best illustrated graphically. A constant variance for prediction errors is shown in the top half of Figure 19.12, while the bottom half shows a violation of the assumption, with prediction errors increasing in magnitude as X increases.

This assumption is also not terribly stringent, for seldom is there a reason why our prediction accuracy should get better or worse as the value of X changes. If age or education helps us predict income, is there any reason we should be able to predict income more (or less) accurately for low values of the independent variables than for high ones? With only a few exceptions, the answer to this question is no, and regression is a fairly safe procedure to use.

Robustness of Regression

The regression statistic makes other assumptions as well, but they are either fairly simple or important only in advanced analyses. The three assumptions discussed above are not very severe. The first is common to all measures of association, the second is actually less restrictive than the assumption of Pear-

Errors with a constant variance:

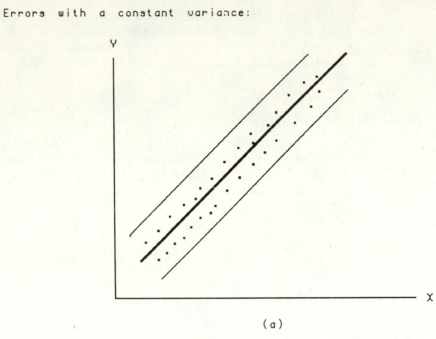

(a)

Errors without a constant variance

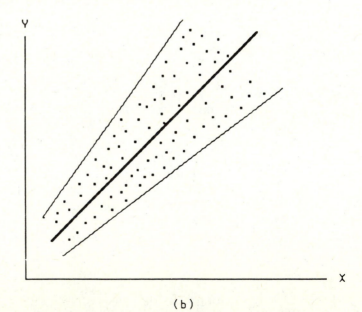

(b)

Figure 19.12 The constant-variance assumption.

son's *r*, and the third does not appear to be too difficult to meet. This is another reason for the popularity of regression among statisticians: not only is it powerful, but also its assumptions are ones we can often live with quite comfortably.

Regression has another attractive feature, its robustness. Some statistics are very sensitive to any violation of the assumptions they require. Even a modest violation may lead the statistic to produce wildly unreliable estimates of the statistical significance or substantive size of a relationship. Other statistics can endure quite a few violations of their assumptions and still produce sample results quite close to the population parameters. The latter statistics are described as **robust statistics**—they are able to "take a licking and keep on ticking." Even with robust statistics, major violations of assumptions will call the sample results into question, but one or more minor violations are not a serious cause for concern.

Regression is robust. We could manufacture an artificial population and create a relationship between some variables that we know violates one or more regression assumptions. If we were then to take repeated samples from this "population" and analyze the relationships with regression, the regression statistics would come pretty close to identifying the true population relationships. Obviously, a robust procedure has considerable value, and regression is such a procedure.

SPSS/PC+ AND RELEASE 4

With both SPSS/PC+ and Release 4, the DESCRIPTIVES subcommand does not contain an explicit NONE option, which is redundant anyway. If you do not want any descriptive statistics, do not use the subcommand. In addition, SPSS/PC+ does not have a COLLECT option on the VARIABLES subcommand.

SUMMARY

We have talked about linear relationships in the last few chapters, calculating zero-order and partial correlations based on them and roughly plotting relationships with the PLOT procedure. With REGRESSION, we are finally able to identify a precise line. The REGRESSION procedure goes beyond just identifying the slope and intercept of a line, however, and allows us to also test hypotheses, measure the strength of a relationship, and determine the predictive accuracy of the line. In addition, regression assumptions are easier to satisfy than some of the assumptions required by other statistics.

All in all, regression is an exceptionally powerful research tool. Its power does not stop with the topics explored in this chapter. Besides single hypotheses, regression can evaluate full models of social phenomena. The examination of models is what we look at next with a discussion of multiple regression.

REVIEW

Key Terms

Slope	Goodness-of-fit statistics
Intercept	Y-HAT
Constant	Multiple R
Least-squares line	R
/DEPENDENT =	R square (R^2)
/METHOD subcommand	Standard error of regression
ENTER option	DESCRIPTIVES subcommand
/ENTER	DEFAULTS option
Simple regression	CORR option
Descriptive section	SIG option
Model section	STATISTICS subcommand
Variables section	ZPP option
b coefficient	CI option
alpha (α)	SES option
beta (β)	Error term
Standardized variables	Robust statistics
Beta coefficient	

Exercises

19.1 Correct any errors in the command statements.
  a. REGRESSION VARIABLES = V5 V27 /DEPENDENT = V5
  b. REGRESSION /DEPENDENT = V5 /METHOD = ENTER
  c. REGRESSION VARIABLES = V27 /DEPENDENT = V5 /METHOD = ENTER
  d. REGRESSION VARIABLES = V5 V27 /DEPENDENT = V5 /METHOD ENTER
  e. REGRESSION VARIABLES = V5 V27 /DEPENDENT = V5
       /METHOD = ENTER /STATISTICS DEFAULTS ZPP
  f. REGRESSION VARIABLES = V5 V27 /DEPENDENT = V5 /ENTER
  g. REGRESSION VARIABLES = V5 V27 /DEPENDENT = V5 /ENTER V27
  h. REGRESSION VARIABLES = V5 V27 /STATISTICS DEFAULTS
       CORR /DEPENDENT = V5   /METHOD = ENTER
  i. REGRESSION VARIABLES = COLLECT   /DEPENDENT = V5
       /METHOD = ENTER
  j. REGRESSION VARIABLES = HAPPY RINCOME   /DESCRIPTIVES
       CORR /DEPENDENT = HAPPY   /METHOD = ENTER
  k. REGRESSION VARIABLES = RELIG SEX /DEPENDENT = RELIG
       /METHOD = ENTER
  l. REGRESSION VARIABLES = HAPPY SEX /DEPENDENT =
       HAPPY /METHOD = ENTER

m. REGRESSION VARIABLES = HAPPY SEX /DESCRIPTIVES SIG
/DEPENDENT = HAPPY /ENTER

n. REGRESSION VARIABLES = HAPPY SEX / STATISTICS DEFAULTS CI
/DEPENDENT = HAPPY/ ENTER

o. REGRESSION VARIABLES = HAPPY SEX /DESCRIPTIVES CORR
SIG /STATISTICS ZPP CI SES   /DEPENDENT = HAPPY
/ ENTER

p. REGRESSION VARIABLES = HAPPY SEX /DESCRIPTIVES CORR SIG
/STATISTICS DEFAULTS ZPP CI SES
/DEPENDENT= SEX / METHOD = ENTER

19.2 Do a simple regression between a dependent and an independent variable.

a. Once you have obtained the regression results, use a COMPUTE statement to calculate a predicted Y (YHAT) for every value of X.

b. Use CROSSTABS to create a contingency table between the X variable and your calculated YHAT. You should observe that every value of X is connected with a single value of YHAT, the value determined by the linear equation.

c. Use CORRELATION to produce a zero-order correlation between YHAT and your Y variable. The resulting statistic should be the same as the multiple R from your regression model.

d. Perform a ONEWAY analysis with Y as your dependent variable and YHAT as the independent one. The result should perfectly match the ANOVA table from the regression analysis.

19.3 Below is a table with 10 cases (A through J) and their values on variables X and Y.

a. Calculate the slope and intercept coefficients for the linear relationship between X and Y.

b. Calculate the beta coefficient between X and Y.

c. Calculate the predicted Y value for each case and the sum of the squared differences between Y and $\hat{Y}$, or $\Sigma(Y - \hat{Y})^2$.

d. Use any other line to represent the X-Y relationship (modify the intercept, slope, or both) and again calculate $\hat{Y}$ for each case and $\Sigma(Y - \hat{Y})^2$. Regardless of what line you pick, this sum of squared errors should be larger than the amount calculated in part *c*.

Case	X	Y
A	1	15
B	2	13
C	6	12
D	5	11
E	4	14
F	3	18
G	8	18
H	9	18
I	7	16
J	5	15

19.4 Repeat Exercise 19.3 for this set of 10 cases.

Case	X	Y
A	4	7
B	9	3
C	3	15
D	3	13
E	9	4
F	4	16
G	8	2
H	6	8
I	7	3
J	7	19

SUGGESTED READINGS

Freedman, David, *et al. Statistics,* 2nd ed. (New York: W. W. Norton, 1991) Chapters 10–12.

Levin, Jack and James Alan Fox. *Elementary Statistics in Social Research,* 4th ed. (New York: Harper & Row, 1988) Chapter 14.

May, Richard B., Michael E. J. Masson, and Michael A. Hunter. *Application of Statistics in Behavioral Research* (New York: Harper & Row, 1990) Chapter 7.

Norusis, Marija J., and SPSS Inc. *SPSS/PC+ V2.0 Base Manual* (Chicago: SPSS Inc., 1988) Chapter 17.

SPSS Inc. *SPSS Reference Guide* (Release 4) (Chicago: SPSS Inc., 1990) pages 585–604.

SPSS Inc. *SPSS-X User's Guide,* 3rd ed. (Chicago: SPSS Inc., 1988) Chapter 45.

Chapter 20

Model Building and Multiple Regression

*H*ow often have we posed what we thought was a clear question, only to get the answer, "It depends"? An example might be this conversation between a prospective college student and an academic counselor.

STUDENT: If I attend and earn my bachelor's degree, what sort of salary can I expect to earn upon graduation?

ADVISER: Well, that depends on many things, such as your major and...

STUDENT: I plan on majoring in business.

ADVISER: OK, that is a lucrative field, but employers will look at how well you perform in your coursework.

STUDENT: I am a good student. Let us say I earn a 3.5 GPA.

ADVISER: Well, that will put you in good shape for landing an attractive job, but different industries and companies pay different salaries. You will not earn very much if you go to work for a public service organization such as the Red Cross.

STUDENT: I want to work for a large multinational corporation such as IBM or Standard Oil.

ADVISER: Very ambitious. If you succeed, such an organization would probably offer a business major with a 3.5 GPA a starting salary between $30,000 and $40,000 per year.

The essence of this conversation, and the source of some frustration to the student, is the adviser's recognition that seldom can one factor alone adequately

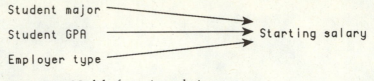

Figure 20.1 Model of starting salaries.

predict another. Reality is just not so simple. This adviser's experience leads her to believe that at least three variables jointly contribute to the starting salaries of graduates—major, GPA, and employer type—represented by the diagram in Figure 20.1. This diagram is called a *model.* The final stop on our tour of introductory statistics is an examination of models, the focus of advanced statistical analysis.

MODELS

Scientists often seek to portray some part of the social or political world with a **model**, which is a description of the major forces at work and how they interact. Models may be described verbally, graphically (as in Figure 20.1), or mathematically. However described, models, like all ideas, need to be tested with data. Before we examine how to conduct such tests, let us get a better feel for how models are related to, yet different from, other research activities discussed in this text.

Models and Hypotheses

Model building and hypothesis testing are related, but not the same. The difference is largely one of logic and perspective. Hypothesis testing is an inherent part of using models, but a model goes beyond individual hypotheses. When stating and testing a hypothesis, we deal with a single bivariate relationship, one independent variable and one dependent variable. Even when a control variable is introduced, we focus on the bivariate independent variable–dependent variable correlation, just purging it of the influence of a confounding variable. When we are examining hypotheses, the independent variable also tends to attract most of our attention. The dependent variable is treated as a given; we know some respondents voted for Bush and others for Dukakis. Our focus is on whether a particular independent variable affects this choice. If we find a statistically significant relationship, say with party identification, we often stop there, content that we have demonstrated that our suspected relationship (the hypothesis) is probably true.

In contrast, a model emphasizes the dependent variable and how we can explain it as fully as possible. We want to identify not just one source of the vote decision, but all important factors influencing it. The adviser in our example knows that student majors, GPAs, and employer types are all correlated with salary. If these were stated as hypotheses, she would confidently reject the null hypothesis of no relationship with salary in each case. No one of these variables alone, however, allows her to make a prediction about starting salaries. She needs information on all three variables together before she can hazard a guess about the salary offers that a student might attract.

A model, even a simple graphic one like Figure 20.1, contains a fount of information. First, the arrows connecting the variables in the model are explicit hypothesized relationships. The diagram claims that there are statistically significant relationships between major, GPA, and employer type with the dependent variable of starting salary. These claims are examined as any other hypotheses are, with statistical significance tests. Second, models are fairly full descriptions of the major forces operating on a dependent variable. With a hypothesis, we claim only that one particular relationship with the dependent variable does exist, not that other relationships do not exist. When we leave variables out of a model, however, we are making the implicit claim that the excluded variables are not significant determinants of the dependent variable. Again, these implicit hypotheses can be examined by testing for statistically significant relationships between the dependent variable and variables not included in the model. Following from a model's purpose to describe all key factors influencing a dependent variable is a third implication. If the model we are using is a good one, we should be able to predict the dependent variable pretty accurately.

Prediction and Parsimony

Some hallmarks of a good model are its completeness and predictive accuracy. We are seeking to identify not just *a* particular cause of the dependent variable (a single hypothesis) but *all* significant influences on it. The model is judged not by the strength of any single relationship between an independent and the dependent variable, but by how well all the variables in unison are able to predict the dependent variable. If, even after knowing a student's GPA, major, and employing organization, we can provide only a very rough salary estimate, say between $25,000 and $60,000, we would not consider the model very useful. If the model could provide a tighter and more precise estimate, such as $30,000 to $40,000, we would consider it to have value.

This does not mean that a good model continually adds more and more independent variables in an attempt to account as fully as possible for differences on the dependent variable. Another indicator of a good model is its **parsimony**, the ability to explain the dependent variable well while using a fairly small number of independent variables. A parsimonious model is preferable for both practical and theoretical reasons. From a practical perspective, trying to include every factor correlated with a given dependent variable is a near impossibility. One personnel officer may have a slight prejudice against red ties while another is hoping to find a qualified candidate who might also contribute to the company's softball team. Virtually all variables are correlated to some extent, but most of these correlations are quite small and contribute very little to explaining any dependent variable. To be practical and usable, a model should include all *important* determinants of the dependent variable, but *only* the important ones. Thus, even if gender, for example, had a statistically significant relationship with salary, it might well be left out of a salary prediction model if its impact was quite small.

A theoretical reason for preferring parsimonious models is the scientific belief that the rules governing nature are really quite simple; the trick is to discover what they are and how they work. This was explicitly stated by a philosopher of the Middle Ages, William of Occam, who propounded a guideline called **Occam's razor**: If you have two explanations for the same phenomenon, the simpler explanation is more likely to be true.

An example can be taken from physics. The physical laws of the universe described by Newton worked well for many years, and the predictions they made about physical behavior were quite accurate. However, as measurement tools became more precise and Newton's laws were applied in a greater variety of situations, discrepancies began to surface between newtonian predictions and the actual behavior of the universe. Working under the belief that Newton was probably correct but had merely overlooked a few key forces, scientists introduced extra variables into Newton's models to bring their predictions back into line. As experiments led to more discrepancies, additional terms were added to the model until it eventually became a complex hodgepodge. As a fictitious example, to evaluate the relationship between matter and energy from a newtonian perspective might have required the formula

$$\sqrt{E^3} = \int_x^y \Delta X - \beta U^{-3} + [X + (X^2 - 1)] + \sin Y$$

Eventually, Einstein proposed an alternative in his famous theory of relativity:

$$E = mc^2$$

Einstein's model predicted behavior as accurately as Newton's. Its simplicity also appealed to scientists' belief that any view of the world which needed to be held together with mathematical Scotch tape and baling wire to produce accurate predictions was probably wrong. A model that is too complex probably does not accurately represent the way the world really works.

MULTIPLE REGRESSION

Anyone can draw a diagram showing probable relationships between variables. More difficult is to estimate the nature of the relationships. How do the independent variables translate to different values on the dependent variable? We cannot just assume that each independent variable has an equal impact, for such an assumption is patently false. Consider a model drawn from the GSS data set in Figure 20.2, positing that education and income are prime determinants of a respondent's happiness. While the two relationships may exist, they are

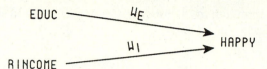

Figure 20.2 Sources of happiness.

probably not of equal importance. Educational differences may lead to sizable changes in happiness while income differences contribute much less, or vice versa.

To use a model for predictive purposes, weights (w_E and w_I in Figure 20.2) must be assigned to each independent variable. The weights tell us how to combine the independent variables into some prediction on the dependent variable. An example of weighting the influence of each variable might be the formula

$$HAPPY = 1.0 + .10 * EDUC + .05 * RINCOME$$

The formula tells us that respondents with zero education and income average 1.0 on the happiness scale. They also increase their happiness by one-tenth of a point for every year of education and one-twentieth of a point for every additional increment of income. If you think this formula looks familiar, you are correct. It is a formula for a line using two independent variables instead of one:

$$HAPPY = a + b_1 * EDUC + b_2 * RINCOME$$

As in Chapter 19, the linear formula is identified by using regression statistics. The only difference is that when the formula contains more than one independent variable, we are performing a **multiple regression** instead of a simple regression.

In describing multiple regression, the first thing to explain is that it is not a new SPSS procedure. Simple regression was explained in Chapter 19 by using the REGRESSION procedure to identify the line connecting a dependent variable and an independent variable. Multiple regression also uses the REGRESSION procedure—the same commands, subcommands, and options. The only procedural difference is that we include more than one independent variable on the variables list. Thus a multiple regression command sequence is

```
REGRESSION VARIABLES = HAPPY EDUC RINCOME
    / DEPENDENT = HAPPY /METHOD = ENTER
```

All three variables are listed on the variables list. Happiness is then identified as the dependent variable with the DEPENDENT subcommand, and both education and income are included as independent variables with the METHOD subcommand.

Although the same SPSS procedure is used for both simple and multiple regressions, the two differ mathematically and conceptually. A simple regression approach to the model in Figure 20.2 would estimate a separate line for each relationship, as in

HAPPY $= a_1 + b_1 *$ EDUC

HAPPY $= a_2 + b_2 *$ RINCOME

Multiple regression, however, estimates only one line with the formula

HAPPY $= a + b_{HE.I} *$ EDUC $+ b_{HI.E} *$ RINCOME

Another difference from the simple regression case is that the b coefficients in multiple regression are **partial b's**; here $b_{HE.I}$ is the relationship between education and happiness while controlling for income, and $b_{HI.E}$ is the relationship between income and happiness while controlling for education. It is necessary to estimate partial relationships in a predictive model to avoid double-counting the impact of each independent variable. We know that education and income are correlated with each other; high scores on the education variable also represent people with high incomes, and respondents with high income values are also likely to have high educational levels. If the coefficient of each variable were calculated in isolation of the other, b_{HE} would represent the impact of education along with some income differences and b_{HI} would reflect the impact of income differences along with some related educational differences. The effect would be similar to taking a 3-hour course that is both required by the university for graduation and required in your major field of study. Just because the course is relevant to two different requirements does not mean you can count it as two courses, for a total of 6 hours.

The formula used to calculate partial b coefficients is too complex to introduce here, but we can roughly illustrate the process. To identify the unique contribution that income makes to happiness, we need to first identify the impact of education on happiness. Thus we start by estimating the education-happiness connection with the formula

HAPPY $= a + b_{HE} *$ EDUC

Having done this, we proceed to remove from the happiness variable the changes connected to different educational levels with the formula

HAPPY$^{**} =$ HAPPY $- (a + b_{HE} *$ EDUC$)$

HAPPY** is a new variable representing the residual or remaining differences in happiness that are not related to educational differences. We can now determine the relationship of income to happiness purged of any effect by education with the formula

HAPPY$^{**} = a + b_{HI.E} *$ RINCOME

where $b_{HI.E}$ is the partial coefficient between income and happiness while controlling for education. We then proceed through this process a second time to identify the relationship between education and happiness purged of any influences due to income.

This process is illustrated graphically in Figure 20.3. The least-squares line between education and happiness is identified in the top part of the figure. Although this line summarizes the two-variable relationship, most cases are scattered around the line rather than falling exactly on it. For any given level of education, some cases will be above the happiness prediction line because they have higher-than-average incomes for that educational group while other cases will fall below the line because they have incomes below average for that educational group. We thus correlate income with these residual prediction errors to see whether income differences partially explain why cases are above or below the education-happiness regression line. Similarly, in the bottom half of Figure 20.3, the same process is carried out to determine whether educational

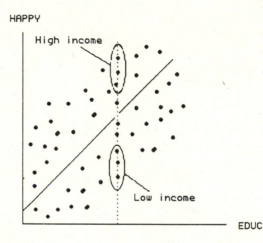

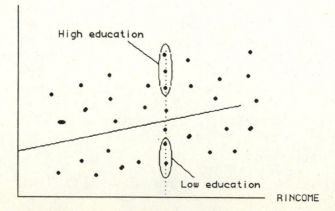

Figure 20.3 A third variable explaining the prediction errors from a two-variable regression line.

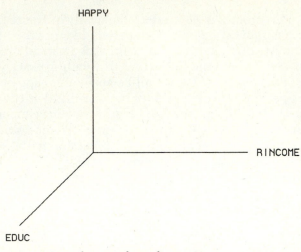

Figure 20.4 A line in three dimensions.

differences explain any of the prediction errors from the happiness-income regression line.

While this illustration makes it appear as if multiple regression estimates different lines for each independent variable, this is not the case. Although it is difficult to illustrate graphically, a linear formula with more than one independent variable is still a formula for a single line. A multiple regression analysis with two independent variables represents an equation for a line in three-dimensional space. As illustrated in Figure 20.4, the happiness and income axes represent the slope of the line in two dimensions, up/down and left/right relative to the page. The third axis, education, represents the extent to which the line lifts off the page into three-dimensional space, much like a pop-up figure in a child's picture book. If the regression model contained three independent variables, it would represent a line moving through four-dimensional space, and a regression model with four independent variables would be a line in five-dimensional space. It is not necessary—indeed, it is impossible—for us to graph lines in more than two dimensions. It is just necessary for us to realize that multiple regression analysis still yields the formula for a single line, but a line created by using more than one independent variable.

Remember, none of the above illustrations are exact descriptions of how partial *b*'s are calculated. They are but simplified examples of the true mathematical processes. Nonetheless, they give us a reasonably accurate perception of how to interpret a multiple regression.

MULTIPLE REGRESSION COMMAND AND OUTPUT

To illustrate the multiple regression command and output, let us return to an analysis performed in the correlation chapters, Chapters 16 and 17, explaining respondents' evaluations of George Bush. In our model, illustrated in Fig-

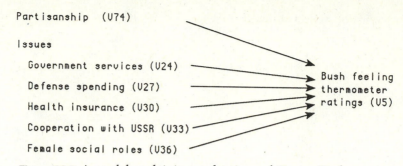

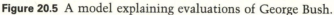

Figure 20.5 A model explaining evaluations of George Bush.

ure 20.5, ratings of Bush were predominantly due to partisanship and respondents' positions on five issue variables. To evaluate this model with multiple regression, these commands would be used:

```
REGRESSION VARIABLES = V5 V24 V27 V30 V33 V36 V74
    / DEPENDENT = V5 / METHOD = ENTER
```

The only difference between these commands and a simple regression command is that more than one independent variable is included on the variables list.

The output from the multiple regression is shown in Figure 20.6. It is similar to the simple regression output except that the descriptive and variables sections now each contain six independent variables instead of only one. The model section is unchanged in appearance, but its interpretation is quite different. In reviewing the interpretation of these statistics, we follow the same format as in Chapter 19, examining first the variables section and then the model section. As in the case of simple regression, the descriptive section is merely a rehashing of how the procedure was performed and so is not discussed further.

Variables Section

The obvious difference in the variables section compared to a simple regression is the number of independent variables contained there. The model in Figure 20.5 argues that evaluations of Bush are predominantly determined by a combination of six independent variables via the formula

$$V5 = a + b_1 * V24 + b_2 * V27 + b_3 * V30 + b_4 * V33 + b_5 * V36 + b_6 * V74$$

The first column of the variables section contains the names of the independent variables (not necessarily in order) as well as the constant. The second column contains the coefficients associated with each. We thus replace the a and b symbols with these coefficients to get the formula

$$V5 = 29.549 - 1.752 * V24 + 4.076 * V27 + .929 * V30 - .033 * V33 + .215 * V36 + 6.489 * V74$$

```
REGRESSION VARIABLES = V5 V24 V27 V30 V33 V36 V74
    /DEPENDENT = V5    /METHOD = ENTER


        * * * *   M U L T I P L E   R E G R E S S I O N   * * * *

LISTWISE DELETION OF MISSING DATA
EQUATION NUMBER 1
DEPENDENT VARIABLE..    V5    FEELING THERMOMETER - BUSH

BEGINNING BLOCK NUMBER  1.    METHOD:  ENTER

VARIABLE(S) ENTERED ON STEP NUMBER
    1..    V74     RESP'S PARTY IDENTIFICATION
    2..    V36     MEN-WOMEN EQUAL ROLES - RESP
    3..    V33     COOPERATE WITH RUSSIA - RESP
    4..    V30     HEALTH INS SCALE - RESP
    5..    V27     DEFENSE SPENDING SCALE - RESP
    6..    V24     GOVT SERVICES SCALE - RESP


MULTIPLE R          0.64882
R SQUARED           0.42096
ADJUSTED R SQUARED  0.41809
STANDARD ERROR      21.30999

ANALYSIS OF VARIANCE
                  DF      SUM OF SQUARES      MEAN SQUARE
REGRESSION         6        399804.78347      66634.13058
RESIDUAL        1211        549934.21571        454.11579
F =   146.73379        SIGNIF F =   0.0000


-------------------- VARIABLES IN THE EQUATION --------------------
VARIABLE        B           SE B          BETA          T      SIG T

V74          6.489171      0.322433      0.487303     20.126   0.0000
V36          0.214647      0.349982      0.013666      0.613   0.5398
V33         -0.033264      0.377319     -0.002060     -0.088   0.9298
V30          0.929199      0.336238      0.066200      2.764   0.0058
V27          4.076461      0.431324      0.225074      9.451   0.0000
V24         -1.752408      0.425439     -0.099177     -4.119   0.0000
(CONSTANT)  29.548902      3.202594                    9.227   0.0000

END BLOCK NUMBER   1    ALL REQUESTED VARIABLES ENTERED.
```

Figure 20.6 Output from a multiple regression.

Partial Coefficients   The a and b coefficients are interpreted essentially the same as in a simple regression. The intercept a is the average Bush rating for respondents with zero on all the independent variables. Each b coefficient is the average change in the dependent variable for each unit change in that independent variable. Thus, every unit increase in partisanship (V74), from 1 to 2 (strong Democrat to weak Democrat) or 5 to 6 (independent Republican to weak Republican), leads to an increase in average evaluations of Bush of 6.489 points on the feeling thermometer. Conversely, the coefficient for V24 is negative, meaning that every unit increase on that variable (preferring increased government services and spending) translates to rating Bush 1.752 units *lower* on the feeling thermometer. This latter result makes sense since candidate Bush proposed fewer services and less spending than his Democratic opponent.

There is one difference between the coefficients in Figure 20.6 and those obtained from a simple regression analysis: They are partial *b*'s. Statistically, this means that each coefficient is calculated while all other independent variables are held constant. From a conceptual standpoint it also means that our interpretation of the *b* coefficients differs somewhat; each is the change in *Y* for every unit change in *X while the model's other independent variables are held constant.* That is, if we could isolate a group of respondents who had identical values on all the variables save one, say, strong Democrats who took the most liberal position on all issues except defense spending, then each 1-unit difference in defense spending preferences among these respondents would lead to a 4.076-unit increase in their ratings of Bush. Similarly, a group of strong Republicans who took the most conservative position on the other four issues would also have a 4.076-unit change in the Bush feeling thermometer placements for every 1-unit difference in defense spending preferences among the respondents.

Hypothesis Testing   A model, like a hypothesis, describes what we believe to be true for the population. The coefficients provided by the REGRESSION procedure are but sample estimates of the population parameters in the model

$$V5 = \alpha + \beta_1 * V24 + \beta_2 * V27 + \beta_3 * V30 + \beta_4 * V33 + \beta_5 * V36 + \beta_6 * V74$$

Thus, our first concern is whether the sample-based estimates of the relationships claimed by the model allow us to conclude that each relationship is different from zero in the population. The standard error of each partial *b* is shown in column 3, while columns 5 and 6 contain a *t* test and report its significance level, respectively. These tests show that two of our variables are suspect. The sample coefficient for the male-female equal-roles scale (V36) has a 54 percent probability of being produced by sampling error from a population where there is not a relationship between this factor and evaluations of Bush (a population β of zero). The *t* test for the cooperation-with-Russia scale (V33) shows a 93 percent probability that the null hypothesis is true for this relationship as well in the population.

When a statistical significance test indicates that we may have erred by including in the model independent variables that are unrelated to the dependent variable, a common practice is to delete these variables from the analysis and then reestimate the model. Since independent variables are often correlated with one another, and since each *b* is a partial *b*, the coefficient estimates will differ as variables are added to or subtracted from the model, even when the added or subtracted variables have little connection with the dependent variable. Thus, if we decide that the correct model includes only four independent variables instead of six, we need to estimate the coefficients by using just these four variables. Although this is not always done by every analyst, it is the preferred practice. Figure 20.7 shows the revised regression statistics.

```
REGRESSION VARIABLES = V5 V24 V27 V30 V74
   / DEPENDENT = V5  / METHOD = ENTER


        * * * *  M U L T I P L E   R E G R E S S I O N  * * * *

LISTWISE DELETION OF MISSING DATA
EQUATION NUMBER 1
DEPENDENT VARIABLE..    V5    FEELING THERMOMETER - BUSH

BEGINNING BLOCK NUMBER  1.   METHOD:   ENTER

VARIABLE(S) ENTERED ON STEP NUMBER
   1..    V74       RESP'S PARTY IDENTIFICATION
   2..    V27       DEFENSE SPENDING SCALE - RESP
   3..    V30       HEALTH INS SCALE - RESP
   4..    V24       GOVT SERVICES SCALE - RESP

MULTIPLE R              0.64912
R SQUARED               0.42136
ADJUSTED R SQUARED      0.41961
STANDARD ERROR         21.33533

ANALYSIS OF VARIANCE
                 DF       SUM OF SQUARES       MEAN SQUARE
REGRESSION        4         437209.72286    109302.43072
RESIDUAL       1319         600403.75750       455.19618
F =  240.12159        SIGNIF F =  0.0000


-------------------- VARIABLES IN THE EQUATION --------------------
VARIABLE          B          SE B         BETA        T      SIG T

V74            6.516221    0.306314     0.490677    21.273   0.0000
V27            4.029540    0.389971     0.224980    10.333   0.0000
V30            0.844555    0.320197     0.060515     2.638   0.0084
V24           -1.763782    0.404801    -0.100005    -4.357   0.0000
(CONSTANT)    29.979830    2.853990                 10.505   0.0000

END BLOCK NUMBER   1    ALL REQUESTED VARIABLES ENTERED.
```

Figure 20.7 Bush evaluations as a function of four independent variables.

Partial Betas   The betas in column 4 of the variables section are also interpreted much as in the simple regression situation. Each b coefficient is affected by not only the strength of the relationship but also the amount of variance possessed by that independent variable. The beta coefficient standardizes the variances of all the variables so that what remains is a measure of only the strength of a relationship. From this column, it is obvious that party identification has the greatest impact on respondents' evaluations of Bush, with respondents' positions on defense spending a distant, but still strong, second in importance.

In a multiple regression, each beta is similar to a partial correlation coefficient. In Figure 20.7, beta for V74 can be interpreted as the correlation between V5 and V74 while controlling for V24, V27, and V30. As mentioned briefly in

Chapter 19, however, the PARTIAL CORR procedure in SPSS actually calculates what is called a "part correlation"—a statistic with a formula slightly different from that for a **partial beta**. Consequently, if you conduct a PARTIAL CORR analysis, using the same variables as in Figure 20.7, you will obtain results close to, but not exactly identical with, the partial betas. Each statistic has its use, but most analysts prefer partial beta to the part correlation.

Model Section

The model section of a multiple regression printout can be quite deceiving. It looks, and indeed is, identical in size and format to the simple regression output in Chapter 19. The analysis conducted in this section is conceptually identical to a simple regression analysis, comparing the predicted Y value to the actual value of Y. What is substantially different is how we determine a predicted value of Y. Since the other statistics in this section utilize the predicted value of Y, they differ as well.

Predicting Y For a simple regression, a predicted value of Y, denoted $\hat{Y}$ (Y-hat), was created for each case by multiplying the b coefficient by each case's value on the X variable and then adding this product to the intercept. The same logic is used for a multiple regression, except that we now have more than one independent variable and associated b coefficient. A case's value on *all* the model's independent variables is used to create a predicted value for that case on the dependent variable. This process is illustrated in Table 20.1. It is not more difficult than calculating $\hat{Y}$ from a simple regression output, just more detailed. SPSS uses this process to create predicted Y values for use in the model section, but does not display those values. If we want to create predicted Y values for our own use, either we could calculate them by hand, following the illustration in Table 20.1, if we are interested in only a few cases, or we could create $\hat{Y}$ values for all cases in the data set with the command

```
COMPUTE BUSHEVAL = 29.980 - 1.764 * V24 + 4.030 * V27 + .845 * V30
   +6.516 * V74
```

Table 20.1 CALCULATING $\hat{Y}$ FROM A MULTIPLE REGRESSION OUTPUT

Case	Actual Y value (V5)	$\hat{Y}$	= Intercept	$+ b_1 * V24$	$+ b_2 * V27$	$+ b_3 * V30$	$+ b_4 * V74$
A	96	100.543	29.980	−1.764 * **1**	4.030 * **6**	+.845 * **3**	6.516 * **7**
B	96	98.828	29.980	−1.764 * **2**	4.030 * **7**	+.845 * **6**	6.516 * **6**
C	50	55.627	29.980	−1.764 * **3**	4.030 * **1**	+.845 * **1**	6.516 * **4**
D	60	70.974	29.980	−1.764 * **4**	4.030 * **3**	+.845 * **4**	6.516 * **5**
E	55	62.548	29.980	−1.764 * **5**	4.030 * **5**	+.845 * **2**	6.516 * **3**
F	37	44.493	29.980	−1.764 * **7**	4.030 * **4**	+.845 * **5**	6.516 * **1**

Once you grasp that the predicted Y values stem from the joint impact of all the independent variables, interpreting the model section is an easy extension of a simple regression analysis. The model statistics represent the extent to which the entire model, all independent variables combined, accurately predicts the dependent variable. The multiple R is the correlation between the predicted and actual values of Y. The R square is the square of the multiple R, which can be interpreted as the proportion of the variance of the dependent variable explained by the model. The standard error is the average error of the predictions, and the analysis of variance is an ANOVA examination of the relationship between $\hat{Y}$ and Y.

Adjusted R Square   When a multiple regression is carried out, another statistic comes into play that is of little use in a simple regression, the **adjusted R square**. One touchstone of a good model is its predictive power. Thus analysts using multiple regression regularly look at the R-square value of the model, which is a PRE measure of the proportion of variance (error) explained (reduced) by the model.

Let us say we have two competing models to explain the same dependent variable. The first is the one we have been using, claiming that respondents' evaluations of Bush are predominantly determined by issues and partisanship only. Another researcher might argue that the public is heavily influenced by the personalities of the candidates as well. He thus proposes an alternative model including three personality variables: respondents' perceptions of Bush as a strong leader (V11), whether he cares for people like the respondent (V12), and perceptions of Bush's honesty (V13). A regression analysis of this alternative model is shown in Figure 20.8. All the personality variables pass the statistical significance test, and the R square from this model is substantially higher than that for the prior one (.630 versus .421). Does this mean that we should accept this model and reject the prior one? Not necessarily.

A number of criteria are used to evaluate models, some theoretical and others statistical. On the statistical side, predictive ability is certainly an important criterion, but we face a mathematical quirk when using R square to compare models. Every time extra variables are introduced into the model, R square necessarily increases, even if the variables are not substantially related to the dependent variable. This is because, at a minimum, each extra variable can be used to predict at least one case more accurately.

Consider an extreme example, a data set with only five cases. We develop a regression model to predict our dependent variable, evaluations of Bush, using four completely nonsensical independent variables, such as a person's height, shoe size, age, and weight. Despite the apparent silliness of the model, it will predict the dependent variable with 100 percent accuracy ($R^2 = 1.0$). The computer will simply select an intercept matching the Bush rating for case A, a b coefficient for height perfectly predicting the dependent-variable value for case B, a b coefficient for shoe size perfectly predicting the evaluation of Bush for case C, and so on. In short, each additional variable will add to a model's R square because no matter how irrelevant it is, it can be used to improve our prediction

```
REGRESSION VARIABLES = V5 V24 V27 V30 V74 V11 V12 V13
   /DEPENDENT = V5 /ENTER


      * * * *   M U L T I P L E   R E G R E S S I O N   * * * *

LISTWISE DELETION OF MISSING DATA
EQUATION NUMBER 1
DEPENDENT VARIABLE..   V5   FEELING THERMOMETER - BUSH

BEGINNING BLOCK NUMBER  1.   METHOD:  ENTER

VARIABLE(S) ENTERED ON STEP NUMBER
   1..    V13      DESCRIBES BUSH - HONEST
   2..    V24      GOVT SERVICES SCALE - RESP
   3..    V27      DEFENSE SPENDING SCALE - RESP
   4..    V30      HEALTH INS SCALE - RESP
   5..    V74      RESP'S PARTY IDENTIFICATION
   6..    V11      DESCRIBES BUSH - STRONG LEADER
   7..    V12      DESCRIBES BUSH-CARES FR PEOPLE LIK ME

MULTIPLE R          0.79390
R SQUARED           0.63027
ADJUSTED R SQUARED  0.62805
STANDARD ERROR      17.38329

ANALYSIS OF VARIANCE
                 DF      SUM OF SQUARES      MEAN SQUARE
REGRESSION        7        599083.86183      85583.40883
RESIDUAL       1163        351433.89735        302.17876
F =   283.22113      SIGNIF F =  0.0000


-------------------- VARIABLES IN THE EQUATION --------------------
VARIABLE       B            SE B          BETA          T      SIG T

V13        -5.882496     0.810961     -0.177682     -7.254    0.0000
V24        -1.609870     0.351371     -0.090167     -4.582    0.0000
V27         2.131423     0.347721      0.116330      6.130    0.0000
V30         0.067298     0.278675      0.004762      0.241    0.8092
V74         3.156197     0.299530      0.234599     10.537    0.0000
V11        -9.799089     0.781706     -0.288646    -12.536    0.0000
V12        -5.942738     0.821365     -0.190170     -7.235    0.0000
(CONSTANT) 102.954736    3.774392                   27.277    0.0000

END BLOCK NUMBER    1    ALL REQUESTED VARIABLES ENTERED.
```

Figure 20.8 A regression analysis with personality variables added.

for at least one case in the data set. This is called a **statistical artifact**, a result produced by a mathematical quirk, not a real relationship between variables.

   This mathematical quirk becomes important when we compare two models via their respective R-square values. A marginally higher R square for one model may be due solely to its use of more independent variables, not because it better identifies important determinants of the dependent variable. Consequently, the model section includes an adjusted R square, a statistic which compensates for the number of independent variables in a model. This number is comparable across regression models with different quantities of independent variables. Comparing the adjusted R-square values of the models in Figures 20.7 and 20.8 (.420 versus .628) tells us that the latter model indeed predicts ratings of Bush more accurately, even after compensating for its additional independent variables.

There is one other item of note in Figure 20.8: The relationship between V30 (the health insurance scale) and the dependent variable is no longer statistically significant. Probably this variable originally reflected respondents' views of Bush's personality, perhaps sentiments about Bush's compassion. Once the personality characteristics have been included in the model, and thus controlled for, no relationship remains between respondents' views of health insurance and their evaluations of candidate Bush.

USING MULTIPLE REGRESSION

We will not spend a lot of time discussing either the assumptions of, or subcommands for, multiple regression. Both are the same as for a simple regression. Instead we explore how the versatility and power of regression analysis lead to its frequent use with multiple research questions.

Being such a powerful statistical tool, regression is often intimidating to those new to quantitative analysis. Beginners tend to opt for simpler procedures that they feel they understand better. This is not necessarily a bad tactic, for one should not use procedures that he or she does not fully understand. The power and flexibility of regression analysis, however, have led to its widespread application in an enormous variety of situations. You are likely to encounter it repeatedly, and it is worth the effort to become more familiar with it. Below we examine a number of situations and how regression might be used in each.

One Independent Variable

You might be exploring only one hypothesis, with one independent variable and one dependent variable, each measured at the interval level. Regression can be used to analyze a simple relationship since the beta coefficient is equal to the Pearson correlation between the variables. In this case, however, most analysts prefer the CORRELATION procedure because its output is much simpler to interpret. A simple regression leads to a large number of statistics in both the model section and the variables section that duplicate one another. If you need to plot the correlation line, you must use regression to obtain the linear formula, but otherwise a Pearson correlation will do quite nicely.

Control Variables

Say you are interested in a single bivariate relationship but deem it necessary to control for one or more possibly confounding variables. PARTIAL CORR can perform such an analysis, but so can REGRESSION. Simply include the control variable(s) in the regression procedure. If you are not particularly interested in the confounding variables, other than controlling for them, you do not need to pay any attention to their b or beta coefficients.

This is a very common use of regression analysis. An analyst is concerned with a specific X-Y relationship, but feels it is necessary to control for variables A, B, and C. All the variables are included in a regression analysis, but the analyst focuses on only the coefficient for variable X, a coefficient produced while controlling for A, B, and C. The model section is largely ignored for this type of analysis since the question being addressed involves the existence of the relationship, which the t test in the variables section will answer.

Multiple Independent Variables

Whenever you examine how more than one independent variable is related to a single dependent variable, you are using a model, implicitly or explicitly. For multiple independent variables, multiple regression is almost a must. If each independent variable is completely independent of (uncorrelated with) the others, a simple CORRELATION analysis will suffice. Most of the time, however, several independent variables will have some correlation with one another—sometimes small and other times large. When this is true, you cannot identify any variable's unique relationship with the dependent variable unless you have controlled for the other variables. PARTIAL CORR will accomplish this, but REGRESSION is far simpler and adds the model section to evaluate how well all the variables jointly explain the dependent variable.

Dummy Variables

While exploring models, analysts often need to incorporate some nominal variables into the model. Say we feel there are two prime determinants of a person's happiness, income and marital status. Being nominal, marital status cannot be included in any interval analysis. We can, however, recode MARITAL into a dichotomous variable, and dichotomies are always interval. When a variable is transformed to a dichotomy, it is typically called a **dummy variable**. Just as a ventriloquist's dummy is a stark simplification of a person, we are using a simplified dichotomy instead of the variable in its original format.

Dummy variables are a common feature of regression analysis, for we often desire to examine how a categorical characteristic, such as race or religious preference, affects some dependent variable. In this case, we are interested in how being married affects a person's happiness level, so MARITAL is recoded to 1 (married) and 0 (separated, widowed, divorced, or never married). Figure 20.9 is the output from the regression of happiness on income and the dummy variable MARITAL. Both are apparent determinants of happiness since each has a t value significance level below .05.

When using dummy variables, we interpret the b coefficient just a little bit differently. For instance, Figure 20.9 shows that each 1-unit increase in income produces a .007-unit increase in happiness (the lowest code number on HAPPY is highest happiness, which is why the signs are negative). For MARITAL, each

```
TEMPORARY
RECODE MARITAL (2,3,4,5=0)
REGRESSION VARIABLES = HAPPY RINCOME MARITAL
    /DEPENDENT = HAPPY /ENTER


      * * * *   M U L T I P L E   R E G R E S S I O N   * * * *

LISTWISE DELETION OF MISSING DATA
EQUATION NUMBER 1       DEPENDENT VARIABLE..    HAPPY     GENERAL HAPPINESS

BEGINNING BLOCK NUMBER  1.   METHOD:   ENTER

VARIABLE(S) ENTERED ON STEP NUMBER
   1..    MARITAL     MARITAL STATUS
   2..    RINCOME     RESPONDENT'S INCOME

MULTIPLE R          0.26787
R SQUARED           0.07176
ADJUSTED R SQUARED  0.06977
STANDARD ERROR      0.57223

ANALYSIS OF VARIANCE
                DF        SUM OF SQUARES      MEAN SQUARE
REGRESSION       2           23.69287         11.84643
RESIDUAL       936 .         306.49457         0.32745
F =  36.17768          SIGNIF F =  0.0000


------------------------ VARIABLES IN THE EQUATION ---------------------
VARIABLE          B            SE B          BETA          T       SIG T

MARITAL      -0.300859      0.037736      -0.252432     -7.973    0.0000
RINCOME      -0.007674      0.003615      -0.067222     -2.123    0.0340
(CONSTANT)    1.998269      0.046328                    43.133    0.0000

END BLOCK NUMBER    1    ALL REQUESTED VARIABLES ENTERED.
```

Figure 20.9 Using a dummy variable.

unit increase produces .301 increased units of happiness. As a dichotomous variable, however, MARITAL can change by only 1 unit, from 0 (not married) to 1 (married). The *b* coefficient thus represents the difference in average happiness levels between the two groups—married respondents are .301 units happier than nonmarried respondents.

We are not limited to creating only one dummy variable from a series of nominal categories. MARITAL has five values: married (1), widowed (2), divorced (3), separated (4), and never married (5). From these five categories, we can create four dummy variables to represent different marital states, examining, for instance, the impact of being divorced, widowed, separated, or married as determinants of happiness.

First, we create four new variables with the COMPUTE command, each of which is merely a carbon copy of the original MARITAL variable:

```
COMPUTE MAR = MARITAL

COMPUTE DIV = MARITAL

COMPUTE WID = MARITAL

COMPUTE SEP = MARITAL
```

Second, the new variables are recoded so that the value 1 represents a different characteristic on each—separated respondents for variable SEP, married respondents for variable MAR, and so on:

```
RECODE MAR (1 = 1) (2, 3, 4, 5 = 0) / DIV (2 = 1) (1, 3, 4, 5 = 0)
    / WID (3 = 1) (1, 2, 4, 5 = 0) / SEP (4 = 1) (1, 2, 3, 5 = 0)
```

Figure 20.10 includes these new dummy variables in the regression analysis. Only the coefficient for the dummy variable MAR is statistically significant. We cannot conclude that the widowed, separated, or divorced respondents are any different in the population from the nonmarried respondents. For illustrative purposes, however, we will treat these coefficients as if they were statistically significant.

Notice that while MARITAL has five values, we created only four dummy variables. This is necessary for conceptual and statistical reasons. The coefficient for each dummy variable is the difference in average happiness between the group coded 1 on the dummy variable and the **baseline group**. The baseline group consists of the respondents with a score of zero on all four dummy variables. Our baseline group contains the respondents who have never been married, those with a value of 5 on MARITAL. Thus, married respondents are .253 unit happier than the never-married group while separated respondents are .185 unit less happy than the baseline group.

Statistically, for any variable with m value codes, we can create no more than $m - 1$ dummy variables. We could always create less than this number, but never more than it. If we had created five dummy variables from the MARITAL variable, not only would we have no baseline group for comparison, but also we would have created a situation known as **perfect multicollinearity**. Perfect multicollinearity occurs when one or more independent variables perfectly predicts (R square equals 1.0) another independent variable. With five dummy variables created from a five-category variable, knowing a case value on any four of them would allow us to perfectly predict its value on the fifth. If case A had a value of 0 on the first four variables, its value on the fifth would have to be 1. If case B had a value of 1 on any of the first four variables, its value on the fifth would have to be 0. When perfect multicollinearity exists among the independent variables of a regression model, regression statistics cannot be calculated. Without presenting any of the mathematics, what perfect multicollinearity does is require the computer to divide by zero—a mathematical impossibility—when it attempts to calculate the b coefficients. As long as we avoid perfect multicollinearity, we can use dummy variables to incorporate any number of nominal characteristics into an interval regression analysis.

```
COMPUTE  MAR  =  MARITAL
COMPUTE  DIV  =  MARITAL
COMPUTE  WID  =  MARITAL
COMPUTE  SEP  =  MARITAL
RECODE MAR  (1=1)  (2,3,4,5=0)  /  WID  (2=1)(1,3,4,5=0)
     /  DIV  (3=1)(1,2,4,5=0)
     /  SEP  (4=1)(1,2,3,5=0)
REGRESSION  VARIABLES  =  HAPPY  RINCOME  MAR  WID  DIV  SEP
     /DEPENDENT  =  HAPPY  /ENTER
```

```
                * * * *   M U L T I P L E   R E G R E S S I O N   * * * *

LISTWISE  DELETION  OF  MISSING  DATA
EQUATION  NUMBER  1        DEPENDENT  VARIABLE..     HAPPY     GENERAL  HAPPINESS
BEGINNING  BLOCK  NUMBER   1.    METHOD:    ENTER

VARIABLE(S)  ENTERED  ON  STEP  NUMBER
     1..      SEP
     2..      WID
     3..      RINCOME      RESPONDENT'S  INCOME
     4..      DIV
     5..      MAR

MULTIPLE  R               0.27516
R  SQUARED                0.07571
ADJUSTED  R  SQUARED      0.07076
STANDARD  ERROR           0.57193

ANALYSIS  OF  VARIANCE
                     DF          SUM  OF  SQUARES        MEAN  SQUARE
REGRESSION            5               24.99958             4.99992
RESIDUAL            933              305.18785             0.32710
F  =   15.28541          SIGNIF  F  =    0.0000

--------------------- VARIABLES  IN  THE  EQUATION ---------------------
VARIABLE           B            SE  B           BETA          T        SIG  T

SEP           0.184844      0.108466        0.056555      1.704     0.0887
WID           0.049889      0.095665        0.017587      0.521     0.6021
RINCOME      -0.008144      0.003646       -0.071339     -2.234     0.0257
DIV           0.088629      0.063318        0.052600      1.400     0.1619
MAR          -0.252801      0.047081       -0.212110     -5.369     0.0000
(CONSTANT)    1.955535      0.052608                     37.172     0.0000

END  BLOCK  NUMBER     1     ALL  REQUESTED  VARIABLES  ENTERED.
```

Figure 20.10 Using multiple dummy variables.

The *R*-Square and *b* Statistics

Everything we have discussed above can be performed with the CORRELA-TION and PARTIAL CORR procedures. Even dummy variables can be created and included in both procedures. There are two statistics which are unique to, and can only be obtained from, a regression analysis. First is R square. The procedures mentioned above consider simple bivariate relationships only, with or without controlling for another variable. None identifies the combined impact of a group of independent variables on a dependent variable. Only the R-square statistic from a regression will give us this information. The second unique product of regression is the b coefficient, the amount of change in the dependent variable for every unit change in an independent variable. Other procedures will give us the strength of a relationship, but none tells us what the strength means in terms of how the dependent variable changes. The b coefficient does, and regression analysis is often used for this purpose alone—to identify how an independent variable modifies a dependent one.

SUMMARY

We are now at the end of our journey. We began by looking at the notion of the research process—to suggest answers (hypotheses) to some questions. We then looked at a number of ways to calculate statistical significance—T-TEST, ONEWAY, and the chi-square statistic—determining from our sample data whether the null or research hypothesis was probably true for the population. From statistical significance we moved on to substantive importance by reviewing measures of association available with CROSSTABS and CORRELATION. Then we examined confounding variables and how to control for them with CROSSTABS and PARTIAL CORR. Finally, we touched briefly on modeling and evaluating models with REGRESSION.

All in all, we have covered a lot of territory. The topics examined in this text should allow you to perform your own basic statistical analyses and, just as important, properly interpret statistics that regularly bombard us from all directions. When pollsters tell us which candidate the public supports in a campaign with a certain margin of error, we know that they are talking about a mean and its confidence interval. When we encounter graphics, such as television viewing habits by age group, we should recognize them as merely another form of contingency table. When an analyst predicts the annual crop size in a region, he is using a predictive model like regression—based on estimates of the amount of rainfall, sunshine, and number of acres being farmed, a prediction about crop yields can be made.

No matter what the topic or statistical strategy, the goal is the same—to examine social reality in a rigorous, systematic, and objective manner. Sometimes we succeed and other times we do not, but success or failure is only a part of the story. We do the best we can with the tools at hand, and that is the other part of the story. Many people do not even try and are willing to wallow in subjective predispositions without attempting to objectively confirm or deny them. The scholar must do more, and the tools of research offer a way to do so. As long as we are doing the best we can with available technology, we deserve the title of social scientist.

REVIEW

Key Terms

Model
parsimony
Occam's razor
Multiple regression
Partial *b*'s
Partial beta

Adjusted *R* square
Statistical artifact
Dummy variable
Baseline group
Perfect multicollinearity

Exercises

20.1 Correct any errors in the command statements.
  a. REGRESSION VARIABLES = V5 V24 V27 V30 /DEPENDENT = V5
      /METHOD = ENTER V24 V27 V30
  b. REGRESSION /DEPENDENT = V5 /METHOD = ENTER V24 V27 V30
  c. REGRESSION VARIABLES = V5 V24 V27 V30 /DEPENDENT = V5
      /ENTER V24 V27
  d. REGRESSION VARIABLES = V5 V24 V27 V30 /DEPENDENT = V5
      /METHOD = ENTER /STATISTICS DEFAULTS ZPP
  e. REGRESSION VARIABLES = COLLECT /DEPENDENT = V5 /ENTER V24
      V27 V30
  f. REGRESSION VARIABLES = HAPPY RINCOME EDUC SPEDUC
      /DESCRIPTIVES CORR /DEPENDENT = HAPPY /METHOD = ENTER
  g. REGRESSION VARIABLES = HAPPY RINCOME EDUC SPEDUC
      /DESCRIPTIVES CORR /DEPENDENT = HAPPY /METHOD = ENTER
      /STATISTICS DEFAULTS ZPP CI SES
  h. REGRESSION VARIABLES = HAPPY RINCOME EDUC SPEDUC
      /STATISTICS CORR SIG /DEPENDENT = HAPPY
      /METHOD = ENTER
  i. REGRESSION VARIABLES = HAPPY RINCOME EDUC SPEDUC
      /DEPENDENT = HAPPY /ENTER RINCOME EDUC
      /DEPENDENT = HAPPY /ENTER RINCOME SPEDUC
  j. REGRESSION VARIABLES = HAPPY SEX /STATISTICS DEFAULTS CI
      /DEPENDENT = HAPPY /ENTER RINCOME EDUC
      /DEPENDENT = HAPPY /ENTER RINCOME SPEDUC
  k. REGRESSION VARIABLES = AIDSADS AIDSIDS AIDSSCH AIDSSXED SEX
      /DEPENDENT = AIDSADS /ENTER SEX
      /DEPENDENT = AIDSIDS /ENTER SEX
      /DEPENDENT = AIDSSCH /ENTER SEX
      /DEPENDENT = AIDSSXED /ENTER SEX

20.2 Do a multiple regression, using one dependent and multiple independent variables.
  a. Once you have obtained the regression results, use a COMPUTE statement to calculate a predicted $\hat{Y}$ (YHAT) for every case.
  b. Use CROSSTABS to create a contingency table between an X variable and your calculated $\hat{Y}$. In contrast with the simple regression case, there should not be an

exact match between the values of any single independent variable and specific $\hat{Y}$ values since all the independent variables are used to produce $\hat{Y}$.

c. Use CORRELATION to produce a zero-order correlation between $\hat{Y}$ and your Y variable. The resulting statistic should be the same as the multiple R from your regression model.

d. Perform a ONEWAY analysis with Y as your dependent variable and $\hat{Y}$ as the independent one. The results should match the ANOVA table from the regression analysis.

SUGGESTED READINGS

Achen, Christopher H. *Interpreting and Using Regression*, Quantitative Applications in the Social Sciences, Sage University Papers Series No. 29 (Newbury Park, Calif.: Sage Publications, 1982).

Berry, William D. and Stanley Feldman. *Multiple Regression in Practice*, Quantitative Applications in the Social Sciences, Sage University Papers Series No. 50 (Newbury Park, Calif.: Sage Publications, 1985).

Lewis-Beck, Michael S. *Applied Regression*, Quantitative Applications in the Social Sciences, Sage University Papers Series No. 22 (Newbury Park, Calif.: Sage Publications, 1980).

Codebook: 1988 American National Election Survey

Variable Name: V1   **Record:** 1   **Column(s):** 1–4

Question Asked: None. This is an arbitrarily selected number from 1 to 2040 uniquely identifying each respondent in the data set.

Code No.	Response
1.	First respondent
2.	Second respondent
.	.
.	.
.	.
2040	Last respondent

1988 VOTE

Variable Name: V2   **Record:** 1   **Column(s):** 5

Question Asked: Did you vote for a candidate for president in the 1988 election? If so, whom did you vote for?

Code No.	Response
1.	George Bush
2.	Michael Dukakis
3.	Third-party/Independent candidate
8.	Did not vote
9.	NA
0.	INAP

Variable Name: V3   **Record:** 1   **Column(s):** 6

Question Asked: How about the election for the House of Representatives in Washington? Did you vote for a candidate for the House of Representatives? Whom did you vote for?

Code No.	Response
1.	Democratic candidate
2.	Republican candidate
3.	Third-party/Independent candidate
7.	Did not vote
8.	DK
9.	NA
0.	INAP

Variable Name: V4   **Record:** 1   **Column(s):** 7

Question Asked: How about the election for the U.S. Senate? Did you vote for a candidate for the U.S. Senate? Whom did you vote for?

Code No.	Response
1.	Democratic candidate
2.	Republican candidate
3.	Third-party/Independent candidate
6.	Did not vote
7.	No Senate race
8.	DK
9.	NA
0.	INAP

EVALUATION OF PERSONAL CHARACTERISTICS OF PRESIDENTIAL CANDIDATES

Variable Name: V5   **Record:** 1   **Column(s):** 8–10

Question Asked: I'd like to get your feelings toward some of our political leaders and other people who are in the news these days.

I'll read the name of a person, and I'd like you to rate that person, using something we call the feeling thermometer. Ratings between 50 degrees and 100 degrees mean that you feel favorable and warm toward the person.

Ratings between 0 degrees and 50 degrees mean that you don't feel favorable toward the person and that you don't care too much for that person.

You would rate the person at the 50 degree mark if you didn't feel particularly warm or cold toward the person. If we come to a person whose name you don't recognize, you don't need to rate that person. Just tell me, and we'll move on to the next one.

Our first person is George Bush. How would you rate him, using the thermometer?

Code No.	Response
000.	Cold, hostile
.	.
.	.
.	.

Code No.	Response
050.	Neutral
.	.
.	.
.	.
100.	Warm, friendly
997.	Respondent doesn't recognize name.
998.	DK. Can't rate.
999.	NA

Variable Name: V6   **Record:** 1   **Column(s):** 11–13

Question Asked: How would you rate Michael Dukakis?

Code No.	Response
000.	Cold, hostile
.	.
.	.
.	.
050.	Neutral
.	.
.	.
100.	Warm, friendly
997.	Respondent doesn't recognize name.
998.	DK. Can't rate.
999.	NA

Variable Name: V7   **Record:** 1   **Column(s):** 14–16

Question Asked: How would you rate Lloyd Bentsen?

Code No.	Response
000.	Cold, hostile
.	.
.	.
.	.
050.	Neutral
.	.
.	.
.	.
100.	Warm, friendly
997.	Respondent doesn't recognize name.
998.	DK. Can't rate.
999.	NA

Variable Name: V8   **Record:** 1   **Column(s):** 17–19

Question Asked: How would you rate Dan Quayle?

Code No.	Response
000.	Cold, hostile
.	.

Code No.	Response
.	.
.	.
050.	Neutral
.	.
.	.
.	.
100.	Warm, friendly
997.	Respondent doesn't recognize name.
998.	DK. Can't rate.
999.	NA

Variable Name: V9   **Record:** 1   **Column(s):** 20

Question Asked: I am going to read a list of words and phrases that people may use to describe political figures. For each, tell me whether the word or phrase describes the candidate I name.

Think about George Bush. In your opinion does the phrase "he is compassionate" describe George Bush extremely well, quite well, not too well, or not well at all?

Code No.	Response
1.	Extremely well
2.	Quite well
3.	Not too well
4.	Not well at all
8.	DK
9.	NA

Variable Name: V10   **Record:** 1   **Column(s):** 21

Question Asked: How well does "inspiring" describe George Bush?

Code No.	Response
1.	Extremely well
2.	Quite well
3.	Not too well
4.	Not well at all
8.	DK
9.	NA

Variable Name: V11   **Record:** 1   **Column(s):** 22

Question Asked: How well does "strong leader" describe George Bush?

Code No.	Response
1.	Extremely well
2.	Quite well
3.	Not too well
4.	Not well at all
8.	DK
9.	NA

Variable Name: V12   **Record:** 1   **Column(s):** 23

Question Asked: How well does "cares for people like me" describe George Bush?

Code No.   Response

1.	Extremely well
2.	Quite well
3.	Not too well
4.	Not well at all
8.	DK
9.	NA

Variable Name: V13   **Record:** 1   **Column(s):** 24

Question Asked: How well does "honest" describe George Bush?

Code No.   Response

1.	Extremely well
2.	Quite well
3.	Not too well
4.	Not well at all
8.	DK
9.	NA

Variable Name: V14   **Record:** 1   **Column(s):** 25

Question Asked: Now let's turn to Michael Dukakis. How well does the term "compassionate" describe Michael Dukakis?

Code No.   Response

1.	Extremely well
2.	Quite well
3.	Not too well
4.	Not well at all
8.	DK
9.	NA

Variable Name: V15   **Record:** 1   **Column(s):** 26

Question Asked: How well does "inspiring" describe Michael Dukakis?

Code No.   Response

1.	Extremely well
2.	Quite well
3.	Not too well
4.	Not well at all
8.	DK
9.	NA

Variable Name: V16   **Record:** 1   **Column(s):** 27

Question Asked: How well does "strong leader" describe Michael Dukakis?

Code No.	Response
1.	Extremely well
2.	Quite well
3.	Not too well
4.	Not well at all
8.	DK
9.	NA

Variable Name: V17   **Record:** 1   **Column(s):** 28

Question Asked: How well does "cares for people like me" describe Michael Dukakis?

Code No.	Response
1.	Extremely well
2.	Quite well
3.	Not too well
4.	Not well at all
8.	DK
9.	NA

Variable Name: V18   **Record:** 1   **Column(s):** 29

Question Asked: How well does "honest" describe Michael Dukakis?

Code No.	Response
1.	Extremely well
2.	Quite well
3.	Not too well
4.	Not well at all
8.	DK
9.	NA

COMPARISON OF RESPONDENT AND PRESIDENTIAL CANDIDATE ON ISSUES

Variable Name: V19   **Record:** 1   **Column(s):** 30

Question Asked: We hear a lot of talk these days about liberals and conservatives. Here is a seven-point scale on which the political views that people might hold are arranged from extremely liberal to extremely conservative.

Where would place yourself on this scale, or haven't you thought much about this?

Code No.	Response
1.	Extremely liberal
2.	Liberal
3.	Slightly liberal
4.	Moderate, middle of the road
5.	Slightly conservative
6.	Conservative
7.	Extremely conservative

Code No.	Response
8.	DK
9.	NA
0.	Haven't thought much

Variable Name: V20   **Record:** 1   **Column(s):** 31

Question Asked: Where would you place Michael Dukakis on this scale?

Code No.	Response
1.	Extremely liberal
2.	Liberal
3.	Slightly liberal
4.	Moderate, middle of the road
5.	Slightly conservative
6.	Conservative
7.	Extremely conservative
8.	DK
9.	NA
0.	INAP

Variable Name: V21   **Record:** 1   **Column(s):** 32

Question Asked: Where would you place George Bush on this scale?

Code No.	Response
1.	Extremely liberal
2.	Liberal
3.	Slightly liberal
4.	Moderate, middle of the road
5.	Slightly conservative
6.	Conservative
7.	Extremely conservative
8.	DK
9.	NA
0.	INAP

Variable Name: V22   **Record:** 1   **Column(s):** 33

Question Asked: Where would you place the Republican Party?

Code No.	Response
1.	Extremely liberal
2.	Liberal
3.	Slightly liberal
4.	Moderate, middle of the road
5.	Slightly conservative
6.	Conservative
7.	Extremely conservative
8.	DK
9.	NA
0.	INAP

Variable Name: V23   **Record:** 1   **Column(s):** 34

Question Asked: Where would you place the Democratic Party?

Code No.   Response
_____

   1.   Extremely liberal
   2.   Liberal
   3.   Slightly liberal
   4.   Moderate, middle of the road
   5.   Slightly conservative
   6.   Conservative
   7.   Extremely conservative
   8.   DK
   9.   NA
   0.   INAP

Variable Name: V24   **Record:** 1   **Column(s):** 35

Question Asked: Some people think the government should provide fewer services, even in areas such as health and education, in order to reduce spending. Suppose these people are at one end of the scale at point 1. Other people feel it is important for the government to provide many more services even if it means an increase in spending. Suppose these people are at the other end, at point 7. And of course, some other people have opinions somewhere in between at points 2, 3, 4, 5, or 6.

Where would you place yourself on this scale, or haven't you thought much about this?

Code No.   Response
_____

   1.   A lot fewer services and less government spending
   .   .
   .   .
   .   .
   7.   A lot more services and more government spending
   8.   DK
   9.   NA
   0.   Haven't thought much

Variable Name: V25   **Record:** 1   **Column(s):** 36

Question Asked: Where would you place Michael Dukakis on this scale?

Code No.   Response
_____

   1.   A lot fewer services and less government spending
   .   .
   .   .
   .   .
   7.   A lot more services and more government spending
   8.   DK
   9.   NA
   0.   INAP

Variable Name: V26   **Record:** 1   **Column(s):** 37

Question Asked: Where would you place George Bush on this scale?

Code No.	Response
1.	A lot fewer services and less government spending
.	.
.	.
.	.
7.	A lot more services and more government spending
8.	DK
9.	NA
0.	INAP

Variable Name: V27   **Record:** 1   **Column(s):** 38

Question Asked: Some people believe that we should spend much less money for defense. Others feel that defense spending should be greatly increased. Where would you place yourself on this scale, or haven't you thought much about this?

Code No.	Response
1.	Greatly decrease defense spending
.	.
.	.
.	.
7.	Greatly increase defense spending
8.	DK
9.	NA
0.	Haven't thought much

Variable Name: V28   **Record:** 1   **Column(s):** 39

Question Asked: Where would you place Michael Dukakis on this scale?

Code No.	Response
1.	Greatly decrease defense spending
.	.
.	.
.	.
7.	Greatly increase defense spending
8.	DK
9.	NA
0.	INAP

Variable Name: V29   **Record:** 1   **Column(s):** 40

Question Asked: Where would you place George Bush on this scale?

Code No.	Response
1.	Greatly decrease defense spending
.	.
.	.
.	.
7.	Greatly increase defense spending
8.	DK
9.	NA
0.	INAP

Variable Name: V30   **Record:** 1   **Column(s):** 41

Question Asked: There is much concern about the rapid rise in medical and hospital costs. Some people feel there should be a government insurance plan which would cover all medical and hospital expenses for everyone. Others feel that all medical expenses should be paid by individuals and through private insurance plans such as Blue Cross or other company-paid plans.

Where would you place yourself on this scale, or haven't you thought much about this?

Code No.	Response
1.	Favor a government insurance plan
.	.
.	.
.	.
7.	Favor a private-sector insurance plan
8.	DK
9.	NA
0.	Haven't thought much

Variable Name: V31   **Record:** 1   **Column(s):** 42

Question Asked: Where would you place Michael Dukakis on this scale?

Code No.	Response
1.	Favor a government insurance plan
.	.
.	.
.	.
7.	Favor a private-sector insurance plan
8.	DK
9.	NA
0.	INAP

Variable Name: V32   **Record:** 1   **Column(s):** 43

Question Asked: Where would you place George Bush on this scale?

Code No.	Response
1.	Favor a government insurance plan
.	.
.	.
.	.
7.	Favor a private-sector insurance plan
8.	DK
9.	NA
0.	INAP

Variable Name: V33   **Record:** 1   **Column(s):** 44

Question Asked: Some people feel it is important for us to try to cooperate more with Russia, while others believe we should be much tougher in our dealings with Russia. Where would you place yourself on this scale, or haven't you thought much about this?

Code No.	Response
1.	Try to cooperate more with Russia.
.	.
.	.
.	.
7.	Get much tougher with Russia.
8.	DK
9.	NA
0.	Haven't thought much.

Variable Name: V34   **Record:** 1   **Column(s):** 45

Question Asked: Where would you place Michael Dukakis on this scale?

Code No.	Response
1.	Try to cooperate more with Russia.
.	.
.	.
.	.
7.	Get much tougher with Russia.
8.	DK
9.	NA
0.	Haven't thought much.

Variable Name: V35   **Record:** 1   **Column(s):** 46

Question Asked: Where would you place George Bush on this scale?

Code No.	Response
1.	Try to cooperate more with Russia.
.	.
.	.
.	.
7.	Get much tougher with Russia.
8.	DK
9.	NA
0.	Haven't thought much.

Variable Name: V36   **Record:** 1   **Column(s):** 47

Question Asked: Recently there has been a lot of talk about women's rights. Some people feel that women should have an equal role with men in running business, industry, and government. Others feel that women's place is in the home. Where would you place yourself on this scale, or haven't you thought much about this?

Code No.	Response
1.	Men and women should have equal roles in society.
.	.
.	.
.	.
7.	A woman's place is in the home.
8.	DK
9.	NA
0.	Haven't thought much.

Variable Name: V37   **Record:** 1   **Column(s):** 48

Question Asked: Where would you place Michael Dukakis on this scale?

Code No.   Response

   1.   Men and women should have equal roles in society.
   .   .
   .   .
   .   .
   7.   A woman's place is in the home.
   8.   DK
   9.   NA
   0.   Haven't thought much.

Variable Name: V38   **Record:** 1   **Column(s):** 49

Question Asked: Where would you place George Bush on this scale?

Code No.   Response

   1.   Women and men should have equal roles in society.
   .   .
   .   .
   .   .
   7.   A woman's place is in the home.
   8.   DK
   9.   NA
   0.   Haven't thought much.

SPENDING PRIORITIES

Variable name V39 not used.

Variable Name: V40   **Record:** 1   **Column(s):** 51

Question Asked: Should federal spending for aid to the Contras in Nicaragua be increased, decreased, or kept about the same?

Code No.   Response

   1.   Increased
   2.   Same
   3.   Decreased
   7.   Cut out entirely (VOL)*
   8.   DK
   9.   NA

Variable Name: V41   **Record:** 1   **Column(s):** 52

Question Asked: Should federal spending on the strategic defense initiative (Star Wars) be increased, decreased, or kept about the same?

---

*VOL means the respondent volunteered this answer, but it was not one of the choices on the close-ended questionnaire.

Code No.	Response
1.	Increased
2.	Same
3.	Decreased
7.	Cut out entirely (VOL)
8.	DK
9.	NA

Variable names V42, V43, V44, and V45 not used.

Variable Name: V46   **Record:** 1   **Column(s):** 57

Question Asked: Should federal spending for public schools be increased, decreased, or kept about the same?

Code No.	Response
1.	Increased
2.	Same
3.	Decreased
7.	Cut out entirely (VOL)
8.	DK
9.	NA

Variable Name: V47   **Record:** 1   **Column(s):** 58

Question Asked: Should federal spending to aid the homeless be increased, decreased, or kept about the same?

Code No.	Response
1.	Increased
2.	Same
3.	Decreased
7.	Cut out entirely (VOL)
8.	DK
9.	NA

POLITICAL EFFICACY

Variable Name: V48   **Record:** 1   **Column(s):** 59

Question Asked: Please tell me how much you agree or disagree with the statements below.

People like me don't have any say about what the government does.

Code No.	Response
1.	Agree strongly
2.	Agree somewhat
3.	Neither agree nor disagree
4.	Disagree somewhat
5.	Disagree strongly
8.	DK
9.	NA
0.	INAP

Variable Name: V49   **Record:** 1   **Column(s):** 60

Question Asked: I don't think public officials care much what people like me think.

Code No.   Response

  1.   Agree strongly
  2.   Agree somewhat
  3.   Neither agree nor disagree
  4.   Disagree somewhat
  5.   Disagree strongly
  8.   DK
  9.   NA
  0.   INAP

Variable names V50 and V51 not used.

PUBLIC MORALS

Variable Name: V52   **Record:** 1   **Column(s):** 63

Question Asked: Here are several more statements. As before, please tell me how strongly you agree or disagree with them.

The world is always changing, and we should adjust our view of moral behavior to those changes.

Code No.   Response

  1.   Agree strongly
  2.   Agree somewhat
  3.   Neither agree nor disagree
  4.   Disagree somewhat
  5.   Disagree strongly
  8.   DK
  9.   NA
  0.   INAP

Variable Name: V53   **Record:** 1   **Column(s):** 64

Question Asked: We should be more tolerant of people who choose to live according to their own moral standards, even if they are very different from our own.

Code No.   Response

  1.   Agree strongly
  2.   Agree somewhat
  3.   Neither agree nor disagree
  4.   Disagree somewhat
  5.   Disagree strongly
  8.   DK
  9.   NA
  0.   INAP

Variable Name: V54   **Record:** 1   **Column(s):** 65

Question Asked: The newer lifestyles are contributing to the breakdown of our society.

Code No.	Response
1.	Agree strongly
2.	Agree somewhat
3.	Neither agree nor disagree
4.	Disagree somewhat
5.	Disagree strongly
8.	DK
9.	NA
0.	INAP

RACE

Variable Name: V55   **Record:** 1   **Column(s):** 66

Question Asked: Now here are some different statements. Again, please tell me how strongly you agree or disagree with them.

Irish, Italian, Jewish, and many other minorities overcame prejudice and worked their way up. Blacks should do the same without any special favors.

Code No.	Response
1.	Agree strongly
2.	Agree somewhat
3.	Neither agree nor disagree
4.	Disagree somewhat
5.	Disagree strongly
8.	DK
9.	NA
0.	INAP

Variable Name: V56   **Record:** 1   **Column(s):** 67

Question Asked: Over the past few years blacks have gotten less than they deserve.

Code No.	Response
1.	Agree strongly
2.	Agree somewhat
3.	Neither agree nor disagree
4.	Disagree somewhat
5.	Disagree strongly
8.	DK
9.	NA
0.	INAP

Variable Name: V57   **Record:** 1   **Column(s):** 68

Question Asked: It's really a matter of some people not trying hard enough; if blacks would only try harder, they could be just as well off as whites.

Code No.   Response

Code No.	Response
1.	Agree strongly
2.	Agree somewhat
3.	Neither agree nor disagree
4.	Disagree somewhat
5.	Disagree strongly
8.	DK
9.	NA
0.	INAP

Variable name V58 not used.

MISCELLANEOUS ISSUES

Variable Name: V59   **Record:** 1   **Column(s):** 70

Question Asked: We are interested in how people are getting along financially these days. Would you say that you (and your family living here) are better off or worse off financially than you were a year ago? Is that much (better/worse) off or somewhat (better/worse) off?

Code No.	Response
1.	Much better off
2.	Somewhat better off
3.	Same
4.	Somewhat worse off
5.	Much worse off
8.	DK
9.	NA
0.	INAP

Variable Name: V60   **Record:** 1   **Column(s):** 71

Question Asked: There's a lot of talk these days about the budget deficit that has resulted because the federal government has spent more money than it has taken in. Do you personally feel the budget deficit is a very serious problem, a somewhat serious problem, or not much of a problem?

Code No.	Response
1.	Very serious
2.	Somewhat serious
3.	Not much of a problem
8.	DK
9.	NA

Variable Name: V61   **Record:** 1   **Column(s):** 72

Question Asked: During the past year, would you say that the U.S. position in the world has grown weaker, stayed about the same, or grown stronger?

Code No.   Response

1.	Grown weaker
3.	Stayed the same
5.	Grown stronger
8.	DK
9.	NA
0.	INAP

Variable Name: V62   **Record:** 1   **Column(s):** 73

Question Asked: There has been some discussion about abortion during recent years. Which one of the opinions on this page best agrees with your view?

Code No.   Response

1.	By law, abortion should never be permitted.
2.	The law should permit abortion only in case of rape, incest, or when the woman's life is in danger.
3.	The law should permit abortion for reasons other than rape, incest, or danger to the woman's life, but only after the need for the abortion has been clearly established.
4.	By law, a woman should always be able to obtain an abortion as a matter of personal choice.
7.	Other, specify
8.	DK
9.	NA

Variable Name: V63   **Record:** 1   **Column(s):** 74

Question Asked: Do you favor or oppose laws to protect homosexuals against job discrimination? Do you (favor/oppose) such laws strongly or not strongly?

Code No.   Response

1.	Favor strongly
2.	Favor, but not too strongly
3.	Depends
4.	Oppose, but not too strongly
7.	Oppose strongly
8.	DK
9.	NA
0.	INAP

Variable Name: V64   **Record:** 1   **Column(s):** 75

Question Asked: Do you favor or oppose the death penalty for persons convicted of murder? Do you (favor/oppose) the death penalty for persons convicted of murder strongly or not strongly?

Code No.   Response

1.	Favor strongly
2.	Favor, but not too strongly
3.	Depends

Code No.	Response
4.	Oppose, but not too strongly
7.	Oppose strongly
8.	DK
9.	NA
0.	INAP

Variable Name: V65   **Record:** 1   **Column(s):** 76

Question Asked: Which of the following views comes closest to your opinion on the issue of school prayer?

Code No.	Response
1.	By law, prayers should not be allowed in public schools.
2.	The law should allow public schools to schedule time when children can pray silently if they want to.
3.	The law should allow public schools to schedule time when children, as a group, can say a general prayer not tied to a particular religious faith.
4.	By law, public schools should schedule a time when all children would say a chosen Christian prayer.
7.	Other
8.	DK
9.	NA
0.	INAP

Variable Name: V66   **Record:** 1   **Column(s):** 77

Question Asked: I would like you to tell me how much you agree or disagree with the statement: We have gone too far in pushing equal rights in this country.

Code No.	Response
1.	Agree strongly
2.	Agree somewhat
3.	Neither agree nor disagree
4.	Disagree somewhat
5.	Disagree strongly
8.	DK
9.	NA
0.	INAP

Variable name V67 not used.

REAGAN RETROSPECTIVE

Variable Name: V68   **Record:** 1   **Column(s):** 79

Question Asked: Would you say that over the past eight years the economic policies of the Reagan administration have made the nation's economy better, have made it worse, or haven't made much difference either way? Would you say much (better/worse) or somewhat (better/worse)?

Code No.	Response
1.	Much better
2.	Somewhat better
3.	Same
4.	Somewhat worse
5.	Much worse
8.	DK
9.	NA
0.	INAP

Variable Name: V69   **Record:** 1   **Column(s):** 80

Question Asked: Have the policies of the Reagan administration made the United States more secure or less secure from its foreign enemies than it was in 1980, or hasn't this changed very much? Is that much or somewhat (more/less) secure?

Code No.	Response
1.	Much more secure
2.	Somewhat more secure
3.	Same
4.	Somewhat less secure
5.	Much less secure
8.	DK
9.	NA
0.	INAP

(NOTE: Columns 1–4 of record 2 repeat the respondent's four-digit ID number.)

Variable Name: V70   **Record:** 2   **Column(s):** 5

Question Asked: Are the people running the federal government now more honest or less honest than those who were running the government in 1980, or hasn't this changed much? Is that much or somewhat (more/less) honest?

Code No.	Response
1.	Much more honest
2.	Somewhat more honest
3.	Same
4.	Somewhat less honest
5.	Much less honest
8.	DK
9.	NA
0.	INAP

Variable Name: V71   **Record:** 2   **Column(s):** 6

Question Asked: Overall, do you approve or disapprove of the way Ronald Reagan has handled his job as president? Do you (approve/disapprove) strongly or not strongly?

Code No.	Response
1.	Approve strongly
2.	Approve not strongly
4.	Disapprove not strongly

Code No.	Response
5.	Disapprove strongly
8.	DK
9.	NA
0.	INAP

RESPONDENT'S BACKGROUND AND BEHAVIOR

Variable Name: V72   **Record:** 2   **Column(s):** 7

Question Asked: Some people don't pay much attention to political campaigns. How about you? Would you say that you have been very much interested, somewhat interested, or not much interested in the political campaigns so far this year?

Code No.	Response
1.	Very much interested
3.	Somewhat interested
5.	Not much interested
8.	DK
9.	NA

Variable Name: V73   **Record:** 2   **Column(s):** 8

Question Asked: How much attention did you pay to news on TV about the campaign for president—a great deal, quite a bit, some, very little, or none?

Code No.	Response
1.	A great deal
2.	Quite a bit
3.	Some
4.	Very little
5.	None
6.	Respondent doesn't watch TV news.
8.	DK
9.	NA
0.	INAP

Variable Name: V74   **Record:** 2   **Column(s):** 9

Question Asked: Generally speaking, do you usually think of yourself as a Republican, a Democrat, an Independent, or what? (If Democrat or Republican) Would you call yourself a strong or a not very strong (Democrat/Republican)? (If Independent) Do you think of yourself as closer to the Republican Party or to the Democratic Party?

Code No.	Response
0.	Strong Democrat
1.	Weak Democrat
2.	Independent, leaning toward Democrat
3.	Independent, Independent
4.	Independent, leaning toward Republican
5.	Weak Republican

Code No.	Response
6.	Strong Republican
7.	Other—minor party, refused to say
8.	Apolitical
9.	NA

Variable Name: V75   **Record:** 2   **Column(s):** 10

Question Asked: Some people seem to follow what's going on in government and public affairs most of the time, whether there's an election going on or not. Others aren't that interested. Would you say you follow what's going on in government and public affairs most of the time, some of the time, only now and then, or hardly at all?

Code No.	Response
1.	Most of the time
2.	Some of the time
3.	Only now and then
4.	Hardly at all
8.	DK
9.	NA
0.	INAP

Variable Name: V76   **Record:** 2   **Column(s):** 11

Question Asked: Here are four statements about the Bible, and I'd like you to tell me which is closest to your own view. Just give me the number of your choice.

Code No.	Response
1.	The Bible is God's word, and all it says is true.
2.	The Bible was written by men inspired by God, but it contains some human errors.
3.	The Bible is a good book because it was written by wise men, but God had nothing to do with it.
4.	The Bible was written by men who lived so long ago that it is worth very little today.
7.	Other
8.	DK
9.	NA
0.	INAP

Variable Name: V77   **Record:** 2   **Column(s):** 12

Question Asked: About how often do you pray—several times a day, once a day, a few times a week, once a week or less, or never?

Code No.	Response
1.	Several times a day
2.	Once a day
3.	A few times a week
4.	Once a week or less
5.	Never
8.	DK
9.	NA
0.	INAP

Variable Name: V78   **Record:** 2   **Column(s):** 13–14

Question Asked: Respondent's age, calculated from questions about month and year respondent was born.

Code No.	Response
17.	17 years old
.	.
.	.
.	.
99.	99 years or older
00.	NA

Variable Name: V79   **Record:** 2   **Column(s):** 15

Question Asked: Are you married now and living with your (husband/wife); or are you widowed, divorced, or separated; or have you never been married?

Code No.	Response
1.	Married and living with spouse
2.	Never married
3.	Divorced
4.	Separated
5.	Widowed
7.	Living with a partner, not married (VOL)
9.	NA

Variable Name: V80   **Record:** 2   **Column(s):** 16–17

Question Asked: What is the highest grade of school or year of college you have completed?

Code No.	Response
00.	None, no grades completed
.	.
.	.
.	.
16.	16 years (4 years of college completed)
17.	17 years or more
98.	DK
99.	NA

Variable Name: V81   **Record:** 2   **Column(s):** 18–19

Question Asked: Please look at this page and tell me the letter of the income group that includes the combined income, before taxes, of all members of your family living here in 1987. This figure should include salaries, wages, pensions, dividends, interest, and all other income. (If uncertain: what would be your best guess?)

Code No.	Response
1.	None or less than $2,999
2.	$3,000–$4,999
3.	$5,000–$6,999
4.	$7,000–$8,999
5.	$9,000–$9,999

Code No.	Response
6.	$10,000–$10,999
7.	$11,000–$11,999
8.	$12,000–$12,999
9.	$13,000–$13,999
10.	$14,000–$14,999
11.	$15,000–$16,999
12.	$17,000–$19,999
13.	$20,000–$21,999
14.	$22,000–$24,999
15.	$25,000–$29,999
16.	$30,000–$34,999
17.	$35,000–$39,999
18.	$40,000–$44,999
19.	$45,000–$49,999
20.	$50,000–$59,999
21.	$60,000–$74,999
22.	$75,000–$89,999
23.	$90,000 and over
88.	DK
98.	Respondent refused to answer.
99.	NA

Variable Name: V82   **Record:** 2   **Column(s):** 20–21

Question Asked: Now we are interested in the income that you yourself received in 1987, not including any of the income received by (your spouse and) the rest of your family. Please look at this page and tell me the income you yourself had in 1987 before taxes. This figure should include salaries, wages, pensions, dividends, interest, and all other income.

Code No.	Response
1.	None or less than $2,999
2.	$3,000–$4,999
3.	$5,000–$6,999
4.	$7,000–$8,999
5.	$9,000–$9,999
6.	$10,000–$10,999
7.	$11,000–$11,999
8.	$12,000–$12,999
9.	$13,000–$13,999
10.	$14,000–$14,999
11.	$15,000–$16,999
12.	$17,000–$19,999
13.	$20,000–$21,999
14.	$22,000–$24,999
15.	$25,000–$29,999
16.	$30,000–$34,999
17.	$35,000–$39,999
18.	$40,000–$44,999
19.	$45,000–$49,999
20.	$50,000–$59,999

Code No.	Response
21.	$60,000–$74,999
22.	$75,000–$89,999
23.	$90,000 and over
88.	DK
98.	Respondent refused to answer.
99.	NA

Variable Name: V83   **Record:** 2   **Column(s):** 22–24

Question Asked: Is your religious preference Protestant, Roman Catholic, Jewish, or something else? What church or denomination is that?

Code No.	Response
100.	Protestant, no denomination given
101.	Nondenominational Protestant church
102.	Community church (no denominational basis)
109.	Other Protestant (not listed below)

Protestant, reformation era

110.	Presbyterian
111.	Lutheran (except Missouri Synod or AME)
112.	Congregational
113.	Evangelical and Reformed
114.	Reformed, Dutch Reformed, or Christian Reformed
115.	United Church of Christ (not Church of Christ)
116.	Episcopalian, Anglican, Church of England

Protestant, Pietistic

120.	Methodist (except Free Methodist)
121.	African Methodist Episcopal
122.	United Brethren; Evangelical Brethren
123.	Baptist (not Southern Baptist)
124.	Disciples of Christ
125.	"Christian"
126.	Mennonite; Amish
127.	Church of the Brethren

Protestant, Neofundamentalist

130.	United Missionary; Protestant Missionary
131.	Church of God; Holiness
132.	Nazarene; Free Methodist
133.	Church of God in Christ
134.	Plymouth Brethren
135.	Pentecostal; Assembly of God
136.	Church of Christ
137.	Salvation Army
138.	Primitive, Free Will, Missionary Fundamentalist, Gospel Baptist
139.	Seventh Day Adventist
140.	Southern Baptist
141.	Missouri Synod Lutheran
149.	Other fundamentalists

Code No.	Response
Nontraditional Christian	
150.	Christian Scientist
151.	Spiritualist
152.	Mormon, Latter Day Saints
153.	Unitarian; Universalist
154.	Jehovah's Witness
155.	Quaker
156.	Unity
Catholic	
200.	Roman Catholic
Jewish	
300.	Jewish
Greek Rite Catholic	
700.	Greek Rite Catholic
Eastern Orthodox	
710.	Greek Orthodox
711.	Russian Orthodox
712.	Rumanian Orthodox
713.	Serbian Orthodox
719.	Other Eastern Orthodox
Non-Christians, other than Jewish	
720.	Muslim; Mohammedan
721.	Buddhist
722.	Hindu
723.	Bahai
729.	Other non-Judeo-Christian religions
790.	Other religions, including religious/ethical cults
Other	
800.	Agnostics, Atheists
996.	Refused
998.	DK; None; No preference
999.	NA

Variable Name: V84   **Record:** 2   **Column(s):** 25

Question Asked: (If any religious preference) Do you go to church or synagogue every week, almost every week, once or twice a month, a few times a year, or never?

Code No.	Response
1.	Every week
2.	Almost every week
3.	Once or twice a month
4.	A few times a year
5.	Never
8.	DK
9.	NA
0.	INAP, 996 to 999 in V83

Variable Name: V85   **Record:** 2   **Column(s):** 26

Question Asked: Respondent's race is:

Code No.	Response
1.	White
2.	Black
3.	American Indian or Alaskan Native
4.	Asian or Pacific Islander
7.	Other
9.	NA

Variable Name: V86   **Record:** 2   **Column(s):** 27

Question Asked: Are you of Spanish or Hispanic origin or descent? If so, please tell me which of the categories below best describes your Hispanic origin.

Code No.	Response
0.	No, not Hispanic
1.	Mexican
2.	Puerto Rican
3.	Cuban
4.	Latin American
5.	Central American
6.	Spanish
7.	Other
8.	DK
9.	NA

Variable Name: V87   **Record:** 2   **Column(s):** 28

Question Asked: Respondent's sex is:

Code No.	Response
1.	Male
2.	Female

Codebook: 1988 General Social Survey

RESPONDENT'S GENERAL BACKGROUND

Variable Name: ID   **Record:** 1   **Column(s):** 1–4

Question Asked: None. This is an arbitrarily selected number from 1 to 1481 uniquely identifying each respondent in the data set.

Code No.	Response
1.	First respondent
2.	Second respondent
.	.
.	.
.	.
1481	Last respondent

Variable Name: MARITAL   **Record:** 1   **Column(s):** 5

Question Asked: Are you currently married, widowed, divorced, or separated, or have you never been married?

Code No.	Response
1.	Married
2.	Widowed
3.	Divorced
4.	Separated
5.	Never married
9.	No answer

Variable Name: CHILDS   **Record:** 1   **Column(s):** 6

Question Asked: How many children have you ever had? Please count all that were born alive at any time (including any you had from a previous marriage).

Code No.	Response
0.	None
1.	One
2.	Two
3.	Three
4.	Four
5.	Five
6.	Six
7.	Seven
8.	Eight or more
9.	No answer

Variable Name: AGE   **Record:** 1   **Column(s):** 7–8

Question Asked: NOTE: Respondents were asked, ''What is your date of birth?'' Coders then used this information to determine the respondent's age, the information contained in this variable.

Code No.	Response
18.	Actual age in years
.	.
.	.
.	.
89.	89 or more years old
99.	No answer. Don't know.

Variable Name: EDUC   **Record:** 1   **Column(s):** 9–10

Question Asked: NOTE: Calculated by the coders from the responses to the following three separate questions. What is the highest grade in elementary school or high school that you finished and got credit for? Did you complete one or more years of college for credit—not including schooling such as business college, technical or vocational school? If yes, How many years did you complete?

Code No.	Response
00.	No formal schooling
01.	1st grade
02.	2d grade
03.	3d grade
04.	4th grade
05.	5th grade
06.	6th grade
07.	7th grade
08.	8th grade
09.	9th grade
10.	10th grade
11.	11th grade
12.	12th grade
13.	1 year of college

Code No.	Response
14.	2 years of college
15.	3 years of college
16.	4 years of college
17.	5 years of college
18.	6 years of college
19.	7 years of college
20.	8 or more years of college
98.	Don't know
99.	No answer

Variable Name: SPEDUC   **Record:** 1   **Column(s):** 11–12

Question Asked: NOTE: This variable was calculated by the coders from the responses to the following three separate questions. What is the highest grade in elementary school or high school that your spouse finished and got credit for? Did (he/she) complete one or more years of college for credit—not including schooling such as business college, technical or vocational school? If yes, how many years did (he/she) complete?

Code No.	Response
00.	No formal schooling
01.	1st grade
02.	2d grade
03.	3d grade
04.	4th grade
05.	5th grade
06.	6th grade
07.	7th grade
08.	8th grade
09.	9th grade
10.	10th grade
11.	11th grade
12.	12th grade
13.	1 year of college
14.	2 years of college
15.	3 years of college
16.	4 years of college
17.	5 years of college
18.	6 years of college
19.	7 years of college
20.	8 years of college
97.	Not applicable (not married)
98.	Don't know

Variable Name: SEX   **Record:** 1   **Column(s):** 13

Question Asked: None, coded by interviewer.

Code No.	Response
1.	Male
2.	Female

Variable Name: RACE   **Record:** 1   **Column(s):** 14

Question Asked: What race do you consider yourself? NOTE: If there was *no* doubt in the interviewer's mind, the response code was entered by the interviewer without asking the question.

Code No.	Response
1.	White
2.	Black
3.	Other

Variable Name: WRKSTAT   **Record:** 1   **Column(s):** 15

Question Asked: Last week were you working full-time, working part-time, going to school, keeping house, or what?

Code No.	Response
1.	Working full-time
2.	Working part-time
3.	With a job, but not at work because of temporary illness, vacation, strike
4.	Unemployed, laid off, looking for work
5.	Retired
6.	In school
7.	Keeping house
8.	Other

Variable Name: RINCOME   **Record:** 1   **Column(s):** 16–17

Question Asked: Did you earn any income from your occupation last year? If yes, in which of these groups did your income fall last year, before taxes, that is? Just tell me the letter. NOTE: Respondent shown card with income groups on it.

Code No.	Response
01.	Under $1,000
02.	$1,000 to $2,999
03.	$3,000 to $3,999
04.	$4,000 to $4,999
05.	$5,000 to $5,999
06.	$6,000 to $6,999
07.	$7,000 to $7,999
08.	$8,000 to $9,999
09.	$10,000 to $12,499
10.	$12,500 to $14,999
11.	$15,000 to $17,499
12.	$17,500 to $19,999
13.	$20,000 to $22,499
14.	$22,500 to $24,999
15.	$25,000 to $29,999
16.	$30,000 to $34,999
17.	$35,000 to $39,999
18.	$40,000 to $49,999
19.	$50,000 to $59,999
20.	$60,000 and over
97.	Refused
98.	Don't know
99.	No answer

Variable Name: SPWRKSTA   **Record:** 1   **Column(s):** 18–19

Question Asked: Last week was your (wife/husband) working full-time, part-time, going to school, keeping house, or what?

Code No.	Response
1.	Working full-time
2.	Working part-time
3.	With a job, but not at work because of temporary illness, vacation, strike
4.	Unemployed, laid off, looking for work
5.	Retired
6.	In school
7.	Keeping house
8.	Other
9.	No answer
−1.	Not applicable—no spouse (codes 2–5 on MARITAL)

Variable Name: FINCOME   **Record:** 1   **Column(s):** 20–21

Question Asked: In which of these groups did your total *family* income, from *all* sources, fall last year, before taxes that is? Just tell me the letter. *Note:* Respondent shown card with income groups on it.

Code No.	Response
01.	Under $1,000
02.	$1,000 to $2,999
03.	$3,000 to $3,999
04.	$4,000 to $4,999
05.	$5,000 to $5,999
06.	$6,000 to $6,999
07.	$7,000 to $7,999
08.	$8,000 to $9,999
09.	$10,000 to $12,499
10.	$12,500 to $14,999
11.	$15,000 to $17,499
12.	$17,500 to $19,999
13.	$20,000 to $22,499
14.	$22,500 to $24,999
15.	$25,000 to $29,999
16.	$30,000 to $34,999
17.	$35,000 to $39,999
18.	$40,000 to $49,999
19.	$50,000 to $59,999
20.	$60,000 and over
97.	Refused
98.	Don't know
99.	No answer

Variable Name: WORDSUM   **Record:** 1   **Column(s):** 22–23

Question Asked: Respondents were given a 10-word vocabulary test. For each of the 10 words provided, respondents were provided a choice of 5 other words and asked to pick the one closest to the original word in meaning. Below is the number of vocabulary words they were able to correctly match. This simple vocabulary test has been found to be a reasonable and reliable indicator of the respondent's IQ.

Code No.	Response
00.	None correct
01.	One correct
02.	Two correct
03.	Three correct
04.	Four correct
05.	Five correct
06.	Six correct
07.	Seven correct
08.	Eight correct
09.	Nine correct
10.	All ten correct
99.	No answer, did not try
−1.	Not applicable

RESPONDENT'S RELIGIOUS BELIEFS OR BEHAVIOR

Variable Name: RELIG   **Record:** 1   **Column(s):** 24

Question Asked: What is your religious preference? Is it Protestant, Catholic, Jewish, some other religion, or no religion?

Code No.	Response
1.	Protestant
2.	Catholic
3.	Jewish
4.	None
5.	Other
9.	No answer

Variable Name: SPREL   **Record:** 1   **Column(s):** 25–26

Question Asked: What is your spouse's religious preference? Is it Protestant, Catholic, Jewish, some other religion, or no religion?

Code No.	Response
1.	Protestant
2.	Catholic
3.	Jewish
4.	None
5.	Other
8.	Don't know
9.	No answer
−1.	Not applicable (not currently married)

Variable Name: ATTEND   **Record:** 1   **Column(s):** 27

Question Asked: How often do you attend religious services?

Code No.	Response
0.	Never
1.	Less than once a year

Code No.	Response
2.	About once or twice a year
3.	Several times a year
4.	About once a month
5.	2–3 times a month
6.	Nearly every week
7.	Every week
8.	Several times a week
9.	Don't know, no answer

Variable Name: SPATTEND   **Record:** 1   **Column(s):** 28–29

Question Asked: How often does your spouse attend religious services?

Code No.	Response
0.	Never
1.	Less than once a year
2.	About once or twice a year
3.	Several times a year
4.	About once a month
5.	2–3 times a month
6.	Nearly every week
7.	Every week
8.	Several times a week
9.	Don't know, no answer
−1.	Not applicable (never married)

Variable Name: PRAY   **Record:** 1   **Column(s):** 30

Question Asked: About how often do you pray?

Code No.	Response
1.	Several times a day
2.	Once a day
3.	Several times a week
4.	Once a week
5.	Less than once a week
6.	Never
8.	Don't know
9.	No answer

Variable Name: TITHING   **Record:** 1   **Column(s):** 31–35

Question Asked: About how much do you contribute to your religion every year (not including school tuition)?

Code No.	Response
0.	None
.	Actual dollars contributed
.	.
.	.
.	.
.	.

Code No.	Response
5000	5000 dollars or more
99998	Don't know
99999	No answer

MORAL ISSUES

Variable Name: ROTAPPLE   **Record:** 1   **Column(s):** 36

Question Asked: Do you strongly agree, agree, disagree, or strongly disagree that immoral actions by one person can corrupt society in general?

Code No.	Response
1.	Strongly agree
2.	Agree
3.	Disagree
4.	Strongly disagree
5.	Don't know
6.	No answer

Variable Name: PERMORAL   **Record:** 1   **Column(s):** 37

Question Asked: Do you strongly agree, agree, disagree, or strongly disagree that morality is a personal matter and society should not force everyone to follow one standard?

Code No.	Response
1.	Strongly agree
2.	Agree
3.	Disagree
4.	Strongly disagree
5.	Don't know
6.	No answer

RESPONDENT'S ATTITUDES ON SEXUAL ISSUES

Variable Name: PILLOK   **Record:** 1   **Column(s):** 38

Question Asked: Do you strongly agree, agree, disagree, or strongly disagree that methods of birth control should be available to teenagers between the ages and 14 and 16 if their parents do not approve?

Code No.	Response
1.	Strongly agree
2.	Agree
3.	Disagree
4.	Strongly disagree
5.	Don't know
6.	No answer
0.	Not applicable

Variable Name: PREMARSX   **Record:** 1   **Column(s):** 39

Question Asked: There's been a lot of discussion about the way morals and attitudes about sex are changing in this country. If a man and woman have sex relations before marriage, do you think it is always wrong, almost always wrong, wrong only sometimes, or not wrong at all?

Code No.	Response
1.	Always wrong
2.	Almost always wrong
3.	Wrong only sometimes
4.	Not wrong at all
8.	Don't know
9.	No answer
0.	Not applicable

Variable Name: TEENSEX   **Record:** 1   **Column(s):** 40

Question Asked: What if they are in their early teens, say 14 to 16 years old? In that case, do you think sex relations before marriage are always wrong, almost always wrong, wrong only sometimes, or not wrong at all?

Code No.	Response
1.	Always wrong
2.	Almost always wrong
3.	Wrong only sometimes
4.	Not wrong at all
8.	Don't know
9.	No answer
0.	Not applicable

Variable Name: HOMOSEX   **Record:** 1   **Column(s):** 41

Question Asked: What about sexual relations between two *adults* of the same sex—do you think it is always wrong, almost always wrong, wrong only sometimes, or not wrong at all?

Code No.	Response
1.	Always wrong
2.	Almost always wrong
3.	Wrong only sometimes
4.	Not wrong at all
8.	Don't know
9.	No answer
0.	Not applicable

Variable Name: PORNLAW   **Record:** 1   **Column(s):** 42

Question Asked: Which of these statements comes closest to your feelings about pornography laws?

Code No.	Response
1.	There should be laws against the distribution of pornography whatever the age.
2.	There should be laws against the distribution of pornography to persons under 18.
3.	There should be no laws forbidding the distribution of pornography.
8.	Don't know
9.	No answer
0.	Not applicable

RESPONDENT'S ATTITUDES ON GENDER ISSUES

Variable Name: FEHOME   **Record:** 1   **Column(s):** 43

Question Asked: Tell me if you agree or disagree with this statement: Women should take care of running their homes and leave running the country to men.

Code No.	Response
1.	Agree
2.	Disagree
8.	Not sure
9.	No answer
0.	Not applicable

Variable Name: FEPOL   **Record:** 1   **Column(s):** 44

Question Asked: Tell me if you agree or disagree with this statement: Most men are better suited emotionally for politics than are most women.

Code No.	Response
1.	Agree
2.	Disagree
8.	Not sure
9.	No answer
0.	Not applicable

Variable Name: FEFAM   **Record:** 1   **Column(s):** 45

Question Asked: Tell me if you agree or disagree with this statement: It is much better for everyone involved if the man is the achiever outside the home and the woman takes care of the home and family.

Code No.	Response
1.	Strongly agree
2.	Agree
3.	Disagree
4.	Strongly disagree
8.	Don't know
9.	No answer
0.	Not applicable

Variable Name: FEPRESCH   **Record:** 1   **Column(s):** 46

Question Asked: Tell me if you agree or disagree with this statement: A preschool child is likely to suffer if her or his mother works.

Code No.	Response
1.	Strongly agree
2.	Agree
3.	Disagree
4.	Strongly disagree
8.	Don't know
9.	No answer
0.	Not applicable

RESPONDENT'S VIEW OF PERSONAL SITUATION

Variable Name: HAPPY   **Record:** 1   **Column(s):** 47

Question Asked: Taken all together, how would you say things are these days—would you say that you are very happy, pretty happy, or not too happy?

Code No.	Response
1.	Very happy
2.	Pretty happy
3.	Not too happy
9.	No answer

Variable Name: HAPMAR   **Record:** 1   **Column(s):** 48

Question Asked: Taking things all together, how would you describe your marriage? Would you say that your marriage is very happy, pretty happy, or not too happy?

Code No.	Response
1.	Very happy
2.	Pretty happy
3.	Not too happy
8.	Don't know
9.	No answer
0.	Not applicable (not currently married)

Variable Name: SATFIN   **Record:** 1   **Column(s):** 49

Question Asked: We are interested in how people are getting along financially these days. So far as you and your family are concerned, would you say that you are pretty well satisfied with your present financial situation, more or less satisfied, or not satisfied at all?

Code No.	Response
1.	Pretty well satisfied
2.	More or less satisfied
3.	Not satisfied at all
8.	Don't know
9.	No answer

Variable Name: SATFAM   **Record:** 1   **Column(s):** 50

Question Asked: How much satisfaction do you get from your family life?

Code No.	Response
1.	A very great deal
2.	A great deal
3.	Quite a bit
4.	A fair amount
5.	Some
6.	A little
7.	None
8.	Don't know
9.	No answer
0.	Not applicable

Variable Name: SATJOB   **Record:** 1   **Column(s):** 51

Question Asked: On the whole, how satisfied are you with the work you do—would you say you are very satisfied, moderately satisfied, a little dissatisfied, or very dissatisfied?

Code No.	Response
1.	Very satisfied
2.	Moderately satisfied
3.	A little dissatisfied
4.	Very dissatisfied
8.	Don't know
9.	No answer
0.	Not applicable (coded 5, 6, or 8 on WRKSTAT)

Variable Name: LIFE   **Record:** 1   **Column(s):** 52

Question Asked: In general, do you find life exciting, pretty routine, or dull?

Code No.	Response
1.	Exciting
2.	Pretty routine
3.	Dull
8.	No opinion
9.	No answer
0.	Not applicable

RESPONDENT'S VIEW OF OTHER PEOPLE

Variable Name: HELPFUL   **Record:** 1   **Column(s):** 53

Question Asked: Would you say that most of the time people try to be helpful or that they are mostly just looking out for themselves?

Code No.	Response
1.	Try to be helpful
2.	Just look out for themselves
3.	Depends (volunteered)*
8.	Don't know
9.	No answer
0.	Not applicable

Variable Name: FAIR   **Record:** 1   **Column(s):** 54

Question Asked: Do you think most people would try to take advantage of you if they got a chance, or would they try to be fair?

Code No.	Response
1.	Would take advantage of you
2.	Would try to be fair
3.	Depends (volunteered)*
8.	Don't know
9.	No answer
0.	Not applicable

Variable Name: TRUST   **Record:** 1   **Column(s):** 55

Question Asked: Generally speaking, would you say that most people can be trusted or that you can't be too careful in dealing with people?

Code No.	Response
1.	Most people can be trusted
2.	Can't be too careful
3.	Other, depends (volunteered)*
8.	Don't know
9.	No answer
0.	Not applicable

RACE ISSUES

Variable Name: RACCHNG   **Record:** 1   **Column(s):** 56

Question Asked: If you and your friends belonged to a social club that would not let blacks join, would you try to change the rules so that blacks could join?

Code No.	Response
1.	Yes
2.	No
8.	Don't know
9.	No answer
0.	Not applicable

Variable Name: RACDIF2   **Record:** 1   **Column(s):** 57

Question Asked: On the average, blacks have worse jobs, income, and housing than whites. Do you think these differences are because most blacks have less inborn ability to learn?

Code No.	Response
1.	Yes
2.	No
8.	Don't know
9.	No answer
0.	Not applicable

Variable Name: RACDIF4   **Record:** 1   **Column(s):** 58

Question Asked: On the average, blacks have worse jobs, income, and housing than whites. Do you think these differences are because most blacks just don't have the motivation or will power to pull themselves up out of poverty?

Code No.	Response
1.	Yes
2.	No
8.	Don't know
9.	No answer
0.	Not applicable

*Volunteered means the respondent volunteered this answer, but it was not one of the choices on the close-ended questionnaire.

Variable Name: RACSCHL   **Record:** 1   **Column(s):** 59

Question Asked: Would you yourself have any objection to sending your children to a school where some of the children are black?

Code No.	Response
1.	Yes, if a few of the children are black.
2.	Yes, if half of the children are black.
3.	Yes, if more than half of the children are black.
4.	No, do not object to any of the above.
7.	Not applicable
8.	Don't know
9.	No answer

MISCELLANEOUS ATTITUDES

Variable Name: DRUNK   **Record:** 1   **Column(s):** 60

Question Asked: Do you sometimes drink more than you think you should?

Code No.	Response
1.	Yes
2.	No
3.	Not appropriate (respondent does not drink)
8.	Don't know
9.	No answer
0.	Not applicable

Variable Name: XMOVIE   **Record:** 1   **Column(s):** 61

Question Asked: Have you seen an X-rated movie in the last year?

Code No.	Response
1.	Yes
2.	No
8.	Don't know
9.	No answer
0.	Not applicable

Variable Name: TVHOURS   **Record:** 1   **Column(s):** 62–63

Question Asked: On the average day, about how many hours do you personally watch television?

Code No.	Response
00.	0 hours
.	.
.	Actual number of hours coded
.	.
20.	20 or more hours per day
98.	Don't know
99.	No answer
−1.	Not applicable

Variable Name: POLVIEWS   **Record:** 1   **Column(s):** 64

Question Asked: We hear a lot of talk these days about liberals and conservatives. I'm going to show you a seven-point scale on which the political views that people might hold are arranged from extremely liberal—point 1—to extremely conservative—point 7. Where would you place yourself on this scale?

Code No.	Response
1.	Extremely liberal
2.	Liberal
3.	Slightly liberal
4.	Moderate, middle of the road
5.	Slightly conservative
6.	Conservative
7.	Extremely conservative
8.	Don't know
9.	No answer

ATTITUDES TOWARD CHILDREN

Variable Name: OBEY   **Record:** 1   **Column(s):** 65

Question Asked: If you had to choose, which thing on this list would you pick as the most important for a child to learn to prepare him or her for life? Which comes next in importance? Third? Fourth?
To obey.

Code No.	Response
1.	Most important
2.	Second
3.	Third
4.	Fourth
5.	Least important
9.	No answer
0.	Not applicable

Variable Name: POPULAR   **Record:** 1   **Column(s):** 66

Question Asked: To be well liked or popular.

Code No.	Response
1.	Most important
2.	Second
3.	Third
4.	Fourth
5.	Least important
9.	No answer
0.	Not applicable

Variable Name: THNKSELF   **Record:** 1   **Column(s):** 67

Question Asked: To think for herself or himself.

Code No.	Response
1.	Most important
2.	Second
3.	Third
4.	Fourth
5.	Least important
9.	No answer
0.	Not applicable

Variable Name: WORKHARD   **Record:** 1   **Column(s):** 68

Question Asked: To work hard.

Code No.	Response
1.	Most important
2.	Second
3.	Third
4.	Fourth
5.	Least important
9.	No answer
0.	Not applicable

Variable Name: HELPOTH   **Record:** 1   **Column(s):** 69

Question Asked: To help others when they need help.

Code No.	Response
1.	Most important
2.	Second
3.	Third
4.	Fourth
5.	Least important
9.	No answer
0.	Not applicable

Variable Name: SPANKING   **Record:** 1   **Column(s):** 70

Question Asked: Do you strongly agree, agree, disagree, or strongly disagree that it is sometimes necessary to discipline a child with a good, hard spanking?

Code No.	Response
1.	Strongly agree
2.	Agree
3.	Disagree
4.	Strongly disagree
8.	Don't know
9.	No answer
0.	Not applicable

ATTITUDES TOWARD ABORTION

Variable Name: ABDEFECT   **Record:** 1   **Column(s):** 71

Question Asked: Please tell me whether you think it should be possible for a pregnant woman to obtain a legal abortion in the following situations.

There is a strong chance of serious defect in the baby.

Code No.	Response
1.	Yes
2.	No
8.	Don't know
9.	No answer
0.	Not applicable

Variable Name: ABPOOR   **Record:** 1   **Column(s):** 72

Question Asked: The family has a very low income and cannot afford any more children.

Code No.	Response
1.	Yes
2.	No
8.	Don't know
9.	No answer
0.	Not applicable

Variable Name: ABRAPE   **Record:** 1   **Column(s):** 73

Question Asked: She became pregnant as a result of rape.

Code No.	Response
1.	Yes
2.	No
8.	Don't know
9.	No answer
0.	Not applicable

Variable Name: ABANY   **Record:** 1   **Column(s):** 74

Question Asked: The woman wants it for any reason.

Code No.	Response
1.	Yes
2.	No
8.	Don't know
9.	No answer
0.	Not applicable

ATTITUDES TOWARD SCIENCE

Variable Name: SCISOLVE   **Record:** 1   **Column(s):** 75

Question Asked: Here are some things that have been said about science. Do you tend to agree or disagree with them? Science will solve our social problems such as crime and mental illness.

Code No.	Response
1.	Agree
2.	Disagree
8.	Don't know
9.	No answer
0.	Not applicable

Variable Name: SCICHNG   **Record:** 1   **Column(s):** 76

Question Asked: One trouble with science is that it makes our way of life change too fast.

Code No.	Response
1.	Agree
2.	Disagree
8.	Don't know
9.	No answer
0.	Not applicable

Variable Name: SCIPRY   **Record:** 1   **Column(s):** 77

Question Asked: Scientists always seem to be prying into things that they really ought to stay out of.

Code No.	Response
1.	Agree
2.	Disagree
8.	Don't know
9.	No answer
0.	Not applicable

Variable Name: SCIMORAL   **Record:** 1   **Column(s):** 78

Question Asked: One of the bad effects of science is that it breaks down people's ideas of right and wrong.

Code No.	Response
1.	Agree
2.	Disagree
8.	Don't know
9.	No answer
0.	Not applicable

ATTITUDES TOWARD AIDS

Variable Name: AIDSSCH   **Record:** 1   **Column(s):** 79

Question Asked: Do you support or oppose the following measures to deal with AIDS?

Prohibit students with the AIDS virus from attending public school.

Code No.	Response
1.	Support
2.	Oppose
8.	No opinion
9.	No answer
0.	Not applicable

Variable Name: AIDSADS　　　　　　　　**Record:** 1　　　　　　　　**Column(s):** 80

Question Asked: Develop a governmental information program to promote safe sex practices, such as the use of condoms.

Code No.	Response
1.	Support
2.	Oppose
8.	No opinion
9.	No answer
0.	Not applicable

Variable Name: AIDSSXED　　　　　　　　**Record:** 2　　　　　　　　**Column(s):** 1

Question Asked: Require the teaching of safe sex practices, such as the use of condoms, in sex education courses in public schools.

Code No.	Response
1.	Support
2.	Oppose
8.	No opinion
9.	No answer
0.	Not applicable

Variable Name: AIDSIDS　　　　　　　　**Record:** 2　　　　　　　　**Column(s):** 2

Question Asked: Require people with the AIDS virus to wear identification tags that look like those carried by people with allergies or diabetes.

Code No.	Response
1.	Support
2.	Oppose
8.	No opinion
9.	No answer
0.	Not applicable

Note: The two questions below were self-administered. Instead of the interviewer's asking the questions, respondents were handed a card and asked to check the correct answer.

Variable Name: PARTNERS　　　　　　　　**Record:** 2　　　　　　　　**Column(s):** 3–4

Question Asked: How many sex partners have you had in the last 12 months?

Code No.	Response
0.	No partners
1.	1 partner
2.	2 partners
3.	3 partners
4.	4 partners
5.	5–10 partners
6.	11–20 partners
7.	21–100 partners
8.	More than 100 partners
−2.	One or more, don't know the number
−1.	Not applicable

Variable Name: SEXSEX   **Record:** 2   **Column(s):** 5

Question Asked: Have your sex partners in the last 12 months been . . .

Code No.	Response
1.	Exclusively male
2.	Both male and female
3.	Exclusively female
9.	No answer
0.	Not applicable

Appendix C

Answers to Selected Exercises

Page 511

2.3 *a.* Yes, southerners, but you need to be more precise than this. What does one mean by a southerner? Usually, the U.S. South is identified as the states of the old Confederacy, although occasionally other states are included as well.

   c. Note that the question talks about voters only, not all people in the United States. So the population relevant to this question is the group that voted in the 1988 presidential election.

   e. This is tricky. The question focuses on gay people and your first reaction might be to define the population as all gays. However, the question really asks whether gays are different from non-gays and thus both groups must be included in the study, or the entire U.S. population.

4.2 *a.* There is no slash between the DATA LIST term and the name of the first variable.

   c. Two problems. First, the term DATA is misspelled as DATE. This will not cause a problem for SPSS/PC+ because the misspelling occurs after the third letter of the command. Second, there is no END DATA statement, which will lead SPSS to try to read the FREQUENCIES command as data rather than a command.

   d. The FREQUENCIES command refers to variable N2 which is not defined on the DATA LIST.

   g. There is a typing error on DATA LIST. The name of the second variable is supposed to be A3, but it is typed with spaces between the A and the 3 (A 3). This will cause SPSS to read the second variable as one named A located in column 3. Then SPSS will try to read the later column designation (4-7) as the name of the next variable which will produce an error message because this "variable name" neither begins with a letter nor is followed by a column location.

    i. The name of the second variable, GT, is an SPSS reserved term that cannot be used as a variable name.

5.2 *a.* Some of the concepts that might be measured by these operational variables are:
RACSCHL, a person's level of racism
PREMARSX, a person's level of social conservatism or moral traditionalism
SPANKING, a person's authoritarian personality or tendency toward violence or parental strictness
TITHING, a person's level of religious commitment or personal wealth

5.3 *a.* The file name is not enclosed in quotation marks. This might work, but only if the file is in the current directory.
  c. There is no slash between the file name and the list of variables.
  d. For IBM computers using JCL, the file name should *not* be enclosed in quotation marks.
  f. No problem.
  h. The FILE HANDLE must come before any reference to the file on a DATA LIST or other command.

6.3 *a.* The label is enclosed in single quotes, so the apostrophe in RESP'S will be considered the end of the first label.
  c. There is no slash separating the labels for variables RACE and AGE.
  e. Only three values can be declared as missing for any variable.
  g. The term FILE is missing.

7.1 V1: Mode = 1 and 7, median = 6, range = 9. When we are dealing with the mode, it is possible for a variable to have two modes (called bimodal) or even more.
    V2: Mode = 7, median = 7, mean = 5.73.
    V3: Median = 3, mean = 3, variance = 2.0, standard deviation = 1.41.

7.2 *b.* You cannot ask for both a BARCHART and a HISTOGRAM on the same FREQUENCIES command. SPSS will give you a warning message and then produce bar charts only if they can fit on one page of output; otherwise it will produce a histogram.
  e. You are requesting the default statistics, which are interval-level statistics, for a nominal variable.
  f. You cannot split the name of a variable (SPWRKSTA) between two lines.

7.5 SEX is a dichotomy, which means interval statistics (mean and standard deviation) can be used. The mode is also an acceptable statistic for dichotomies, but neither the median nor the range is very useful.
  MARITAL is nominal. Only the mode is a useful measure of central tendency, and there is no useful measure of dispersion.
  PERMORAL is a judgment call. The conceptual variable being measured is a continuum ranging from seeing morality as completely a personal concern to seeing it as completely a concern of society. Do the values of this operational variable seem to represent equal distances apart on the conceptual variable? If so, interval statistics can be used. If not, only ordinal statistics are appropriate.
  RINCOME. The income variables in both data sets illustrate well how an operational variable's character—nominal, ordinal, or interval—depends on what conceptual variable it is used to measure. Dollars of income seem like an obvious interval measure, but look at how this operational variable is coded. The difference between code numbers 3 and 4 is a distance of $1000. Between code numbers

16 and 17 is a distance of $5000. If we are measuring dollars of income, the current coding system is ordinal. If, however, we are measuring standard of living, it is probably interval. To a person making $2000 or $3000 a year, an extra $1000 in income is a substantial change in the person's standard of living. To people making $50,000 a year, their income needs to increase by $5000 to $10,000 before they experience a similar change in standard of living.

V2 is nominal, and only the mode is useful.

V40. Like PERMORAL above, it is a judgment call as to whether this operational variable is an ordinal or interval measure of the conceptual variable. This variable has a quirk to it. The Increased, Same, Decreased responses might be equal distances apart on the conceptual variable. However, a number of respondents volunteered that spending should be cut entirely, a response that may be extremely far away from the others on the conceptual variable.

V82. Same as RINCOME above.

8.1 *b.* Each group can be recoded into only one new value. What new value will SPSS give these cases, 4 or 5?

    d. The command asks for two inconsistent conditions to be met simultaneously—that a person have both 8 years and 12 years of education.

    f. Except for Release 4, the condition is specified with the logical operator EQ, not a mathematical symbol, and setting a new variable equal to a value uses mathematical symbols, not logical operators.

    h. Each IF or other data modification command must begin on a new line. Observe that, if done properly, the impact of the two IF commands would be the same as the command

       RECODE AGE (0 THRU 39 = 1) (40 THRU 89 = 2)

    j. The number of cases in the data set is omitted.

    k. This command will work, but it does not really accomplish anything since you are asking for a 100 percent (1.0) sample, or the exact same cases you already have in your active file.

8.3   There may be more than one way to develop each answer. Below are some ways to develop the variables requested.

    b. We want the new variable to have negative numbers if the husband attends more frequently, positive numbers if the wife does (or vice versa), and a zero if both attend at the same level of frequency. This can be done by largely duplicating the strategy displayed in Table 8.7, substituting the ATTEND and SPATTEND variables for EDUC and SPEDUC.

    d. RECODE V74 (0,6 = 6) (1,5 = 5) (2,4 = 4). The variable desired is one that has people strongly committed to any political party (regardless of which one) at one end of the spectrum (high or low) and those independent of any party at the other. The command above groups Republican and Democratic identifiers together based on the strength of their commitment.

    f. This exercise requires the variable to be changed to an either/or dichotomy, but which original values are grouped together depends on exactly what is being sought. Do you want a variable showing whether people are *currently* single? If so, all married respondents should be in one group and all the single, widowed, divorced, etc., respondents in another group. If, however, you are trying to identify only those who have never been married at all, the never-married category comprises one group while all those currently or formerly married make up a second group.

h. As discussed in the answers for Chapter 7, the income variables are probably close to interval measures of each respondent's standard of living, but not of her or his actual income earned. The difference between code numbers 4 and 5 on RINCOME is a distance of $1000 in income earned, while the difference between code numbers 15 and 16 is a distance of $5000 in earned income.

This can be changed by revising the operational variable's code numbers to match actual distances apart in dollars of income. The simplest way to do this is to recode the operational variable's code numbers to the midpoint of the income group that they represent. Code numbers 4 and 5 would be recoded to 4500 and 5500, respectively, code numbers 15 and 16 would become 27500 and 32500, and so on. Then the code numbers would match distances apart on the conceptual variable of income in dollars, although the recoded variable would no longer well represent distances apart in standard of living.

9.1   There are 36 possible outcomes from tossing a pair of dice, all listed in Table 9.1. Of these outcomes, 6 are doubles. Thus, the probability of obtaining doubles from any single roll of the dice is $\frac{6}{36}$, or $\frac{1}{6}$.

9.6   AGE: 95% CI = 45.374 ± .935
SPEDUC: 95% CI = 12.676 ± .208
V6: 95% CI = 56.762 ± 1.184
V8: 99% CI = 45.863 ± 1.561

9.7   You can't. We have discussed confidence intervals only for population means. Religious preference is a nominal variable for which the mean has no significance or interpretation. A confidence interval for a statistic without meaning is also without value.

10.1   *b.* Directional, negative. Increases in age are related to decreases in support for premarital sex.
e. Directional, positive.
g. Directional, negative.
h. Directional, positive.

10.2   The answers below are merely illustrations. Any phrasing is acceptable as long as the null hypothesis is written to be the opposite of the research hypothesis.
a. Race is not related to voting.
c. Increasingly favorable reactions to Dan Quayle are not related to less favorable reactions to Lloyd Bentsen.
d. A person's age is not related to his or her income.
f. More frequent church attenders have the same or lower levels of opposition to abortion as less frequent church attenders.
h. Democrats are not more liberal than Republicans.

11.1   *a.* There is no GROUPS = statement.
c. The command syntax is correct, but is the operational variable HAPPY an interval measure of the concept, a person's level of happiness? This could be argued either way, but you need to make a decision before determining if this command makes sense.
d. Three code numbers are used for the GROUPS statement.
f. RELIG and SPREL are nominal variables.
h. There is no VARIABLES = statement.
k. No code numbers are identified for the grouping variable.

> m. The PAIRS part of the command is correct, but VARIABLES = V6 does not belong on this command.
>
> o. The command has a space between "T" and "TEST."

11.2 b. No. The independent variable, level of education, does not refer to just two groups.

> d. Yes.
>
> f. No. Marital status includes many different groups, not just two. The hypothesis would need to be rephrased, such as comparing married with single respondents or the widowed to the divorced.
>
> g. Yes. Education can be recoded into groups with and without a college degree. In addition, the science variables SCISOLVE to SCIMORAL are dichotomies, which qualifies them as interval variables.
>
> h. Yes. You can use the paired version of the T-TEST to compare how the two parties are perceived, V22 and V23.
>
> j. Yes. Use a paired T-TEST on variables V11 and V16.
>
> k. No. Race is not just two categories. Voting is, but that is the dependent variable, not the independent one.

12.1 a. There is no BY keyword separating the dependent and independent variables. No option is selected for the RANGES subcommand.

> c. The BTUKEY option works only with PC+. It will create an error message in SPSS-X and in some versions of Release 4.
>
> e. Two independent variables are listed after the BY statement. Only one independent variable can be analyzed per ONEWAY command.
>
> g. The command used is ANOVA, not ONEWAY. There is an SPSS command called ANOVA, so you will obtain a printout, but not the analysis-of-variance test described in this chapter.
>
> i. The RANGES subcommand requests the TUKEY comparison instead of TUKEYB. Since a TUKEY comparison does exist, you will obtain a printout but containing a different statistic.
>
> k. Using the FORMAT = LABELS subcommand makes sense only when some part of the printout will list the independent-variable groups, only when descriptive statistics or the Tukey *b* comparison is requested. Adding it to this command will not hurt anything, but it will not do any good either.
>
> m. The OPTIONS request will work only on SPSS/PC+. For SPSS-X version 2, the OPTIONS subcommand must begin in column 1.
>
> o. Both the OPTIONS and STATISTICS subcommands must begin in column 1, and thus obviously on different lines, in SPSS-X and no slashes are used. For SPSS/PC+, the OPTIONS statement must begin with a slash.
>
> q. No problem.

12.2 a. No problem.

> c. The dependent variable V4, vote in the Senate election, is nominal.
>
> e. The independent variable V87, sex, contains only two values. It is legitimate to use a dichotomous independent variable in an analysis of variance, but the T-TEST provides more information than does ANOVA and is preferable when the independent variable is dichotomous.
>
> g. Probably OK. One must assume that V24, respondent's position on scale of government provision of social services, is an interval measure of the conceptual variable, an assumption that can be argued but is not unreasonable.

i. No. Religious preference, V83, contains a large number of possible responses, some of which will have been selected by only a few cases. This variable can be used only after recoding is done to make sure all the groups are sizable.

k. To begin with, V85 is nominal, but the logic of this analysis also is faulty. Attending church more or less frequently (V84, the independent variable) causes you to change your race (V85, the dependent variable)? The dependent and independent variables are probably switched.

m. Probably OK, but the nonwhite categories of the RACE variable may not contain enough cases for a legitimate analysis. This should be checked by either running a FREQUENCIES on RACE or using the STATISTICS DESCRIPTIVES subcommand.

o. OK, as long as you can reasonably assume that PILLOK is an interval measure of the concept of attitudes toward birth control.

q. Technically OK, but the validity of the analysis depends on the theory's justifying the hypothesis. The logic of the analysis is that being happy leads to differences in income. Most people would argue that the cause-effect relationship is the reverse, but you might be able to make a theoretical case for treating HAPPY as the independent variable (e.g., happy people work better and thus earn higher incomes).

s. Technically OK since dichotomies (XMOVIE) are interval. However, variables with only a few values are better analyzed with contingency tables, discussed in Chapter 13.

12.4 *a.* $\bar{X} = 40$, $\bar{G}_1 = 28$, $\bar{G}_2 = 42$, $\bar{G}_3 = 48$. For illustration, a calculation table is filled out below for the first three cases of groups 1 and 2.

Case	$X_i - \bar{X}$	$(X_i - \bar{X})^2$	$\bar{G}_j - \bar{X}$	$(\bar{G}_j - \bar{X})^2$	$X_i - \bar{G}_j$	$(X_i - \bar{G}_j)^2$
1	$10 - 40 = -30$	900	$28 - 40 = -12$	144	$10 - 28 = -18$	324
2	$8 - 40 = -32$	1024	$28 - 40 = -12$	144	$8 - 28 = -20$	400
3	$37 - 40 = -3$	9	$28 - 40 = -12$	144	$37 - 28 = 9$	81
11	$30 - 40 = -10$	100	$42 - 40 = 2$	4	$30 - 42 = -12$	144
12	$17 - 40 = -23$	529	$42 - 40 = 2$	4	$17 - 42 = -25$	635
13	$75 - 40 = 35$	1225	$42 - 40 = 2$	4	$75 - 42 = 33$	1089

The ANOVA table would then be:

Source of variance	Degrees of freedom	Sums of squares	Mean square	F ratio
Between groups (TRSS)	2	2,480	1,240	4.01
Within groups (RSSE)	27	8,346	309.11	
Total (TSSE)	29	10,826		

From Table 12.4, when the numerator has 2 degrees of freedom and the denominator has 25 (the closest number to our 27 degrees of freedom), *F* ratios up to 3.38 can be found in samples through sample error only. The *F* ratio above of

4.01 is larger than this critical value, allowing us to reject sampling error at a .05 significance level.

13.1 *a.* There is no TABLES = statement. This command may work because the TABLES = statement is optional in some cases.

c. No BY keyword separates the independent and dependent variables.

e. No options have been selected for the CELLS subcommand.

g. This will work, but it is redundant. COUNT is the default if no CELLS subcommand is used.

i. No problem.

k. This will work, but do you want it to? We used the RESID option only to illustrate the chi-square calculation. It normally is unnecessary and adds to the clutter in each cell.

m. There are two problems. First, EDUC has a lot of values, will produce a very large table, and may lead to some small cells with associated problems in calculating chi-square. SEX as the dependent variable here is irrational. A high school diploma leads you to have a sex-change operation?

o. Technically OK, but this will not give you column n's, just percentages. Adding the COUNT option is preferred.

q. The OPTIONS subcommand must begin in column 1 except in SPSS/PC+ where it must be preceded by a slash.

s. Will work only with SPSS/PC+. SPSS-X version 2 does not use slashes before the OPTIONS and STATISTICS subcommands.

13.2 *a.*

	COUNT EXP VAL RESIDUAL	EDUC			
		LOW *1*	MEDIUM *2*	HIGH *3*	ROW TOTAL
RINCOME					
LOW	1	15 9 −6	10 10.5 .5	5 10.5 5.5	30 30.0%
MEDIUM	2	10 12 2	20 14 −6	10 14 4	40 40.0%
HIGH	3	5 9 4	5 10.5 5.5	20 10.5 −9.5	30 30.0%
COLUMN TOTAL		30 30.0%	35 35.0%	35 35.0%	100 100.0%

Chi square is 24.20 (rounding to two decimal places during all calculations). Degrees of freedom = $(r - 1)*(c - 1) = 4$. Critical chi square with 4 degrees of freedom (.05 significance level) is 9.488. Since the calculated chi square is larger than this, we reject the null hypothesis.

14.1 *a.* There is no slash before the STATISTICS subcommand.

c. Tau-b is for square tables. This will be a rectangular one.

e. The printout for gamma does not include a statistical significance level. You will need CHISQ as well.

    g. No problem.

    i. Gamma and tau-*c* are for ordinal variables. RACE is nominal.

    k. PARTNERS and SEX are both at least ordinal (if a dichotomy like SEX is interval, it is also ordinal). Use ordinal statistics. Phi and the contingency coefficient are usable, but not efficient for this relationship.

    m. There is no such statistic as CV. Cramer's *V* is automatically calculated when you request phi if the table is not 2 by 2.

    o. This command will work well, but when you request that many statistics, it is easier to use the ALL keyword.

    q. No problem.

    s. SPSS requires a slash before the STATISTICS subcommand and that it not begin in column 1. Version 2 of SPSS-X requires the subcommand to begin in column 1, but you need to use numbers for the statistics, not keywords.

    u. No problem. The ALL keyword is acceptable in version 2 of SPSS-X.

14.2 *a.* Phi = .17227, CC = .16977.

    c. Phi = .08292, CC = .08264. (*Note:* For 2 by 2 tables, use the "before Yates correction" chi square for calculating the measures of association.)

    e. V = .25284, CC = .40115.

14.3 *a.* Yes. A negative relationship means that seeing George Bush as getting tougher with Russia leads him to be perceived as a stronger leader.

    c. No. Both variables have reverse coding.

    e. Yes. A negative relationship means greater prayer frequency is associated with greater opposition to abortion.

    f. It had better not. RACE is a nominal variable, and relationships involving it cannot be thought of as positive or negative.

15.1 *a.* There are no BY keywords in the command.

    c. This is a third-order partial correlation which will probably create too many tables, each with a small number of cases. Technically, however, it is an acceptable SPSS command.

    e. No problem.

    g. No problem.

    i. There is no second BY keyword; thus no controls will be performed.

    k. Controlling for POLVIEWS is probably unreasonable. The zero-order relationship is to determine if women are more liberal on women's issues, so controlling for their degree of liberalism or conservatism is controlling for the independent variable.

    m. There is no STATISTICS subcommand, so no partial correlations will be produced.

15.2 *a.* None without any BY keywords.

    c. Third-order.

    e. First-order.

    g. First-order.

    i. Zero-order.

    k. First-order.

    m. None without a STATISTICS subcommand, first-order with one.

15.3 *a.* It is probably a spurious relationship; differences in defense spending attitudes make no difference to the vote but originally picked up partisanship with Democrats being in the less-defense-spending category and Republicans wanting more. One might argue that party identification was an intervening variable, but past research strongly supports the view of party identifications being formed early in life with specific attitudes, such as concerning defense spending, coming later.

c. The use of this control variable makes no sense. Why should views about Bush's health insurance position affect the relationship between perceptions on Dukakis' leadership qualities and position on defense? The three variables are probably correlated, and thus controlling for the third will affect the relationship between the first two; but there is no strong theory to justify this control variable and thus no logic being tested.

e. Sex was partially suppressing the impact of partisanship on preferences for government policies toward the homeless.

g. Education is strongly correlated with income for those working full-time but, quite reasonably, correlated little, if at all, with income for those working only part-time or unemployed. This is a conditional interpretation of the original hypothesis.

i. Sex does not intervene between education and premarital sex attitudes, so the original relationship was probably spurious, produced by gender differences among the educational groups.

k. Age, negatively correlated with education (older people were raised during a time when few went to college) and positively with income, was suppressing the strength of the education-income connection.

16.1 a. Only one variable is mentioned on the command.

c. The two FORMAT options are inconsistent, asking for both serial and matrix formats.

e. Unless you have recoded V2 into a dichotomy, it is not an interval variable.

g. If you are using the PEARSON CORR command, it is probably because you are working with version 2 of SPSS-X. If so, you need to use OPTION 6 to request serial printing of the correlations.

i. No problem.

k. No problem technically, but you are overworking yourself. The subcommand requests the default option, the same one in effect if you add no subcommands. So why bother?

m. DESCRIPTIVES is an option with the STATISTICS subcommand, not PRINT.

16.2 a.   The filled-in table and formulas are:

Case	X	Y	x	y	x * y	x^2	y^2
A	1	15	−4	0	0	16	0
B	2	13	−3	−2	6	9	4
C	6	12	1	−3	−3	1	9
D	5	11	0	−4	0	0	16
E	4	14	−1	−1	1	1	1
F	3	18	−2	3	−6	4	9
G	8	18	3	3	9	9	9
H	9	18	4	3	12	16	9
I	7	16	2	1	2	4	1
J	5	15	0	0	0	0	0
	$\overline{X} = 5$	$\overline{Y} = 15$			$\Sigma(x * y) = 21$	$\Sigma x^2 = 60$	$\Sigma y^2 = 58$

$$r = \frac{21}{\sqrt{60 * 58}} = \frac{21}{\sqrt{3480}} = \frac{21}{58.9915} = .3560$$

17.1 *a.* There is no control variable or inclusion level.

  c. No problem.

  e. The inclusion level is higher than the number of variables on the control list.

  g. There is no slash before the FORMAT subcommand.

  i. Technically OK, but the inclusion level is very high, leading to a sizable chance of violating the multivariate normal assumption.

  k. No problem.

  m. Technically acceptable, but it is preferable to request a zero-order correlation matrix whenever pairwise deletion is used.

  o. Technically acceptable, but there is no reason to include the /MISSING = LISTWISE subcommand since this is the default.

  q. The TWOTAIL option is requested with the SIGNIFICANCE subcommand in PARTIAL CORR.

  s. MARITAL is a nominal variable and should not be used with either CORRELATION or PARTIAL CORR unless it is first recoded into an interval dichotomy.

18.1 *a.* There is no /PLOT subcommand

  c. No problem. You can change just one axis (VSIZE) without having to change both. Similarly, you can use either the HORIZONTAL or the VERTICAL subcommand without having to use the other.

  e. No /PLOT subcommand or variables to be plotted.

  g. No problem. HSIZE reduces the printed space used by the graph, but does not change a variable's code numbers. Variable V6 still contains values from 0 to 100, and a reference line can be drawn at value 50.

  i. There is no REFERENCE specification for the /HORIZONTAL subcommand.

  k. Subcommands, such as /FORMAT, need to come before the /PLOT subcommand. This will probably not produce an error message, but any subcommand after /PLOT will be applied only to later /PLOT subcommands—in this case not at all since there is no second /PLOT subcommand.

  m. Technically no problem, but HAPPY has only three values—not enough for an interpretable scatterplot.

  o. Two control variables are listed. The PLOT procedure allows for only one.

18.2 *a.* The plot is not a problem, but first you must create variables measuring husband's and wife's educational levels. The IF statements below can accomplish this.

   IF (SEX EQ 1) HED = EDUC

   IF (SEX EQ 2) HED = SPEDUC

   IF (SEX EQ 1) WED = SPEDUC

   IF (SEX EQ 2) WED = EDUC

18.3 *a.* Income would have to be the dependent variable (higher incomes cannot cause you to become younger or older) and thus should be on the horizontal axis.

 b–d. There should be a visible upward linear pattern when the variables are plotted in their original form, a pattern that tends to disappear as the variables are recoded into a smaller number of values.

19.1 *a.* There is no METHOD subcommand.

  c. V5 is not contained on the variables list.

  e. Subcommands, such as STATISTICS, need to come before the DEPENDENT and METHOD subcommands.

  g. Acceptable. With the ENTER option, it is not necessary to include the name of the subcommand (METHOD), and specific independent variables may be listed after ENTER as long as they are contained on the variables list.

i. The COLLECT option is acceptable as a substitute for naming variables on the variables list (see Table 19.1), but you must explicitly name the independent variables after the ENTER specification. This option is not available with SPSS/PC+.

k. RELIG is a nominal variable. It cannot be used in regression unless it is recoded into a dichotomy.

m. There is no point to the SIG option on DESCRIPTIVES unless CORR is requested also.

o. Technically OK, but usually you will want to request the default statistics as well as the additional ones.

19.3 *a, b.* The necessary formulas are:

$$b = \frac{\Sigma xy}{\Sigma x^2} \qquad a = \overline{Y} - b * \overline{X} \qquad \text{Beta} = b * \frac{S_X}{S_Y}$$

Proceed by creating a table similar to the one used to calculate the correlation coefficient. The completed table is:

Case	X	Y	x	y	$x * y$	x^2	y^2
A	1	15	−4	0	0	16	0
B	2	13	−3	−2	6	9	4
C	6	12	1	−3	−3	1	9
D	5	11	0	−4	0	0	16
E	4	14	−1	−1	1	1	1
F	3	18	−2	3	−6	4	9
G	8	18	3	3	9	9	9
H	9	18	4	3	12	16	9
I	7	16	2	1	2	4	1
J	5	15	0	0	0	0	0
	$\overline{X} = 5$	$\overline{Y} = 15$			$\Sigma(x * y) = 21$	$\Sigma x^2 = 60$	$\Sigma y^2 = 58$

$$b = \frac{\Sigma xy}{\Sigma x^2} = \frac{21}{60} = .35 \qquad a = \overline{Y} - b * \overline{X} = 15 - (.35 * 5) = 15 - 1.75 = 13.25$$

so $Y = 13.25 + .35X$

$$S_X^2 = \frac{\Sigma x^2}{n} = \frac{60}{10} = 6 \qquad S_X = \sqrt{S_X^2} = \sqrt{6} = 2.4495$$

$$S_Y^2 = \frac{\Sigma y^2}{n} = \frac{58}{10} = 5.8 \qquad S_Y = \sqrt{S_Y^2} = \sqrt{5.8} = 2.4083$$

$$\text{Beta} = b * \frac{S_X}{S_Y} = .35 * \frac{2.4495}{2.4083} = .35 * 1.0171 = .3560$$

20.1 *a.* No problem.

c. It is technically acceptable for the ENTER command to refer to less than all the independent variables. Unless it is done for a good reason, it is usually not advisable since listwise deletion of missing data will delete cases with missing values on V30 even though this variable is not currently being analyzed.

e. Perfectly acceptable.

g. The STATISTICS subcommand needs to come before the DEPENDENT and

METHOD subcommands. *Note*: This will not produce an error message, but neither will any optional statistics be calculated.

i. It is perfectly acceptable to have several DEPENDENT and ENTER commands, and this is one of the reasons why a variables list may contain more variables than are analyzed in a single model. This is usually done, instead of repeating the main REGRESSION command, if you want all regression models calculated from the same cases—listwise deletion based on the variables list. This subcommand series will produce two regression analyses, a separate one for each model.

k. This will not work. Recall from the Pearson correlation chapters (Chapters 16 and 17) that the AIDS variables were used on different halves of the sample. Listwise deletion of missing data will produce no cases left for analysis. You will need to either use separate REGRESSION commands for each model or add the /MISSING = PAIRWISE subcommand.

Glossary of Terms

Active window   The section of the computer screen where the cursor currently resides and where you can enter information or commands.

Addition rule   The probability that any one of a group of possible outcomes may happen is the sum of the individual probabilities.

Adjusted R-square   The R square from a regression analysis that has been adjusted slightly downward to account for the number of independent variables in the regression equation.

ALL   The keyword that refers to all specifications for a particular subcommand (STATISTICS = ALL) or all variables in a data set (VARIABLES = ALL).

Alpha variable   A variable whose values for at least one case in the data set contain a letter or other non-numeric character.

Alphanumeric variable   See *alpha variable*.

Alternative hypothesis   See *research hypothesis*.

Analysis of variance   A test comparing the means of three or more groups on the same dependent variable to determine if at least one of the group means is different from the others at a statistically significant level.

AND connector   A keyword used on IF and SELECT IF statements that identifies an operation to be performed only if two or more conditions are met; for example, IF SEX EQ 1 <u>AND</u> RACE EQ 1.

ANOVA   Acronym for an analysis of variance.

Asymmetric statistic   A statistic that is calculated differently depending upon which variable is independent and which dependent.

b coefficient   An unstandardized regression coefficient that shows how much, and in what direction, the dependent variable changes for each unit change in an independent variable.

Barchart   The distribution for a single variable represented as bars on a graph rather than the number of cases with each of a variable's possible values.

Batch processing   Entering and executing a batch of SPSS commands as a group instead of each single command being carried out as soon as it is completed. The opposite of *interactive processing.*

BEGIN DATA   A command required immediately before lines of data so SPSS will not try to read the data as commands.

Beta coefficient   The standardized *b* coefficient; that is, the sample estimate when using standardized variables. Not the same as the Greek letter β (beta) which refers to the population parameter of which the *b* coefficient is a sample estimate.

Case   A single member of a sample from which information has been obtained, for example, a single person responding to a public opinion survey or a single book in a sample of library books.

Central limit theorem   A theorem (conclusion based on a mathematical proof) about the distribution of a sample statistic over an infinite number of samples. For sample means, the theorem states that the distribution's average will be the true population mean; the distribution's dispersion will be $\sigma_{\bar{x}} = \sigma/\sqrt{n}$; and the distribution will be normally shaped.

Central tendency   The average or middle value of a variable's distribution, calculated differently depending upon the variable's level of measurement.

Chi square   A statistical significance test used to evaluate the probability that any sample relationship observed might be due solely to sampling error.

Close-ended questions   Survey questions with a predetermined set of answers from which a respondent chooses one.

Codebook   Any document describing the variables in a data set; what each variable is (the question asked or characteristic being measured); and what that variable's code numbers represent.

Command   Any single instruction or set of instructions that a software program (for example, SPSS or an operating system) "understands" and can execute.

Command driven   An operating system or software program where you must type in commands for operations to be performed.

Command generator   A menu in most implementations of Release 4 of SPSS allowing you to select commands which are then automatically pasted into the input window.

Command terminator   A period used in many forms of SPSS which is entered at the end of a completed command informing the software that the command is complete.

COMMENT   An SPSS command that indicates that any typed material following the command is merely a comment to be printed on the output, not an instruction to be carried out.

COMPUTE   An SPSS command that performs some mathematical operation on the values of one or more variables for each case in the data set.

Concept   An idea or mental image of some abstraction we believe exists but often cannot measure directly, for example, a person's level of prejudice or respect for a political candidate.

Conceptual definition   A definition for a concept that clarifies its meaning by defining it in words. A dictionary type of definition.

Conditional hypothesis   A relationship we believe to be true only for a particular group in the population, not necessarily for everyone. For example, for Catholics (the condition or group), increased church attendance leads to decreased support for abortion. Both the research and null hypotheses apply to the identified group only with no claims being made about other members of the population.

Confidence interval   A range of values that we believe (with a certain level of confidence or probability) contains a population parameter.

Confounding variable   A third variable that interferes with our ability to identify the independent variable–dependent variable relationship. It must be controlled for to remove its interference.

Constant   Any characteristic that is the same for all cases in the data set, for example, in a survey of college students, all cases would have the occupational status "student." Sometimes also used to refer to the intercept in a regression equation.

Contingency table   A table showing the contingent or joint distribution of two variables to evaluate whether a relationship exists between them.

Contingent distribution   The distribution of one variable, like income, for each value of a second variable, like education.

Continuous distribution   The distribution of a continuous variable, that is, one that can take on an infinite number of values. Age, for example, could be measured in minutes, seconds, and so on, depending on the precision of measurement. A continuous distribution is represented by a smooth curve.

Control plot   A scatterplot between two variables while holding a third variable constant.

Control variable   A variable being held constant (that is controlled for) so as not to interfere with an examination of the independent variable–dependent variable relationship.

Controlled experiment   A scientific experiment comparing, at least, an experimental group receiving the stimulus and a control group that does not to determine what response the stimulus produces.

Correlation   Any measure of association between variables. Unless otherwise indicated, it usually refers to the Pearson correlation coefficient.

CORRELATION   An SPSS procedure that produces a Pearson correlation between variables.

Correlation matrix   A matrix (rows and columns) with variable names listed both down the rows and across the columns. The correlation between any two variables is found where the row for one variable intersects the column for another.

Covariance   The extent to which two variables vary together, that is, when cases above the mean on one variable are likely to be consistently above (or below) the mean on the other variable. A step in measuring the relationship between variables.

Critical value   The value of a statistical significance test above which we reject the null hypothesis. Using a probability distribution, like chi square, we know that, with 9 degrees of freedom, we might find chi-square values up to 16.92 just by sampling error only. Anything above this critical value is unlikely to be sampling error and provides strong evidence that two variables are related.

CROSSTABS   An SPSS procedure that produces contingency tables.

Data definition commands   SPSS commands that define a data file but do not perform any analysis of the data.

Data file   Any computer file containing only the data obtained from some data generation technique.

DATA LIST   An SPSS command that identifies the name, location, and type of variables in a data file.

Data modification   Some form of change to the data in use, such as recoding a variable or analyzing only selected cases.

Default   Any practice normally followed by the SPSS software unless we specifically instruct it via subcommands to do something different.

Degrees of freedom   A statistical compensation used to avoid drawing inaccurate conclusions from a sample to the population.

Dependent variable   A variable influenced by an independent variable. The effect in a cause-effect relationship.

Deviation format   A measuring scale for interval variables in which each case is measured by its distance above or below the sample mean.

Dichotomy   A variable that has only two values.

Direction of a relationship   The positive or negative sign of the measure of association.

Directional hypothesis   A hypothesis that states a specific (positive or negative) relationship between variables.

Discrete distribution   The distribution of a variable that has a finite and countable number of categories, represented graphically by box or line charts rather than a smooth curve.

Disk operating system   See *DOS*.

Dispersion   How widely spread cases are around the average value of a variable.

Distribution   A graphic or tabular portrayal of how cases are arrayed on a single variable—e.g., how many cases are age 18, how many age 19, and so on.

DOS   An operating system used on IBM and compatible microcomputers.

Dummy variables   Another name for dichotomous variables, often created through data massaging from multicategory variables.

Editor   A software program allowing you to type material into a computer file and to correct any mistakes.

Elaboration   The process of expanding upon a two-variable relationship by controlling for a third variable. Interpreting the results constitutes elaborating upon your discussion of a relationship.

Empirical   Based on the senses.

Empirical distribution   A distribution based on observed results (as from a sample), not predicted based on probability rules as with a known distribution.

END DATA   An SPSS command that must appear immediately after lines of data.

Error   Any difference between a value predicted for a case and that case's actual value on some variable.

Error, SPSS   Any inability to carry out a command. Produces an error message describing the problem.

Error term   In regression, the variation in the dependent variable unexplained by the regression model.

Exact sample   A subsample of a precise number of cases drawn using the SAMPLE command.

Exaggerated relationship   A relationship that appears larger than it actually is because of the influence of a confounding variable.

Expected frequencies   The frequencies (number of cases) we would expect to find in each cell of a contingency table if the null hypothesis were true.

Expected value   The value of a variable or mathematical operation we would expect to find in most circumstances. Usually the average or mean value.

Explained sum of squares   In an analysis of variance, the sum of squared errors in predicting a dependent variable explained or accounted for by its relationship with an independent variable.

Extended menus   Menus that include all possible options or commands in SPSS implementations that use menus.

External file   Any file, usually a data file, referred to in a program but not actually included as a part of that program.

***F* ratio**   The ratio of two variances. This ratio has a known distribution and can be used in statistical significance tests.

File   Any collection of commands, data, or other information stored in a computer with a unique name.

FILE HANDLE   A command used in some implementations of SPSS which both identifies an external file and gives it a nickname to use when referring to the file later in the program.

First-order statistics   Statistics produced while controlling for one other variable.

FREQUENCIES   An SPSS procedure that displays the univariate distribution of a variable.

GET FILE   An SPSS command used to access an SPSS system file.

Glossary   A feature of many SPSS implementations that provides an on-screen description of statistical and SPSS terminology.

Help menu   A feature of many SPSS implementations that provides on-screen assistance with using the software and its commands.

Hypothesis   A statement of a relationship between two variables that can be tested to determine if it is true or false.

IBM/CMS   An operating system for IBM mainframe computers.

IBM/OS   An operating system for IBM mainframe computers.

IF   An SPSS command that performs some mathematical operation on one or more variables only if a particular condition is first determined to be true.

INCLUDE   An SPSS command which fetches and executes an external file of SPSS commands.

Independent variable   The variable believed to have led to cases having different values on a dependent variable. The cause in a cause-effect relationship.

Inferential statistics   Statistics allowing conclusions to be drawn from sample information to the entire population from which the sample was drawn.

Input window   The window in some implementations of SPSS where commands are entered.

Interactive processing   The processing of commands carried out one at a time. The opposite of *batch processing.*

Intercept   Where a regression line crosses the Y axis. Also called the constant in a regression equation.

Interval estimate   An estimate about a population parameter which is not a single number but a range (interval) of numbers.

Interval variable   A variable whose values represent distances apart on a concept to be measured.

Intervening variable   A variable that operates between a dependent and an independent variable that represents the process through which the independent and dependent variables are related. For example, higher education (*independent variable*) leads to higher income (*intervening variable*) which leads to higher levels of conservatism (*dependent variable*).

JCL (Job Control Language)   Command statements used on IBM mainframe computers that both precede and follow an SPSS program. JCL statements identify the user and software program to the central processing unit along with any external files being accessed or saved by SPSS commands.

Job Control Language   See *JCL.*

Journal file   A file automatically created by some implementations of SPSS containing a copy of all commands entered (and sometimes the output they produce) during an SPSS session.

Known distribution   The distribution of a variable that can be predicted using the rules of probability.

Least-squares line   A line representing a relationship between two interval variables drawn to produce the smallest sum of squared errors when using values of one variable to predict values of the other.

Levels of measurement   What an operational variable's code numbers represent as measures of a conceptual variable.

Linear relationship   A relationship between two interval variables that can be summarized or graphically portrayed with a straight line.

LIS file   A file automatically created by some implementations of SPSS containing the output produced during an SPSS session.

LIST   An SPSS command which lists the cases in a data set and their values on one or more variables.

Listwise deletion   A method for deleting missing data from an analysis. A case with missing data on any variable mentioned on the command will be deleted from all analyses produced by the command.

LOG file   A file automatically created by some implementations of SPSS containing the commands entered during an SPSS session.

Logical operator   AND and OR terms used to represent logical conditions on IF and SELECT IF commands.

Long string   A string variable more than 8 characters long.

Marginals   The univariate distribution of any single variable. Displayed in a frequencies table or in the margins next to a contingency table.

Mathematical operators   Two-letter terms (for example, EQ) or mathematical symbols (for example, =) used to describe mathematical operations on IF, SELECT IF, or COMPUTE commands.

Mean   The measure of central tendency for interval variables.

Measures of association   Statistics that measure the strength and often the direction of a relationship between variables.

Measures of dispersion   Statistics that measure how widely spread cases are around the average value of a variable.

Median   The measure of central tendency for ordinal variables.

Menu driven   An operating system or SPSS implementation where commands can be selected from menus on the screen rather than having to be typed in.

Menu/help system   Used by some versions of SPSS/PC+ and equivalent to the command generator.

Missing value   A value or code number that represents some type of missing information for a variable.

MISSING VALUES   An SPSS command that identifies the values of a variable used to represent missing information.

Mode   The measure of central tendency for nominal variables.

Model   A description of all the important determinants of a single dependent variable.

Monotonic relationship   A relationship between variables in which increases of the independent variable are consistently related to increases (or decreases) on the dependent variable, though not necessarily at the constant rate true of linear relationships.

Multiple regression   A regression analysis that includes two or more independent variables.

Multiplication rule   The probability that two or more events may all occur is determined by multiplying together the probabilities of each individual event.

Multivariate analysis   Any analysis in which more than two variables are involved to calculate a single statistic.

Negative relationship   A relationship in which increases on one variable produce decreases on another.

Nominal variable   One whose code numbers only represent different categories of a variable but in no particular order.

Nondirectional hypothesis   A hypothesis that states a relationship between variables without indicating whether the relationship is positive or negative.

Normal curve   A smooth curve that has a single peak at its mean and each side of which gradually slopes down to the bottom axis. One side of the normal curve is the mirror image of the other side.

Normal distribution   A distribution having the shape of a normal curve.

Note, SPSS   An SPSS message that informs the user of an unusual circumstance encountered by the software. Does not stop the processing of commands; does not necessarily mean there is an error.

Null hypothesis   A statement of no relationship between variables. The opposite of the research hypothesis and the object of statistical significance tests.

One-tailed test   A statistical significance test using only one side or tail of a probability distribution. Used to test directional hypotheses.

ONEWAY   An SPSS procedure that performs an analysis of variance.

Open-ended question   A survey question without preset answers.

Operating system   Basic software of all computers that controls the storage and manipulation of files as well as how software is executed.

Operational definition   The definition of a concept that identifies precise procedures to follow for measurement purposes. The operational definition produces the values of an operational variable.

OR connector   A keyword used on IF and SELECT IF statements that identifies an operation to be performed if any of two or more conditions are met; for example, IF SEX EQ 1 OR RACE EQ 1.

Ordinal variable   A variable whose code numbers represent a high-to-low order on a conceptual variable.

OS/2   An operating system used on IBM PS/2 model microcomputers.

Output window   An on-screen window where the results of commands are displayed. Available on some implementations of SPSS.

Pairwise deletion   A method to delete cases with missing data from an analysis. Only cases with missing values on the particular variables being used to produce a specific statistic are deleted. Cases with missing values on other variables listed on the command, but not involved in calculating this particular statistic, are not deleted.

Parameter   The value of a particular summary measure (mean, gamma, and so forth) for the entire population, not just the sample. That which is estimated using sample statistics.

Partial coefficients   Measures of association produced while controlling for one or more variables.

PARTIAL CORR   An SPSS procedure to produce Pearson correlations while controlling for one or more variables.

PEARSON CORR   An SPSS procedure to produce Pearson correlations between variables. Renamed CORRELATION in later versions of the software.

PLOT   An SPSS procedure to produce scatterplots between variables.

Point estimate   A single number, instead of an interval, used as an estimate of a population parameter.

Population   The entire group about which conclusions are drawn.

Positive relationship   A relationship where increases in value on one variable are related to increases in value on another.

PRE   Acronym for proportional reduction of error. A family of measures of association based on the logic of using the independent variable to predict the dependent variable.

Probability distribution   The distribution of a variable based on the rules of probability rather than on the observation of a number of outcomes.

Probability level   The probability that something is true. Often used interchangeably on SPSS output with significance level and can be interpreted as the probability that the null hypothesis is true.

Procedure commands   SPSS commands that process data and produce some statistics.

Prompted session   The SPSS term that refers to interactive processing.

RECODE   An SPSS command that allows the modification of the code numbers that exist for a variable.

Record   A line of data for a single case. Cases may require more than one record in a data file to enter all the information obtained.

REGRESSION   An SPSS procedure to produce regression lines and regression statistics.

Release 4   The latest version of SPSS; it works similarly on all types of computers.

Replicability   The ability of an experiment or statistical analysis to be replicated by other scholars. A test for objectivity.

Research focus   A general topic of the research, such as racism, sexism, voting behavior, or political ideology.

Research hypothesis   A relationship between variables that is believed to exist.

Research question   In a general sense, that which statistical research tries to answer; for example, Why are some people less likely to vote than others?

Reserved words   Some SPSS keywords that cannot be used as names for variables.

Residual sum of squared errors (RSSE)   In an analysis of variance, the sum of squared prediction errors that remain after the impact of the independent variable has been accounted for.

Reverse coding   A common occurrence on operational variables where low code numbers represent high levels of something and high code numbers low amounts of some concept. Not a problem as long as the analyst is aware of them and appropriately interprets a measure of association's sign.

REVIEW   A text editor included in the SPSS/PC+ software.

Robust statistic   Any statistic that can produce reasonably accurate estimates of a population parameter even when the assumptions made by the statistics are violated.

RSSE   See *Residual sum of squared errors.*

Sample   A small group selected for analysis from a larger population.

Sampling distribution   The probability distribution of a sample statistic over an infinite number of samples.

SAVE   An SPSS command used to save a raw data or SPSS system file for use in later analyses.

Scatterplot   A graphic portrayal of relationships between interval variables. Produced by plotting each case on a graph using that case's value on the independent and dependent variables (the axes of the graph).

Secondary analysis   The analysis of any data that were collected by someone else.

Seed number   A number used by SPSS as a starting point for creating random numbers or drawing random samples.

SELECT IF   An SPSS command used to select only certain cases for analysis.

SET SEED   An SPSS command used to change the default seed number.

SET WIDTH   An SPSS command used to change the width of the output.

Short strings   Any string variable with 8 or less characters.

Significance level   The statistical significance level calculated by SPSS procedures; also often called the probability level on SPSS output. Interpreted as the probability that the null hypothesis is true.

Simple regression   A regression equation using only one independent variable.

Specifications   Alternatives available on SPSS subcommands.

SPSS/PC+   A version of SPSS for use on DOS microcomputers.

SPSS-X   An earlier version of SPSS used on mainframe computers.

Spurious relationship   A relationship that does not really exist in a causal sense, but appears in statistics because of the influence of a confounding variable.

Standard deviation   A measure of dispersion for interval variables.

Standard error   A measure of dispersion for a sampling distribution. The standard deviation of a sampling distribution.

Standard menus   Menus that list the most commonly used (but not all) SPSS commands, subcommands, and options. Available only on SPSS implementations that use menus.

Standard scores   The values of a variable once it has been standardized. A case's value above or below the variable's mean expressed in standard deviation units.

Standardized variable   A variable whose measurement system has been changed into standard scores. The distribution of the variable has a mean of zero and a standard deviation of 1.

Statistic   Any summary measure obtained from a sample, as opposed to a parameter— the same summary measure for an entire population.

Statistical artifact   Any statistic produced by a mathematical quirk rather than the representation of something real. For example, a regression equation including as many variables as there are cases in the data set will always perfectly predict the dependent variable (R square = 1.0) even if the variables have no causal connection.

Statistical significance   An evaluation of whether a relationship discovered in a sample might be produced by sampling error.

String variable   An alpha variable.

Strong relationship   Variables that are very closely related so that the independent variable highly and accurately predicts the values of a dependent variable.

Subcommands   Additions to SPSS commands that describe in more detail how a procedure is carried out and the output to be produced.

Substantive significance   An evaluation of whether a relationship is important substantively; that is, whether the variables are strongly or weakly related to one another.

Suppressed relationship   A relationship made to appear weaker than it actually is due to the impact of a confounding variable.

Surveys   Any generation of data from cases in their normal state as opposed to a controlled experiment where a stimulus is manipulated by the researcher.

Symmetric statistic   A statistic that is the same regardless of which variable is independent and which dependent.

Syntax   The "grammar" of the SPSS language. The subcommands and specifications that are available with each command and how they must be entered.

Syntax window   A window available on some SPSS implementations that displays the syntax of commands.

SYSMIS   An SPSS keyword that refers to system missing values. Renamed $SYSMIS in Release 4.

System file   A file containing data and the SPSS descriptions of the data.

System missing value   A missing value designation (a period) created by the SPSS software due to errors in the data file or performing some mathematical operation on a variable containing missing values.

T-TEST   An SPSS procedure that compares the means of two groups to determine if the sample difference between the means is statistically significant.

TEMPORARY   A command instructing SPSS to treat any data modifications following the command and before the next procedure as temporary. After the next procedure has been carried out, the data modifications will be erased from computer memory.

Text file   A file containing anything being created or modified with an editor. Called a text file because the editor treats everything in the file as text to be edited, not as commands to be carried out or data to be analyzed.

Theoretical distributions   Distributions of variables determined by the laws of probability rather than by the actual examination of a variable in a sample or population.

THRU   An SPSS keyword used with the RECODE and some other commands to refer to a group or range of adjacent values, such as RECODE V1 (1 THRU 6 = 2).

TO   An SPSS keyword used on any command to refer to a group or range of adjacent variables such as RECODE V1 TO V6 (1 = 2).

Total sum of squared error (TSSE)   In an analysis of variance, the sum of each case's squared deviation from the mean of a specific variable.

Treatment sum of squares (TRSS)   In an analysis of variance, that part of the total sum of squared error produced by the impact of the independent variable.

TRSS   See *Treatment sum of squares.*

TSSE   See *Total sum of squared error.*

Two-tailed test   A statistical significance test for a nondirectional hypothesis using both tails of a sampling distribution.

Type I error   In statistical inference, the decision to reject the null hypothesis when it is in fact true for the population.

Type II error   In statistical inference, the decision to accept the null hypothesis when it is actually false for the population.

Univariate analysis   Any analysis that examines only one variable at a time.

Value   A characteristic of a case on a variable.

VALUE LABELS   An SPSS command that attaches printing labels to the values of a variable.

Variable   Any attribute (for example, gender, age, or political ideology) that varies across cases and is divided into both mutually exclusive and exhaustive categories.

VARIABLE LABELS   An SPSS command attaching printing labels to the name of a variable.

Variable name   Any unique term used to represent a variable to the SPSS software. The name must begin with a letter and be no more than 8 characters long.

Variable type   Whether a variable is numeric or alphanumeric.

Variance   A measure of dispersion for interval variables.

Version   Any edition of a software program.

Video display terminal (VDT)   A television-type screen used both to enter data or commands and to review the results of computer actions.

VMS   An operating system used on VAX mainframe computers.

Warning   An SPSS message that indicates the action SPSS took when it encountered a situation it did not fully "understand;" for example, the substituting of a system missing value for blanks in a data file.

Window   A section of a computer screen displaying different activities or operations from other sections of the computer screen.

WITH   An SPSS keyword often used to separate one group of variables from another on a procedure command.

Y-HAT   A value for a case on a dependent variable (Y) calculated using the coefficients estimated for a regression equation.

Yates correction   A correction to the chi-square value sometimes used for 2 by 2 contingency tables.

Z scores   A synonym for standard scores.

Zero-order correlation   A correlation between variables not involving any control variables.

Bibliography

Achen, Christopher H. *Interpreting and Using Regression*, Quantitative Applications in the Social Sciences, Sage University Papers Series No. 29 (Newbury Park, California: Sage Publications, 1982)

Babbie, Earl. *The Practice of Social Research*, Fifth Edition (Belmont, California: Wadsworth, 1989)

Berry, William D. and Stanley Feldman. *Multiple Regression in Practice*, Quantitative Applications in the Social Sciences, Sage University Papers Series No. 50 (Newbury Park, California: Sage Publications, 1985)

Converse, Jean M. and Stanley Presser. *Survey Questions*, Quantitative Applications in the Social Sciences, Sage University Papers Series No. 63 (Newbury Park, California: Sage Publications, 1986)

Freedman, David, *et al.*, *Statistics*, Second Edition (New York: W. W. Norton, 1991)

Henkel, Ramon E. *Tests of Significance*, Quantitative Applications in the Social Sciences, Sage University Papers Series No. 4 (Newbury Park, California: Sage Publications, 1976)

Hoover, Kenneth, R. *The Elements of Social Scientific Thinking*, Fourth Edition (New York: St. Martin's Press, 1988)

Hildebrand, David K., James D. Laing and Howard Rosenthal. *Analysis of Ordinal Data*, Quantitative Applications in the Social Sciences, Sage University Papers Series No. 8 (Newbury Park, California: Sage Publications, 1977)

Iversen, Gudmund R. and Helmut Norpoth. *Analysis of Variance*, Second Edition, Quantitative Applications in the Social Sciences, Sage University Papers Series No. 1 (Newbury Park, California: Sage Publications, 1976)

Kalton, Graham. *Introduction to Survey Sampling*, Quantitative Applications in the Social Sciences, Sage University Papers Series No. 35 (Newbury Park, California: Sage Publications, 1983)

Kiecolt, J. Jill and Laura E. Nathan. *Secondary Analysis of Survey Data*, Quantitative

Applications in the Social Sciences, Sage University Papers Series No. 53 (Newbury Park, California: Sage Publications, 1985)

Levin, Jack and James Alan Fox. *Elementary Statistics in Social Research*, Fourth Edition (New York: Harper & Row, 1988)

Lewis-Beck, Michael S. *Applied Regression*, Quantitative Applications in the Social Sciences, Sage University Papers Series No. 22 (Newbury Park, California: Sage Publications, 1980)

Liebetrau, Albert M. *Measures of Association*, Quantitative Applications in the Social Sciences, Sage University Papers Series No. 32 (Newbury, California: Sage Publications, 1983)

May, Richard B., Michael E. J. Masson, and Michael A. Hunter. *Application of Statistics in Behavioral Research* (New York: Harper & Row, 1990)

Mohr, Lawrence B. *Understanding Significance Testing*, Quantitative Applications in the Social Sciences, Sage University Papers Series No. 73 (Newbury Park, California: Sage Publications, 1990)

Nachmias, David and Chava Nachmias. *Research Methods in the Social Sciences*, Third Edition (New York: St. Martin's Press, 1987)

Norusis, Marija J., and SPSS Inc. *SPSS/PC+ V2.0 Base Manual* (Chicago: SPSS Inc., 1988)

Reynolds, H. T. *Analysis of Nominal Data*, Quantitative Applications in the Social Sciences, Sage University Papers Series No. 7 (Newbury California: Sage Publications, 1977)

Spector, Paul E. *Research Designs*, Quantitative Applications in the Social Sciences, Sage University Papers Series No. 23 (Newbury Park, California: Sage Publications, 1981)

SPSS Inc. *Getting Started with SPSS-X on VAX/VMS* (Chicago: SPSS, Inc., 1989)

SPSS Inc. *SPSS for IBM CMS: Operations Guide* (Chicago: SPSS Inc., 1990)

SPSS Inc. *SPSS for OS/2: Operations Guide* (Chicago: SPSS Inc., 1990)

SPSS Inc. *SPSS for the Macintosh: Operations Guide* (Chicago: SPSS Inc., 1990)

SPSS Inc. *SPSS for UNIX: Operations Guide* (Chicago: SPSS Inc., 1990)

SPSS Inc. *SPSS for VAX/VMS: Operations Guide* (Chicago: SPSS Inc., 1990)

SPSS Inc. *SPSS Reference Guide* (Release 4) (Chicago: SPSS Inc., 1990)

SPSS Inc. *SPSS-X User's Guide*, Third Edition (Chicago, SPSS Inc., 1988)

Index